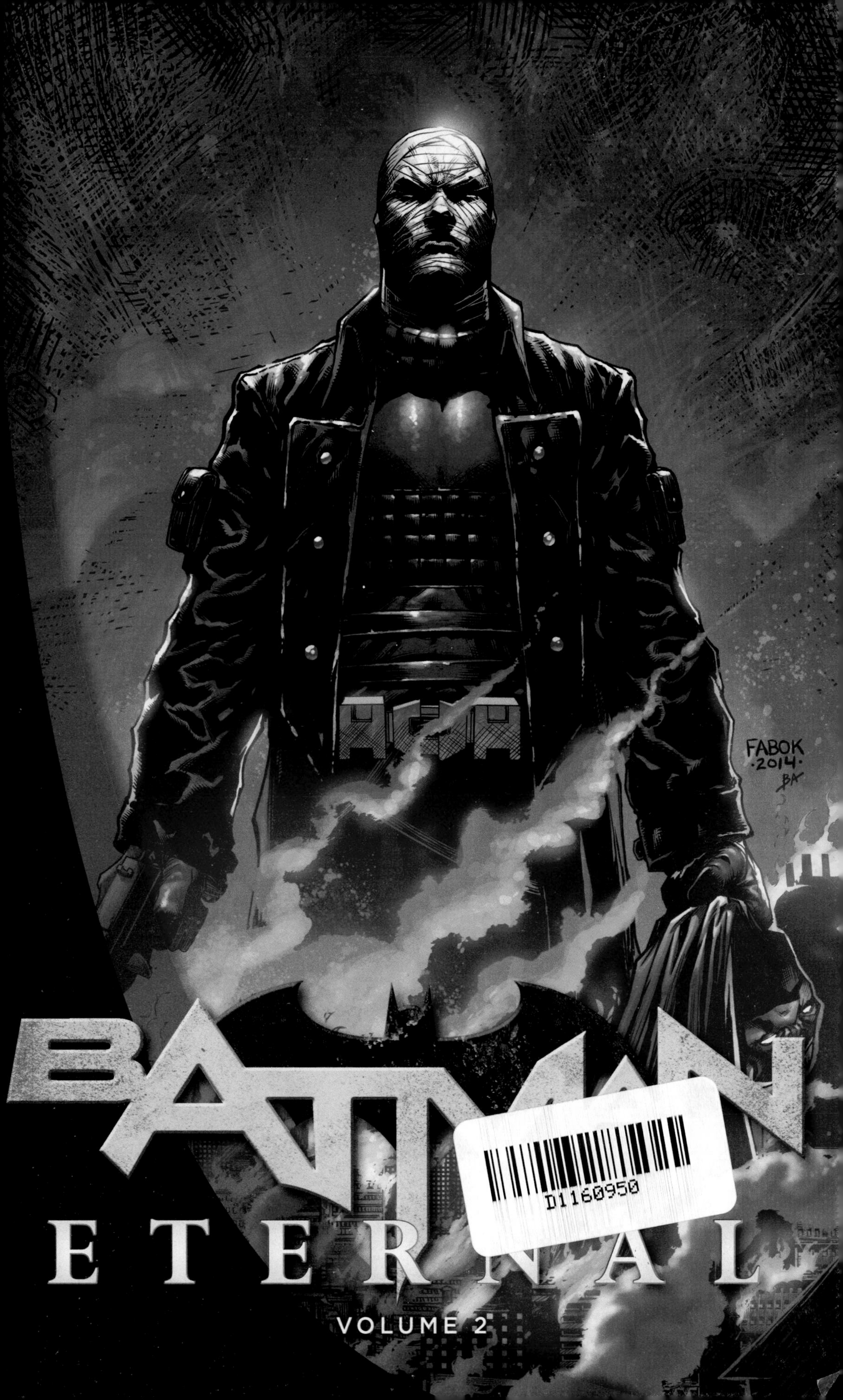
FABOK
·2014·
BA

# BATMAN ETERNAL

VOLUME 2

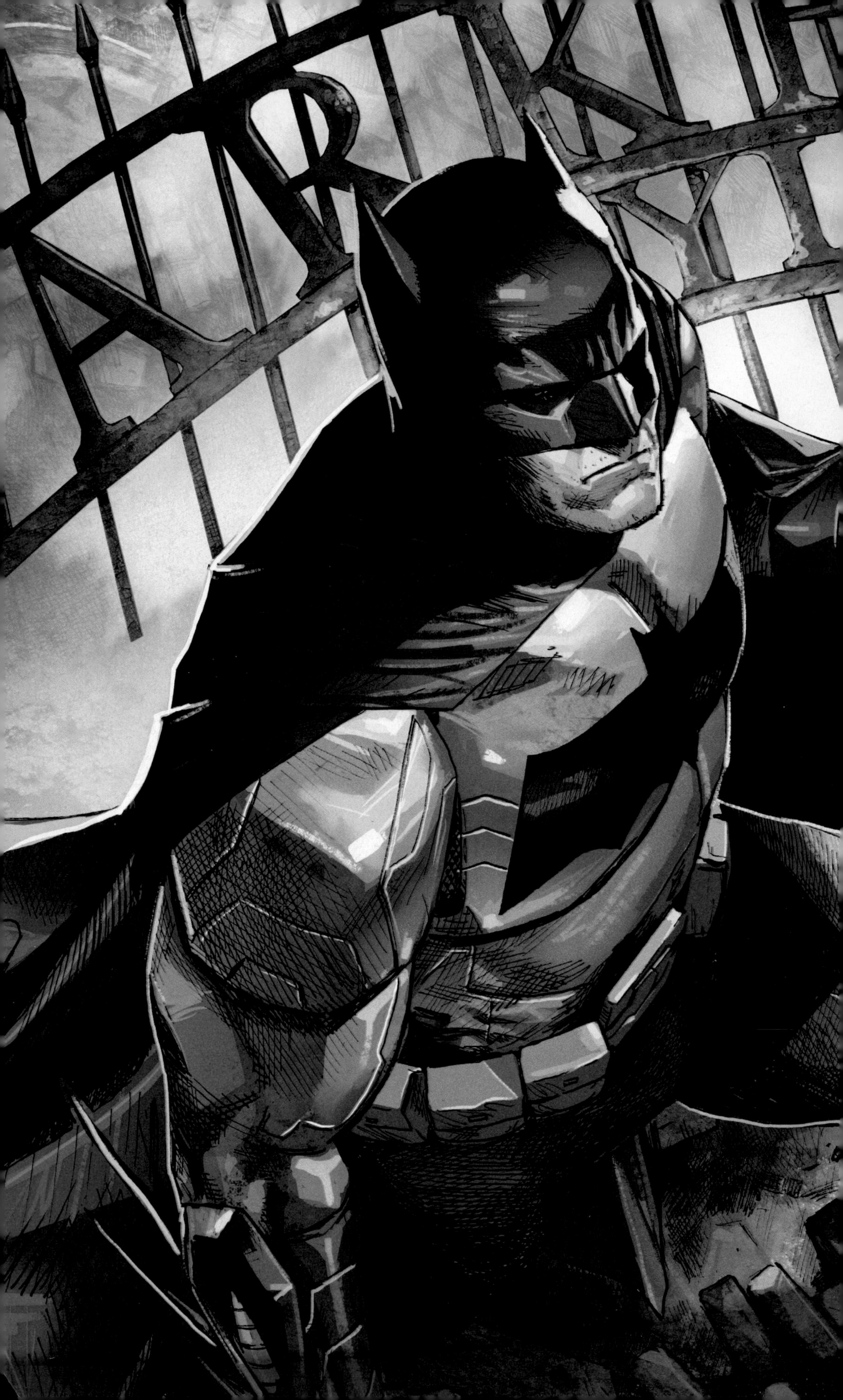

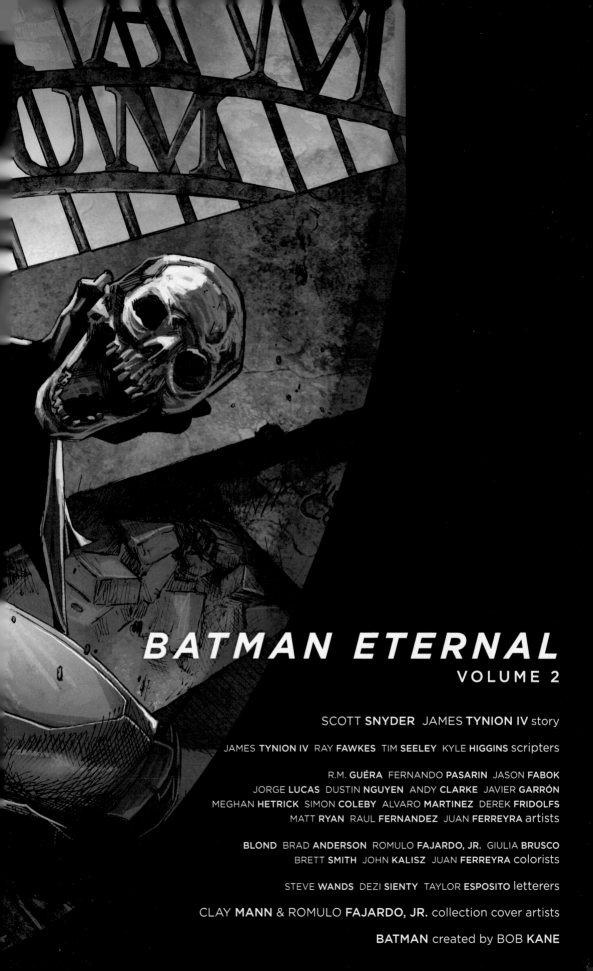

# BATMAN ETERNAL
## VOLUME 2

SCOTT **SNYDER**   JAMES **TYNION IV** story

JAMES **TYNION IV**   RAY **FAWKES**   TIM **SEELEY**   KYLE **HIGGINS** scripters

R.M. **GUÉRA**   FERNANDO **PASARIN**   JASON **FABOK**
JORGE **LUCAS**   DUSTIN **NGUYEN**   ANDY **CLARKE**   JAVIER **GARRÓN**
MEGHAN **HETRICK**   SIMON **COLEBY**   ALVARO **MARTINEZ**   DEREK **FRIDOLFS**
MATT **RYAN**   RAUL **FERNANDEZ**   JUAN **FERREYRA** artists

**BLOND**   BRAD **ANDERSON**   ROMULO **FAJARDO, JR.**   GIULIA **BRUSCO**
BRETT **SMITH**   JOHN **KALISZ**   JUAN **FERREYRA** colorists

STEVE **WANDS**   DEZI **SIENTY**   TAYLOR **ESPOSITO** letterers

CLAY **MANN** & ROMULO **FAJARDO, JR.** collection cover artists

**BATMAN** created by BOB **KANE**

CHRIS CONROY Editor – Original Series  DAVE WIELGOSZ  MATT HUMPHREYS Assistant Editors – Original Series
ROBIN WILDMAN Editor  ROBBIN BROSTERMAN Design Director – Books  ROBBIE BIEDERMAN Publication Design

BOB HARRAS Senior VP – Editor-in-Chief, DC Comics

DIANE NELSON President  DAN DIDIO and JIM LEE Co-Publishers  GEOFF JOHNS Chief Creative Officer
AMIT DESAI Senior VP – Marketing and Franchise Management
AMY GENKINS Senior VP – Business and Legal Affairs  NAIRI GARDINER Senior VP – Finance
JEFF BOISON VP – Publishing Planning  MARK CHIARELLO VP – Art Direction and Design
JOHN CUNNINGHAM VP – Marketing  TERRI CUNNINGHAM VP – Editorial Administration
LARRY GANEM VP – Talent Relations and Services  ALISON GILL Senior VP – Manufacturing and Operations
HANK KANALZ Senior VP – Vertigo and Integrated Publishing  JAY KOGAN VP – Business and Legal Affairs, Publishing
JACK MAHAN VP – Business Affairs, Talent  NICK NAPOLITANO VP – Manufacturing Administration  SUE POHJA VP – Book Sales
FRED RUIZ VP – Manufacturing Operations  COURTNEY SIMMONS Senior VP – Publicity  BOB WAYNE Senior VP – Sales

BATMAN ETERNAL VOLUME 2

DC Comics, 4000 Warner Blvd., Burbank, CA 91522
A Warner Bros. Entertainment Company.
Printed by RR Donnelley, Owensville, MO, USA. 6/12/15. First Printing.

ISBN: 978-1-4012-5231-1

Library of Congress Cataloging-in-Publication Data

Snyder, Scott, author.
Batman eternal volume 2 / Scott Snyder, writer ; Jason Fabok, Tim Seeley.
pages cm
ISBN 978-1-4012-5231-1 (paperback)
1.  Graphic novels.  I. Snyder, Scott, author. II. Fabok, Jason. III. Seeley, Tim. IV. Title.

PN6728.B36S659 2014
741.5'973—dc23

2014026870

SUSTAINABLE
FORESTRY
INITIATIVE

Certified Chain of Custody
20% Certified Forest Content,
80% Certified Sourcing
www.sfiprogram.org
SFI-01042
APPLIES TO TEXT STOCK ONLY

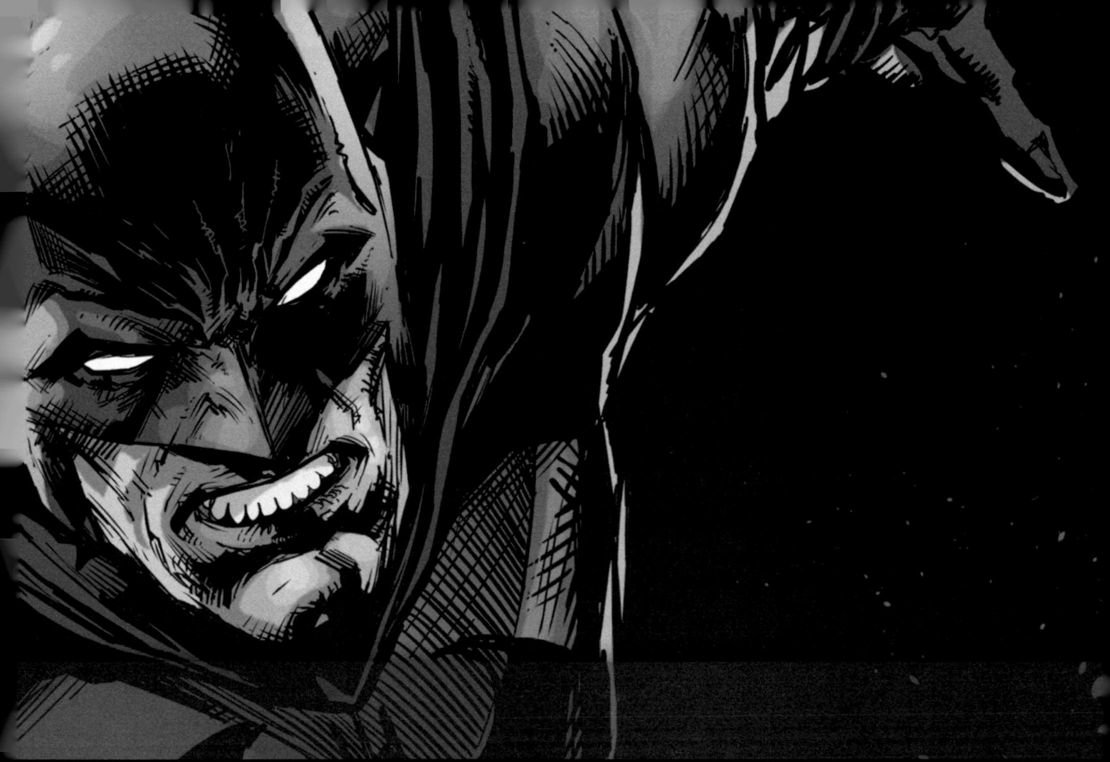

## THE STORY SO FAR

On the night Lieutenant Jason Bard arrived in Gotham, the young recruit's first act as a GCPD officer was to arrest his hero for manslaughter. Commissioner James Gordon had fired at what he thought was an armed assailant, but the bullet passed right through the target to hit a transformer causing a train collision that killed 162 people.

Batman uncovered that the man Gordon shot was a member of Carmine "The Roman" Falcone's gang. After five years away, Falcone had returned to rid Gotham of its "costumed freaks" and reclaim it as his own. It wasn't long before he had Mayor Sebastian Hady and the interim police commissioner, Jack Forbes, in his pocket, and he set about going to war with the Penguin. As the gang war brewed, Commissioner Forbes' GCPD was more interested in bringing down the Bat than The Roman.

Elsewhere in Gotham, young Stephanie Brown stumbled upon a plot by a group of villains led by her father, Cluemaster, and Red Robin teamed with wannabe hero Harper Row to track an infection of nanobots affecting Gotham's poorest children. And deep under Arkham Asylum Batwing and Jim Corrigan found Joker's Daughter using Arkham inmates to power a summoning to resurrect Deacon Blackfire and unleash literal hell on Earth.

With Gotham in chaos, Bard hatched a plan with Batman, Harvey Bullock, Maggie Sawyer, and Gotham Gazette reporter Vicki Vale. Together they tricked Forbes, Falcone, and Penguin into revealing their criminal activities. Bard was promoted to commissioner, and Falcone was granted extradition back to Hong Kong, where a criminal empire awaited him. Convinced Falcone had a role in framing Gordon, Batman confronted him. But Falcone revealed that he had been told of Gordon's impending fall by someone else, the real mastermind behind all these events.

Batgirl, Red Hood, and Batwoman traveled all the way to Brazil to track the men who framed Jim Gordon and eventually gathered enough evidence to free the former commissioner. However when Batman gave Bard the evidence absolving Gordon, Bard instead delivered release papers for Zachary Gate, The Architect!

At the same time, an intruder entered Wayne Manor and injected Alfred with a derivative of Scarecrow's fear toxin. As Bard destroyed the evidence that could free Gordon, he called Alfred's attacker, the man orchestrating all that had befallen Gotham: Hush! And the chaos that has

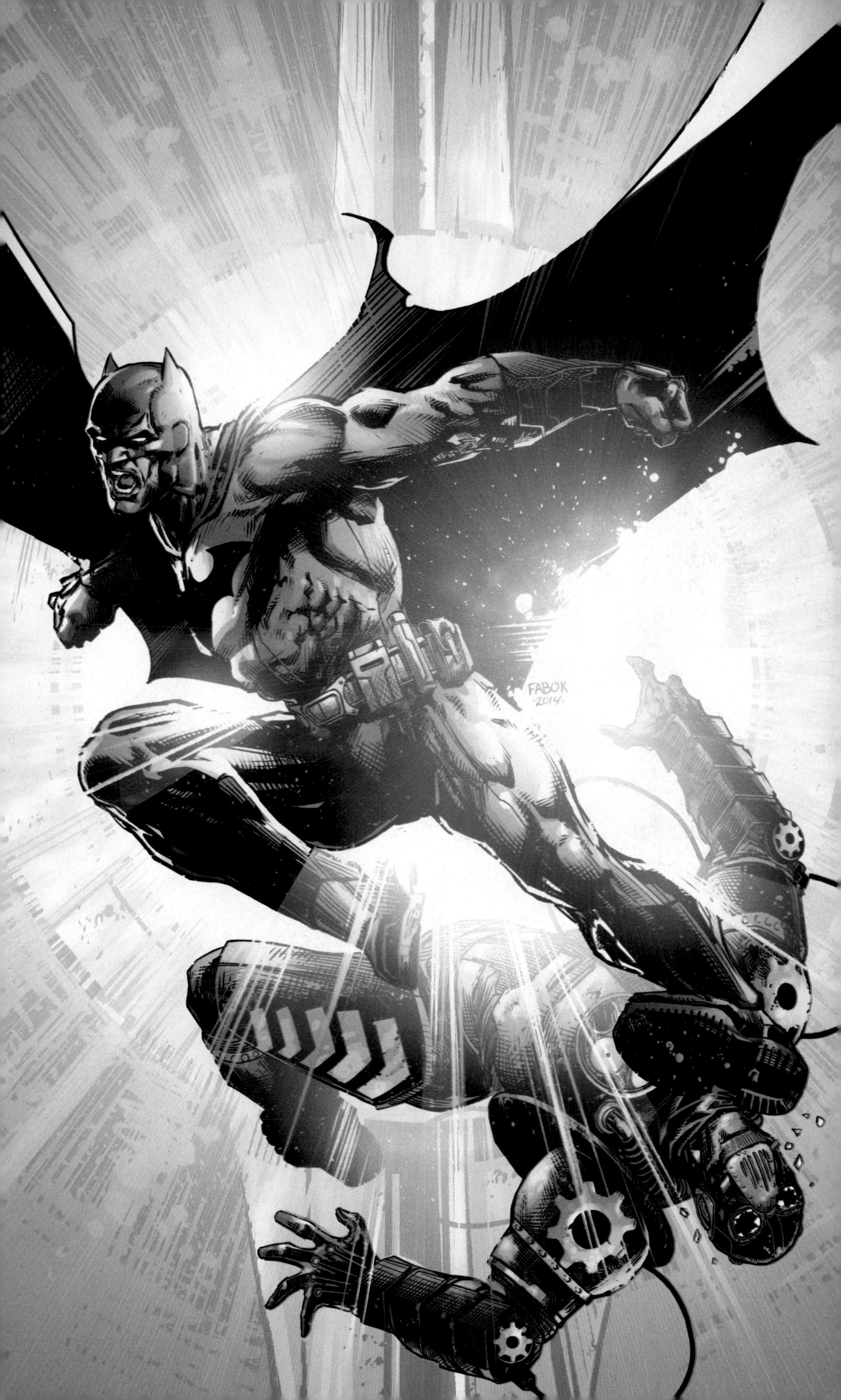
FABOK
2014

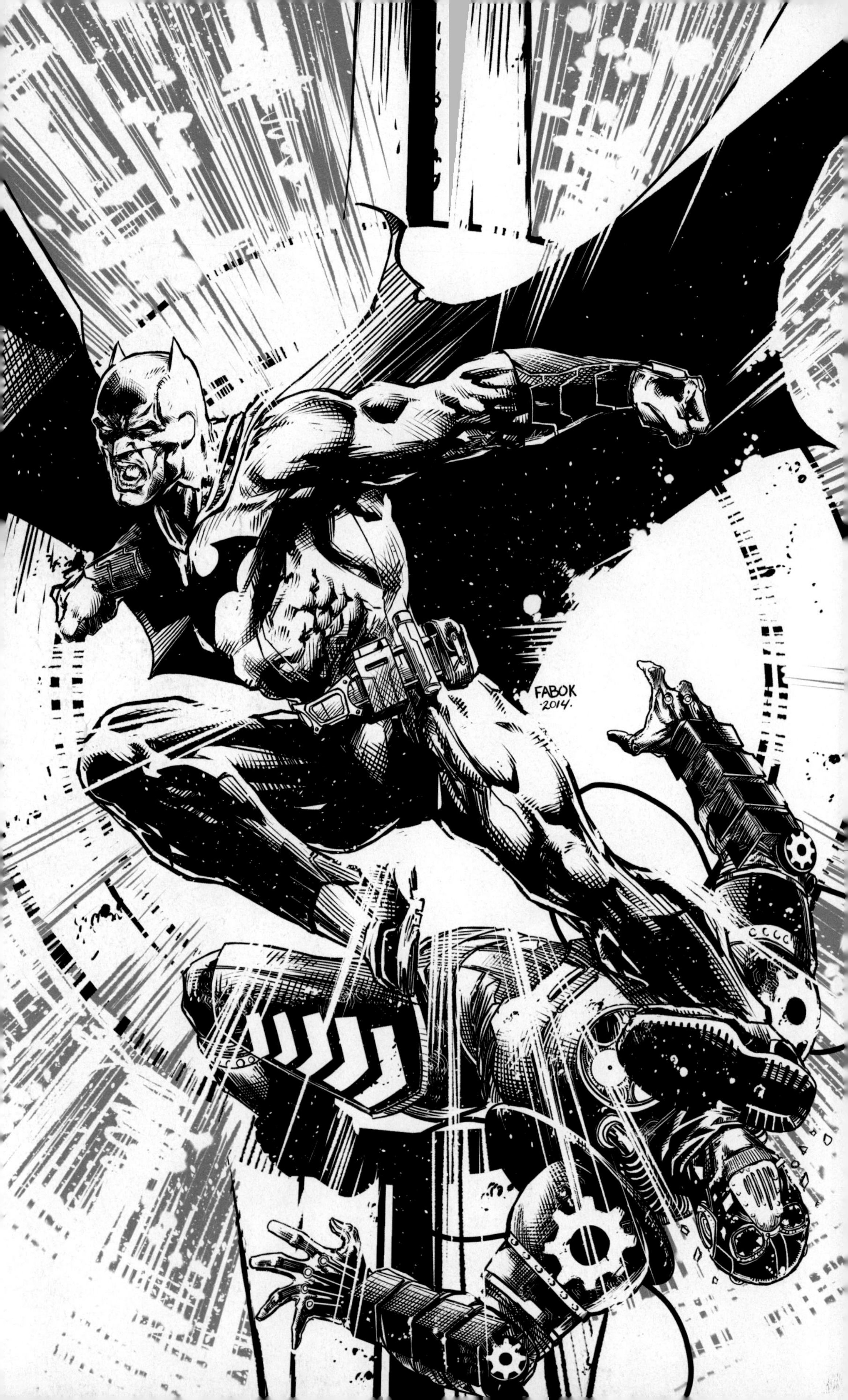
FABOK
2014

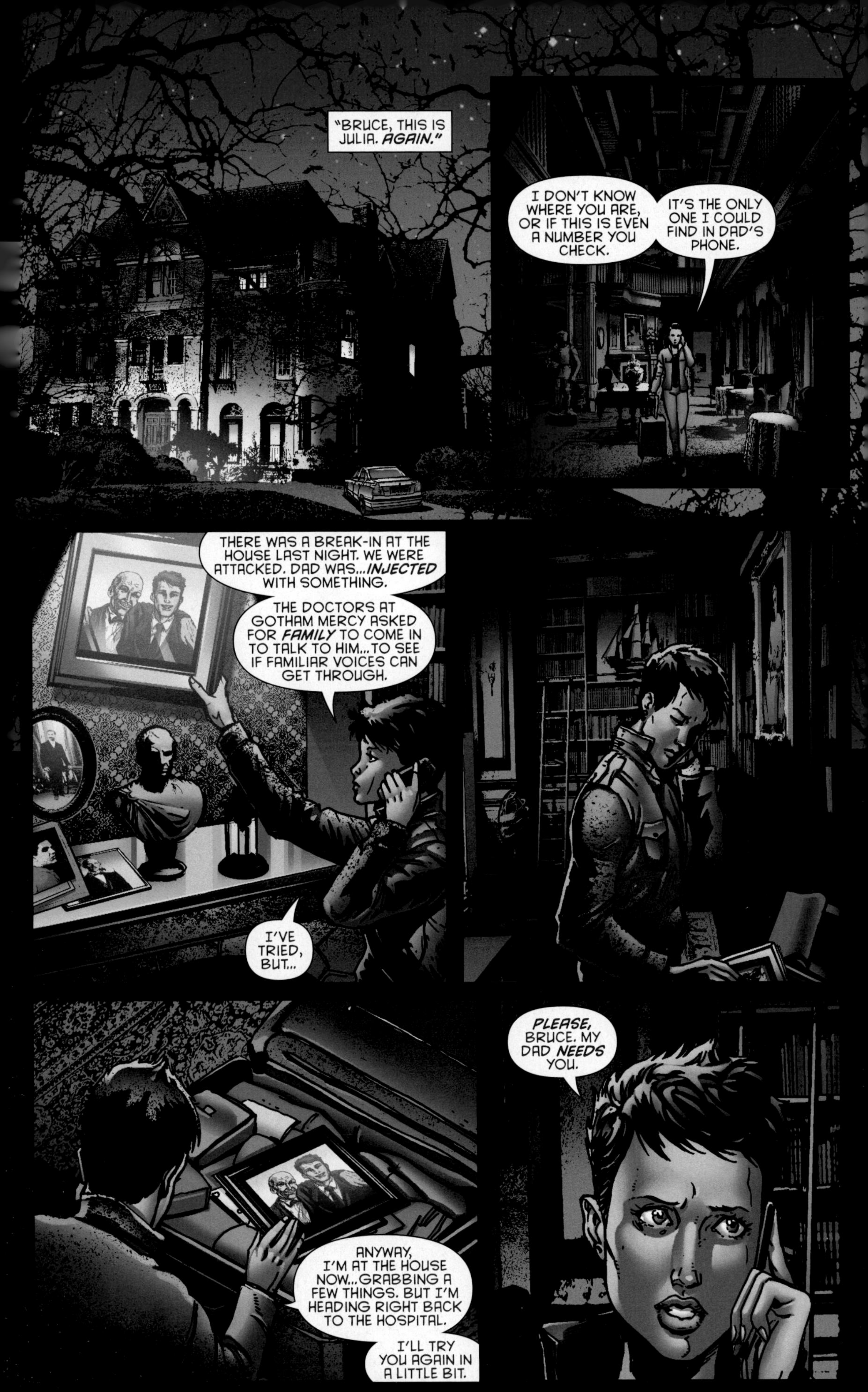
"BRUCE, THIS IS JULIA. AGAIN."
I DON'T KNOW WHERE YOU ARE, OR IF THIS IS EVEN A NUMBER YOU CHECK.
IT'S THE ONLY ONE I COULD FIND IN DAD'S PHONE.
THERE WAS A BREAK-IN AT THE HOUSE LAST NIGHT. WE WERE ATTACKED. DAD WAS...INJECTED WITH SOMETHING.
THE DOCTORS AT GOTHAM MERCY ASKED FOR FAMILY TO COME IN TO TALK TO HIM...TO SEE IF FAMILIAR VOICES CAN GET THROUGH.
I'VE TRIED, BUT...
ANYWAY, I'M AT THE HOUSE NOW...GRABBING A FEW THINGS. BUT I'M HEADING RIGHT BACK TO THE HOSPITAL.
I'LL TRY YOU AGAIN IN A LITTLE BIT.
PLEASE, BRUCE. MY DAD NEEDS YOU.

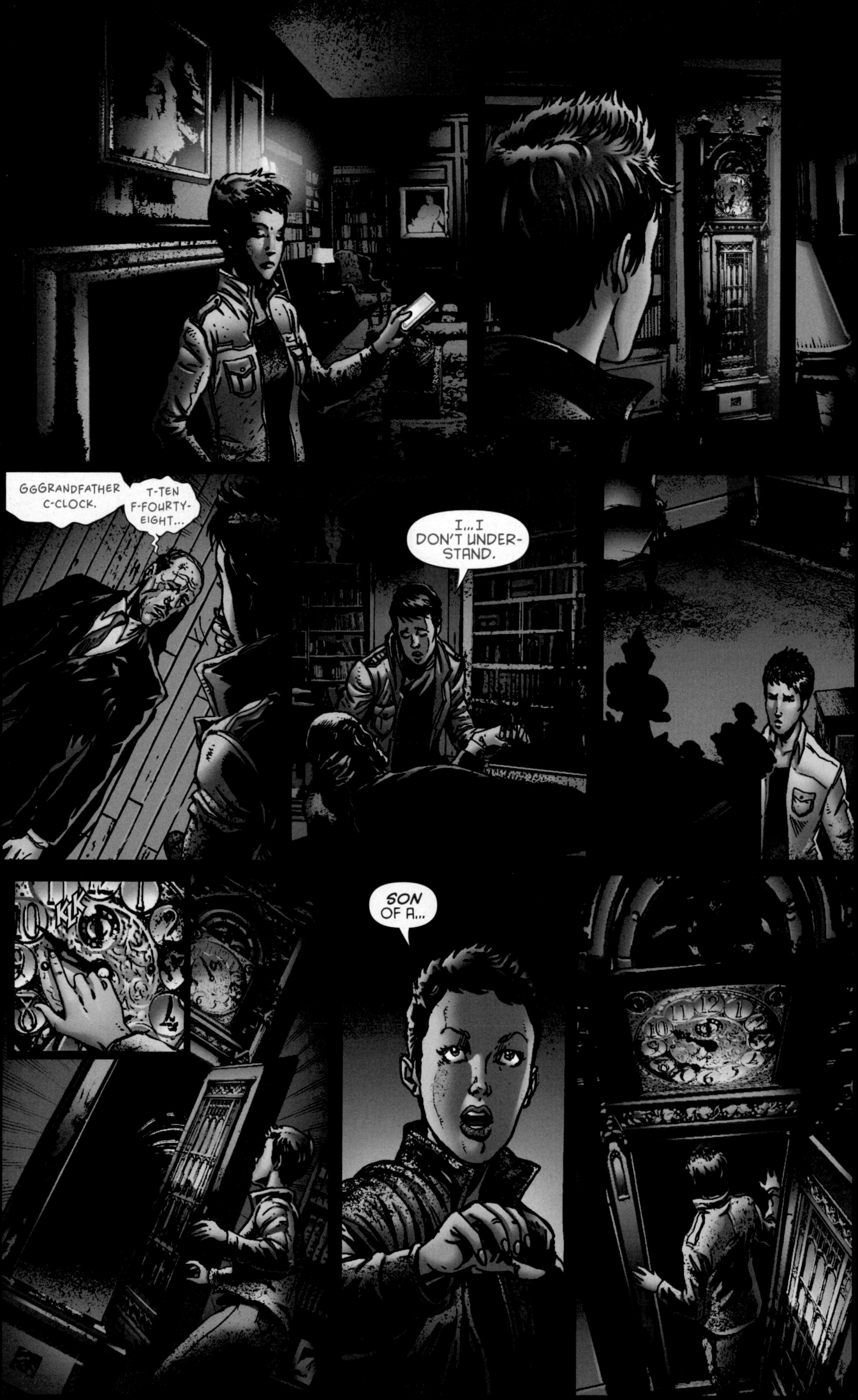
GGGRANDFATHER C-CLOCK.
T-TEN F-FOURTY-EIGHT...
I...I DON'T UNDER-STAND.
KLK
SON OF A...

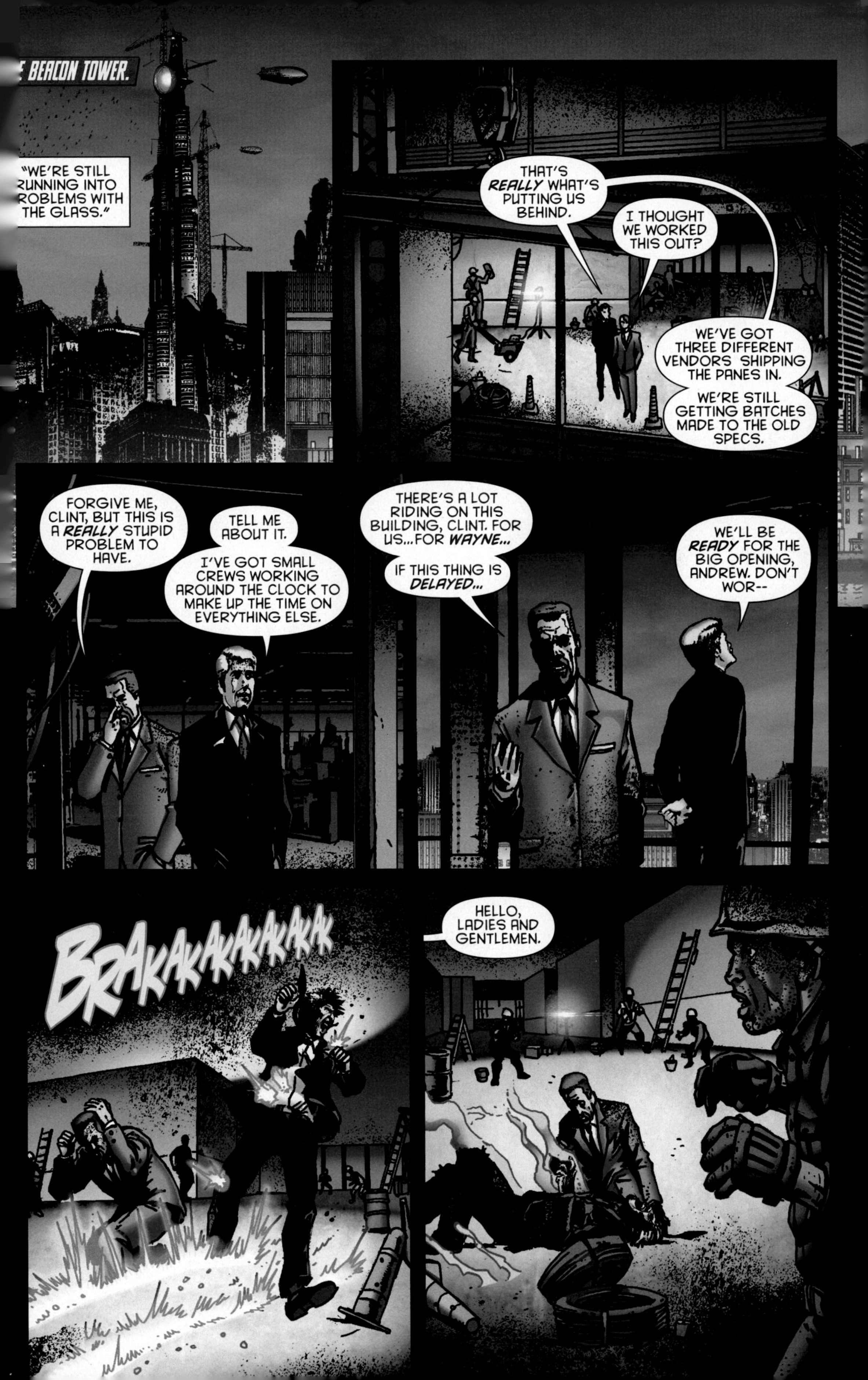
E BEACON TOWER.
"WE'RE STILL RUNNING INTO ROBLEMS WITH THE GLASS."
THAT'S REALLY WHAT'S PUTTING US BEHIND.
I THOUGHT WE WORKED THIS OUT?
WE'VE GOT THREE DIFFERENT VENDORS SHIPPING THE PANES IN.
WE'RE STILL GETTING BATCHES MADE TO THE OLD SPECS.
FORGIVE ME, CLINT, BUT THIS IS A REALLY STUPID PROBLEM TO HAVE.
TELL ME ABOUT IT.
I'VE GOT SMALL CREWS WORKING AROUND THE CLOCK TO MAKE UP THE TIME ON EVERYTHING ELSE.
THERE'S A LOT RIDING ON THIS BUILDING, CLINT. FOR US...FOR WAYNE...
IF THIS THING IS DELAYED...
WE'LL BE READY FOR THE BIG OPENING, ANDREW. DON'T WOR--
BRAKAKAKAKAKAKAK
HELLO, LADIES AND GENTLEMEN.

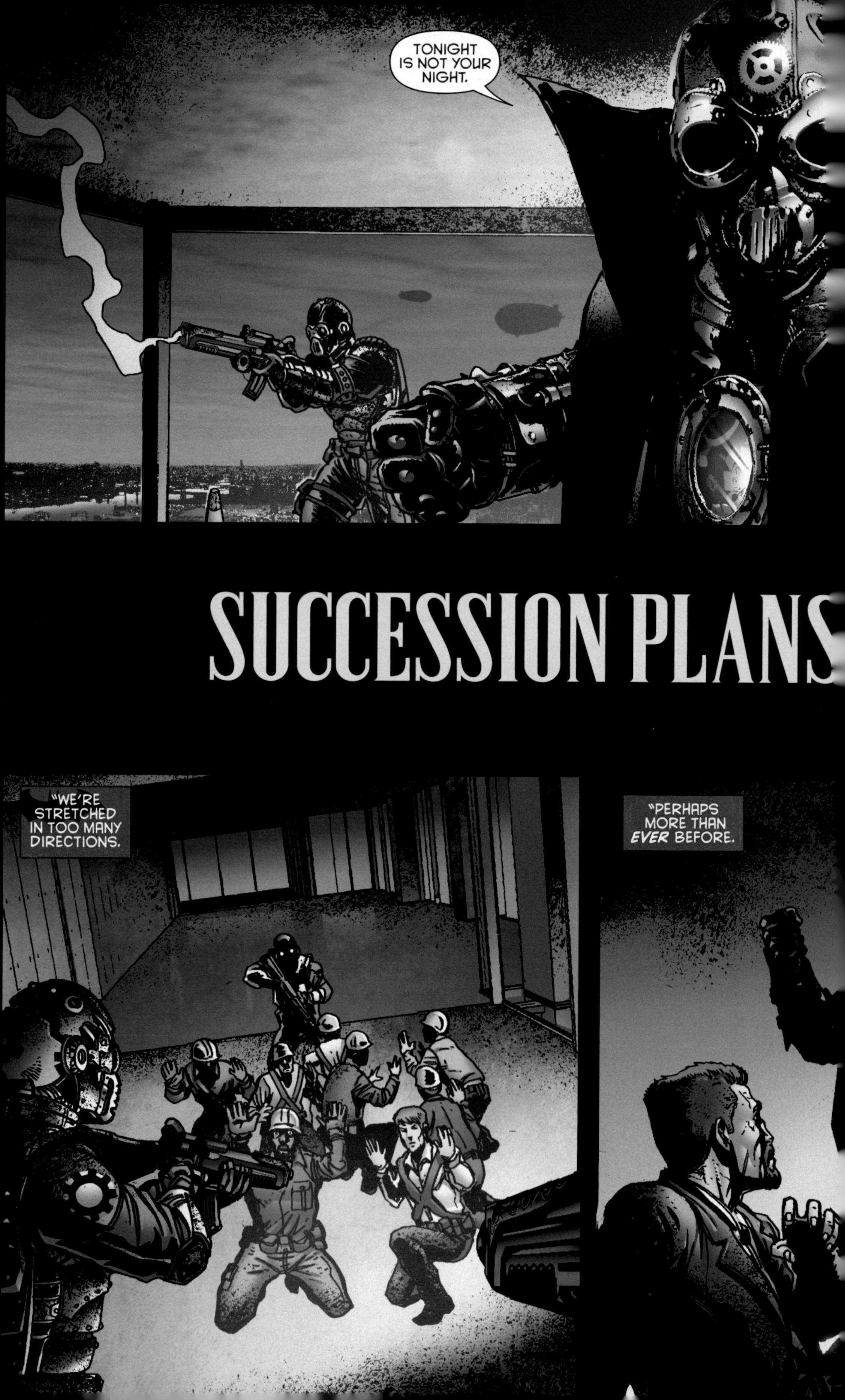
TONIGHT IS NOT YOUR NIGHT.
SUCCESSION PLANS
"WE'RE STRETCHED IN TOO MANY DIRECTIONS.
"PERHAPS MORE THAN *EVER* BEFORE.

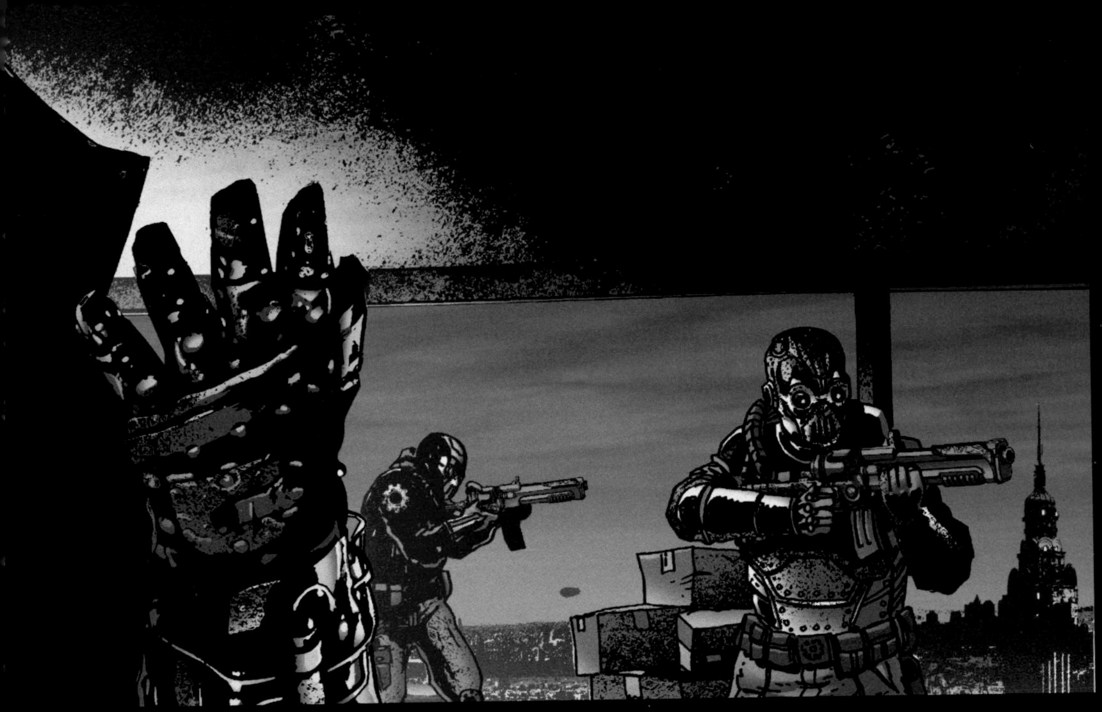

SCOTT SNYDER & JAMES TYNION IV STORY KYLE HIGGINS SCRIPT
RAY FAWKES & TIM SEELEY CONSULTING WRITERS JORGE LUCAS ART
BRETT SMITH COLORS DEZI SIENTY LETTERS JAY FABOK & BRAD ANDERSON COVER

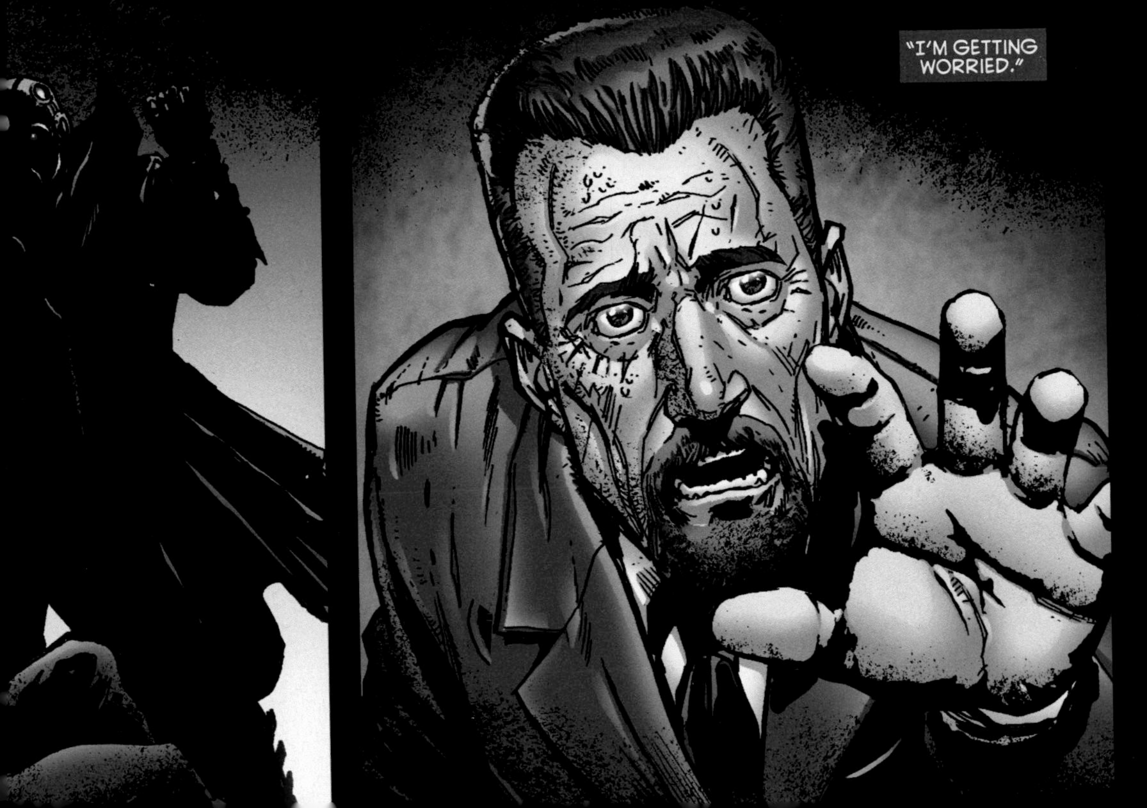
"I'M GETTING WORRIED."

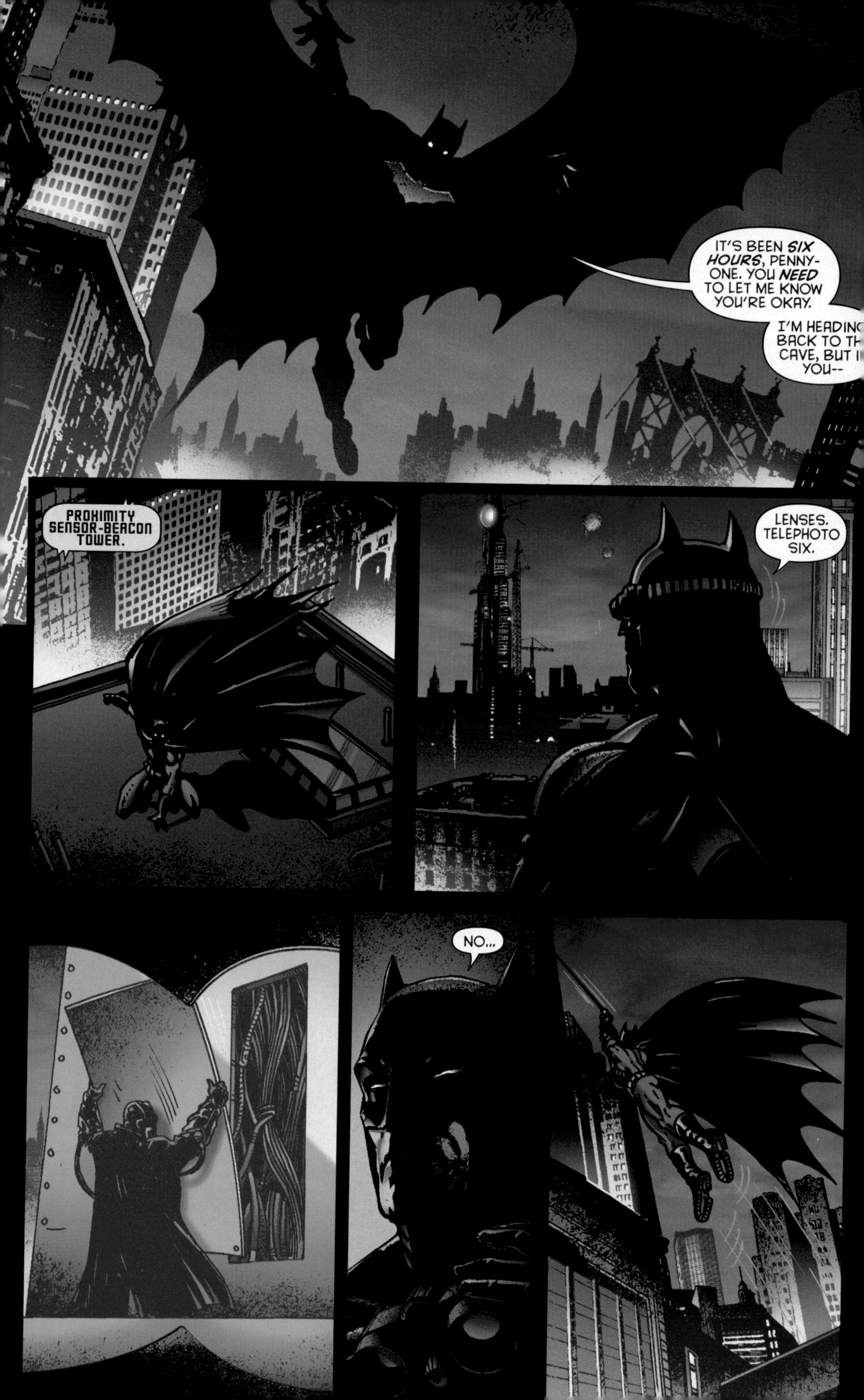
IT'S BEEN SIX HOURS, PENNY-ONE. YOU NEED TO LET ME KNOW YOU'RE OKAY.
I'M HEADING BACK TO THE CAVE, BUT IF YOU--
PROXIMITY SENSOR-BEACON TOWER.
LENSES. TELEPHOTO SIX.
NO...

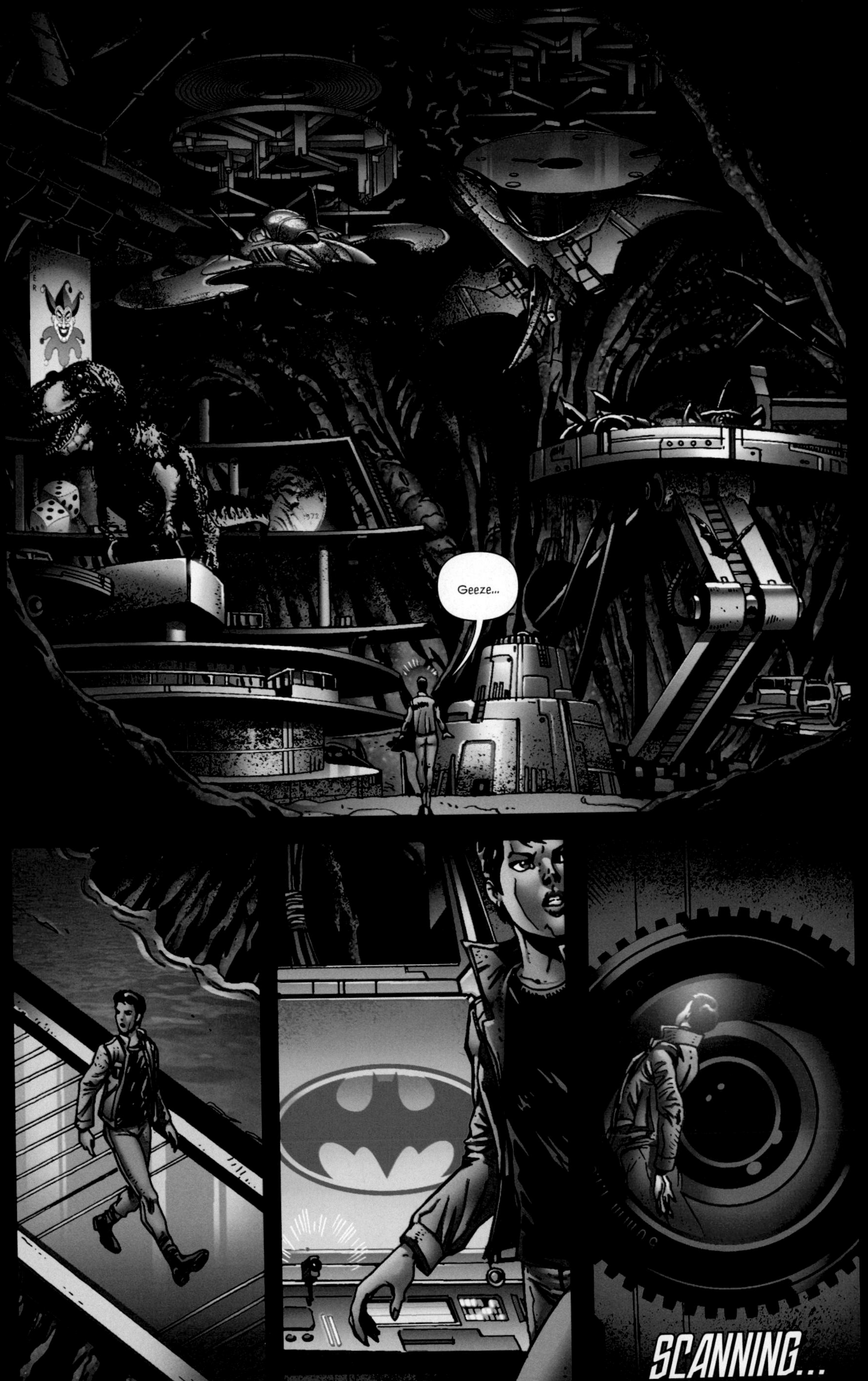
Geeze...
SCANNING...

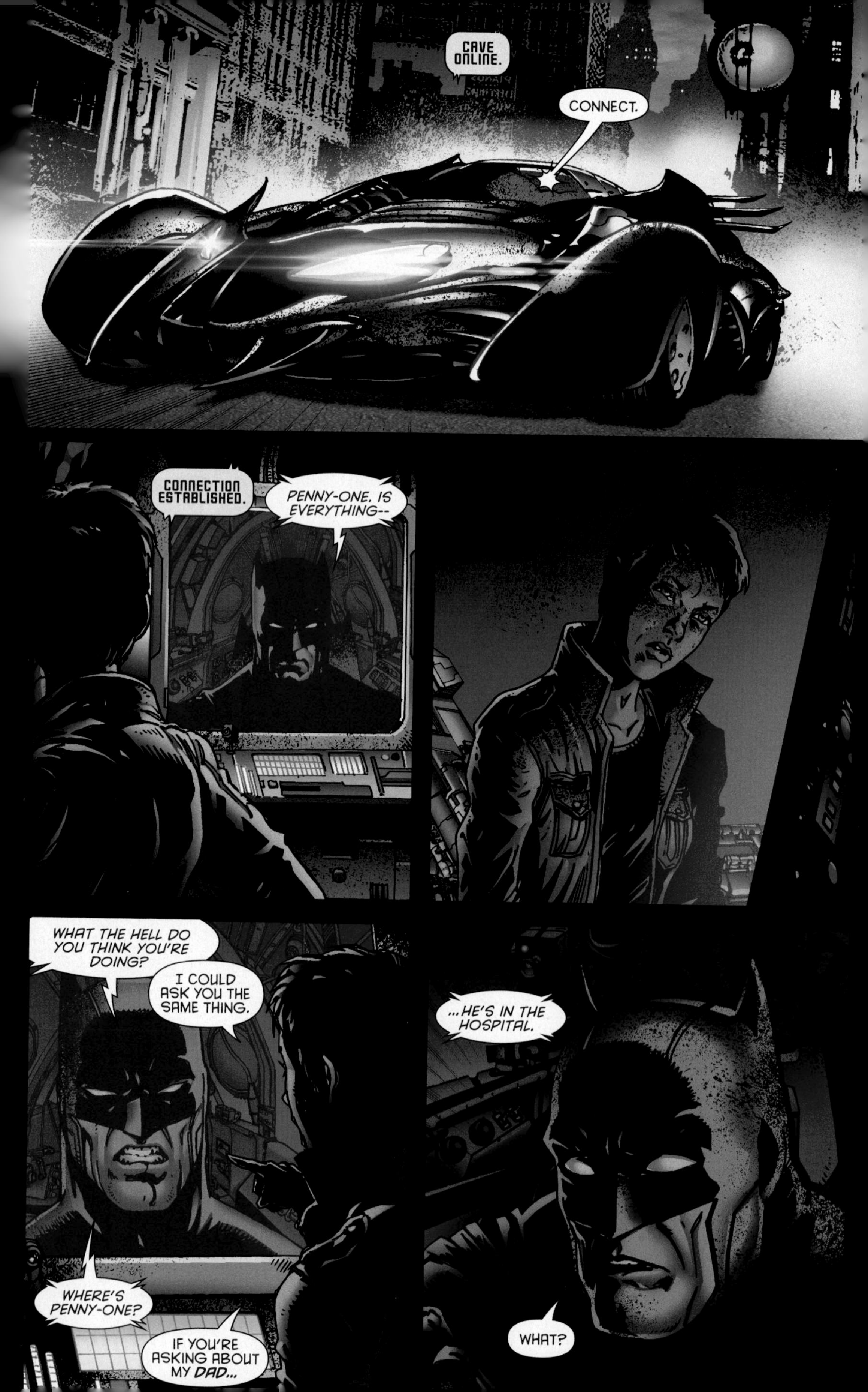

CAVE ONLINE.
CONNECT.
CONNECTION ESTABLISHED.
PENNY-ONE. IS EVERYTHING--
WHAT THE HELL DO YOU THINK YOU'RE DOING?
I COULD ASK YOU THE SAME THING.
WHERE'S PENNY-ONE?
IF YOU'RE ASKING ABOUT MY DAD...
...HE'S IN THE HOSPITAL.
WHAT?

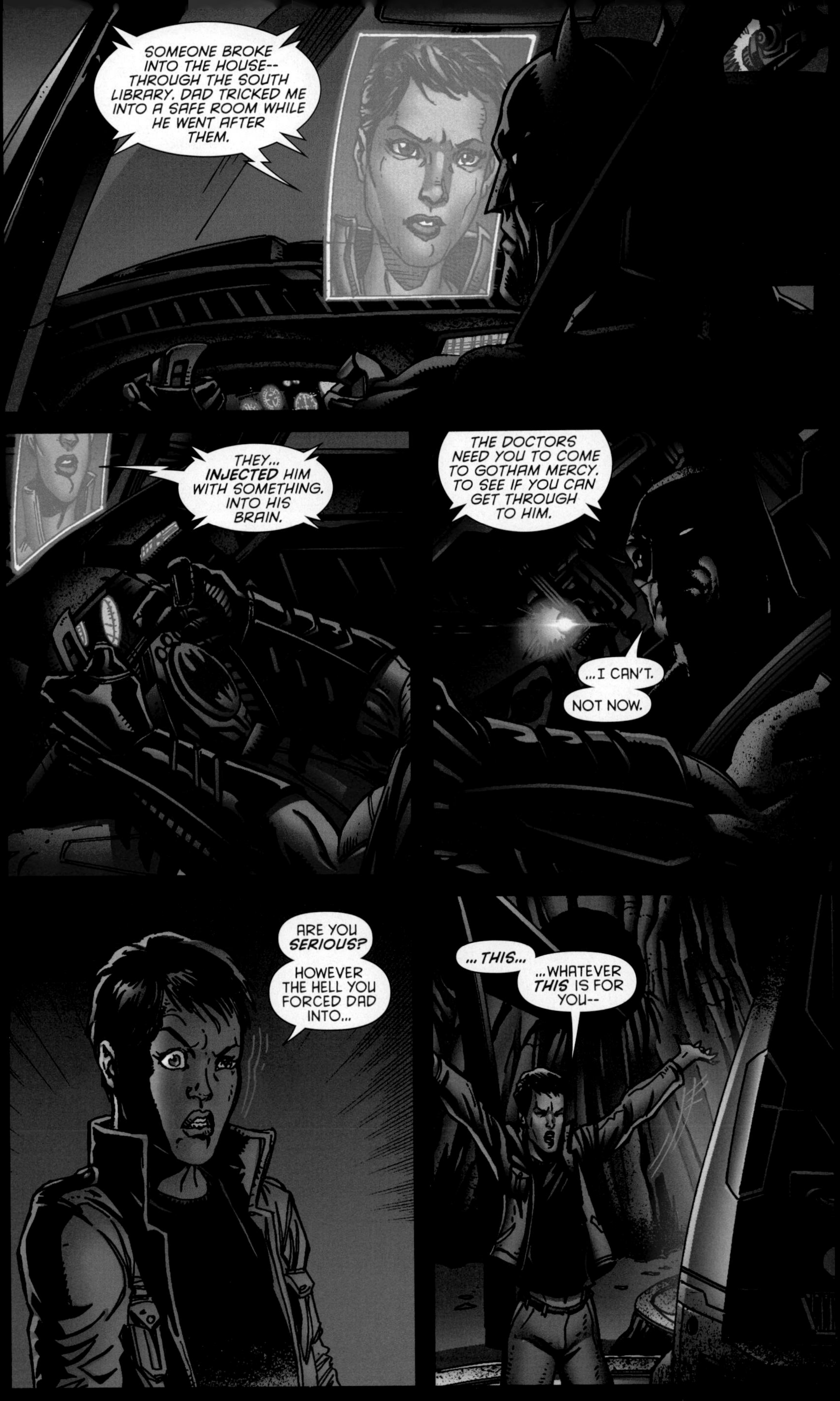
SOMEONE BROKE INTO THE HOUSE-- THROUGH THE SOUTH LIBRARY. DAD TRICKED ME INTO A SAFE ROOM WHILE HE WENT AFTER THEM.
THEY... INJECTED HIM WITH SOMETHING. INTO HIS BRAIN.
THE DOCTORS NEED YOU TO COME TO GOTHAM MERCY. TO SEE IF YOU CAN GET THROUGH TO HIM.
...I CAN'T.
NOT NOW.
ARE YOU SERIOUS?
HOWEVER THE HELL YOU FORCED DAD INTO...
...THIS...
...WHATEVER THIS IS FOR YOU--

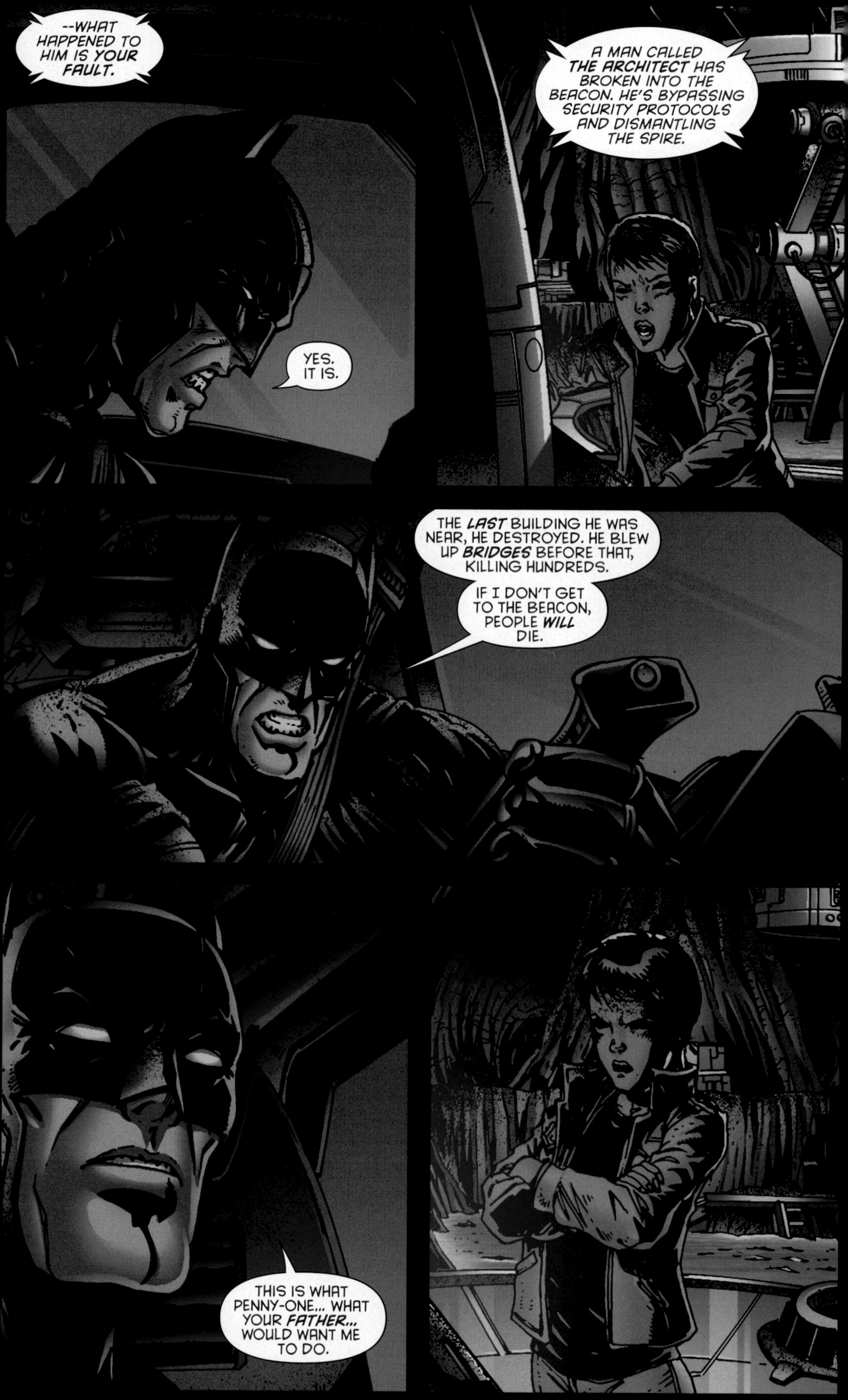
--WHAT HAPPENED TO HIM IS YOUR FAULT.
A MAN CALLED THE ARCHITECT HAS BROKEN INTO THE BEACON. HE'S BYPASSING SECURITY PROTOCOLS AND DISMANTLING THE SPIRE.
YES. IT IS.
THE LAST BUILDING HE WAS NEAR, HE DESTROYED. HE BLEW UP BRIDGES BEFORE THAT, KILLING HUNDREDS.
IF I DON'T GET TO THE BEACON, PEOPLE WILL DIE.
THIS IS WHAT PENNY-ONE... WHAT YOUR FATHER... WOULD WANT ME TO DO.

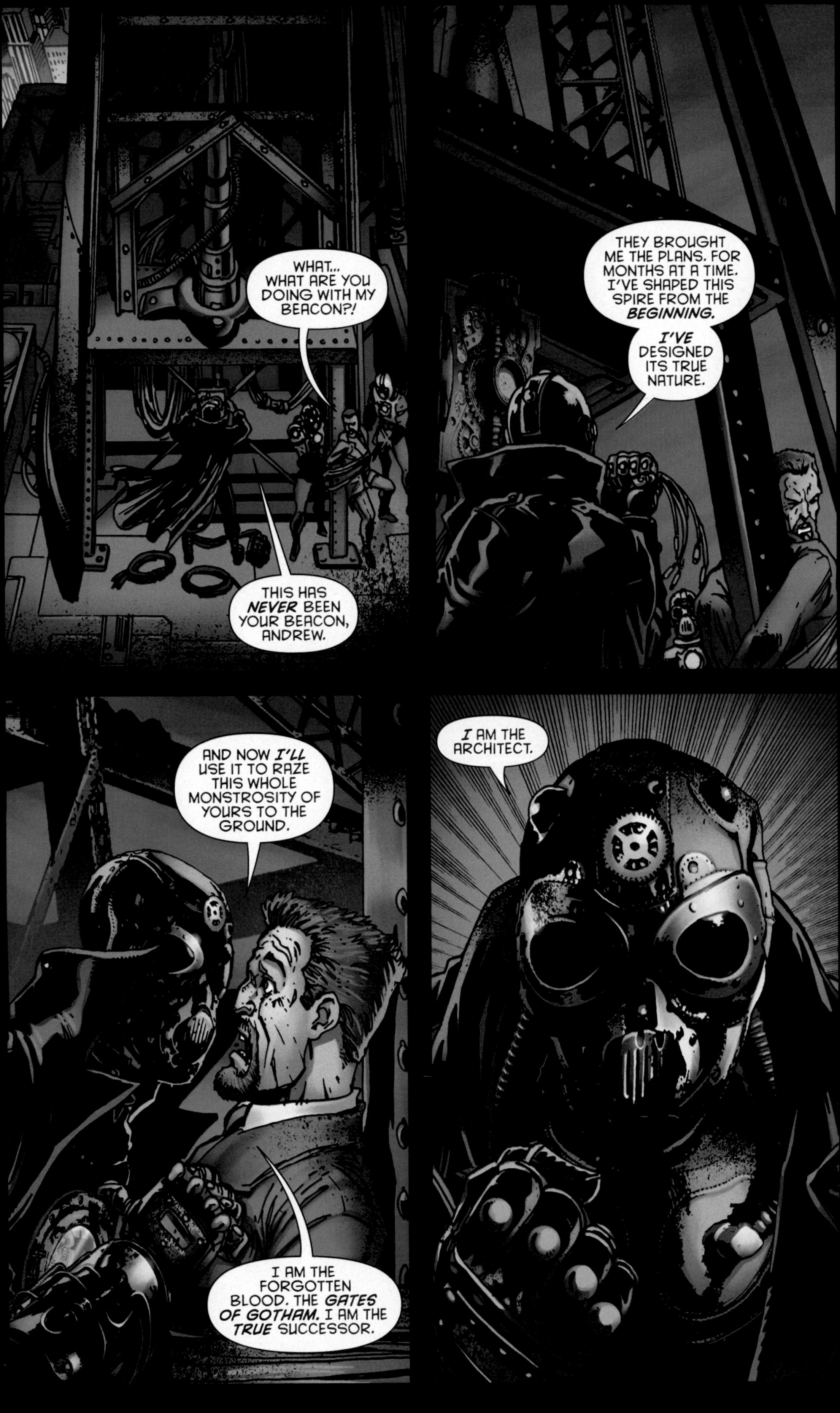
WHAT... WHAT ARE YOU DOING WITH MY BEACON?!
THIS HAS *NEVER* BEEN YOUR BEACON, ANDREW.
THEY BROUGHT ME THE PLANS. FOR MONTHS AT A TIME. I'VE SHAPED THIS SPIRE FROM THE *BEGINNING.*
*I'VE* DESIGNED ITS TRUE NATURE.
AND NOW *I'LL* USE IT TO RAZE THIS WHOLE MONSTROSITY OF YOURS TO THE GROUND.
I AM THE FORGOTTEN BLOOD. THE *GATES OF GOTHAM.* I AM THE *TRUE* SUCCESSOR.
*I* AM THE ARCHITECT.

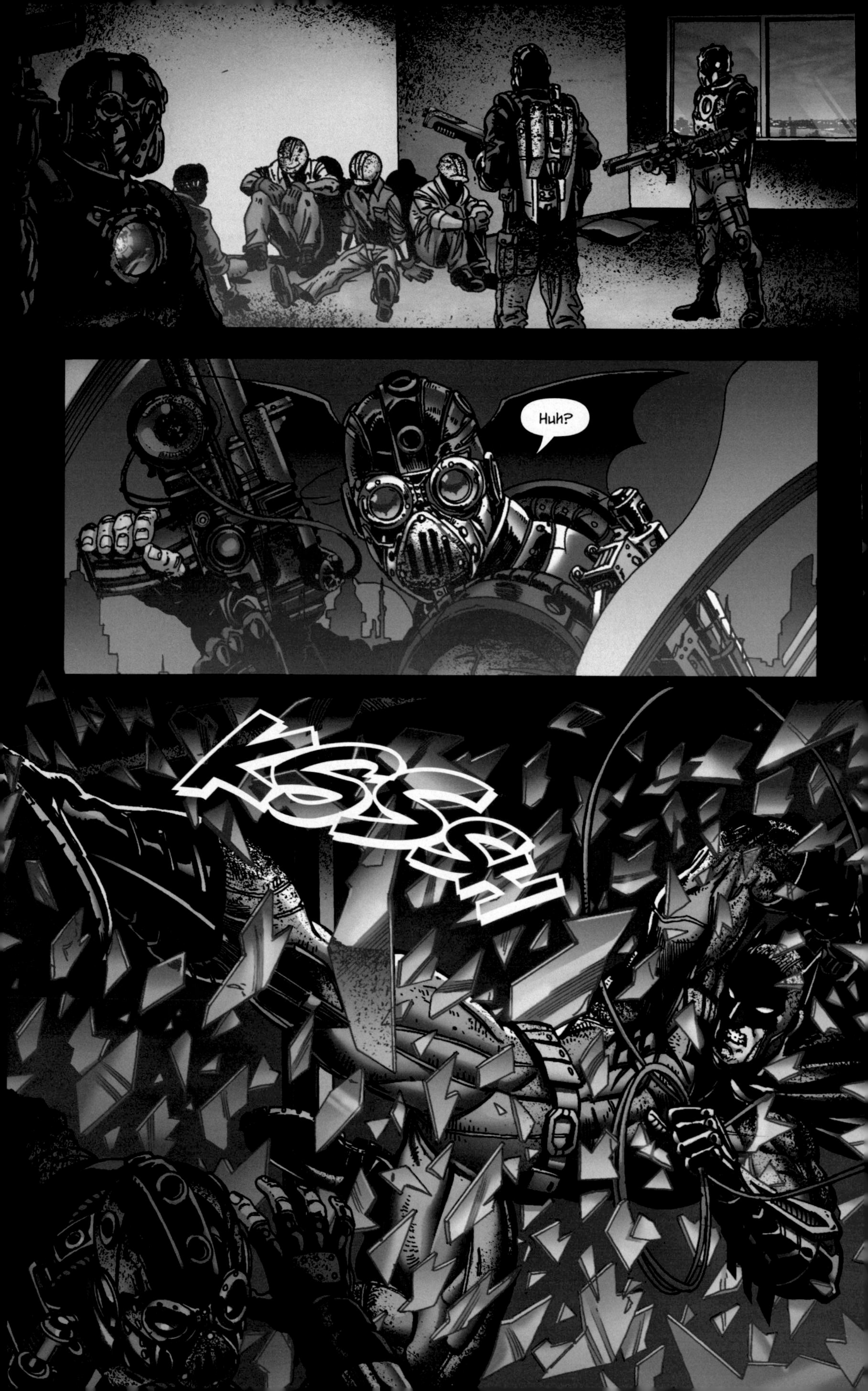
Huh?
KSSSH

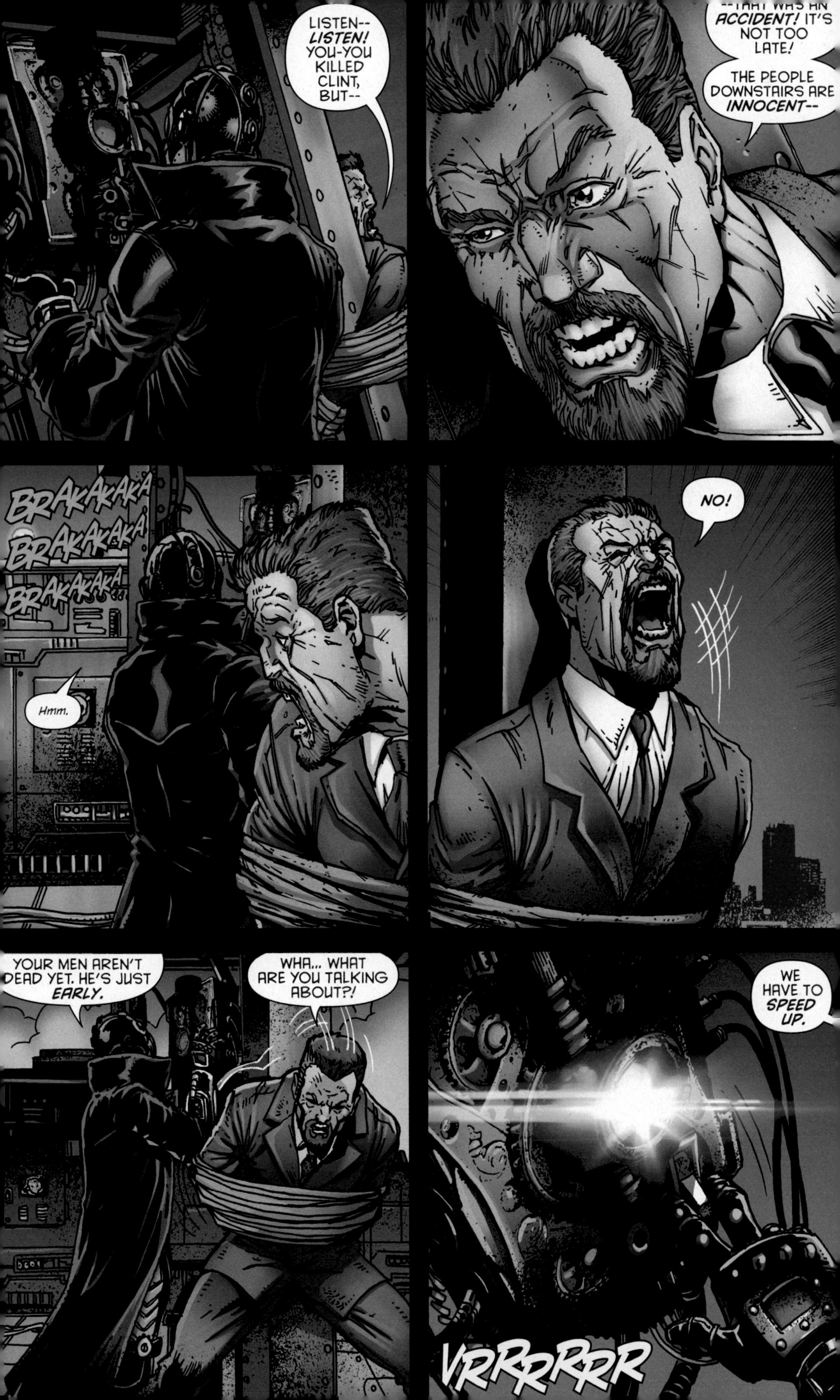
LISTEN-- LISTEN! YOU-YOU KILLED CLINT, BUT--
--THAT WAS AN ACCIDENT! IT'S NOT TOO LATE!
THE PEOPLE DOWNSTAIRS ARE INNOCENT--
BRAKAKAKA BRAKAKAKA BRAKAKAKA
Hmm.
NO!
YOUR MEN AREN'T DEAD YET. HE'S JUST EARLY.
WHA... WHAT ARE YOU TALKING ABOUT?!
WE HAVE TO SPEED UP.
VRRRRRR

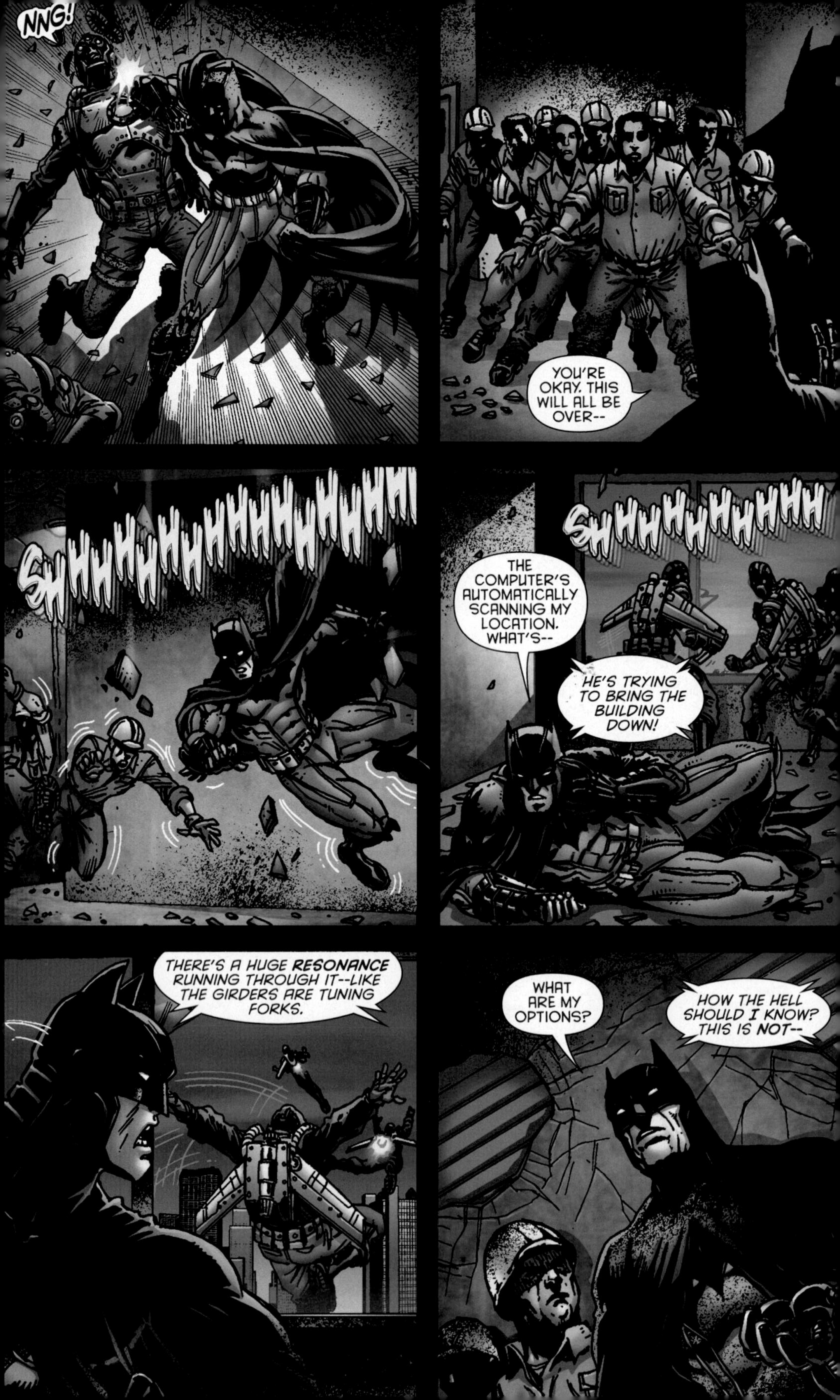
NNG!
YOU'RE OKAY. THIS WILL ALL BE OVER--
SHHHHHHHHHHHHHHHHH
SHHHHHHHHHHHH
THE COMPUTER'S AUTOMATICALLY SCANNING MY LOCATION. WHAT'S--
HE'S TRYING TO BRING THE BUILDING DOWN!
THERE'S A HUGE RESONANCE RUNNING THROUGH IT--LIKE THE GIRDERS ARE TUNING FORKS.
WHAT ARE MY OPTIONS?
HOW THE HELL SHOULD I KNOW? THIS IS NOT--

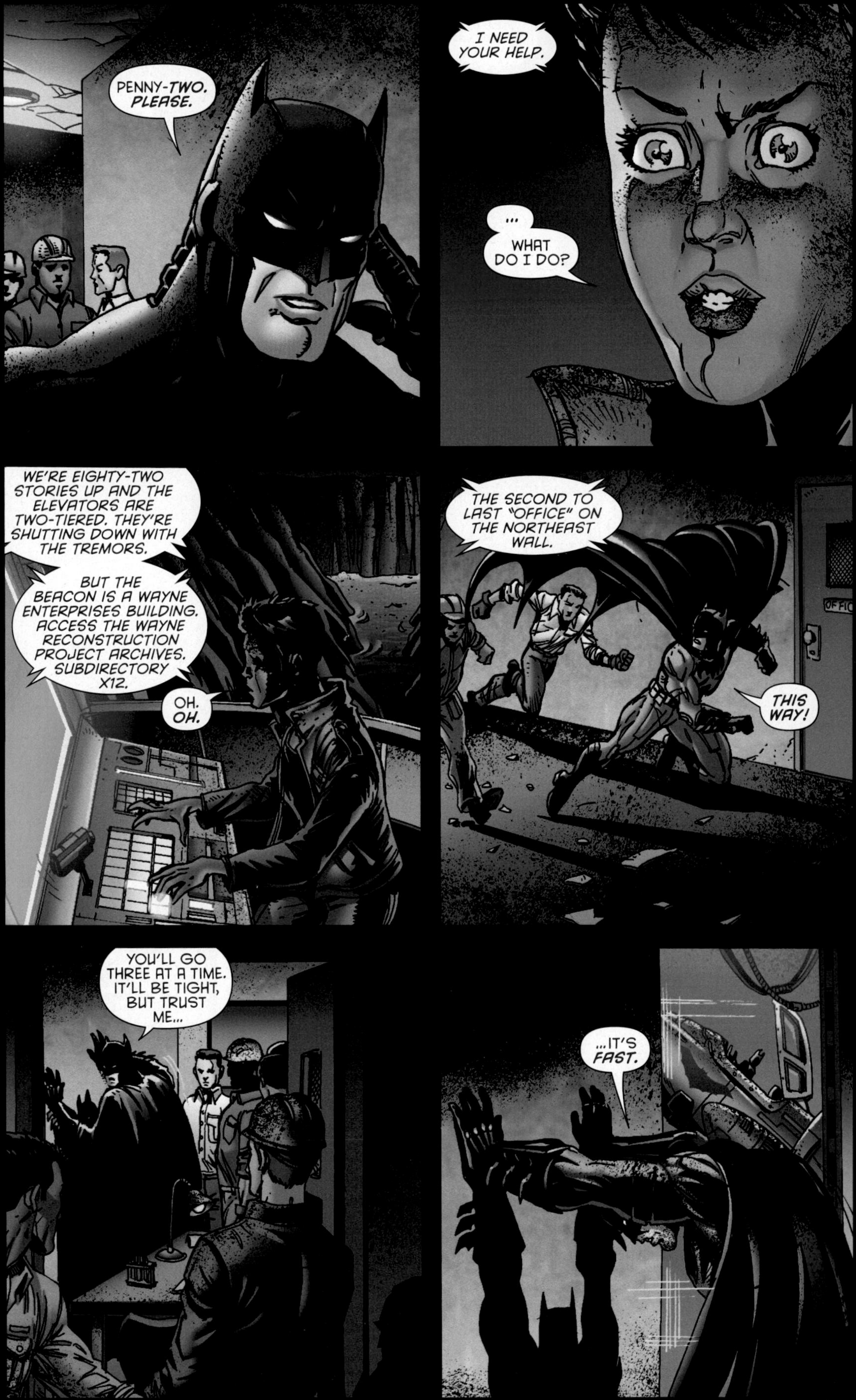
PENNY-TWO. PLEASE.
I NEED YOUR HELP.
... WHAT DO I DO?
WE'RE EIGHTY-TWO STORIES UP AND THE ELEVATORS ARE TWO-TIERED. THEY'RE SHUTTING DOWN WITH THE TREMORS.
BUT THE BEACON IS A WAYNE ENTERPRISES BUILDING. ACCESS THE WAYNE RECONSTRUCTION PROJECT ARCHIVES. SUBDIRECTORY X12.
OH. OH.
THE SECOND TO LAST "OFFICE" ON THE NORTHEAST WALL.
THIS WAY!
YOU'LL GO THREE AT A TIME. IT'LL BE TIGHT, BUT TRUST ME...
...IT'S FAST.

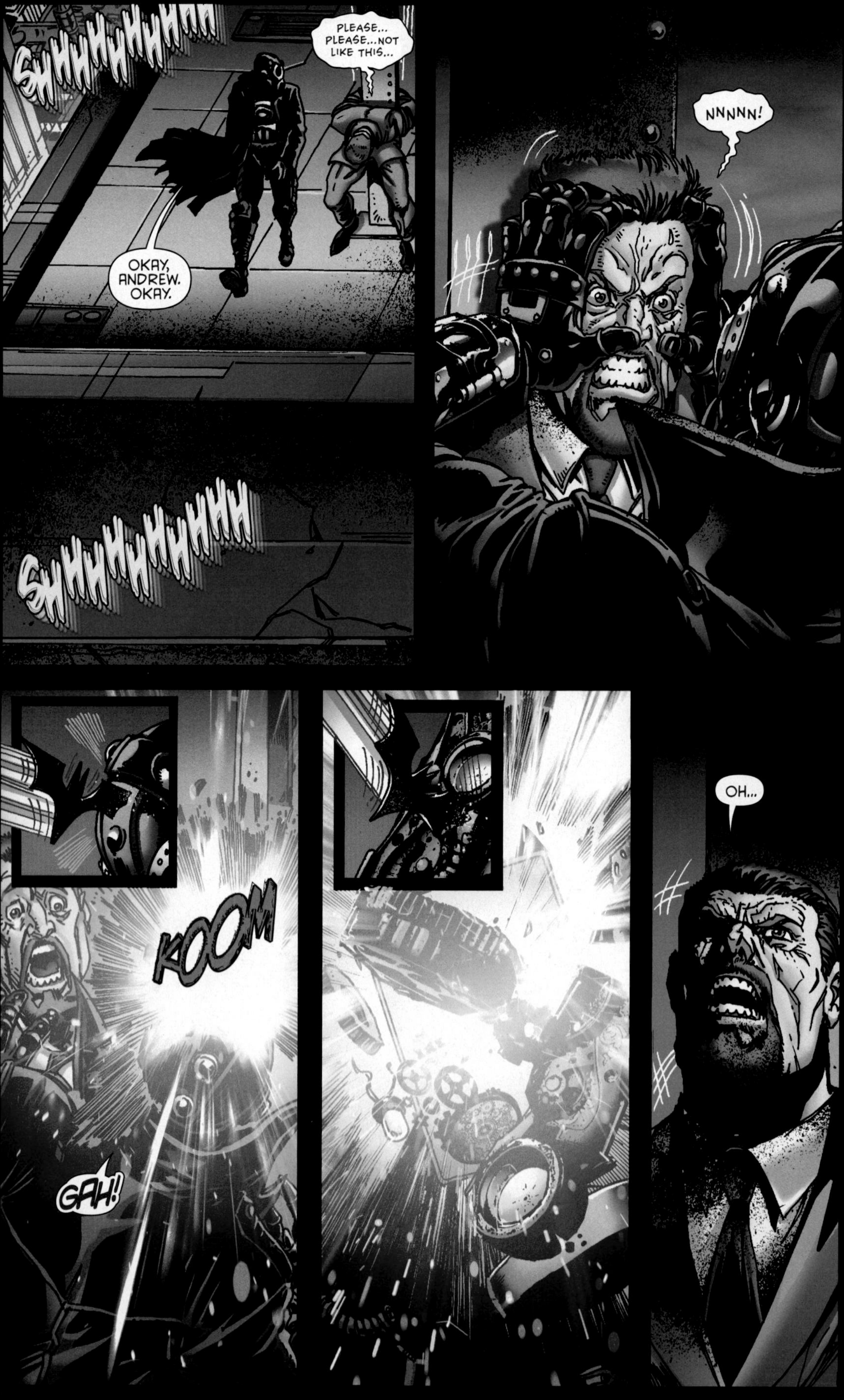
SHHHHHHHHH
PLEASE... PLEASE...NOT LIKE THIS...
OKAY, ANDREW. OKAY.
SHHHHHHHHH
NNNNN!
KOOM
GAH!
OH...

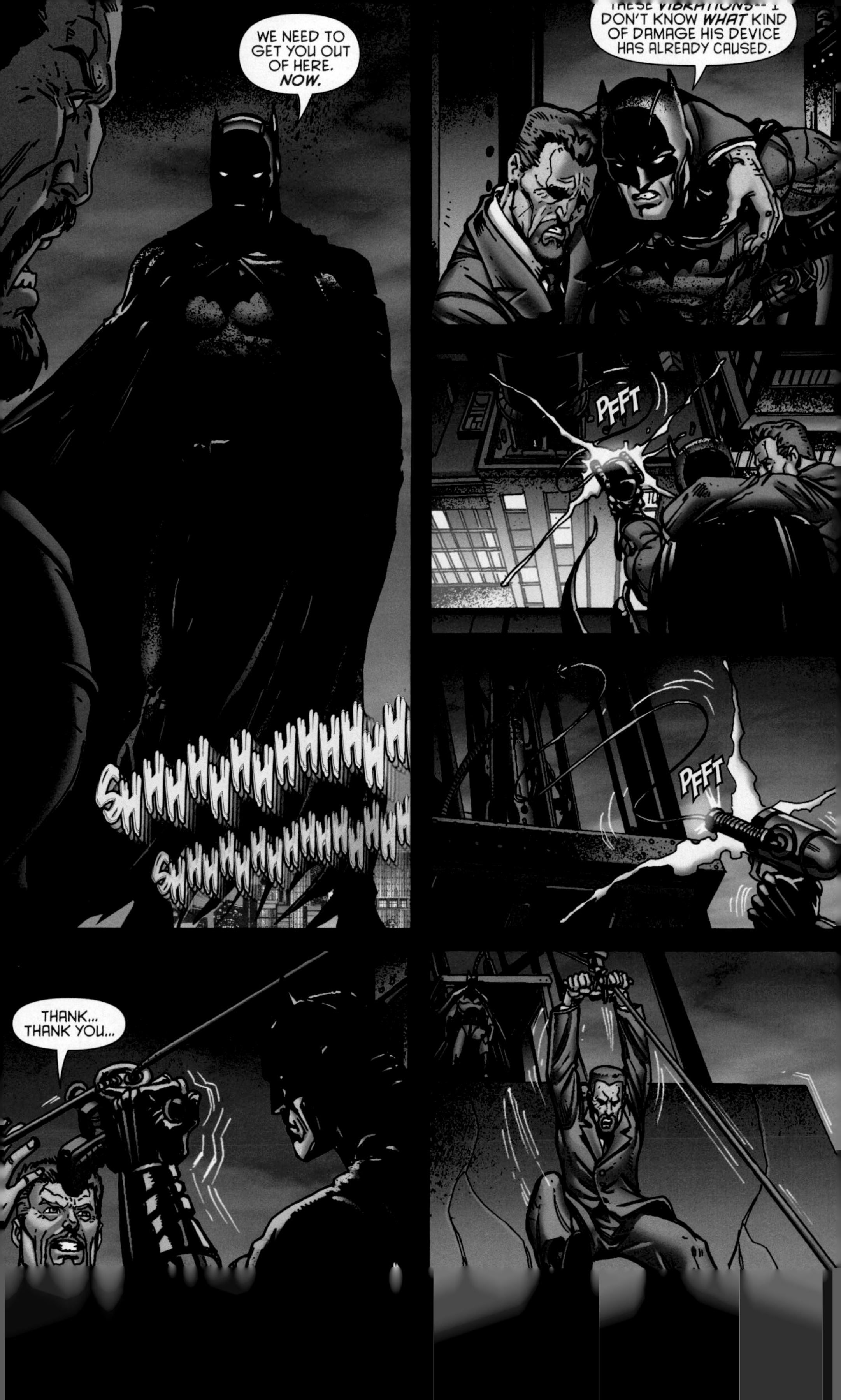
WE NEED TO GET YOU OUT OF HERE. NOW.
SHHHHHHHHHHHHHHHHH
SHHHHHHHHHHHHHHHHH
THESE VIBRATIONS-- I DON'T KNOW WHAT KIND OF DAMAGE HIS DEVICE HAS ALREADY CAUSED.
PFFT
PFFT
THANK... THANK YOU...

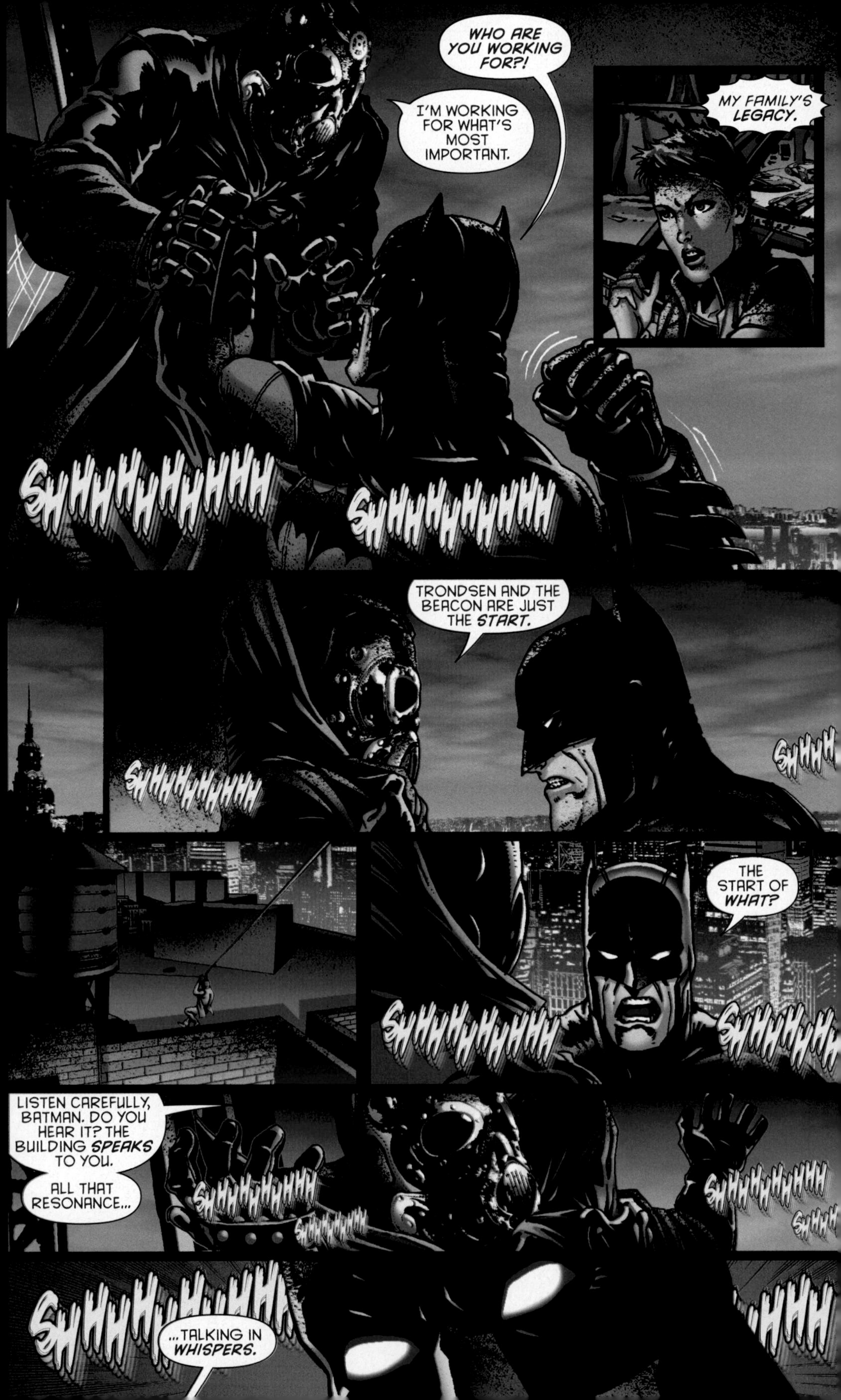

WHO ARE YOU WORKING FOR?!
I'M WORKING FOR WHAT'S MOST IMPORTANT.
MY FAMILY'S LEGACY.
SHHHHHHHHHH
SHHHHHHHHHH
TRONDSEN AND THE BEACON ARE JUST THE START.
SHHHHHHHHH
SHHH
THE START OF WHAT?
SHHHHHHHHHH
SHHHHHHH
LISTEN CAREFULLY, BATMAN. DO YOU HEAR IT? THE BUILDING SPEAKS TO YOU.
ALL THAT RESONANCE...
SHHHHHHHHHH
SHHHHHHHHH
SHHHHHHHHHH
SHHH
...TALKING IN WHISPERS.

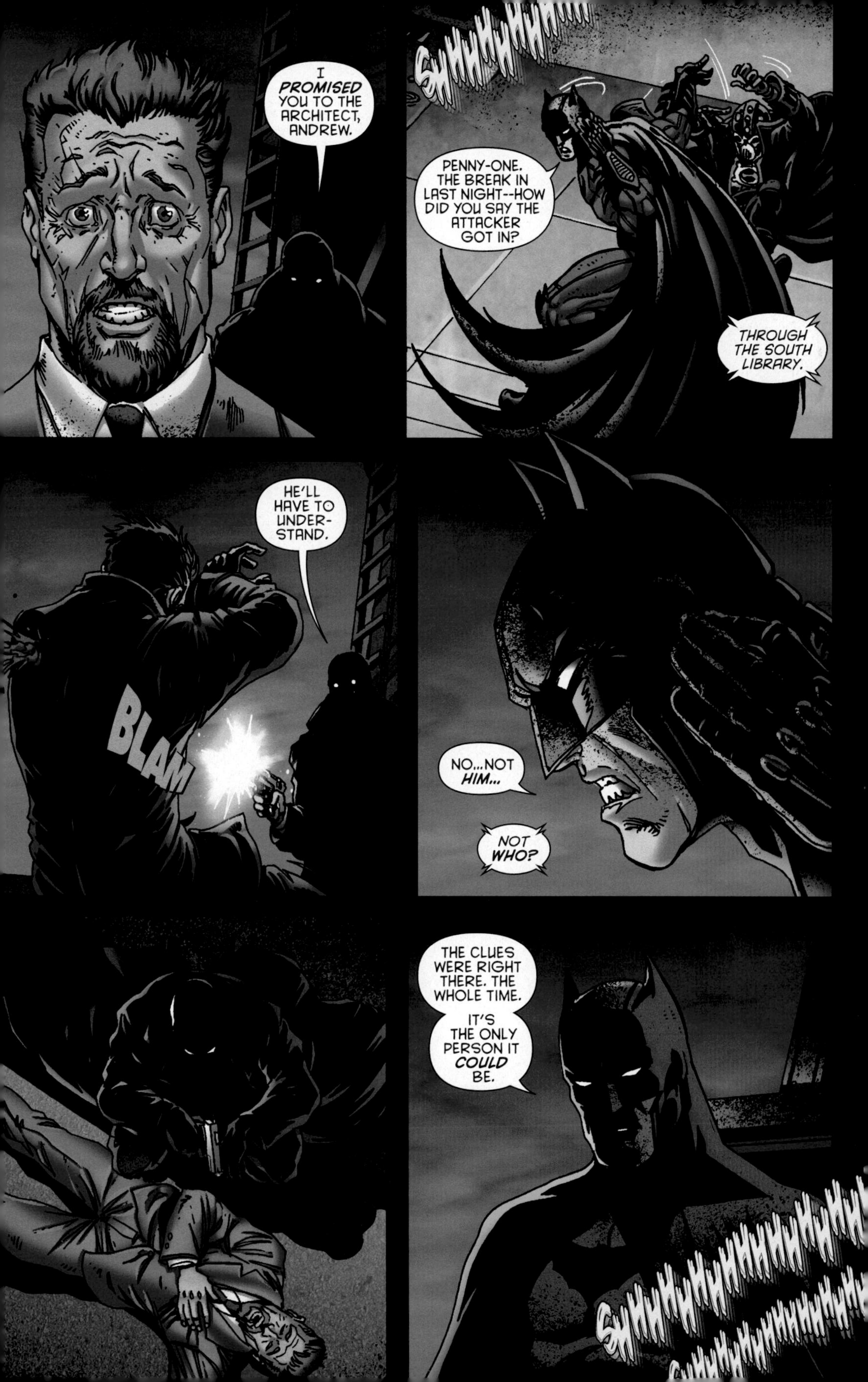

I PROMISED YOU TO THE ARCHITECT, ANDREW.
SHHHHHHHHHH
PENNY-ONE. THE BREAK IN LAST NIGHT--HOW DID YOU SAY THE ATTACKER GOT IN?
THROUGH THE SOUTH LIBRARY.
HE'LL HAVE TO UNDER-STAND.
BLAM
NO...NOT HIM...
NOT WHO?
THE CLUES WERE RIGHT THERE. THE WHOLE TIME.
IT'S THE ONLY PERSON IT COULD BE.
SHHHHHHHHHHHHHHHH

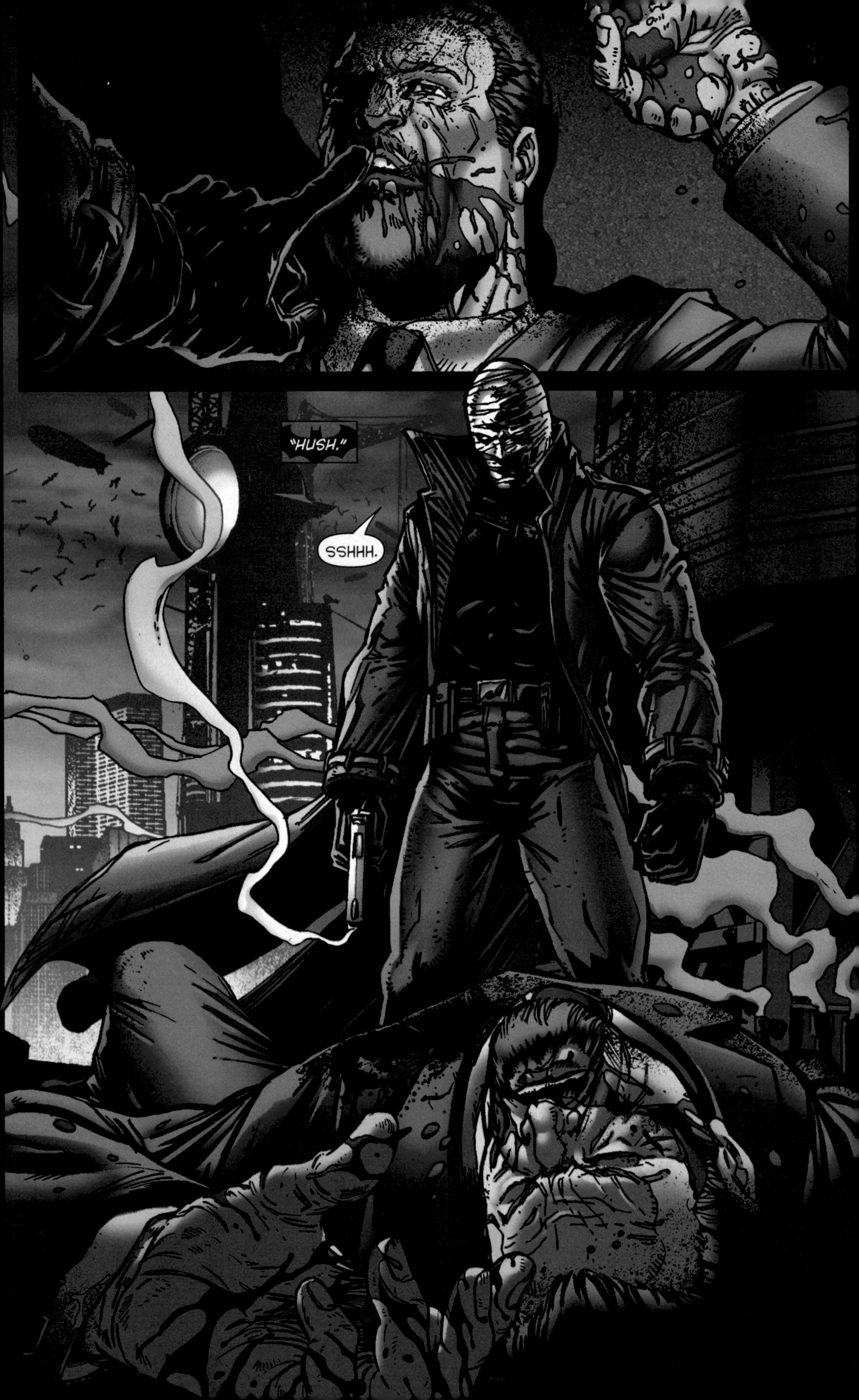
"HUSH."
SSHHH.

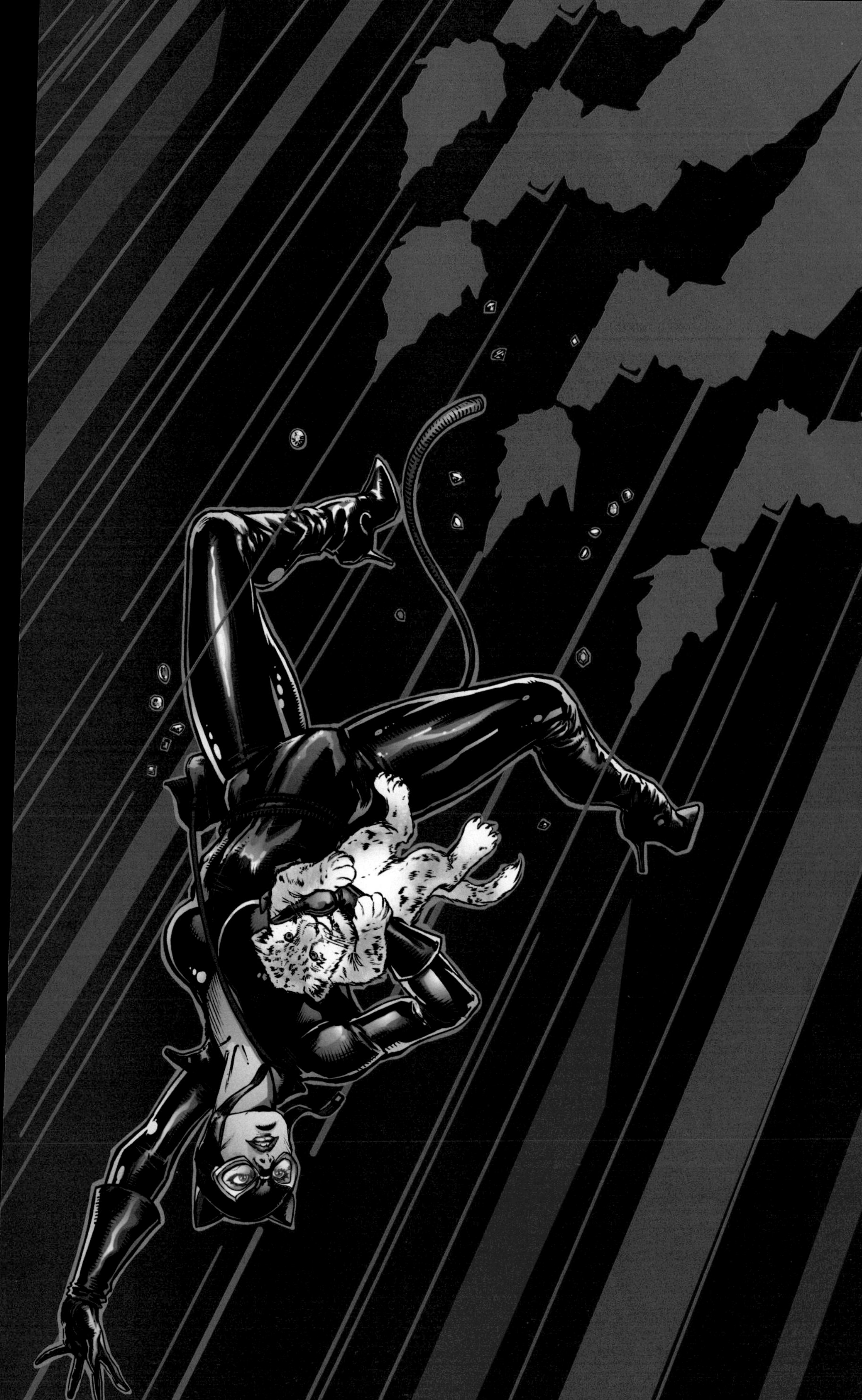

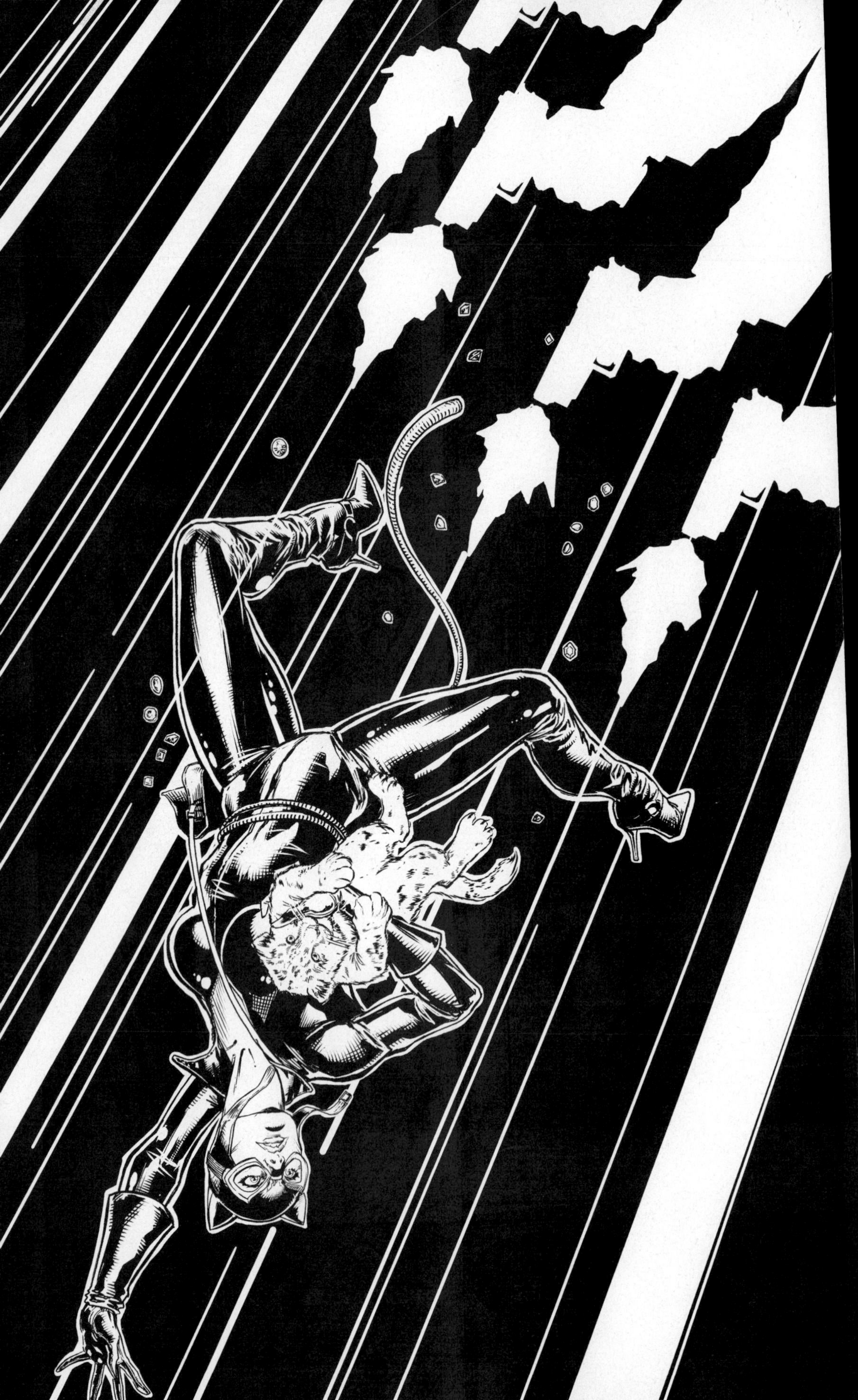

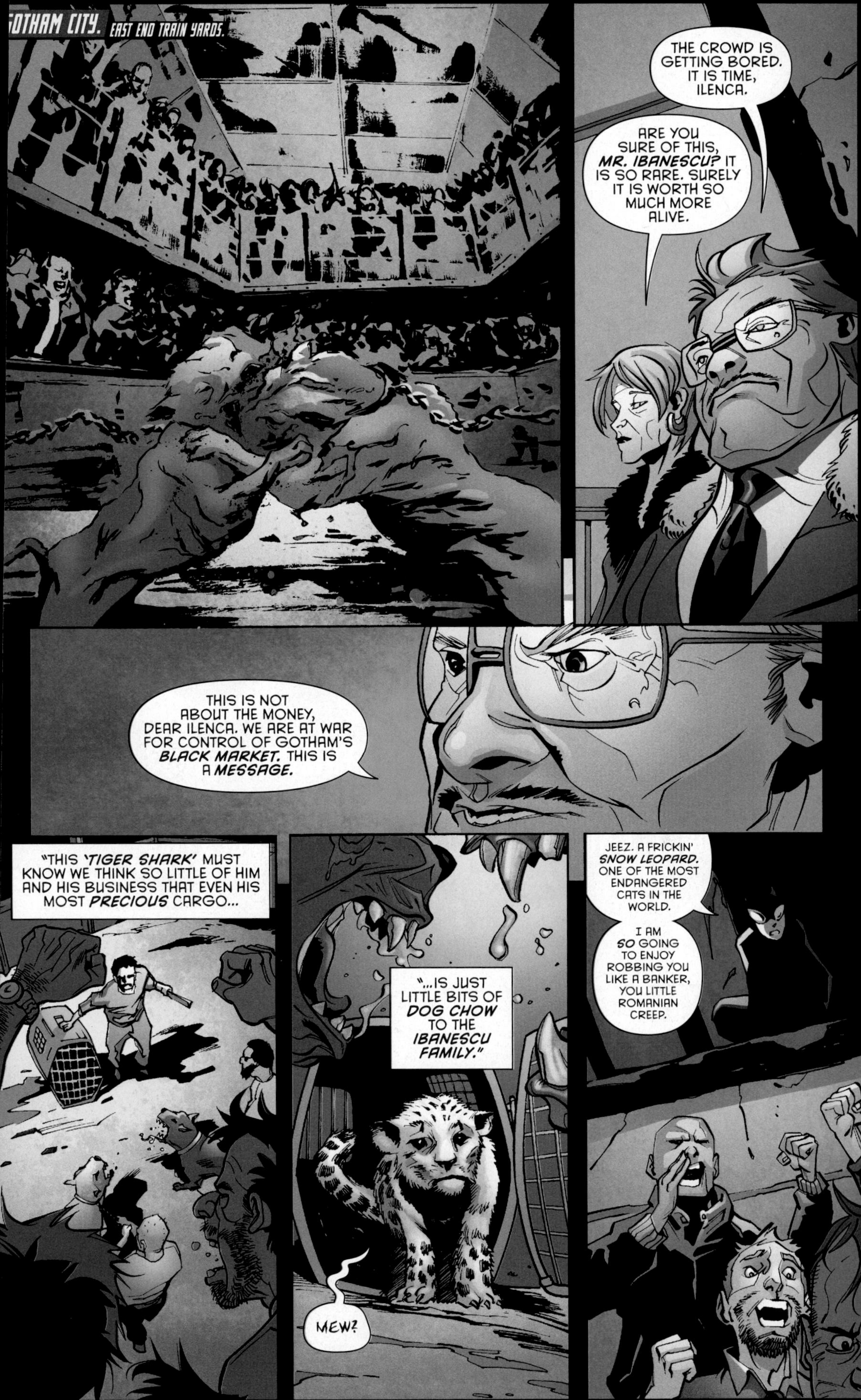
GOTHAM CITY. EAST END TRAIN YARDS.
THE CROWD IS GETTING BORED. IT IS TIME, ILENCA.
ARE YOU SURE OF THIS, MR. IBANESCU? IT IS SO RARE. SURELY IT IS WORTH SO MUCH MORE ALIVE.
THIS IS NOT ABOUT THE MONEY, DEAR ILENCA. WE ARE AT WAR FOR CONTROL OF GOTHAM'S BLACK MARKET. THIS IS A MESSAGE.
"THIS 'TIGER SHARK' MUST KNOW WE THINK SO LITTLE OF HIM AND HIS BUSINESS THAT EVEN HIS MOST PRECIOUS CARGO...
"...IS JUST LITTLE BITS OF DOG CHOW TO THE IBANESCU FAMILY."
MEW?
JEEZ. A FRICKIN' SNOW LEOPARD. ONE OF THE MOST ENDANGERED CATS IN THE WORLD.
I AM SO GOING TO ENJOY ROBBING YOU LIKE A BANKER, YOU LITTLE ROMANIAN CREEP.

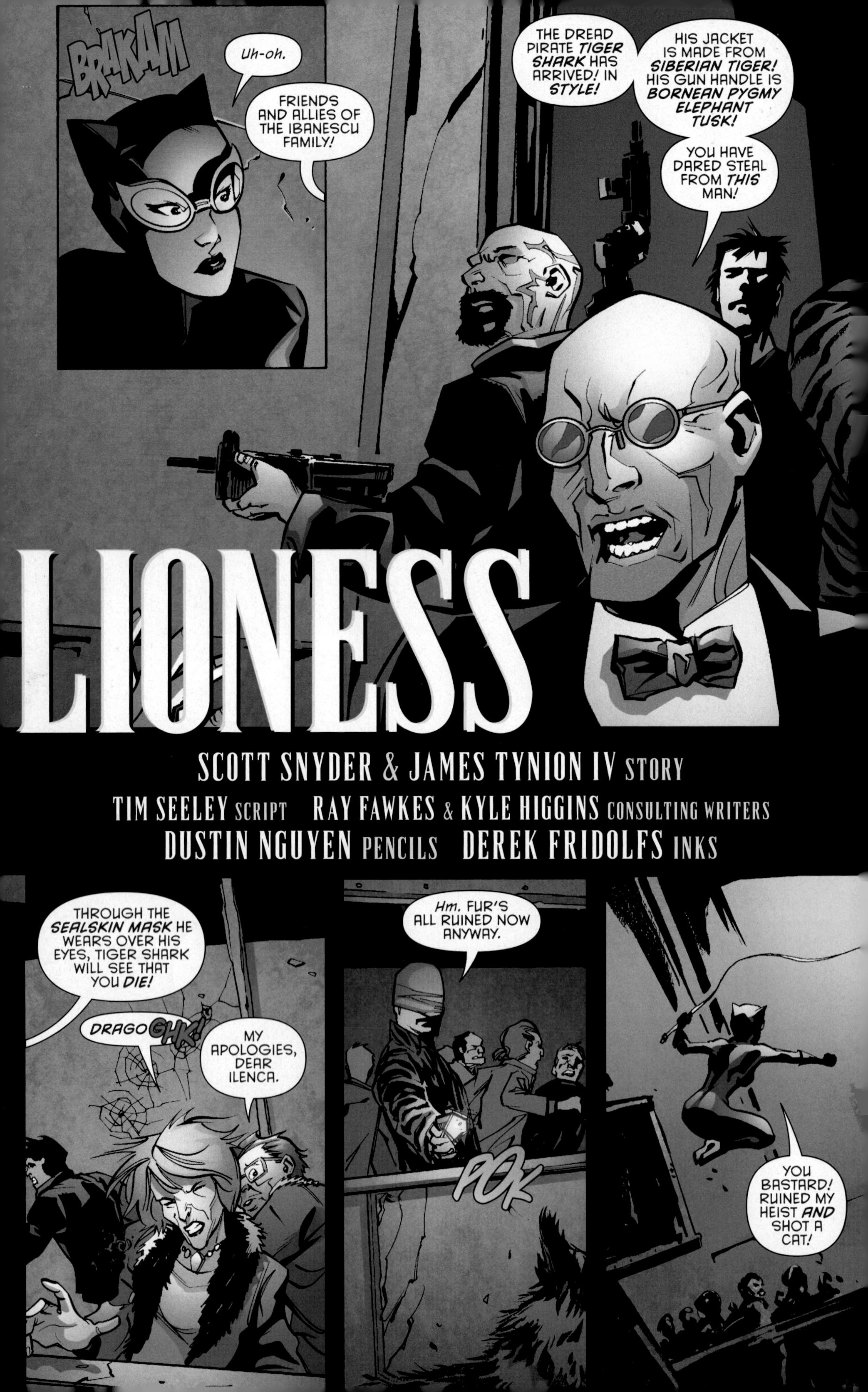
BRAKAM
Uh-oh.
FRIENDS AND ALLIES OF THE IBANESCU FAMILY!
THE DREAD PIRATE TIGER SHARK HAS ARRIVED! IN STYLE!
HIS JACKET IS MADE FROM SIBERIAN TIGER! HIS GUN HANDLE IS BORNEAN PYGMY ELEPHANT TUSK!
YOU HAVE DARED STEAL FROM THIS MAN!
LIONESS
SCOTT SNYDER & JAMES TYNION IV STORY
TIM SEELEY SCRIPT RAY FAWKES & KYLE HIGGINS CONSULTING WRITERS
DUSTIN NGUYEN PENCILS DEREK FRIDOLFS INKS
THROUGH THE SEALSKIN MASK HE WEARS OVER HIS EYES, TIGER SHARK WILL SEE THAT YOU DIE!
DRAGOGHK!
MY APOLOGIES, DEAR ILENCA.
Hm. FUR'S ALL RUINED NOW ANYWAY.
POK
YOU BASTARD! RUINED MY HEIST AND SHOT A CAT!

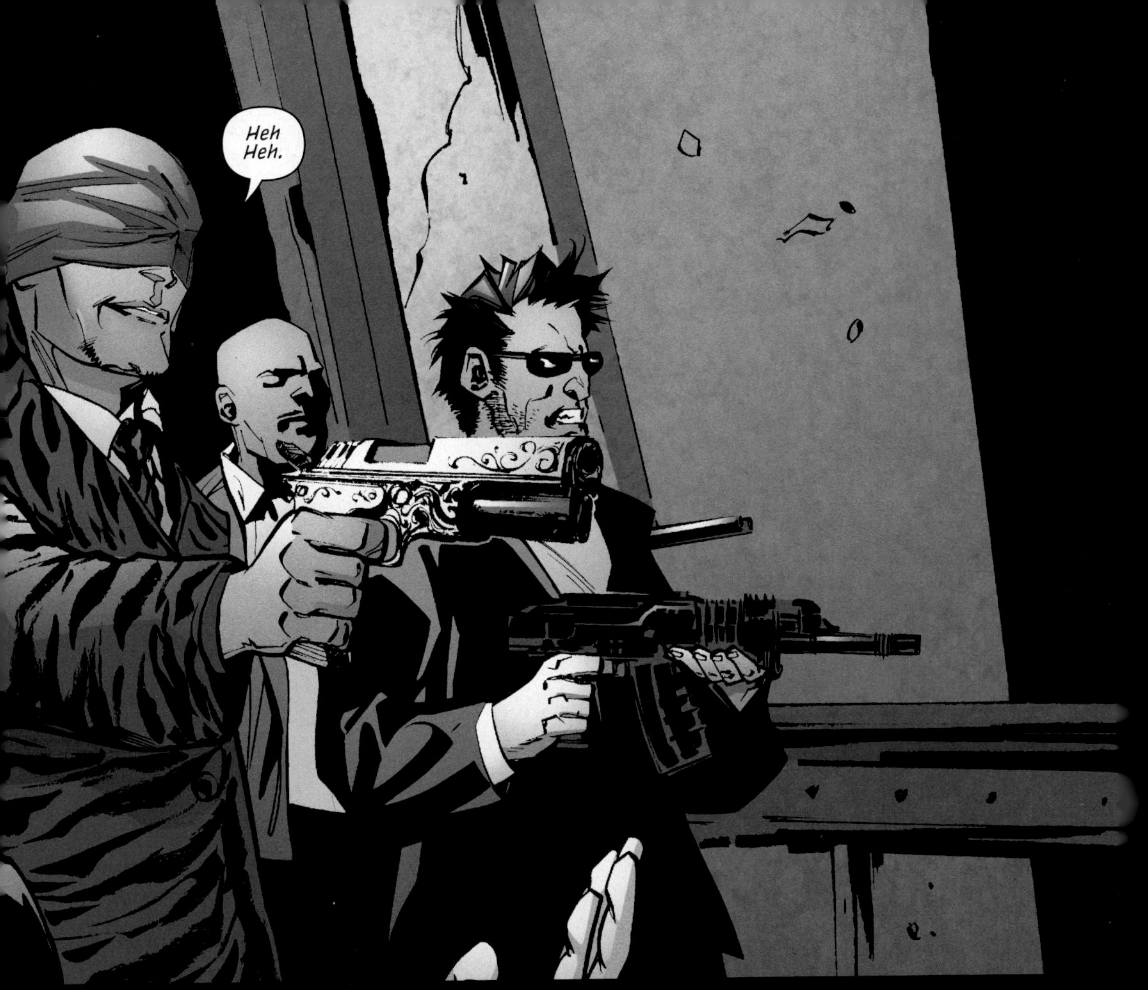
Heh Heh.

JOHN KALISZ COLORS STEVE WANDS LETTERS
JASON FABOK & BRAD ANDERSON COVER

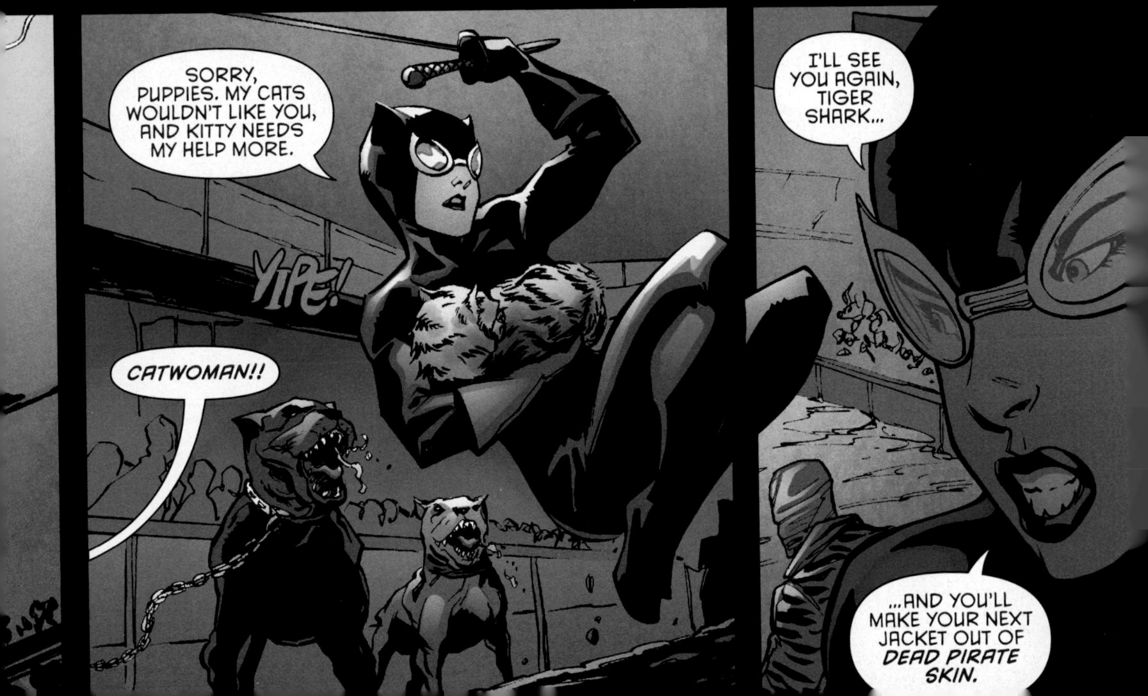
SORRY, PUPPIES. MY CATS WOULDN'T LIKE YOU, AND KITTY NEEDS MY HELP MORE.
YIPE!
CATWOMAN!!
I'LL SEE YOU AGAIN, TIGER SHARK...
...AND YOU'LL MAKE YOUR NEXT JACKET OUT OF *DEAD PIRATE SKIN.*

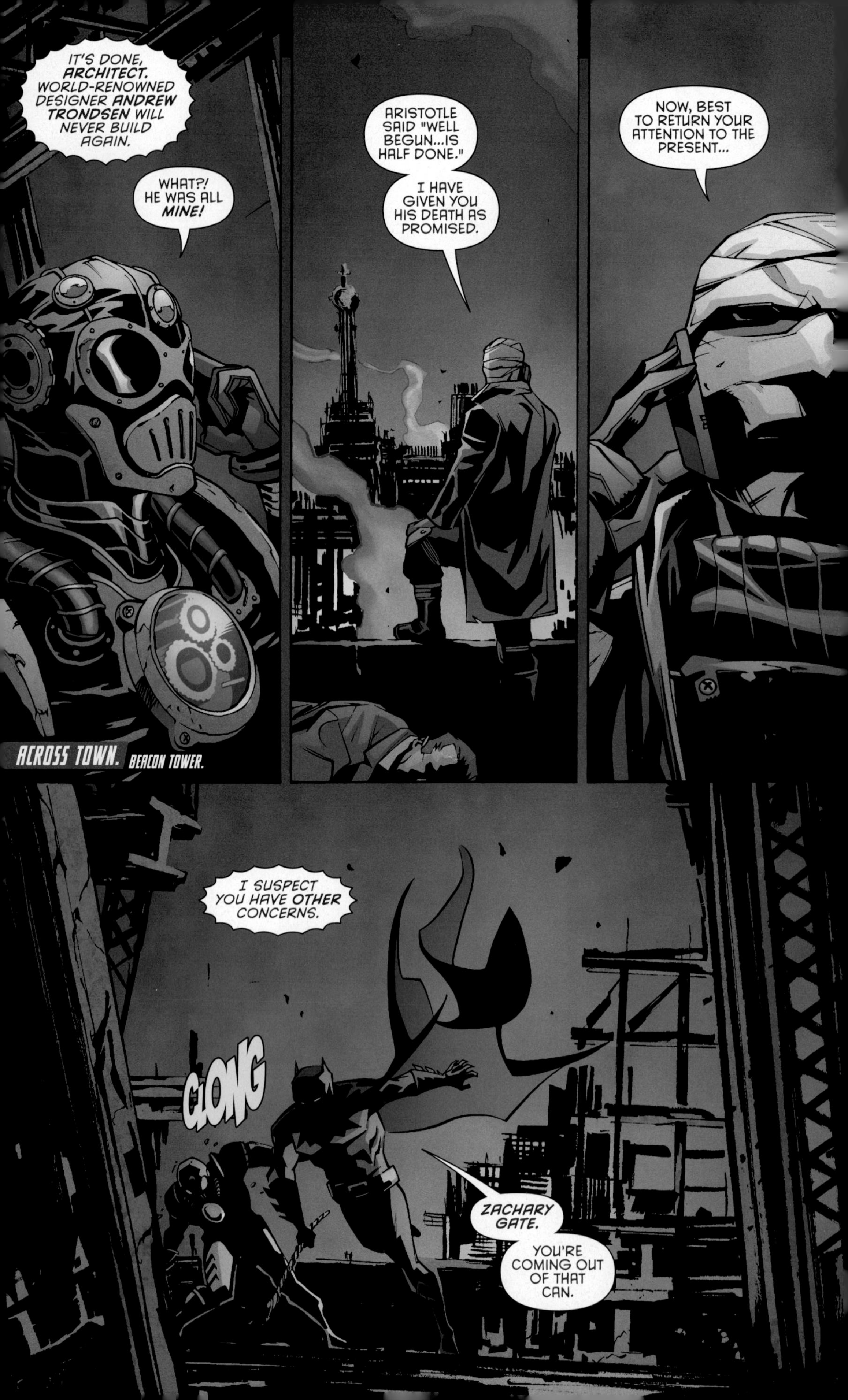
IT'S DONE, ARCHITECT. WORLD-RENOWNED DESIGNER ANDREW TRONDSEN WILL NEVER BUILD AGAIN.
WHAT?! HE WAS ALL MINE!
ACROSS TOWN. BEACON TOWER.
ARISTOTLE SAID "WELL BEGUN...IS HALF DONE."
I HAVE GIVEN YOU HIS DEATH AS PROMISED.
NOW, BEST TO RETURN YOUR ATTENTION TO THE PRESENT...
I SUSPECT YOU HAVE OTHER CONCERNS.
CLONG
ZACHARY GATE.
YOU'RE COMING OUT OF THAT CAN.

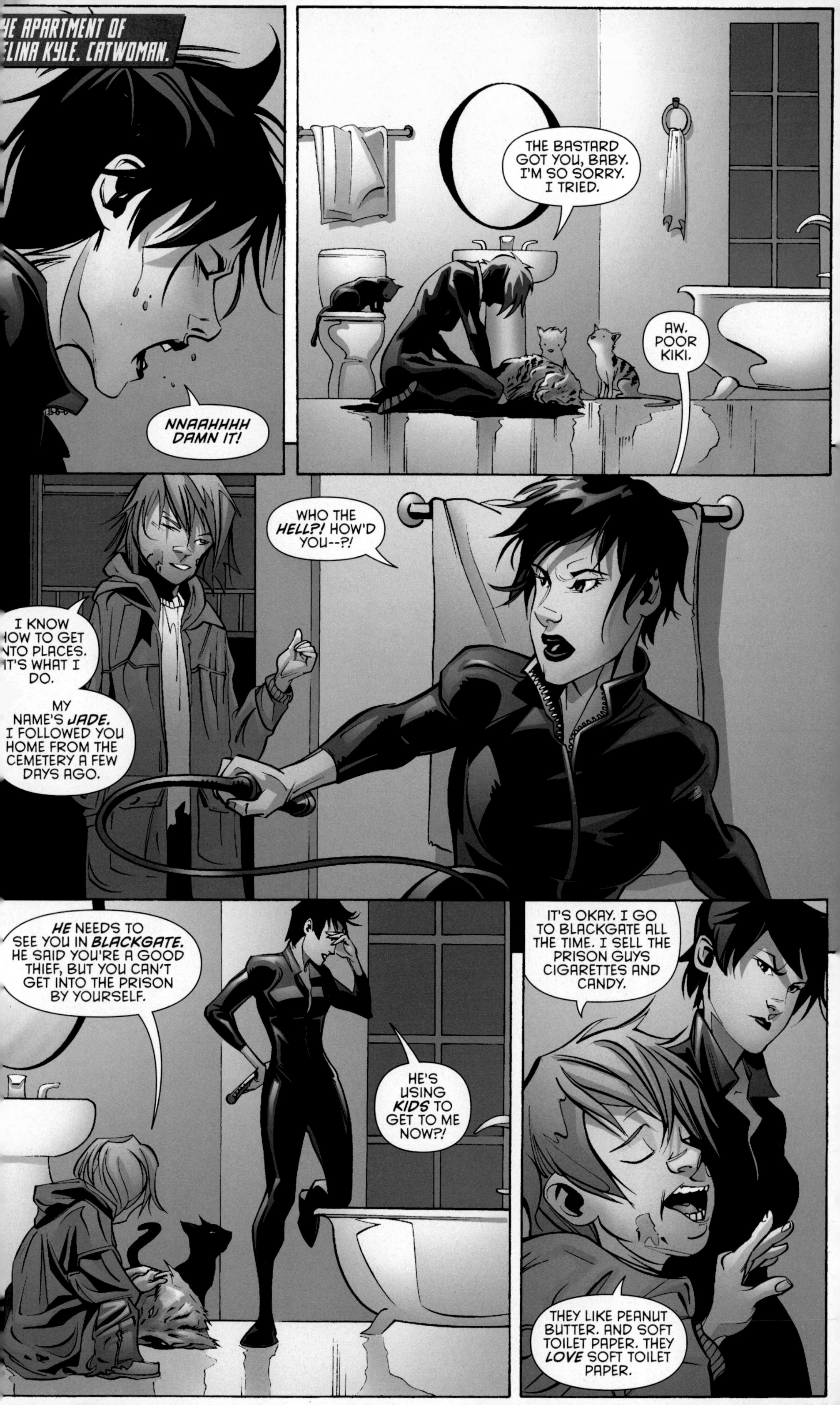

HE APARTMENT OF
ELINA KYLE. CATWOMAN.
NNAAHHHH DAMN IT!
THE BASTARD GOT YOU, BABY. I'M SO SORRY. I TRIED.
AW. POOR KIKI.
WHO THE HELL?! HOW'D YOU--?!
I KNOW HOW TO GET NTO PLACES. IT'S WHAT I DO.
MY NAME'S JADE. I FOLLOWED YOU HOME FROM THE CEMETERY A FEW DAYS AGO.
HE NEEDS TO SEE YOU IN BLACKGATE. HE SAID YOU'RE A GOOD THIEF, BUT YOU CAN'T GET INTO THE PRISON BY YOURSELF.
HE'S USING KIDS TO GET TO ME NOW?!
IT'S OKAY. I GO TO BLACKGATE ALL THE TIME. I SELL THE PRISON GUYS CIGARETTES AND CANDY.
THEY LIKE PEANUT BUTTER. AND SOFT TOILET PAPER. THEY LOVE SOFT TOILET PAPER.

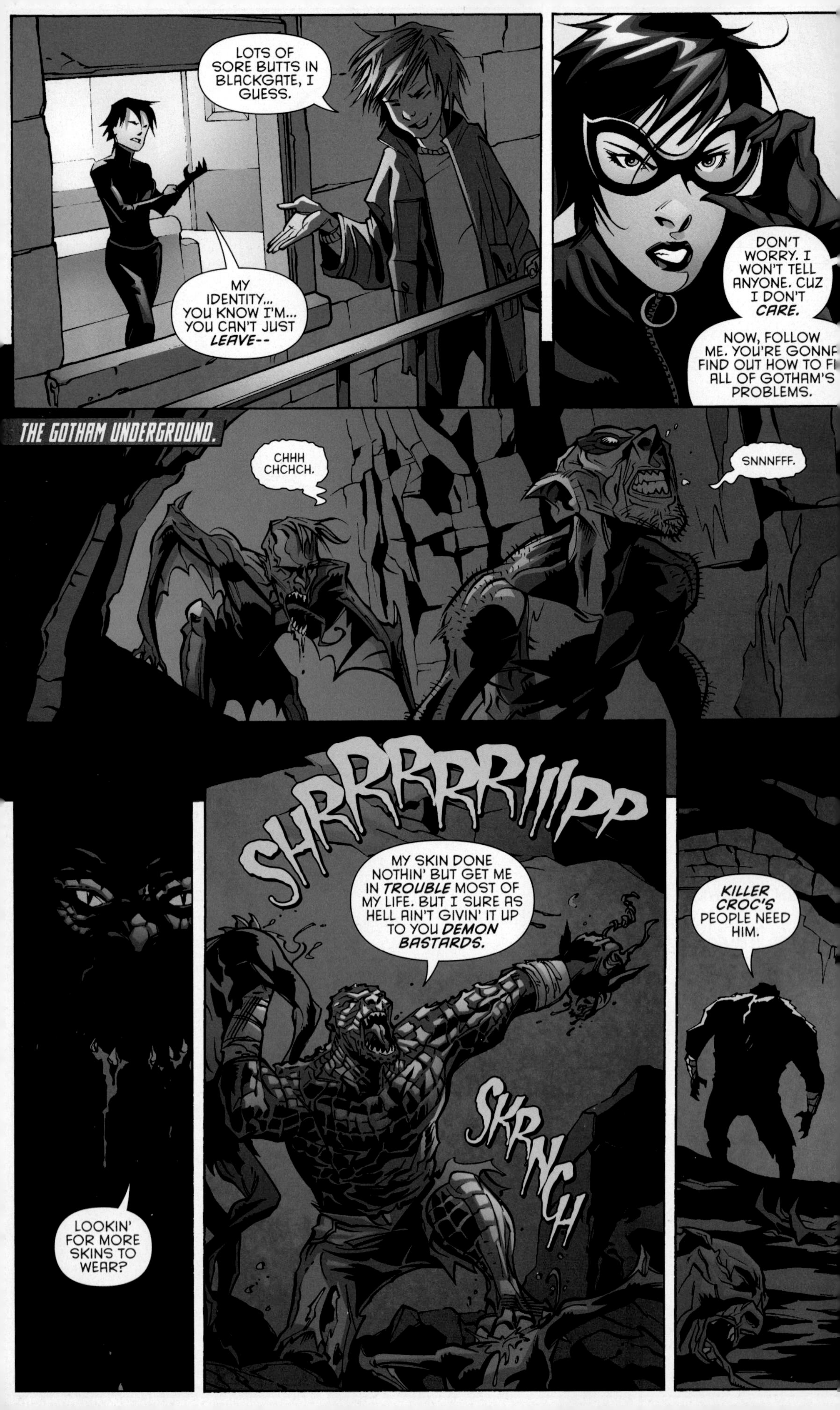

LOTS OF SORE BUTTS IN BLACKGATE, I GUESS.
MY IDENTITY... YOU KNOW I'M... YOU CAN'T JUST LEAVE--
DON'T WORRY. I WON'T TELL ANYONE. CUZ I DON'T CARE.
NOW, FOLLOW ME. YOU'RE GONN FIND OUT HOW TO F ALL OF GOTHAM'S PROBLEMS.
THE GOTHAM UNDERGROUND.
CHHH CHCHCH.
SNNNFFF.
LOOKIN' FOR MORE SKINS TO WEAR?
SHRRRRRIIIPP
MY SKIN DONE NOTHIN' BUT GET ME IN TROUBLE MOST OF MY LIFE. BUT I SURE AS HELL AIN'T GIVIN' IT UP TO YOU DEMON BASTARDS.
SKRNCH
KILLER CROC'S PEOPLE NEED HIM.

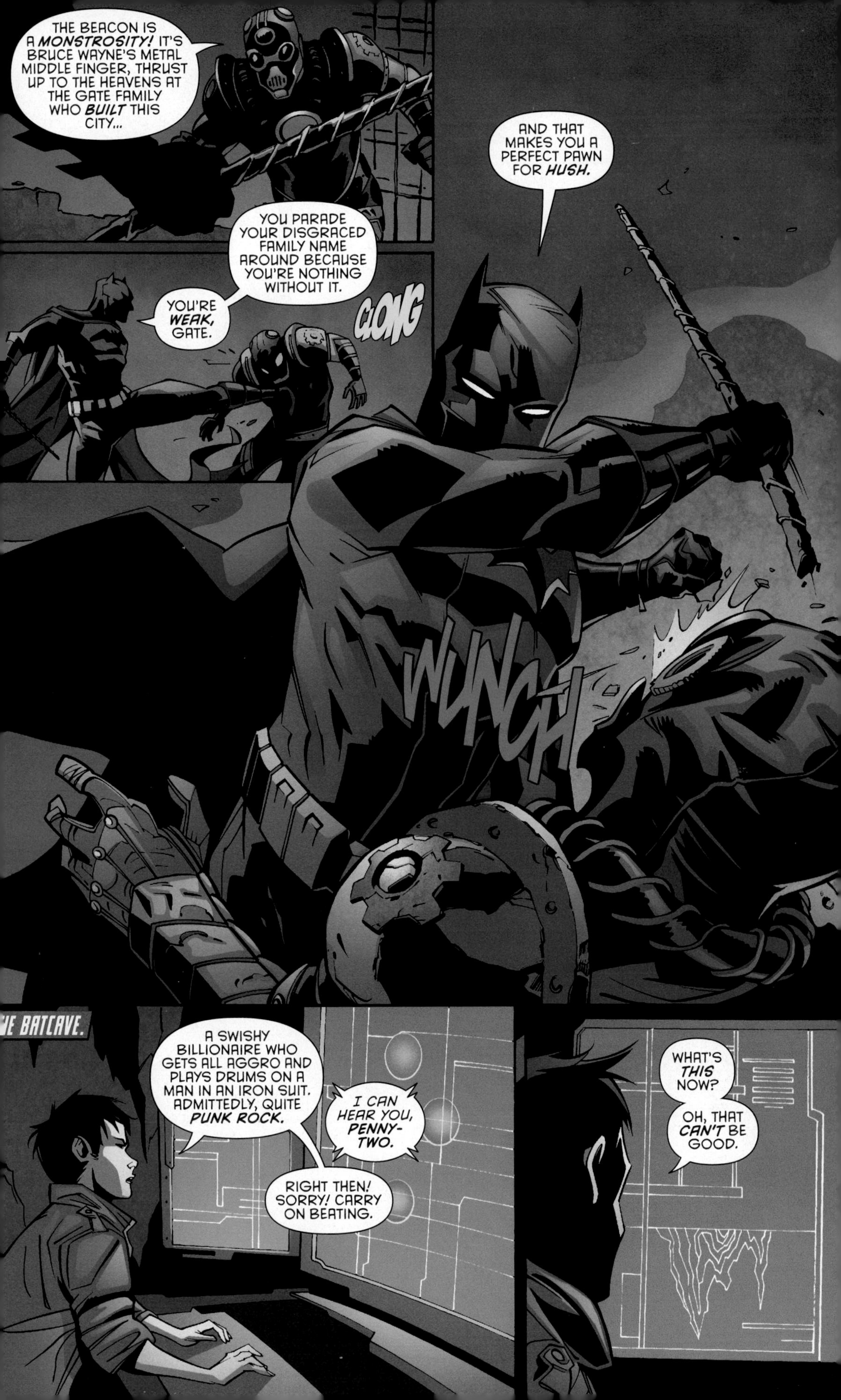
THE BEACON IS A MONSTROSITY! IT'S BRUCE WAYNE'S METAL MIDDLE FINGER, THRUST UP TO THE HEAVENS AT THE GATE FAMILY WHO BUILT THIS CITY...
AND THAT MAKES YOU A PERFECT PAWN FOR HUSH.
YOU PARADE YOUR DISGRACED FAMILY NAME AROUND BECAUSE YOU'RE NOTHING WITHOUT IT.
YOU'RE WEAK, GATE.
CLONG
WUNCH
...E BATCAVE.
A SWISHY BILLIONAIRE WHO GETS ALL AGGRO AND PLAYS DRUMS ON A MAN IN AN IRON SUIT. ADMITTEDLY, QUITE PUNK ROCK.
I CAN HEAR YOU, PENNY-TWO.
RIGHT THEN! SORRY! CARRY ON BEATING.
WHAT'S THIS NOW?
OH, THAT CAN'T BE GOOD.

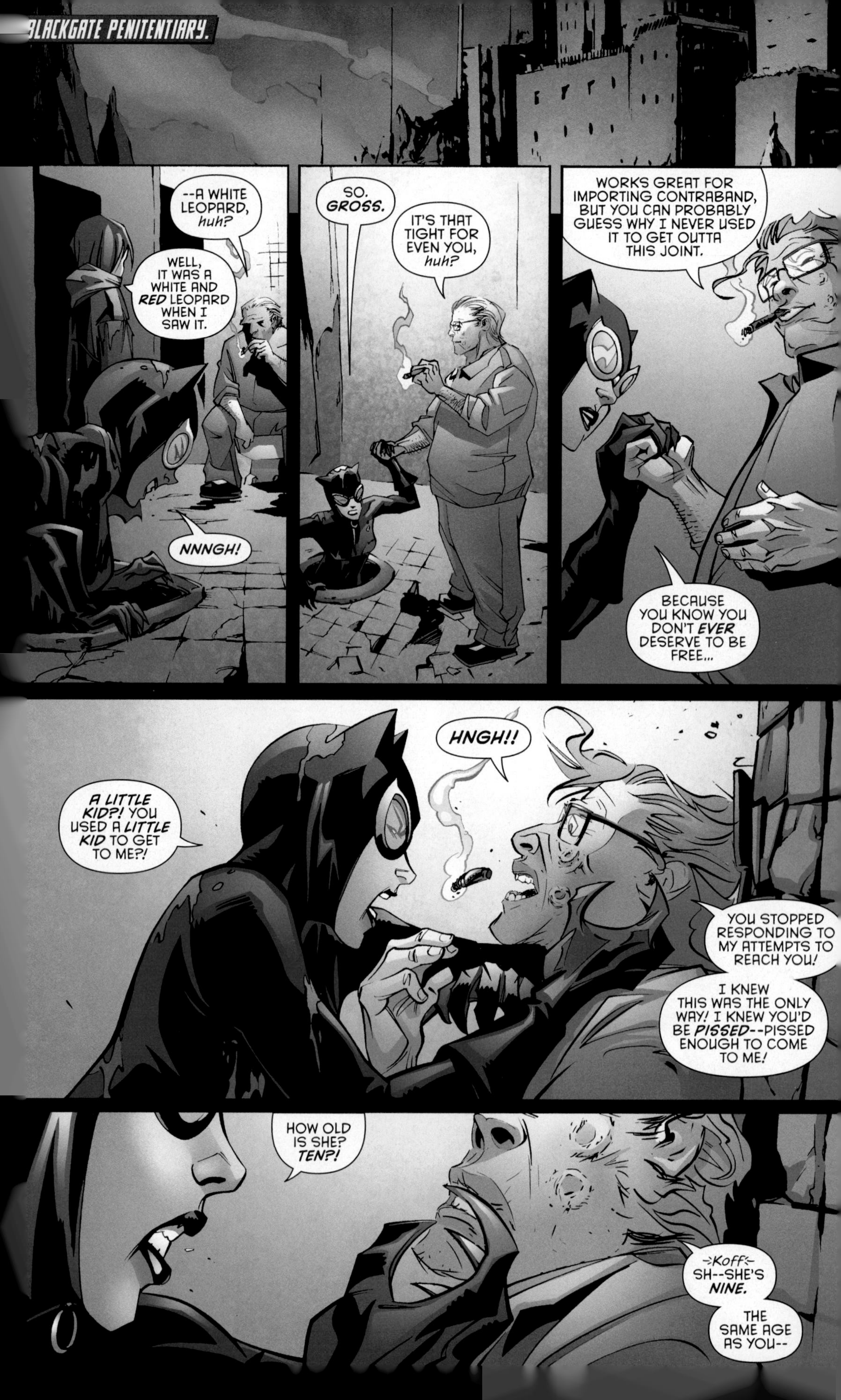
BLACKGATE PENITENTIARY.
--A WHITE LEOPARD, huh?
WELL, IT WAS A WHITE AND RED LEOPARD WHEN I SAW IT.
NNNGH!
SO. GROSS.
IT'S THAT TIGHT FOR EVEN YOU, huh?
WORKS GREAT FOR IMPORTING CONTRABAND, BUT YOU CAN PROBABLY GUESS WHY I NEVER USED IT TO GET OUTTA THIS JOINT.
BECAUSE YOU KNOW YOU DON'T EVER DESERVE TO BE FREE...
HNGH!!
A LITTLE KID?! YOU USED A LITTLE KID TO GET TO ME?!
YOU STOPPED RESPONDING TO MY ATTEMPTS TO REACH YOU!
I KNEW THIS WAS THE ONLY WAY! I KNEW YOU'D BE PISSED--PISSED ENOUGH TO COME TO ME!
HOW OLD IS SHE? TEN?!
Koff SH--SHE'S NINE.
THE SAME AGE AS YOU--

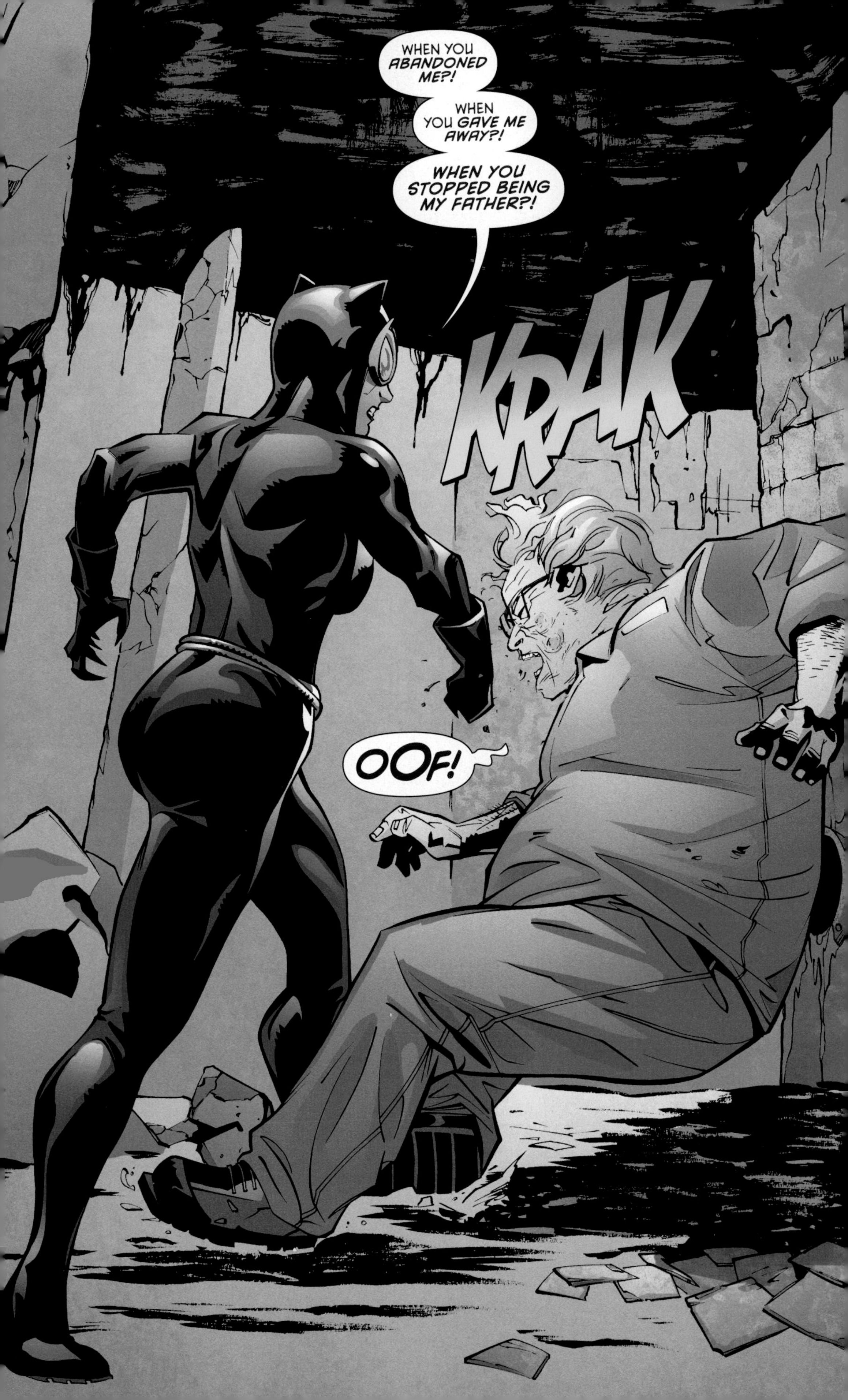
WHEN YOU ABANDONED ME?!
WHEN YOU GAVE ME AWAY?!
WHEN YOU STOPPED BEING MY FATHER?!
KRAK
OOF!

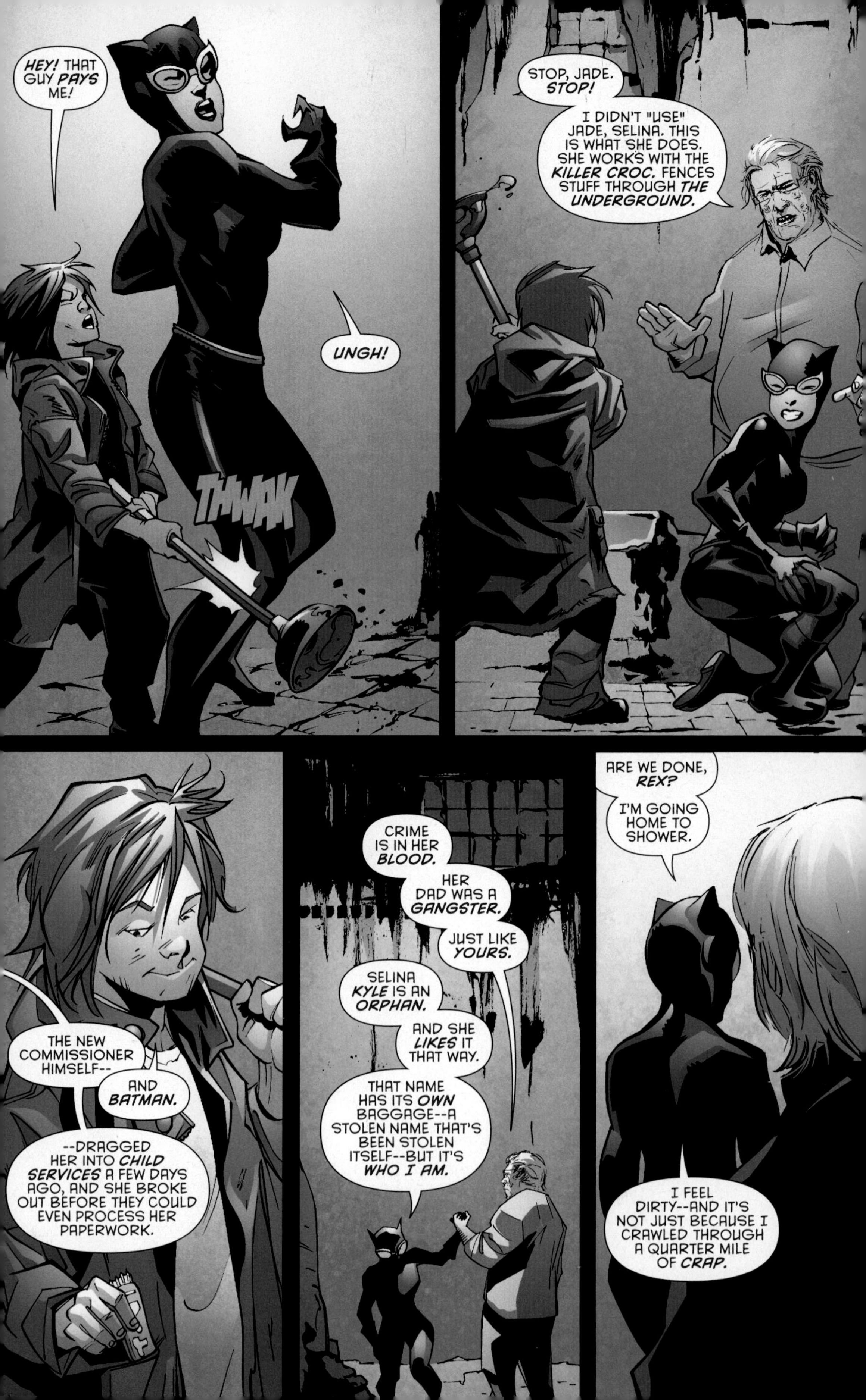
HEY! THAT GUY PAYS ME!
THWAK
UNGH!
STOP, JADE. STOP!
I DIDN'T "USE" JADE, SELINA. THIS IS WHAT SHE DOES. SHE WORKS WITH THE KILLER CROC. FENCES STUFF THROUGH THE UNDERGROUND.
THE NEW COMMISSIONER HIMSELF--
AND BATMAN.
--DRAGGED HER INTO CHILD SERVICES A FEW DAYS AGO, AND SHE BROKE OUT BEFORE THEY COULD EVEN PROCESS HER PAPERWORK.
CRIME IS IN HER BLOOD.
HER DAD WAS A GANGSTER.
JUST LIKE YOURS.
SELINA KYLE IS AN ORPHAN.
AND SHE LIKES IT THAT WAY.
THAT NAME HAS ITS OWN BAGGAGE--A STOLEN NAME THAT'S BEEN STOLEN ITSELF--BUT IT'S WHO I AM.
ARE WE DONE, REX?
I'M GOING HOME TO SHOWER.
I FEEL DIRTY--AND IT'S NOT JUST BECAUSE I CRAWLED THROUGH A QUARTER MILE OF CRAP.

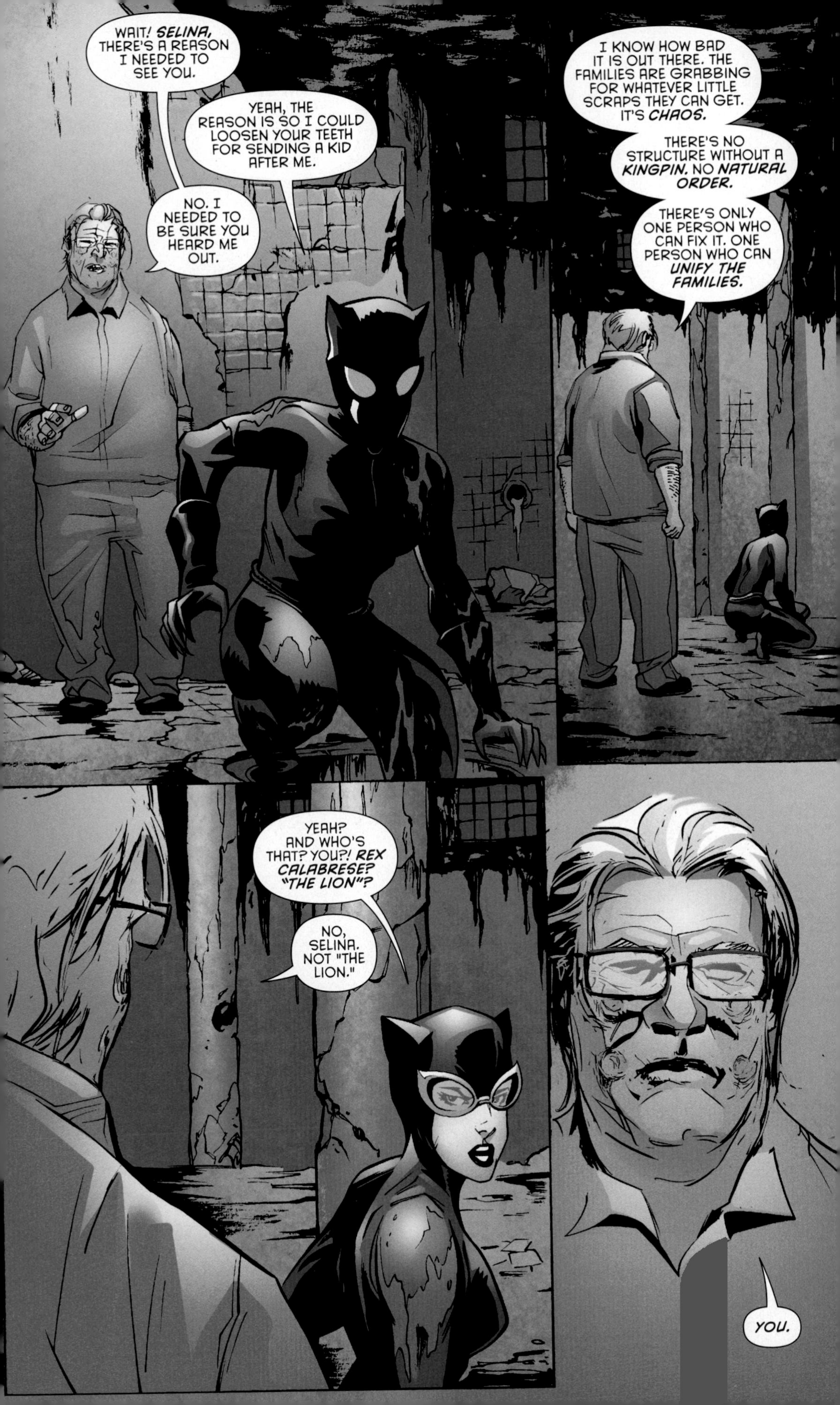
WAIT! SELINA, THERE'S A REASON I NEEDED TO SEE YOU.
YEAH, THE REASON IS SO I COULD LOOSEN YOUR TEETH FOR SENDING A KID AFTER ME.
NO. I NEEDED TO BE SURE YOU HEARD ME OUT.
I KNOW HOW BAD IT IS OUT THERE. THE FAMILIES ARE GRABBING FOR WHATEVER LITTLE SCRAPS THEY CAN GET. IT'S CHAOS.
THERE'S NO STRUCTURE WITHOUT A KINGPIN. NO NATURAL ORDER.
THERE'S ONLY ONE PERSON WHO CAN FIX IT. ONE PERSON WHO CAN UNIFY THE FAMILIES.
YEAH? AND WHO'S THAT? YOU?! REX CALABRESE? "THE LION"?
NO, SELINA. NOT "THE LION."
YOU.

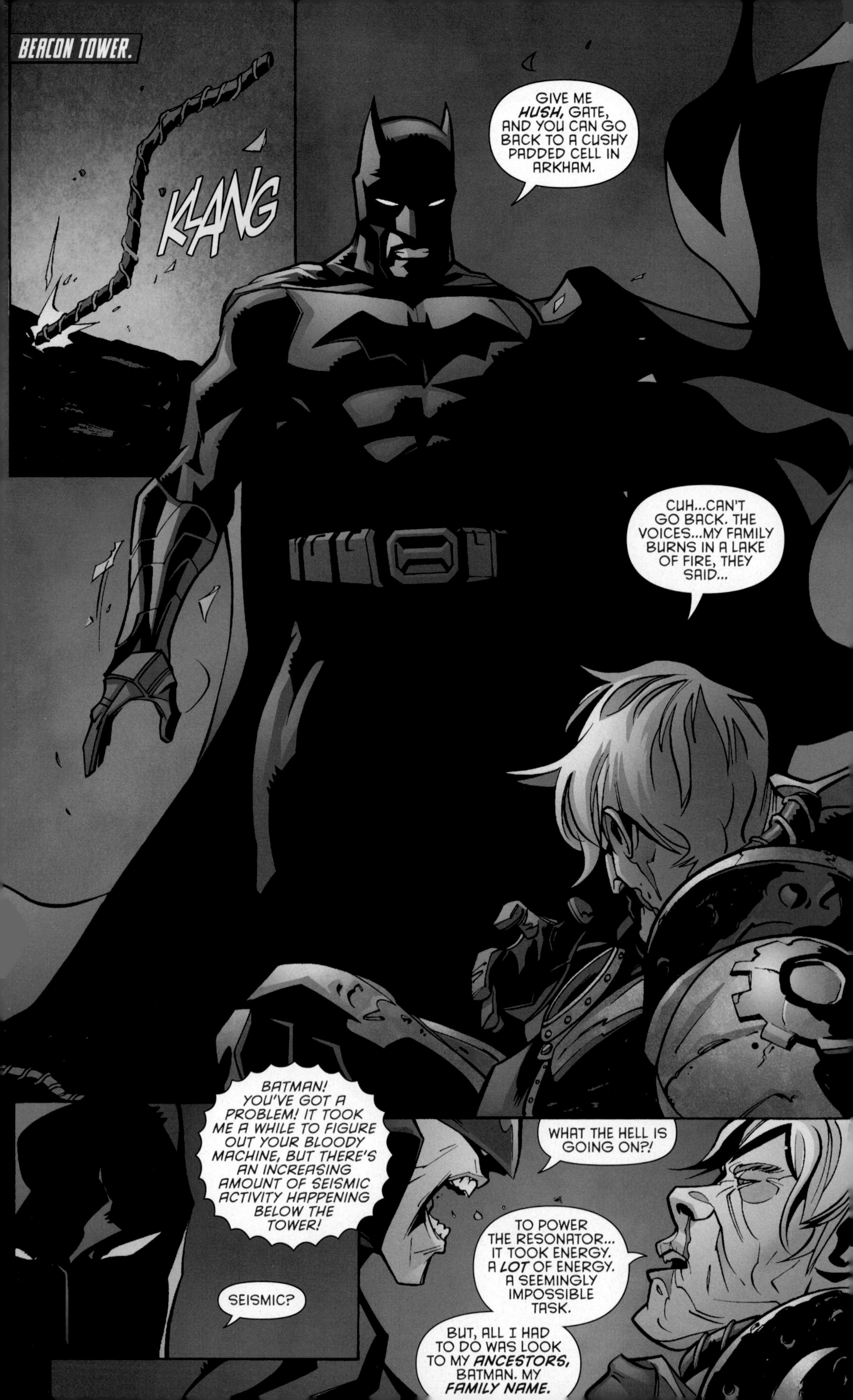
BEACON TOWER.
KLANG
GIVE ME HUSH, GATE, AND YOU CAN GO BACK TO A CUSHY PADDED CELL IN ARKHAM.
CUH...CAN'T GO BACK. THE VOICES...MY FAMILY BURNS IN A LAKE OF FIRE, THEY SAID...
BATMAN! YOU'VE GOT A PROBLEM! IT TOOK ME A WHILE TO FIGURE OUT YOUR BLOODY MACHINE, BUT THERE'S AN INCREASING AMOUNT OF SEISMIC ACTIVITY HAPPENING BELOW THE TOWER!
SEISMIC?
WHAT THE HELL IS GOING ON?!
TO POWER THE RESONATOR... IT TOOK ENERGY. A LOT OF ENERGY. A SEEMINGLY IMPOSSIBLE TASK.
BUT, ALL I HAD TO DO WAS LOOK TO MY ANCESTORS, BATMAN. MY FAMILY NAME.

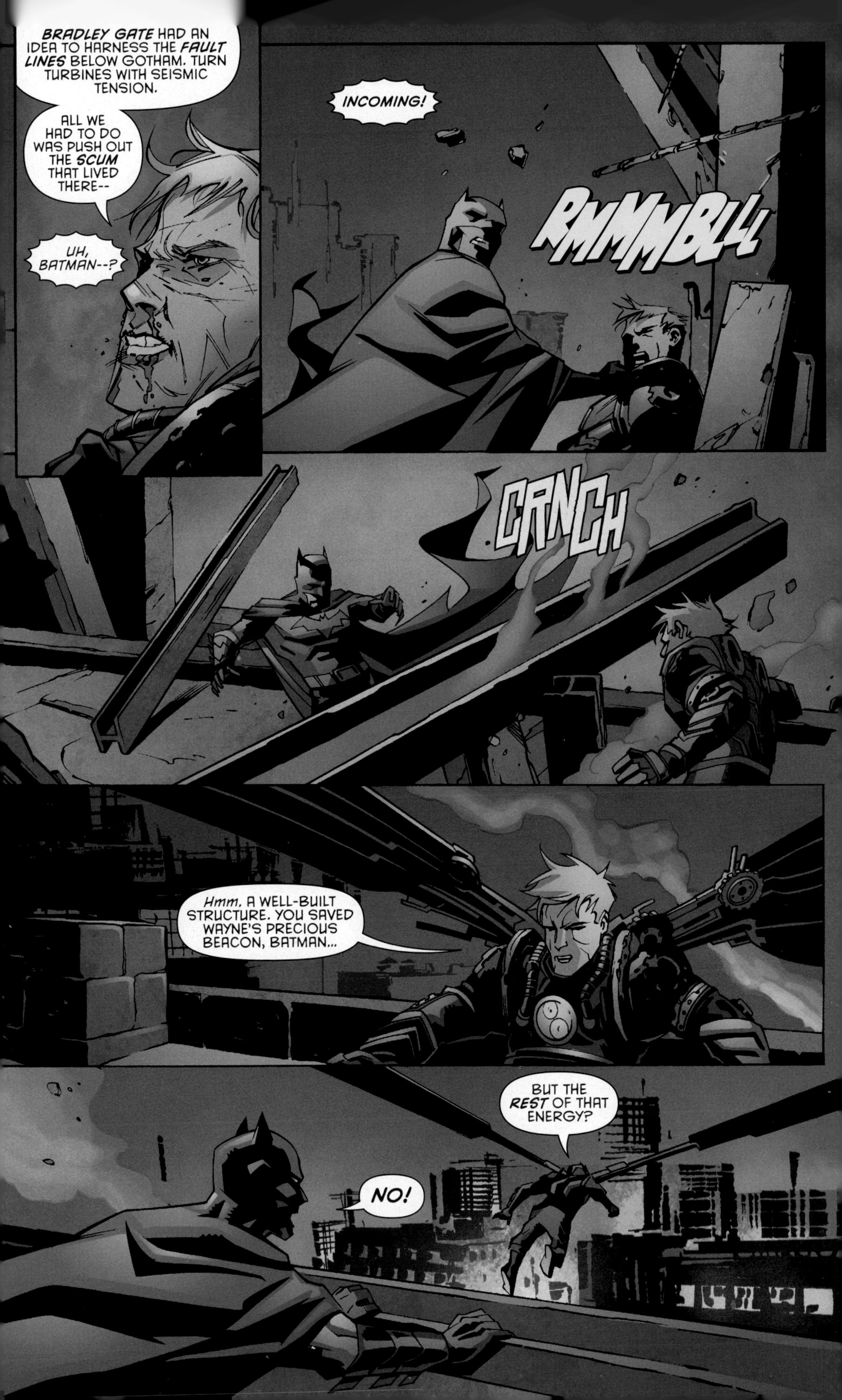
BRADLEY GATE HAD AN IDEA TO HARNESS THE FAULT LINES BELOW GOTHAM. TURN TURBINES WITH SEISMIC TENSION.
ALL WE HAD TO DO WAS PUSH OUT THE SCUM THAT LIVED THERE--
UH, BATMAN--?
INCOMING!
RMMMBLLL
CRNCH
Hmm. A WELL-BUILT STRUCTURE. YOU SAVED WAYNE'S PRECIOUS BEACON, BATMAN...
BUT THE REST OF THAT ENERGY?
NO!

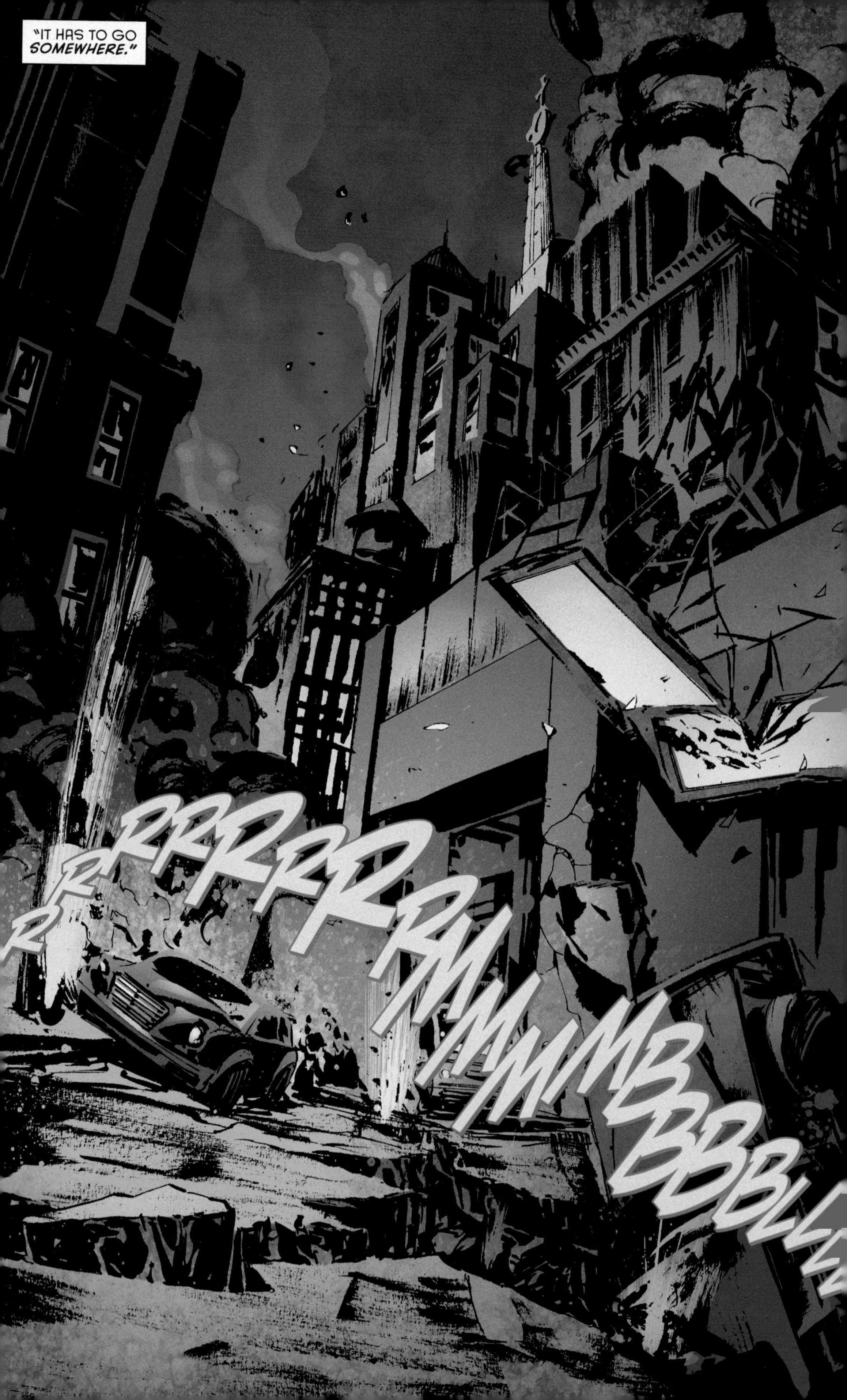
"IT HAS TO GO SOMEWHERE."
RRRRRRRRRMMMMBBBBLLL

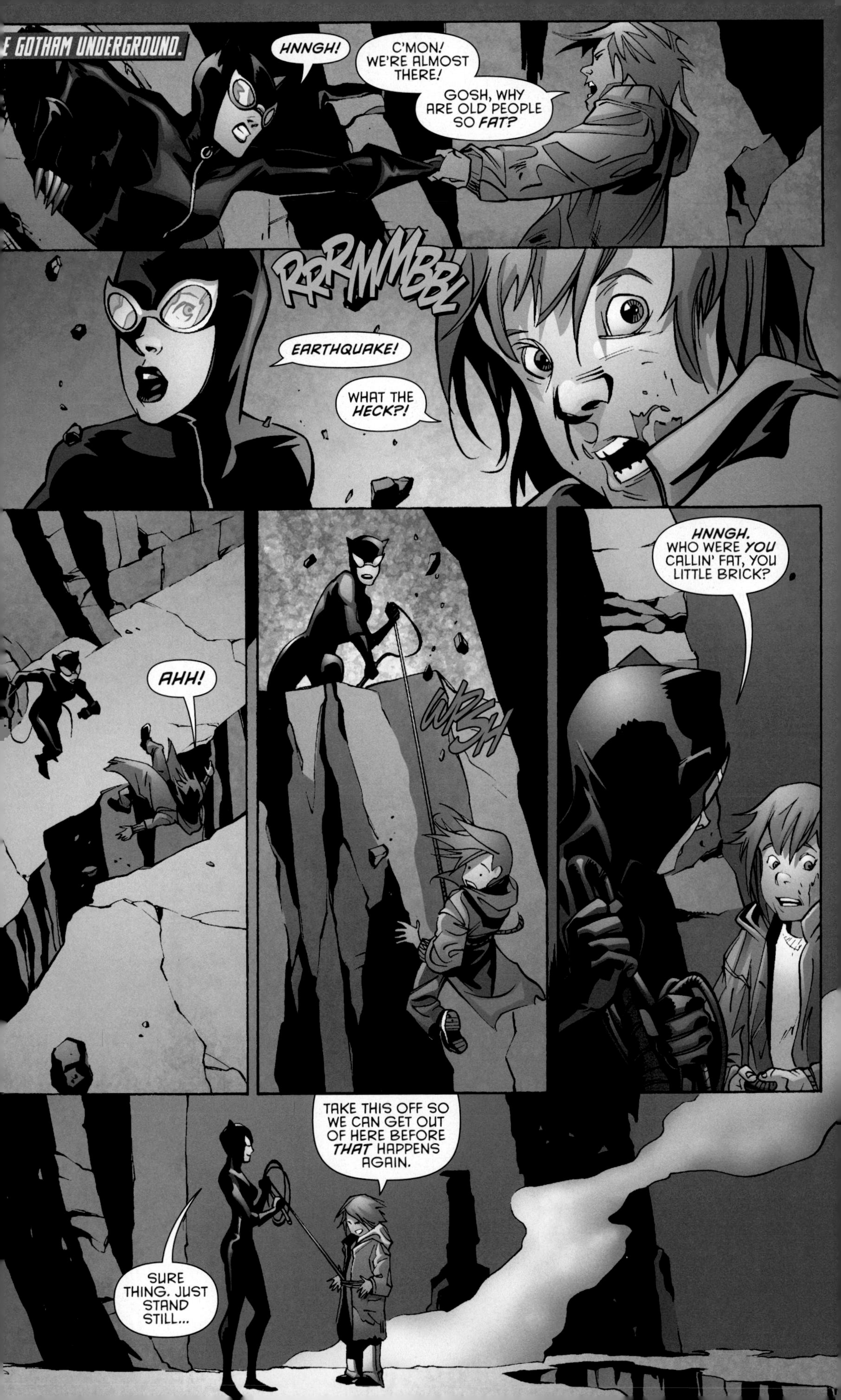
E GOTHAM UNDERGROUND.
HNNGH!
C'MON! WE'RE ALMOST THERE!
GOSH, WHY ARE OLD PEOPLE SO FAT?
RRRMMBBL
EARTHQUAKE!
WHAT THE HECK?!
AHH!
WRSH
HNNGH. WHO WERE YOU CALLIN' FAT, YOU LITTLE BRICK?
TAKE THIS OFF SO WE CAN GET OUT OF HERE BEFORE THAT HAPPENS AGAIN.
SURE THING. JUST STAND STILL...

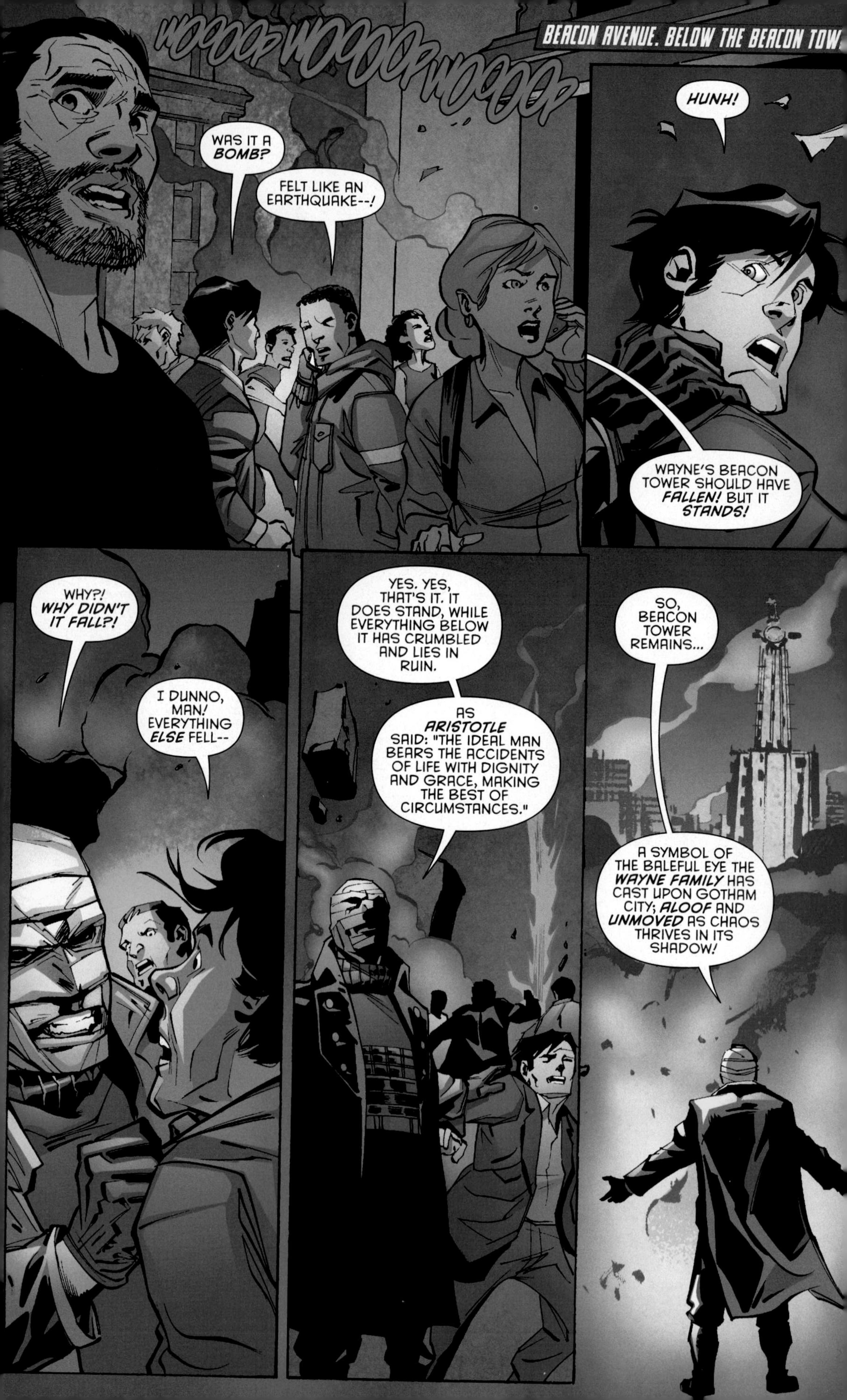

WOOOOOP WOOOOOP WOOOOOP
BEACON AVENUE. BELOW THE BEACON TOW
WAS IT A BOMB?
FELT LIKE AN EARTHQUAKE--!
HUNH!
WAYNE'S BEACON TOWER SHOULD HAVE FALLEN! BUT IT STANDS!
WHY?! WHY DIDN'T IT FALL?!
I DUNNO, MAN! EVERYTHING ELSE FELL--
YES. YES, THAT'S IT. IT DOES STAND, WHILE EVERYTHING BELOW IT HAS CRUMBLED AND LIES IN RUIN.
AS ARISTOTLE SAID: "THE IDEAL MAN BEARS THE ACCIDENTS OF LIFE WITH DIGNITY AND GRACE, MAKING THE BEST OF CIRCUMSTANCES."
SO, BEACON TOWER REMAINS...
A SYMBOL OF THE BALEFUL EYE THE WAYNE FAMILY HAS CAST UPON GOTHAM CITY; ALOOF AND UNMOVED AS CHAOS THRIVES IN ITS SHADOW!

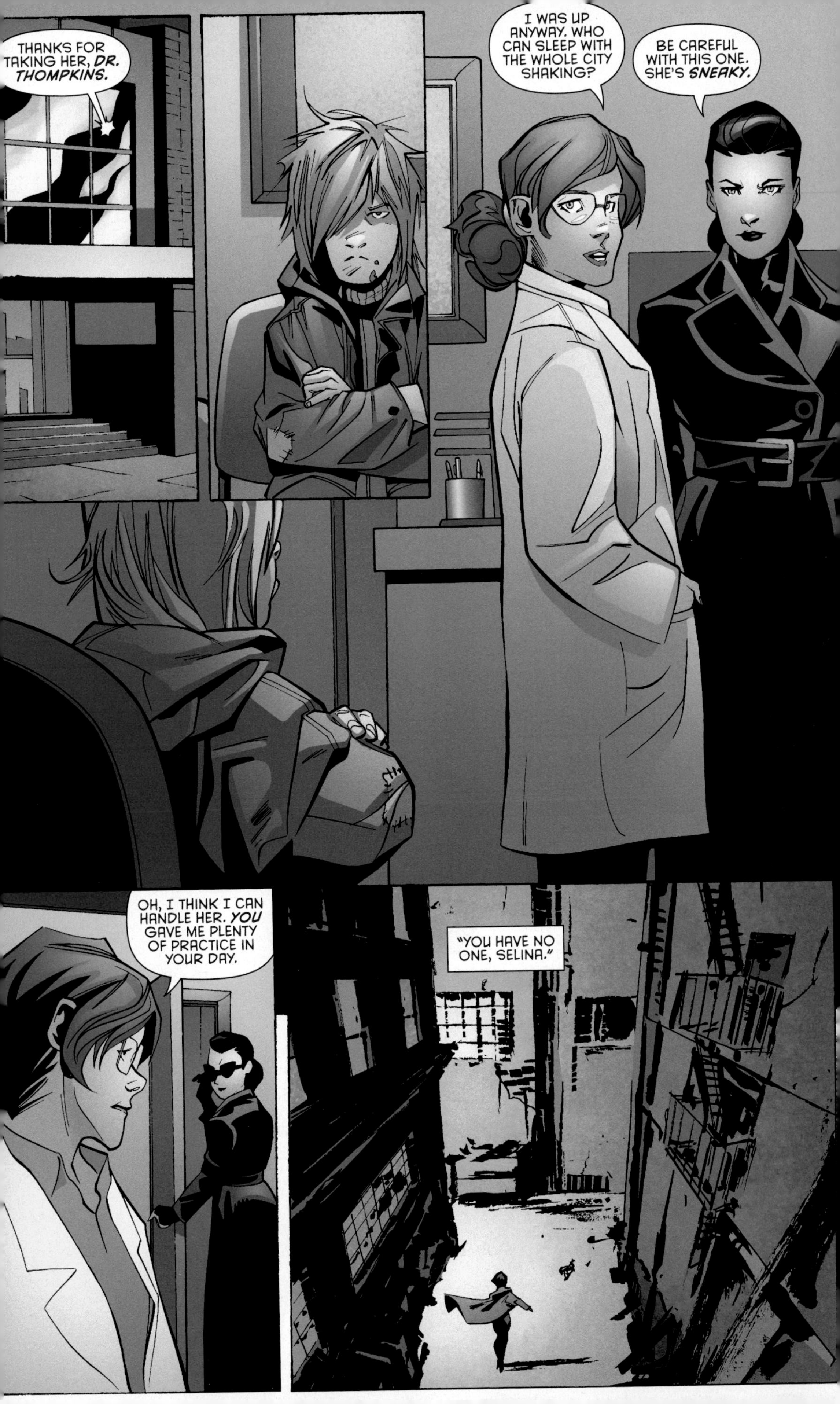
THANKS FOR TAKING HER, DR. THOMPKINS.
I WAS UP ANYWAY. WHO CAN SLEEP WITH THE WHOLE CITY SHAKING?
BE CAREFUL WITH THIS ONE. SHE'S SNEAKY.
OH, I THINK I CAN HANDLE HER. YOU GAVE ME PLENTY OF PRACTICE IN YOUR DAY.
"YOU HAVE NO ONE, SELINA."

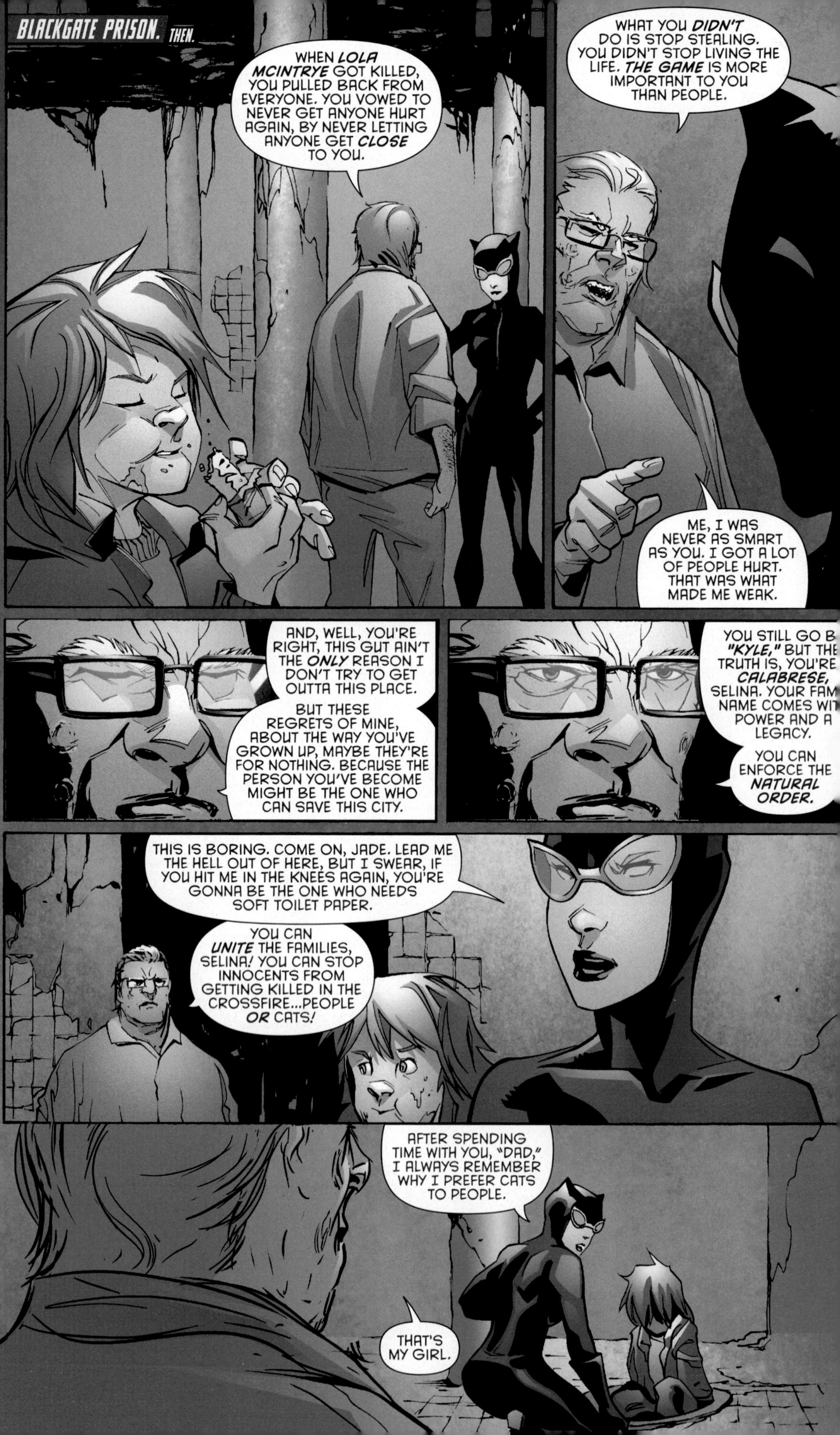

BLACKGATE PRISON. THEN.
WHEN LOLA MCINTRYE GOT KILLED, YOU PULLED BACK FROM EVERYONE. YOU VOWED TO NEVER GET ANYONE HURT AGAIN, BY NEVER LETTING ANYONE GET CLOSE TO YOU.
WHAT YOU DIDN'T DO IS STOP STEALING. YOU DIDN'T STOP LIVING THE LIFE. THE GAME IS MORE IMPORTANT TO YOU THAN PEOPLE.
ME, I WAS NEVER AS SMART AS YOU. I GOT A LOT OF PEOPLE HURT. THAT WAS WHAT MADE ME WEAK.
AND, WELL, YOU'RE RIGHT, THIS GUT AIN'T THE ONLY REASON I DON'T TRY TO GET OUTTA THIS PLACE.
BUT THESE REGRETS OF MINE, ABOUT THE WAY YOU'VE GROWN UP, MAYBE THEY'RE FOR NOTHING. BECAUSE THE PERSON YOU'VE BECOME MIGHT BE THE ONE WHO CAN SAVE THIS CITY.
YOU STILL GO B "KYLE," BUT THE TRUTH IS, YOU'RE CALABRESE, SELINA. YOUR FAM NAME COMES WI POWER AND A LEGACY.
YOU CAN ENFORCE THE NATURAL ORDER.
THIS IS BORING. COME ON, JADE. LEAD ME THE HELL OUT OF HERE, BUT I SWEAR, IF YOU HIT ME IN THE KNEES AGAIN, YOU'RE GONNA BE THE ONE WHO NEEDS SOFT TOILET PAPER.
YOU CAN UNITE THE FAMILIES, SELINA! YOU CAN STOP INNOCENTS FROM GETTING KILLED IN THE CROSSFIRE...PEOPLE OR CATS!
AFTER SPENDING TIME WITH YOU, "DAD," I ALWAYS REMEMBER WHY I PREFER CATS TO PEOPLE.
THAT'S MY GIRL.

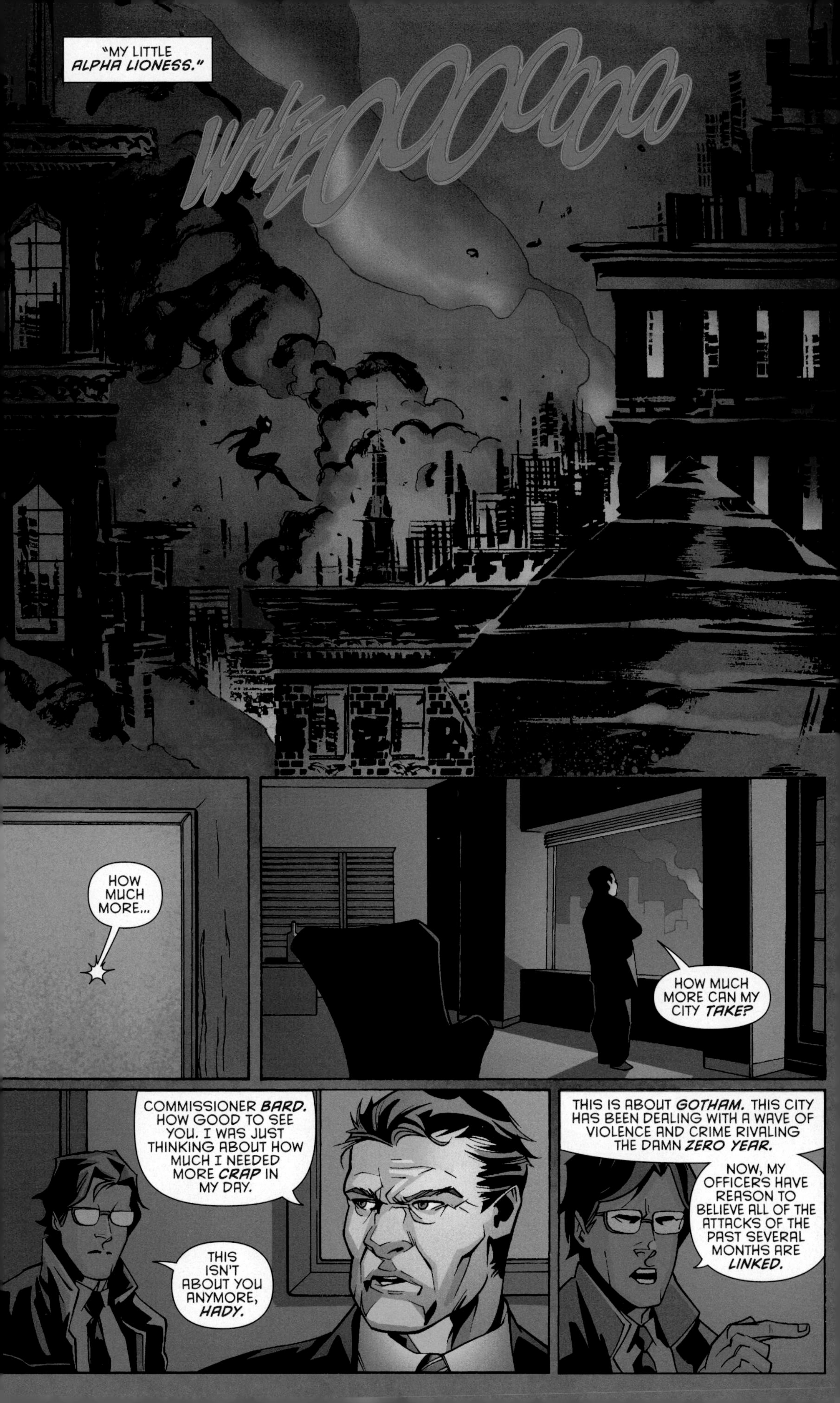

"MY LITTLE ALPHA LIONESS."
WHEEOOOOOOOO
HOW MUCH MORE...
HOW MUCH MORE CAN MY CITY TAKE?
COMMISSIONER BARD. HOW GOOD TO SEE YOU. I WAS JUST THINKING ABOUT HOW MUCH I NEEDED MORE CRAP IN MY DAY.
THIS ISN'T ABOUT YOU ANYMORE, HADY.
THIS IS ABOUT GOTHAM. THIS CITY HAS BEEN DEALING WITH A WAVE OF VIOLENCE AND CRIME RIVALING THE DAMN ZERO YEAR.
NOW, MY OFFICERS HAVE REASON TO BELIEVE ALL OF THE ATTACKS OF THE PAST SEVERAL MONTHS ARE LINKED.

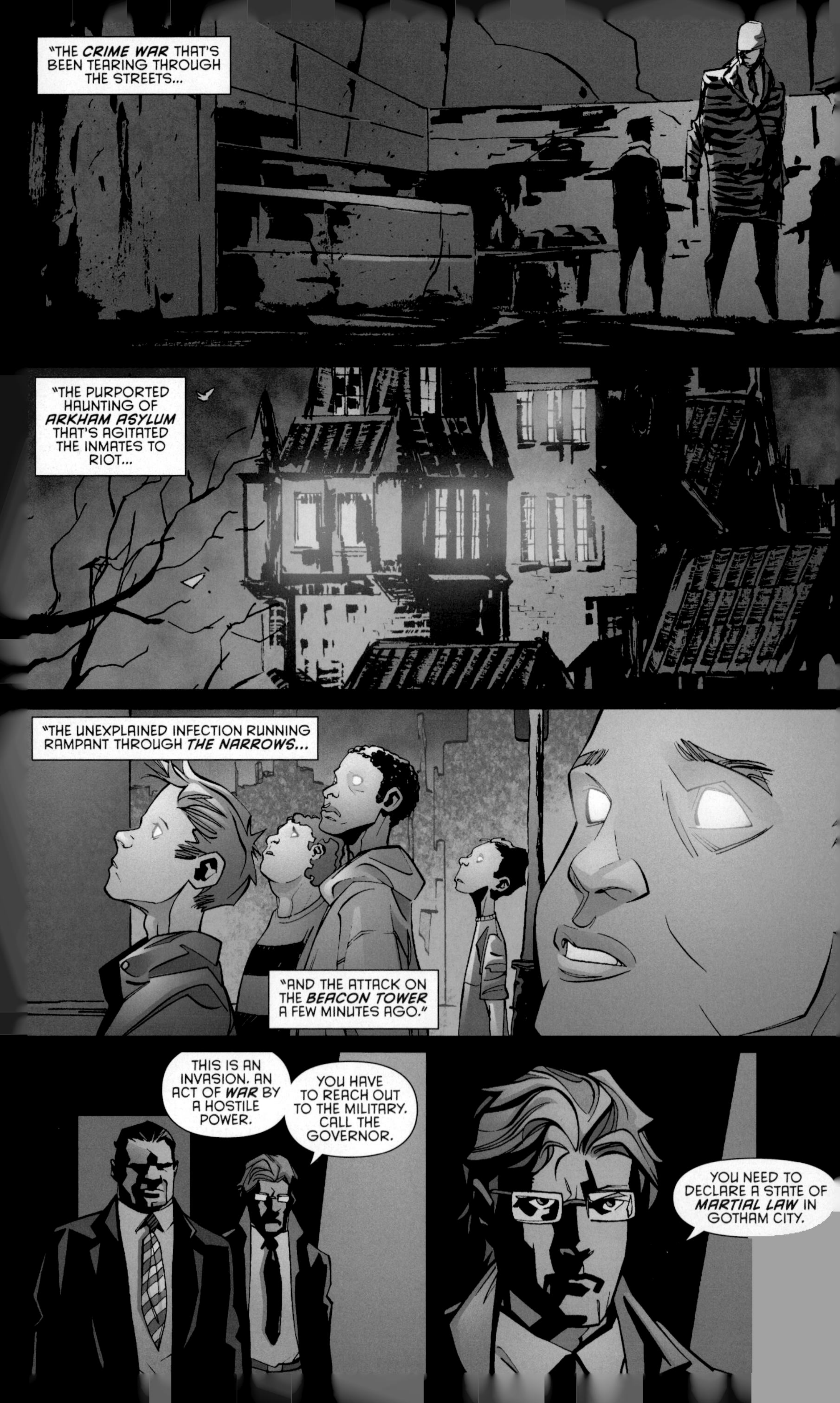
"THE *CRIME WAR* THAT'S BEEN TEARING THROUGH THE STREETS...
"THE PURPORTED HAUNTING OF *ARKHAM ASYLUM* THAT'S AGITATED THE INMATES TO RIOT...
"THE UNEXPLAINED INFECTION RUNNING RAMPANT THROUGH *THE NARROWS*...
"AND THE ATTACK ON THE *BEACON TOWER* A FEW MINUTES AGO."
THIS IS AN INVASION. AN ACT OF *WAR* BY A HOSTILE POWER.
YOU HAVE TO REACH OUT TO THE MILITARY. CALL THE GOVERNOR.
YOU NEED TO DECLARE A STATE OF *MARTIAL LAW* IN GOTHAM CITY.

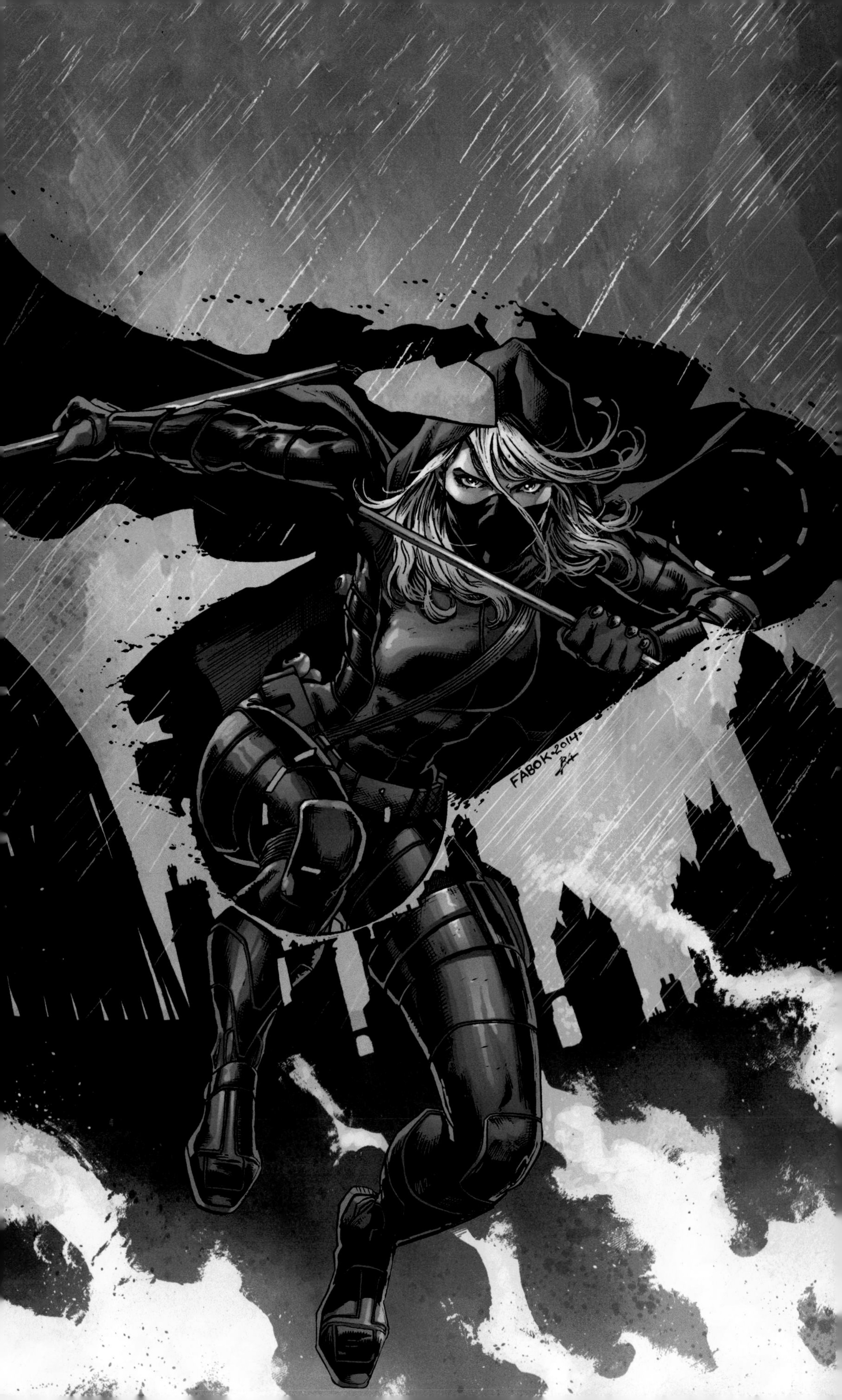

FABOK 2014

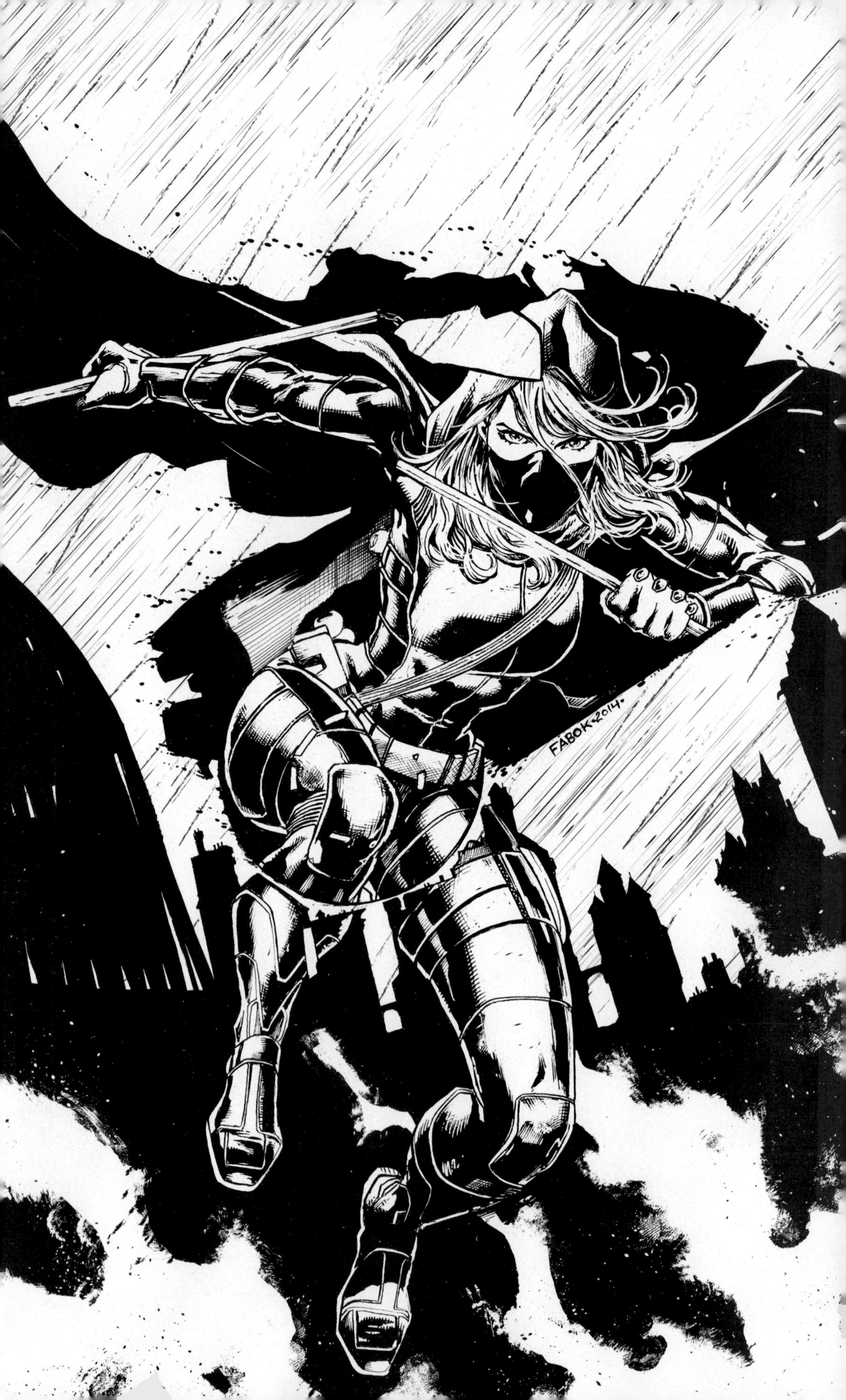
FABOK 2014

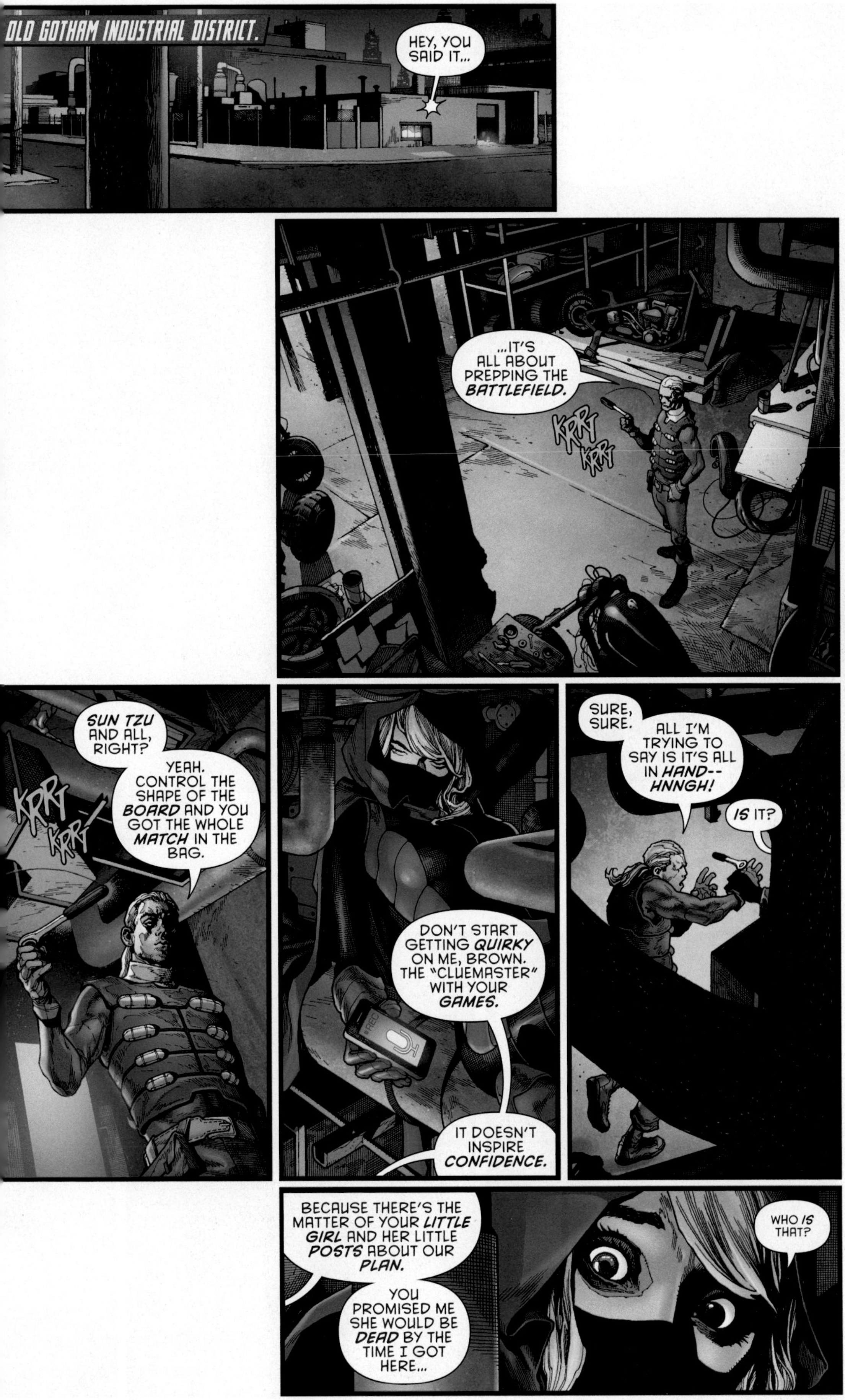

OLD GOTHAM INDUSTRIAL DISTRICT.
HEY, YOU SAID IT...
...IT'S ALL ABOUT PREPPING THE BATTLEFIELD.
KRRT KRRT
SUN TZU AND ALL, RIGHT?
YEAH. CONTROL THE SHAPE OF THE BOARD AND YOU GOT THE WHOLE MATCH IN THE BAG.
KRRT KRRT
DON'T START GETTING QUIRKY ON ME, BROWN. THE "CLUEMASTER" WITH YOUR GAMES.
IT DOESN'T INSPIRE CONFIDENCE.
SURE, SURE.
ALL I'M TRYING TO SAY IS IT'S ALL IN HAND-- HNNGH!
IS IT?
BECAUSE THERE'S THE MATTER OF YOUR LITTLE GIRL AND HER LITTLE POSTS ABOUT OUR PLAN.
YOU PROMISED ME SHE WOULD BE DEAD BY THE TIME I GOT HERE...
WHO IS THAT?

...AND I'M NOT SEEING A *BODY*.

I DON'T CARE IF SHE'S YOUR *DARLING DAUGHTER*. YOU SAID YOU COULD *ELIMINATE* HER.

WE DON'T WANT HER SCREWING THIS UP, BROWN...

DO YOU *HEAR* ME?

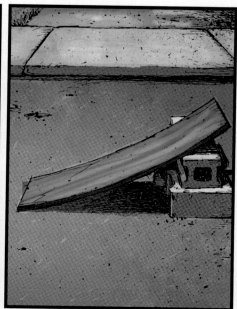

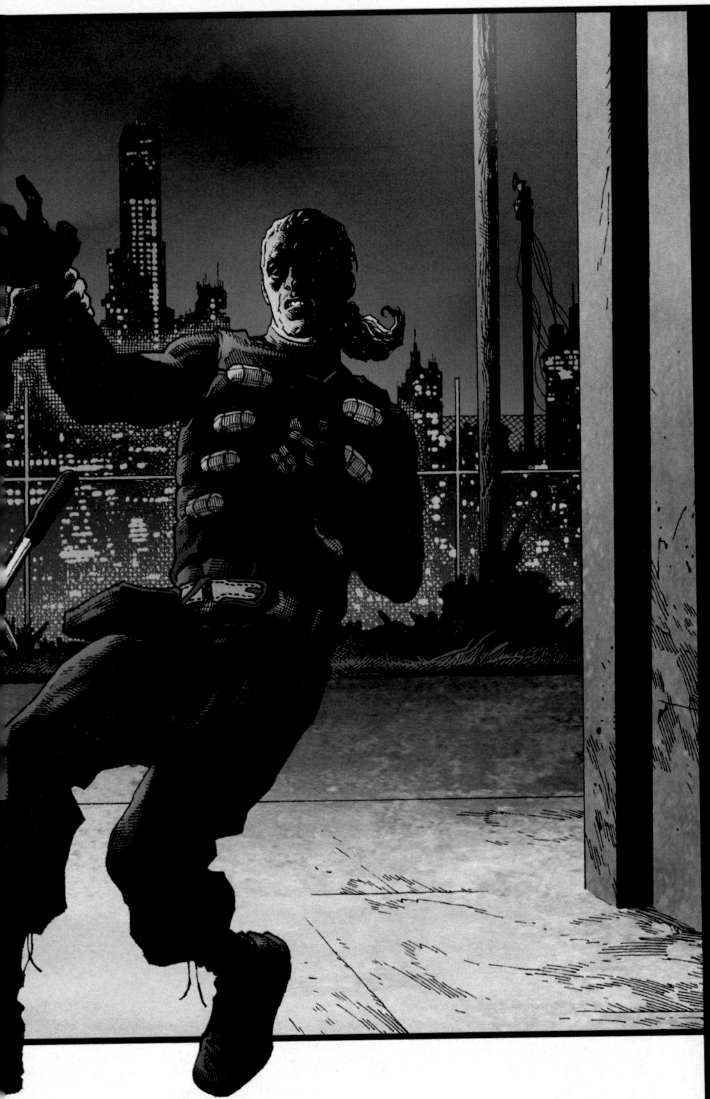

# THE SPOILER

SCOTT SNYDER & JAMES TYNION IV STORY
RAY FAWKES SCRIPT
KYLE HIGGINS & TIM SEELEY CONSULTING WRITERS
ANDY CLARKE ART

BLOND COLORS
STEVE WANDS LETTERS
JASON FABOK & BRAD ANDERSON COVER

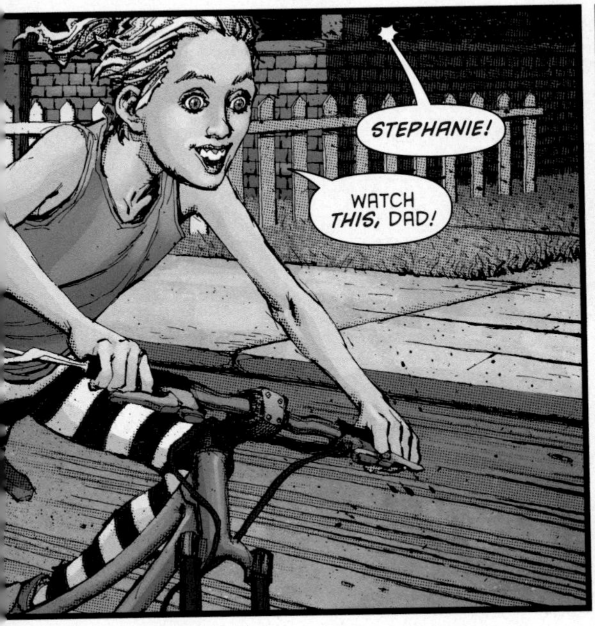
STEPHANIE!
WATCH THIS, DAD!

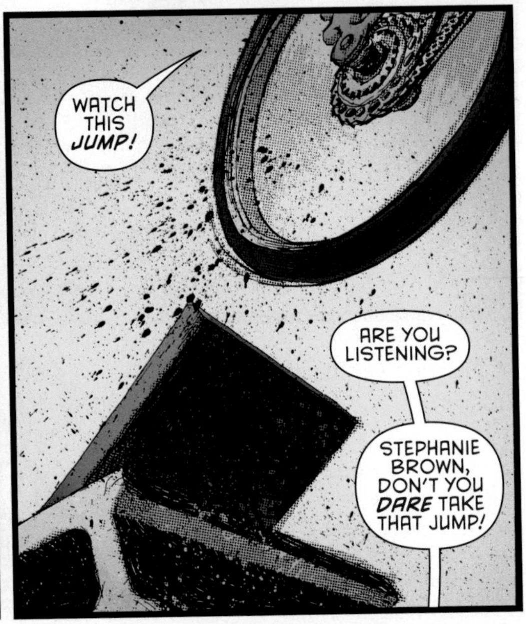
WATCH THIS JUMP!
ARE YOU LISTENING?
STEPHANIE BROWN, DON'T YOU DARE TAKE THAT JUMP!

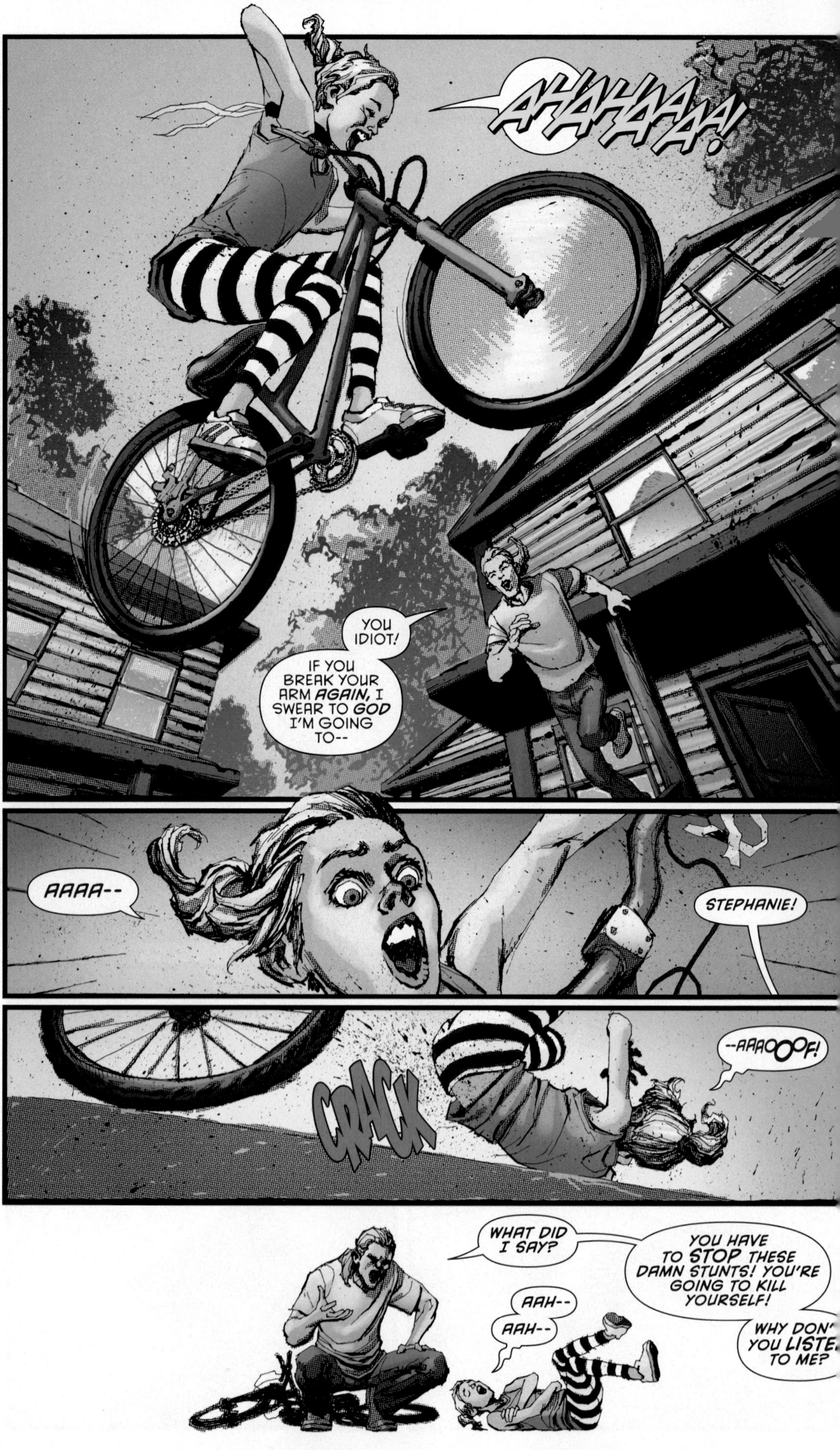
AHAHAAAA!
YOU IDIOT!
IF YOU BREAK YOUR ARM *AGAIN*, I SWEAR TO *GOD* I'M GOING TO--
AAAA--
STEPHANIE!
CRACK
--AAAOOOF!
WHAT DID I SAY?
YOU HAVE TO **STOP** THESE DAMN STUNTS! YOU'RE GOING TO KILL YOURSELF!
AAH--
AAH--
WHY DON' YOU **LISTE** TO ME?

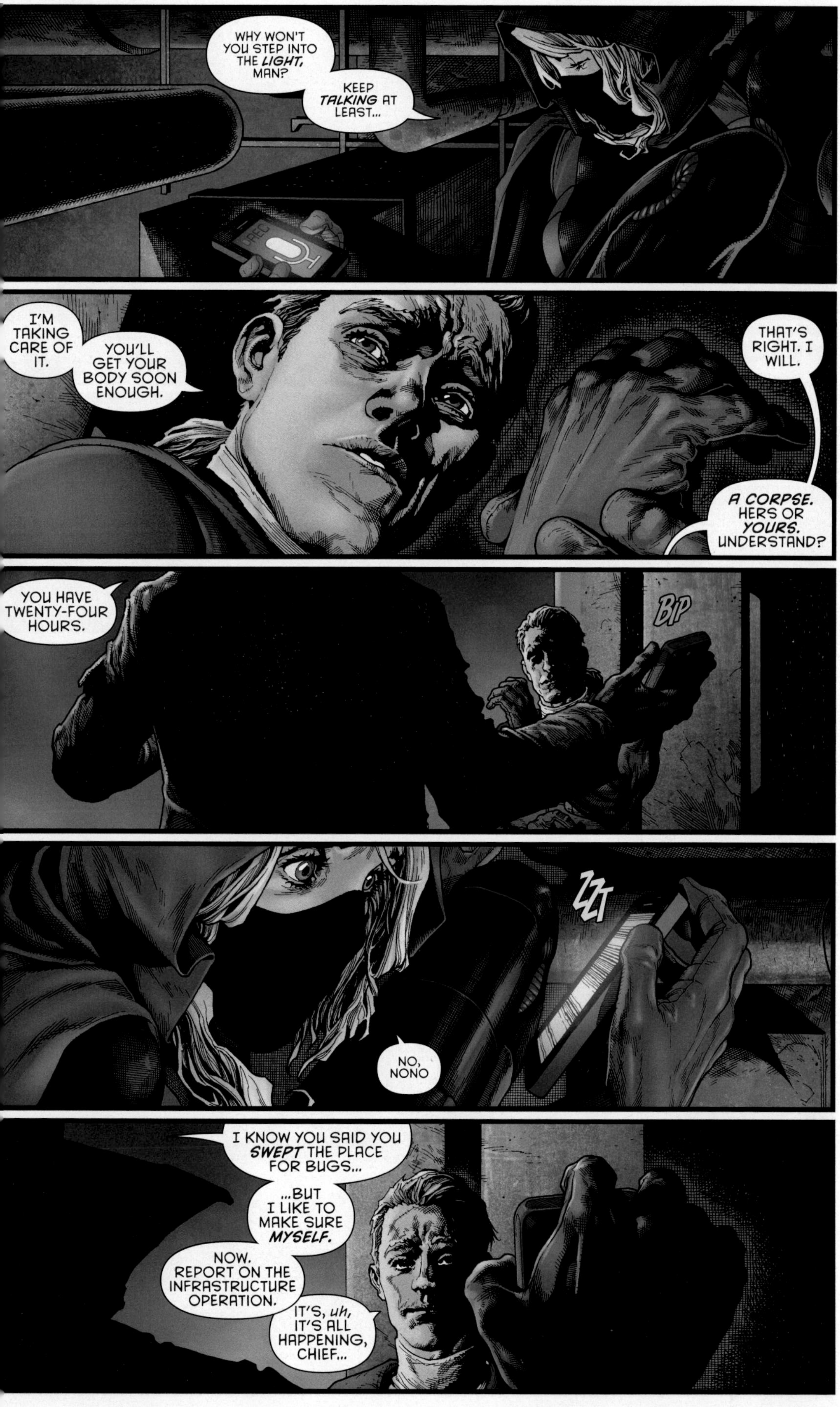
WHY WON'T YOU STEP INTO THE *LIGHT*, MAN?
KEEP *TALKING* AT LEAST...
I'M TAKING CARE OF IT.
YOU'LL GET YOUR BODY SOON ENOUGH.
THAT'S RIGHT. I WILL.
*A CORPSE.* HERS OR *YOURS.* UNDERSTAND?
YOU HAVE TWENTY-FOUR HOURS.
BIP
ZZT
NO, NONO
I KNOW YOU SAID YOU *SWEPT* THE PLACE FOR BUGS...
...BUT I LIKE TO MAKE SURE *MYSELF.*
NOW. REPORT ON THE INFRASTRUCTURE OPERATION.
IT'S, *uh,* IT'S ALL HAPPENING, CHIEF...

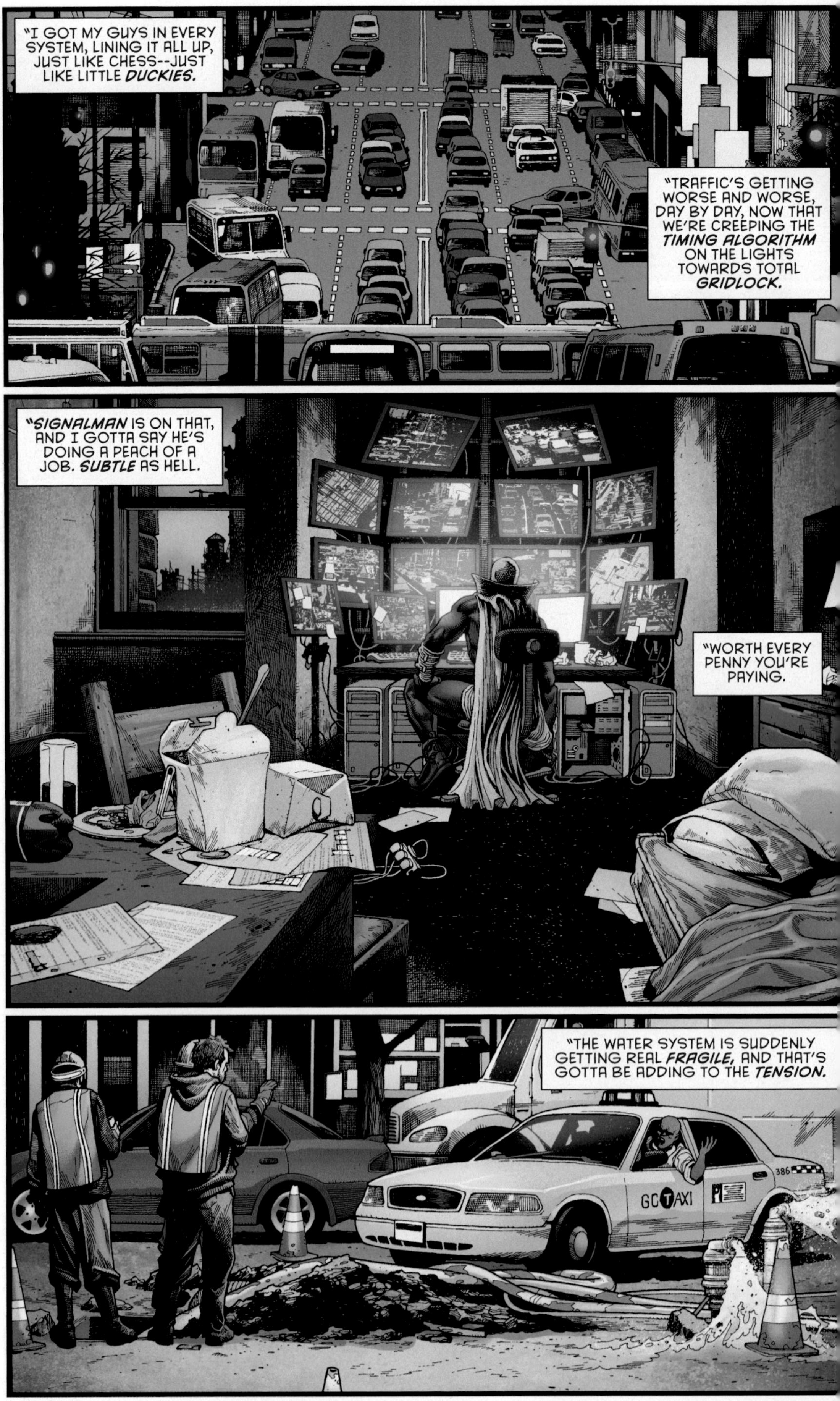
"I GOT MY GUYS IN EVERY SYSTEM, LINING IT ALL UP, JUST LIKE CHESS--JUST LIKE LITTLE *DUCKIES.*
"TRAFFIC'S GETTING WORSE AND WORSE, DAY BY DAY, NOW THAT WE'RE CREEPING THE *TIMING ALGORITHM* ON THE LIGHTS TOWARDS TOTAL *GRIDLOCK.*
"*SIGNALMAN* IS ON THAT, AND I GOTTA SAY HE'S DOING A PEACH OF A JOB. *SUBTLE* AS HELL.
"WORTH EVERY PENNY YOU'RE PAYING.
"THE WATER SYSTEM IS SUDDENLY GETTING REAL *FRAGILE,* AND THAT'S GOTTA BE ADDING TO THE *TENSION.*
GC TAXI
386

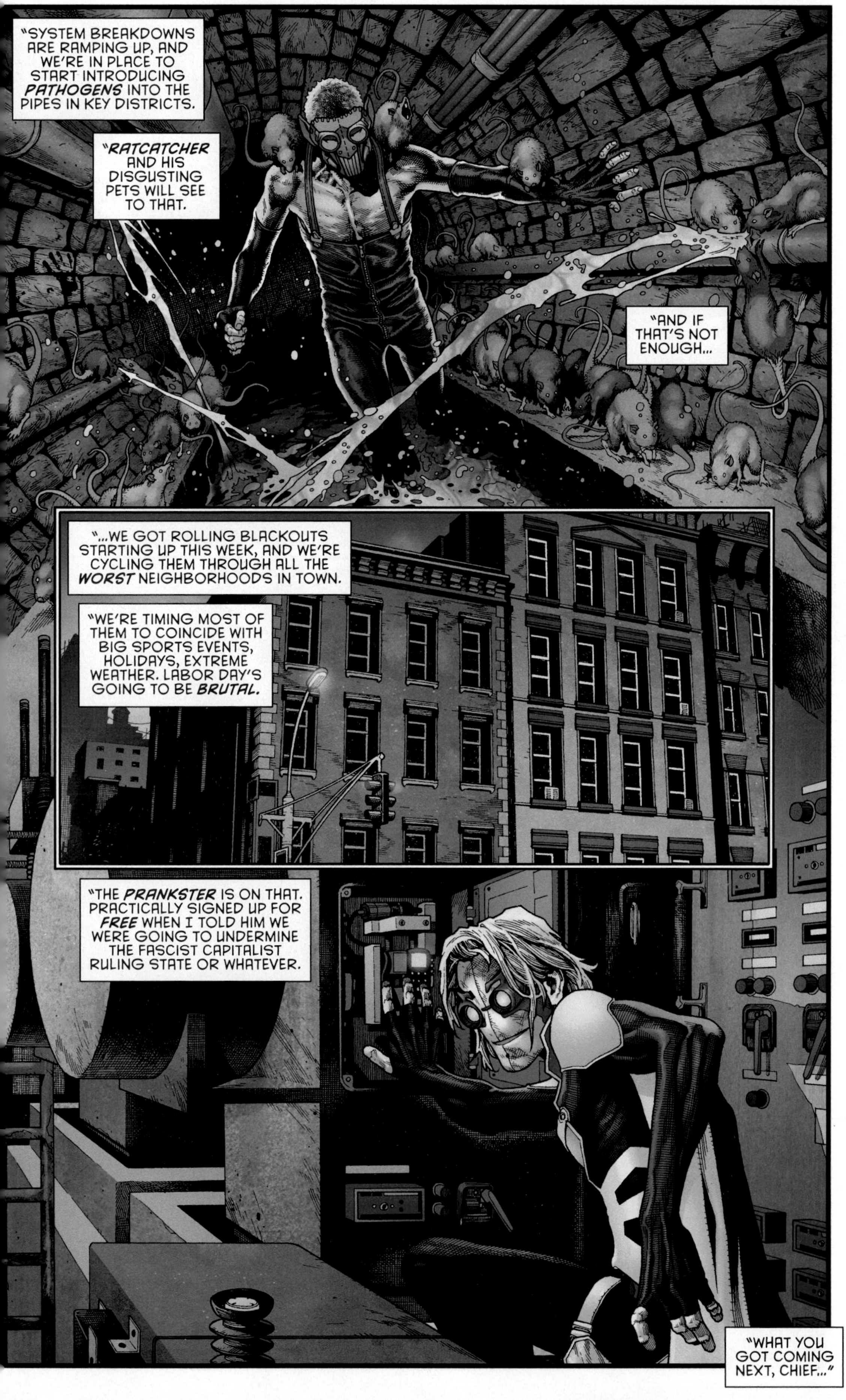
"SYSTEM BREAKDOWNS ARE RAMPING UP, AND WE'RE IN PLACE TO START INTRODUCING *PATHOGENS* INTO THE PIPES IN KEY DISTRICTS.
"*RATCATCHER* AND HIS DISGUSTING PETS WILL SEE TO THAT.
"AND IF THAT'S NOT ENOUGH...
"...WE GOT ROLLING BLACKOUTS STARTING UP THIS WEEK, AND WE'RE CYCLING THEM THROUGH ALL THE *WORST* NEIGHBORHOODS IN TOWN.
"WE'RE TIMING MOST OF THEM TO COINCIDE WITH BIG SPORTS EVENTS, HOLIDAYS, EXTREME WEATHER. LABOR DAY'S GOING TO BE *BRUTAL.*
"THE *PRANKSTER* IS ON THAT. PRACTICALLY SIGNED UP FOR *FREE* WHEN I TOLD HIM WE WERE GOING TO UNDERMINE THE FASCIST CAPITALIST RULING STATE OR WHATEVER.
"WHAT YOU GOT COMING NEXT, CHIEF..."

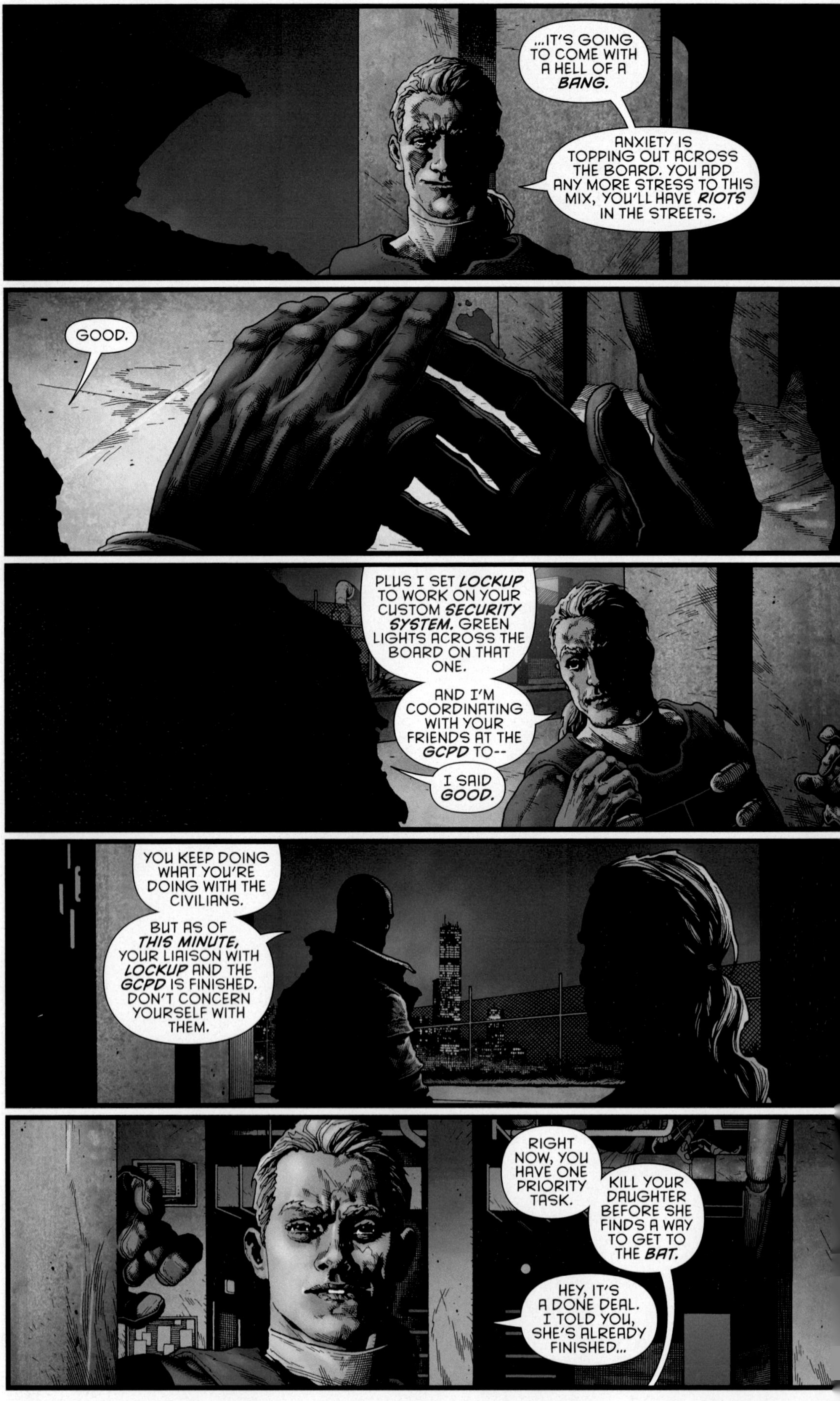

...IT'S GOING TO COME WITH A HELL OF A BANG.
ANXIETY IS TOPPING OUT ACROSS THE BOARD. YOU ADD ANY MORE STRESS TO THIS MIX, YOU'LL HAVE RIOTS IN THE STREETS.
GOOD.
PLUS I SET LOCKUP TO WORK ON YOUR CUSTOM SECURITY SYSTEM. GREEN LIGHTS ACROSS THE BOARD ON THAT ONE.
AND I'M COORDINATING WITH YOUR FRIENDS AT THE GCPD TO--
I SAID GOOD.
YOU KEEP DOING WHAT YOU'RE DOING WITH THE CIVILIANS.
BUT AS OF THIS MINUTE, YOUR LIAISON WITH LOCKUP AND THE GCPD IS FINISHED. DON'T CONCERN YOURSELF WITH THEM.
RIGHT NOW, YOU HAVE ONE PRIORITY TASK.
KILL YOUR DAUGHTER BEFORE SHE FINDS A WAY TO GET TO THE BAT.
HEY, IT'S A DONE DEAL. I TOLD YOU, SHE'S ALREADY FINISHED...

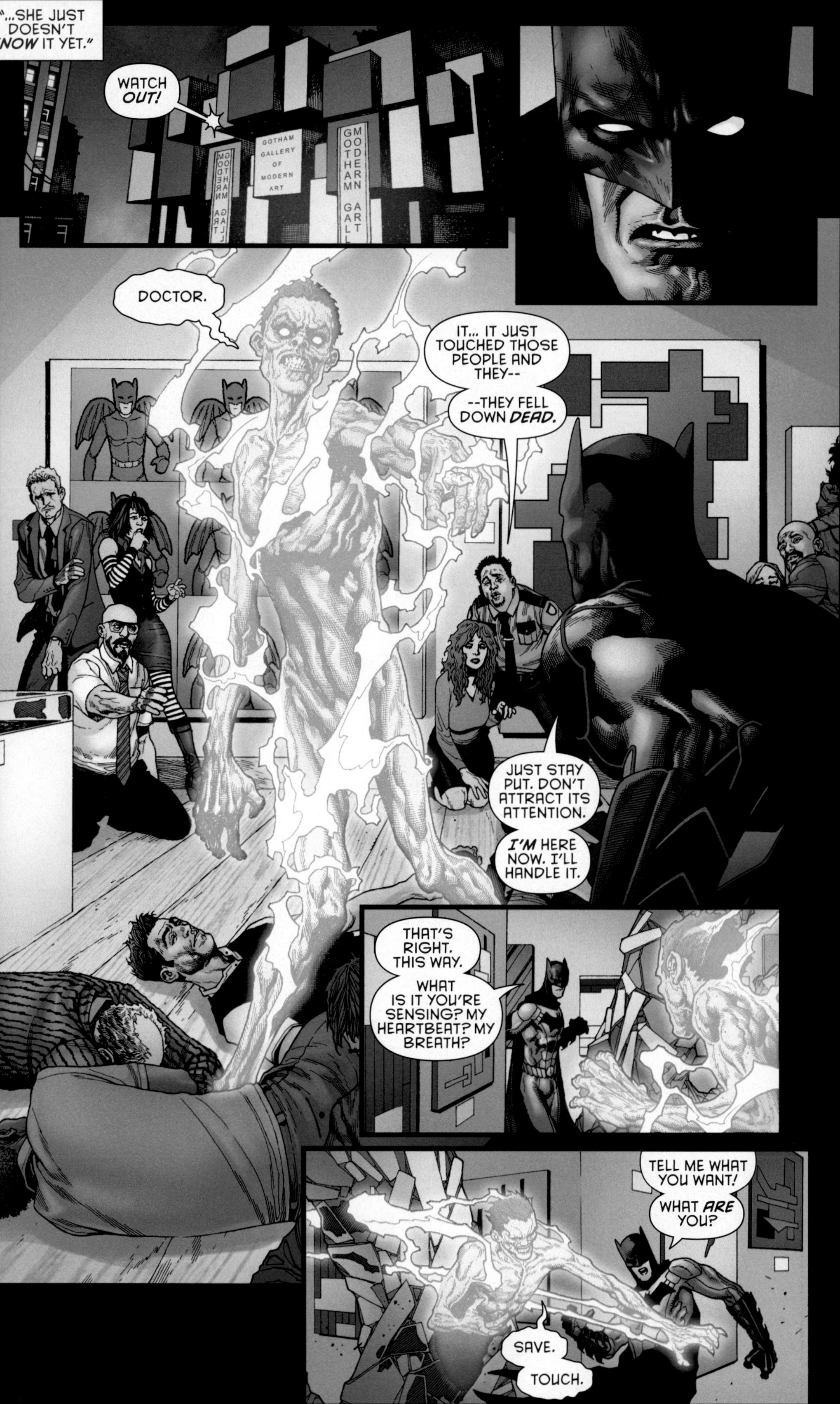
"...SHE JUST DOESN'T NOW IT YET."
WATCH *OUT!*
GOTHAM GALLERY OF MODERN ART
GOTHAM MODERN ART GALL
DOCTOR.
IT... IT JUST TOUCHED THOSE PEOPLE AND THEY--
--THEY FELL DOWN *DEAD.*
JUST STAY PUT. DON'T ATTRACT ITS ATTENTION.
*I'M* HERE NOW. I'LL HANDLE IT.
THAT'S RIGHT. THIS WAY.
WHAT IS IT YOU'RE SENSING? MY HEARTBEAT? MY BREATH?
TELL ME WHAT YOU WANT!
WHAT *ARE* YOU?
SAVE.
TOUCH.

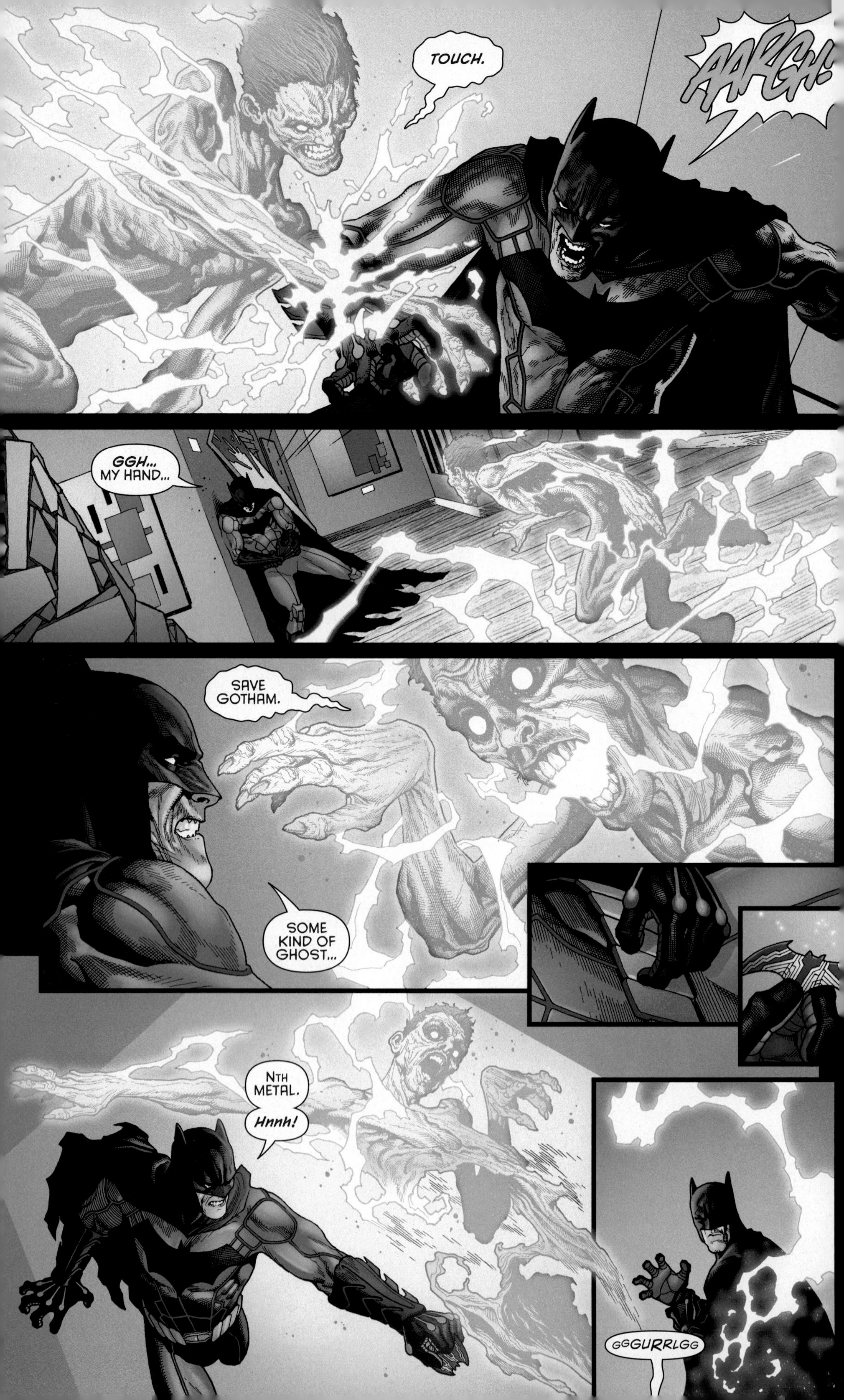
TOUCH.
AARGH!
GGH... MY HAND...
SAVE GOTHAM.
SOME KIND OF GHOST...
NTH METAL.
Hnnh!
GGGURRLGG

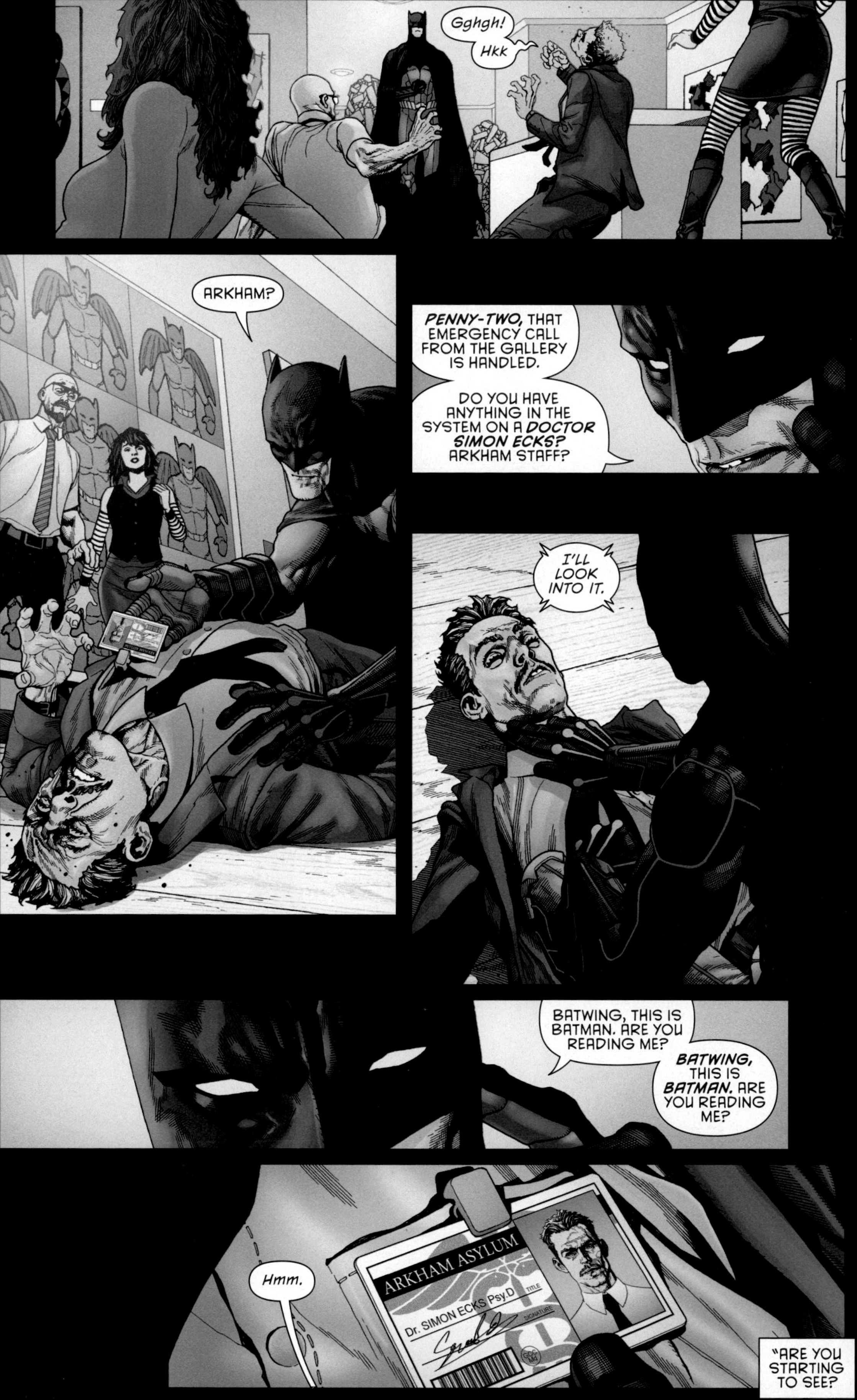

Gghgh!
Hkk
ARKHAM?
PENNY-TWO, THAT EMERGENCY CALL FROM THE GALLERY IS HANDLED.
DO YOU HAVE ANYTHING IN THE SYSTEM ON A DOCTOR SIMON ECKS? ARKHAM STAFF?
I'LL LOOK INTO IT.
BATWING, THIS IS BATMAN. ARE YOU READING ME?
BATWING, THIS IS BATMAN. ARE YOU READING ME?
Hmm.
ARKHAM ASYLUM
Dr. SIMON ECKS Psy.D
"ARE YOU STARTING TO SEE?

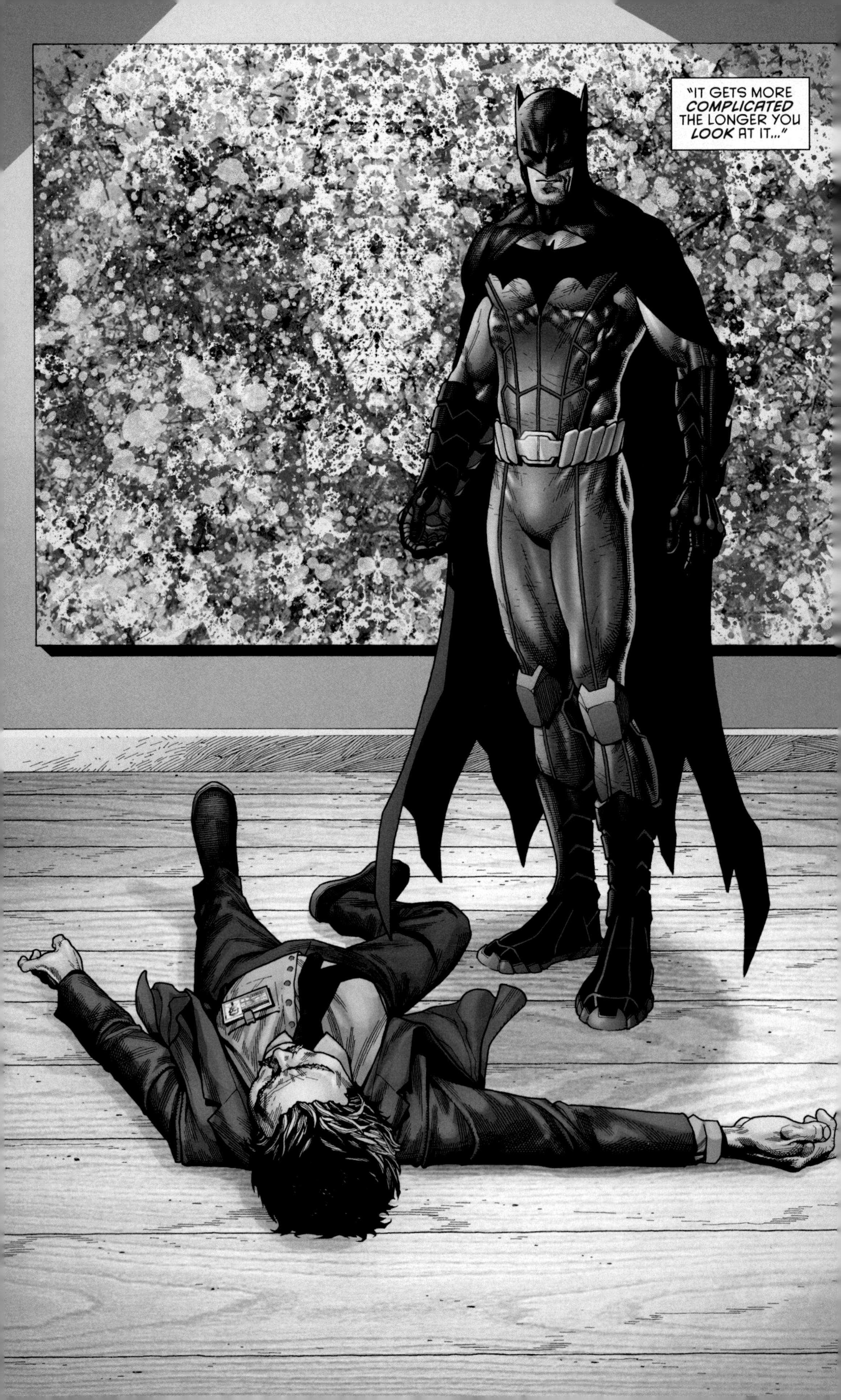
"IT GETS MORE COMPLICATED THE LONGER YOU LOOK AT IT..."

"...BUT IT ALL LEADS TO *ONE* INEVITABLE CONCLUSION."

OWW.

SITTING UP THERE FOR LIKE THREE HOURS...

DAD, DAD...

YOU'VE GONE TOO FAR TO COME *BACK* NOW.

YOU ALWAYS HAD TO LOOK LIKE THE SMARTEST GUY IN THE ROOM...

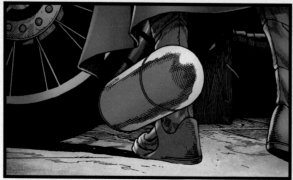

WHUH

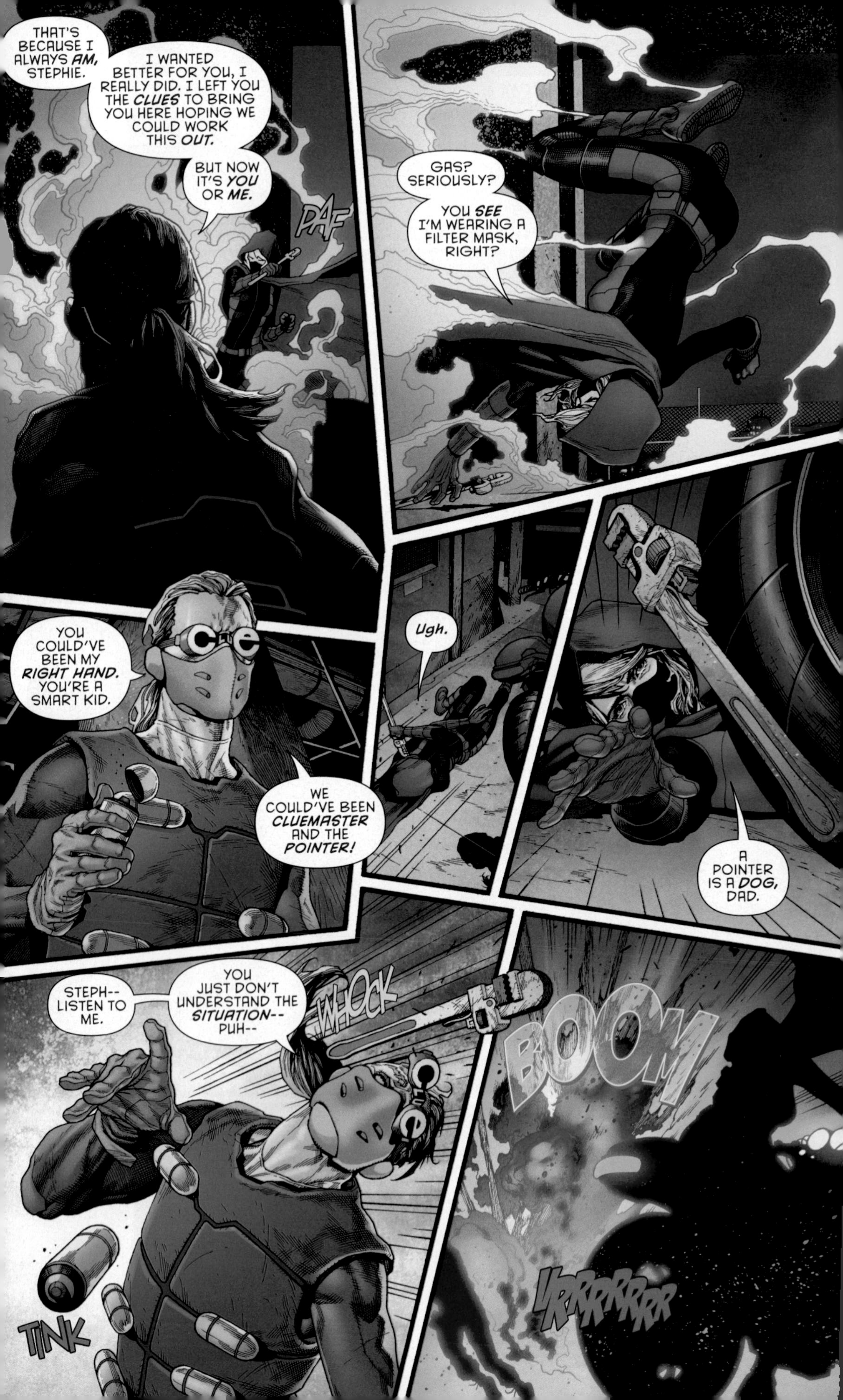
THAT'S BECAUSE I ALWAYS *AM*, STEPHIE.
I WANTED BETTER FOR YOU, I REALLY DID. I LEFT YOU THE *CLUES* TO BRING YOU HERE HOPING WE COULD WORK THIS *OUT.*
BUT NOW IT'S *YOU* OR *ME.*
PAF
GAS? SERIOUSLY?
YOU *SEE* I'M WEARING A FILTER MASK, RIGHT?
YOU COULD'VE BEEN MY *RIGHT HAND.* YOU'RE A SMART KID.
WE COULD'VE BEEN *CLUEMASTER* AND THE *POINTER!*
*Ugh.*
A POINTER IS A *DOG,* DAD.
STEPH-- LISTEN TO ME.
YOU JUST DON'T UNDERSTAND THE *SITUATION--* PUH--
WHOCK
TINK
BOOM
VRRRRRRRR

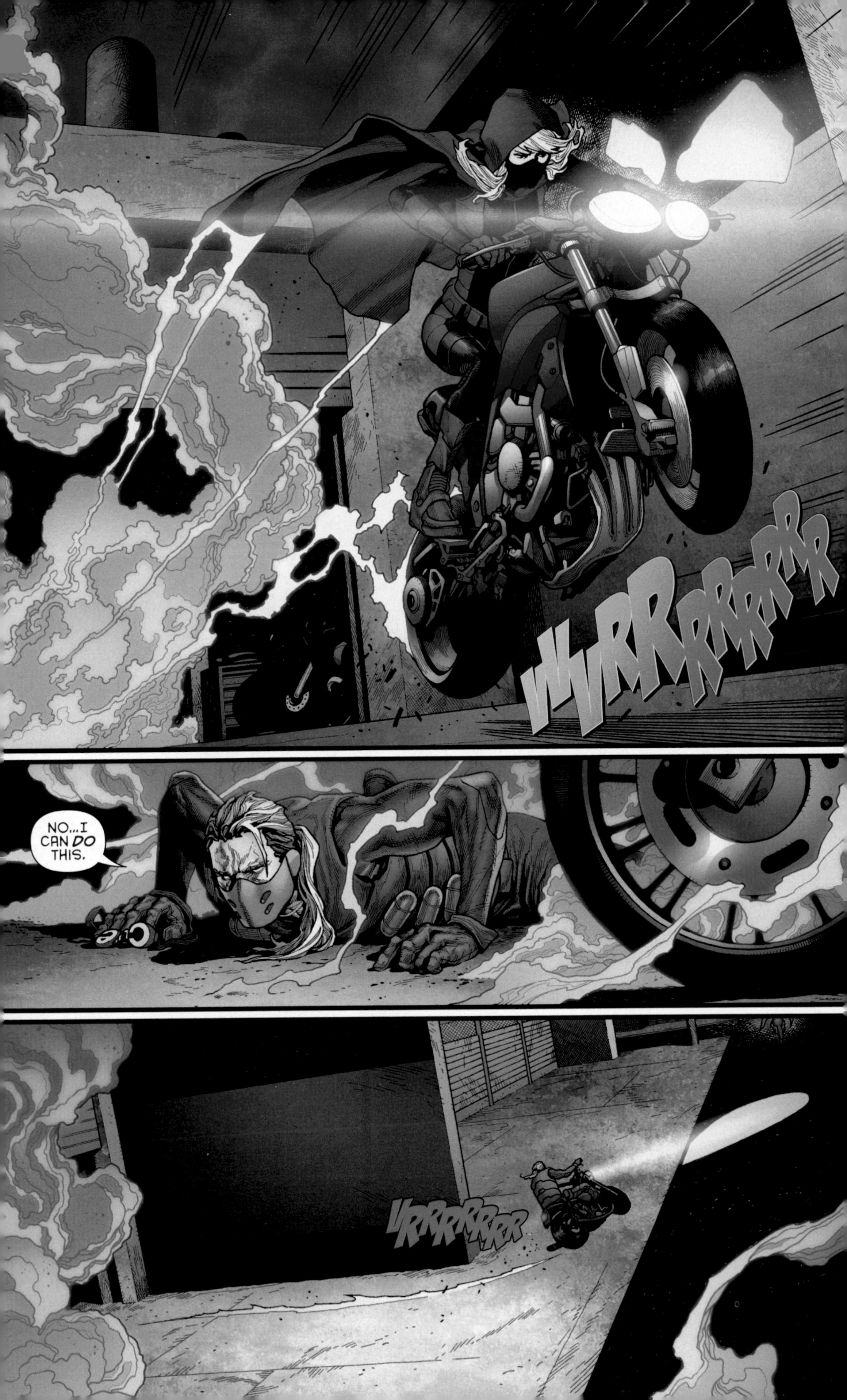
WRRRRRRRR
NO... I CAN DO THIS.
VRRRRRRRR

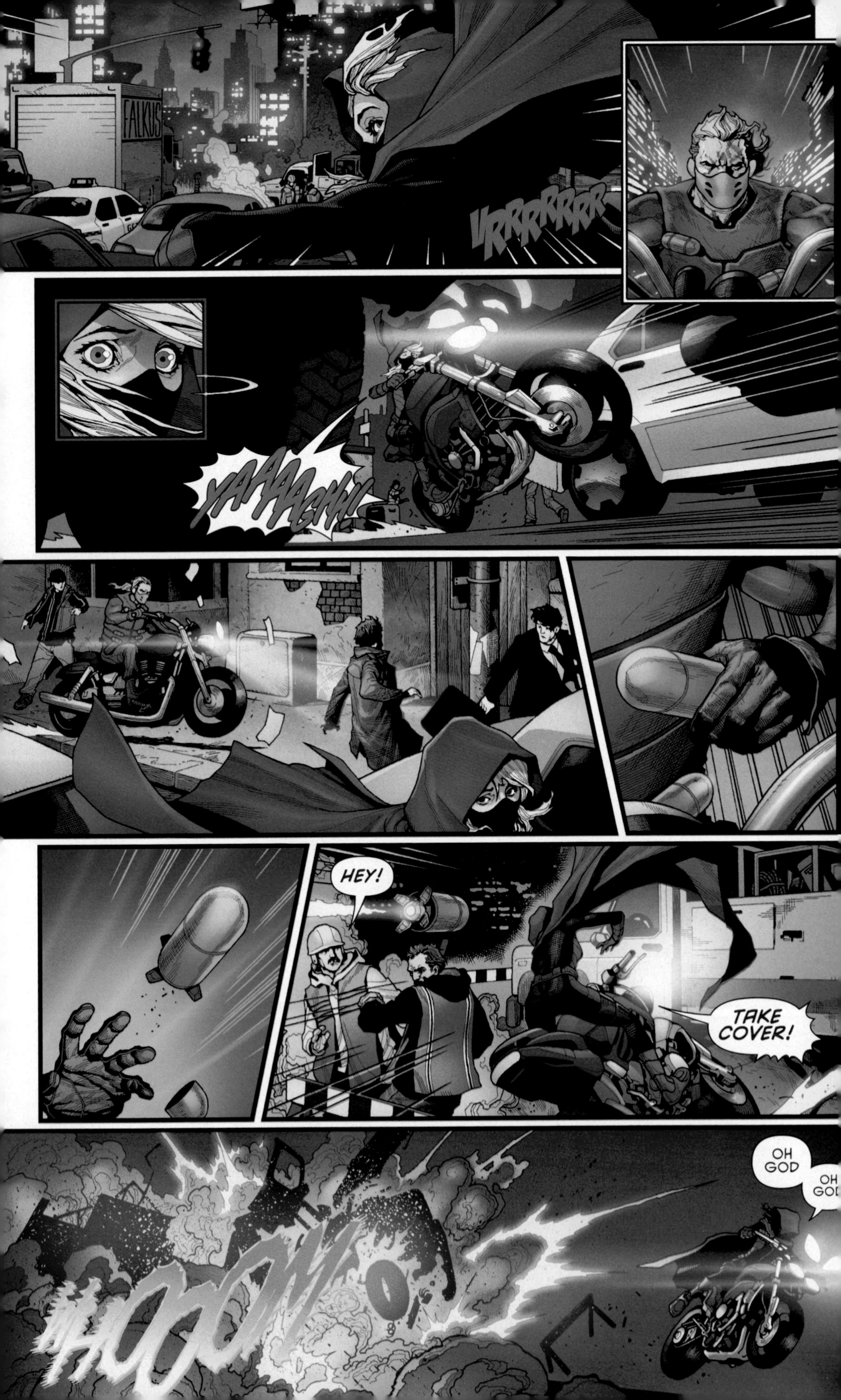
FALKUS
VRRRRRRR
YAAAAAGHH!
HEY!
TAKE COVER!
OH GOD
OH GOD
THOOOM

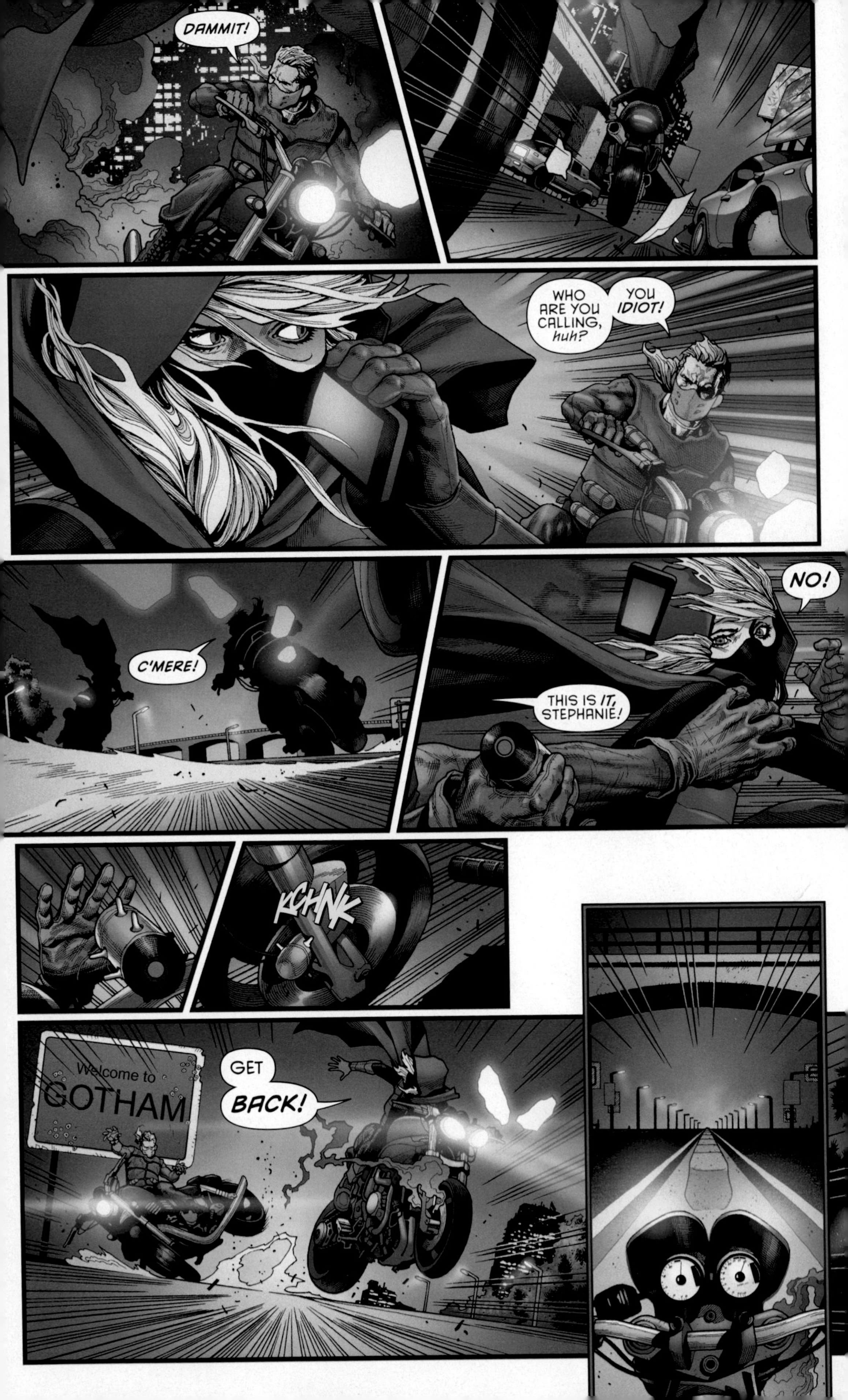
DAMMIT!
WHO ARE YOU CALLING, huh?
YOU IDIOT!
C'MERE!
NO!
THIS IS IT, STEPHANIE!
KCHNK
Welcome to GOTHAM
GET BACK!

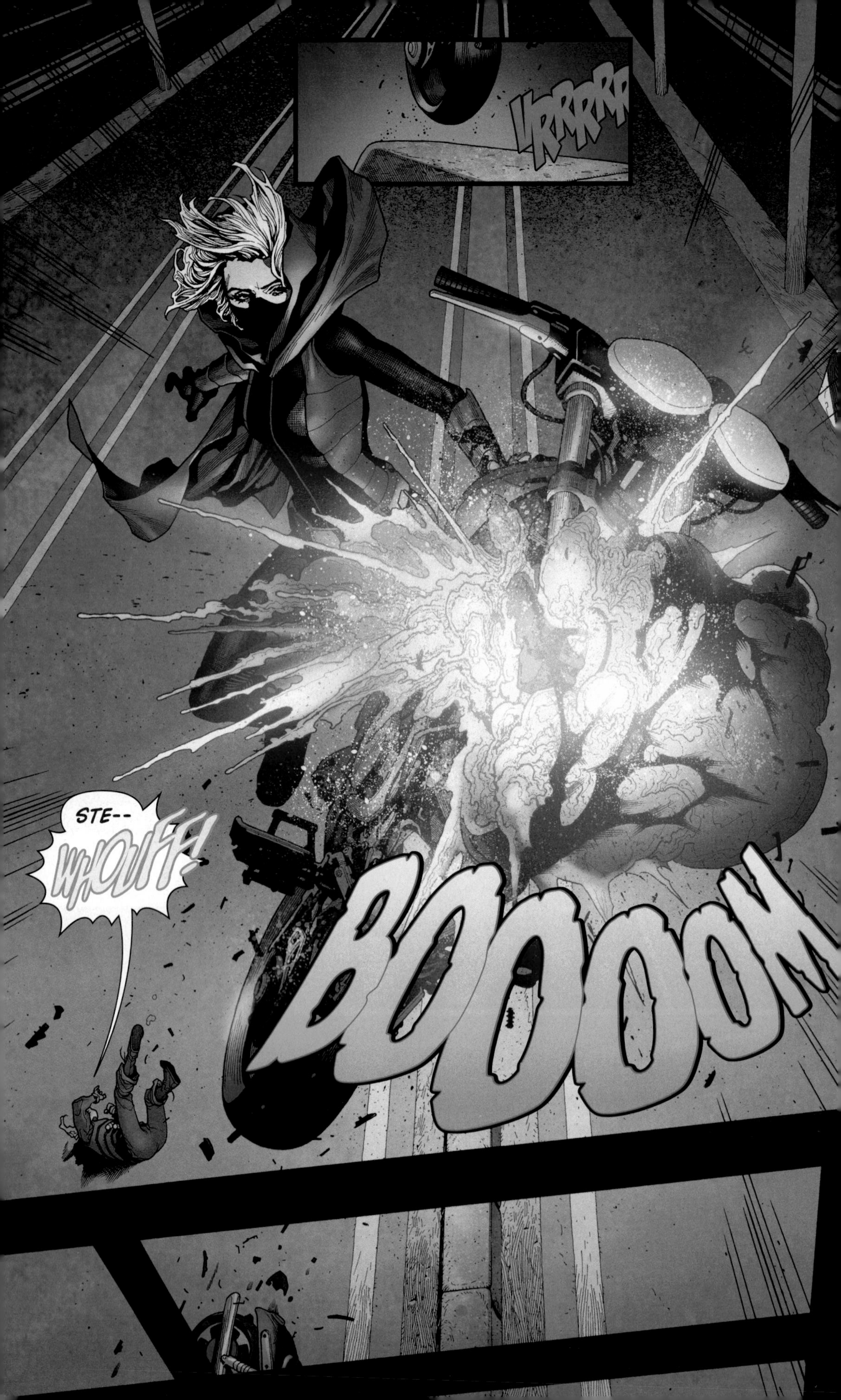
URRRRR
STE--
WHOUFF!
BOOOOM

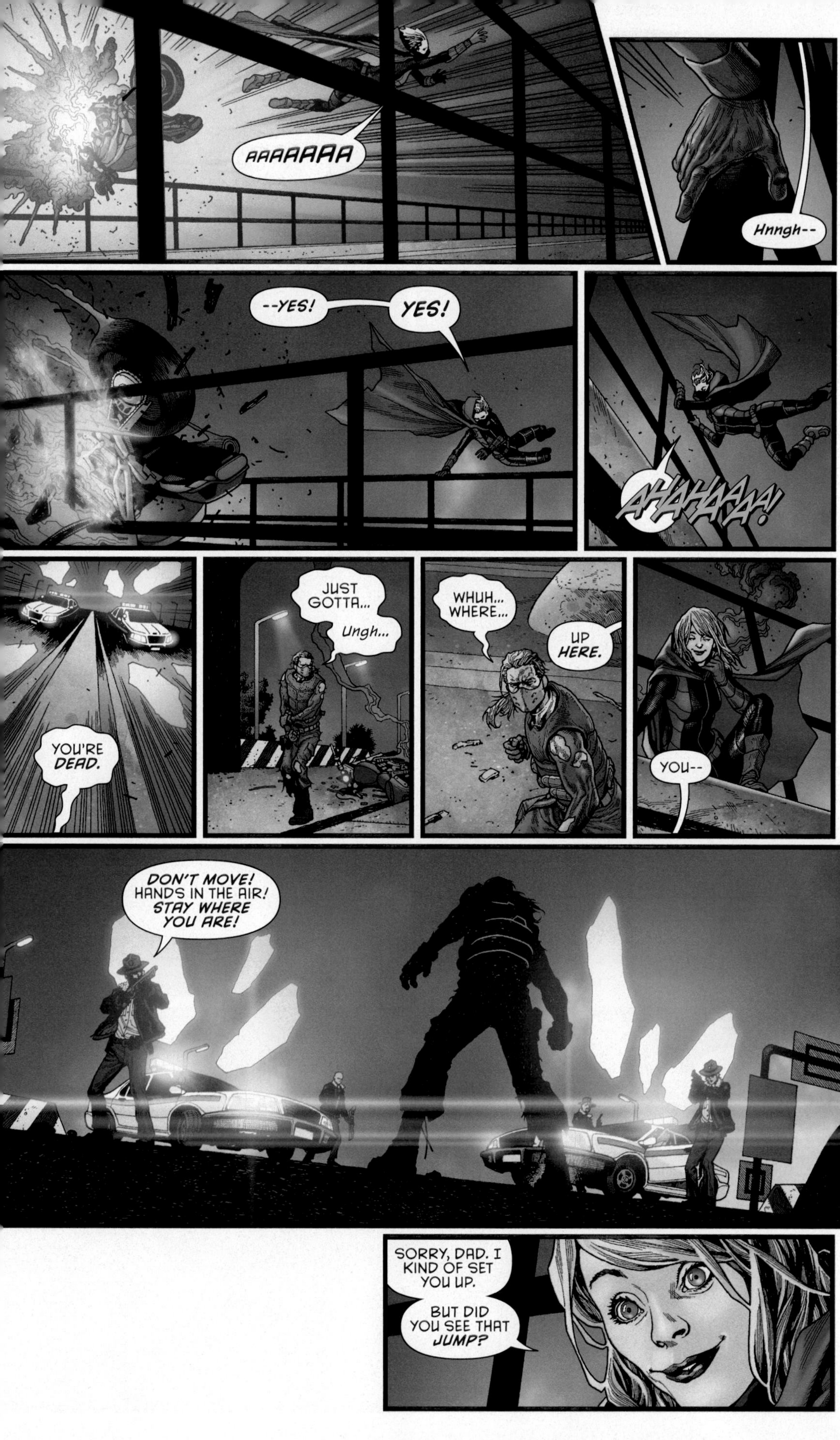
AAAAAAA
Hnngh--
--YES!
YES!
AHAHAAA!
YOU'RE DEAD.
JUST GOTTA... Ungh...
WHUH... WHERE...
UP HERE.
YOU--
DON'T MOVE! HANDS IN THE AIR! STAY WHERE YOU ARE!
SORRY, DAD. I KIND OF SET YOU UP.
BUT DID YOU SEE THAT JUMP?

YOU'RE SIX MILES *OUTSIDE* GOTHAM NOW, SWEETHEART. YOU'RE IN *STATE* CUSTODY, NOT GCPD.

AND YOU DON'T OWN *US.*

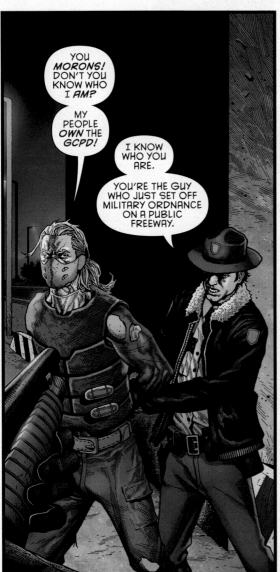

YOU *MORONS!* DON'T YOU KNOW WHO I *AM?*

MY PEOPLE *OWN* THE GCPD!

I KNOW WHO YOU ARE.

YOU'RE THE GUY WHO JUST SET OFF MILITARY ORDNANCE ON A PUBLIC FREEWAY.

STEPHANIE! I'LL *GET* YOU FOR THIS!

YOU THINK YOU CAN *DO* THIS?

YOU'RE *FINISHED*, DO YOU *HEAR* ME? YOU'RE *DONE!*

NO, DAD. *YOU'RE* DONE.

I'M JUST GETTING *STARTED.*

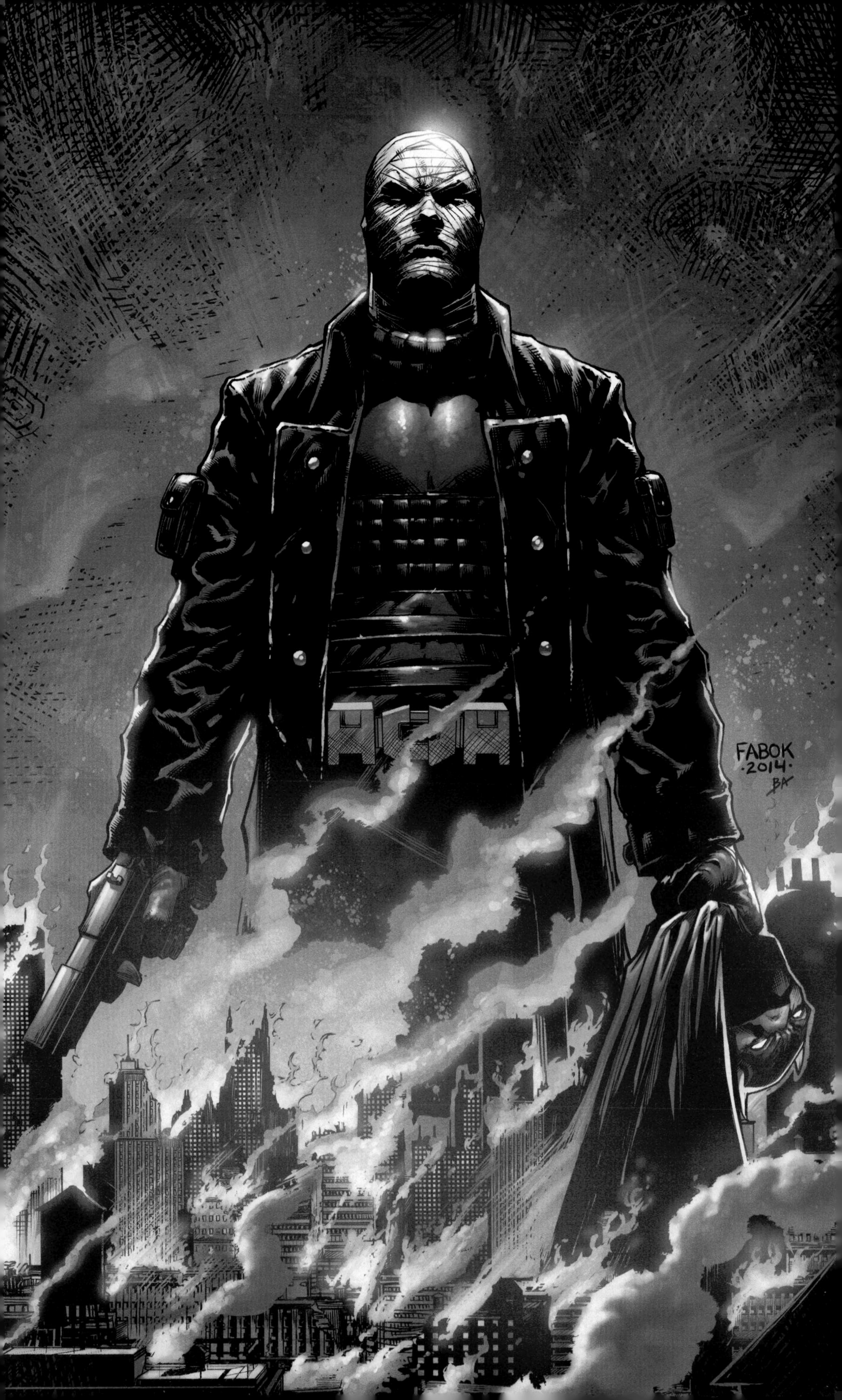
FABOK
·2014·
BA

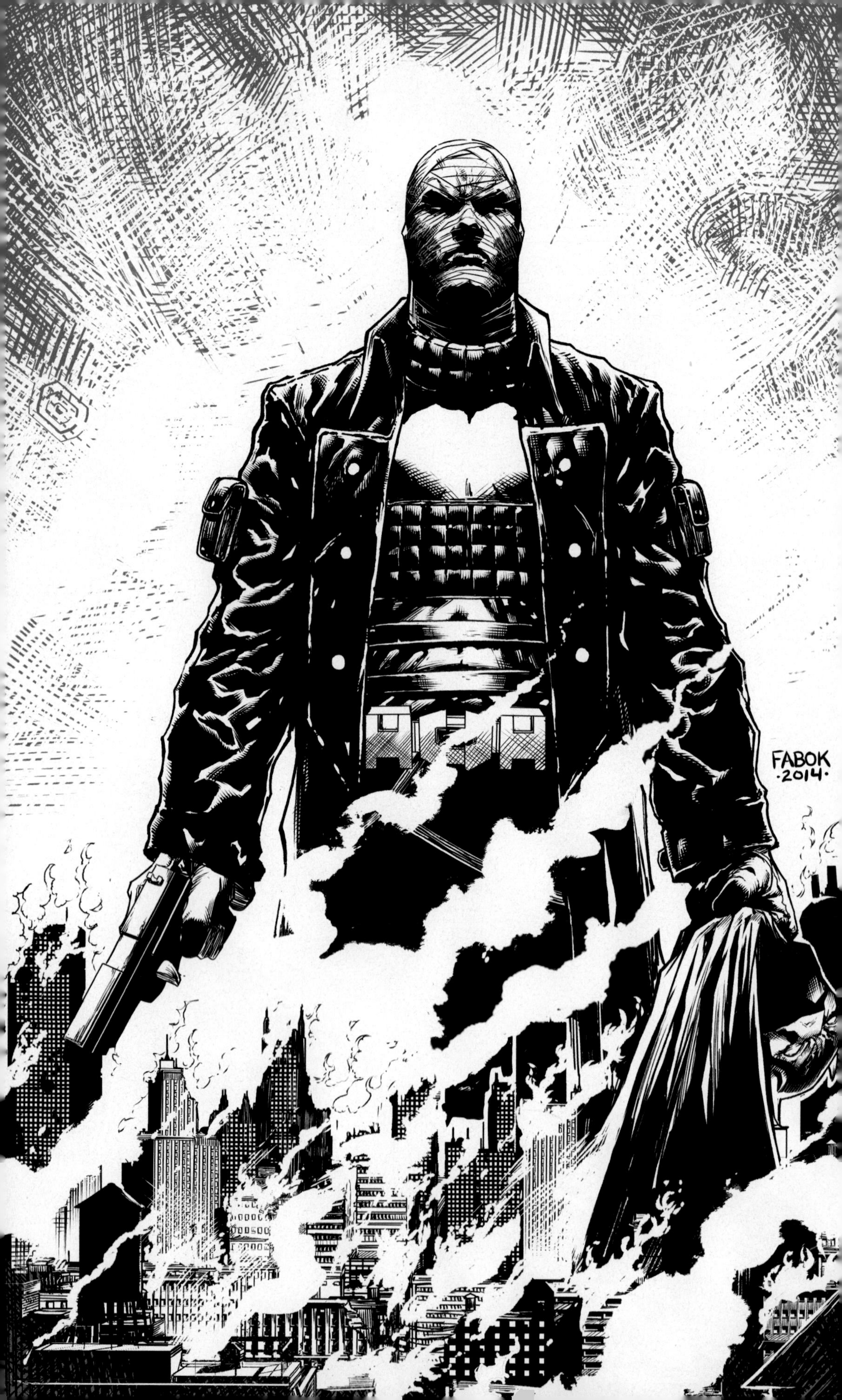
FABOK
·2014·

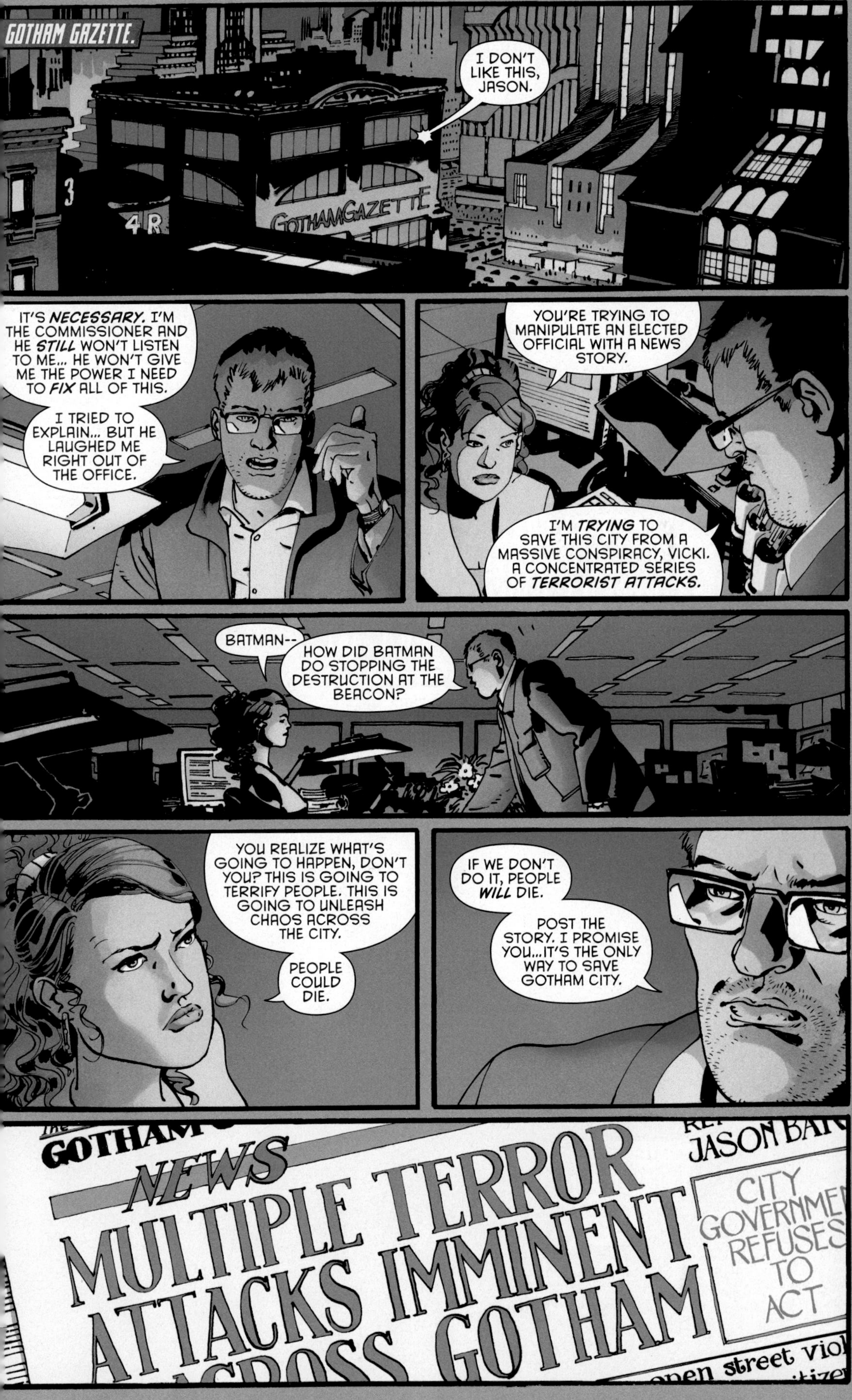
GOTHAM GAZETTE.
I DON'T LIKE THIS, JASON.
GOTHAM GAZETTE
IT'S NECESSARY. I'M THE COMMISSIONER AND HE STILL WON'T LISTEN TO ME... HE WON'T GIVE ME THE POWER I NEED TO FIX ALL OF THIS.
I TRIED TO EXPLAIN... BUT HE LAUGHED ME RIGHT OUT OF THE OFFICE.
YOU'RE TRYING TO MANIPULATE AN ELECTED OFFICIAL WITH A NEWS STORY.
I'M TRYING TO SAVE THIS CITY FROM A MASSIVE CONSPIRACY, VICKI. A CONCENTRATED SERIES OF TERRORIST ATTACKS.
BATMAN--
HOW DID BATMAN DO STOPPING THE DESTRUCTION AT THE BEACON?
YOU REALIZE WHAT'S GOING TO HAPPEN, DON'T YOU? THIS IS GOING TO TERRIFY PEOPLE. THIS IS GOING TO UNLEASH CHAOS ACROSS THE CITY.
PEOPLE COULD DIE.
IF WE DON'T DO IT, PEOPLE WILL DIE.
POST THE STORY. I PROMISE YOU...IT'S THE ONLY WAY TO SAVE GOTHAM CITY.
GOTHAM NEWS
MULTIPLE TERROR ATTACKS IMMINENT ACROSS GOTHAM
JASON BA
CITY GOVERNME REFUSES TO ACT
open street vio

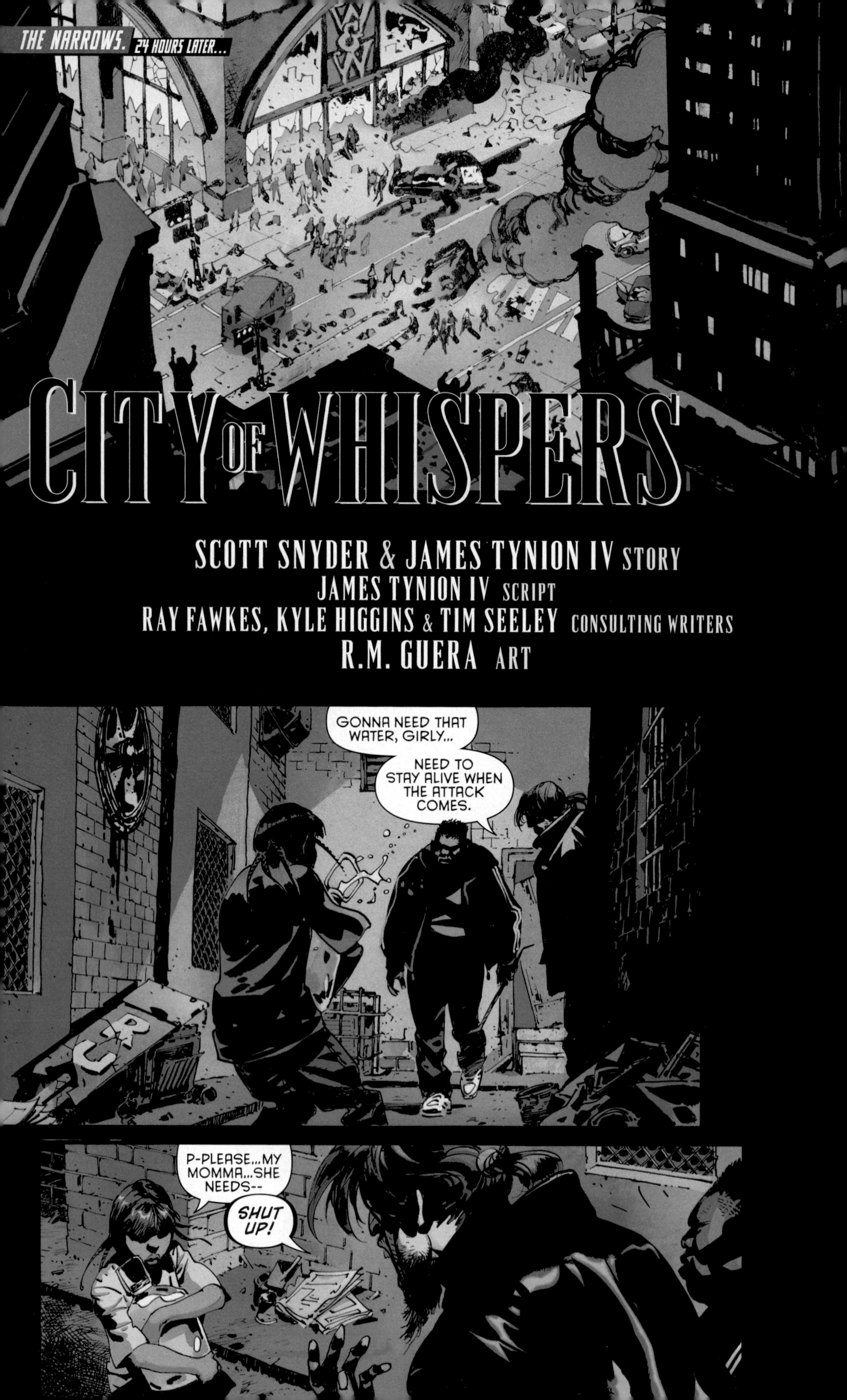
THE NARROWS. 24 HOURS LATER...
CITY OF WHISPERS
SCOTT SNYDER & JAMES TYNION IV STORY
JAMES TYNION IV SCRIPT
RAY FAWKES, KYLE HIGGINS & TIM SEELEY CONSULTING WRITERS
R.M. GUERA ART
GONNA NEED THAT WATER, GIRLY...
NEED TO STAY ALIVE WHEN THE ATTACK COMES.
P-PLEASE...MY MOMMA...SHE NEEDS--
SHUT UP!

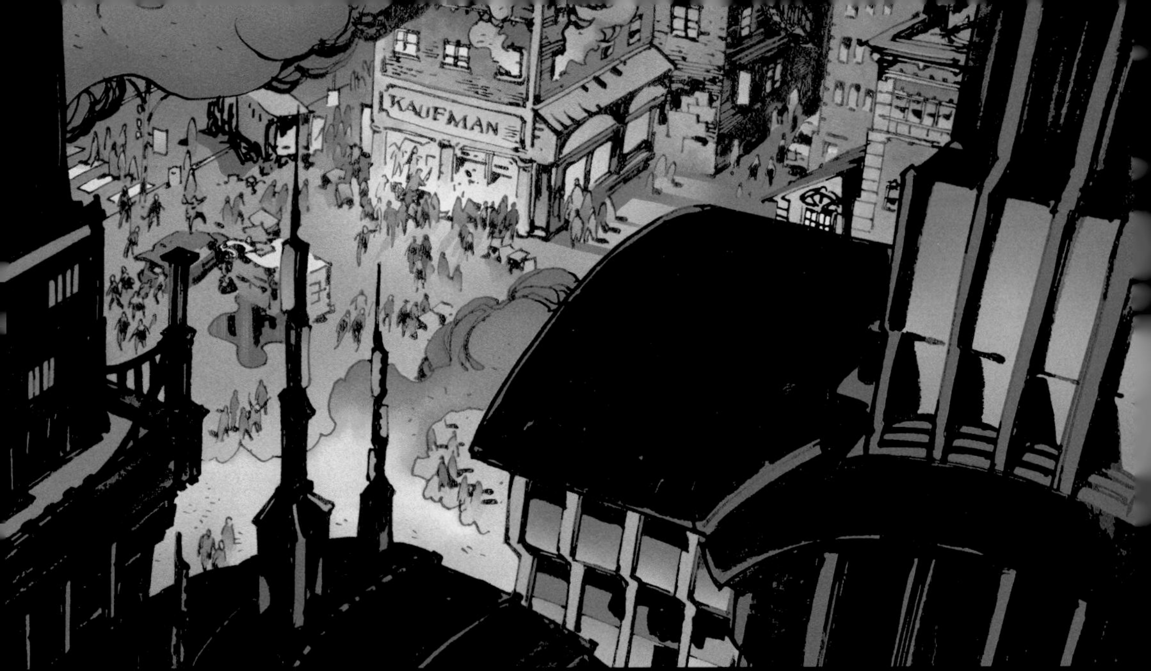
KAUFMAN

GIULIA BRUSCO COLORS STEVE WANDS LETTERS
JASON FABOK & BRAD ANDERSON COVER

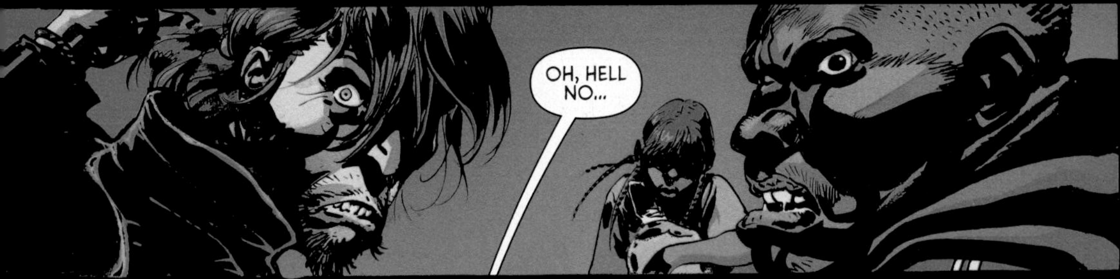
OH, HELL NO...

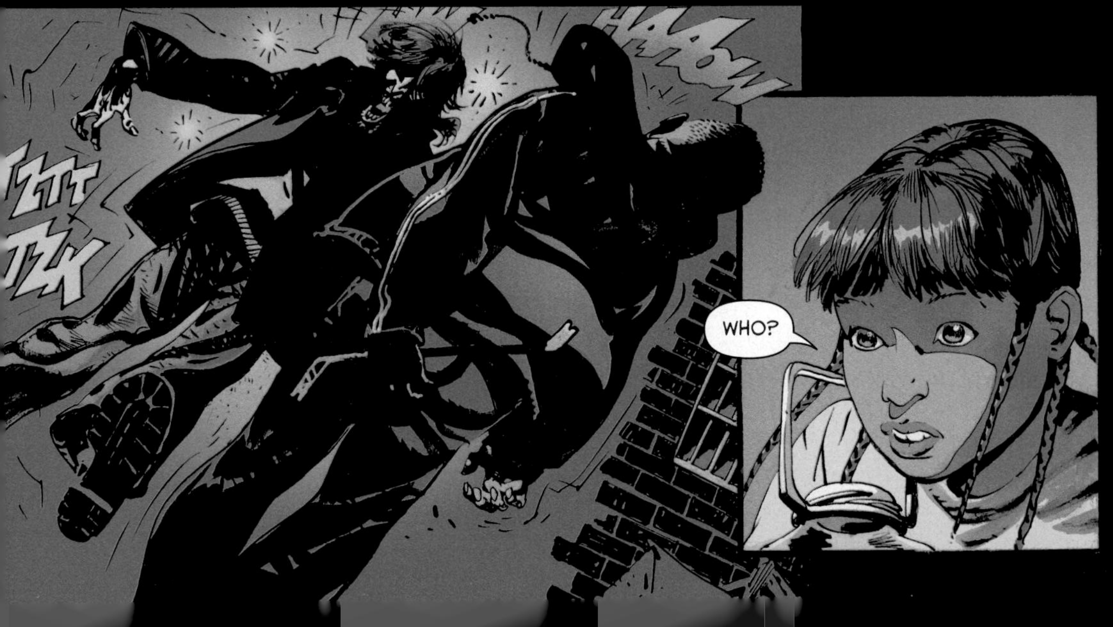
WHO?

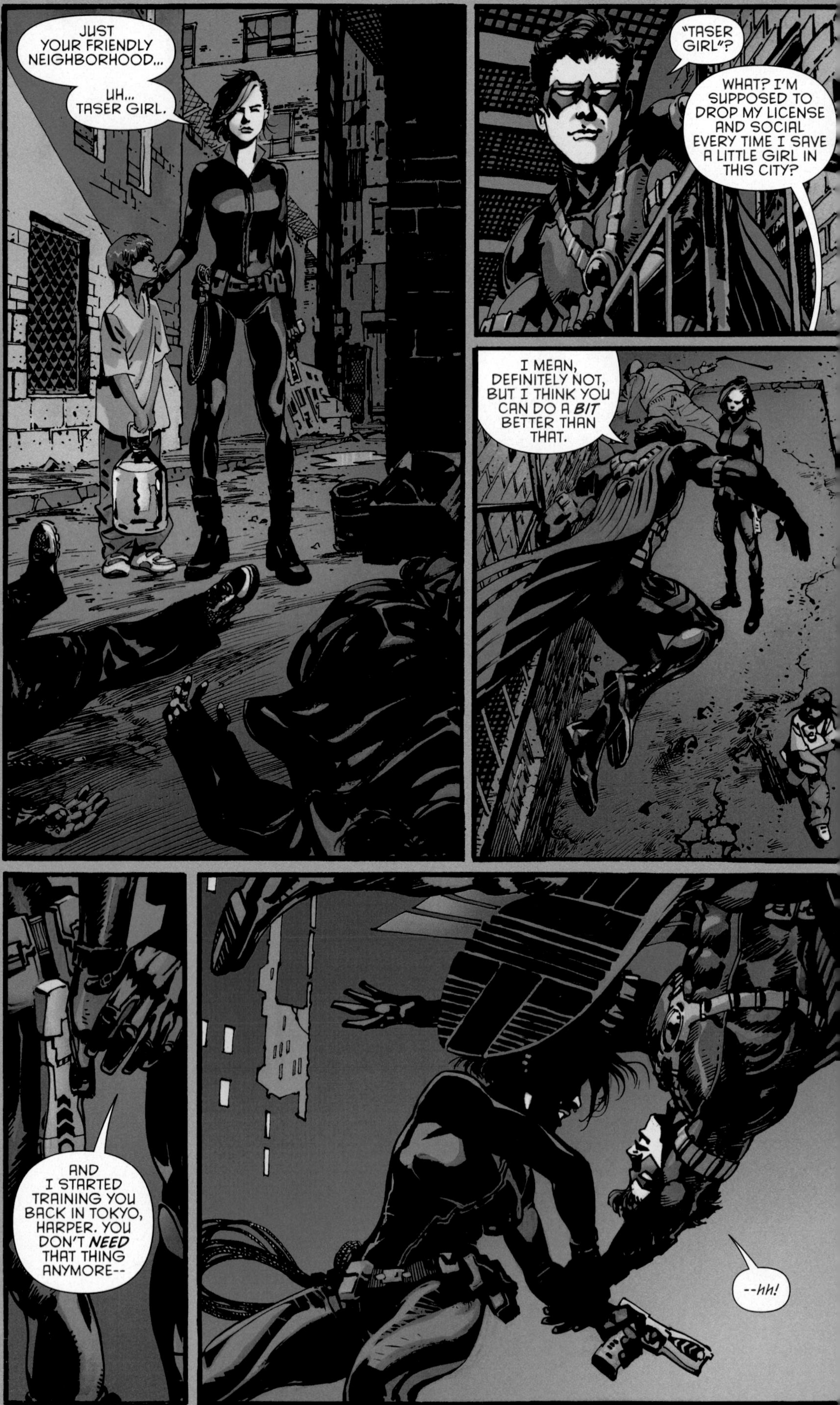
JUST YOUR FRIENDLY NEIGHBORHOOD...
UH... TASER GIRL.
"TASER GIRL"?
WHAT? I'M SUPPOSED TO DROP MY LICENSE AND SOCIAL EVERY TIME I SAVE A LITTLE GIRL IN THIS CITY?
I MEAN, DEFINITELY NOT, BUT I THINK YOU CAN DO A *BIT* BETTER THAN THAT.
AND I STARTED TRAINING YOU BACK IN TOKYO, HARPER. YOU DON'T ***NEED*** THAT THING ANYMORE--
--*hh!*

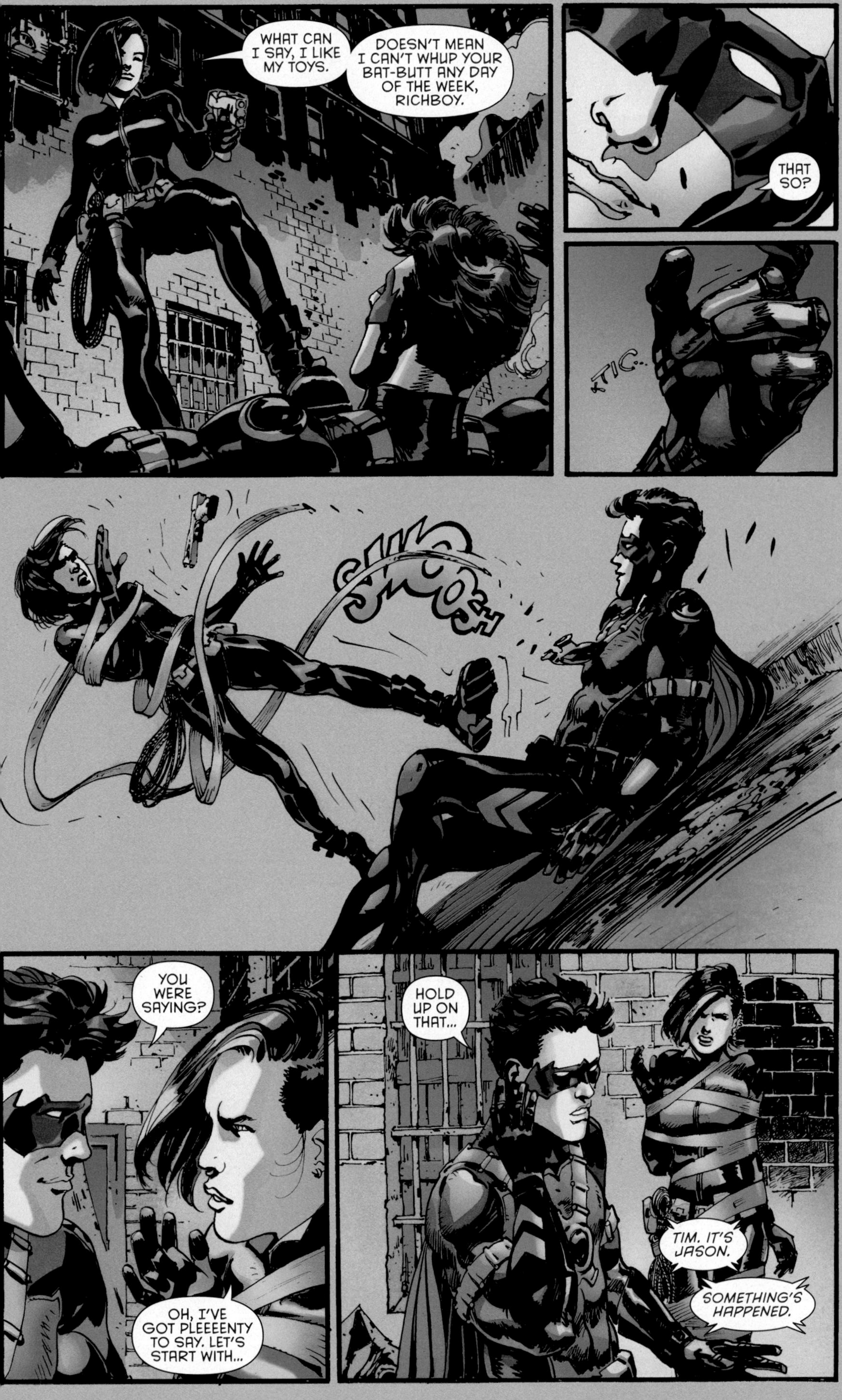
WHAT CAN I SAY, I LIKE MY TOYS.
DOESN'T MEAN I CAN'T WHUP YOUR BAT-BUTT ANY DAY OF THE WEEK, RICHBOY.
THAT SO?
TIC...
YOU WERE SAYING?
OH, I'VE GOT PLEEEENTY TO SAY. LET'S START WITH...
HOLD UP ON THAT...
TIM. IT'S JASON.
SOMETHING'S HAPPENED.

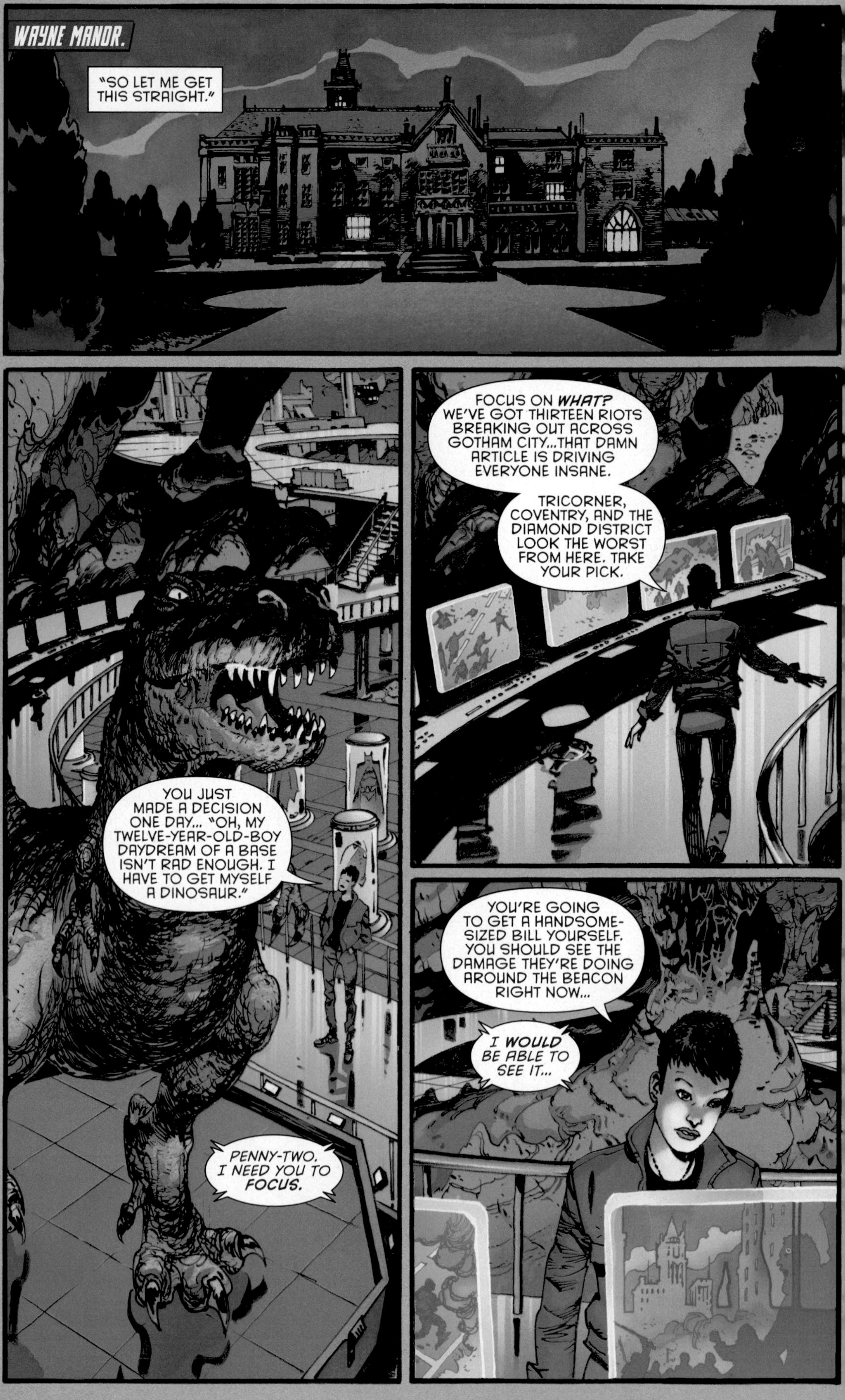
WAYNE MANOR.
"SO LET ME GET THIS STRAIGHT."
YOU JUST MADE A DECISION ONE DAY... "OH, MY TWELVE-YEAR-OLD-BOY DAYDREAM OF A BASE ISN'T RAD ENOUGH. I HAVE TO GET MYSELF A DINOSAUR."
PENNY-TWO. I NEED YOU TO FOCUS.
FOCUS ON WHAT? WE'VE GOT THIRTEEN RIOTS BREAKING OUT ACROSS GOTHAM CITY...THAT DAMN ARTICLE IS DRIVING EVERYONE INSANE.
TRICORNER, COVENTRY, AND THE DIAMOND DISTRICT LOOK THE WORST FROM HERE. TAKE YOUR PICK.
YOU'RE GOING TO GET A HANDSOME-SIZED BILL YOURSELF. YOU SHOULD SEE THE DAMAGE THEY'RE DOING AROUND THE BEACON RIGHT NOW...
I WOULD BE ABLE TO SEE IT...

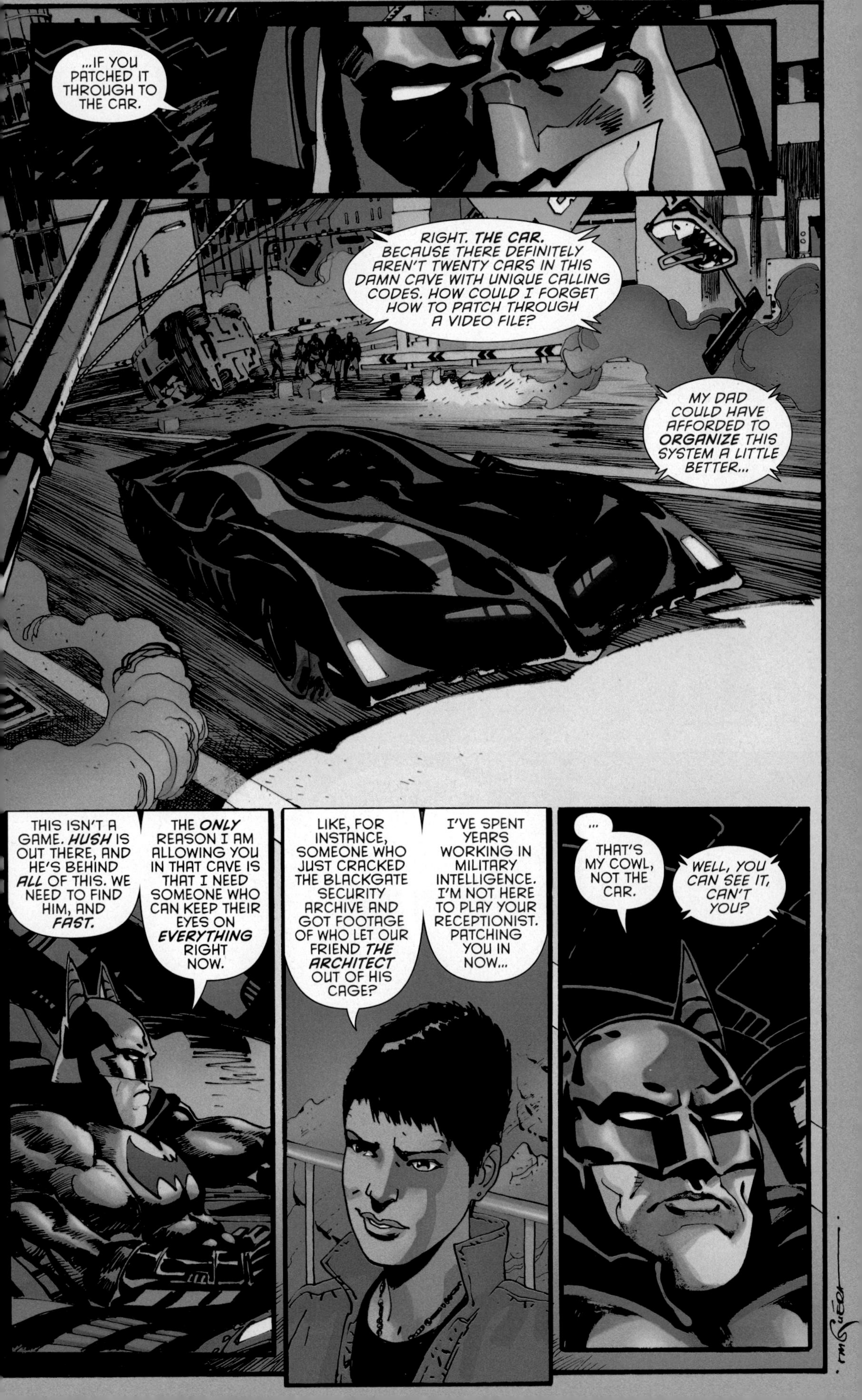

...IF YOU PATCHED IT THROUGH TO THE CAR.
RIGHT. THE CAR. BECAUSE THERE DEFINITELY AREN'T TWENTY CARS IN THIS DAMN CAVE WITH UNIQUE CALLING CODES. HOW COULD I FORGET HOW TO PATCH THROUGH A VIDEO FILE?
MY DAD COULD HAVE AFFORDED TO ORGANIZE THIS SYSTEM A LITTLE BETTER...
THIS ISN'T A GAME. HUSH IS OUT THERE, AND HE'S BEHIND ALL OF THIS. WE NEED TO FIND HIM, AND FAST.
THE ONLY REASON I AM ALLOWING YOU IN THAT CAVE IS THAT I NEED SOMEONE WHO CAN KEEP THEIR EYES ON EVERYTHING RIGHT NOW.
LIKE, FOR INSTANCE, SOMEONE WHO JUST CRACKED THE BLACKGATE SECURITY ARCHIVE AND GOT FOOTAGE OF WHO LET OUR FRIEND THE ARCHITECT OUT OF HIS CAGE?
I'VE SPENT YEARS WORKING IN MILITARY INTELLIGENCE. I'M NOT HERE TO PLAY YOUR RECEPTIONIST. PATCHING YOU IN NOW...
...
THAT'S MY COWL, NOT THE CAR.
WELL, YOU CAN SEE IT, CAN'T YOU?

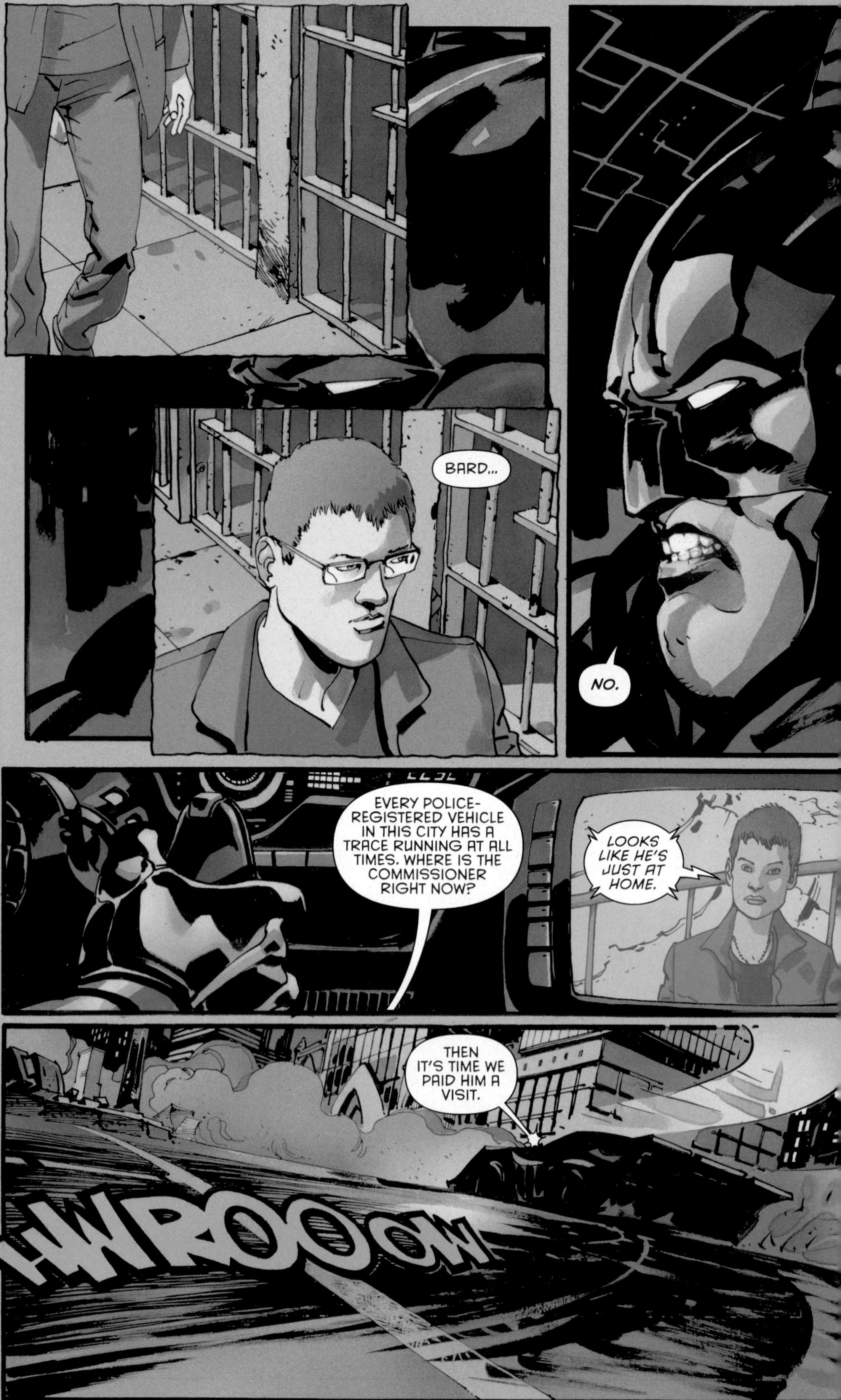
BARD...
NO.
EVERY POLICE-REGISTERED VEHICLE IN THIS CITY HAS A TRACE RUNNING AT ALL TIMES. WHERE IS THE COMMISSIONER RIGHT NOW?
LOOKS LIKE HE'S JUST AT HOME.
THEN IT'S TIME WE PAID HIM A VISIT.
HWROOOM

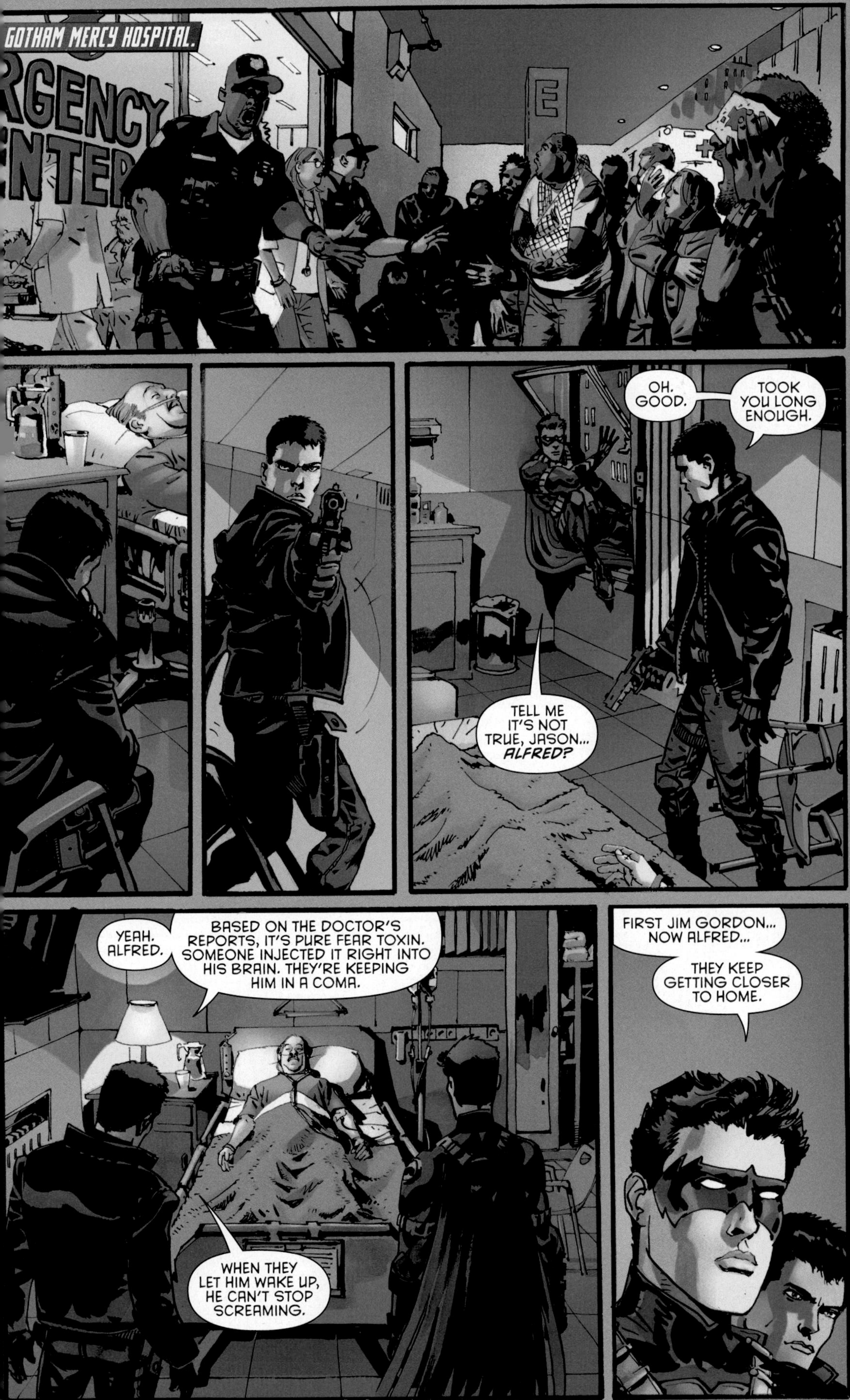
GOTHAM MERCY HOSPITAL.
RGENCY
ENTER
E
OH. GOOD.
TOOK YOU LONG ENOUGH.
TELL ME IT'S NOT TRUE, JASON... ALFRED?
YEAH. ALFRED.
BASED ON THE DOCTOR'S REPORTS, IT'S PURE FEAR TOXIN. SOMEONE INJECTED IT RIGHT INTO HIS BRAIN. THEY'RE KEEPING HIM IN A COMA.
WHEN THEY LET HIM WAKE UP, HE CAN'T STOP SCREAMING.
FIRST JIM GORDON... NOW ALFRED...
THEY KEEP GETTING CLOSER TO HOME.

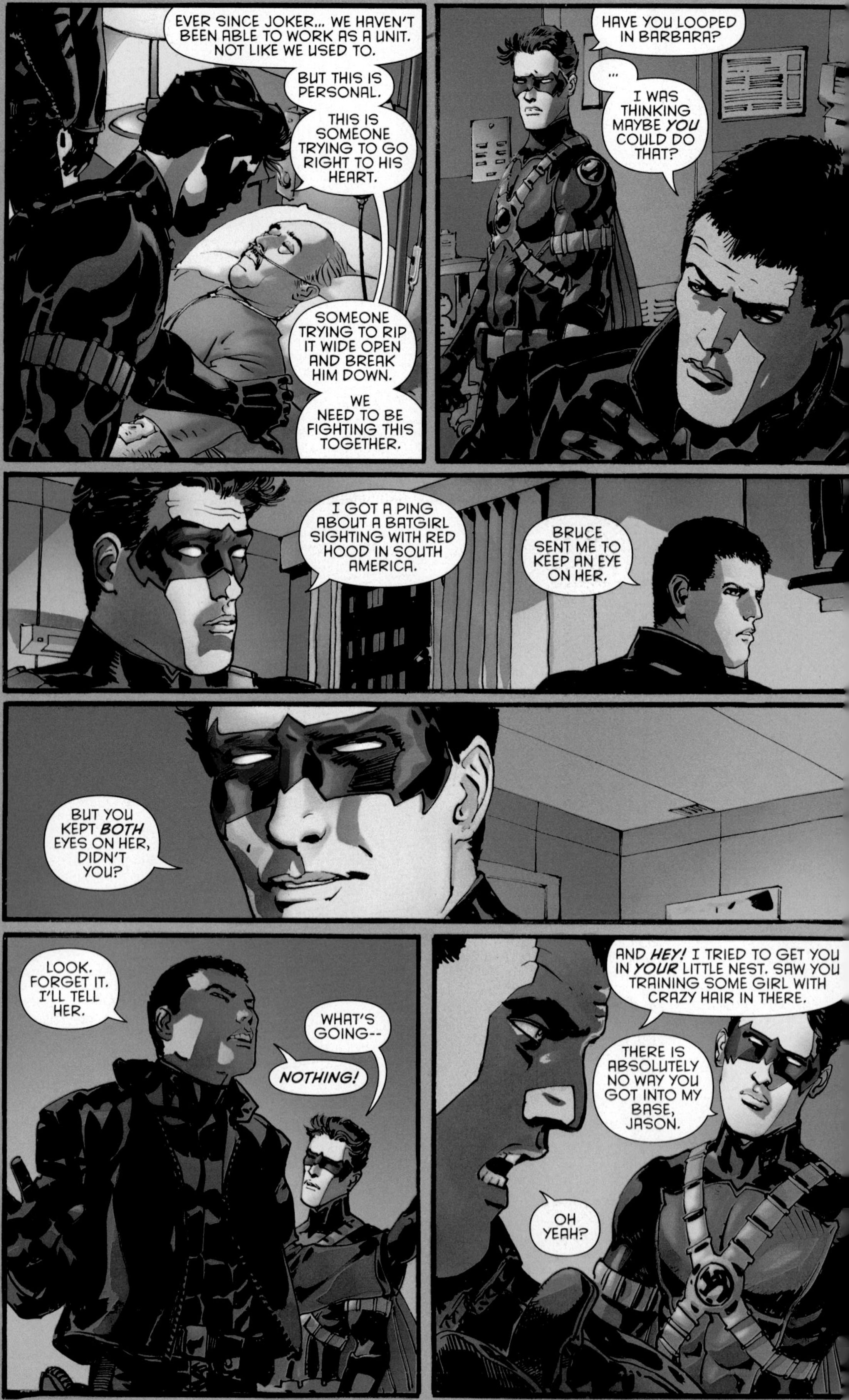
EVER SINCE JOKER... WE HAVEN'T BEEN ABLE TO WORK AS A UNIT. NOT LIKE WE USED TO.
BUT THIS IS PERSONAL.
THIS IS SOMEONE TRYING TO GO RIGHT TO HIS HEART.
SOMEONE TRYING TO RIP IT WIDE OPEN AND BREAK HIM DOWN.
WE NEED TO BE FIGHTING THIS TOGETHER.
HAVE YOU LOOPED IN BARBARA?
...
I WAS THINKING MAYBE *YOU* COULD DO THAT?
I GOT A PING ABOUT A BATGIRL SIGHTING WITH RED HOOD IN SOUTH AMERICA.
BRUCE SENT ME TO KEEP AN EYE ON HER.
BUT YOU KEPT *BOTH* EYES ON HER, DIDN'T YOU?
LOOK. FORGET IT. I'LL TELL HER.
WHAT'S GOING--
*NOTHING!*
AND *HEY!* I TRIED TO GET YOU IN *YOUR* LITTLE NEST. SAW YOU TRAINING SOME GIRL WITH CRAZY HAIR IN THERE.
THERE IS ABSOLUTELY NO WAY YOU GOT INTO MY BASE, JASON.
OH YEAH?

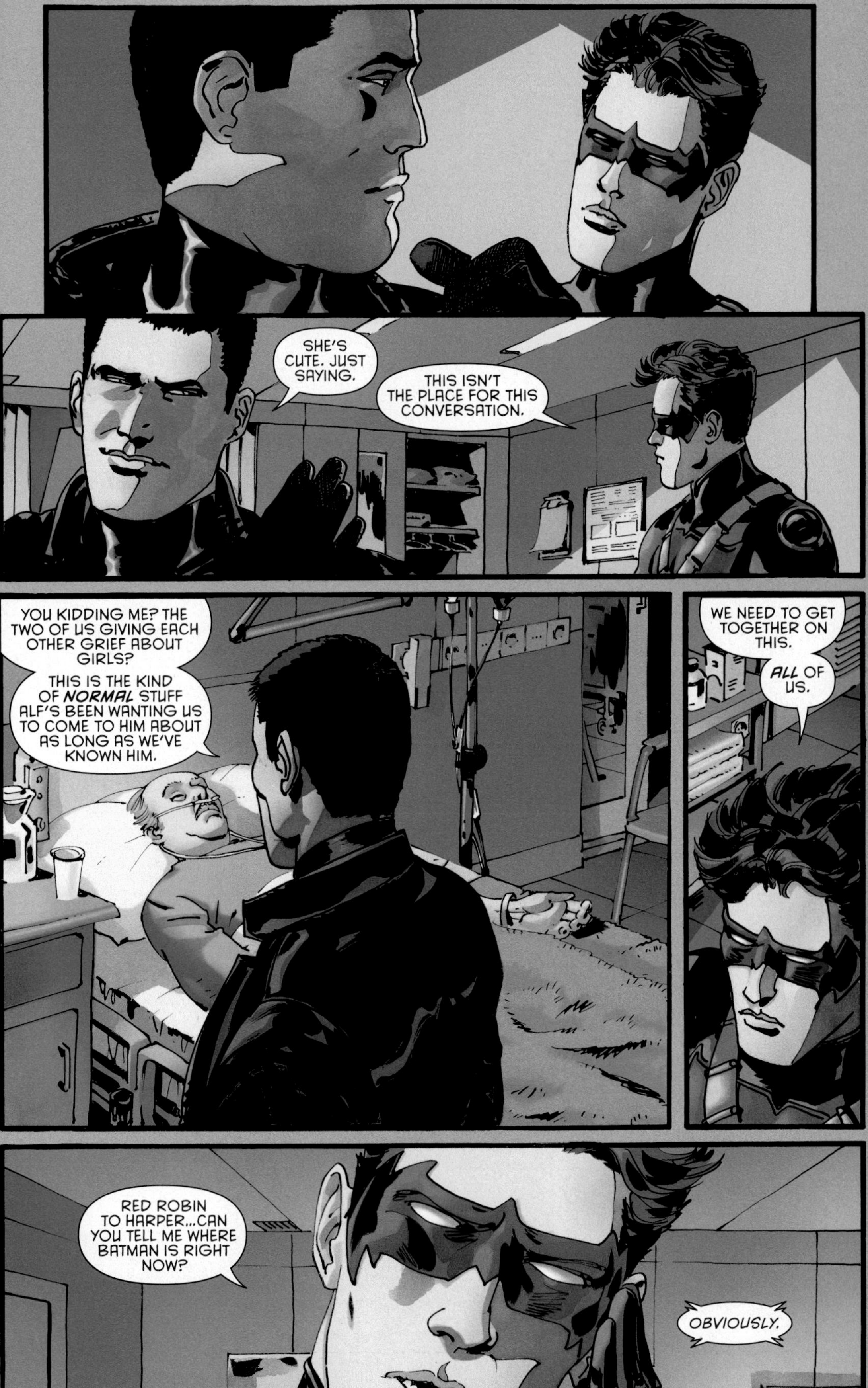
SHE'S CUTE. JUST SAYING.
THIS ISN'T THE PLACE FOR THIS CONVERSATION.
YOU KIDDING ME? THE TWO OF US GIVING EACH OTHER GRIEF ABOUT GIRLS?
THIS IS THE KIND OF NORMAL STUFF ALF'S BEEN WANTING US TO COME TO HIM ABOUT AS LONG AS WE'VE KNOWN HIM.
WE NEED TO GET TOGETHER ON THIS.
ALL OF US.
RED ROBIN TO HARPER...CAN YOU TELL ME WHERE BATMAN IS RIGHT NOW?
OBVIOUSLY.

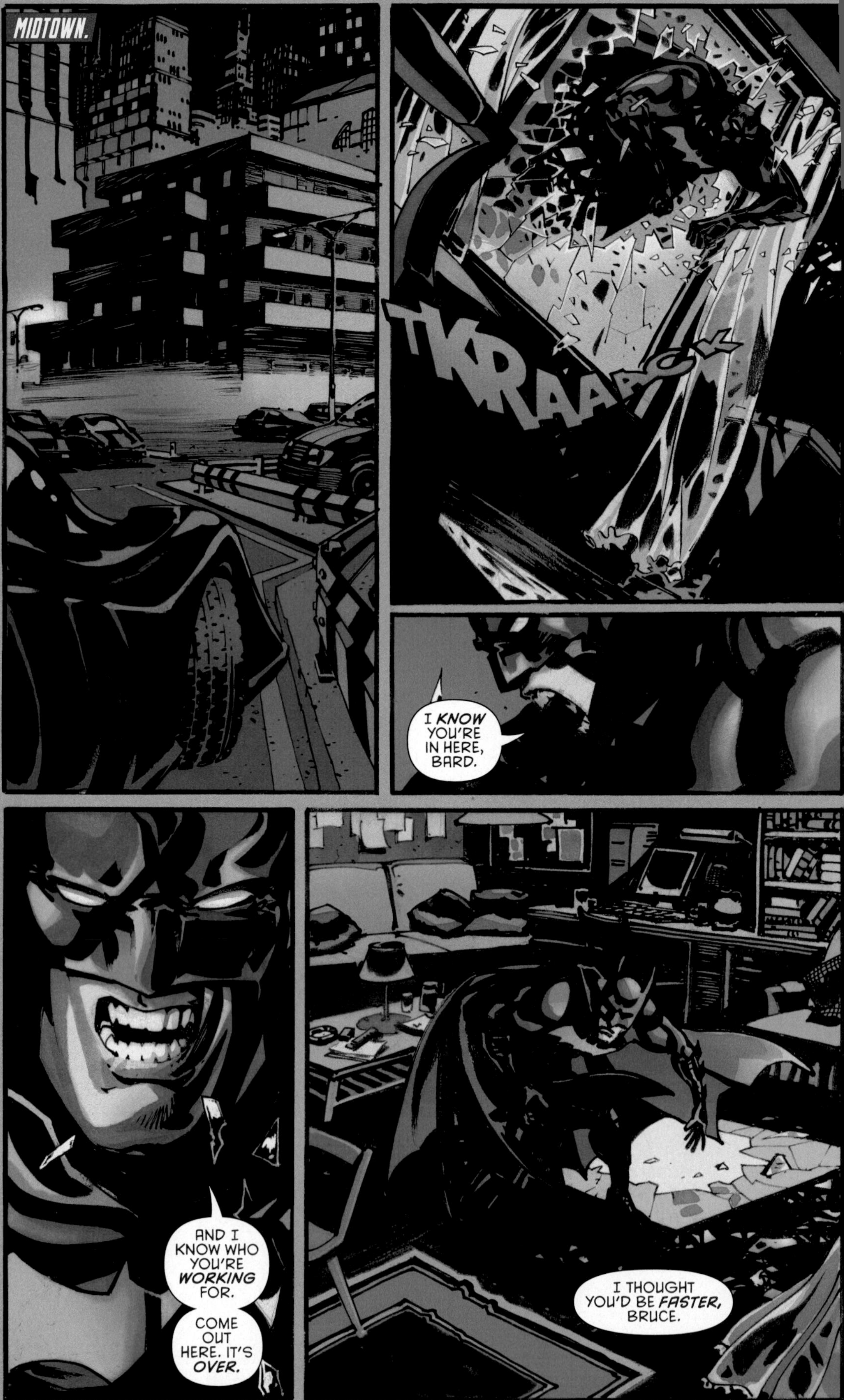
MIDTOWN.
TKRAAAK
I KNOW YOU'RE IN HERE, BARD.
AND I KNOW WHO YOU'RE WORKING FOR.
COME OUT HERE. IT'S OVER.
I THOUGHT YOU'D BE FASTER, BRUCE.

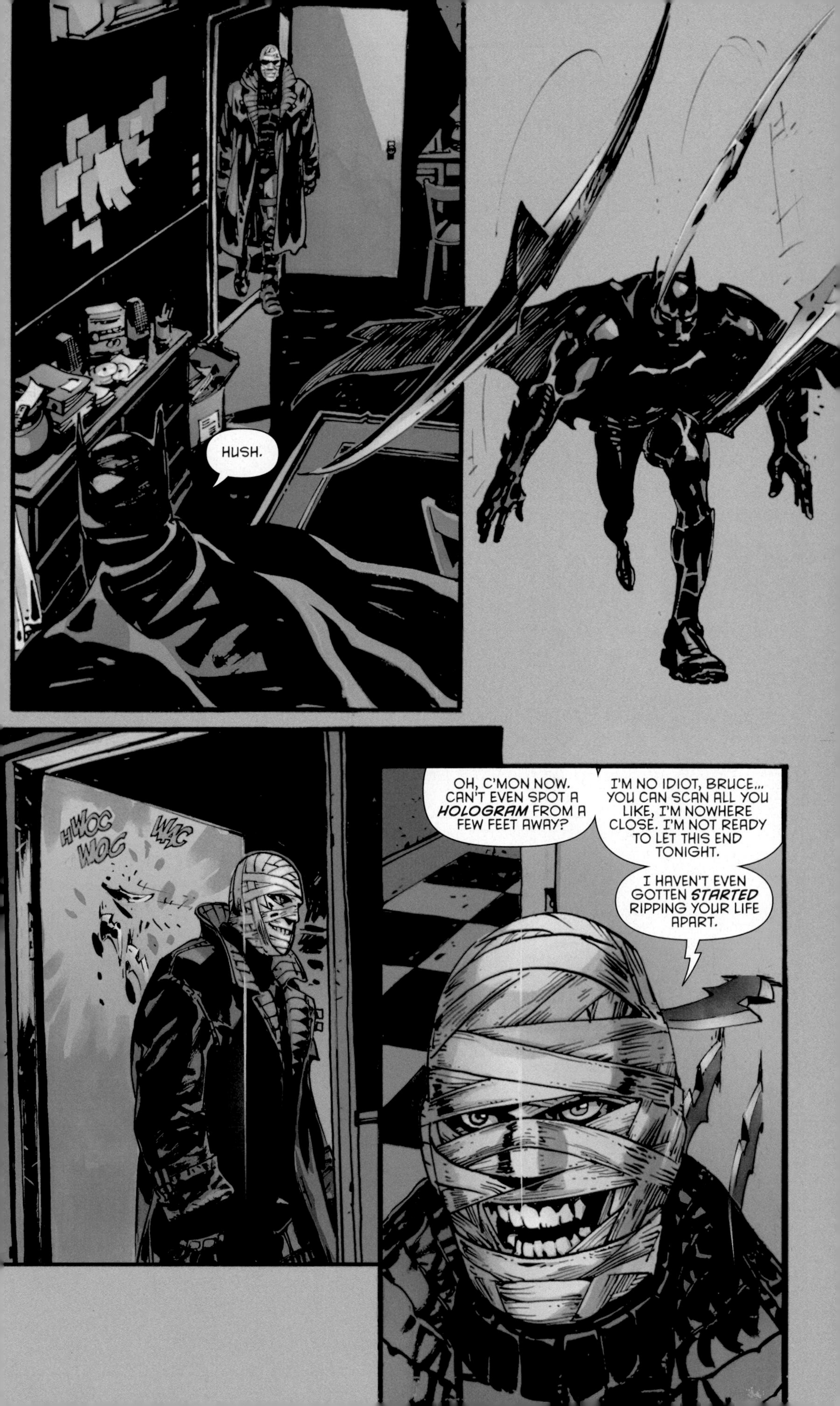
HUSH.
HWOC
WOC
WAC
OH, C'MON NOW. CAN'T EVEN SPOT A ***HOLOGRAM*** FROM A FEW FEET AWAY?
I'M NO IDIOT, BRUCE... YOU CAN SCAN ALL YOU LIKE, I'M NOWHERE CLOSE. I'M NOT READY TO LET THIS END TONIGHT.
I HAVEN'T EVEN GOTTEN ***STARTED*** RIPPING YOUR LIFE APART.

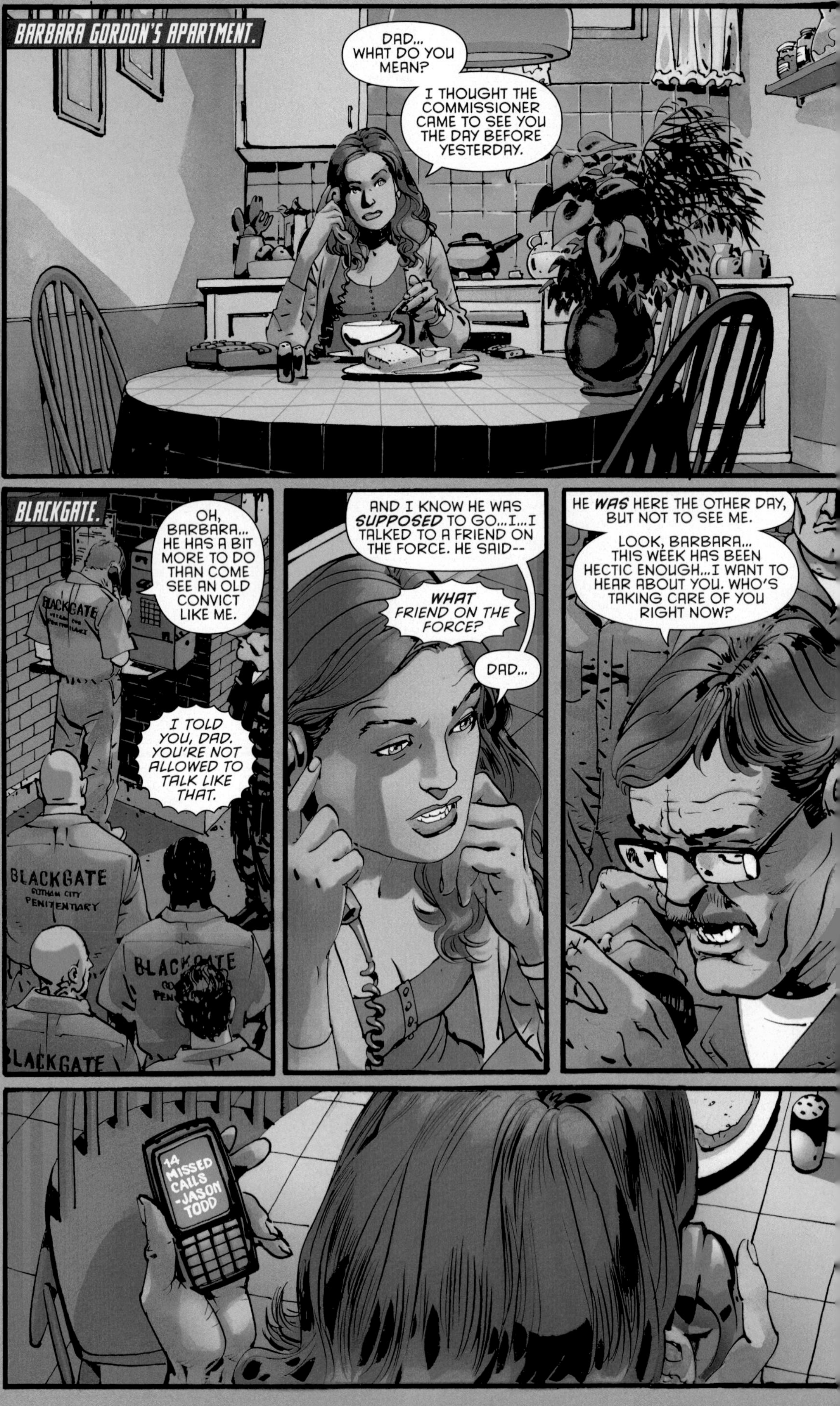
BARBARA GORDON'S APARTMENT.
DAD... WHAT DO YOU MEAN?
I THOUGHT THE COMMISSIONER CAME TO SEE YOU THE DAY BEFORE YESTERDAY.
BLACKGATE.
OH, BARBARA... HE HAS A BIT MORE TO DO THAN COME SEE AN OLD CONVICT LIKE ME.
I TOLD YOU, DAD. YOU'RE NOT ALLOWED TO TALK LIKE THAT.
BLACKGATE
GOTHAM CITY
PENITENTIARY
BLACKGATE
AND I KNOW HE WAS *SUPPOSED* TO GO...I...I TALKED TO A FRIEND ON THE FORCE. HE SAID--
*WHAT* FRIEND ON THE FORCE?
DAD...
HE *WAS* HERE THE OTHER DAY, BUT NOT TO SEE ME.
LOOK, BARBARA... THIS WEEK HAS BEEN HECTIC ENOUGH...I WANT TO HEAR ABOUT YOU. WHO'S TAKING CARE OF YOU RIGHT NOW?
14 MISSED CALLS -JASON TODD

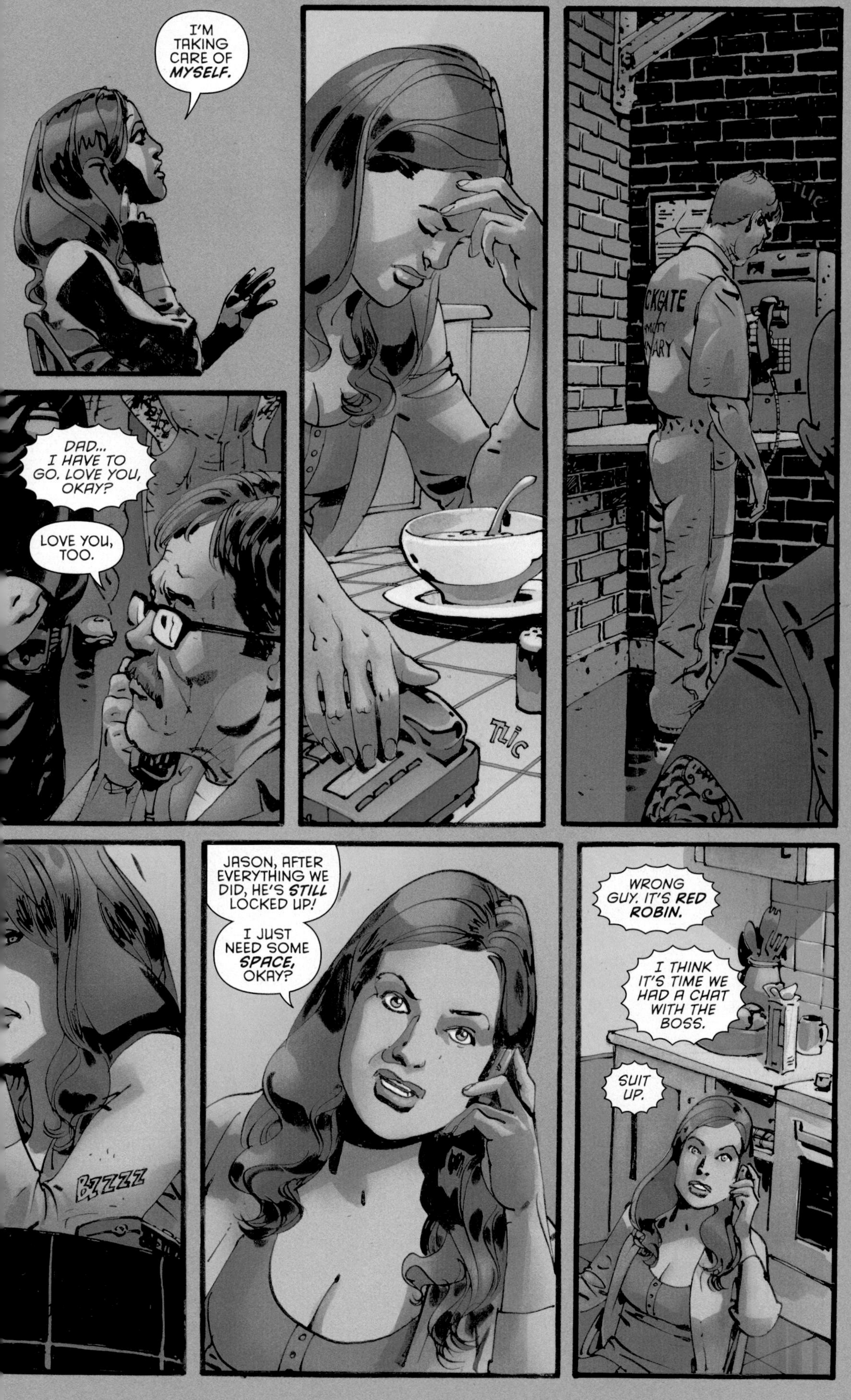

I'M TAKING CARE OF MYSELF.
DAD... I HAVE TO GO. LOVE YOU, OKAY?
LOVE YOU, TOO.
TLIC
TLIC
BZZZZ
JASON, AFTER EVERYTHING WE DID, HE'S STILL LOCKED UP!
I JUST NEED SOME SPACE, OKAY?
WRONG GUY. IT'S RED ROBIN.
I THINK IT'S TIME WE HAD A CHAT WITH THE BOSS.
SUIT UP.

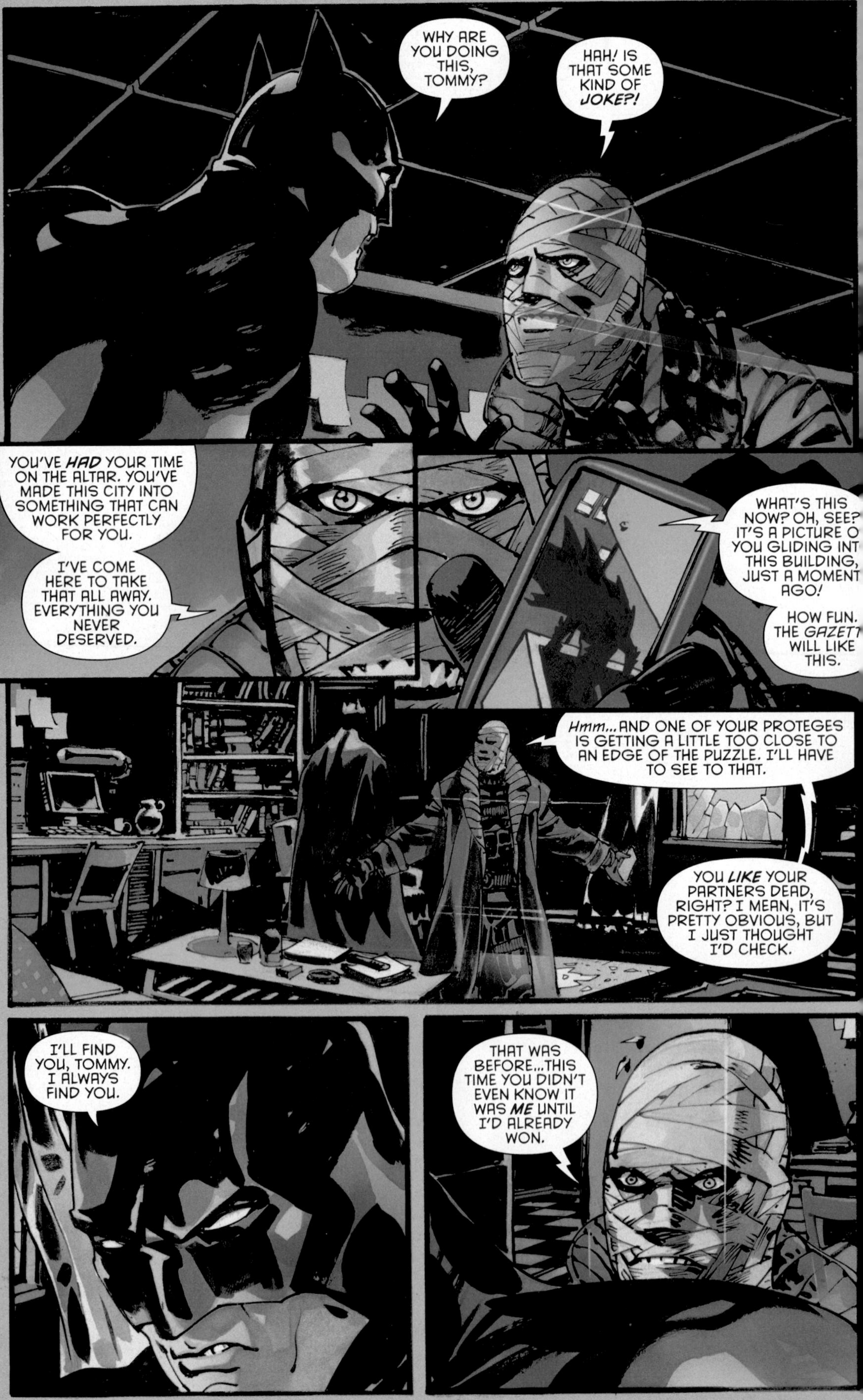
WHY ARE YOU DOING THIS, TOMMY?
HAH! IS THAT SOME KIND OF JOKE?!
YOU'VE HAD YOUR TIME ON THE ALTAR. YOU'VE MADE THIS CITY INTO SOMETHING THAT CAN WORK PERFECTLY FOR YOU.
I'VE COME HERE TO TAKE THAT ALL AWAY. EVERYTHING YOU NEVER DESERVED.
WHAT'S THIS NOW? OH, SEE? IT'S A PICTURE O YOU GLIDING INT THIS BUILDING, JUST A MOMENT AGO!
HOW FUN. THE GAZETT WILL LIKE THIS.
Hmm... AND ONE OF YOUR PROTEGES IS GETTING A LITTLE TOO CLOSE TO AN EDGE OF THE PUZZLE. I'LL HAVE TO SEE TO THAT.
YOU LIKE YOUR PARTNERS DEAD, RIGHT? I MEAN, IT'S PRETTY OBVIOUS, BUT I JUST THOUGHT I'D CHECK.
I'LL FIND YOU, TOMMY. I ALWAYS FIND YOU.
THAT WAS BEFORE... THIS TIME YOU DIDN'T EVEN KNOW IT WAS ME UNTIL I'D ALREADY WON.

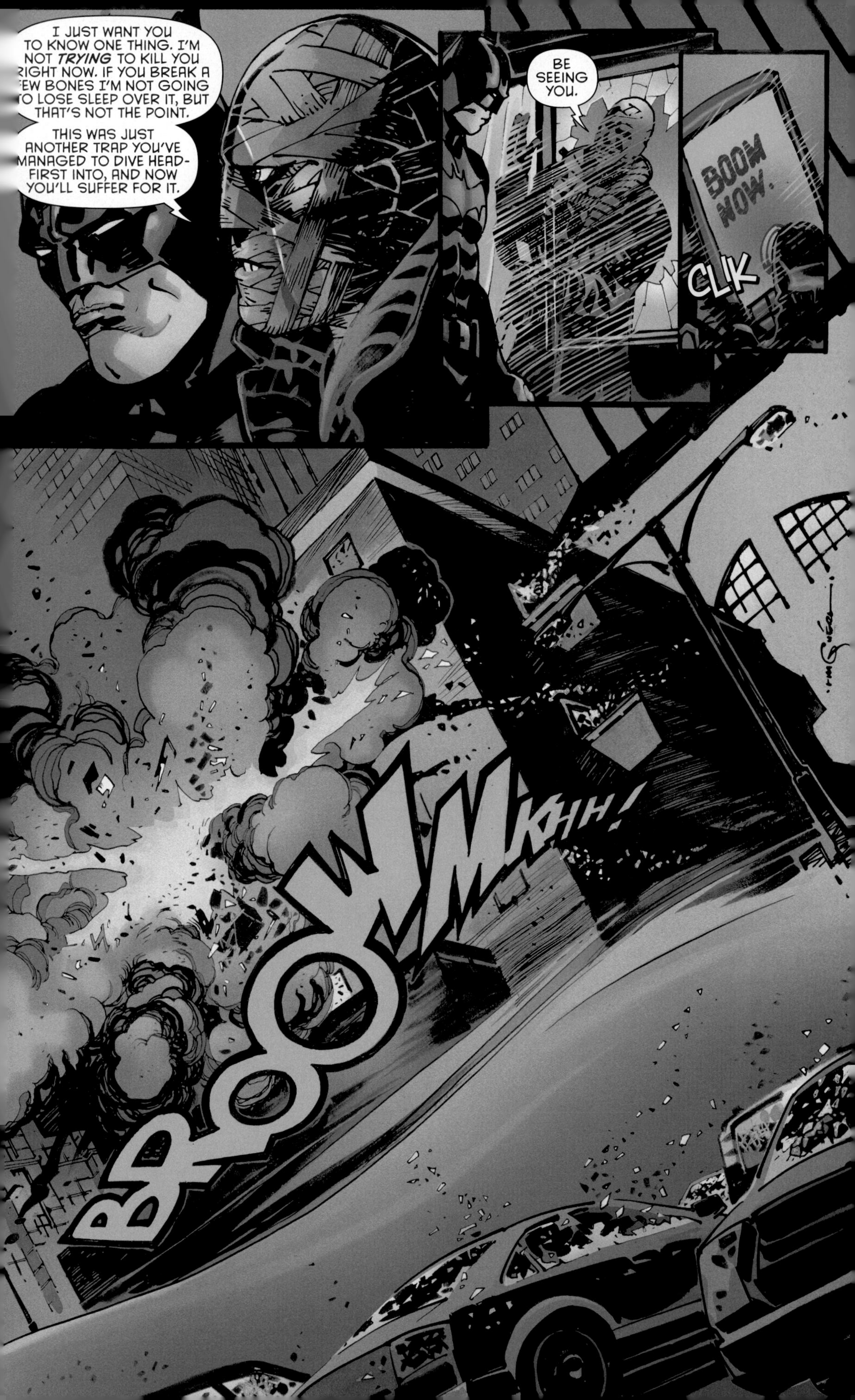
I JUST WANT YOU TO KNOW ONE THING. I'M NOT *TRYING* TO KILL YOU RIGHT NOW. IF YOU BREAK A FEW BONES I'M NOT GOING TO LOSE SLEEP OVER IT, BUT THAT'S NOT THE POINT.
THIS WAS JUST ANOTHER TRAP YOU'VE MANAGED TO DIVE HEAD-FIRST INTO, AND NOW YOU'LL SUFFER FOR IT.
BE SEEING YOU.
BOOM NOW.
CLIK
BROOOWMKHH!

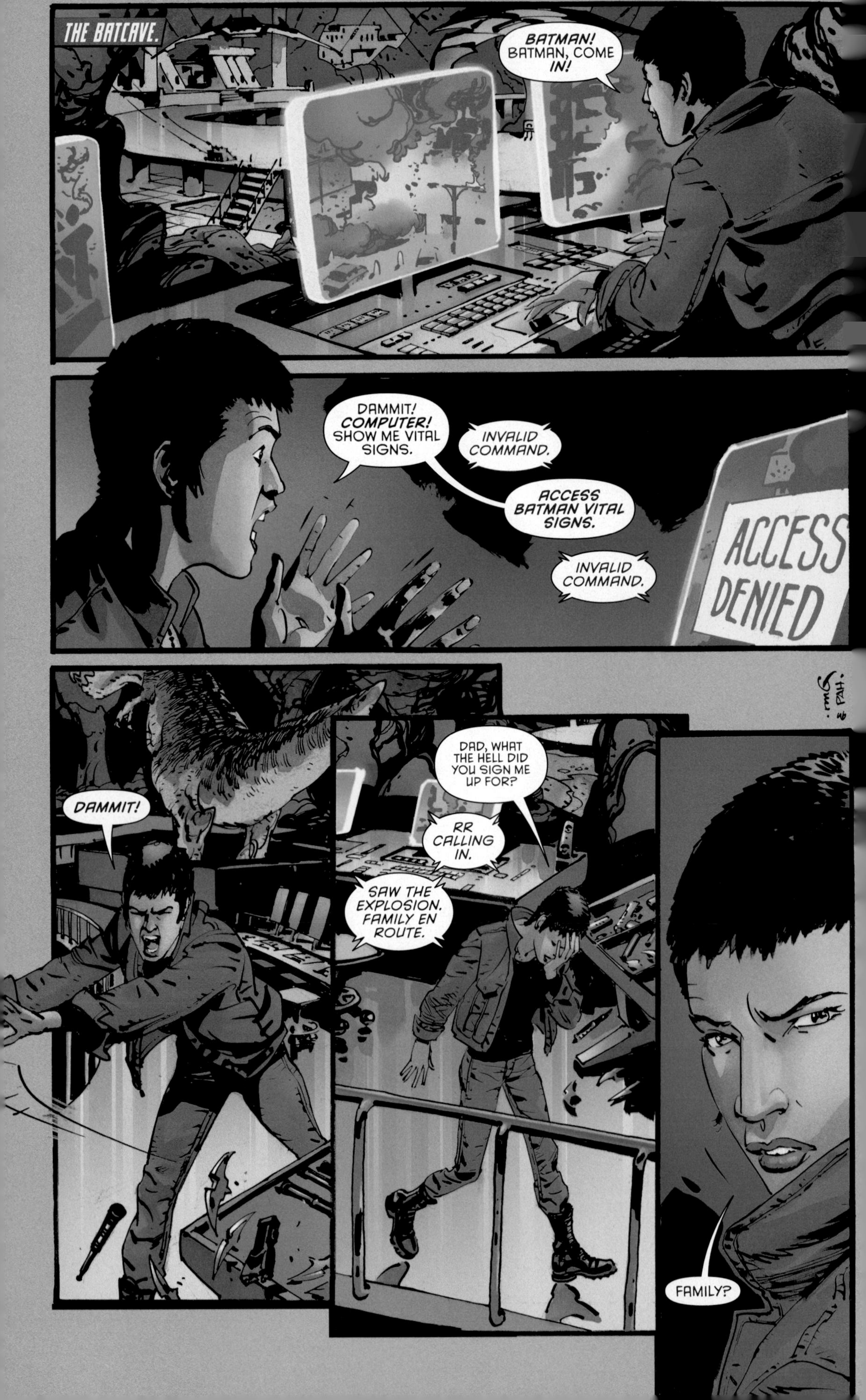
THE BATCAVE.
BATMAN! BATMAN, COME IN!
DAMMIT! COMPUTER! SHOW ME VITAL SIGNS.
INVALID COMMAND.
ACCESS BATMAN VITAL SIGNS.
INVALID COMMAND.
ACCESS DENIED
DAMMIT!
DAD, WHAT THE HELL DID YOU SIGN ME UP FOR?
RR CALLING IN.
SAW THE EXPLOSION. FAMILY EN ROUTE.
FAMILY?

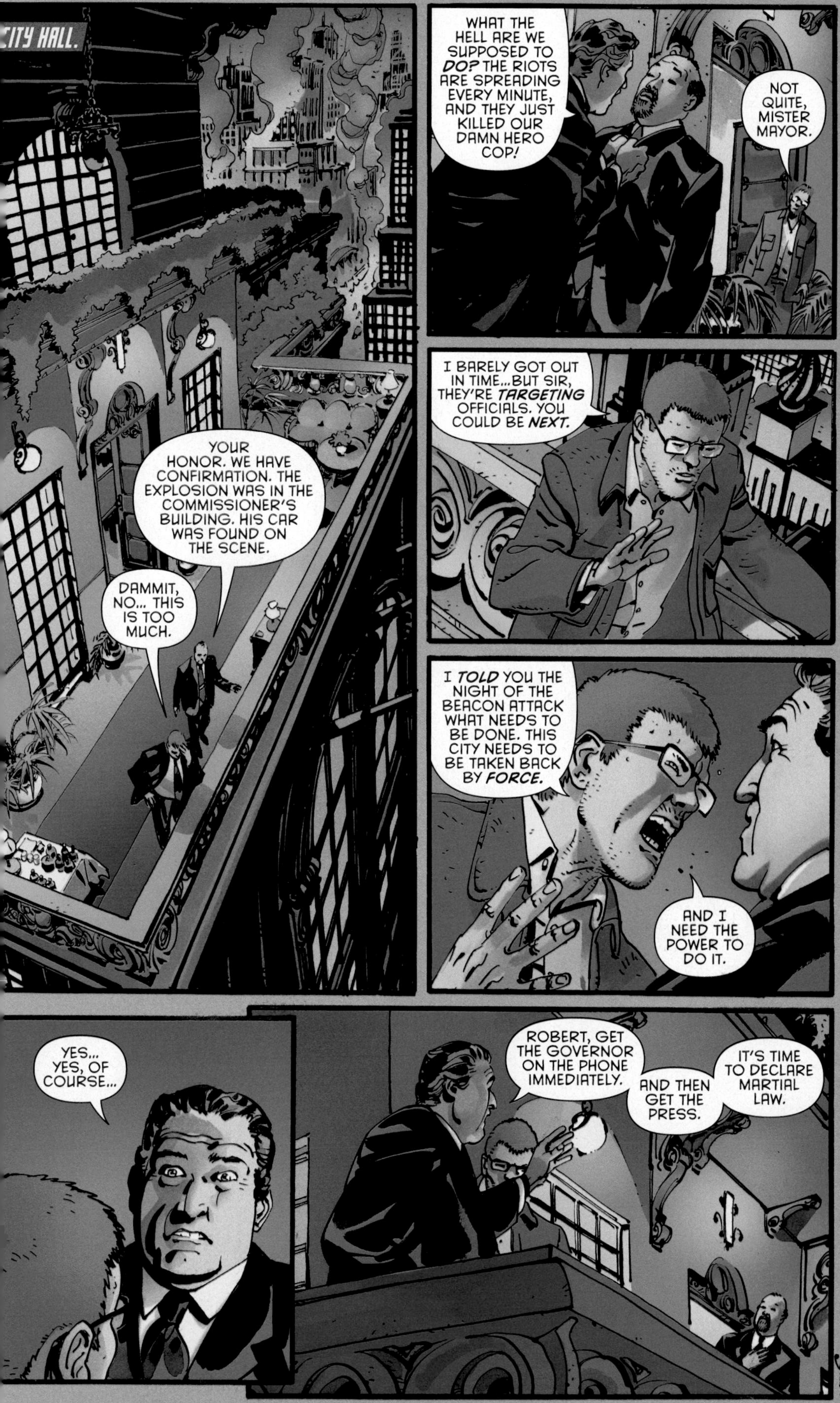
CITY HALL.
YOUR HONOR. WE HAVE CONFIRMATION. THE EXPLOSION WAS IN THE COMMISSIONER'S BUILDING. HIS CAR WAS FOUND ON THE SCENE.
DAMMIT, NO... THIS IS TOO MUCH.
WHAT THE HELL ARE WE SUPPOSED TO DO? THE RIOTS ARE SPREADING EVERY MINUTE, AND THEY JUST KILLED OUR DAMN HERO COP!
NOT QUITE, MISTER MAYOR.
I BARELY GOT OUT IN TIME...BUT SIR, THEY'RE TARGETING OFFICIALS. YOU COULD BE NEXT.
I TOLD YOU THE NIGHT OF THE BEACON ATTACK WHAT NEEDS TO BE DONE. THIS CITY NEEDS TO BE TAKEN BACK BY FORCE.
AND I NEED THE POWER TO DO IT.
YES... YES, OF COURSE...
ROBERT, GET THE GOVERNOR ON THE PHONE IMMEDIATELY.
AND THEN GET THE PRESS.
IT'S TIME TO DECLARE MARTIAL LAW.

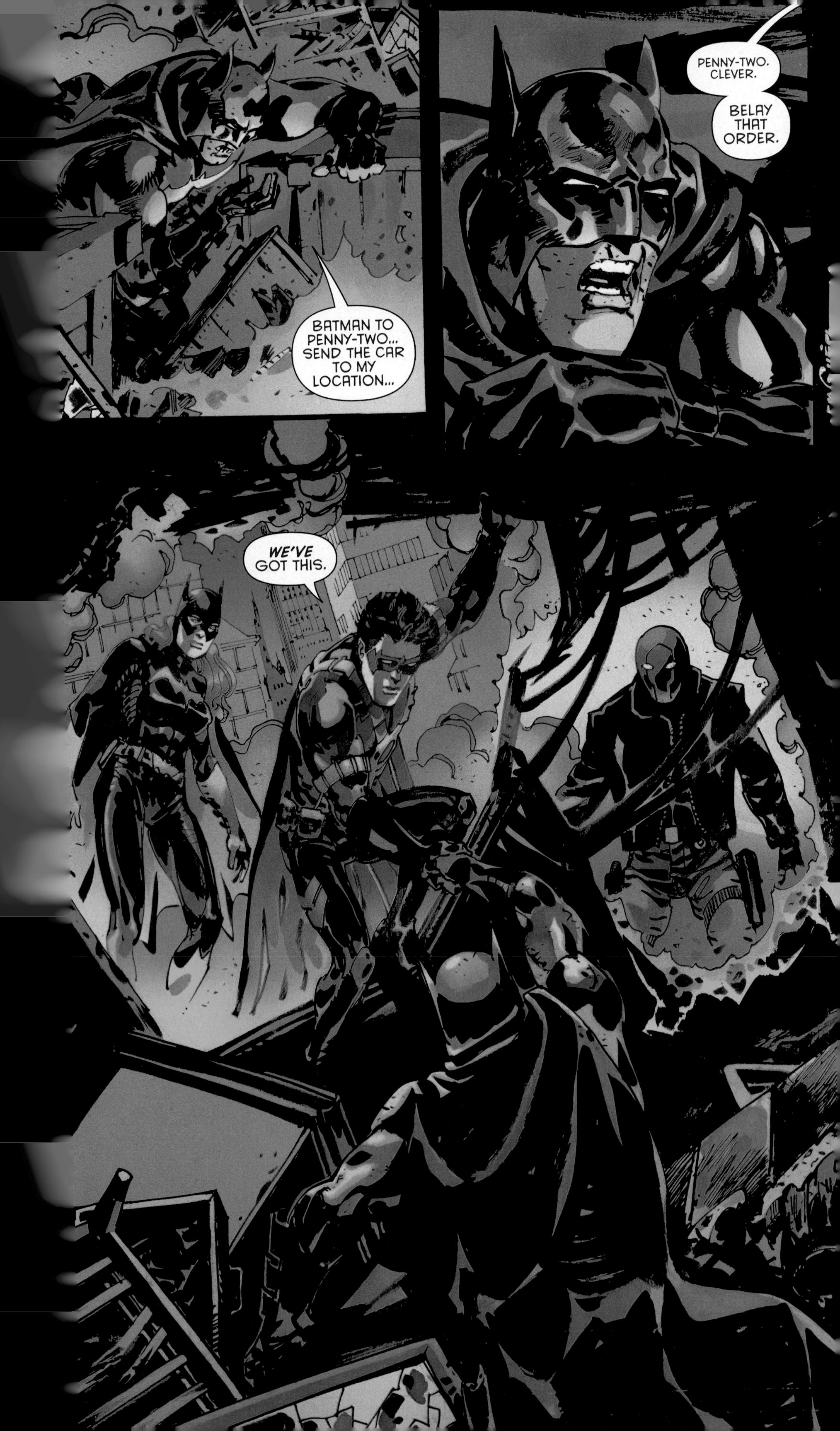
BATMAN TO PENNY-TWO... SEND THE CAR TO MY LOCATION...
PENNY-TWO. CLEVER.
BELAY THAT ORDER.
*WE'VE* GOT THIS.

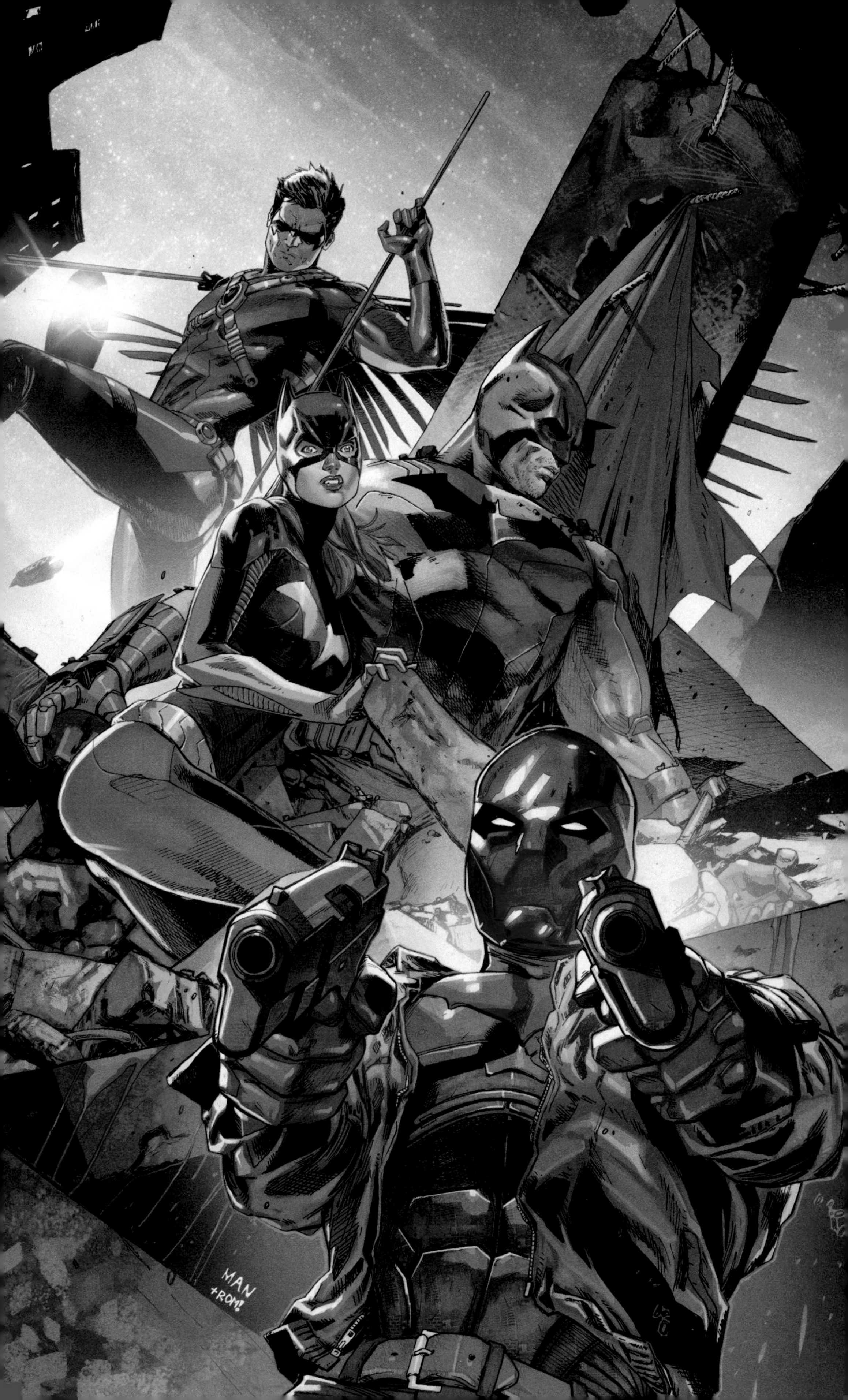
MAN
+ROM!

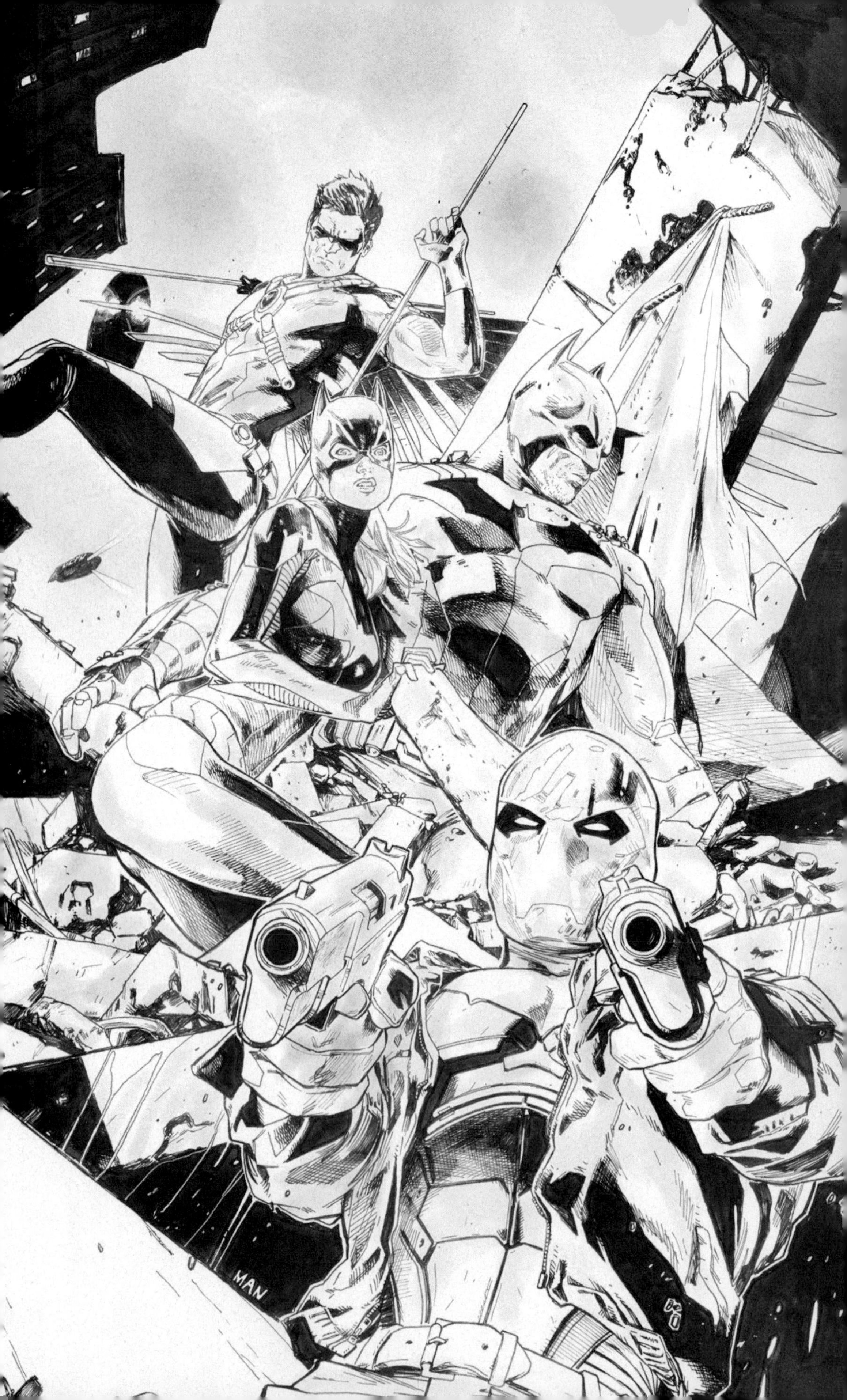
MAN

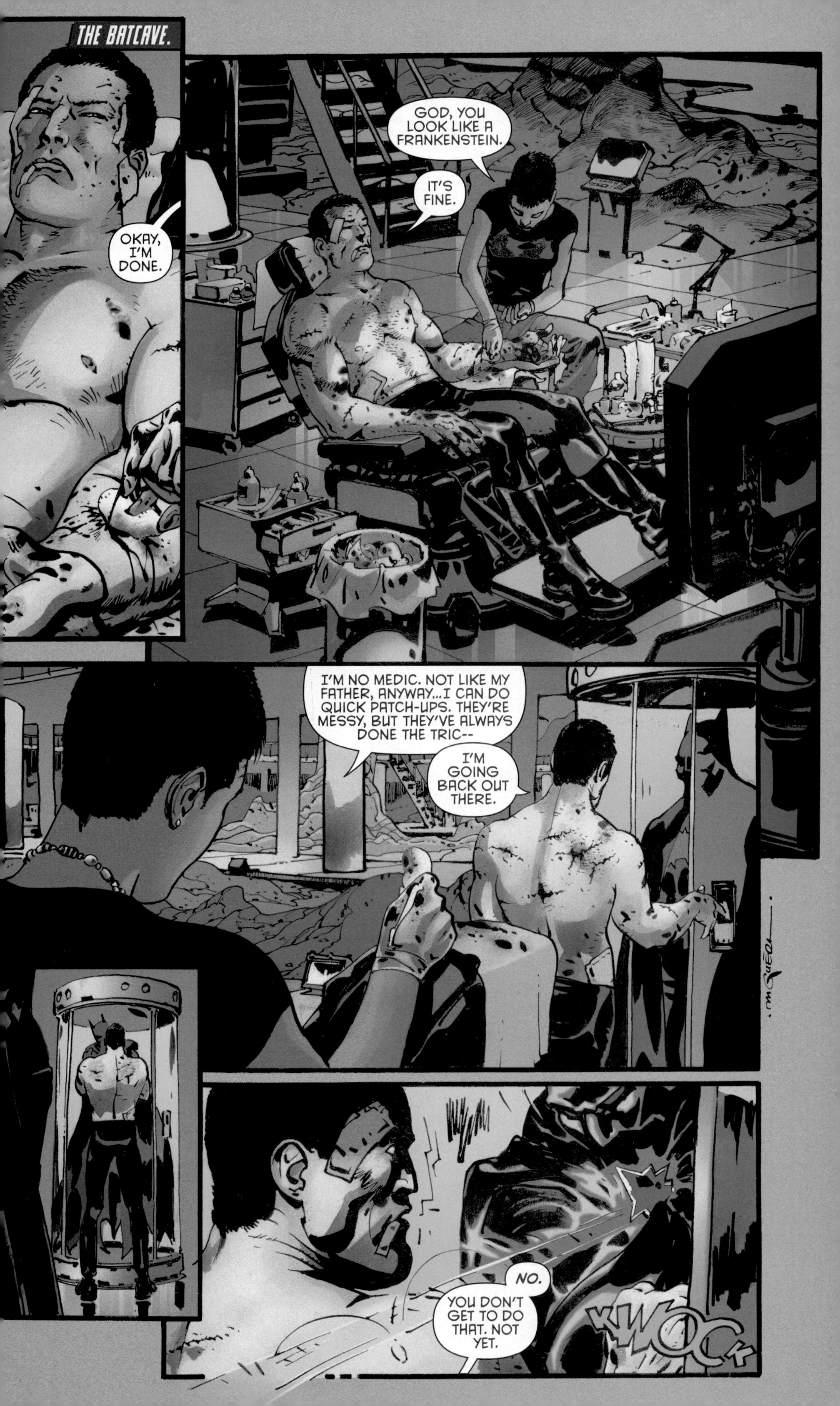

THE BATCAVE.
OKAY, I'M DONE.
GOD, YOU LOOK LIKE A FRANKENSTEIN.
IT'S FINE.
I'M NO MEDIC. NOT LIKE MY FATHER, ANYWAY...I CAN DO QUICK PATCH-UPS. THEY'RE MESSY, BUT THEY'VE ALWAYS DONE THE TRIC--
I'M GOING BACK OUT THERE.
NO.
YOU DON'T GET TO DO THAT. NOT YET.
KWOCK

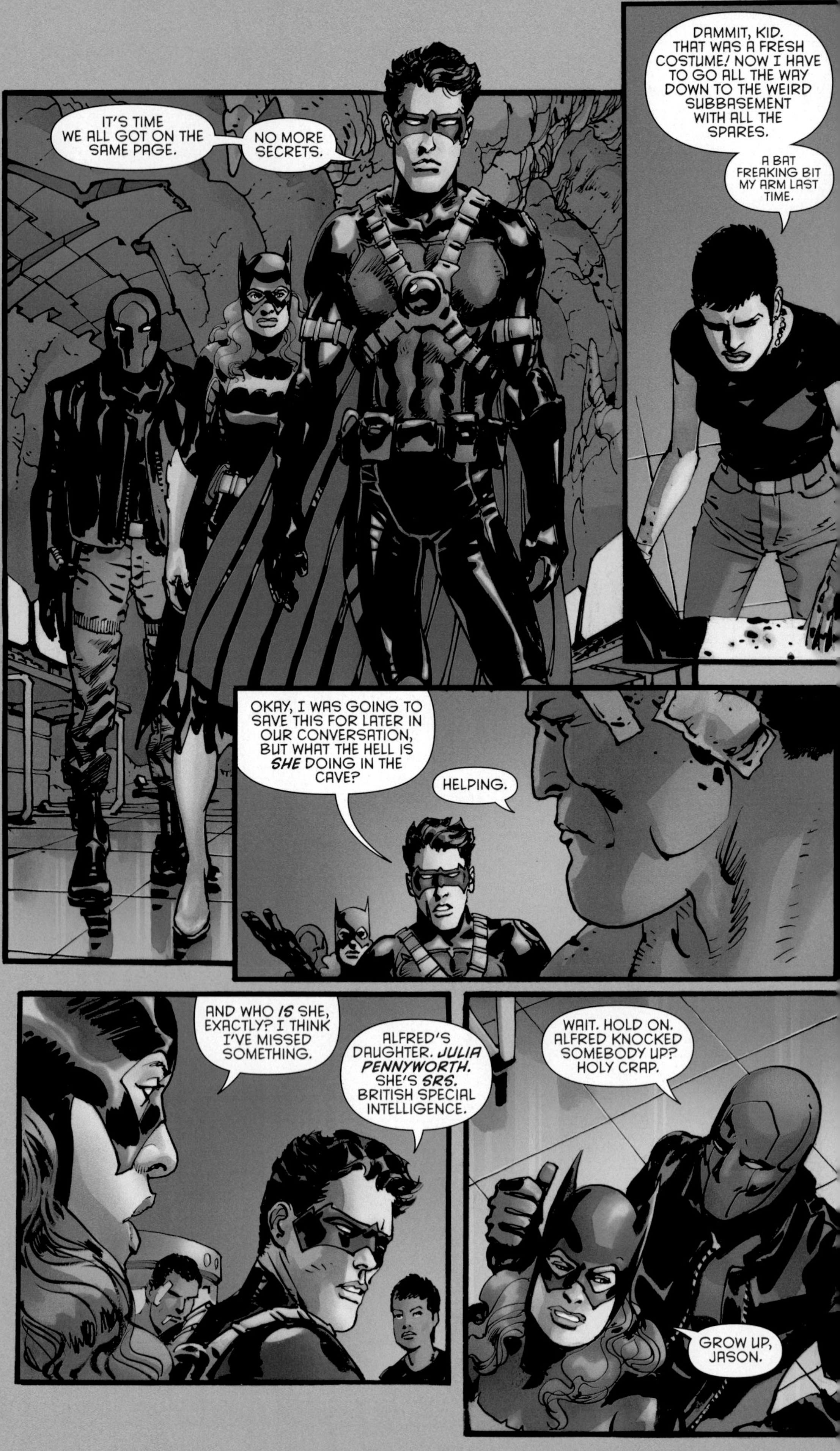
IT'S TIME WE ALL GOT ON THE SAME PAGE.
NO MORE SECRETS.
DAMMIT, KID. THAT WAS A FRESH COSTUME! NOW I HAVE TO GO ALL THE WAY DOWN TO THE WEIRD SUBBASEMENT WITH ALL THE SPARES.
A BAT FREAKING BIT MY ARM LAST TIME.
OKAY, I WAS GOING TO SAVE THIS FOR LATER IN OUR CONVERSATION, BUT WHAT THE HELL IS *SHE* DOING IN THE CAVE?
HELPING.
AND WHO *IS* SHE, EXACTLY? I THINK I'VE MISSED SOMETHING.
ALFRED'S DAUGHTER. *JULIA PENNYWORTH.* SHE'S *SRS.* BRITISH SPECIAL INTELLIGENCE.
WAIT. HOLD ON. ALFRED KNOCKED SOMEBODY UP? HOLY CRAP.
GROW UP, JASON.

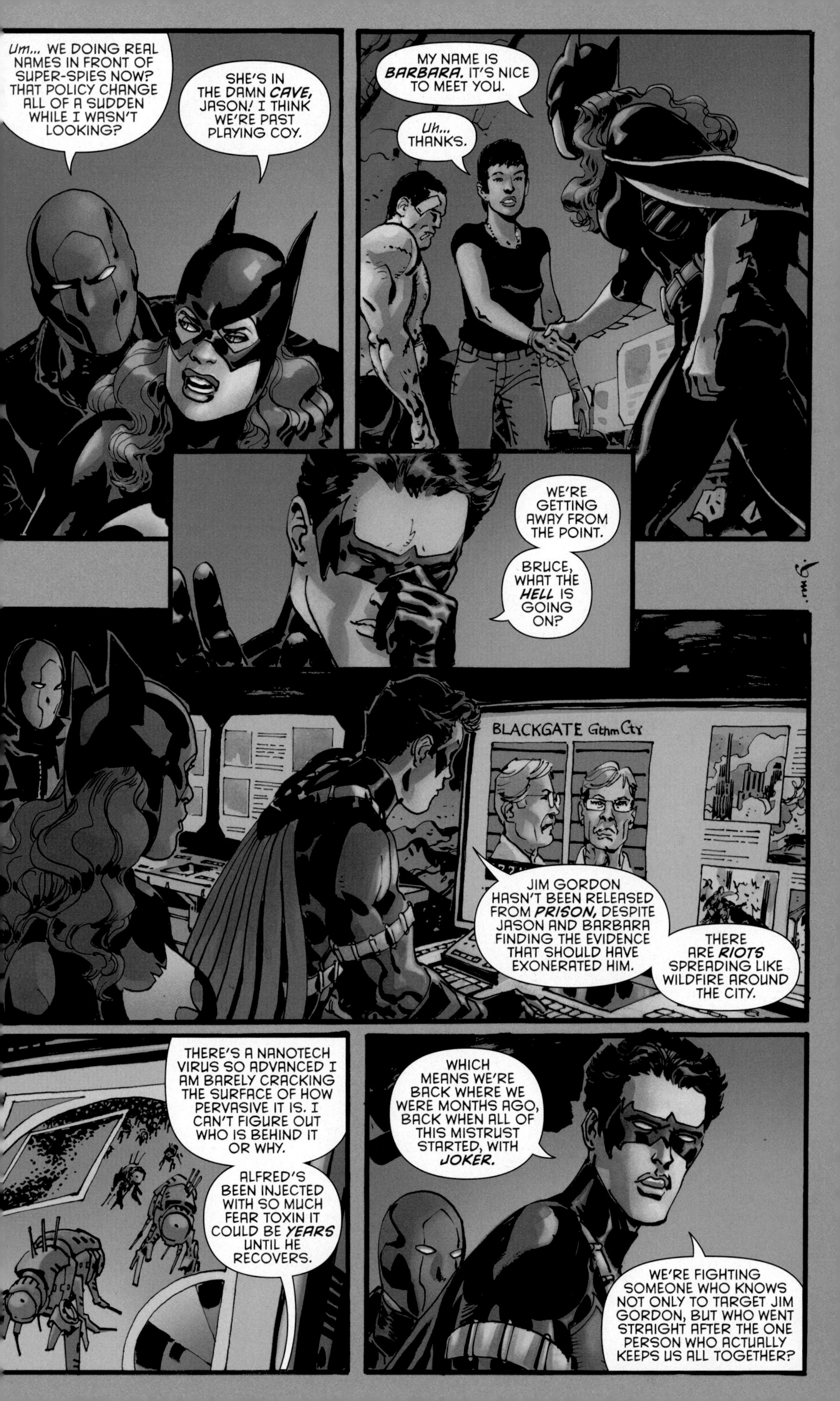
UM... WE DOING REAL NAMES IN FRONT OF SUPER-SPIES NOW? THAT POLICY CHANGE ALL OF A SUDDEN WHILE I WASN'T LOOKING?
SHE'S IN THE DAMN CAVE, JASON! I THINK WE'RE PAST PLAYING COY.
MY NAME IS BARBARA. IT'S NICE TO MEET YOU.
UH... THANKS.
WE'RE GETTING AWAY FROM THE POINT.
BRUCE, WHAT THE HELL IS GOING ON?
BLACKGATE Gthm Cty
JIM GORDON HASN'T BEEN RELEASED FROM PRISON, DESPITE JASON AND BARBARA FINDING THE EVIDENCE THAT SHOULD HAVE EXONERATED HIM.
THERE ARE RIOTS SPREADING LIKE WILDFIRE AROUND THE CITY.
THERE'S A NANOTECH VIRUS SO ADVANCED I AM BARELY CRACKING THE SURFACE OF HOW PERVASIVE IT IS. I CAN'T FIGURE OUT WHO IS BEHIND IT OR WHY.
ALFRED'S BEEN INJECTED WITH SO MUCH FEAR TOXIN IT COULD BE YEARS UNTIL HE RECOVERS.
WHICH MEANS WE'RE BACK WHERE WE WERE MONTHS AGO, BACK WHEN ALL OF THIS MISTRUST STARTED, WITH JOKER.
WE'RE FIGHTING SOMEONE WHO KNOWS NOT ONLY TO TARGET JIM GORDON, BUT WHO WENT STRAIGHT AFTER THE ONE PERSON WHO ACTUALLY KEEPS US ALL TOGETHER?

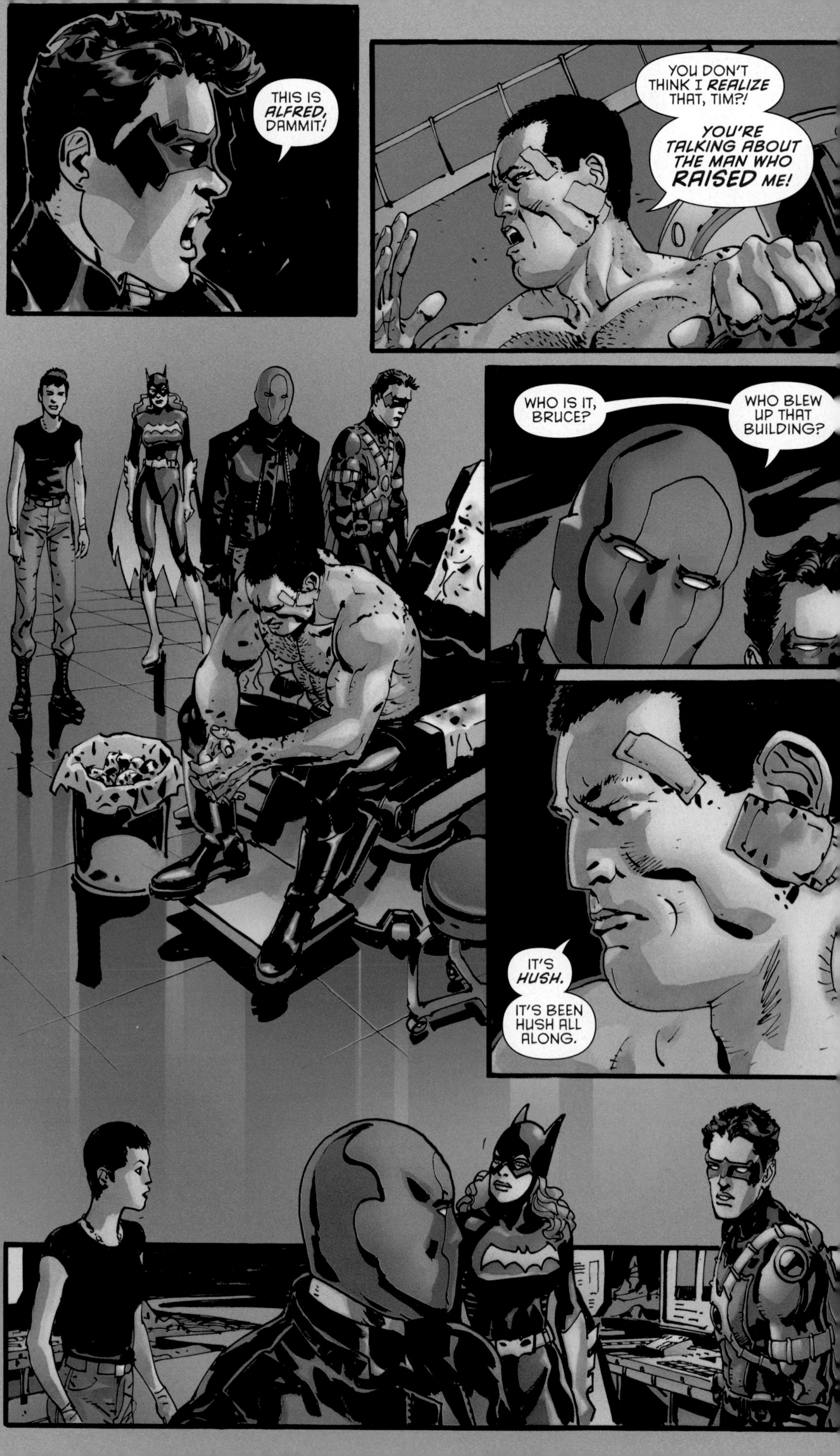

THIS IS ALFRED, DAMMIT!
YOU DON'T THINK I REALIZE THAT, TIM?!
YOU'RE TALKING ABOUT THE MAN WHO RAISED ME!
WHO IS IT, BRUCE?
WHO BLEW UP THAT BUILDING?
IT'S HUSH.
IT'S BEEN HUSH ALL ALONG.

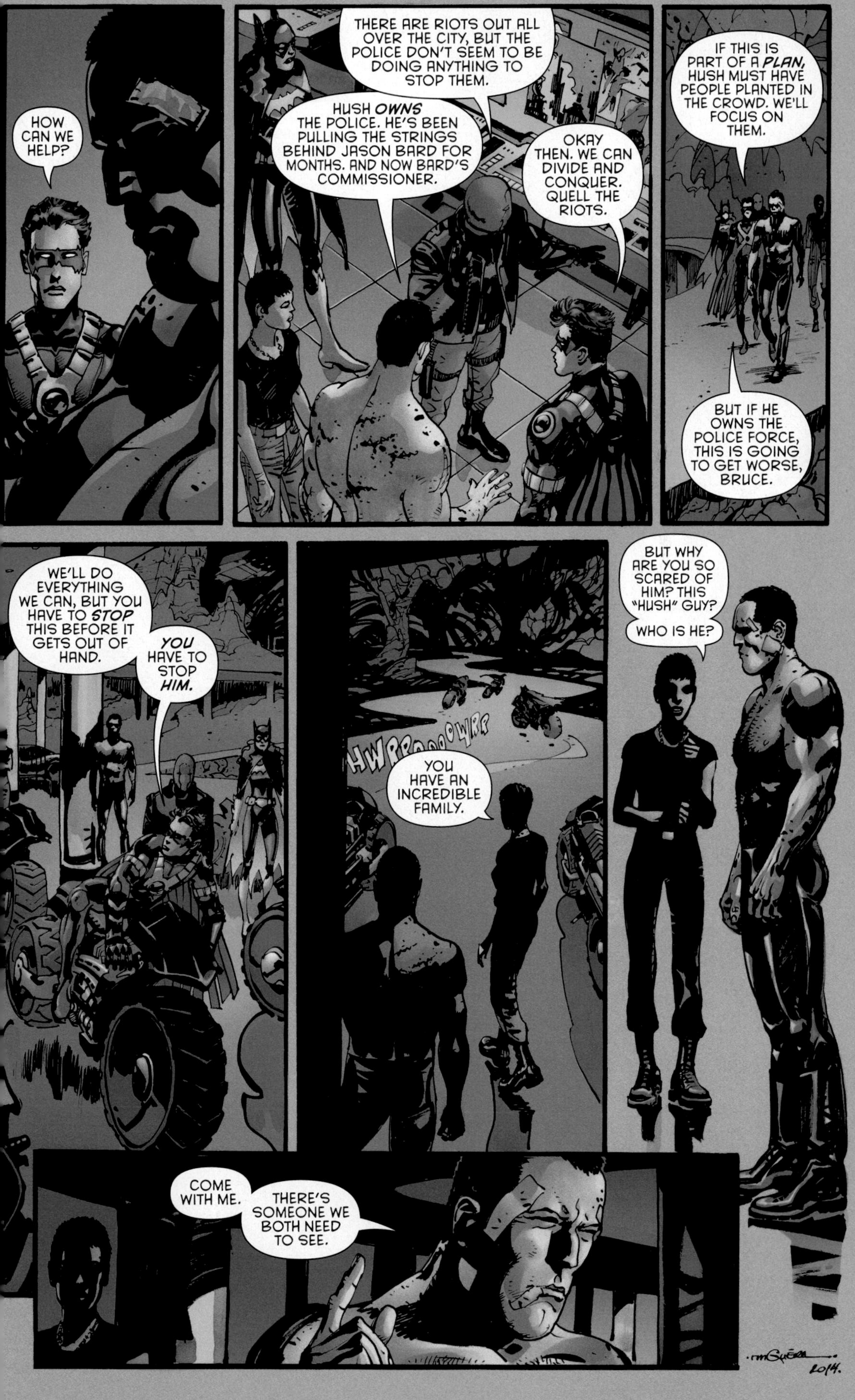
HOW CAN WE HELP?
THERE ARE RIOTS OUT ALL OVER THE CITY, BUT THE POLICE DON'T SEEM TO BE DOING ANYTHING TO STOP THEM.
HUSH *OWNS* THE POLICE. HE'S BEEN PULLING THE STRINGS BEHIND JASON BARD FOR MONTHS. AND NOW BARD'S COMMISSIONER.
OKAY THEN. WE CAN DIVIDE AND CONQUER. QUELL THE RIOTS.
IF THIS IS PART OF A *PLAN*, HUSH MUST HAVE PEOPLE PLANTED IN THE CROWD. WE'LL FOCUS ON THEM.
BUT IF HE OWNS THE POLICE FORCE, THIS IS GOING TO GET WORSE, BRUCE.
WE'LL DO EVERYTHING WE CAN, BUT YOU HAVE TO *STOP* THIS BEFORE IT GETS OUT OF HAND.
*YOU* HAVE TO STOP *HIM.*
HWRRROOOOWRR
YOU HAVE AN INCREDIBLE FAMILY.
BUT WHY ARE YOU SO SCARED OF HIM? THIS "HUSH" GUY?
WHO IS HE?
COME WITH ME.
THERE'S SOMEONE WE BOTH NEED TO SEE.
2014.

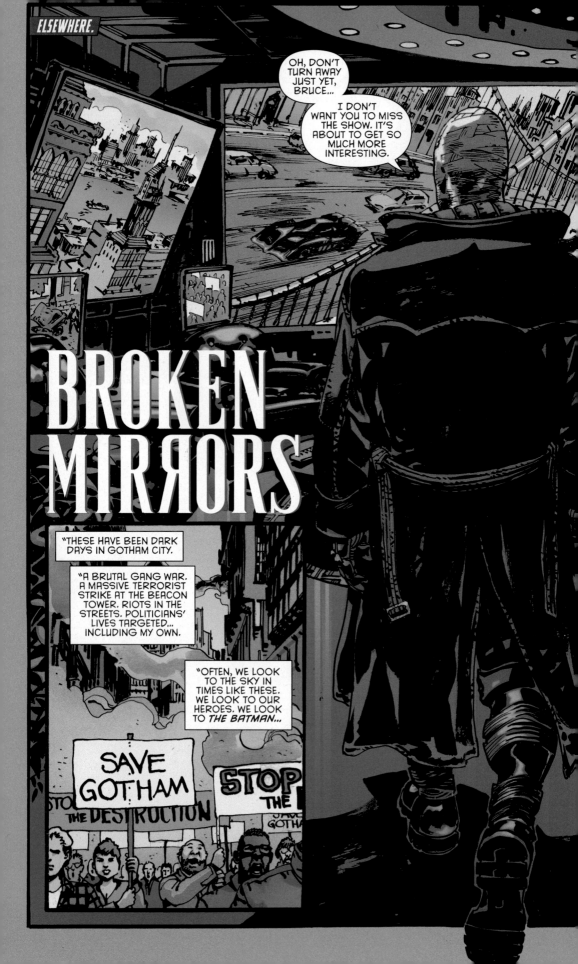

OH, DON'T TURN AWAY JUST YET, BRUCE...

I DON'T WANT YOU TO MISS THE SHOW. IT'S ABOUT TO GET SO MUCH MORE INTERESTING.

# BROKEN MIRRORS

"THESE HAVE BEEN DARK DAYS IN GOTHAM CITY.

"A BRUTAL GANG WAR. A MASSIVE TERRORIST STRIKE AT THE BEACON TOWER. RIOTS IN THE STREETS. POLITICIANS' LIVES TARGETED... INCLUDING MY OWN.

"OFTEN, WE LOOK TO THE SKY IN TIMES LIKE THESE. WE LOOK TO OUR HEROES. WE LOOK TO *THE BATMAN*...

SAVE GOTHAM

STOP THE DESTRUCTION

STOP THE

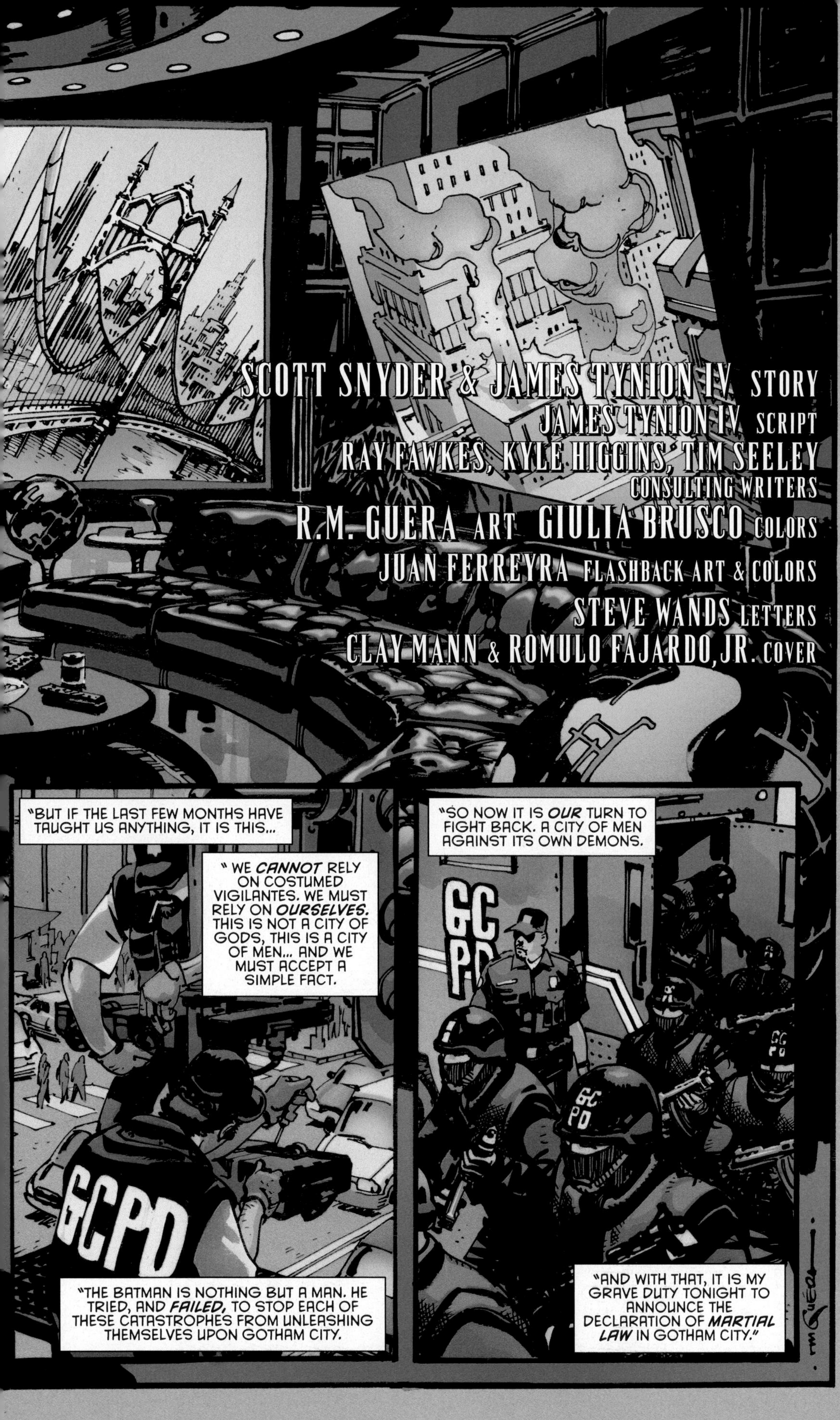
SCOTT SNYDER & JAMES TYNION IV STORY
JAMES TYNION IV SCRIPT
RAY FAWKES, KYLE HIGGINS, TIM SEELEY CONSULTING WRITERS
R.M. GUERA ART GIULIA BRUSCO COLORS
JUAN FERREYRA FLASHBACK ART & COLORS
STEVE WANDS LETTERS
CLAY MANN & ROMULO FAJARDO, JR. COVER
"BUT IF THE LAST FEW MONTHS HAVE TAUGHT US ANYTHING, IT IS THIS...
"WE CANNOT RELY ON COSTUMED VIGILANTES. WE MUST RELY ON OURSELVES. THIS IS NOT A CITY OF GODS, THIS IS A CITY OF MEN... AND WE MUST ACCEPT A SIMPLE FACT.
GCPD
"THE BATMAN IS NOTHING BUT A MAN. HE TRIED, AND FAILED, TO STOP EACH OF THESE CATASTROPHES FROM UNLEASHING THEMSELVES UPON GOTHAM CITY.
"SO NOW IT IS OUR TURN TO FIGHT BACK. A CITY OF MEN AGAINST ITS OWN DEMONS.
GC PD
"AND WITH THAT, IT IS MY GRAVE DUTY TONIGHT TO ANNOUNCE THE DECLARATION OF MARTIAL LAW IN GOTHAM CITY."
rm GUERA

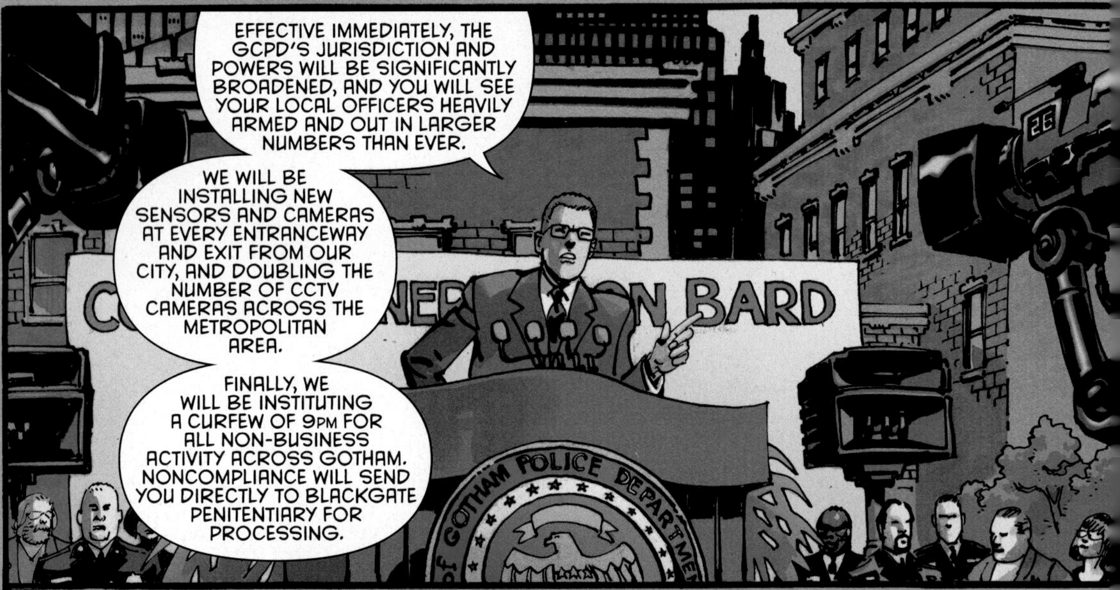
EFFECTIVE IMMEDIATELY, THE GCPD'S JURISDICTION AND POWERS WILL BE SIGNIFICANTLY BROADENED, AND YOU WILL SEE YOUR LOCAL OFFICERS HEAVILY ARMED AND OUT IN LARGER NUMBERS THAN EVER.
WE WILL BE INSTALLING NEW SENSORS AND CAMERAS AT EVERY ENTRANCEWAY AND EXIT FROM OUR CITY, AND DOUBLING THE NUMBER OF CCTV CAMERAS ACROSS THE METROPOLITAN AREA.
FINALLY, WE WILL BE INSTITUTING A CURFEW OF 9PM FOR ALL NON-BUSINESS ACTIVITY ACROSS GOTHAM. NONCOMPLIANCE WILL SEND YOU DIRECTLY TO BLACKGATE PENITENTIARY FOR PROCESSING.
BARD
GOTHAM POLICE DEPARTMENT

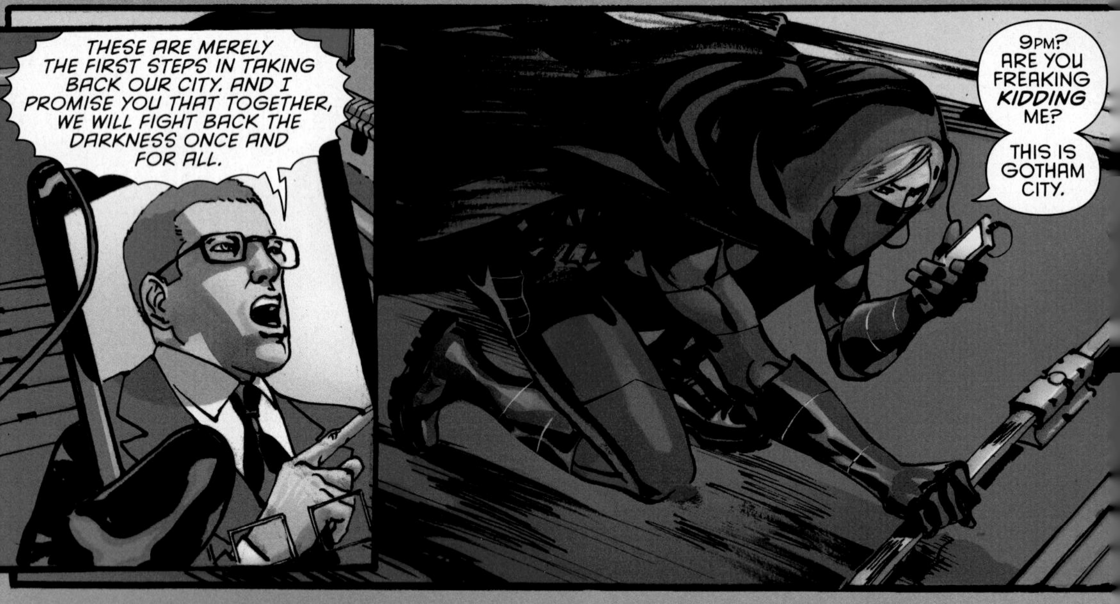
THESE ARE MERELY THE FIRST STEPS IN TAKING BACK OUR CITY. AND I PROMISE YOU THAT TOGETHER, WE WILL FIGHT BACK THE DARKNESS ONCE AND FOR ALL.
9PM? ARE YOU FREAKING *KIDDING* ME?
THIS IS GOTHAM CITY.

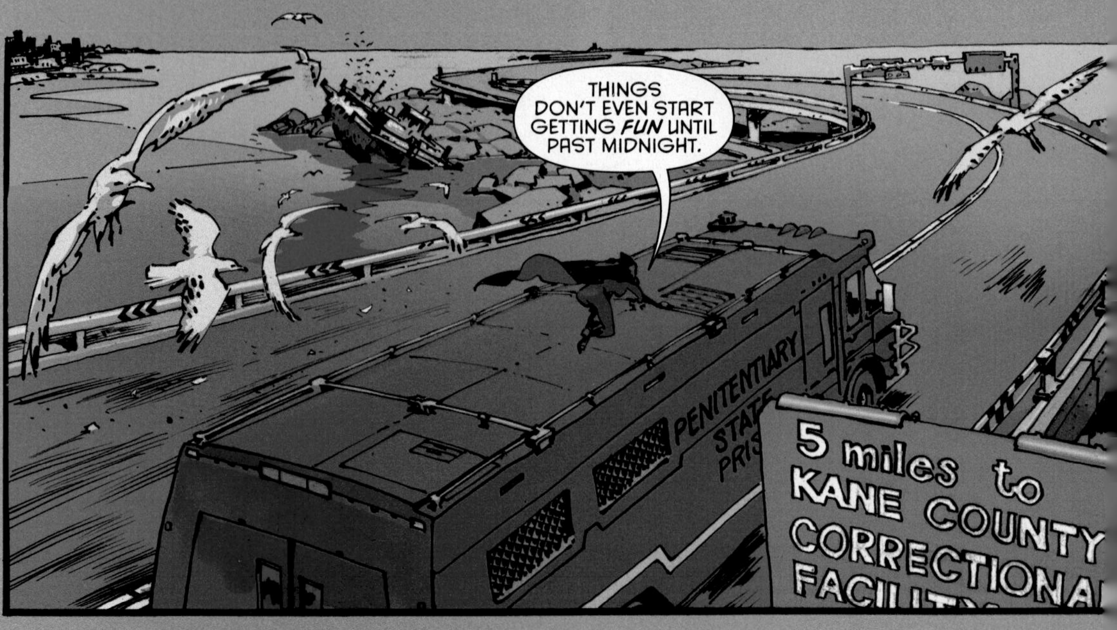
THINGS DON'T EVEN START GETTING *FUN* UNTIL PAST MIDNIGHT.
PENITENTIARY
5 miles to KANE COUNTY CORRECTIONAL

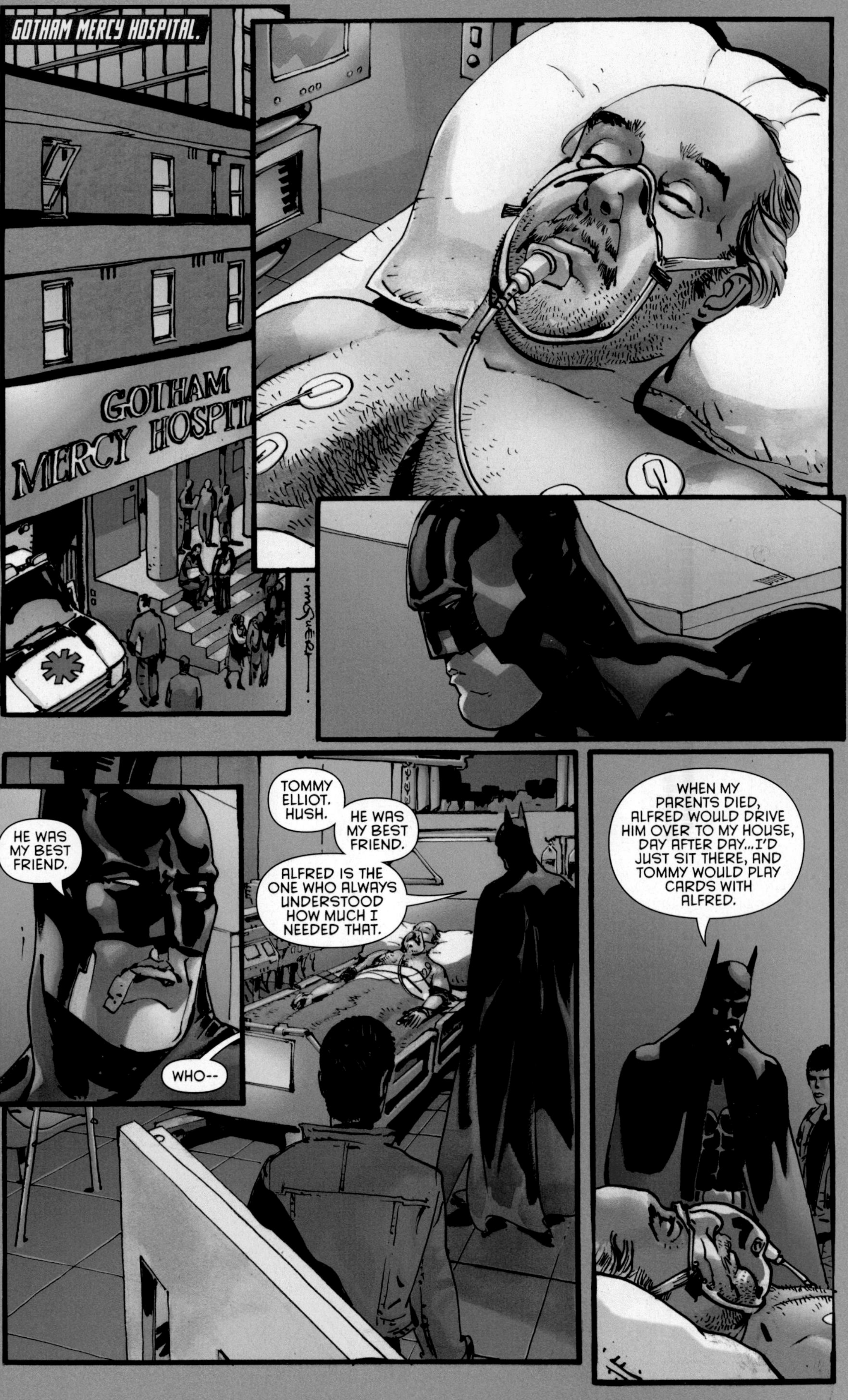
GOTHAM MERCY HOSPITAL.
GOTHAM MERCY HOSPIT
HE WAS MY BEST FRIEND.
WHO--
TOMMY ELLIOT. HUSH.
HE WAS MY BEST FRIEND.
ALFRED IS THE ONE WHO ALWAYS UNDERSTOOD HOW MUCH I NEEDED THAT.
WHEN MY PARENTS DIED, ALFRED WOULD DRIVE HIM OVER TO MY HOUSE, DAY AFTER DAY...I'D JUST SIT THERE, AND TOMMY WOULD PLAY CARDS WITH ALFRED.

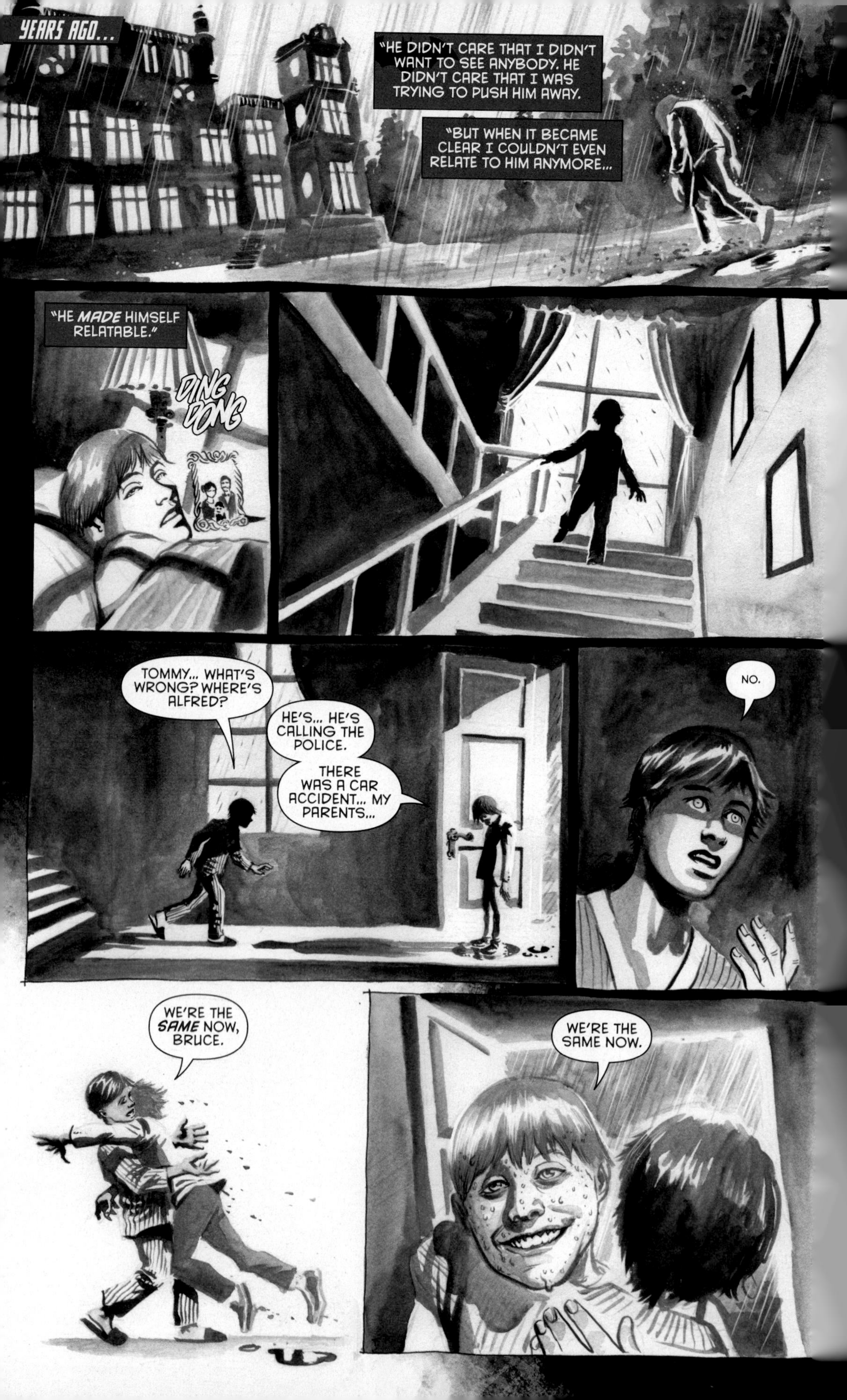
YEARS AGO...
"HE DIDN'T CARE THAT I DIDN'T WANT TO SEE ANYBODY. HE DIDN'T CARE THAT I WAS TRYING TO PUSH HIM AWAY.
"BUT WHEN IT BECAME CLEAR I COULDN'T EVEN RELATE TO HIM ANYMORE...
"HE MADE HIMSELF RELATABLE."
DING DONG
TOMMY... WHAT'S WRONG? WHERE'S ALFRED?
HE'S... HE'S CALLING THE POLICE.
THERE WAS A CAR ACCIDENT... MY PARENTS...
NO.
WE'RE THE SAME NOW, BRUCE.
WE'RE THE SAME NOW.

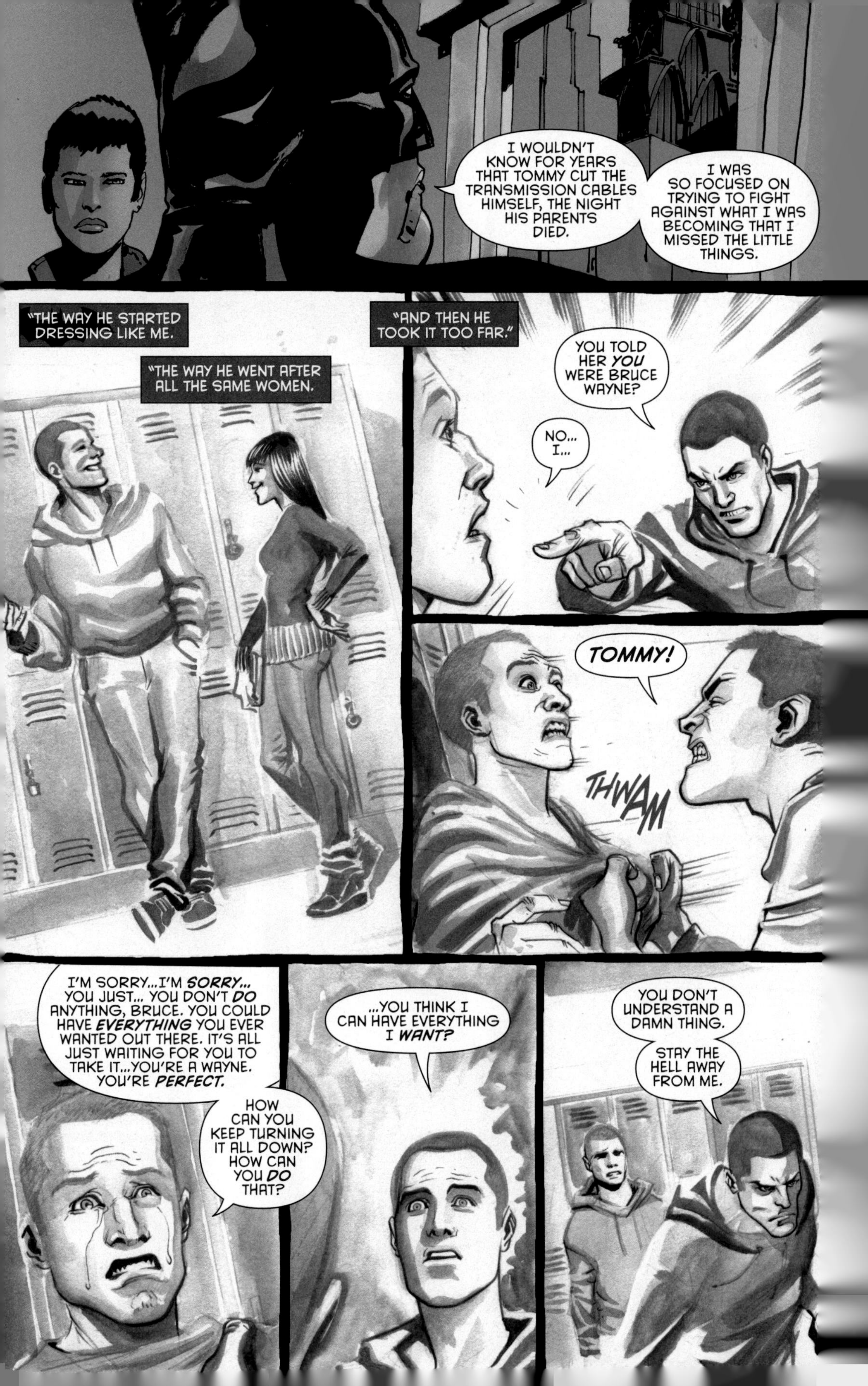
I WOULDN'T KNOW FOR YEARS THAT TOMMY CUT THE TRANSMISSION CABLES HIMSELF, THE NIGHT HIS PARENTS DIED.
I WAS SO FOCUSED ON TRYING TO FIGHT AGAINST WHAT I WAS BECOMING THAT I MISSED THE LITTLE THINGS.
"THE WAY HE STARTED DRESSING LIKE ME.
"THE WAY HE WENT AFTER ALL THE SAME WOMEN.
"AND THEN HE TOOK IT TOO FAR."
YOU TOLD HER *YOU* WERE BRUCE WAYNE?
NO... I...
*TOMMY!*
THWAM
I'M SORRY...I'M *SORRY...* YOU JUST... YOU DON'T *DO* ANYTHING, BRUCE. YOU COULD HAVE *EVERYTHING* YOU EVER WANTED OUT THERE. IT'S ALL JUST WAITING FOR YOU TO TAKE IT...YOU'RE A WAYNE. YOU'RE *PERFECT.*
HOW CAN YOU KEEP TURNING IT ALL DOWN? HOW CAN YOU *DO* THAT?
...YOU THINK I CAN HAVE EVERYTHING I *WANT?*
YOU DON'T UNDERSTAND A DAMN THING.
STAY THE HELL AWAY FROM ME.

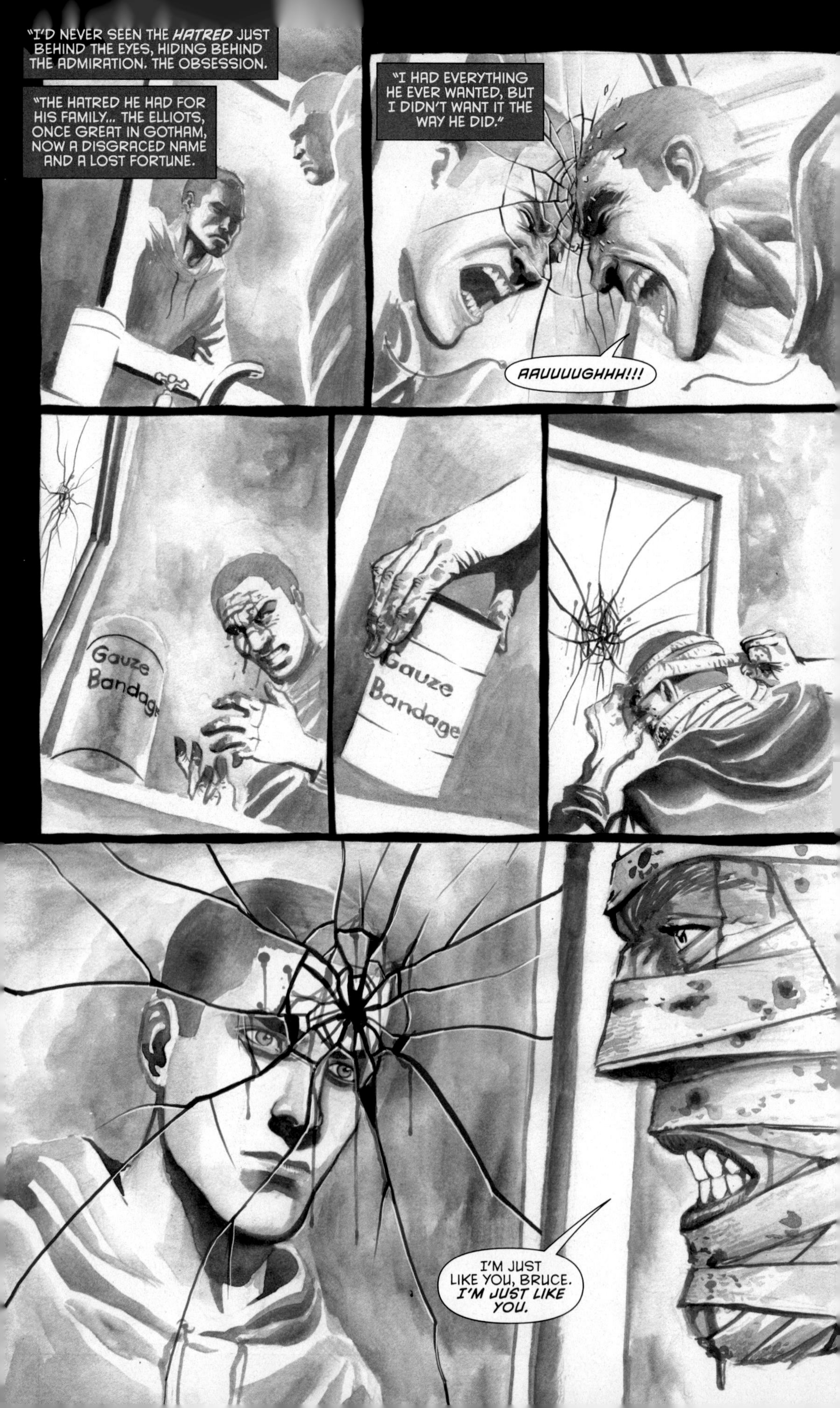
"I'D NEVER SEEN THE HATRED JUST BEHIND THE EYES, HIDING BEHIND THE ADMIRATION. THE OBSESSION.
"THE HATRED HE HAD FOR HIS FAMILY... THE ELLIOTS, ONCE GREAT IN GOTHAM, NOW A DISGRACED NAME AND A LOST FORTUNE.
"I HAD EVERYTHING HE EVER WANTED, BUT I DIDN'T WANT IT THE WAY HE DID."
AAUUUUGHHH!!!
Gauze Bandage
Gauze Bandage
I'M JUST LIKE YOU, BRUCE. I'M JUST LIKE YOU.

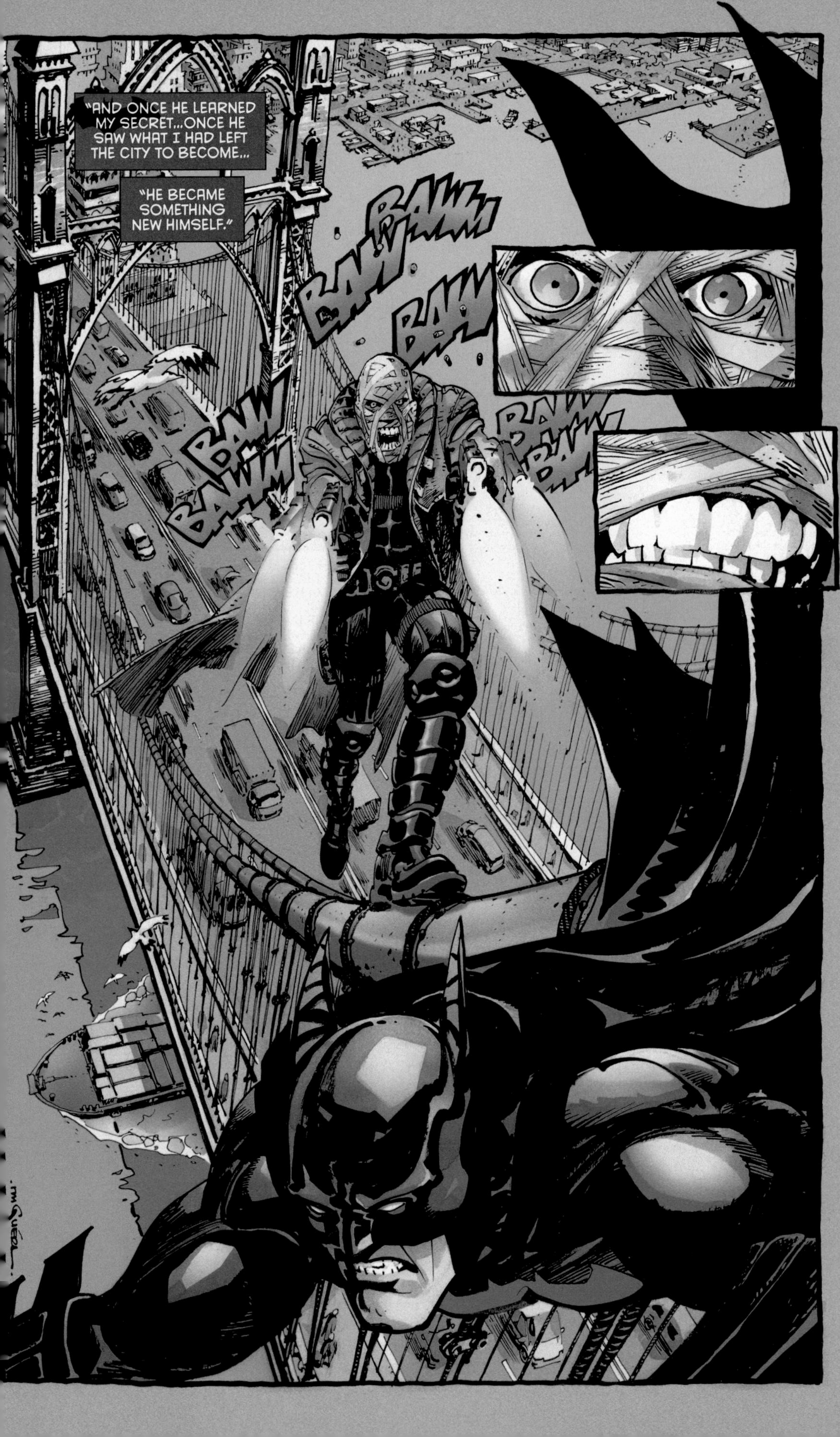
"AND ONCE HE LEARNED MY SECRET...ONCE HE SAW WHAT I HAD LEFT THE CITY TO BECOME...
"HE BECAME SOMETHING NEW HIMSELF."
BAWM BAWM
BAWM
BAWM
BAWM BAWM
BAWM BAWM

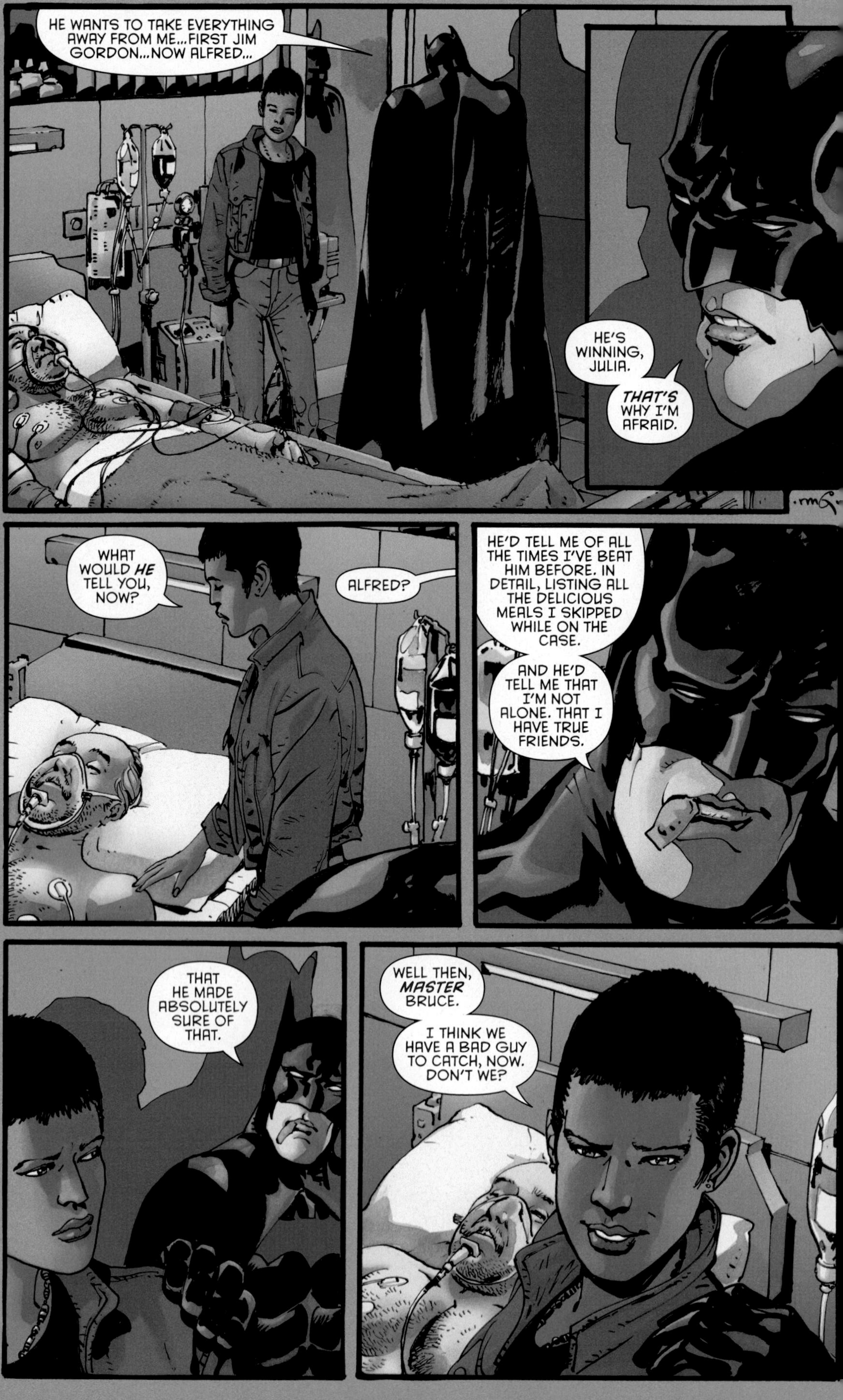
HE WANTS TO TAKE EVERYTHING AWAY FROM ME...FIRST JIM GORDON...NOW ALFRED...
HE'S WINNING, JULIA.
*THAT'S* WHY I'M AFRAID.
WHAT WOULD *HE* TELL YOU, NOW?
ALFRED?
HE'D TELL ME OF ALL THE TIMES I'VE BEAT HIM BEFORE. IN DETAIL, LISTING ALL THE DELICIOUS MEALS I SKIPPED WHILE ON THE CASE.
AND HE'D TELL ME THAT I'M NOT ALONE. THAT I HAVE TRUE FRIENDS.
THAT HE MADE ABSOLUTELY SURE OF THAT.
WELL THEN, *MASTER* BRUCE.
I THINK WE HAVE A BAD GUY TO CATCH, NOW. DON'T WE?

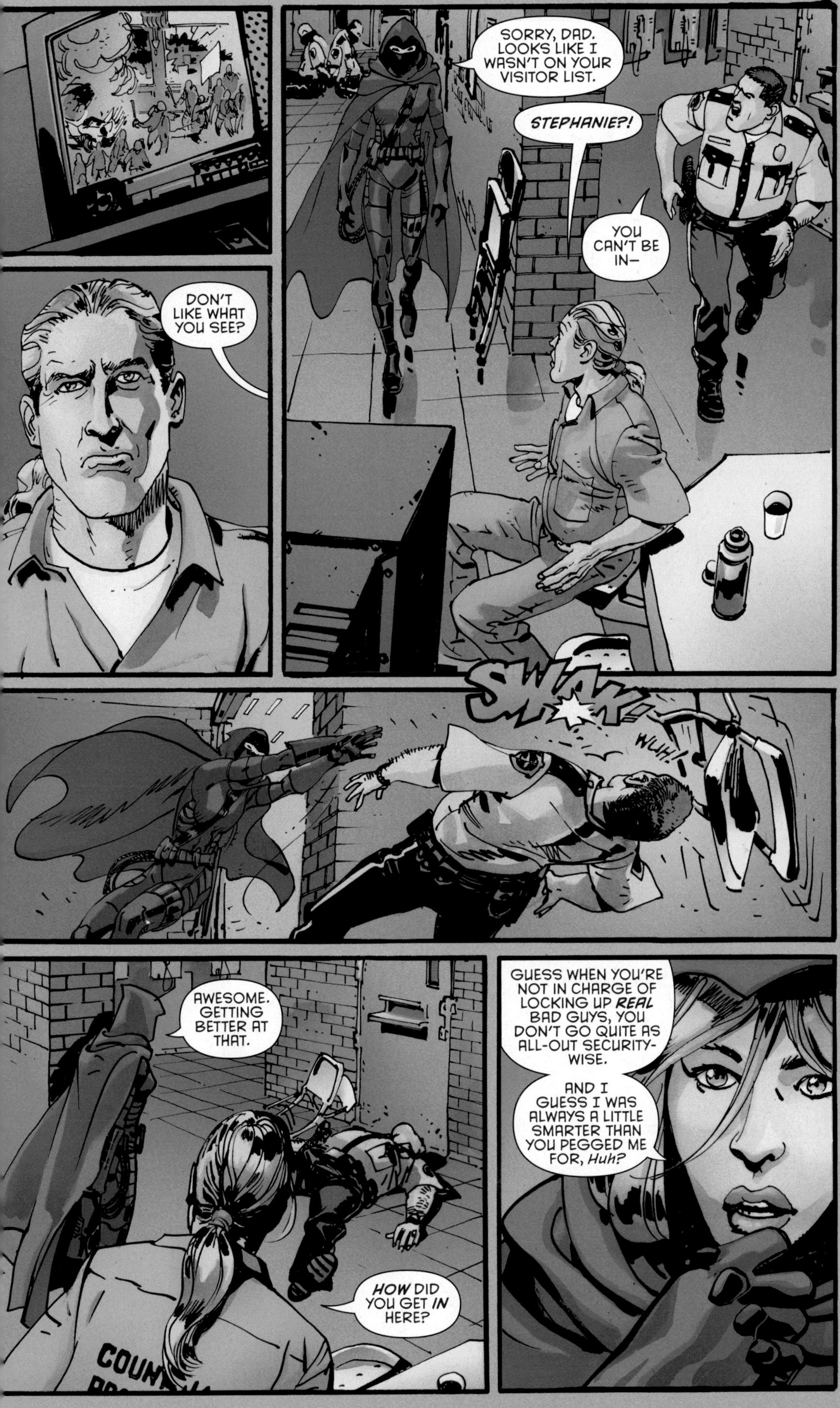
SORRY, DAD. LOOKS LIKE I WASN'T ON YOUR VISITOR LIST.
STEPHANIE?!
YOU CAN'T BE IN—
DON'T LIKE WHAT YOU SEE?
SWAK!
WUH!
AWESOME. GETTING BETTER AT THAT.
HOW DID YOU GET IN HERE?
GUESS WHEN YOU'RE NOT IN CHARGE OF LOCKING UP REAL BAD GUYS, YOU DON'T GO QUITE AS ALL-OUT SECURITY-WISE.
AND I GUESS I WAS ALWAYS A LITTLE SMARTER THAN YOU PEGGED ME FOR, Huh?

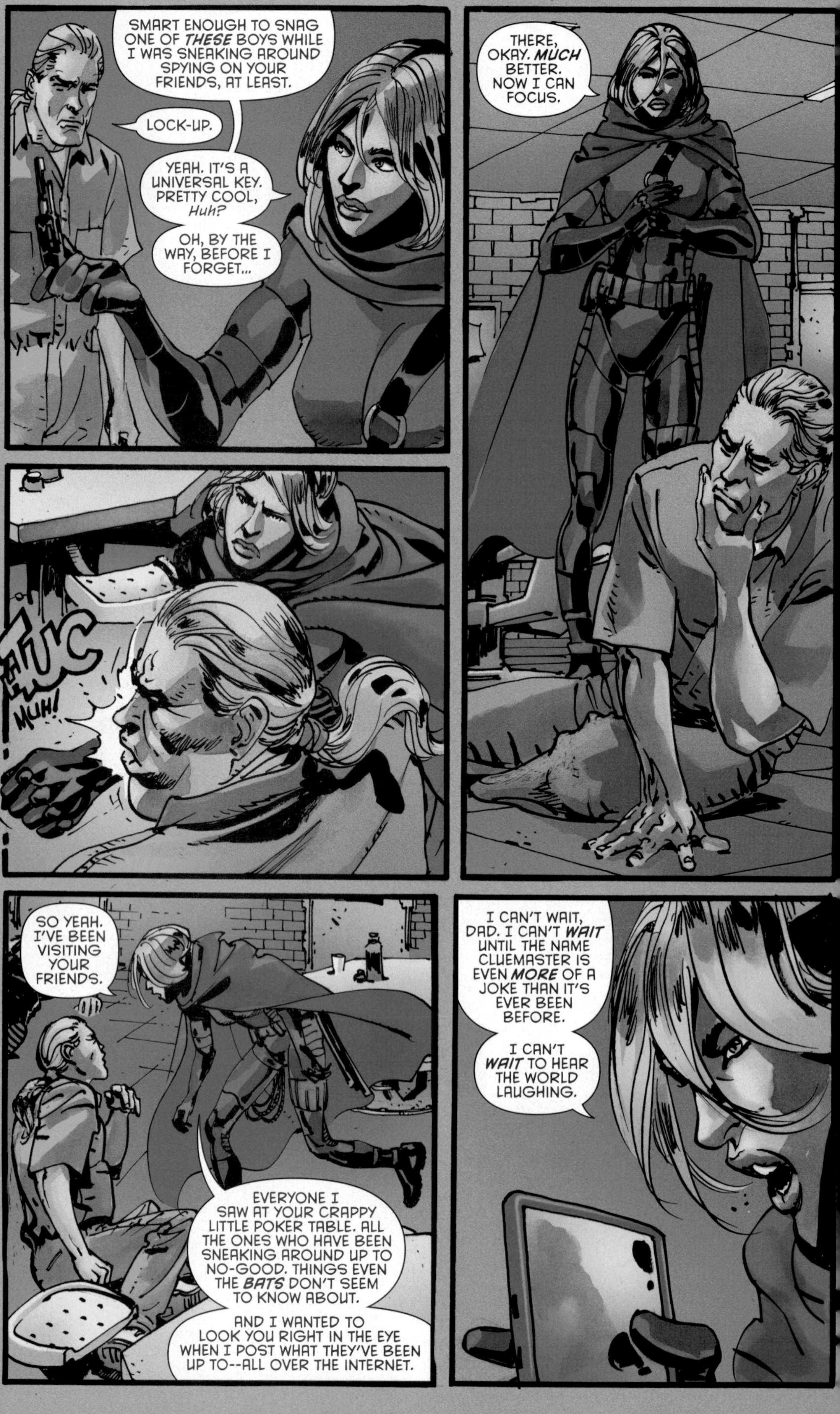
SMART ENOUGH TO SNAG ONE OF THESE BOYS WHILE I WAS SNEAKING AROUND SPYING ON YOUR FRIENDS, AT LEAST.
LOCK-UP.
YEAH. IT'S A UNIVERSAL KEY. PRETTY COOL, Huh?
OH, BY THE WAY, BEFORE I FORGET...
THERE, OKAY. MUCH BETTER. NOW I CAN FOCUS.
THUC
MUH!
SO YEAH. I'VE BEEN VISITING YOUR FRIENDS.
EVERYONE I SAW AT YOUR CRAPPY LITTLE POKER TABLE. ALL THE ONES WHO HAVE BEEN SNEAKING AROUND UP TO NO-GOOD. THINGS EVEN THE BATS DON'T SEEM TO KNOW ABOUT.
AND I WANTED TO LOOK YOU RIGHT IN THE EYE WHEN I POST WHAT THEY'VE BEEN UP TO--ALL OVER THE INTERNET.
I CAN'T WAIT, DAD. I CAN'T WAIT UNTIL THE NAME CLUEMASTER IS EVEN MORE OF A JOKE THAN IT'S EVER BEEN BEFORE.
I CAN'T WAIT TO HEAR THE WORLD LAUGHING.

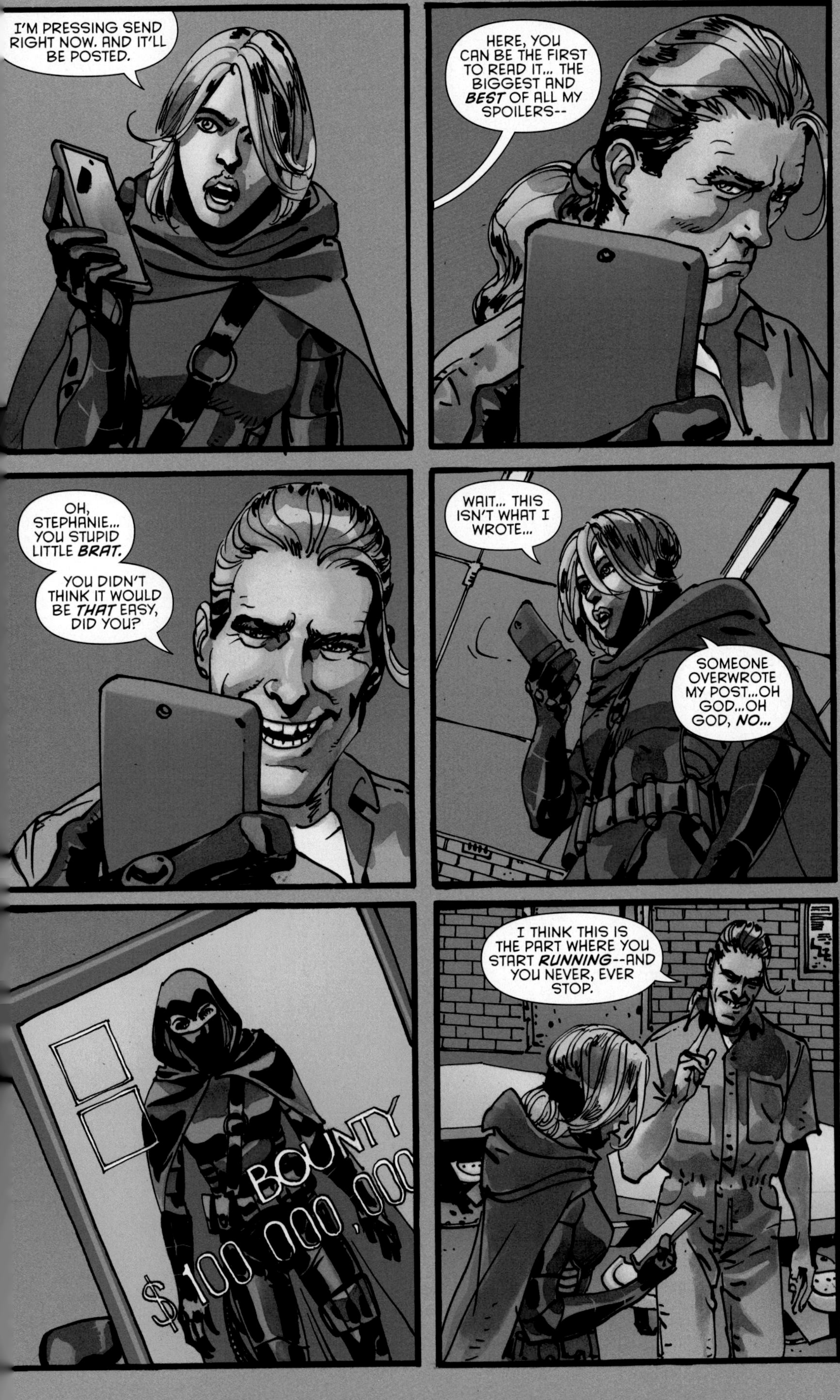

I'M PRESSING SEND RIGHT NOW. AND IT'LL BE POSTED.
HERE, YOU CAN BE THE FIRST TO READ IT... THE BIGGEST AND BEST OF ALL MY SPOILERS--
OH, STEPHANIE... YOU STUPID LITTLE BRAT.
YOU DIDN'T THINK IT WOULD BE THAT EASY, DID YOU?
WAIT... THIS ISN'T WHAT I WROTE...
SOMEONE OVERWROTE MY POST...OH GOD...OH GOD, NO...
BOUNTY
$100,000,000
I THINK THIS IS THE PART WHERE YOU START RUNNING--AND YOU NEVER, EVER STOP.

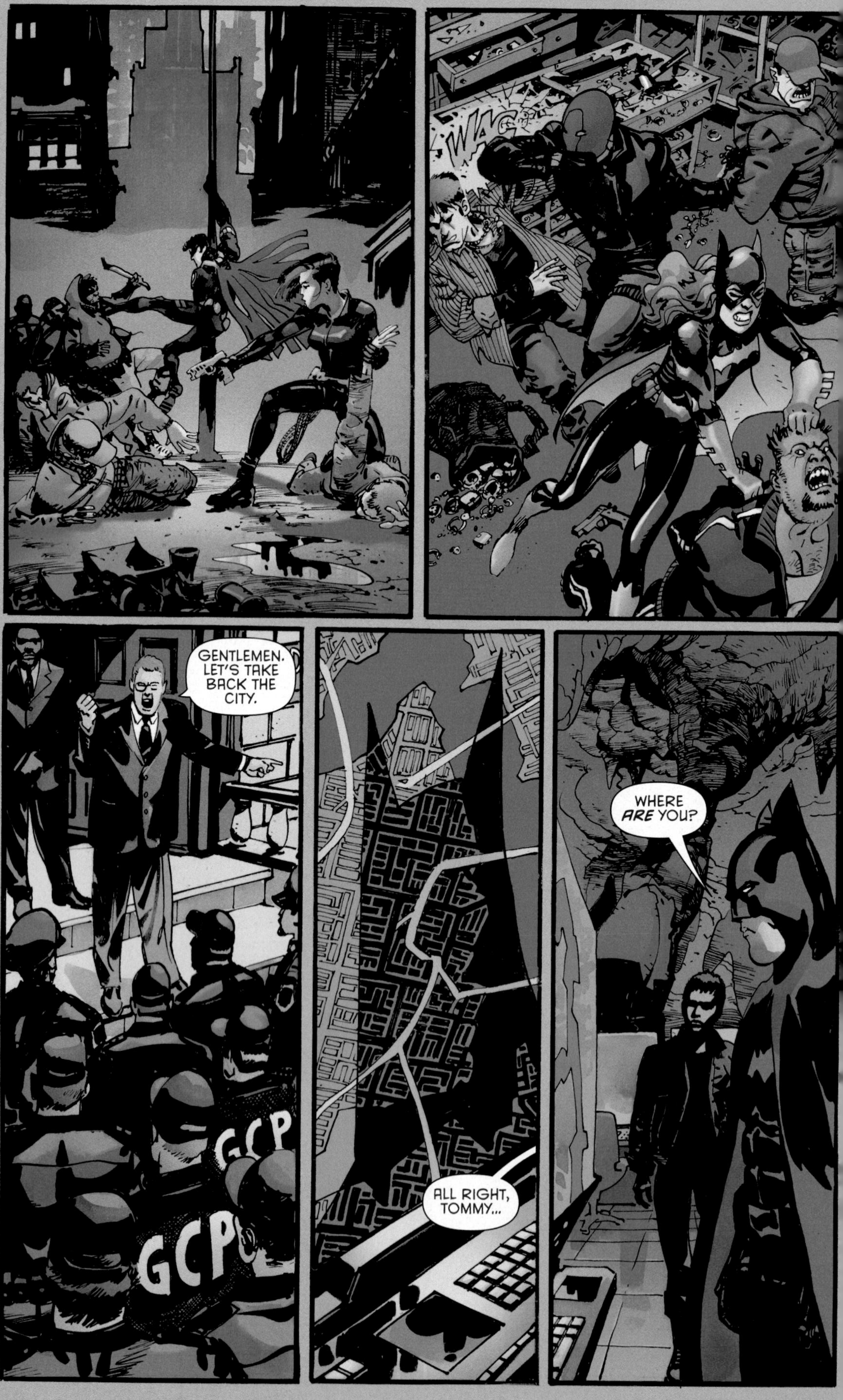
WAG
GENTLEMEN. LET'S TAKE BACK THE CITY.
GCP
GCP
ALL RIGHT, TOMMY...
WHERE *ARE* YOU?

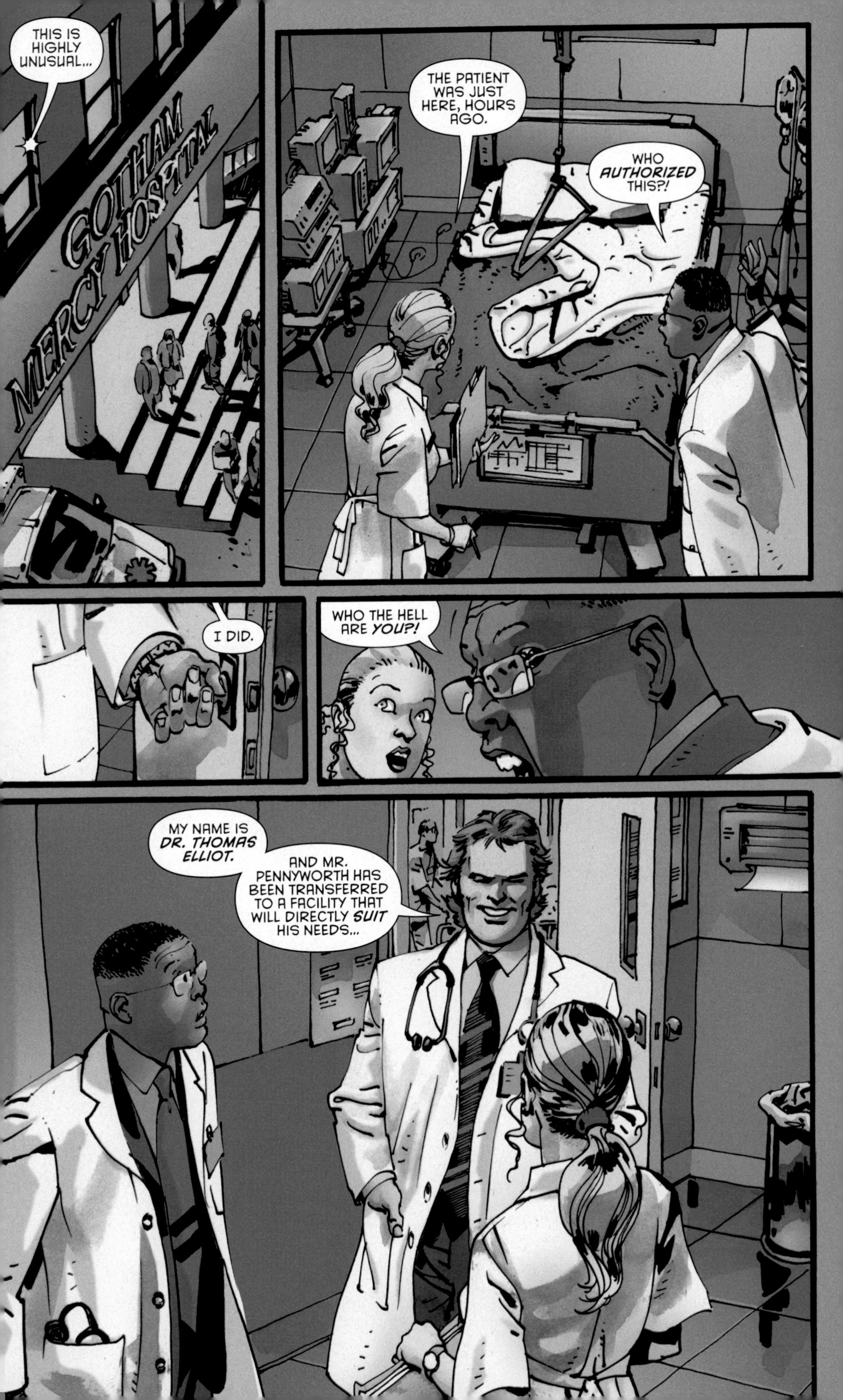
THIS IS HIGHLY UNUSUAL...
GOTHAM MERCY HOSPITAL
THE PATIENT WAS JUST HERE, HOURS AGO.
WHO *AUTHORIZED* THIS?!
I DID.
WHO THE HELL ARE *YOU?!*
MY NAME IS *DR. THOMAS ELLIOT.*
AND MR. PENNYWORTH HAS BEEN TRANSFERRED TO A FACILITY THAT WILL DIRECTLY *SUIT* HIS NEEDS...

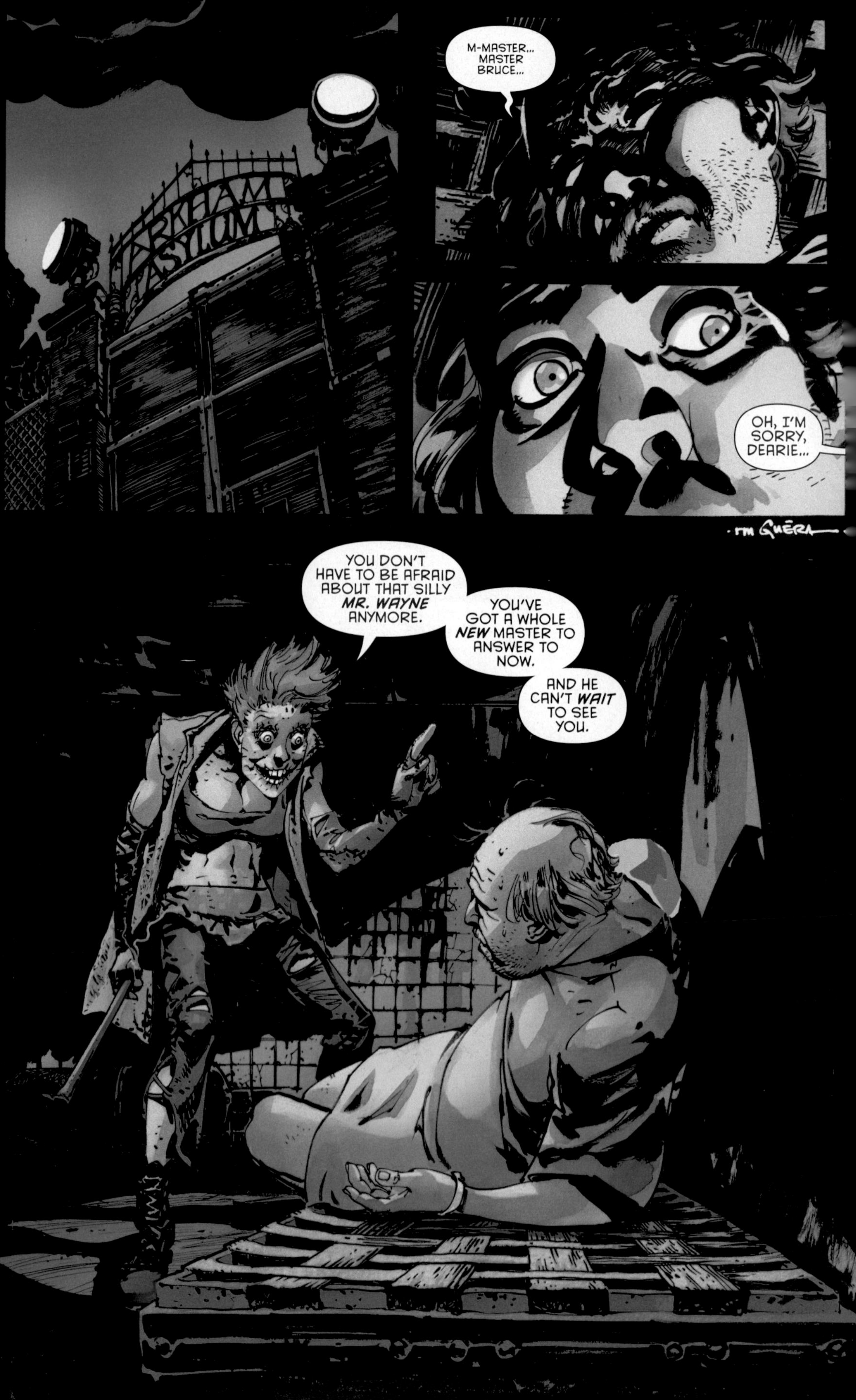
ARKHAM ASYLUM
M-MASTER... MASTER BRUCE...
OH, I'M SORRY, DEARIE...
YOU DON'T HAVE TO BE AFRAID ABOUT THAT SILLY MR. WAYNE ANYMORE.
YOU'VE GOT A WHOLE NEW MASTER TO ANSWER TO NOW.
AND HE CAN'T WAIT TO SEE YOU.

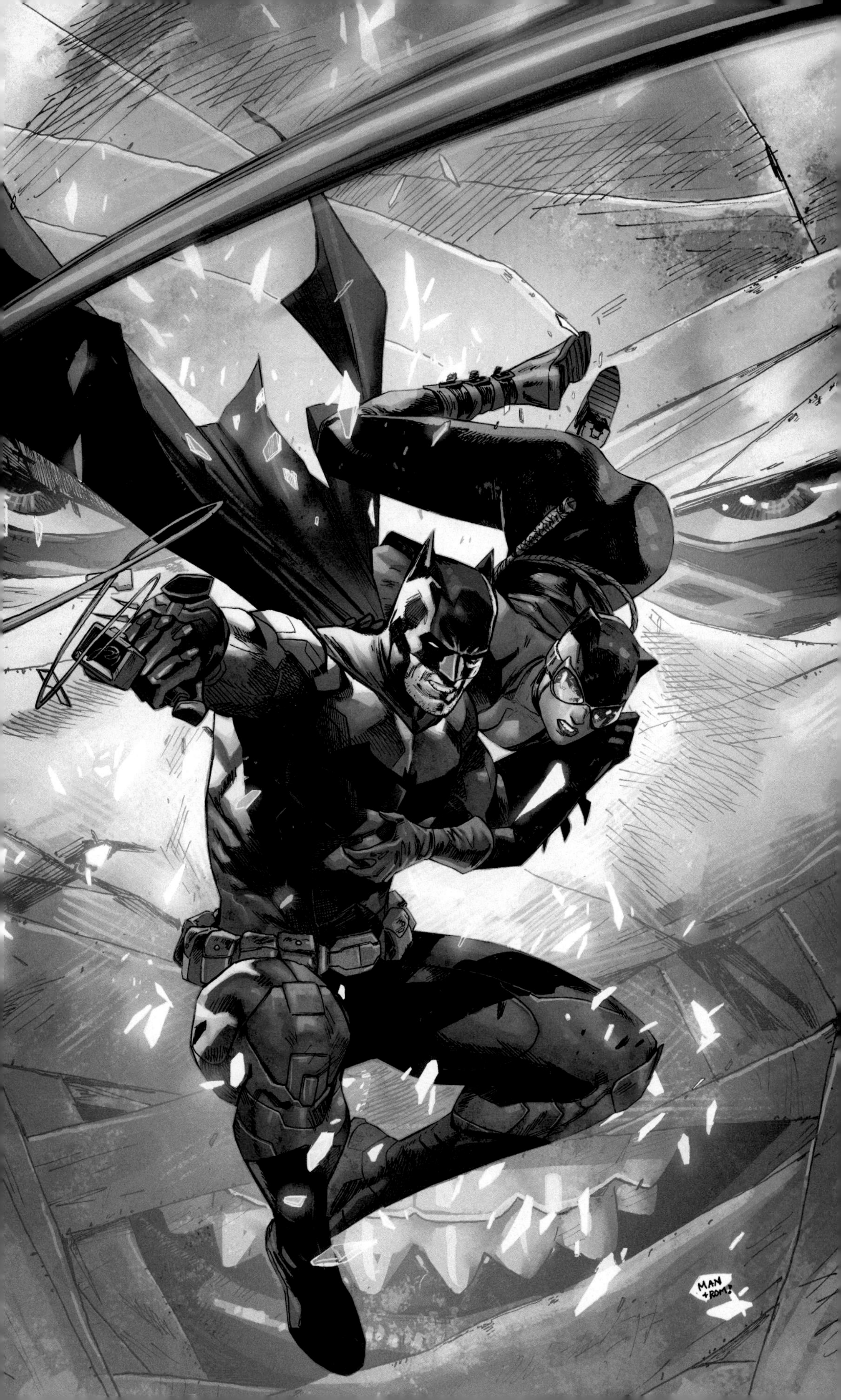
MAN
+ROM.

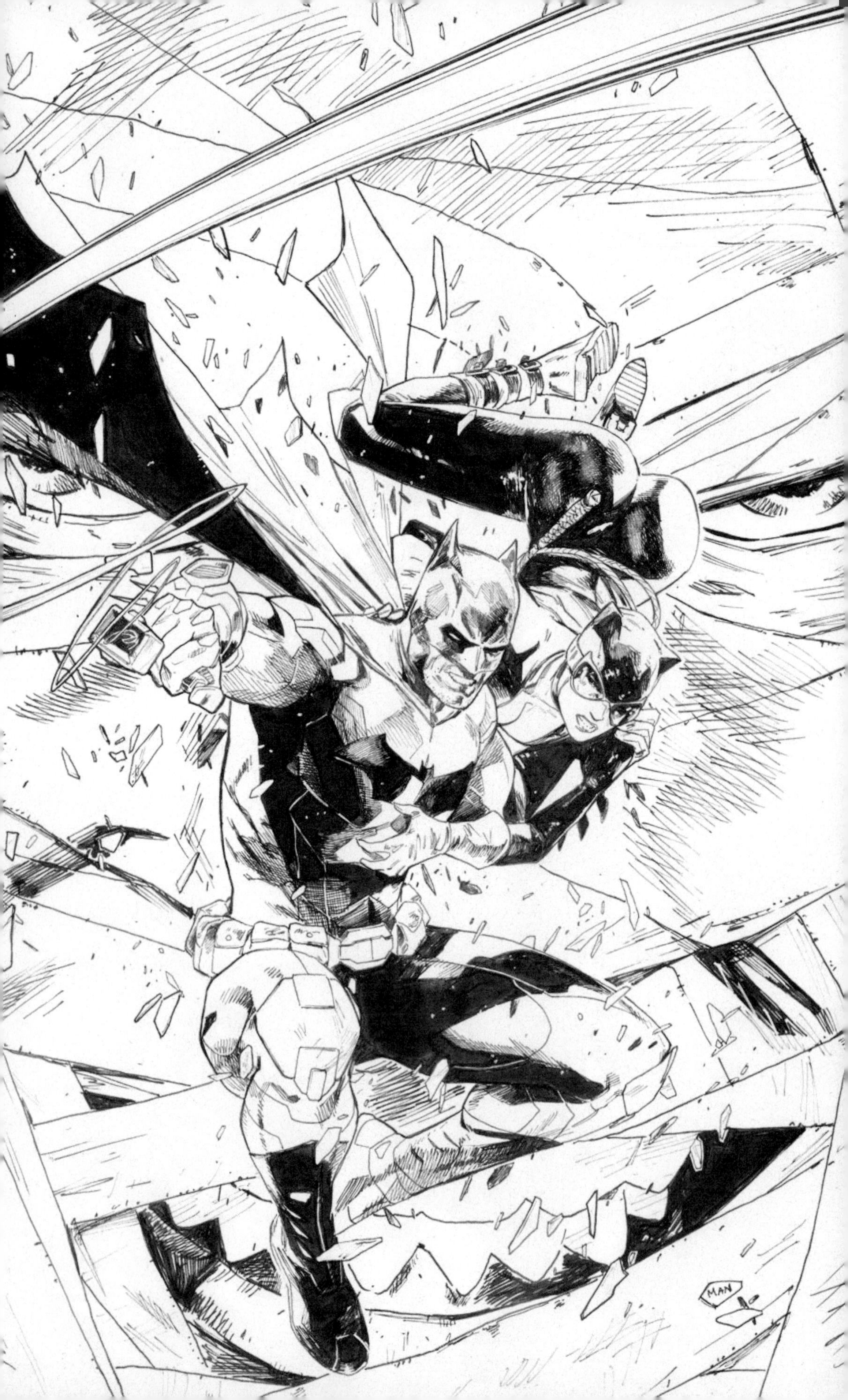
MAN

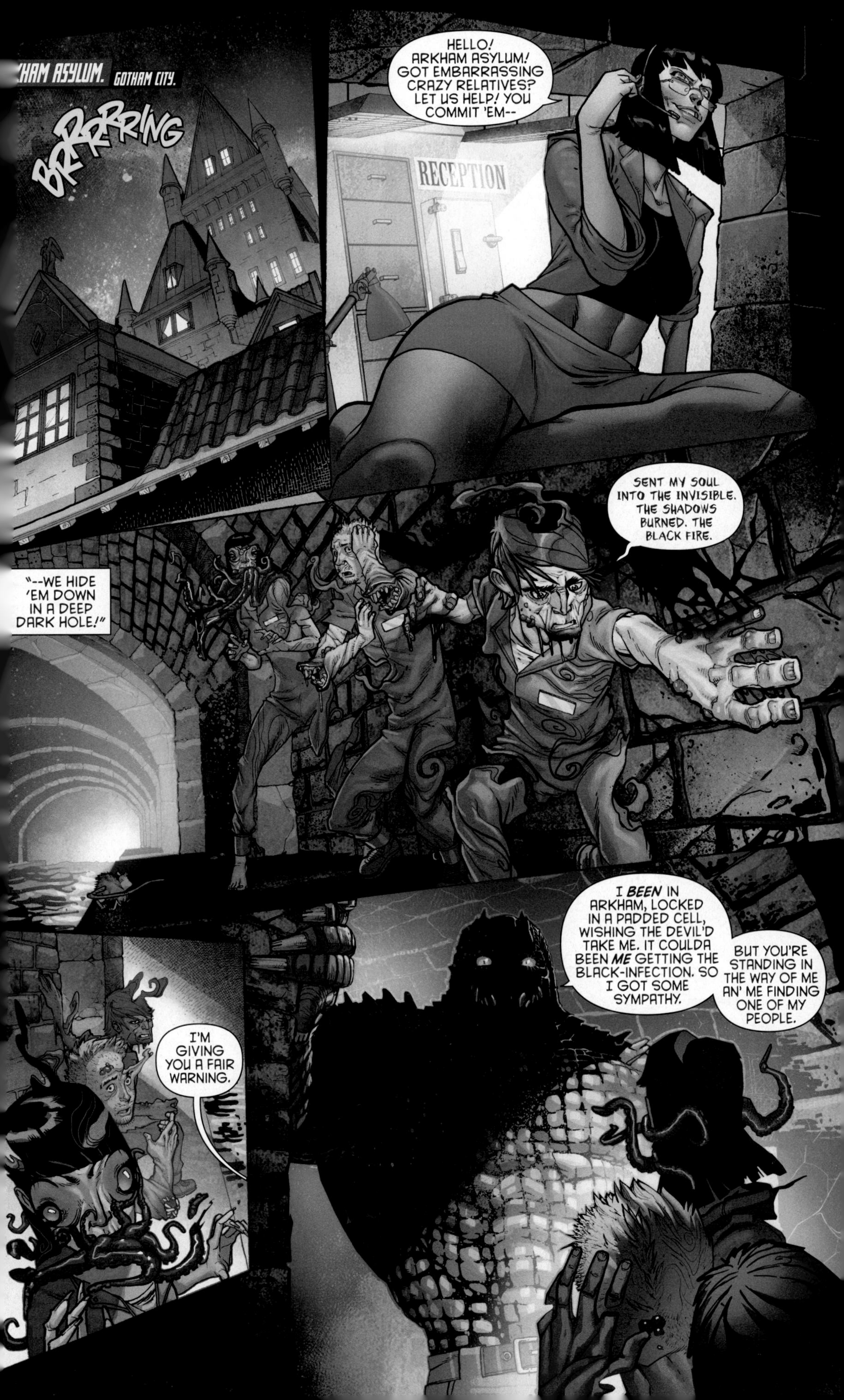
KHAM ASYLUM. GOTHAM CITY.
BRRRRRING
HELLO! ARKHAM ASYLUM! GOT EMBARRASSING CRAZY RELATIVES? LET US HELP! YOU COMMIT 'EM--
RECEPTION
"--WE HIDE 'EM DOWN IN A DEEP DARK HOLE!"
SENT MY SOUL INTO THE INVISIBLE. THE SHADOWS BURNED. THE BLACK FIRE.
I'M GIVING YOU A FAIR WARNING.
I BEEN IN ARKHAM, LOCKED IN A PADDED CELL, WISHING THE DEVIL'D TAKE ME. IT COULDA BEEN ME GETTING THE BLACK-INFECTION. SO I GOT SOME SYMPATHY.
BUT YOU'RE STANDING IN THE WAY OF ME AN' ME FINDING ONE OF MY PEOPLE.

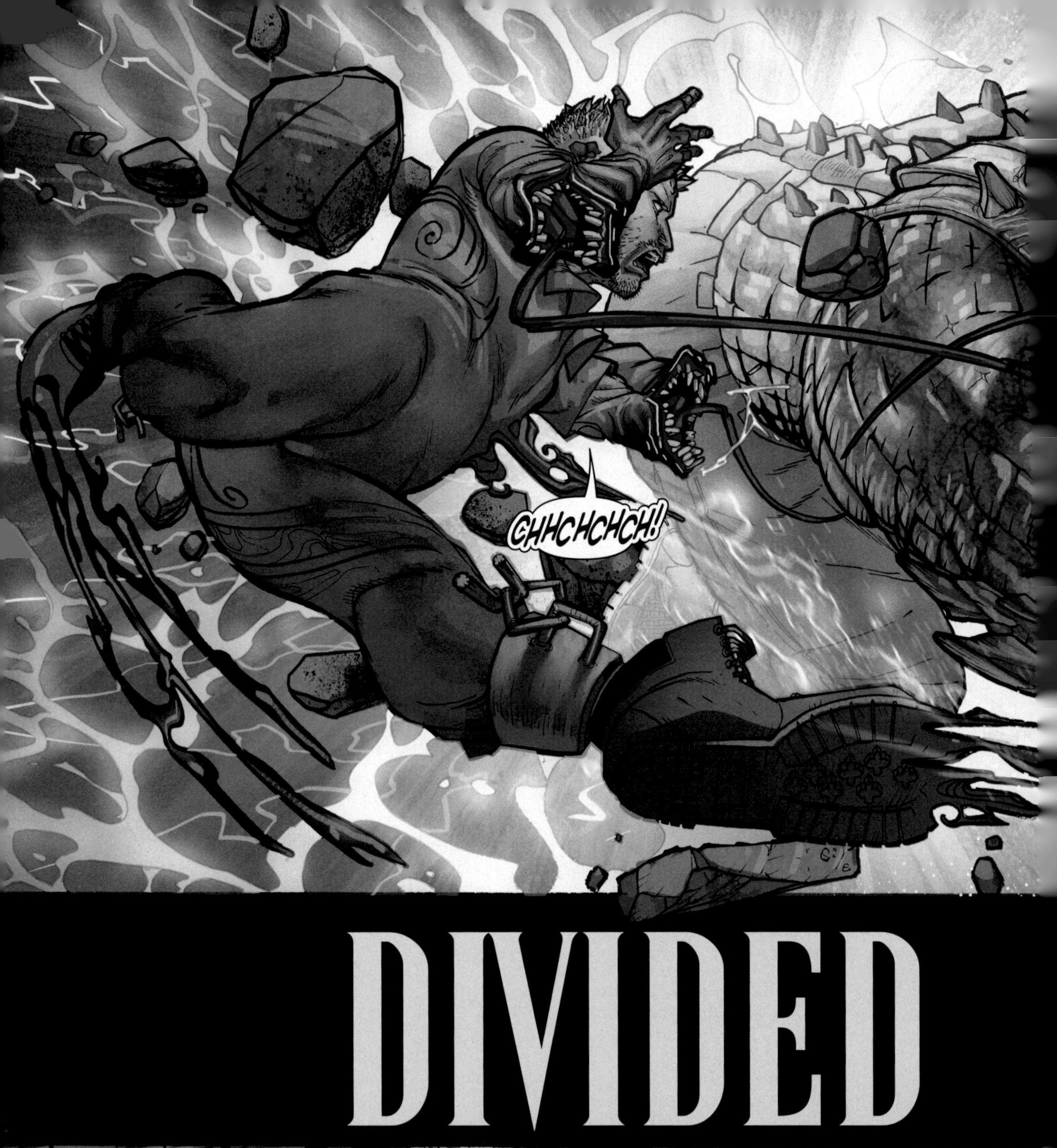
CHHCHCHCH!

# DIVIDED

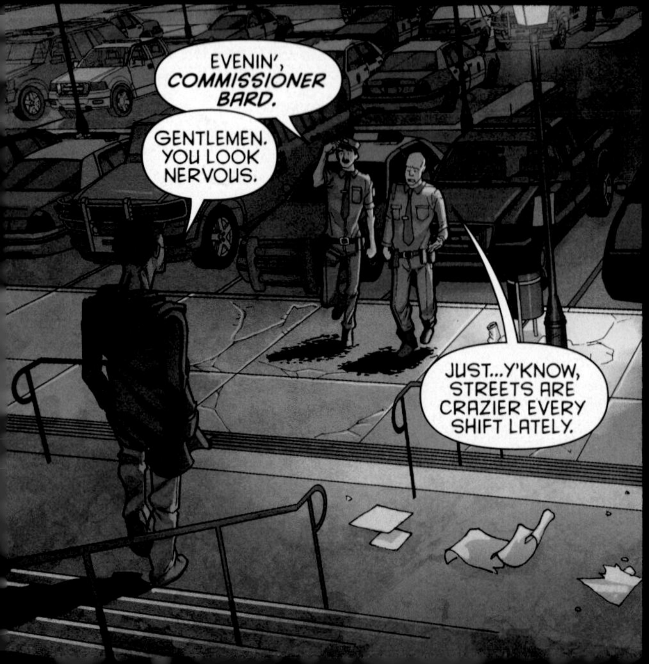
EVENIN', COMMISSIONER BARD.
GENTLEMEN. YOU LOOK NERVOUS.
JUST...Y'KNOW, STREETS ARE CRAZIER EVERY SHIFT LATELY.

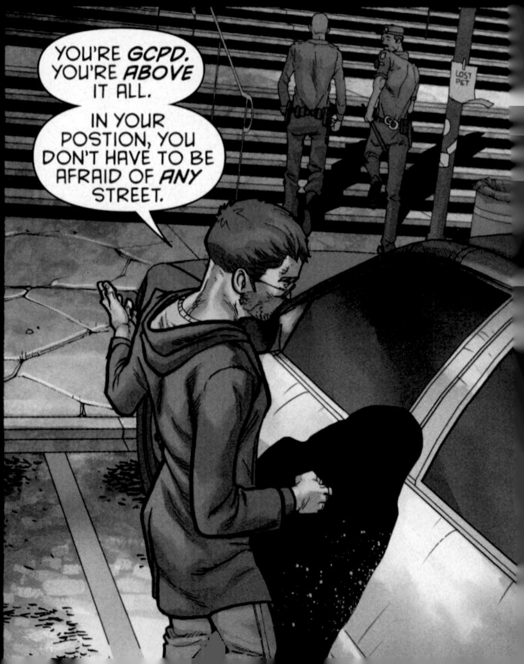
YOU'RE GCPD. YOU'RE ABOVE IT ALL.
IN YOUR POSTION, YOU DON'T HAVE TO BE AFRAID OF ANY STREET.
LOST PET

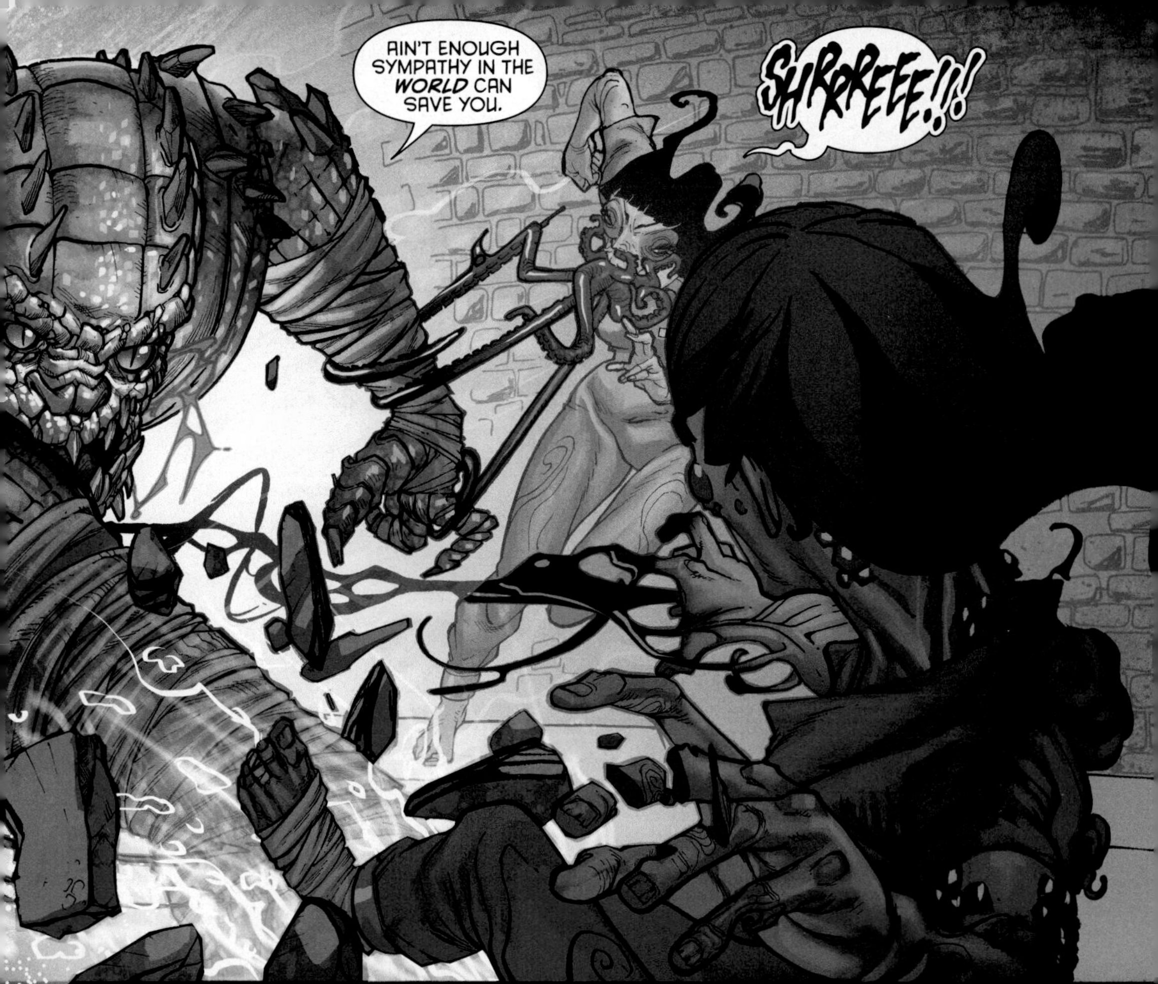
AIN'T ENOUGH SYMPATHY IN THE WORLD CAN SAVE YOU.
SHRRREEE!!!

SCOTT SNYDER & JAMES TYNION IV STORY TIM SEELEY SCRIPT
RAY FAWKES & KYLE HIGGINS CONSULTING WRITERS JAVIER GARRON ART
ROMULO FAJARDO, JR. COLORS DEZI SIENTY LETTERS CLAY MANN AND ROMULO FAJARDO, JR. COVER

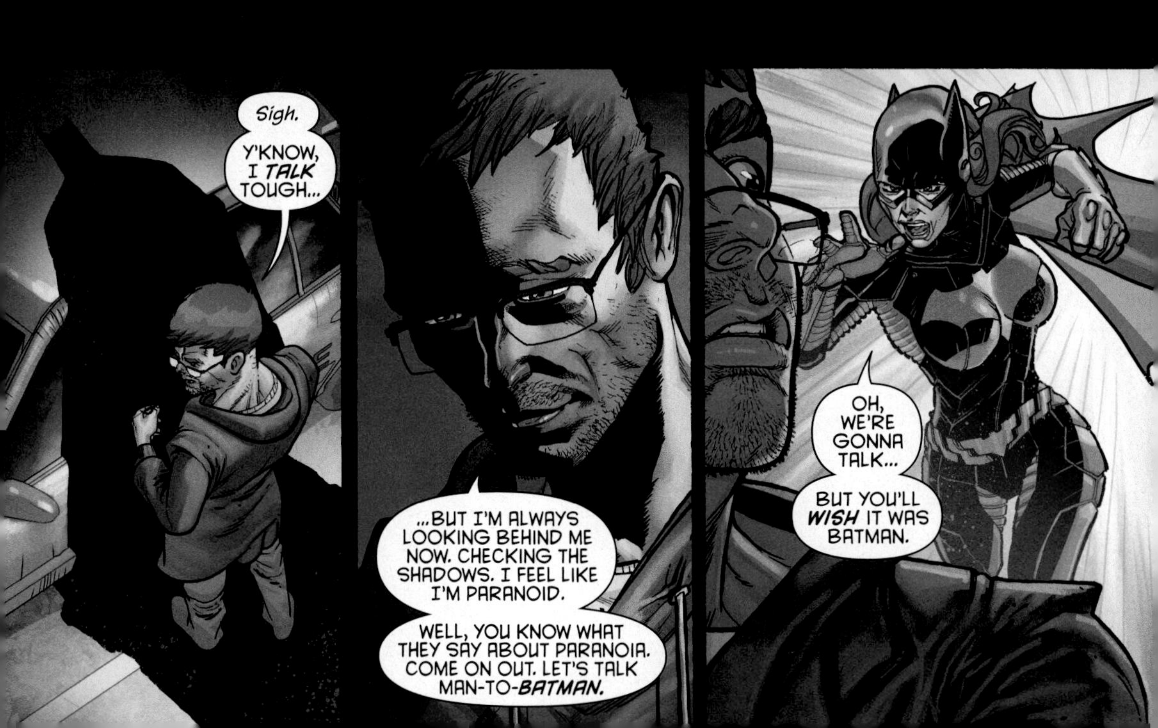
Sigh.
Y'KNOW, I TALK TOUGH...
...BUT I'M ALWAYS LOOKING BEHIND ME NOW. CHECKING THE SHADOWS. I FEEL LIKE I'M PARANOID.
WELL, YOU KNOW WHAT THEY SAY ABOUT PARANOIA. COME ON OUT. LET'S TALK MAN-TO-BATMAN.
OH, WE'RE GONNA TALK...
BUT YOU'LL WISH IT WAS BATMAN.

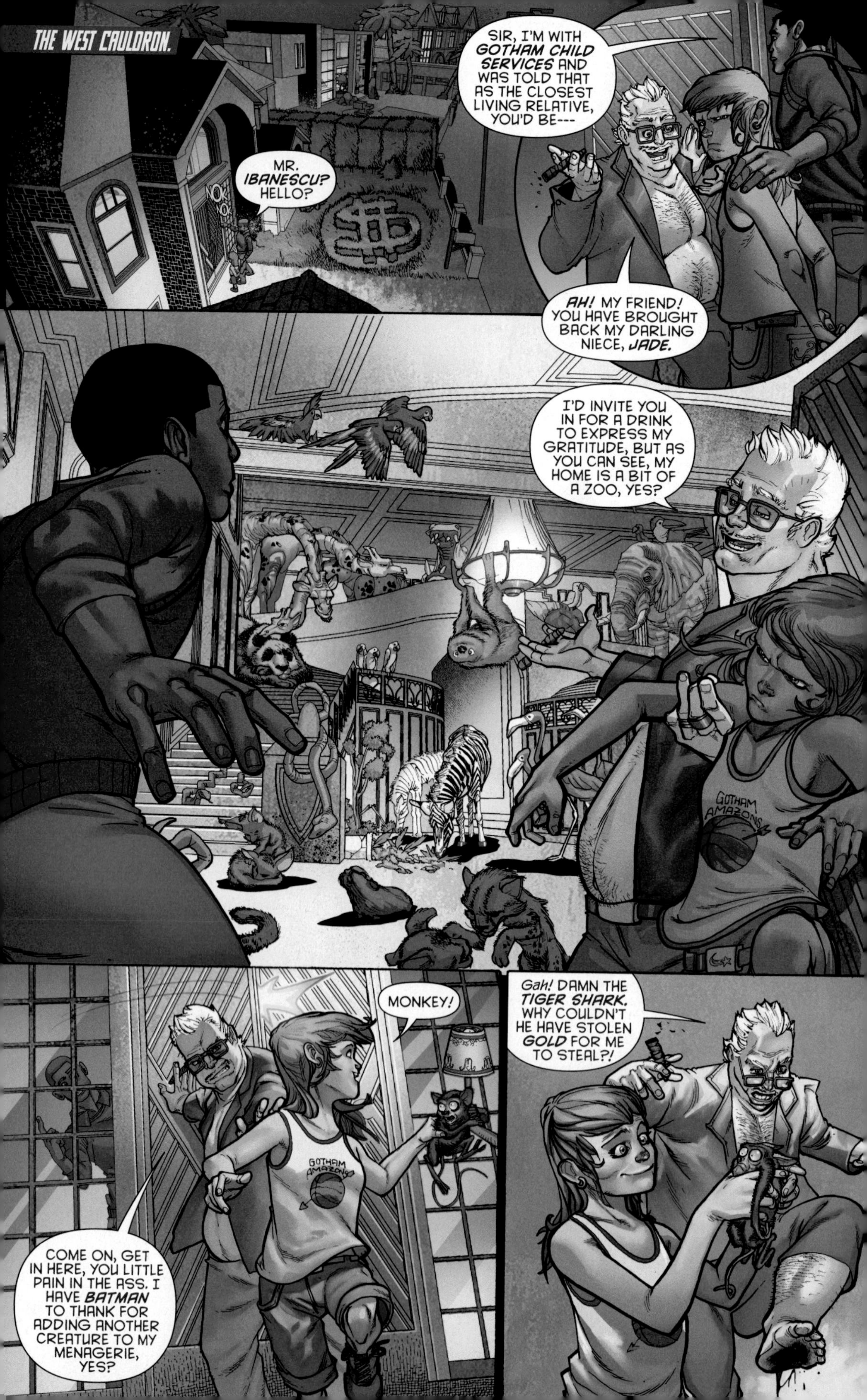
THE WEST CAULDRON.
NOK NOK
MR. IBANESCU? HELLO?
SIR, I'M WITH GOTHAM CHILD SERVICES AND WAS TOLD THAT AS THE CLOSEST LIVING RELATIVE, YOU'D BE---
AH! MY FRIEND! YOU HAVE BROUGHT BACK MY DARLING NIECE, JADE.
I'D INVITE YOU IN FOR A DRINK TO EXPRESS MY GRATITUDE, BUT AS YOU CAN SEE, MY HOME IS A BIT OF A ZOO, YES?
GOTHAM AMAZONS
MONKEY!
COME ON, GET IN HERE, YOU LITTLE PAIN IN THE ASS. I HAVE BATMAN TO THANK FOR ADDING ANOTHER CREATURE TO MY MENAGERIE, YES?
GOTHAM AMAZONS
Gah! DAMN THE TIGER SHARK. WHY COULDN'T HE HAVE STOLEN GOLD FOR ME TO STEAL?!

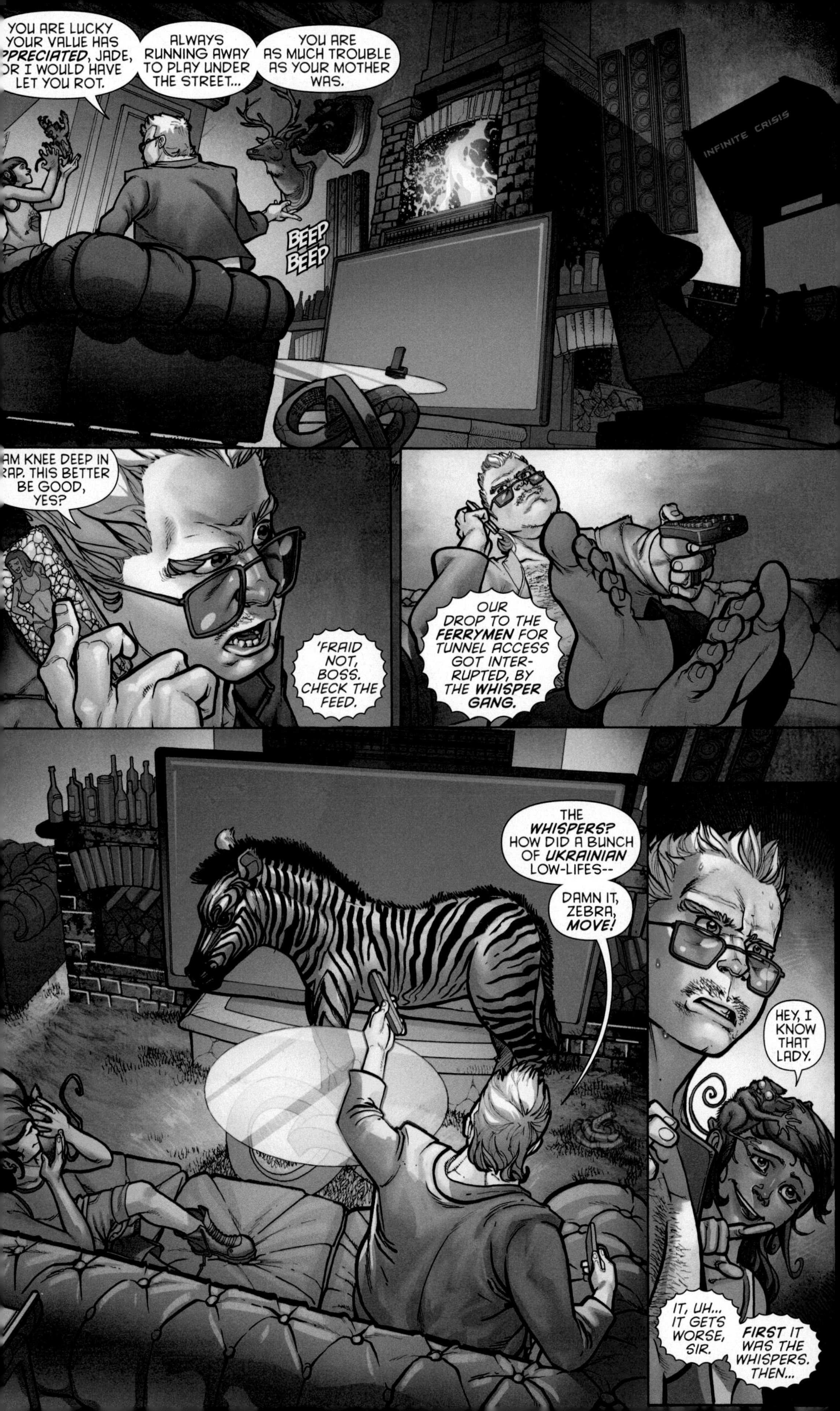
YOU ARE LUCKY YOUR VALUE HAS PPRECIATED, JADE, OR I WOULD HAVE LET YOU ROT.
ALWAYS RUNNING AWAY TO PLAY UNDER THE STREET...
YOU ARE AS MUCH TROUBLE AS YOUR MOTHER WAS.
INFINITE CRISIS
BEEP BEEP
AM KNEE DEEP IN RAP. THIS BETTER BE GOOD, YES?
'FRAID NOT, BOSS. CHECK THE FEED.
OUR DROP TO THE FERRYMEN FOR TUNNEL ACCESS GOT INTER-RUPTED, BY THE WHISPER GANG.
THE WHISPERS? HOW DID A BUNCH OF UKRAINIAN LOW-LIFES--
DAMN IT, ZEBRA, MOVE!
HEY, I KNOW THAT LADY.
IT, UH... IT GETS WORSE, SIR.
FIRST IT WAS THE WHISPERS. THEN...

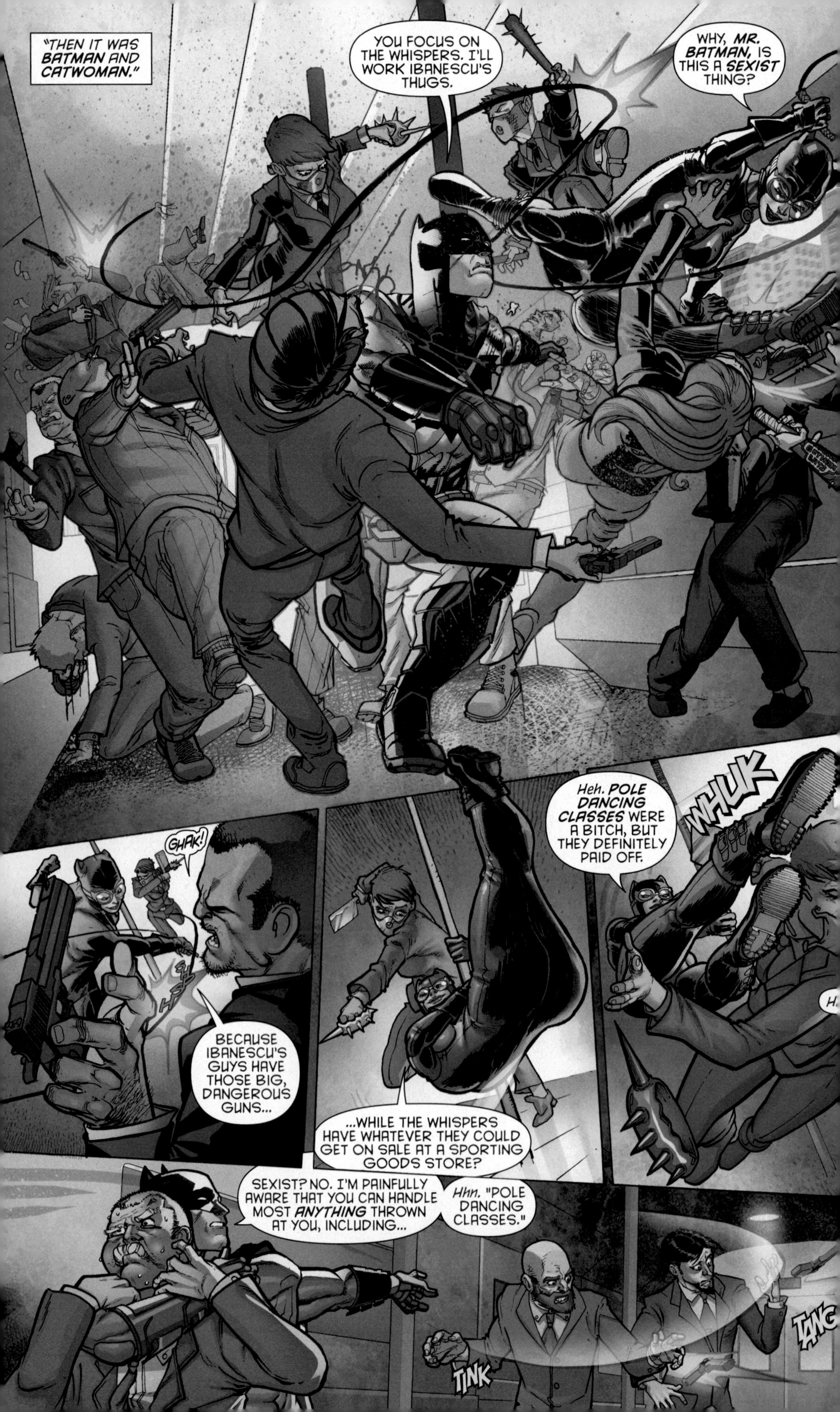
"THEN IT WAS BATMAN AND CATWOMAN."
YOU FOCUS ON THE WHISPERS. I'LL WORK IBANESCU'S THUGS.
WHY, MR. BATMAN, IS THIS A SEXIST THING?
GHAK!
BECAUSE IBANESCU'S GUYS HAVE THOSE BIG, DANGEROUS GUNS...
...WHILE THE WHISPERS HAVE WHATEVER THEY COULD GET ON SALE AT A SPORTING GOODS STORE?
Heh. POLE DANCING CLASSES WERE A BITCH, BUT THEY DEFINITELY PAID OFF.
WHUK
SEXIST? NO. I'M PAINFULLY AWARE THAT YOU CAN HANDLE MOST ANYTHING THROWN AT YOU, INCLUDING...
Hhn. "POLE DANCING CLASSES."
TINK
TANG

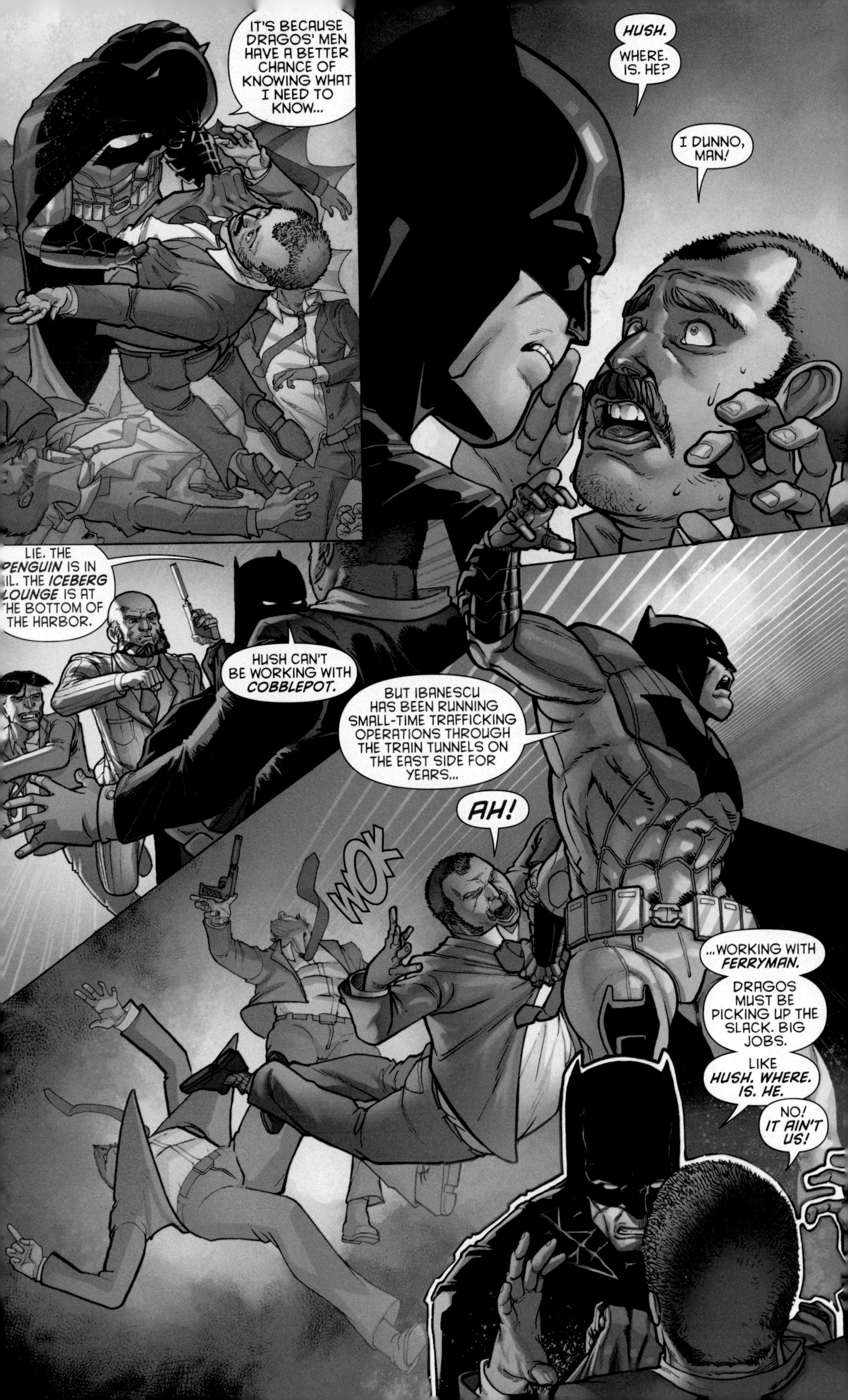
IT'S BECAUSE DRAGOS' MEN HAVE A BETTER CHANCE OF KNOWING WHAT I NEED TO KNOW...
HUSH.
WHERE. IS. HE?
I DUNNO, MAN!
LIE. THE PENGUIN IS IN IL. THE ICEBERG LOUNGE IS AT HE BOTTOM OF THE HARBOR.
HUSH CAN'T BE WORKING WITH COBBLEPOT.
BUT IBANESCU HAS BEEN RUNNING SMALL-TIME TRAFFICKING OPERATIONS THROUGH THE TRAIN TUNNELS ON THE EAST SIDE FOR YEARS...
AH!
WOK
...WORKING WITH FERRYMAN.
DRAGOS MUST BE PICKING UP THE SLACK. BIG JOBS.
LIKE HUSH. WHERE. IS. HE.
NO! IT AIN'T US!

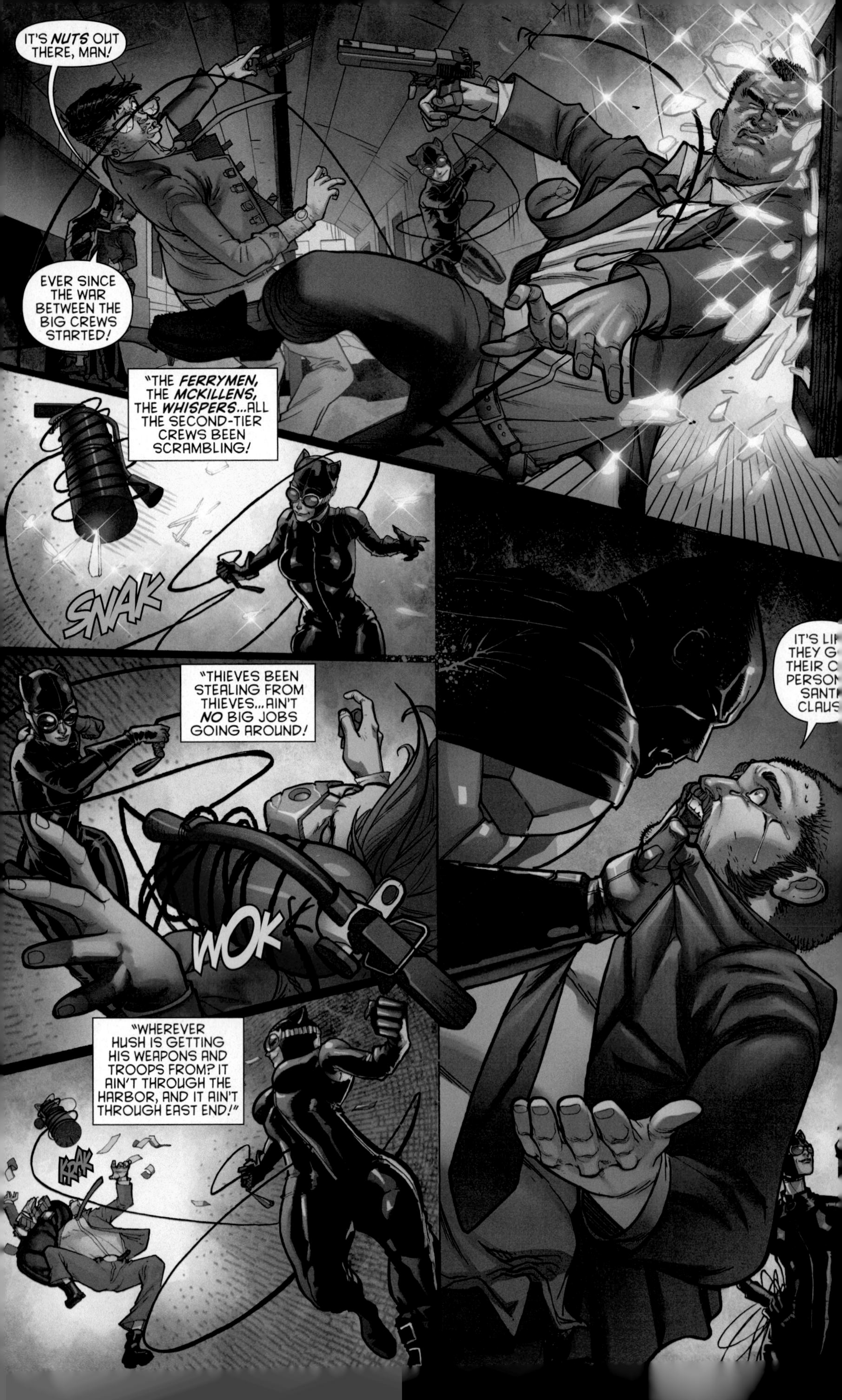
IT'S NUTS OUT THERE, MAN!
EVER SINCE THE WAR BETWEEN THE BIG CREWS STARTED!
"THE FERRYMEN, THE MCKILLENS, THE WHISPERS...ALL THE SECOND-TIER CREWS BEEN SCRAMBLING!
SNAK
"THIEVES BEEN STEALING FROM THIEVES...AIN'T NO BIG JOBS GOING AROUND!
WOK
"WHEREVER HUSH IS GETTING HIS WEAPONS AND TROOPS FROM? IT AIN'T THROUGH THE HARBOR, AND IT AIN'T THROUGH EAST END!"
KRAK

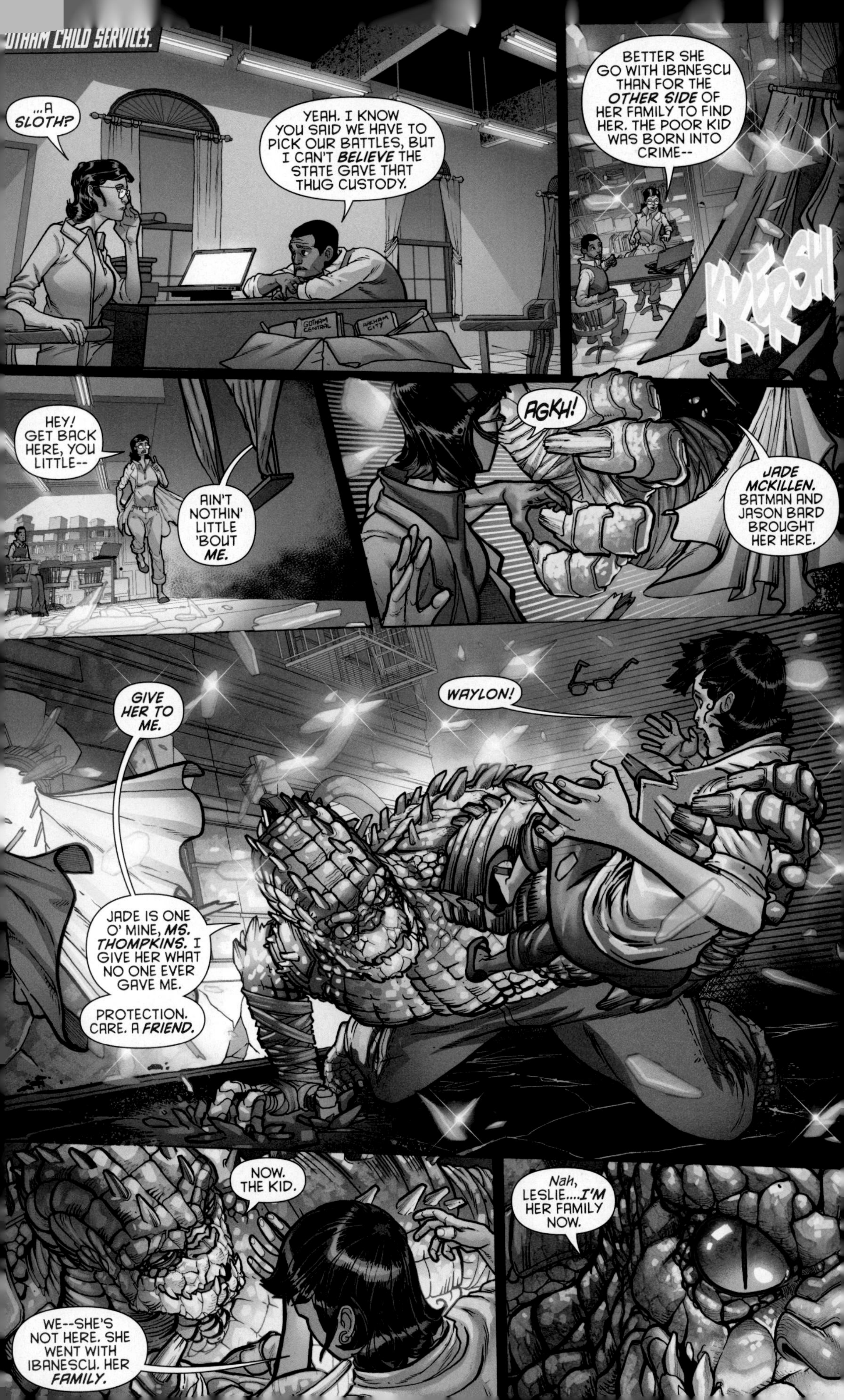

...OTHAM CHILD SERVICES.
...A SLOTH?
YEAH. I KNOW YOU SAID WE HAVE TO PICK OUR BATTLES, BUT I CAN'T BELIEVE THE STATE GAVE THAT THUG CUSTODY.
GOTHAM CENTRAL
ARKHAM CITY
BETTER SHE GO WITH IBANESCU THAN FOR THE OTHER SIDE OF HER FAMILY TO FIND HER. THE POOR KID WAS BORN INTO CRIME--
KKERSH
HEY! GET BACK HERE, YOU LITTLE--
AIN'T NOTHIN' LITTLE 'BOUT ME.
AGKH!
JADE MCKILLEN. BATMAN AND JASON BARD BROUGHT HER HERE.
GIVE HER TO ME.
WAYLON!
JADE IS ONE O' MINE, MS. THOMPKINS. I GIVE HER WHAT NO ONE EVER GAVE ME.
PROTECTION. CARE. A FRIEND.
NOW. THE KID.
WE--SHE'S NOT HERE. SHE WENT WITH IBANESCU. HER FAMILY.
Nah, LESLIE....I'M HER FAMILY NOW.

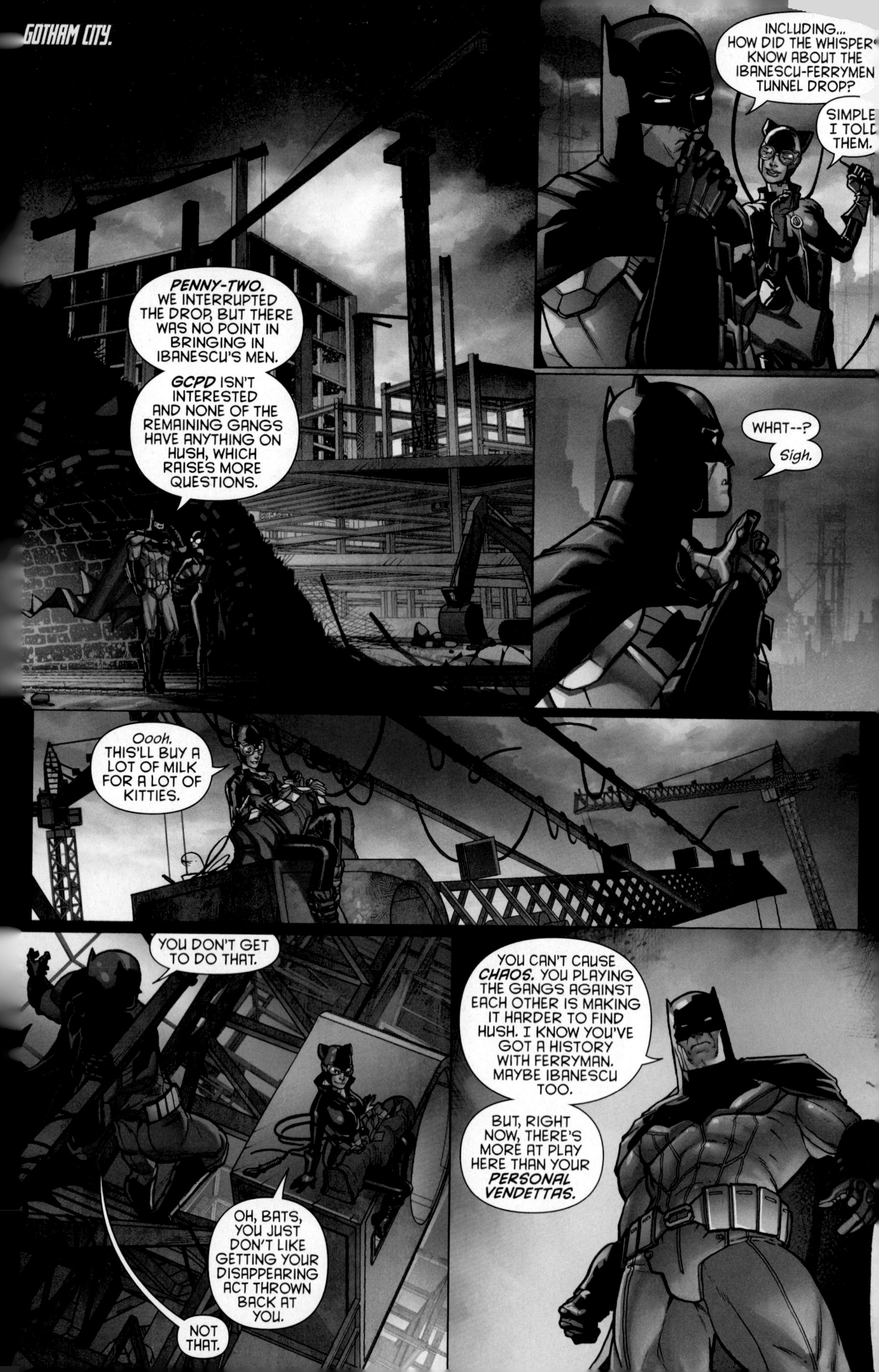
GOTHAM CITY.
PENNY-TWO. WE INTERRUPTED THE DROP, BUT THERE WAS NO POINT IN BRINGING IN IBANESCU'S MEN.
GCPD ISN'T INTERESTED AND NONE OF THE REMAINING GANGS HAVE ANYTHING ON HUSH, WHICH RAISES MORE QUESTIONS.
INCLUDING... HOW DID THE WHISPER KNOW ABOUT THE IBANESCU-FERRYMEN TUNNEL DROP?
SIMPLE I TOLD THEM.
WHAT--? Sigh.
Oooh. THIS'LL BUY A LOT OF MILK FOR A LOT OF KITTIES.
YOU DON'T GET TO DO THAT.
OH, BATS, YOU JUST DON'T LIKE GETTING YOUR DISAPPEARING ACT THROWN BACK AT YOU.
NOT THAT.
YOU CAN'T CAUSE CHAOS. YOU PLAYING THE GANGS AGAINST EACH OTHER IS MAKING IT HARDER TO FIND HUSH. I KNOW YOU'VE GOT A HISTORY WITH FERRYMAN. MAYBE IBANESCU TOO.
BUT, RIGHT NOW, THERE'S MORE AT PLAY HERE THAN YOUR PERSONAL VENDETTAS.

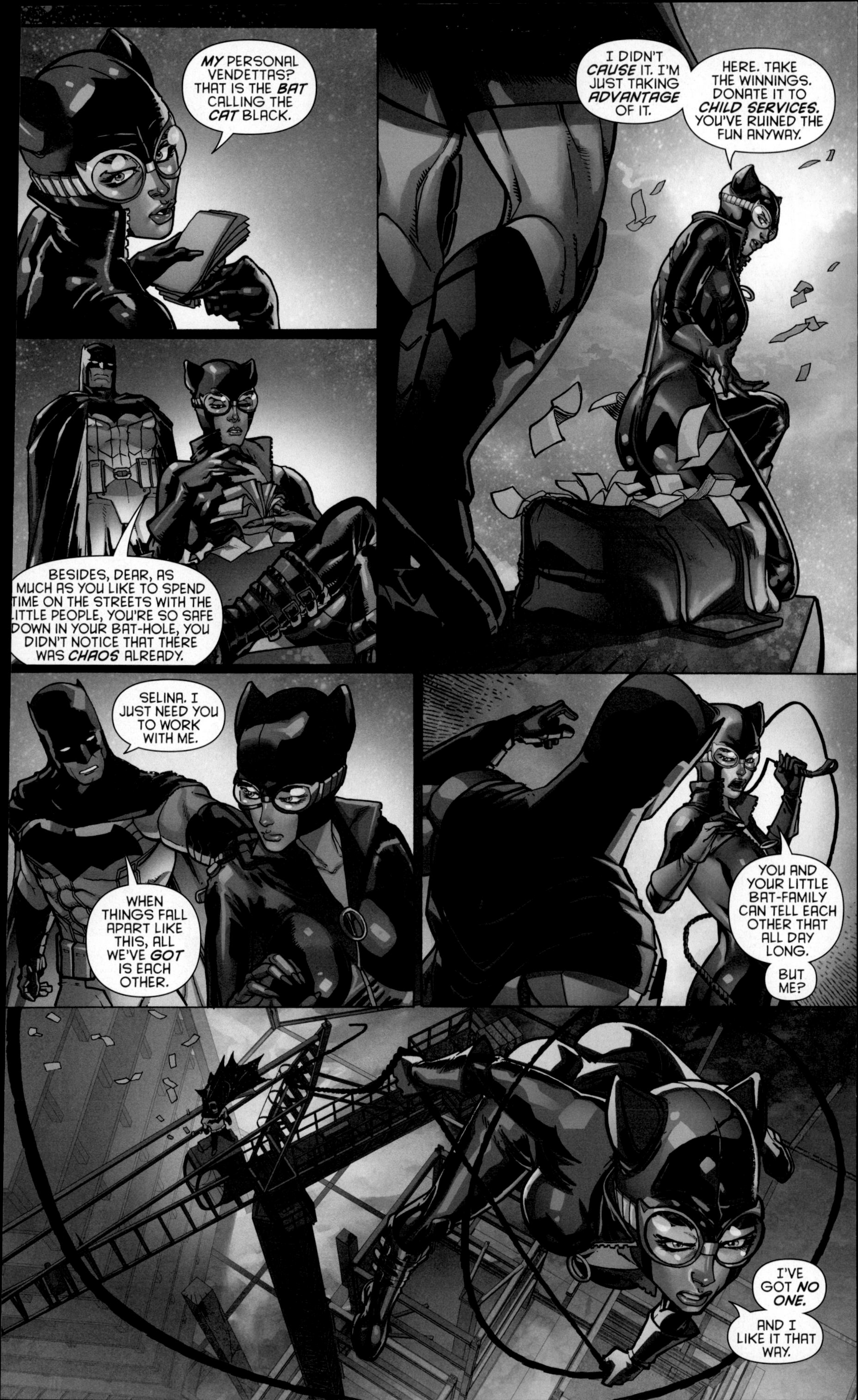
MY PERSONAL VENDETTAS? THAT IS THE BAT CALLING THE CAT BLACK.
BESIDES, DEAR, AS MUCH AS YOU LIKE TO SPEND TIME ON THE STREETS WITH THE LITTLE PEOPLE, YOU'RE SO SAFE DOWN IN YOUR BAT-HOLE, YOU DIDN'T NOTICE THAT THERE WAS CHAOS ALREADY.
I DIDN'T CAUSE IT. I'M JUST TAKING ADVANTAGE OF IT.
HERE. TAKE THE WINNINGS. DONATE IT TO CHILD SERVICES. YOU'VE RUINED THE FUN ANYWAY.
SELINA. I JUST NEED YOU TO WORK WITH ME.
WHEN THINGS FALL APART LIKE THIS, ALL WE'VE GOT IS EACH OTHER.
YOU AND YOUR LITTLE BAT-FAMILY CAN TELL EACH OTHER THAT ALL DAY LONG.
BUT ME?
I'VE GOT NO ONE.
AND I LIKE IT THAT WAY.

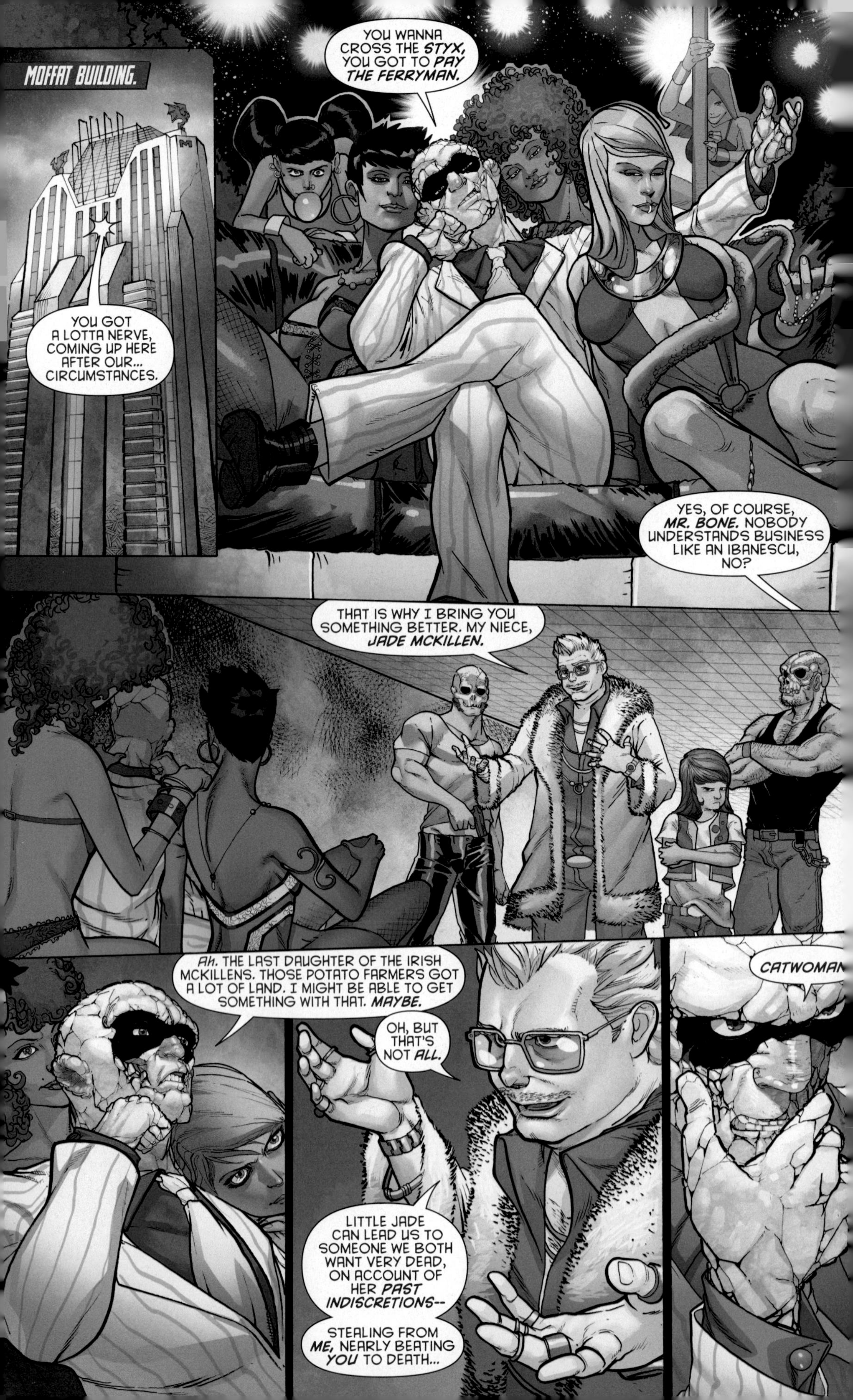
MOFFAT BUILDING.
YOU GOT A LOTTA NERVE, COMING UP HERE AFTER OUR... CIRCUMSTANCES.
YOU WANNA CROSS THE STYX, YOU GOT TO PAY THE FERRYMAN.
YES, OF COURSE, MR. BONE. NOBODY UNDERSTANDS BUSINESS LIKE AN IBANESCU, NO?
THAT IS WHY I BRING YOU SOMETHING BETTER. MY NIECE, JADE MCKILLEN.
AH. THE LAST DAUGHTER OF THE IRISH MCKILLENS. THOSE POTATO FARMERS GOT A LOT OF LAND. I MIGHT BE ABLE TO GET SOMETHING WITH THAT. MAYBE.
OH, BUT THAT'S NOT ALL.
LITTLE JADE CAN LEAD US TO SOMEONE WE BOTH WANT VERY DEAD, ON ACCOUNT OF HER PAST INDISCRETIONS--
STEALING FROM ME, NEARLY BEATING YOU TO DEATH...
CATWOMAN

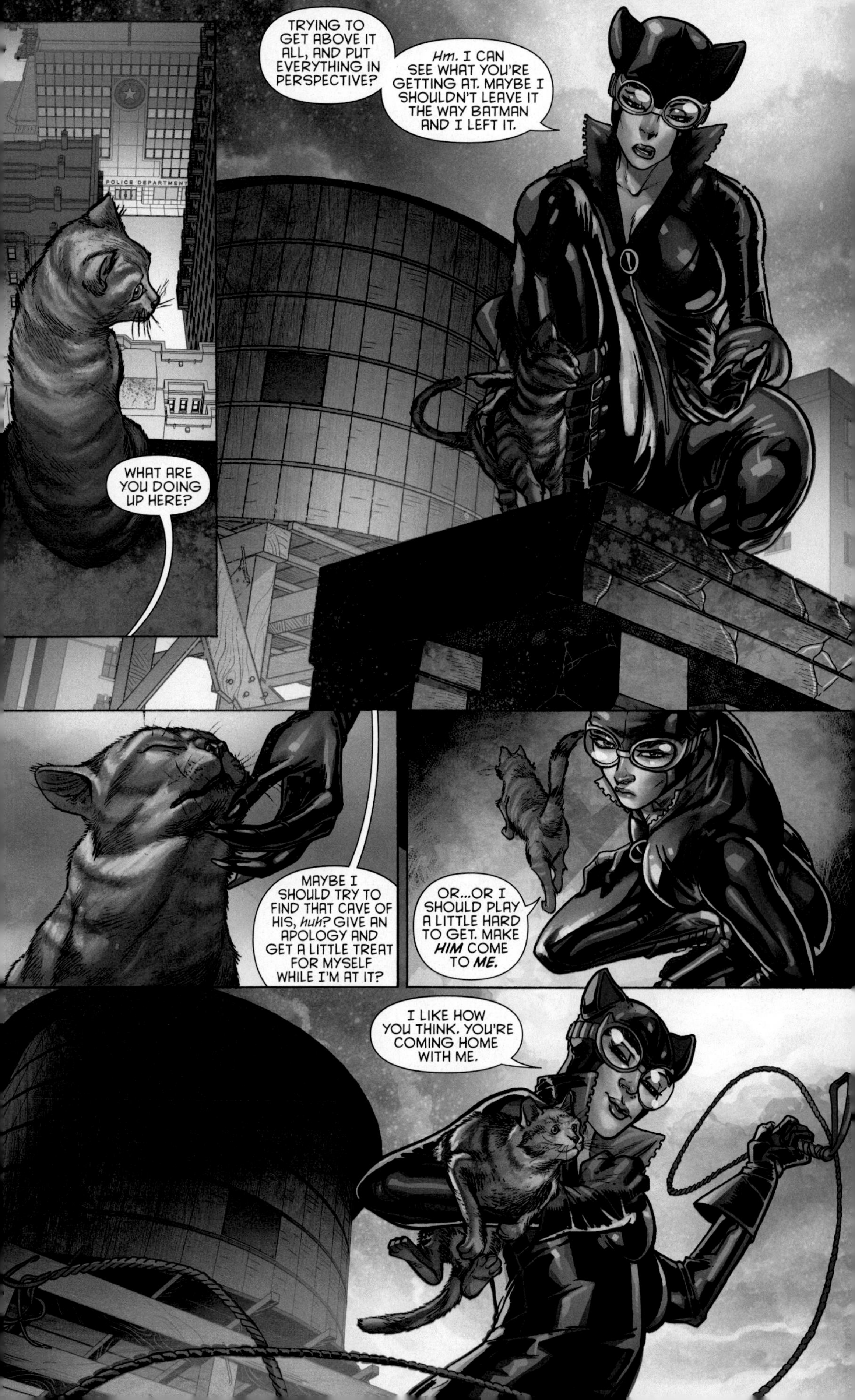
WHAT ARE YOU DOING UP HERE?
TRYING TO GET ABOVE IT ALL, AND PUT EVERYTHING IN PERSPECTIVE?
Hm. I CAN SEE WHAT YOU'RE GETTING AT. MAYBE I SHOULDN'T LEAVE IT THE WAY BATMAN AND I LEFT IT.
POLICE DEPARTMENT
MAYBE I SHOULD TRY TO FIND THAT CAVE OF HIS, huh? GIVE AN APOLOGY AND GET A LITTLE TREAT FOR MYSELF WHILE I'M AT IT?
OR...OR I SHOULD PLAY A LITTLE HARD TO GET. MAKE HIM COME TO ME.
I LIKE HOW YOU THINK. YOU'RE COMING HOME WITH ME.

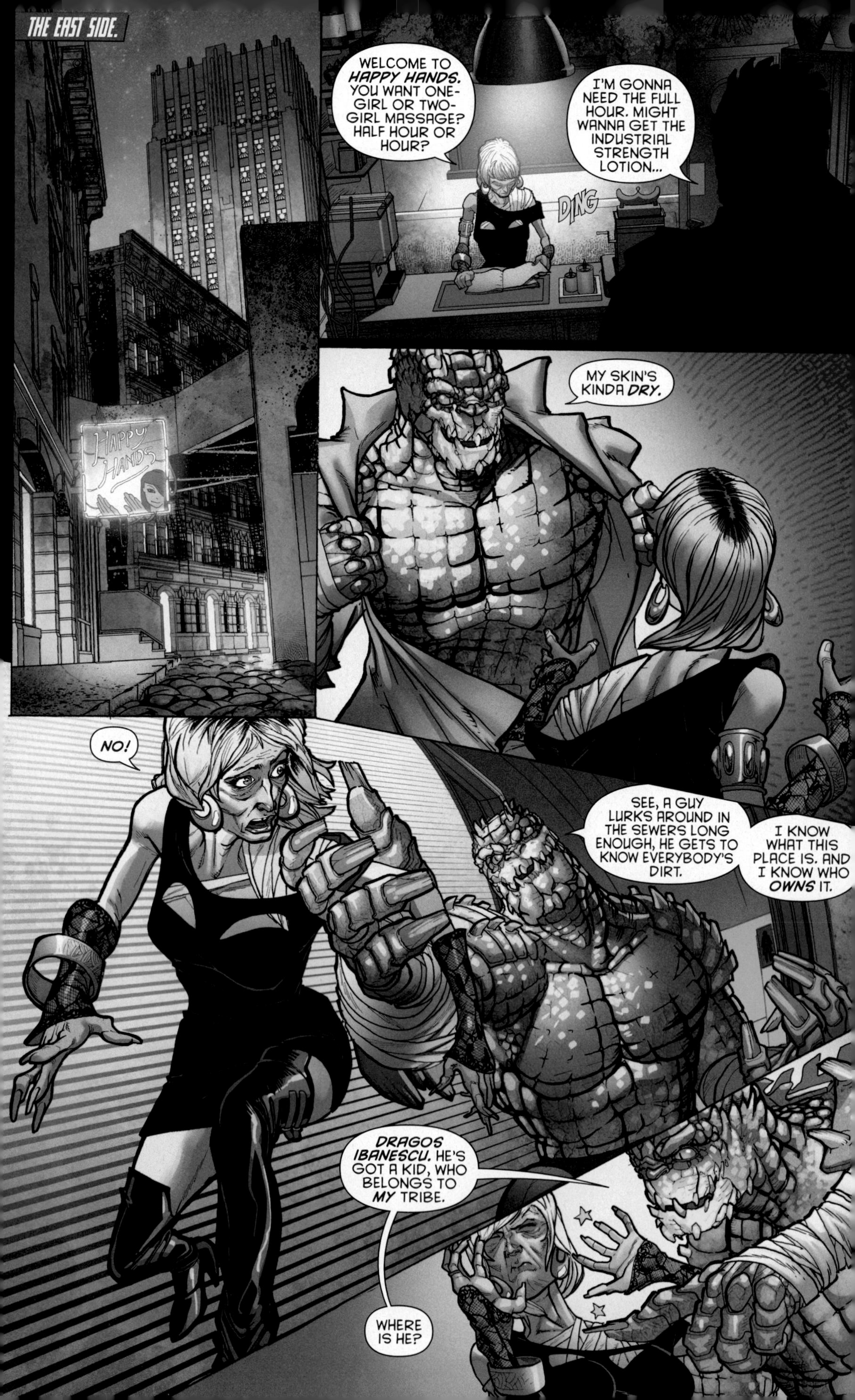
THE EAST SIDE.
HAPPY HANDS
WELCOME TO HAPPY HANDS. YOU WANT ONE-GIRL OR TWO-GIRL MASSAGE? HALF HOUR OR HOUR?
I'M GONNA NEED THE FULL HOUR. MIGHT WANNA GET THE INDUSTRIAL STRENGTH LOTION...
DING
MY SKIN'S KINDA DRY.
NO!
SEE, A GUY LURKS AROUND IN THE SEWERS LONG ENOUGH, HE GETS TO KNOW EVERYBODY'S DIRT.
I KNOW WHAT THIS PLACE IS. AND I KNOW WHO OWNS IT.
DRAGOS IBANESCU. HE'S GOT A KID, WHO BELONGS TO MY TRIBE.
WHERE IS HE?

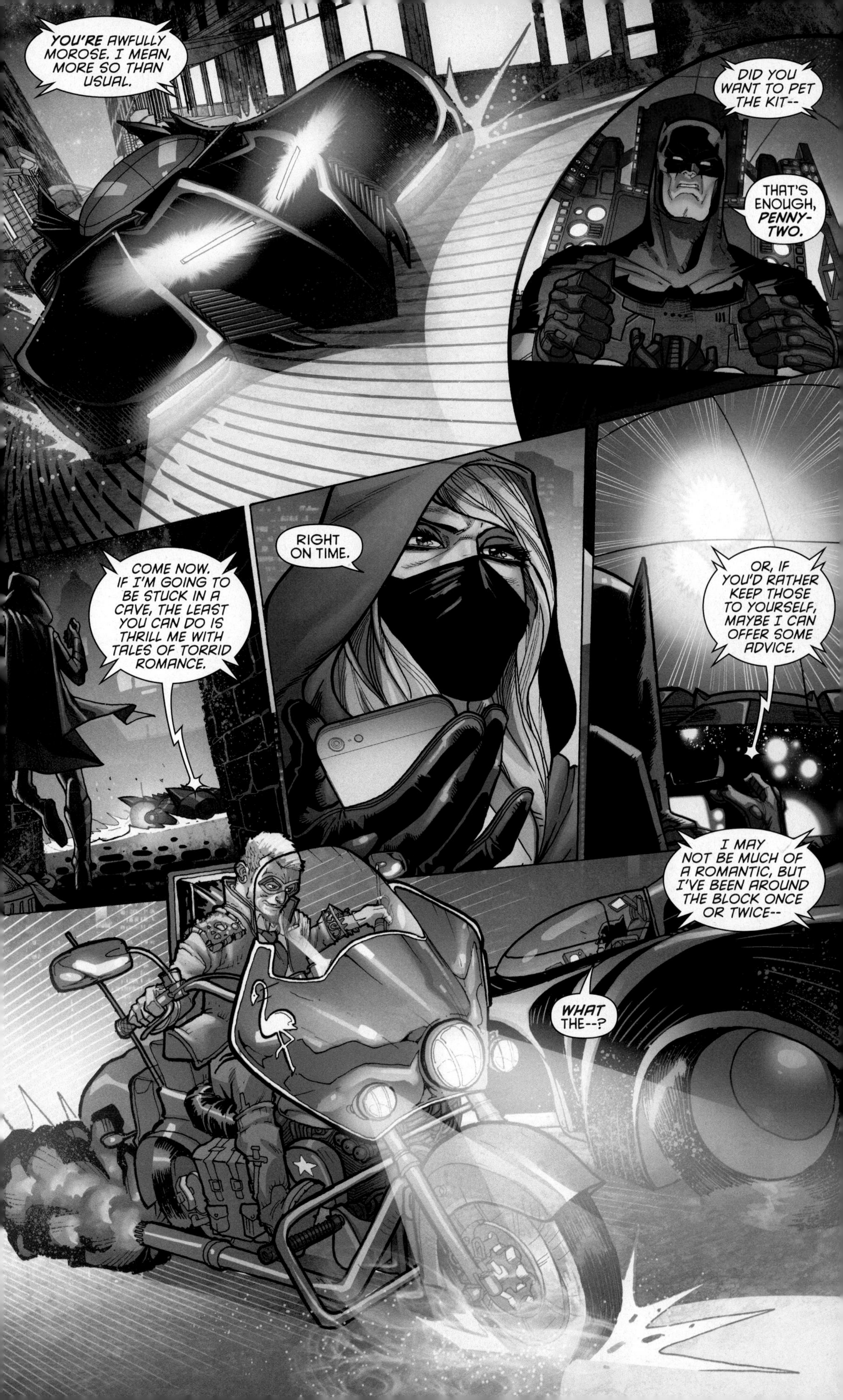
YOU'RE AWFULLY MOROSE. I MEAN, MORE SO THAN USUAL.
DID YOU WANT TO PET THE KIT--
THAT'S ENOUGH, PENNY-TWO.
COME NOW. IF I'M GOING TO BE STUCK IN A CAVE, THE LEAST YOU CAN DO IS THRILL ME WITH TALES OF TORRID ROMANCE.
RIGHT ON TIME.
OR, IF YOU'D RATHER KEEP THOSE TO YOURSELF, MAYBE I CAN OFFER SOME ADVICE.
I MAY NOT BE MUCH OF A ROMANTIC, BUT I'VE BEEN AROUND THE BLOCK ONCE OR TWICE--
WHAT THE--?

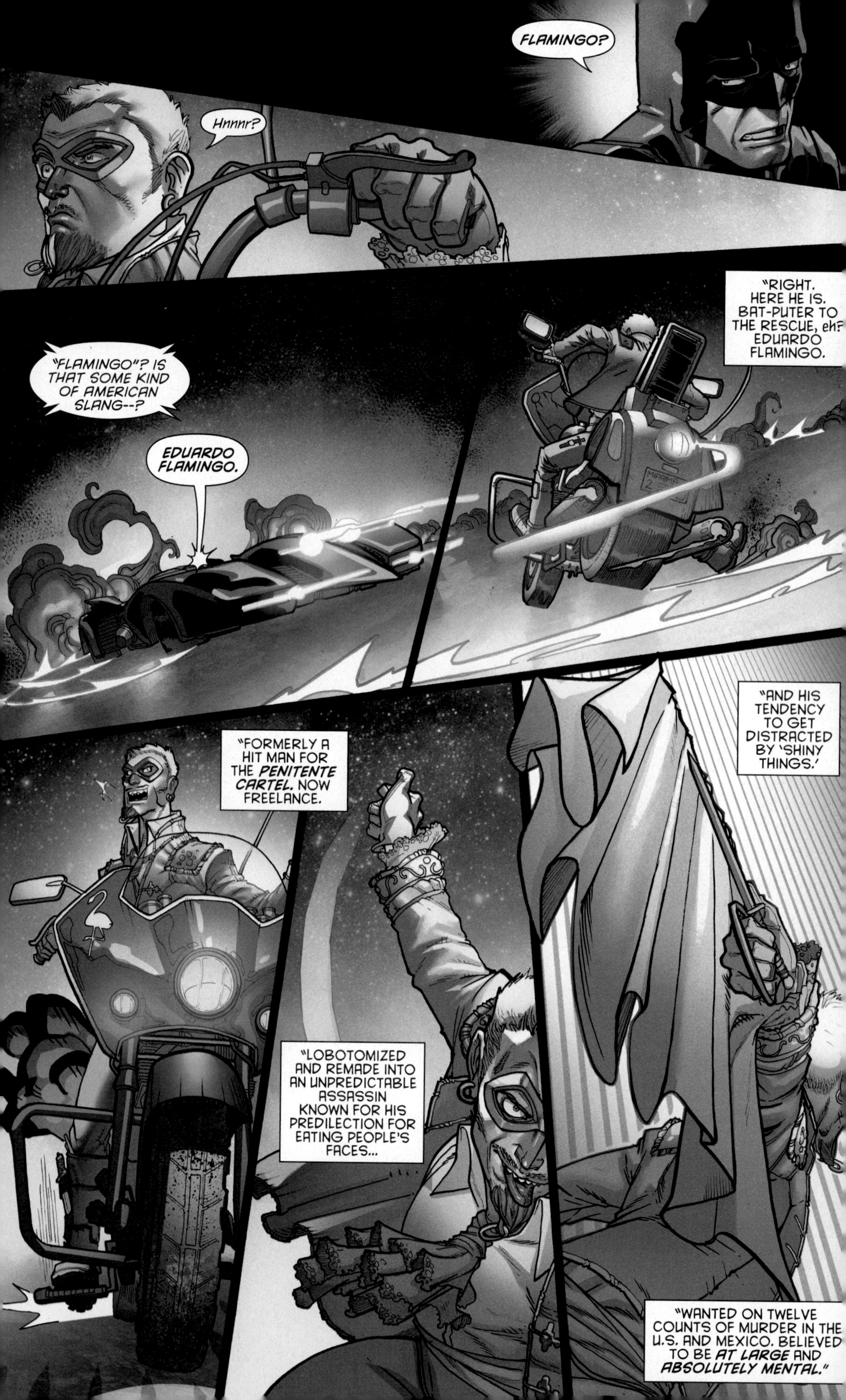

FLAMINGO?
Hnnnr?
"FLAMINGO"? IS THAT SOME KIND OF AMERICAN SLANG--?
*EDUARDO FLAMINGO.*
"RIGHT. HERE HE IS. BAT-PUTER TO THE RESCUE, eh? EDUARDO FLAMINGO.
"FORMERLY A HIT MAN FOR THE *PENITENTE CARTEL.* NOW FREELANCE.
"AND HIS TENDENCY TO GET DISTRACTED BY 'SHINY THINGS.'
"LOBOTOMIZED AND REMADE INTO AN UNPREDICTABLE ASSASSIN KNOWN FOR HIS PREDILECTION FOR EATING PEOPLE'S FACES...
"WANTED ON TWELVE COUNTS OF MURDER IN THE U.S. AND MEXICO. BELIEVED TO BE *AT LARGE* AND *ABSOLUTELY MENTAL.*"

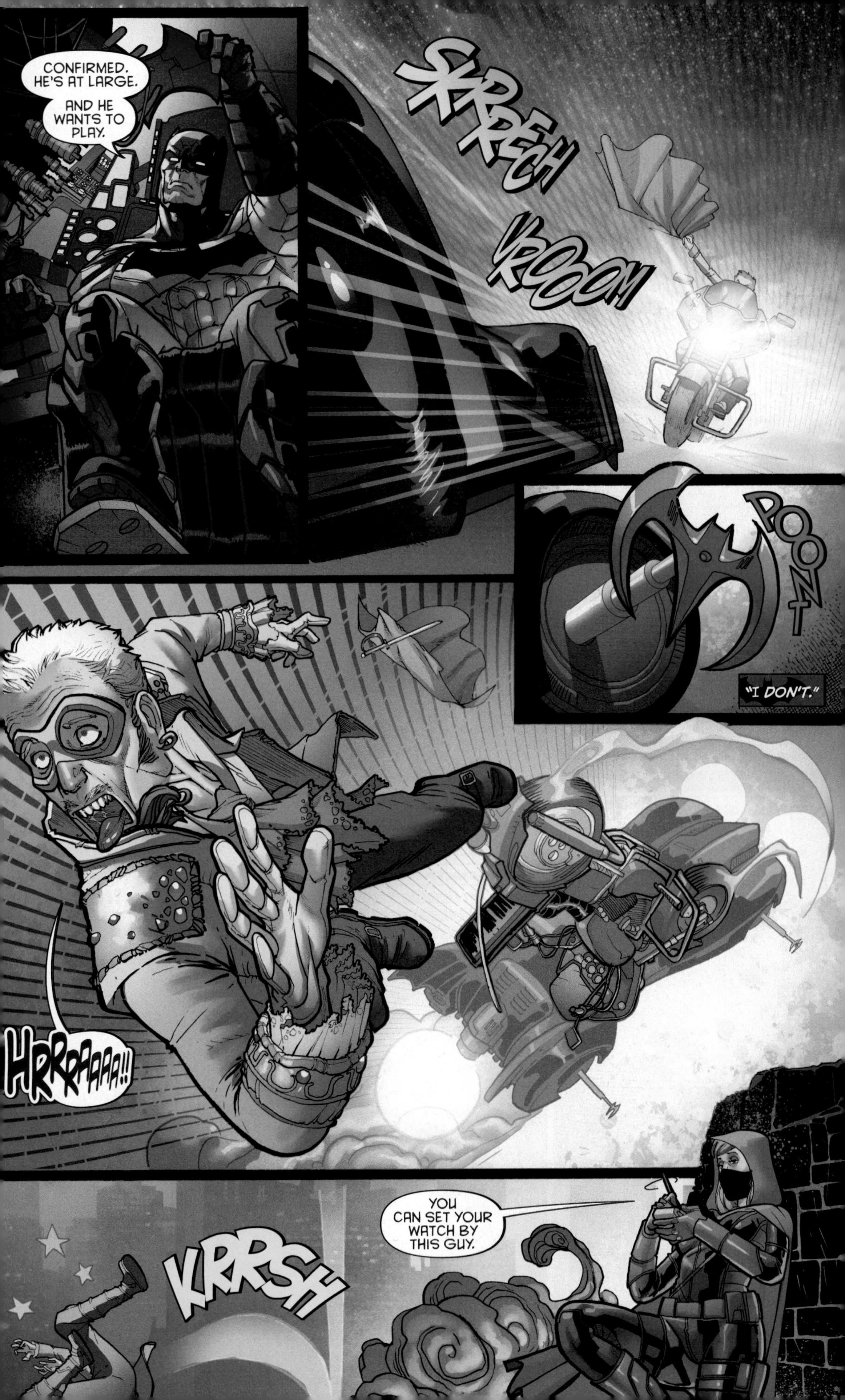
CONFIRMED. HE'S AT LARGE.
AND HE WANTS TO PLAY.
SKREECH
VROOOM
POOONT
"I DON'T."
HRRRAAAA!!
KRRSH
YOU CAN SET YOUR WATCH BY THIS GUY.

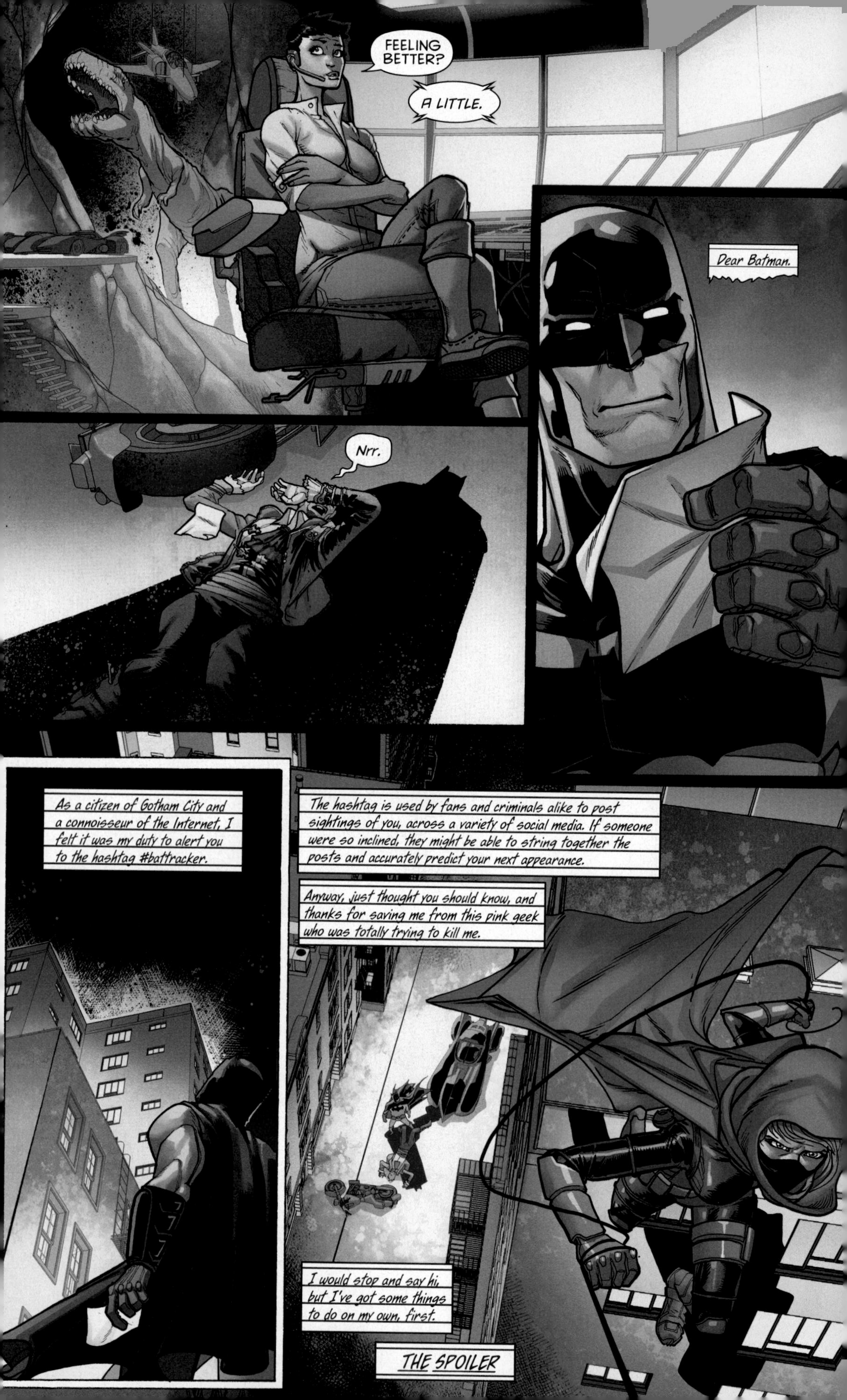
FEELING BETTER?
A LITTLE.
Nrr.
Dear Batman.
As a citizen of Gotham City and a connoisseur of the Internet, I felt it was my duty to alert you to the hashtag #battracker.
The hashtag is used by fans and criminals alike to post sightings of you, across a variety of social media. If someone were so inclined, they might be able to string together the posts and accurately predict your next appearance.
Anyway, just thought you should know, and thanks for saving me from this pink geek who was totally trying to kill me.
I would stop and say hi, but I've got some things to do on my own, first.
THE SPOILER

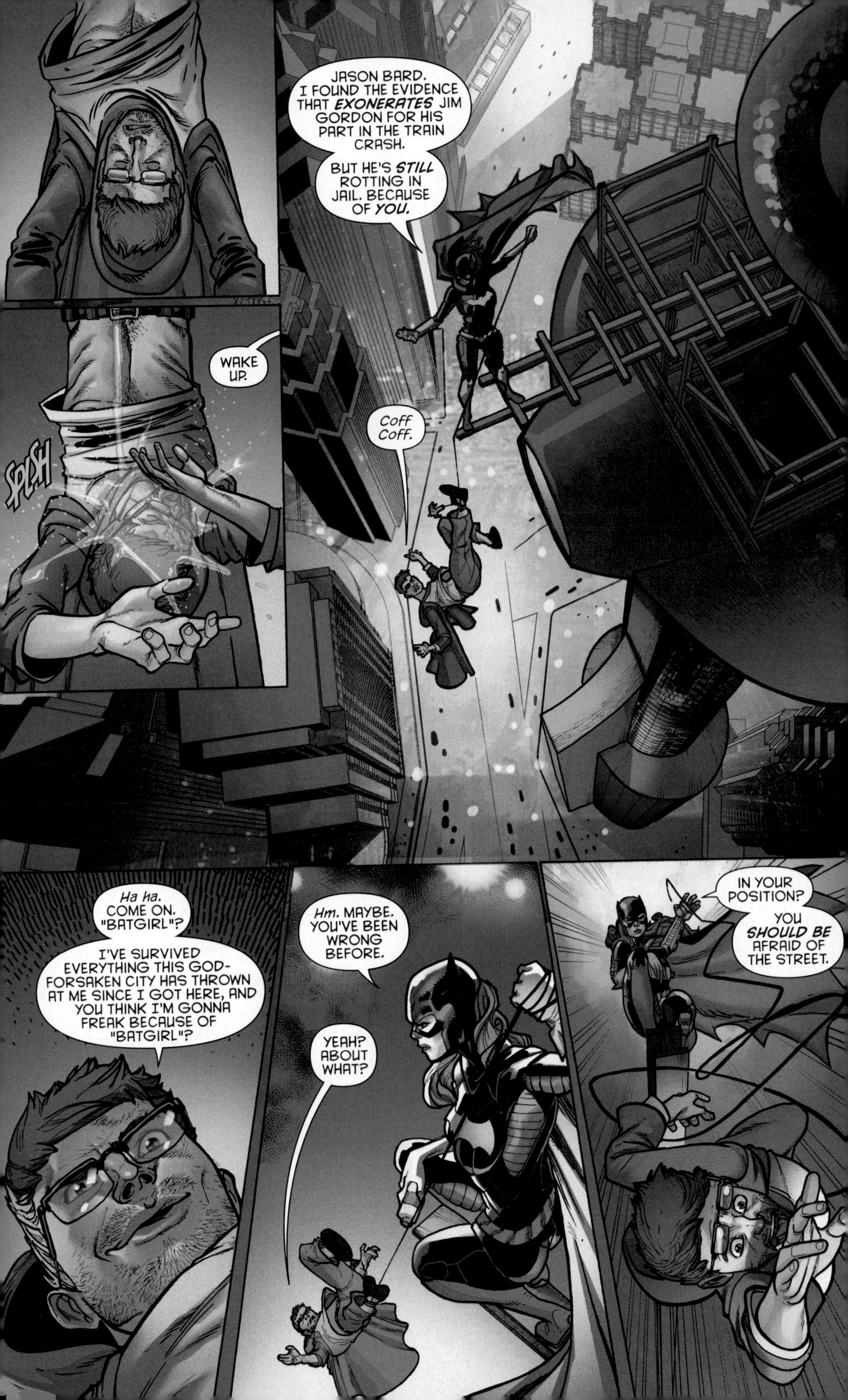

JASON BARD. I FOUND THE EVIDENCE THAT EXONERATES JIM GORDON FOR HIS PART IN THE TRAIN CRASH.
BUT HE'S STILL ROTTING IN JAIL. BECAUSE OF YOU.
WAKE UP.
SPLSH
Coff Coff.
Ha ha. COME ON. "BATGIRL"?
I'VE SURVIVED EVERYTHING THIS GOD-FORSAKEN CITY HAS THROWN AT ME SINCE I GOT HERE, AND YOU THINK I'M GONNA FREAK BECAUSE OF "BATGIRL"?
Hm. MAYBE. YOU'VE BEEN WRONG BEFORE.
YEAH? ABOUT WHAT?
IN YOUR POSITION?
YOU SHOULD BE AFRAID OF THE STREET.

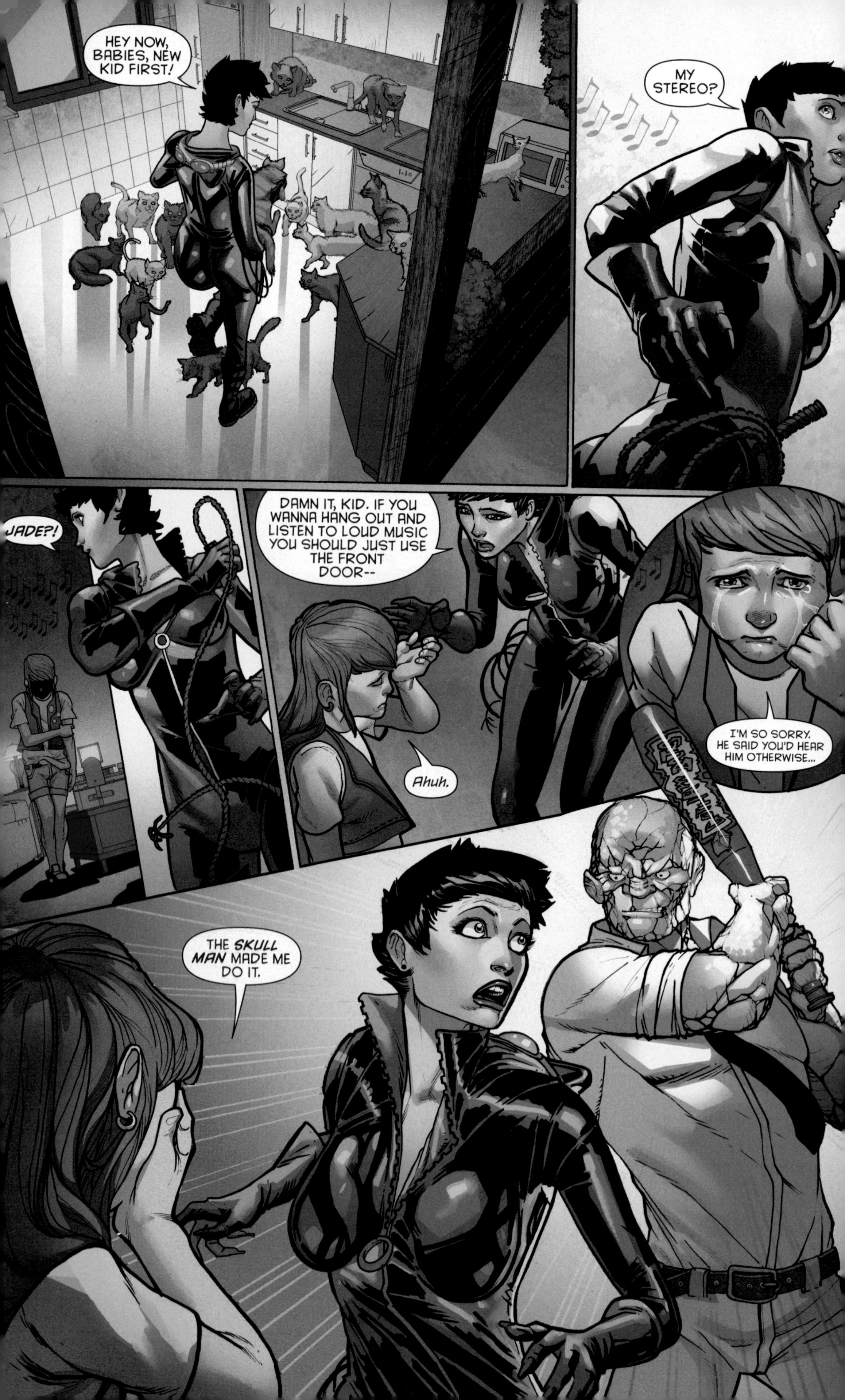
HEY NOW, BABIES, NEW KID FIRST!
MY STEREO?
JADE?!
DAMN IT, KID. IF YOU WANNA HANG OUT AND LISTEN TO LOUD MUSIC YOU SHOULD JUST USE THE FRONT DOOR--
Ahuh.
I'M SO SORRY. HE SAID YOU'D HEAR HIM OTHERWISE...
THE SKULL MAN MADE ME DO IT.

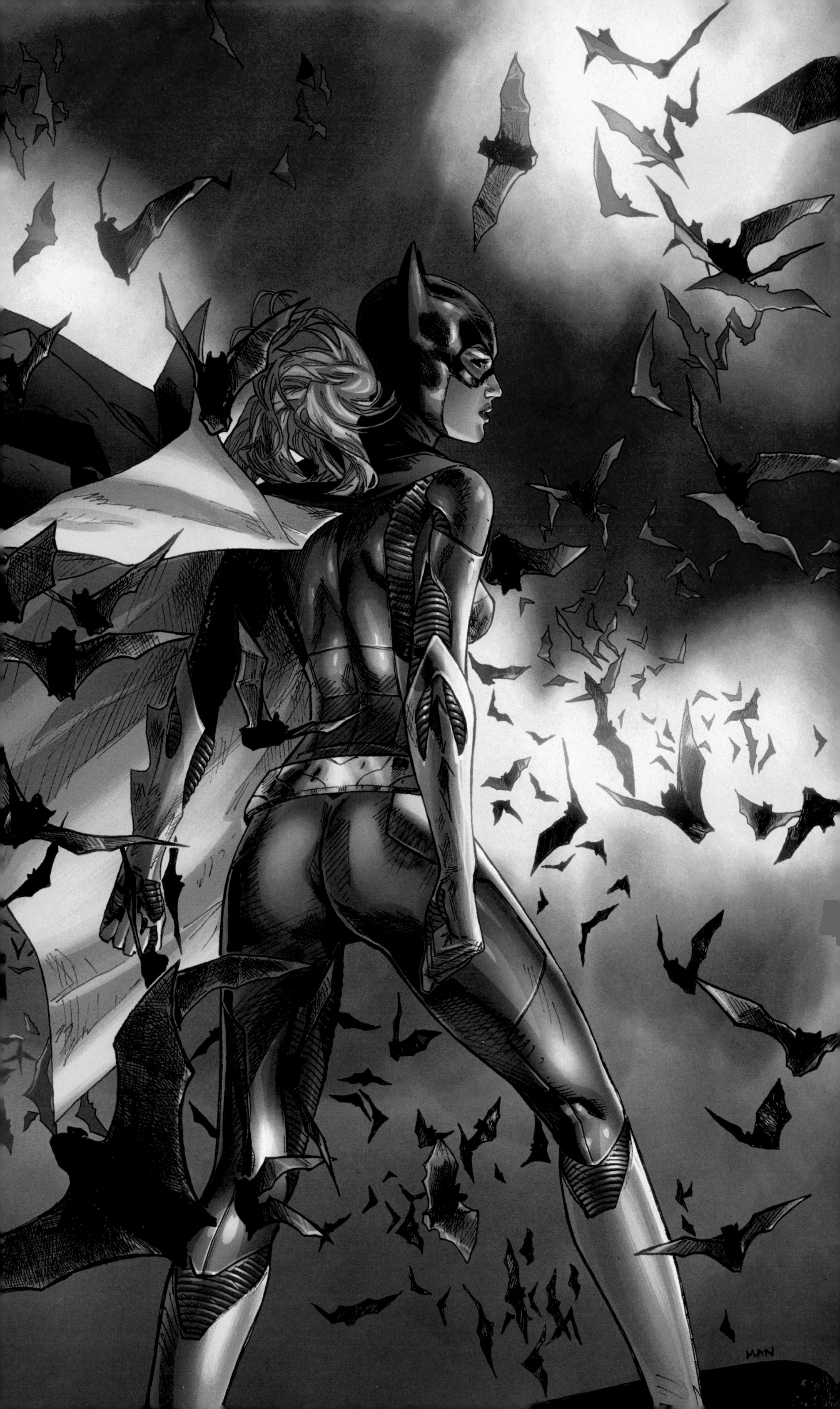
MAN

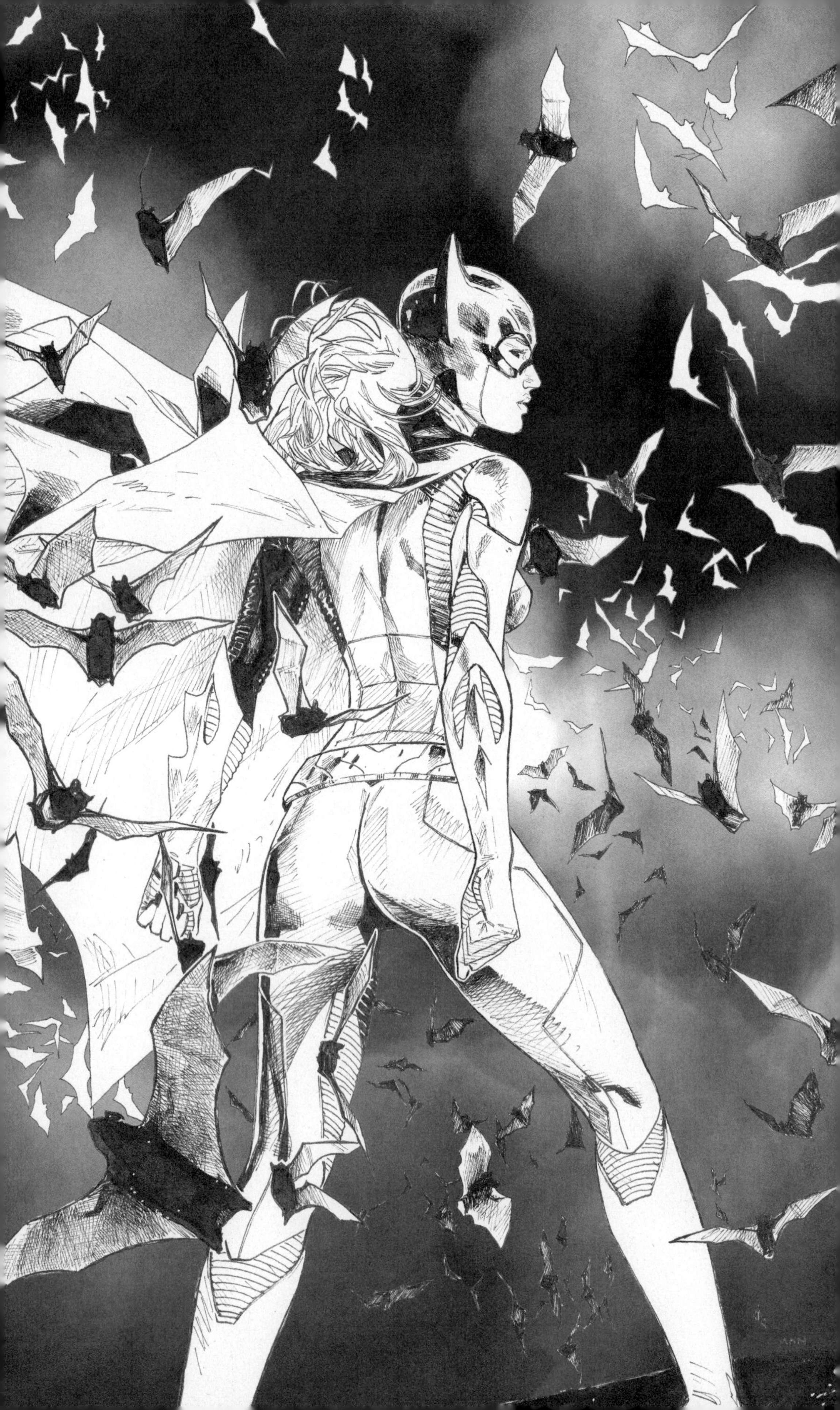

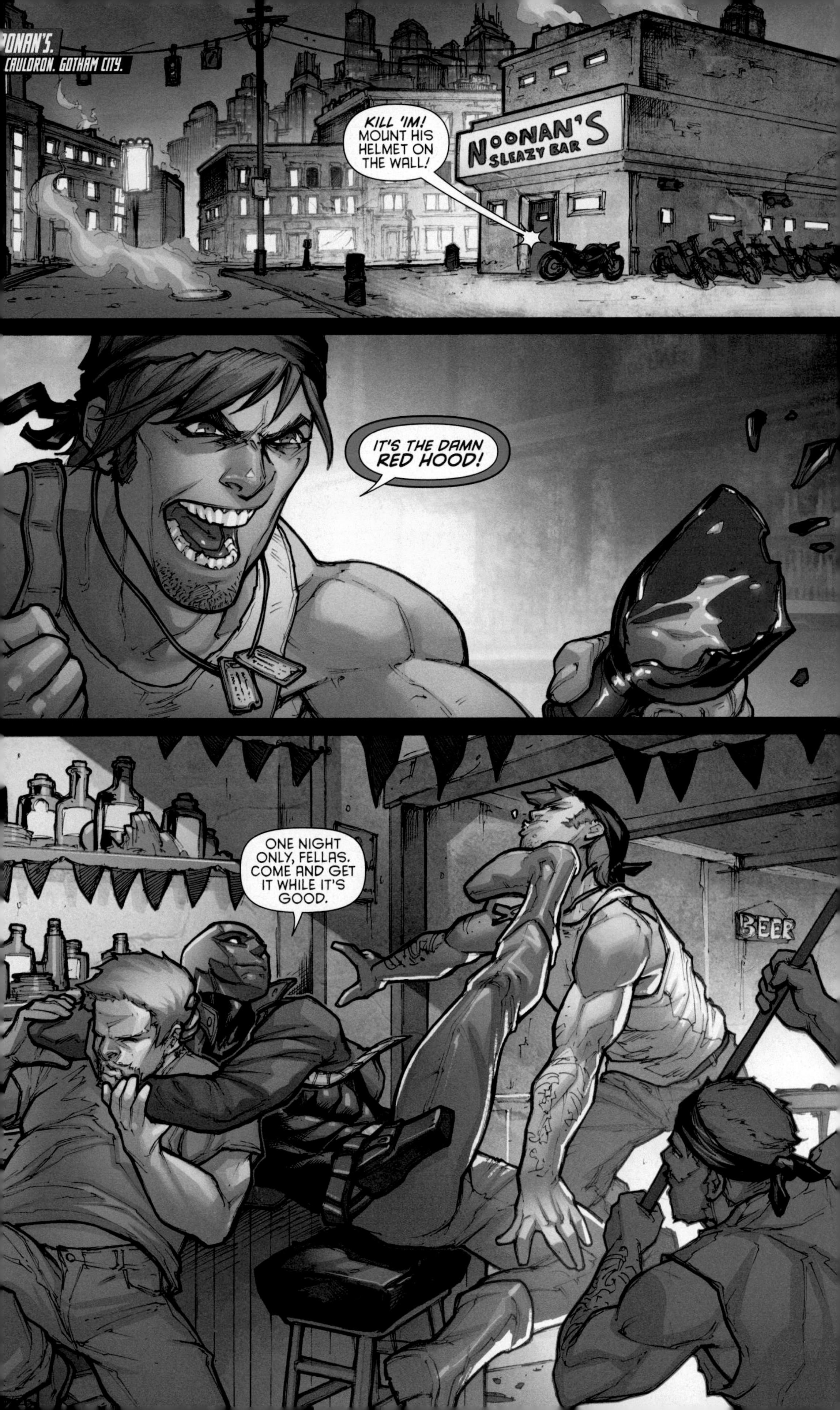

ONAN'S.
CAULDRON. GOTHAM CITY.
KILL 'IM! MOUNT HIS HELMET ON THE WALL!
NOONAN'S SLEAZY BAR
IT'S THE DAMN RED HOOD!
ONE NIGHT ONLY, FELLAS. COME AND GET IT WHILE IT'S GOOD.
BEER

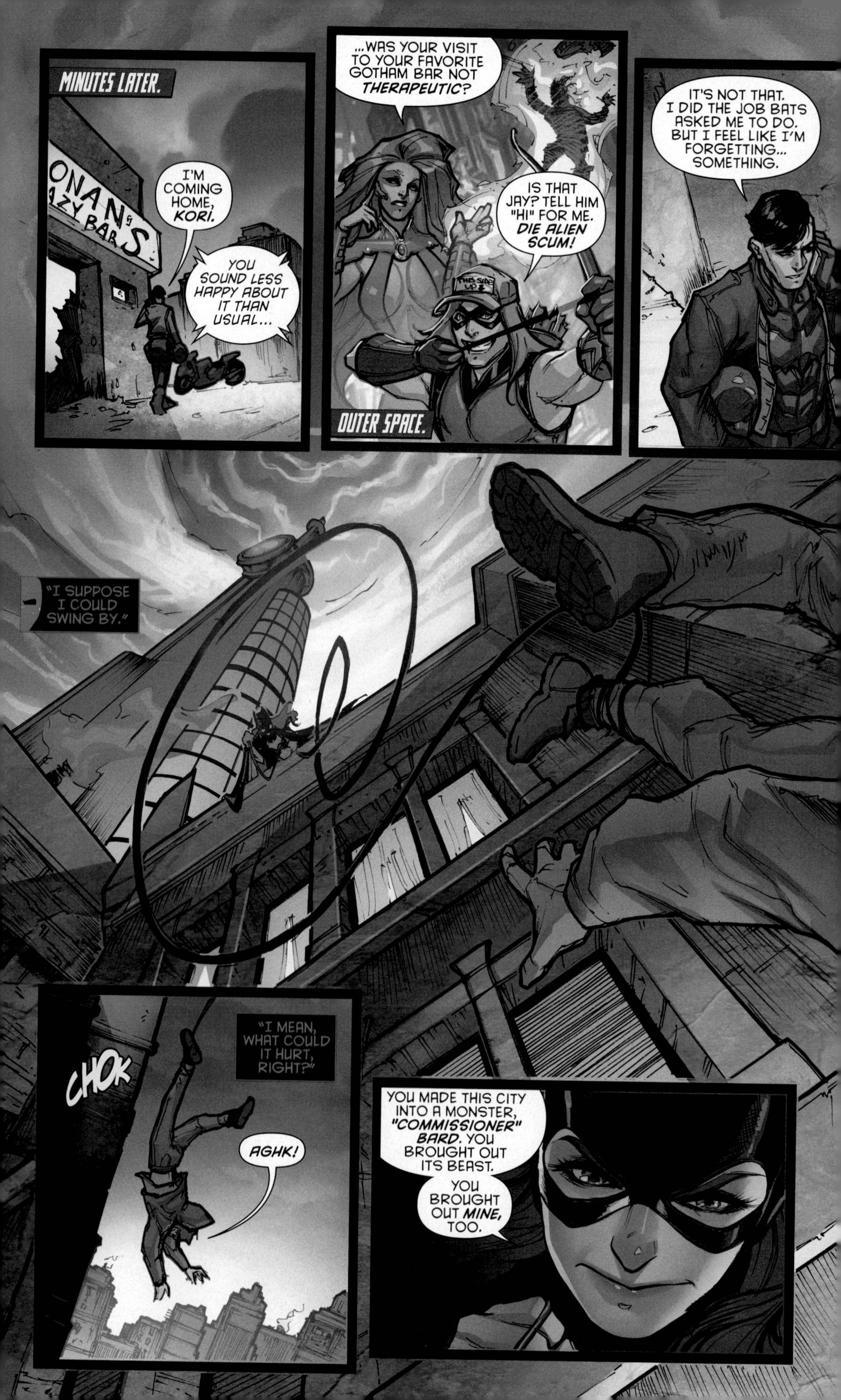
MINUTES LATER.
ONAN'S
AZY BARS
I'M COMING HOME, KORI.
YOU SOUND LESS HAPPY ABOUT IT THAN USUAL...
...WAS YOUR VISIT TO YOUR FAVORITE GOTHAM BAR NOT THERAPEUTIC?
IS THAT JAY? TELL HIM "HI" FOR ME. DIE ALIEN SCUM!
THIS SIDE UP
OUTER SPACE.
IT'S NOT THAT. I DID THE JOB BATS ASKED ME TO DO. BUT I FEEL LIKE I'M FORGETTING... SOMETHING.
"I SUPPOSE I COULD SWING BY."
"I MEAN, WHAT COULD IT HURT, RIGHT?"
CHOK
AGHK!
YOU MADE THIS CITY INTO A MONSTER, "COMMISSIONER" BARD. YOU BROUGHT OUT ITS BEAST.
YOU BROUGHT OUT MINE, TOO.

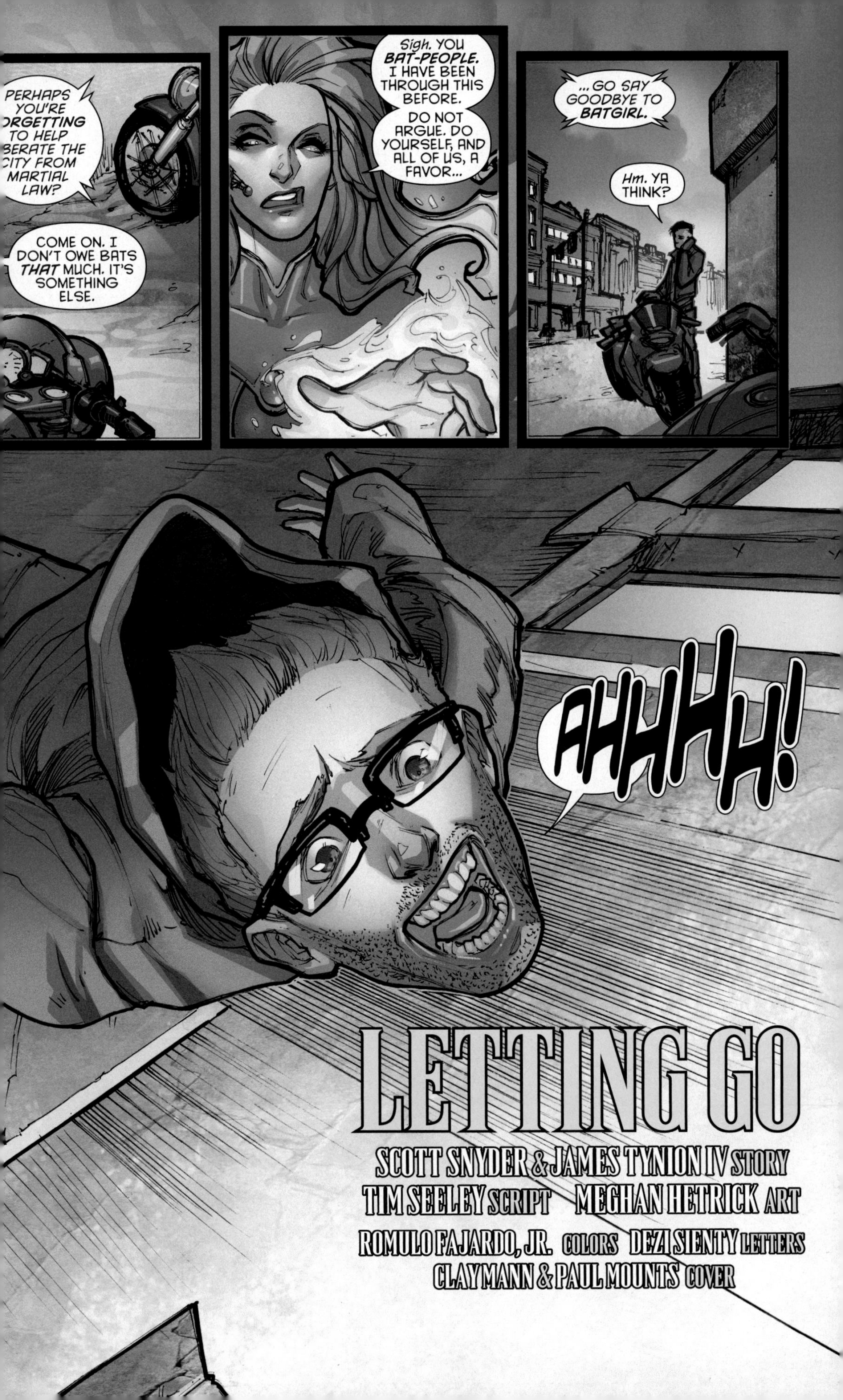
PERHAPS YOU'RE ORGETTING TO HELP IBERATE THE CITY FROM MARTIAL LAW?
COME ON. I DON'T OWE BATS THAT MUCH. IT'S SOMETHING ELSE.
Sigh. YOU BAT-PEOPLE. I HAVE BEEN THROUGH THIS BEFORE.
DO NOT ARGUE. DO YOURSELF, AND ALL OF US, A FAVOR...
...GO SAY GOODBYE TO BATGIRL.
Hm. YA THINK?
AHHHHH!
LETTING GO
SCOTT SNYDER & JAMES TYNION IV STORY
TIM SEELEY SCRIPT MEGHAN HETRICK ART
ROMULO FAJARDO, JR. COLORS DEZI SIENTY LETTERS
CLAY MANN & PAUL MOUNTS COVER

HEY, YOU REMEMBER *ME*, BABY?

NUH...

I MEAN, I REMEMBER *YOU*, AND I'VE HAD SOME *SERIOUS* DAMAGE DONE TO MY BRAIN...

*AW*, NOT AGAIN.

BUT IN CASE YOU FORGOT, I'M *LOUIS FERRYMAN*. THEY CALL ME *BONE*.

NOW, LAST TIME WE WAS TOGETHER, THE ONLY THING THAT KEPT YOU FROM CAVIN' IN MY HEAD WAS *BATMAN*.

Y'KNOW WHAT THE ONLY THING I LIKE *LESS* THAN GETTING MY GOURD BATTED AROUND LIKE A CRICKET BALL IS?

OWING MY *LIFE* TO *BATMAN*.

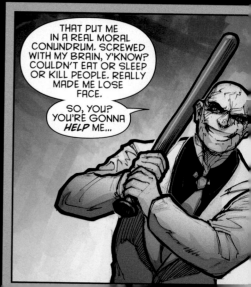

THAT PUT ME IN A REAL MORAL CONUNDRUM. SCREWED WITH MY BRAIN, Y'KNOW? COULDN'T EAT OR SLEEP OR KILL PEOPLE. REALLY MADE ME LOSE FACE.

SO, YOU? YOU'RE GONNA *HELP* ME...

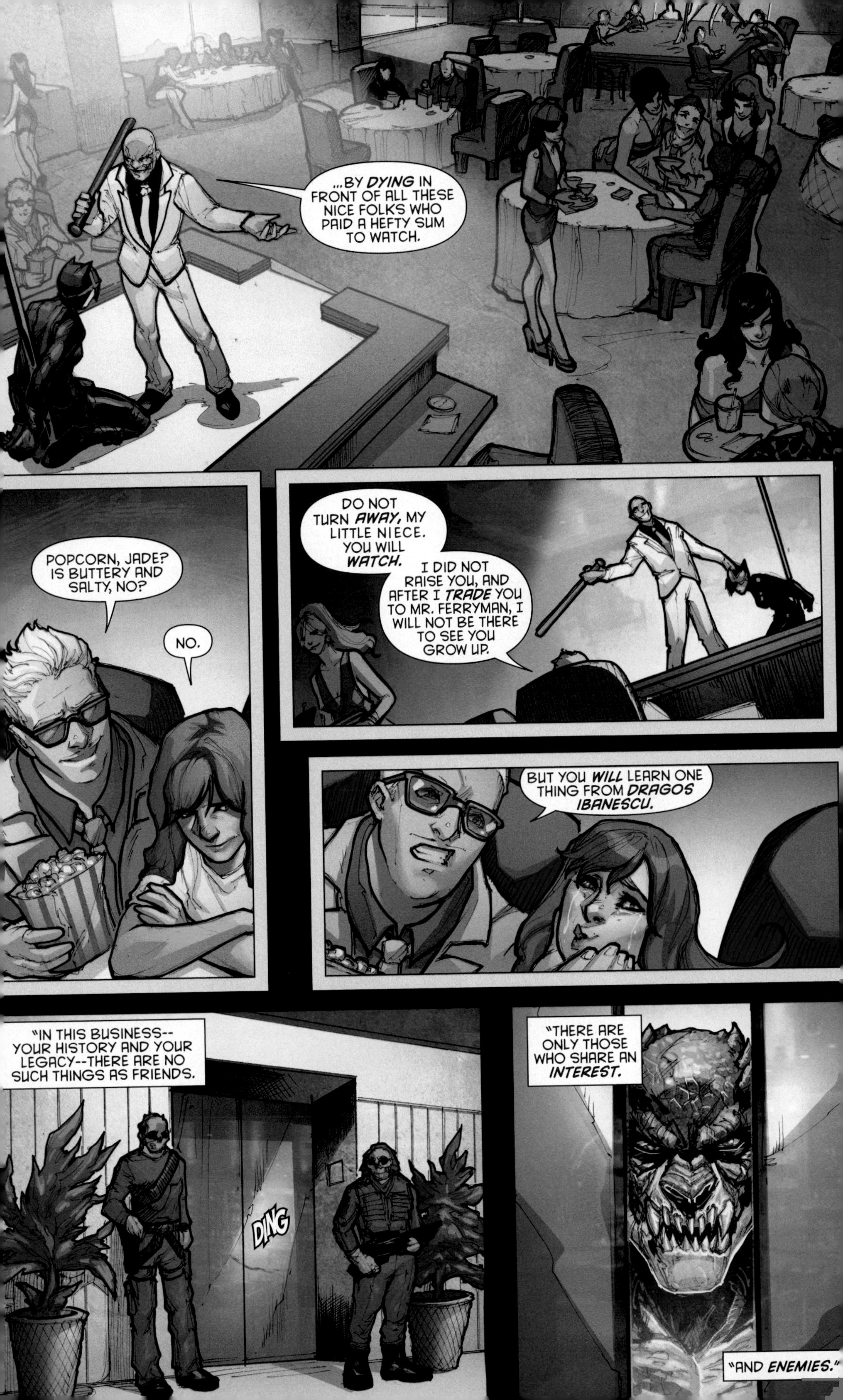
...BY DYING IN FRONT OF ALL THESE NICE FOLKS WHO PAID A HEFTY SUM TO WATCH.
POPCORN, JADE? IS BUTTERY AND SALTY, NO?
NO.
DO NOT TURN AWAY, MY LITTLE NIECE. YOU WILL WATCH.
I DID NOT RAISE YOU, AND AFTER I TRADE YOU TO MR. FERRYMAN, I WILL NOT BE THERE TO SEE YOU GROW UP.
BUT YOU WILL LEARN ONE THING FROM DRAGOS IBANESCU.
"IN THIS BUSINESS-- YOUR HISTORY AND YOUR LEGACY--THERE ARE NO SUCH THINGS AS FRIENDS.
DING
"THERE ARE ONLY THOSE WHO SHARE AN INTEREST.
"AND ENEMIES."

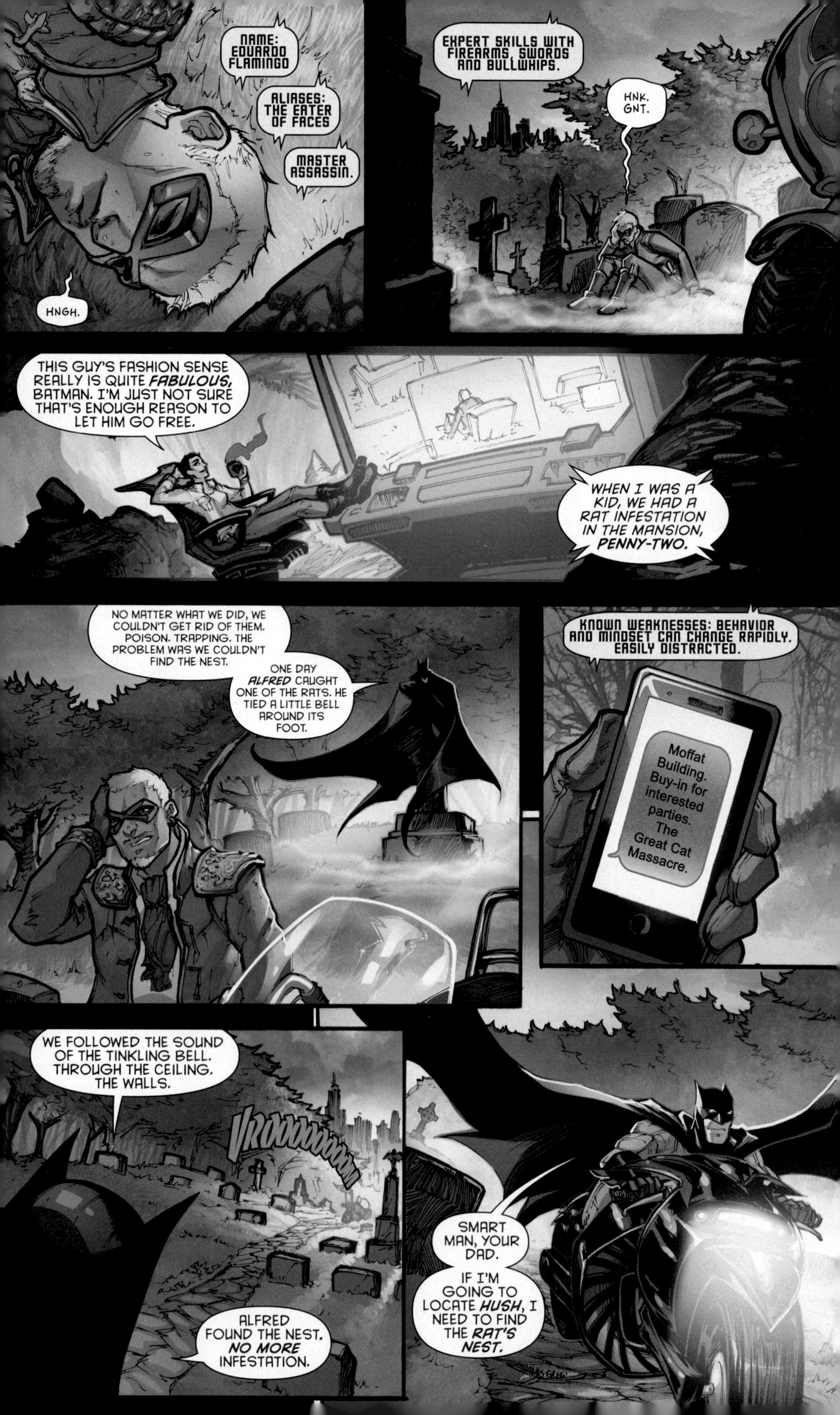
NAME: EDUARDO FLAMINGO
ALIASES: THE EATER OF FACES
MASTER ASSASSIN.
HNGH.
EXPERT SKILLS WITH FIREARMS, SWORDS AND BULLWHIPS.
HNK. GNT.
THIS GUY'S FASHION SENSE REALLY IS QUITE FABULOUS, BATMAN. I'M JUST NOT SURE THAT'S ENOUGH REASON TO LET HIM GO FREE.
WHEN I WAS A KID, WE HAD A RAT INFESTATION IN THE MANSION, PENNY-TWO.
NO MATTER WHAT WE DID, WE COULDN'T GET RID OF THEM. POISON. TRAPPING. THE PROBLEM WAS WE COULDN'T FIND THE NEST.
ONE DAY ALFRED CAUGHT ONE OF THE RATS. HE TIED A LITTLE BELL AROUND ITS FOOT.
KNOWN WEAKNESSES: BEHAVIOR AND MINDSET CAN CHANGE RAPIDLY. EASILY DISTRACTED.
Moffat Building. Buy-in for interested parties. The Great Cat Massacre.
WE FOLLOWED THE SOUND OF THE TINKLING BELL. THROUGH THE CEILING. THE WALLS.
VROOOOOOOOOM
ALFRED FOUND THE NEST. NO MORE INFESTATION.
SMART MAN, YOUR DAD.
IF I'M GOING TO LOCATE HUSH, I NEED TO FIND THE RAT'S NEST.

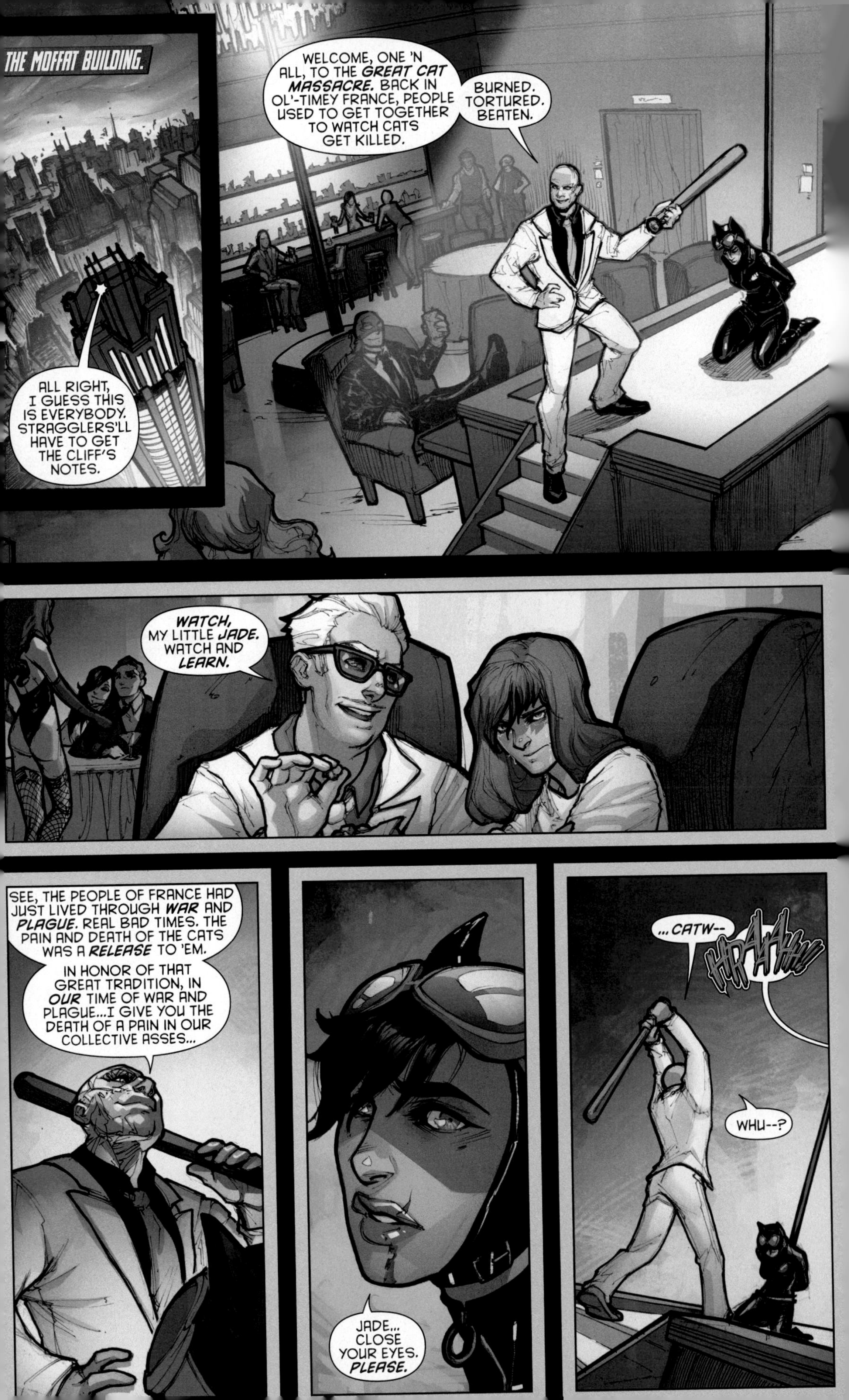
THE MOFFAT BUILDING.
ALL RIGHT, I GUESS THIS IS EVERYBODY. STRAGGLERS'LL HAVE TO GET THE CLIFF'S NOTES.
WELCOME, ONE 'N ALL, TO THE GREAT CAT MASSACRE. BACK IN OL'-TIMEY FRANCE, PEOPLE USED TO GET TOGETHER TO WATCH CATS GET KILLED.
BURNED. TORTURED. BEATEN.
WATCH, MY LITTLE JADE. WATCH AND LEARN.
SEE, THE PEOPLE OF FRANCE HAD JUST LIVED THROUGH WAR AND PLAGUE. REAL BAD TIMES. THE PAIN AND DEATH OF THE CATS WAS A RELEASE TO 'EM.
IN HONOR OF THAT GREAT TRADITION, IN OUR TIME OF WAR AND PLAGUE...I GIVE YOU THE DEATH OF A PAIN IN OUR COLLECTIVE ASSES...
JADE... CLOSE YOUR EYES. PLEASE.
...CATW--
HRAAAHH!!
WHU--?

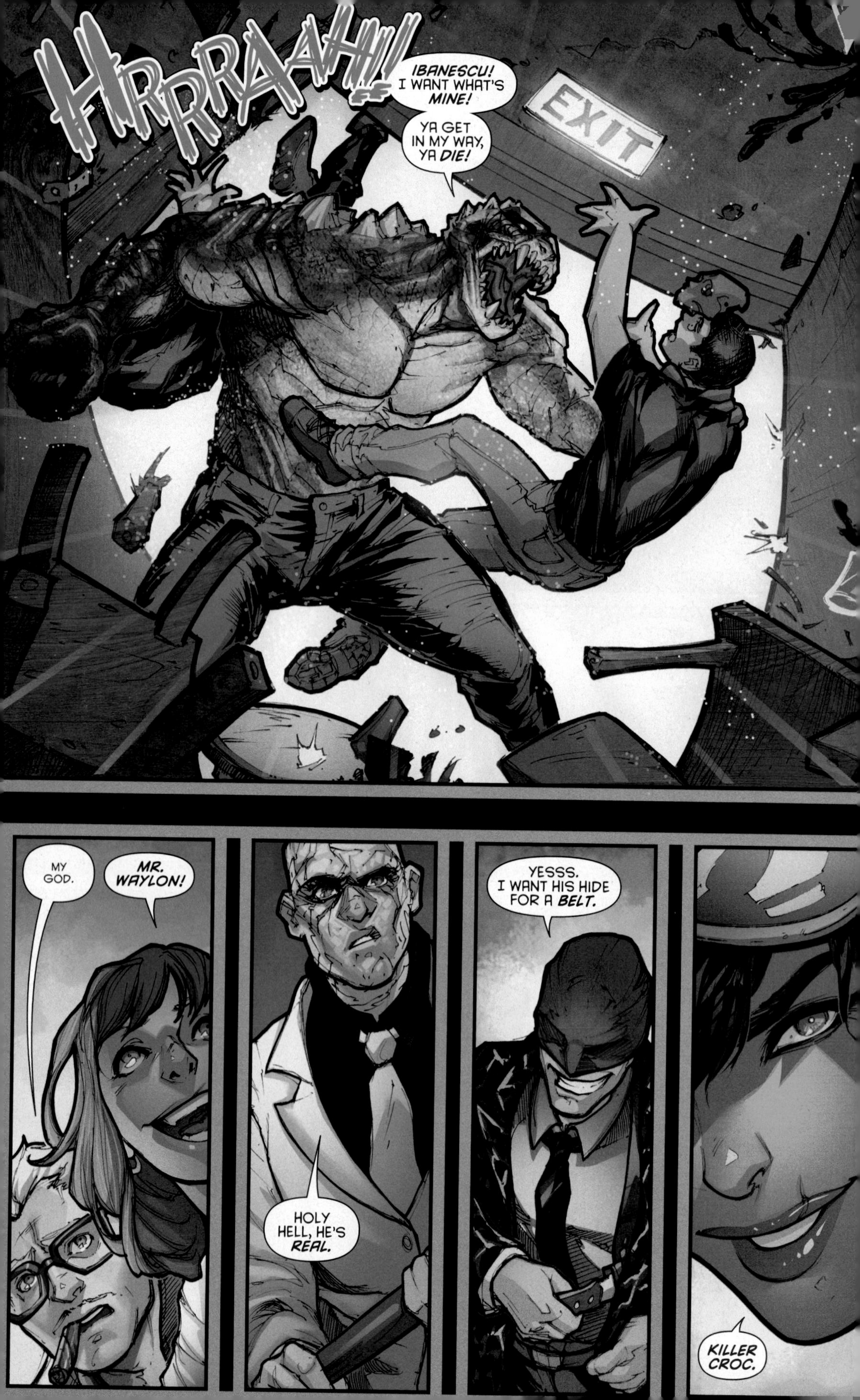
HRRRAAHH!!
IBANESCU! I WANT WHAT'S MINE!
YA GET IN MY WAY, YA DIE!
EXIT
MY GOD.
MR. WAYLON!
HOLY HELL, HE'S REAL.
YESSS. I WANT HIS HIDE FOR A BELT.
KILLER CROC.

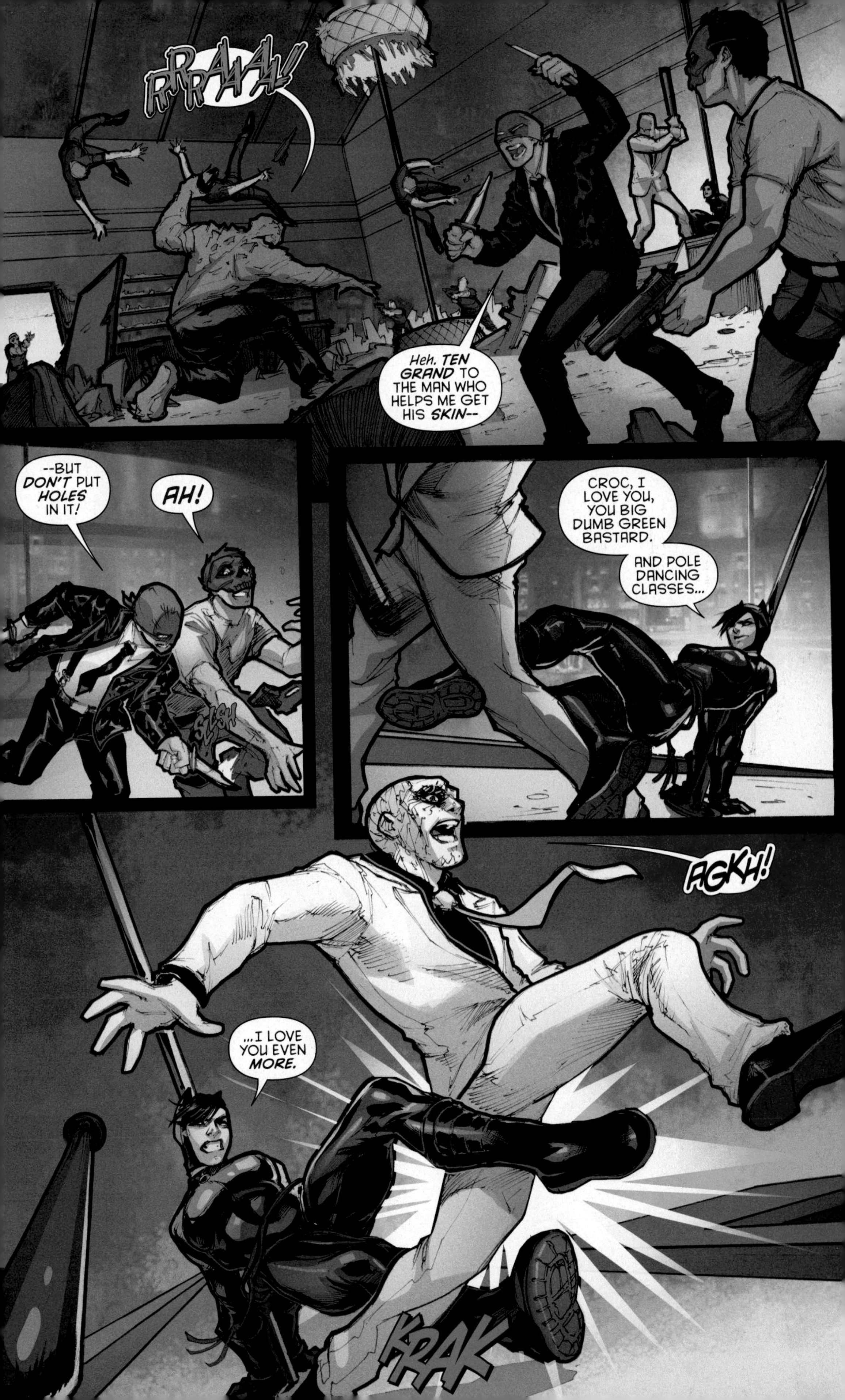
RRRAAAAL!
Heh. TEN GRAND TO THE MAN WHO HELPS ME GET HIS SKIN--
--BUT DON'T PUT HOLES IN IT!
AH!
SLSH
CROC, I LOVE YOU, YOU BIG DUMB GREEN BASTARD.
AND POLE DANCING CLASSES...
AGKH!
...I LOVE YOU EVEN MORE.
KRAK

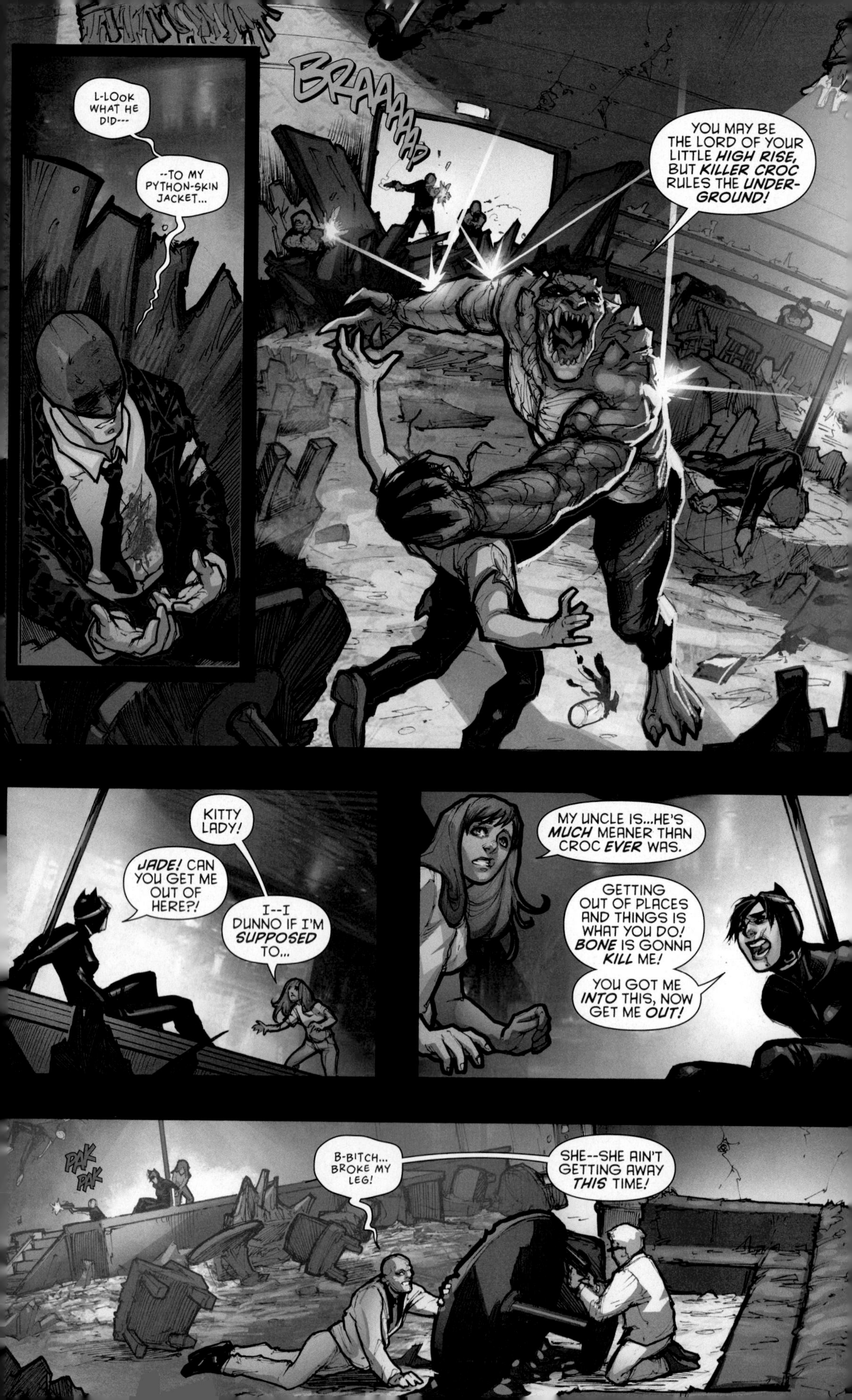
BRAAAAAAP
L-LOOK WHAT HE DID---
--TO MY PYTHON-SKIN JACKET...
YOU MAY BE THE LORD OF YOUR LITTLE HIGH RISE, BUT KILLER CROC RULES THE UNDER-GROUND!
KITTY LADY!
JADE! CAN YOU GET ME OUT OF HERE?!
I--I DUNNO IF I'M SUPPOSED TO...
MY UNCLE IS...HE'S MUCH MEANER THAN CROC EVER WAS.
GETTING OUT OF PLACES AND THINGS IS WHAT YOU DO! BONE IS GONNA KILL ME!
YOU GOT ME INTO THIS, NOW GET ME OUT!
PAK PAK
B-BITCH... BROKE MY LEG!
SHE--SHE AIN'T GETTING AWAY THIS TIME!

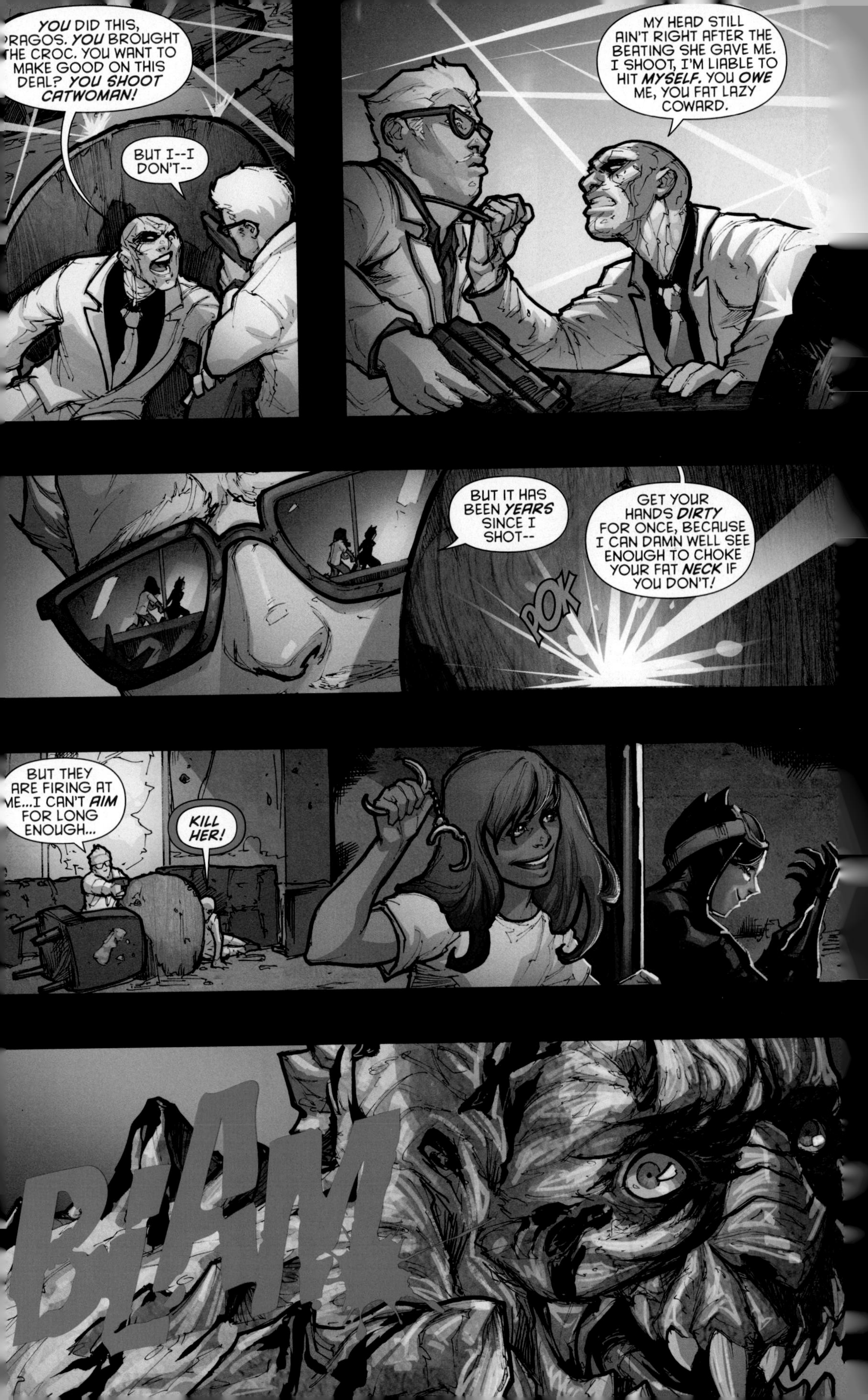
YOU DID THIS, PRAGOS. YOU BROUGHT THE CROC. YOU WANT TO MAKE GOOD ON THIS DEAL? YOU SHOOT CATWOMAN!
BUT I--I DON'T--
MY HEAD STILL AIN'T RIGHT AFTER THE BEATING SHE GAVE ME. I SHOOT, I'M LIABLE TO HIT MYSELF. YOU OWE ME, YOU FAT LAZY COWARD.
BUT IT HAS BEEN YEARS SINCE I SHOT--
GET YOUR HANDS DIRTY FOR ONCE, BECAUSE I CAN DAMN WELL SEE ENOUGH TO CHOKE YOUR FAT NECK IF YOU DON'T!
POK
BUT THEY ARE FIRING AT ME...I CAN'T AIM FOR LONG ENOUGH...
KILL HER!
BLAM

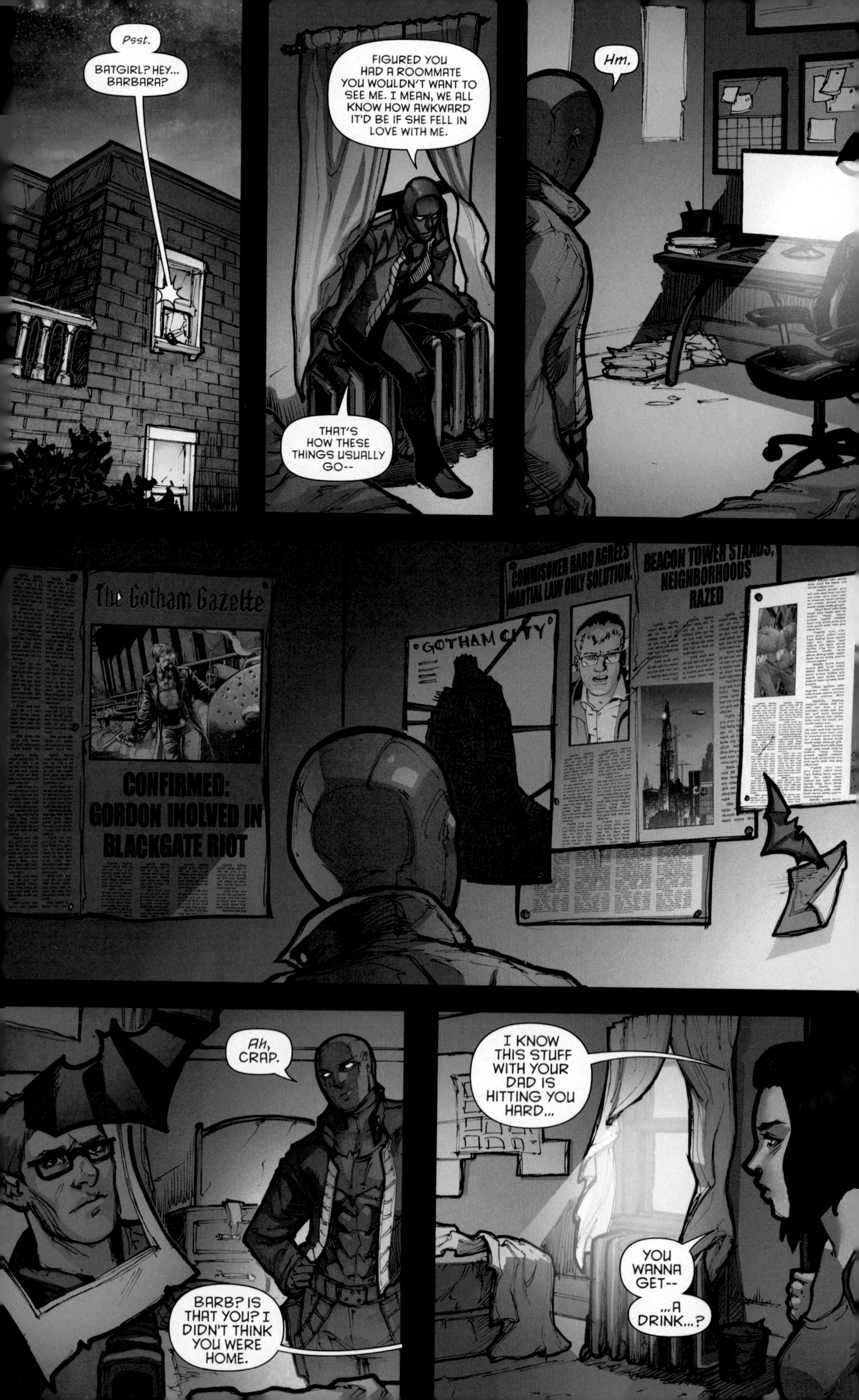
Psst.
BATGIRL? HEY... BARBARA?
FIGURED YOU HAD A ROOMMATE YOU WOULDN'T WANT TO SEE ME. I MEAN, WE ALL KNOW HOW AWKWARD IT'D BE IF SHE FELL IN LOVE WITH ME.
THAT'S HOW THESE THINGS USUALLY GO--
Hm.
The Gotham Gazette
CONFIRMED: GORDON INOLVED IN BLACKGATE RIOT
GOTHAM CITY
COMMISONER BARD AGREES MARTIAL LAW ONLY SOLUTION.
BEACON TOWER STANDS, NEIGHBORHOODS RAZED
Ah, CRAP.
BARB? IS THAT YOU? I DIDN'T THINK YOU WERE HOME.
I KNOW THIS STUFF WITH YOUR DAD IS HITTING YOU HARD...
YOU WANNA GET--
...A DRINK...?

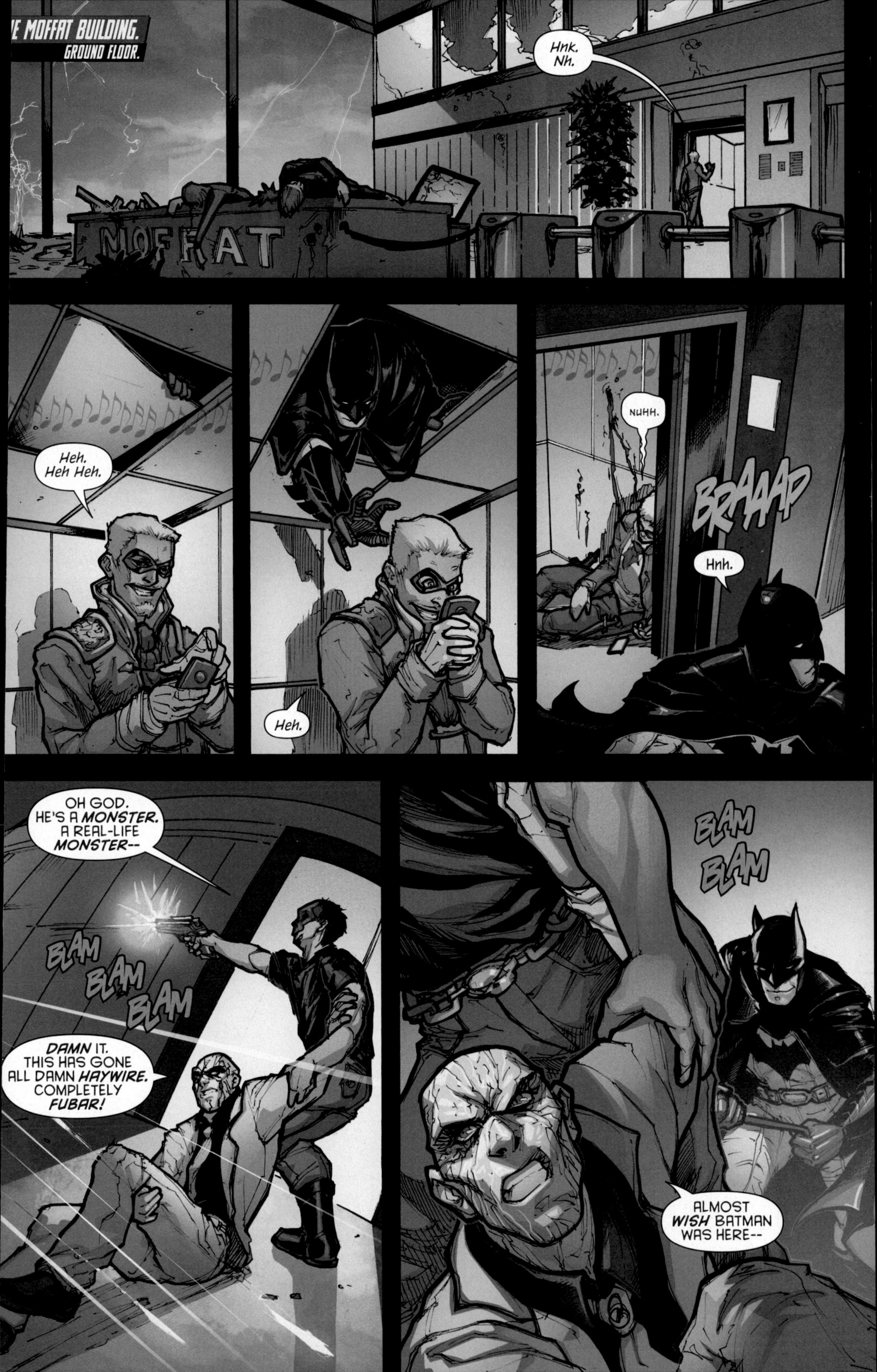
E MOFFAT BUILDING.
GROUND FLOOR.
MOFFAT
Hnk. Nh.
Heh. Heh Heh.
Heh.
NUHH.
BRAAAP
Hnh.
OH GOD. HE'S A MONSTER. A REAL-LIFE MONSTER--
BLAM BLAM BLAM
DAMN IT. THIS HAS GONE ALL DAMN HAYWIRE. COMPLETELY FUBAR!
BLAM BLAM
ALMOST WISH BATMAN WAS HERE--

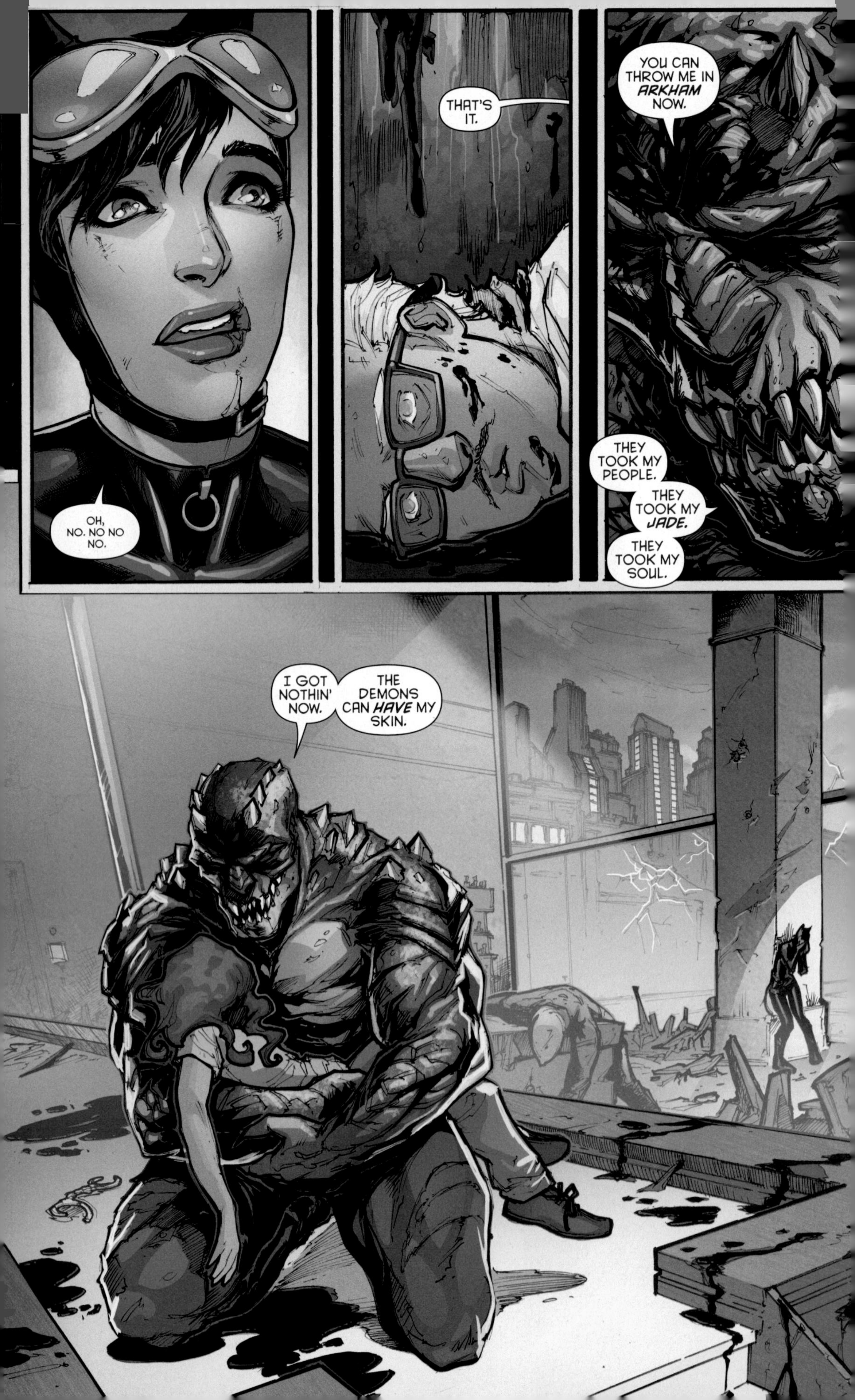
OH, NO. NO NO NO.
THAT'S IT.
YOU CAN THROW ME IN ARKHAM NOW.
THEY TOOK MY PEOPLE.
THEY TOOK MY JADE.
THEY TOOK MY SOUL.
I GOT NOTHIN' NOW.
THE DEMONS CAN HAVE MY SKIN.

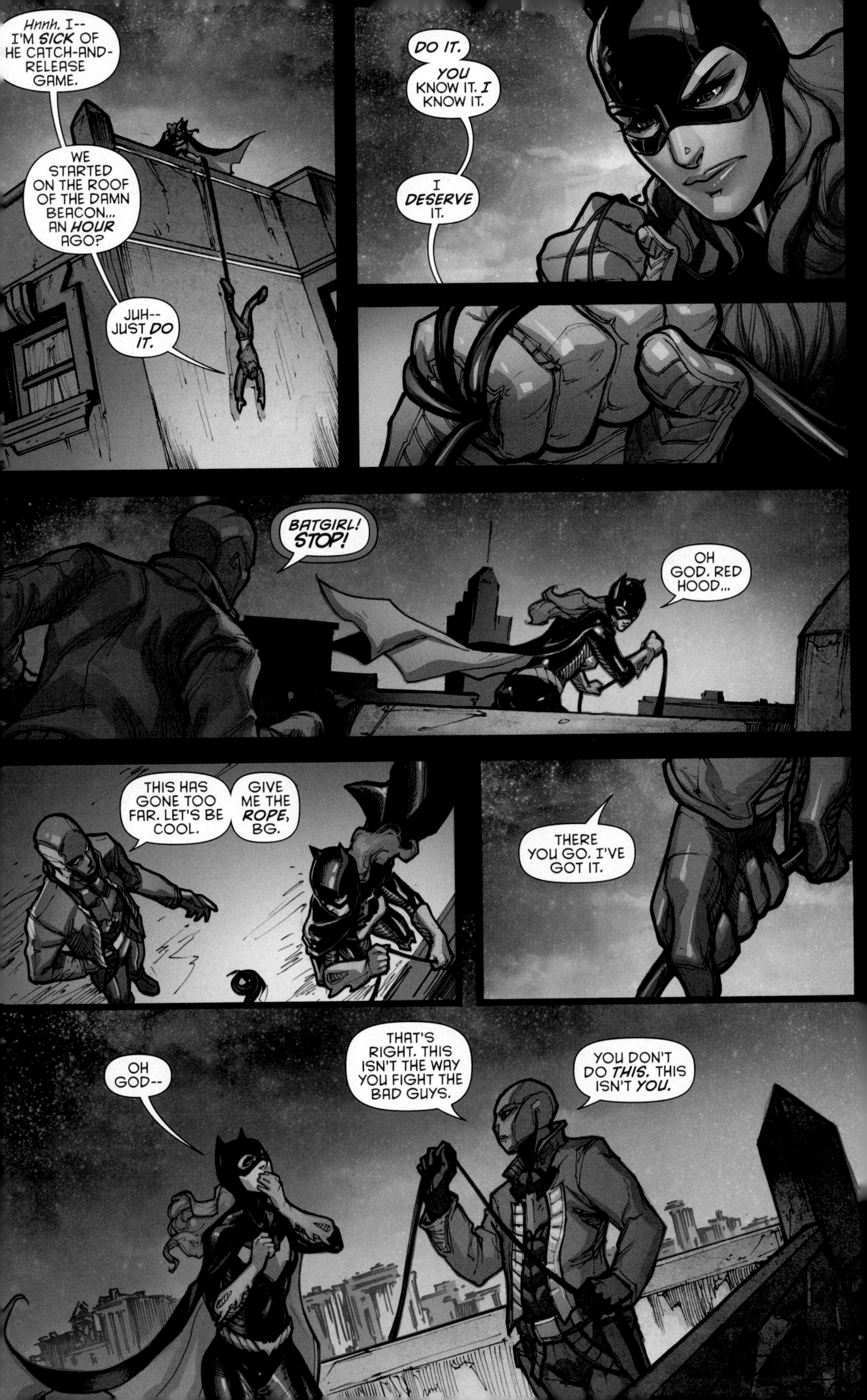
Hnnh. I-- I'M SICK OF HE CATCH-AND-RELEASE GAME.
WE STARTED ON THE ROOF OF THE DAMN BEACON... AN HOUR AGO?
JUH-- JUST DO IT.
DO IT.
YOU KNOW IT. I KNOW IT.
I DESERVE IT.
BATGIRL! STOP!
OH GOD. RED HOOD...
THIS HAS GONE TOO FAR. LET'S BE COOL.
GIVE ME THE ROPE, BG.
THERE YOU GO. I'VE GOT IT.
OH GOD--
THAT'S RIGHT. THIS ISN'T THE WAY YOU FIGHT THE BAD GUYS.
YOU DON'T DO THIS. THIS ISN'T YOU.

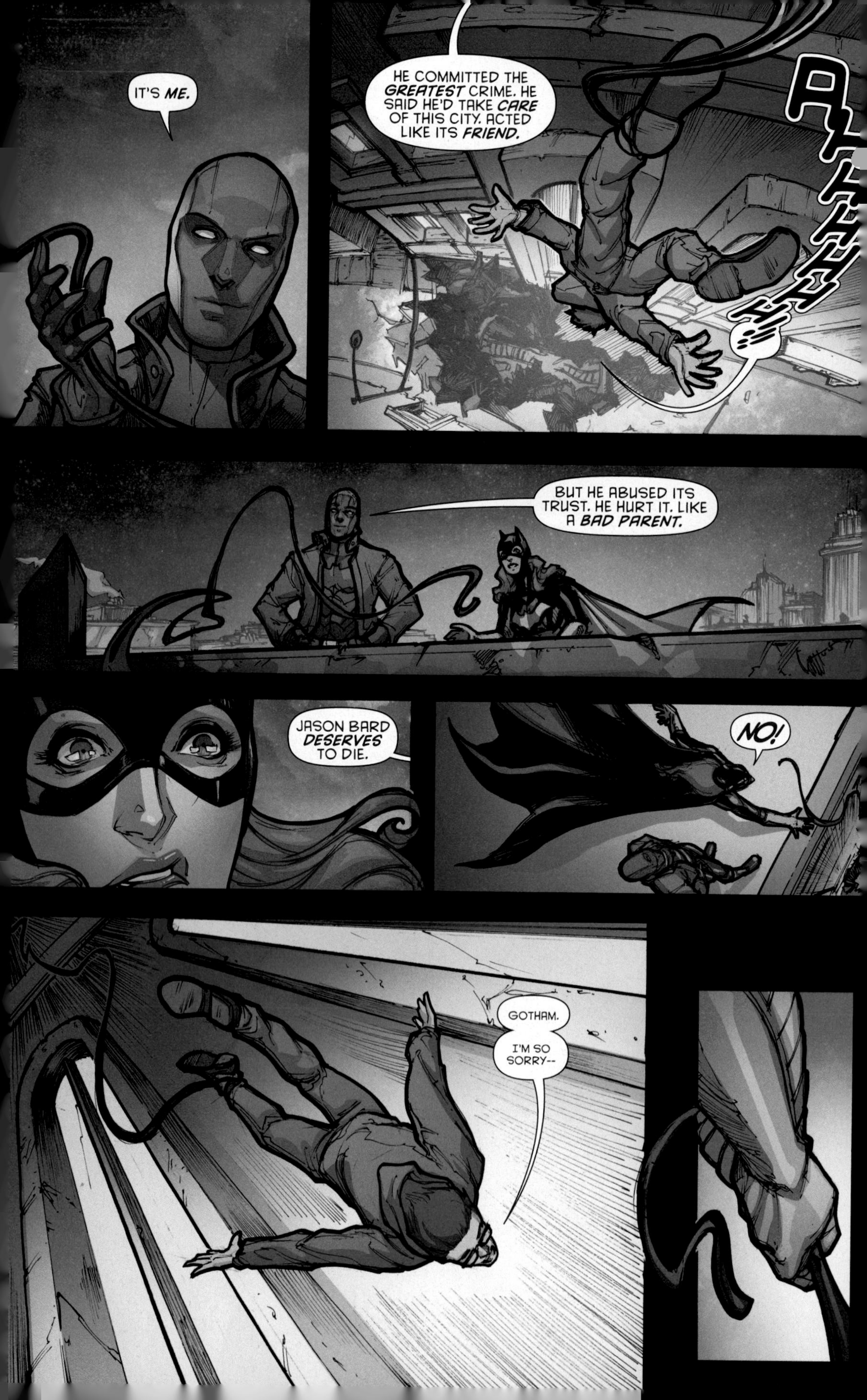
IT'S *ME.*
HE COMMITTED THE *GREATEST* CRIME. HE SAID HE'D TAKE *CARE* OF THIS CITY. ACTED LIKE ITS *FRIEND.*
AAAHHHH!!!
BUT HE ABUSED ITS TRUST. HE HURT IT. LIKE A *BAD PARENT.*
JASON BARD *DESERVES* TO DIE.
*NO!*
GOTHAM.
I'M SO SORRY--

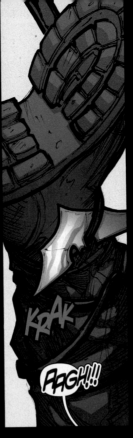

HNNUGH!!

AGH. MY LEG. MY LEG. MY... ...GOD.

I'M ALIVE.

-Huhn-
-huhn-
-huhn-

YOU WERE ALWAYS BETTER THAN ALL OF US ROBINS, *BARB.*

YOU JUST PROVED IT AGAIN...

...YOU'RE *STILL* BETTER THAN *ME.*

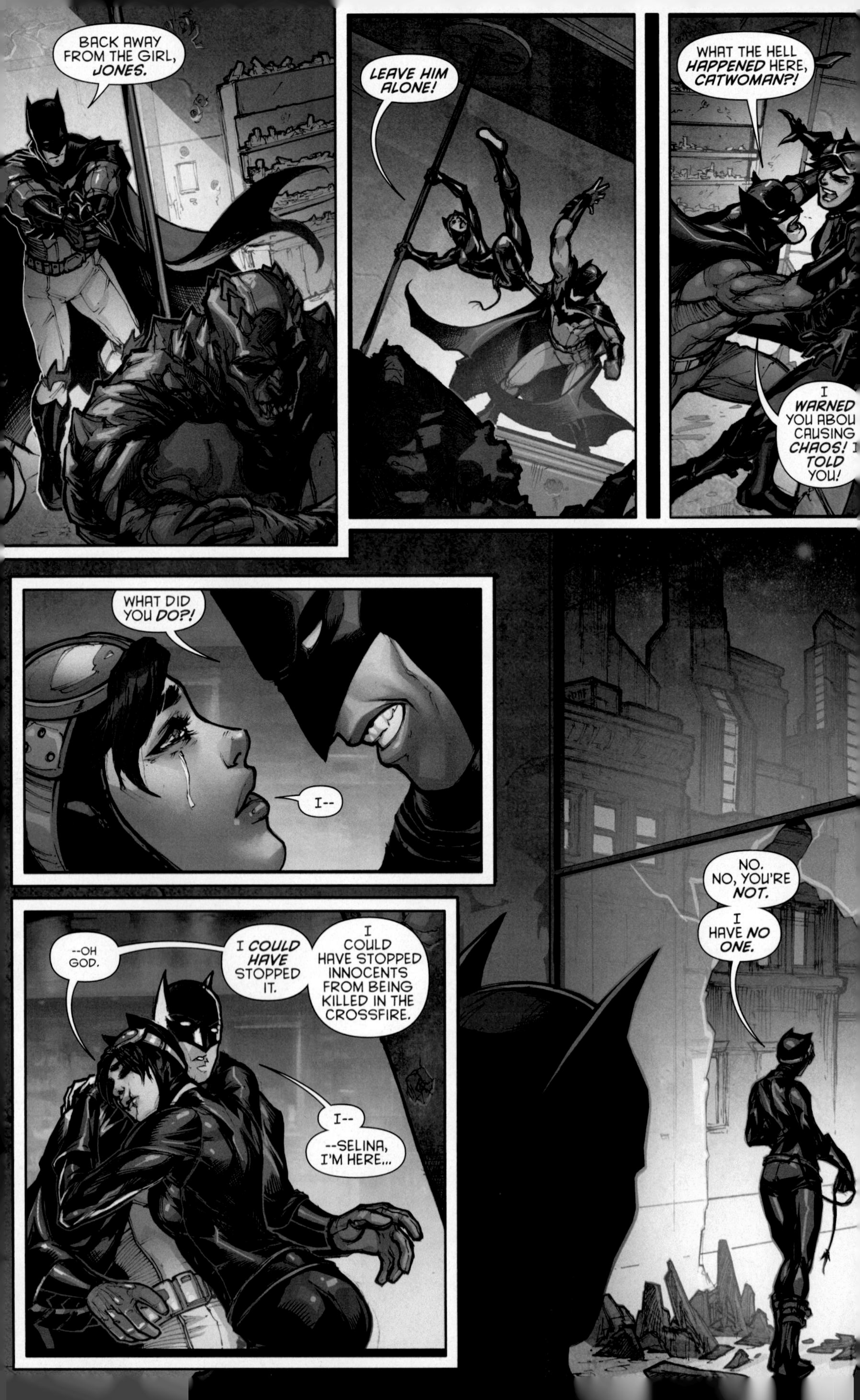
BACK AWAY FROM THE GIRL, *JONES.*
*LEAVE HIM ALONE!*
WHAT THE HELL *HAPPENED* HERE, *CATWOMAN?!*
I *WARNED* YOU ABOU CAUSING *CHAOS!* I *TOLD* YOU!
WHAT DID YOU *DO?!*
I--
--OH GOD.
I *COULD HAVE* STOPPED IT.
I COULD HAVE STOPPED INNOCENTS FROM BEING KILLED IN THE CROSSFIRE.
I--
--SELINA, I'M HERE...
NO. NO, YOU'RE *NOT.*
I HAVE *NO ONE.*

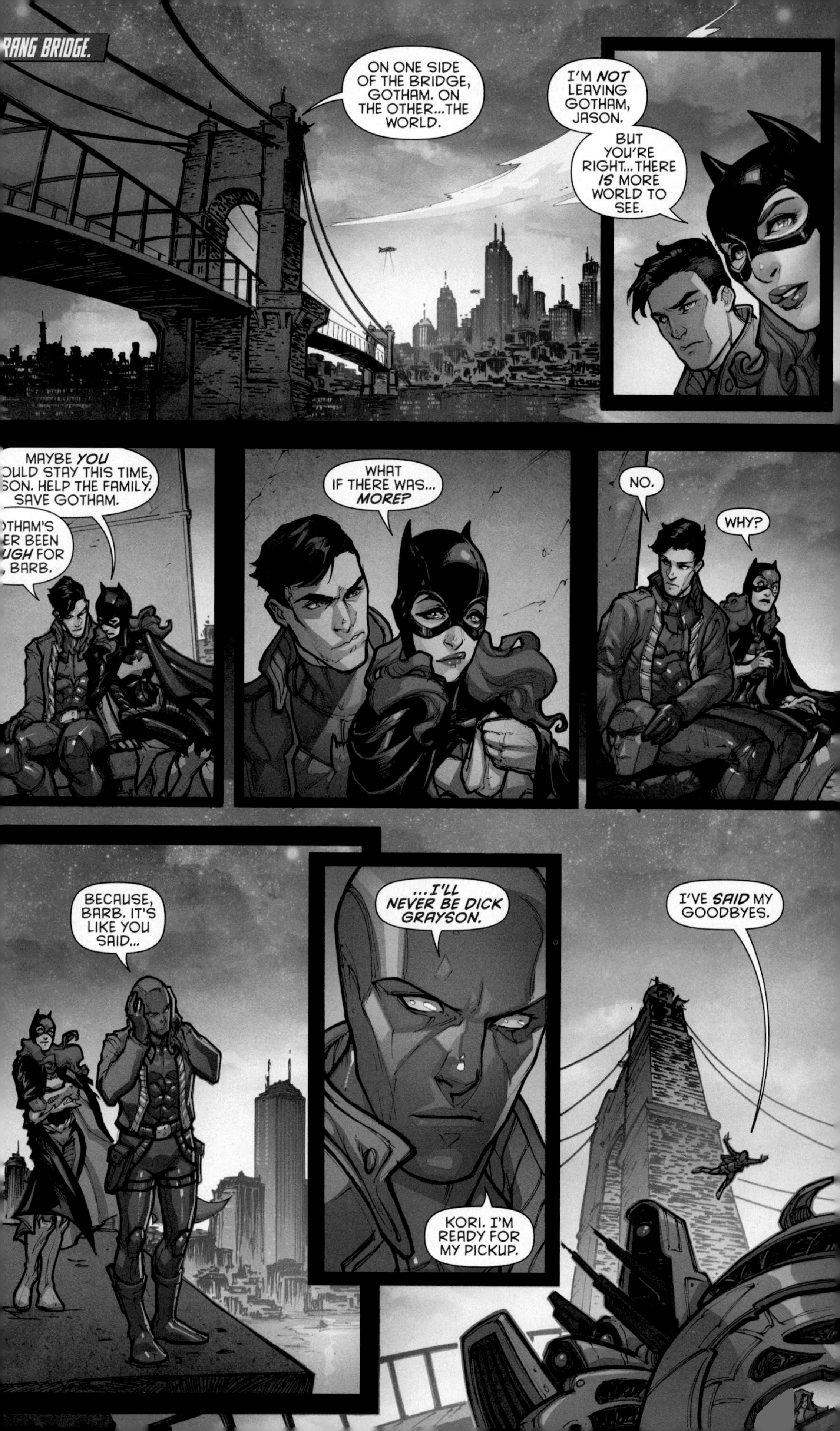
RANG BRIDGE.
ON ONE SIDE OF THE BRIDGE, GOTHAM. ON THE OTHER...THE WORLD.
I'M NOT LEAVING GOTHAM, JASON.
BUT YOU'RE RIGHT...THERE IS MORE WORLD TO SEE.
MAYBE YOU OULD STAY THIS TIME, SON. HELP THE FAMILY. SAVE GOTHAM.
OTHAM'S ER BEEN UGH FOR BARB.
WHAT IF THERE WAS... MORE?
NO.
WHY?
BECAUSE, BARB. IT'S LIKE YOU SAID...
...I'LL NEVER BE DICK GRAYSON.
KORI. I'M READY FOR MY PICKUP.
I'VE SAID MY GOODBYES.

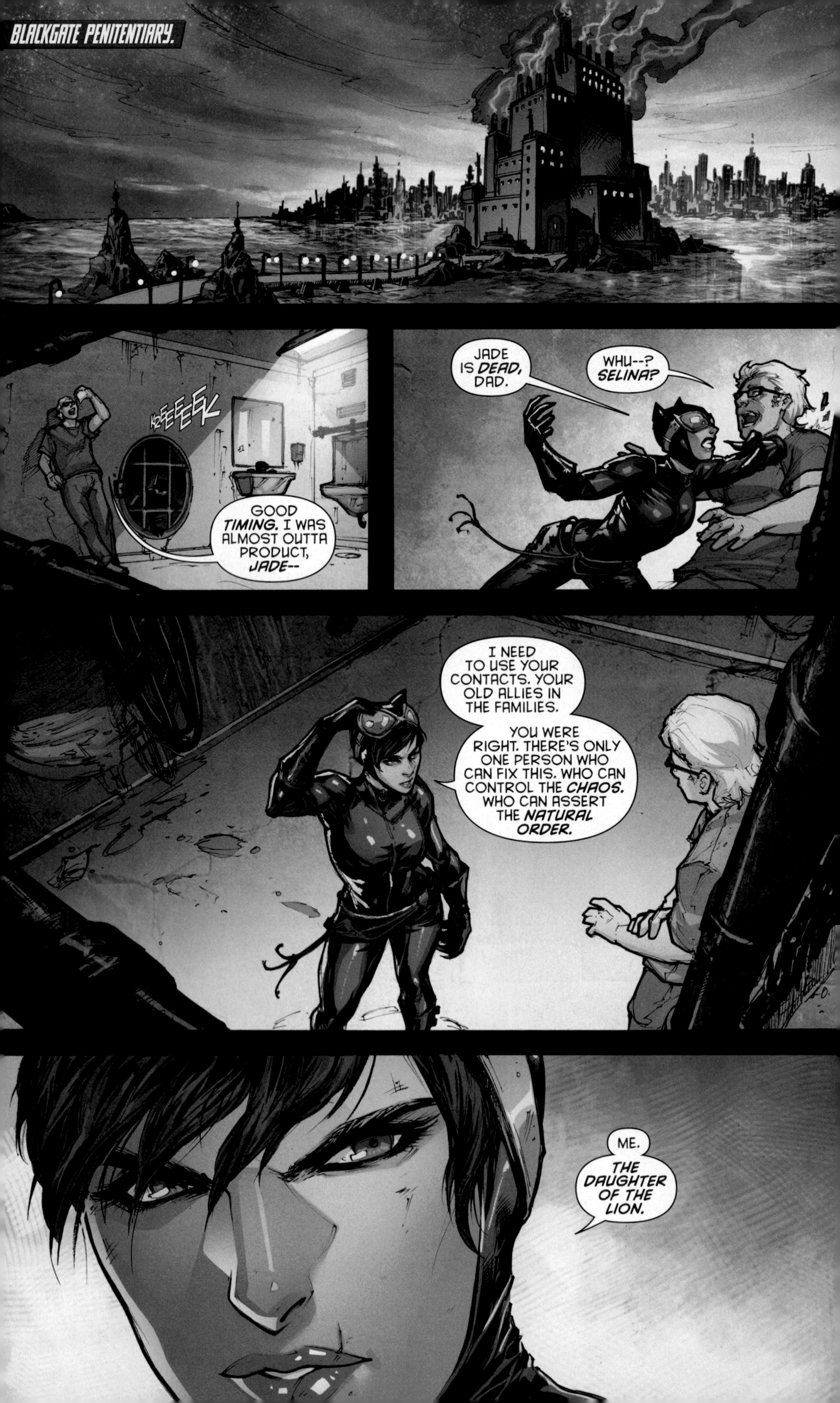
BLACKGATE PENITENTIARY.
KZEEEEEK
GOOD TIMING. I WAS ALMOST OUTTA PRODUCT, JADE--
JADE IS DEAD, DAD.
WHU--? SELINA?
I NEED TO USE YOUR CONTACTS. YOUR OLD ALLIES IN THE FAMILIES.
YOU WERE RIGHT. THERE'S ONLY ONE PERSON WHO CAN FIX THIS. WHO CAN CONTROL THE CHAOS. WHO CAN ASSERT THE NATURAL ORDER.
ME.
THE DAUGHTER OF THE LION.

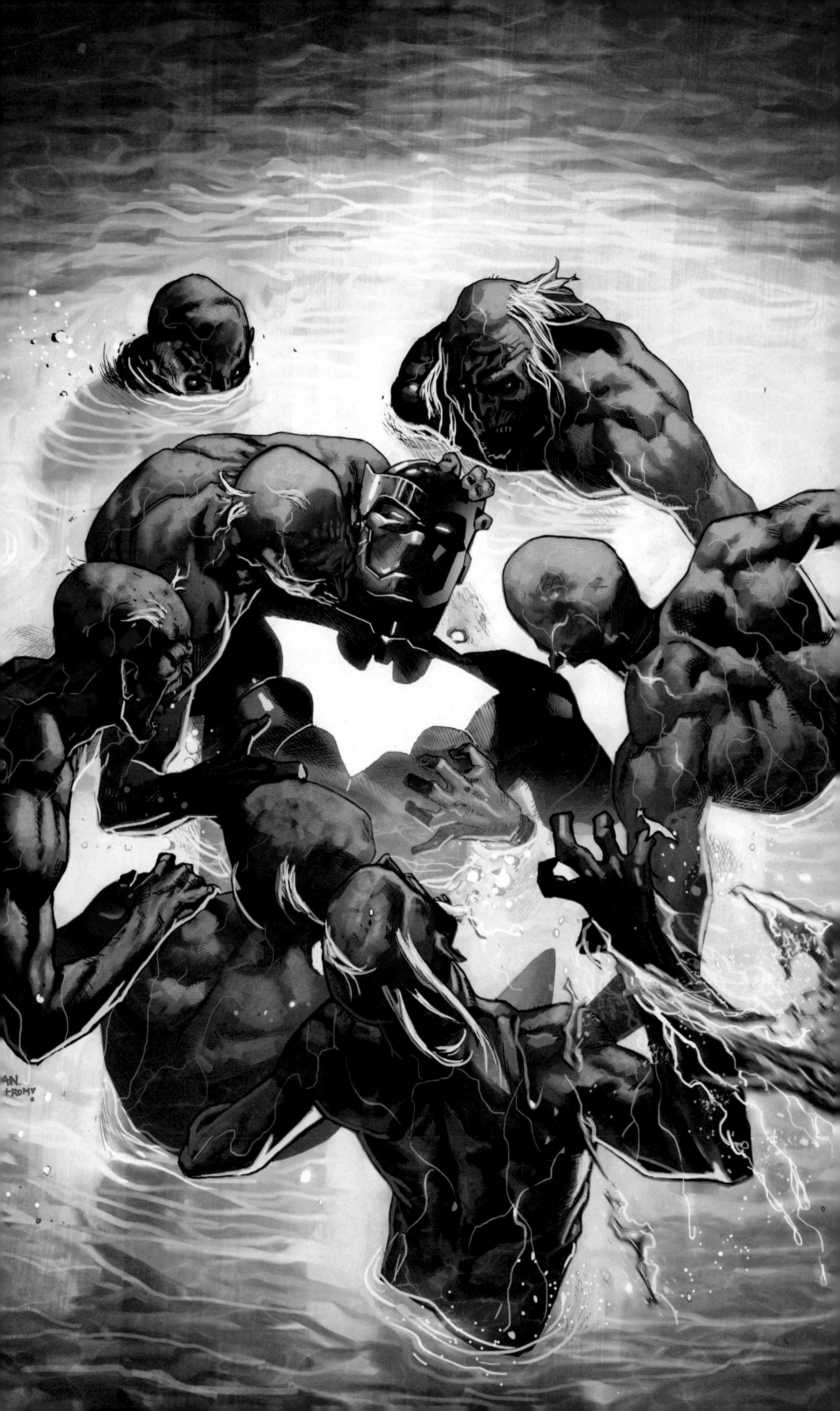

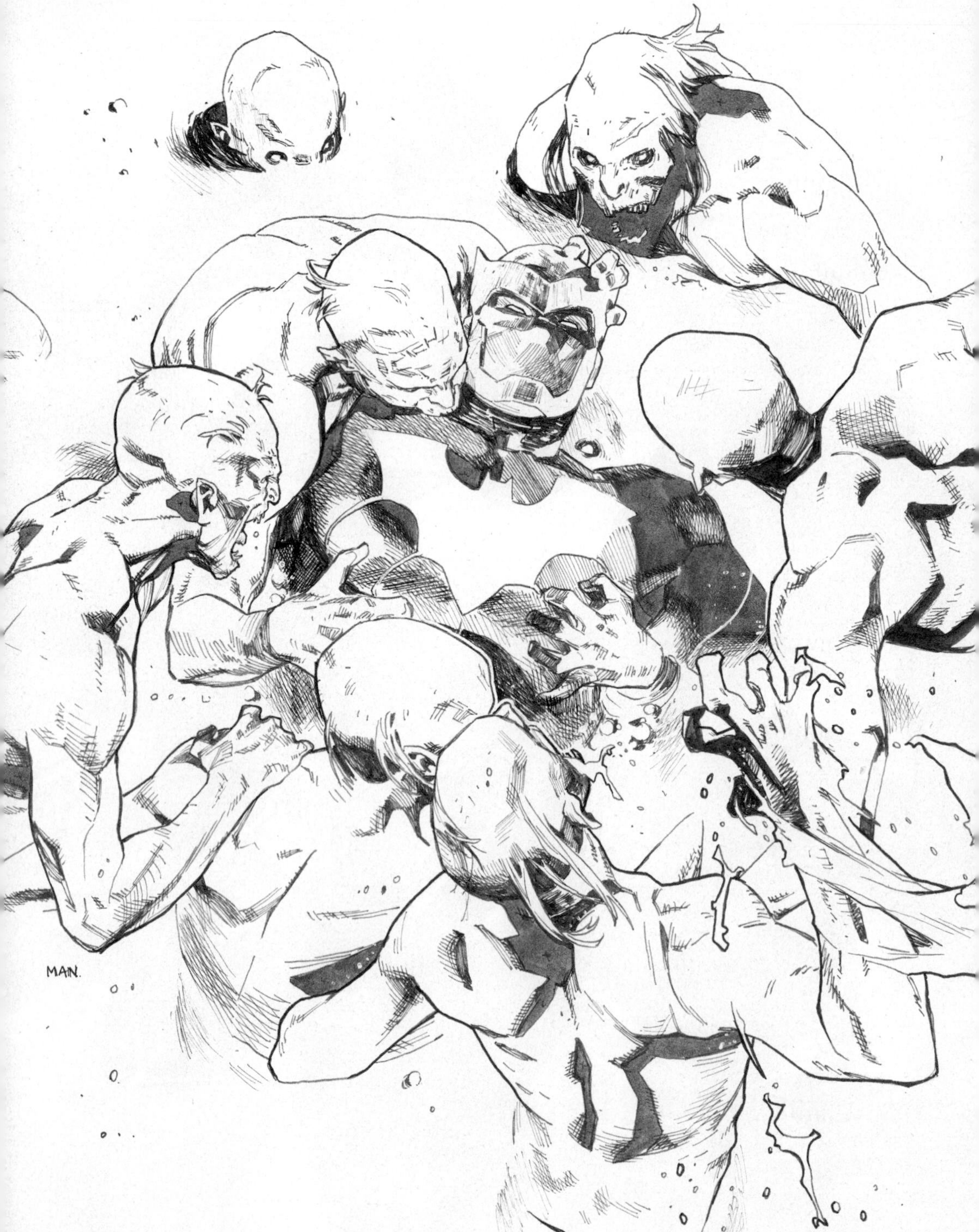
MAIN.

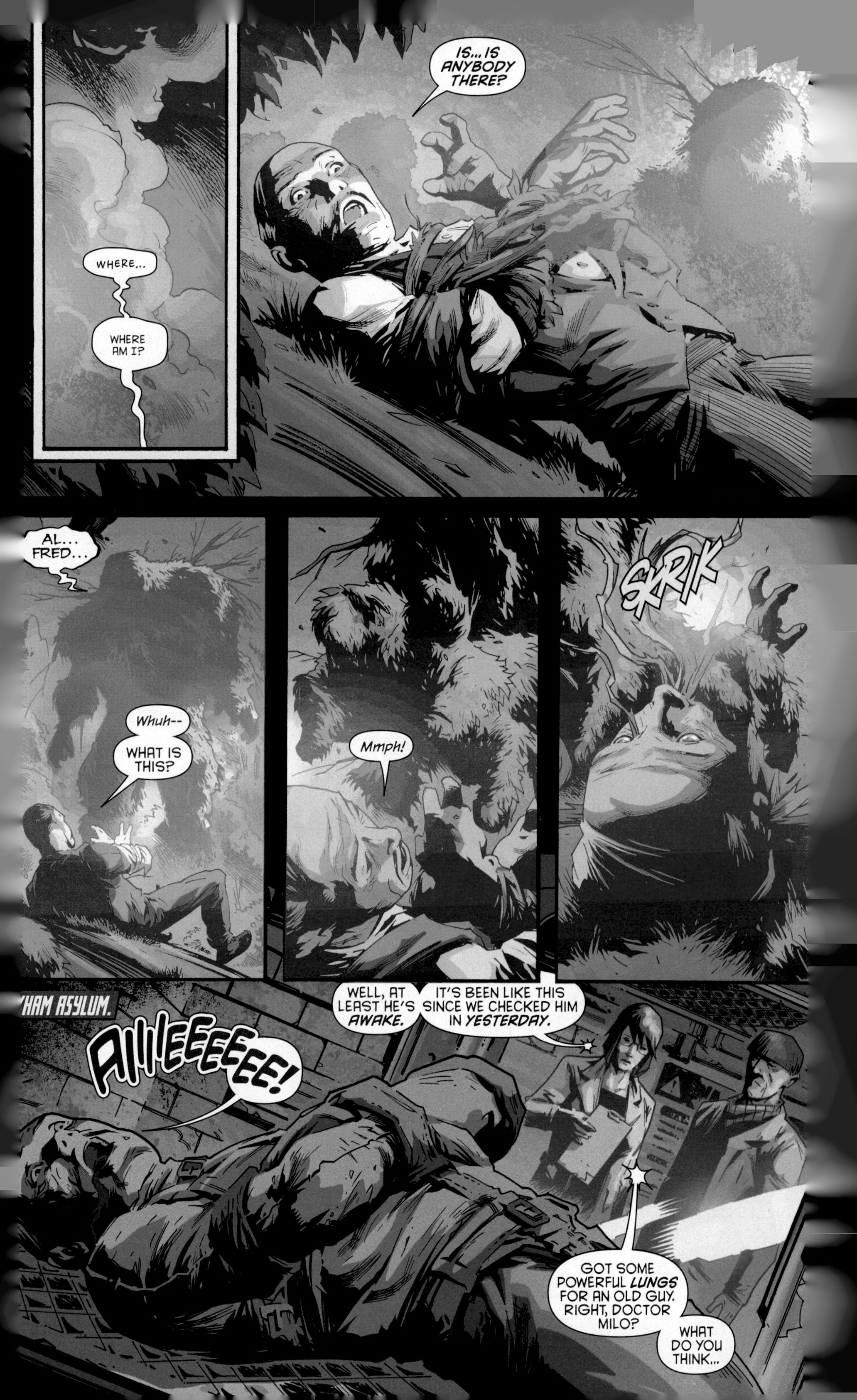
WHERE...
WHERE AM I?
IS... IS ANYBODY THERE?
AL... FRED...
Whuh--
WHAT IS THIS?
Mmph!
SKRIK
HAM ASYLUM.
AIIIEEEEEEE!
WELL, AT LEAST HE'S AWAKE.
IT'S BEEN LIKE THIS SINCE WE CHECKED HIM IN YESTERDAY.
GOT SOME POWERFUL LUNGS FOR AN OLD GUY. RIGHT, DOCTOR MILO?
WHAT DO YOU THINK...

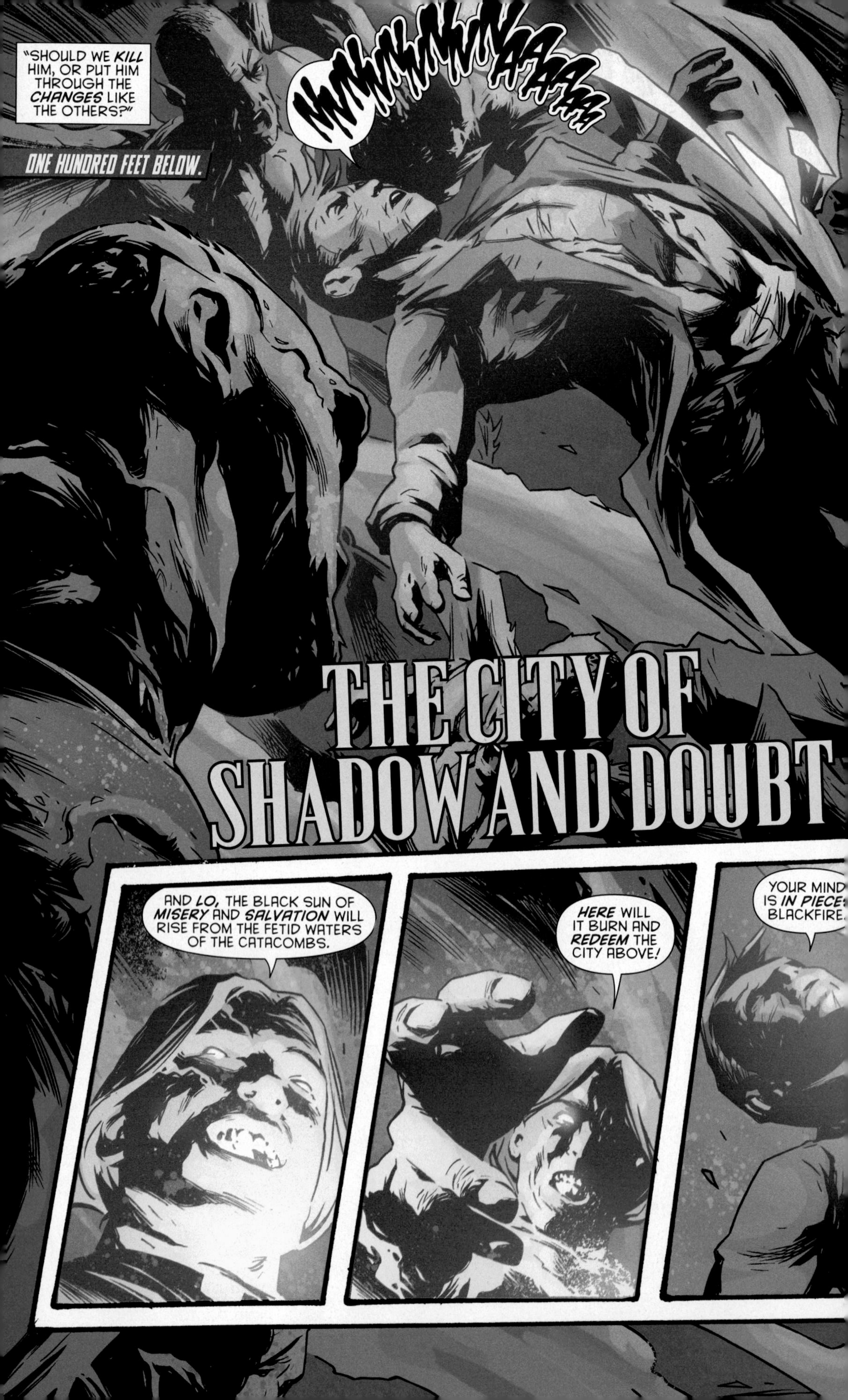
"SHOULD WE KILL HIM, OR PUT HIM THROUGH THE CHANGES LIKE THE OTHERS?"
ONE HUNDRED FEET BELOW.
THE CITY OF SHADOW AND DOUBT
AND LO, THE BLACK SUN OF MISERY AND SALVATION WILL RISE FROM THE FETID WATERS OF THE CATACOMBS.
HERE WILL IT BURN AND REDEEM THE CITY ABOVE!
YOUR MIND IS IN PIECE BLACKFIRE.

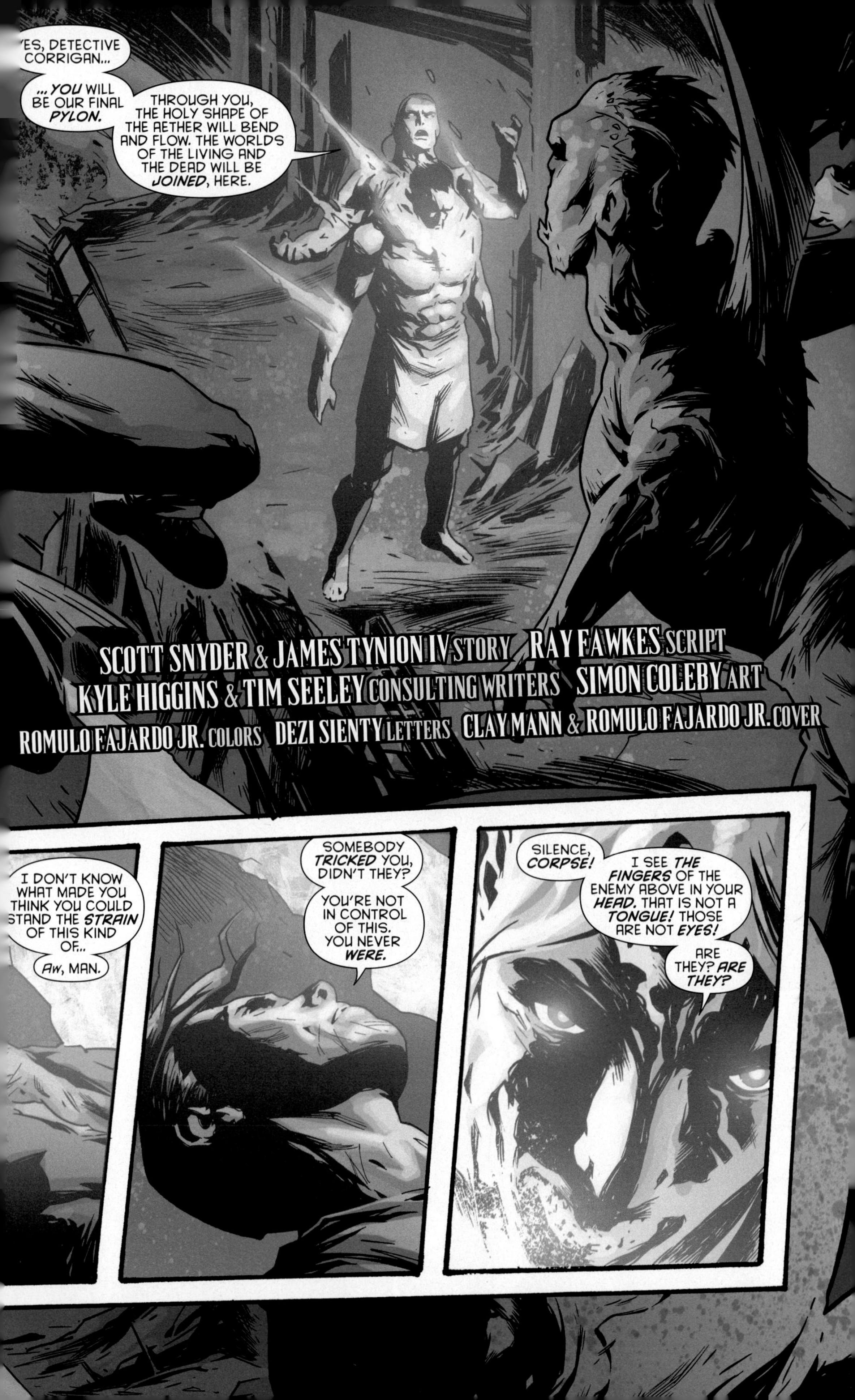
YES, DETECTIVE CORRIGAN...
...YOU WILL BE OUR FINAL PYLON.
THROUGH YOU, THE HOLY SHAPE OF THE AETHER WILL BEND AND FLOW. THE WORLDS OF THE LIVING AND THE DEAD WILL BE JOINED, HERE.
SCOTT SNYDER & JAMES TYNION IV STORY RAY FAWKES SCRIPT
KYLE HIGGINS & TIM SEELEY CONSULTING WRITERS SIMON COLEBY ART
ROMULO FAJARDO JR. COLORS DEZI SIENTY LETTERS CLAY MANN & ROMULO FAJARDO JR. COVER
I DON'T KNOW WHAT MADE YOU THINK YOU COULD STAND THE STRAIN OF THIS KIND OF...
AW, MAN.
SOMEBODY TRICKED YOU, DIDN'T THEY?
YOU'RE NOT IN CONTROL OF THIS. YOU NEVER WERE.
SILENCE, CORPSE!
I SEE THE FINGERS OF THE ENEMY ABOVE IN YOUR HEAD. THAT IS NOT A TONGUE! THOSE ARE NOT EYES!
ARE THEY? ARE THEY?

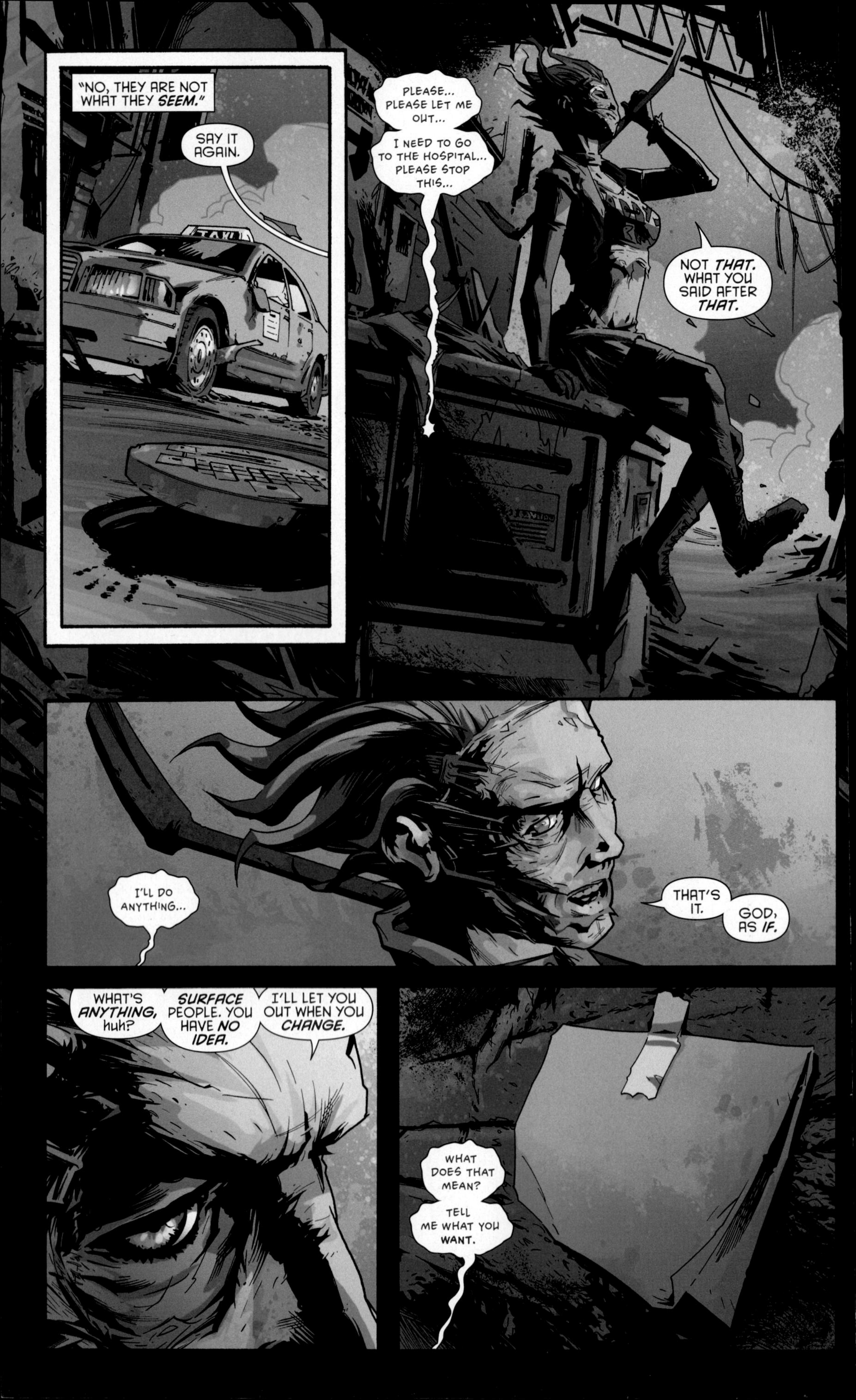
"NO, THEY ARE NOT WHAT THEY *SEEM.*"
SAY IT AGAIN.
PLEASE... PLEASE LET ME OUT...
I NEED TO GO TO THE HOSPITAL... PLEASE STOP THIS...
NOT *THAT.* WHAT YOU SAID AFTER *THAT.*
I'LL DO ANYTHING...
THAT'S IT.
GOD, AS *IF.*
WHAT'S *ANYTHING,* huh?
*SURFACE* PEOPLE. YOU HAVE *NO IDEA.*
I'LL LET YOU OUT WHEN YOU *CHANGE.*
WHAT DOES THAT MEAN?
TELL ME WHAT YOU **WANT.**

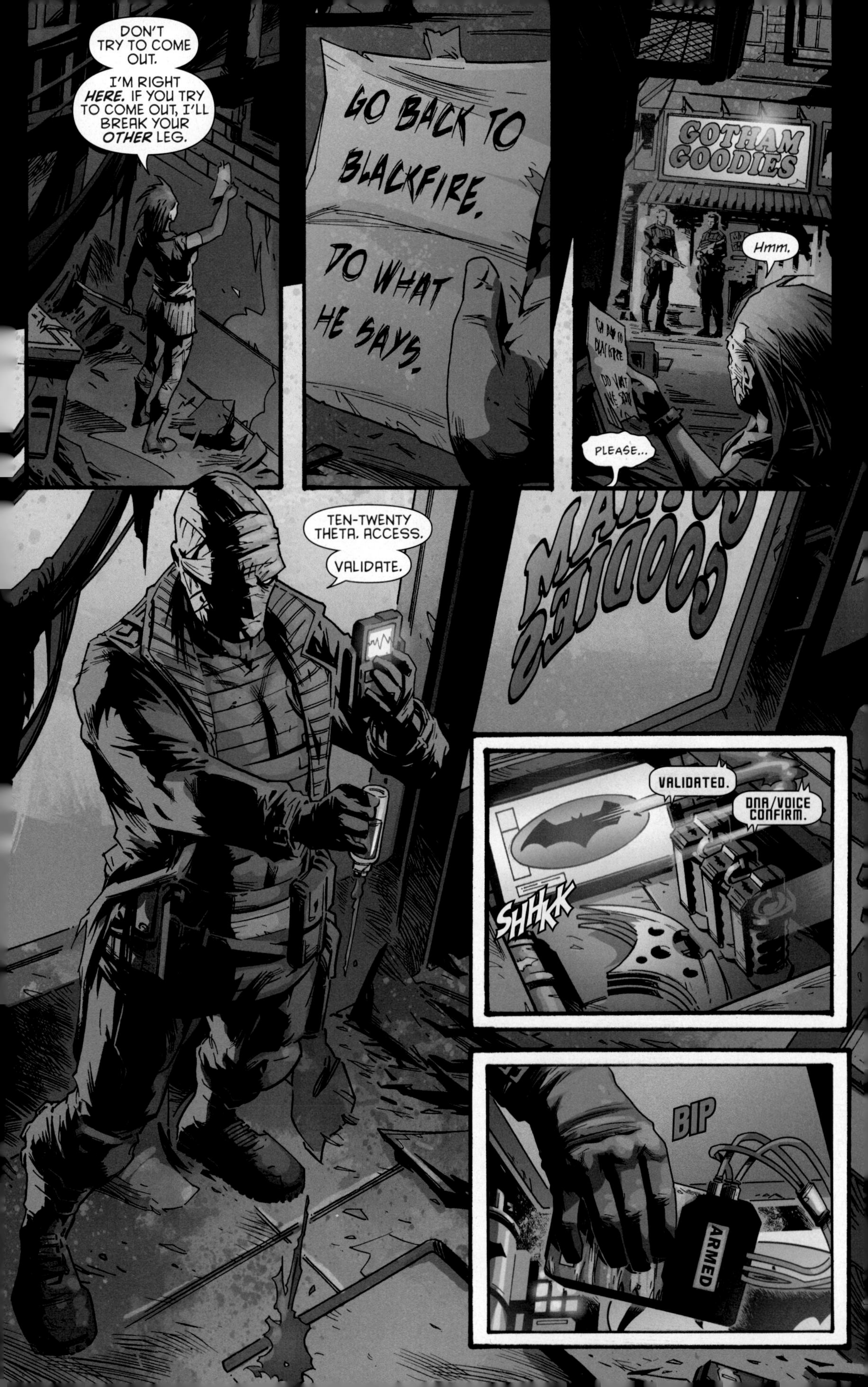
DON'T TRY TO COME OUT.
I'M RIGHT *HERE.* IF YOU TRY TO COME OUT, I'LL BREAK YOUR *OTHER* LEG.
GO BACK TO BLACKFIRE. DO WHAT HE SAYS.
GOTHAM GOODIES
Hmm.
PLEASE...
TEN-TWENTY THETA. ACCESS.
VALIDATE.
VALIDATED.
DNA/VOICE CONFIRM.
SHHKK
BIP
ARMED

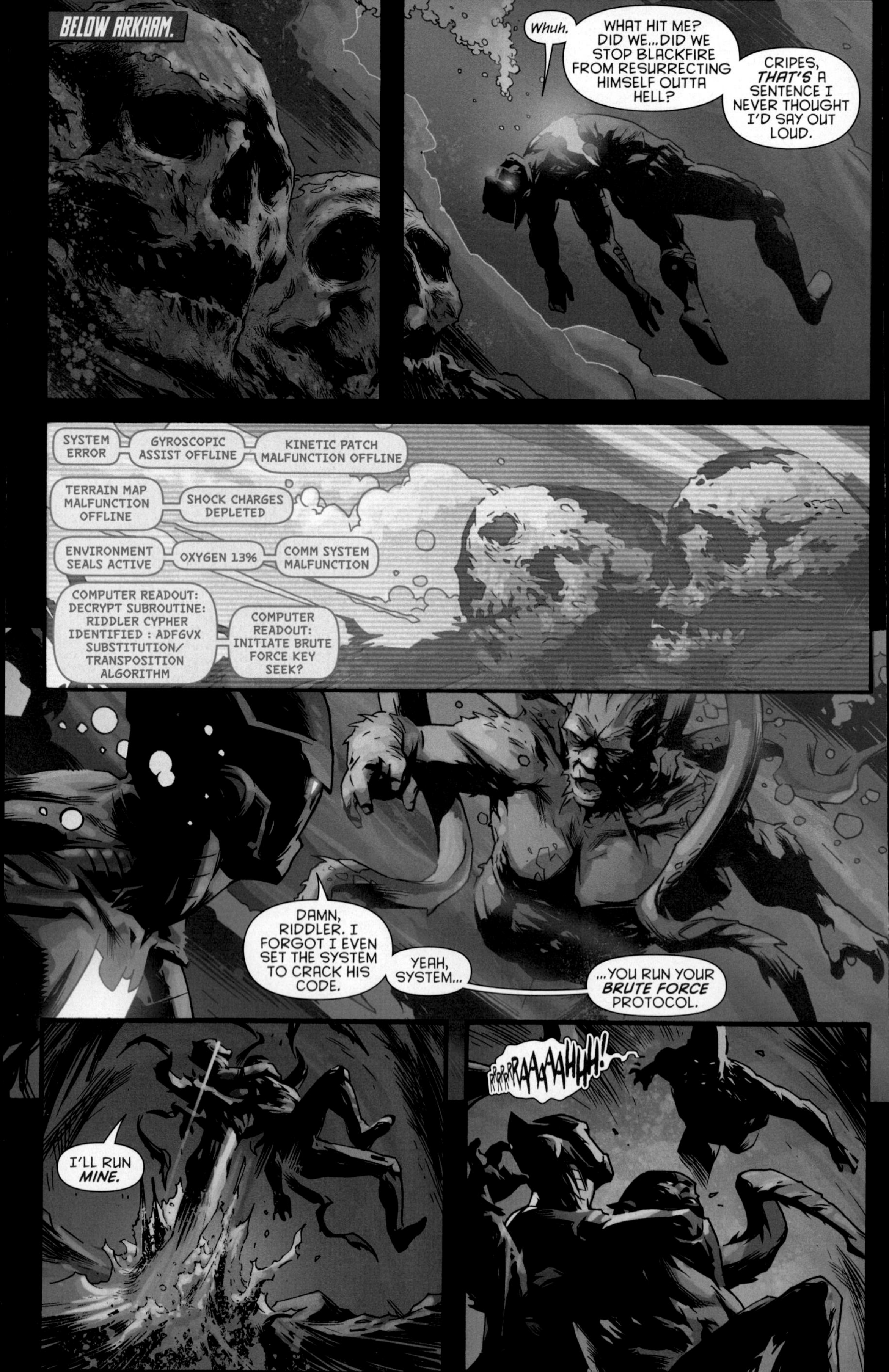
BELOW ARKHAM.
Whuh.
WHAT HIT ME? DID WE...DID WE STOP BLACKFIRE FROM RESURRECTING HIMSELF OUTTA HELL?
CRIPES, THAT'S A SENTENCE I NEVER THOUGHT I'D SAY OUT LOUD.
SYSTEM ERROR
GYROSCOPIC ASSIST OFFLINE
KINETIC PATCH MALFUNCTION OFFLINE
TERRAIN MAP MALFUNCTION OFFLINE
SHOCK CHARGES DEPLETED
ENVIRONMENT SEALS ACTIVE
OXYGEN 13%
COMM SYSTEM MALFUNCTION
COMPUTER READOUT: DECRYPT SUBROUTINE: RIDDLER CYPHER IDENTIFIED : ADFGVX SUBSTITUTION/ TRANSPOSITION ALGORITHM
COMPUTER READOUT: INITIATE BRUTE FORCE KEY SEEK?
DAMN, RIDDLER. I FORGOT I EVEN SET THE SYSTEM TO CRACK HIS CODE.
YEAH, SYSTEM...
...YOU RUN YOUR BRUTE FORCE PROTOCOL.
I'LL RUN MINE.
RRRRRAAAAAHHH!

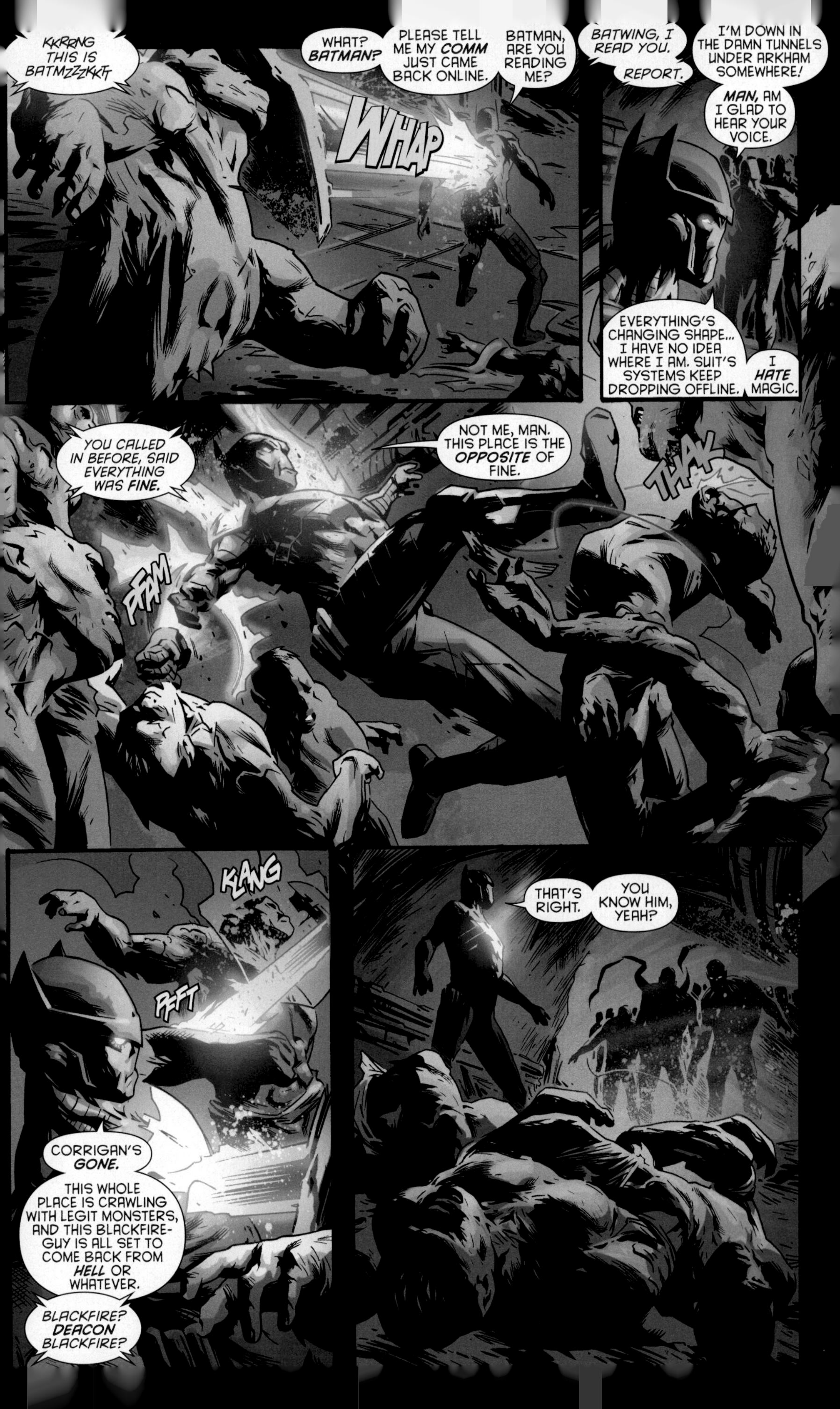
KKRRNG THIS IS BATMZZZKKTT
WHAT? BATMAN?
PLEASE TELL ME MY COMM JUST CAME BACK ONLINE.
BATMAN, ARE YOU READING ME?
WHAP
BATWING, I READ YOU.
REPORT.
I'M DOWN IN THE DAMN TUNNELS UNDER ARKHAM SOMEWHERE!
MAN, AM I GLAD TO HEAR YOUR VOICE.
EVERYTHING'S CHANGING SHAPE... I HAVE NO IDEA WHERE I AM. SUIT'S SYSTEMS KEEP DROPPING OFFLINE.
I HATE MAGIC.
YOU CALLED IN BEFORE, SAID EVERYTHING WAS FINE.
NOT ME, MAN. THIS PLACE IS THE OPPOSITE OF FINE.
THAK
PFAM
KLANG
PFFT
CORRIGAN'S GONE.
THIS WHOLE PLACE IS CRAWLING WITH LEGIT MONSTERS, AND THIS BLACKFIRE-GUY IS ALL SET TO COME BACK FROM HELL OR WHATEVER.
BLACKFIRE? DEACON BLACKFIRE?
THAT'S RIGHT.
YOU KNOW HIM, YEAH?

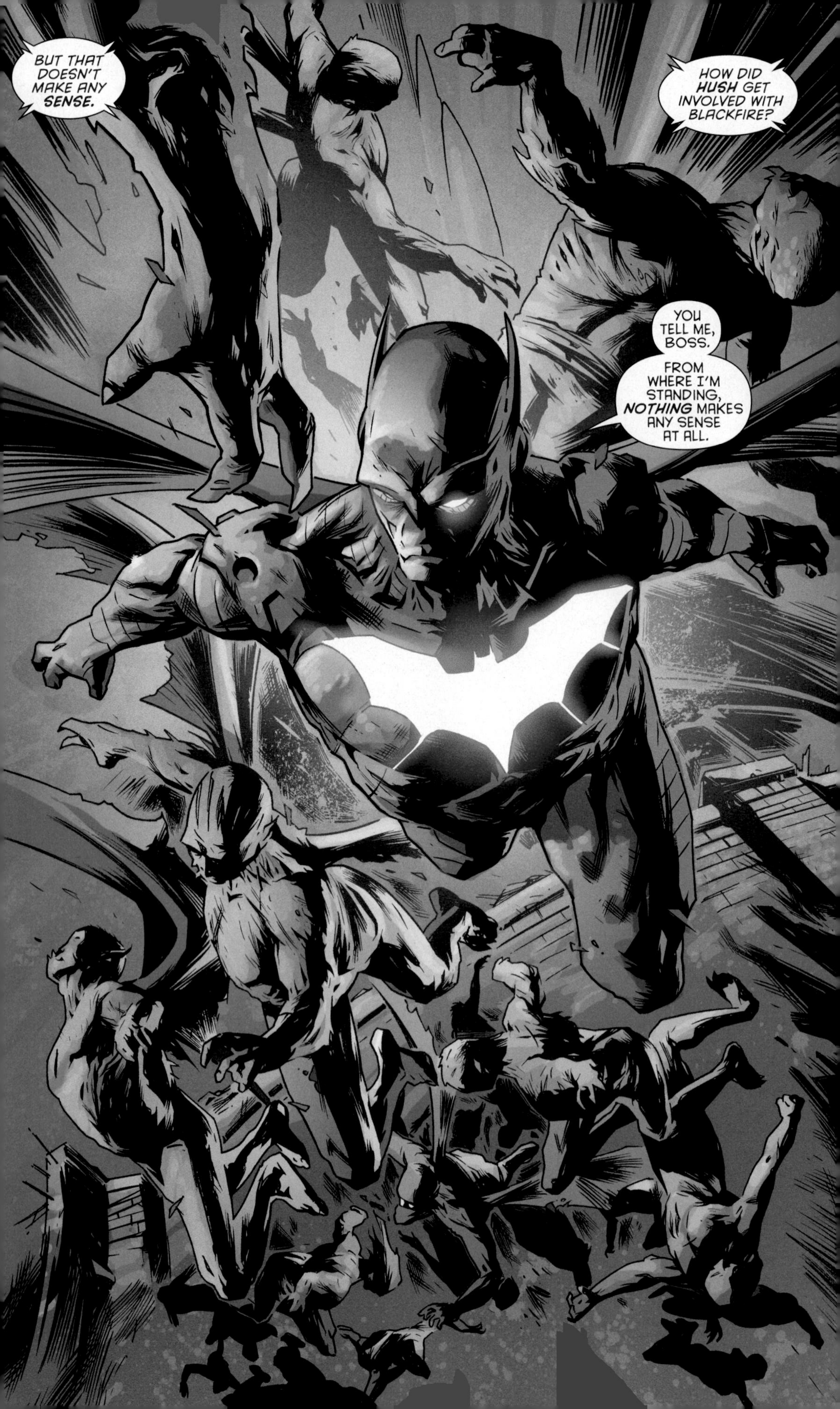

BUT THAT DOESN'T MAKE ANY SENSE.
HOW DID HUSH GET INVOLVED WITH BLACKFIRE?
YOU TELL ME, BOSS.
FROM WHERE I'M STANDING, NOTHING MAKES ANY SENSE AT ALL.

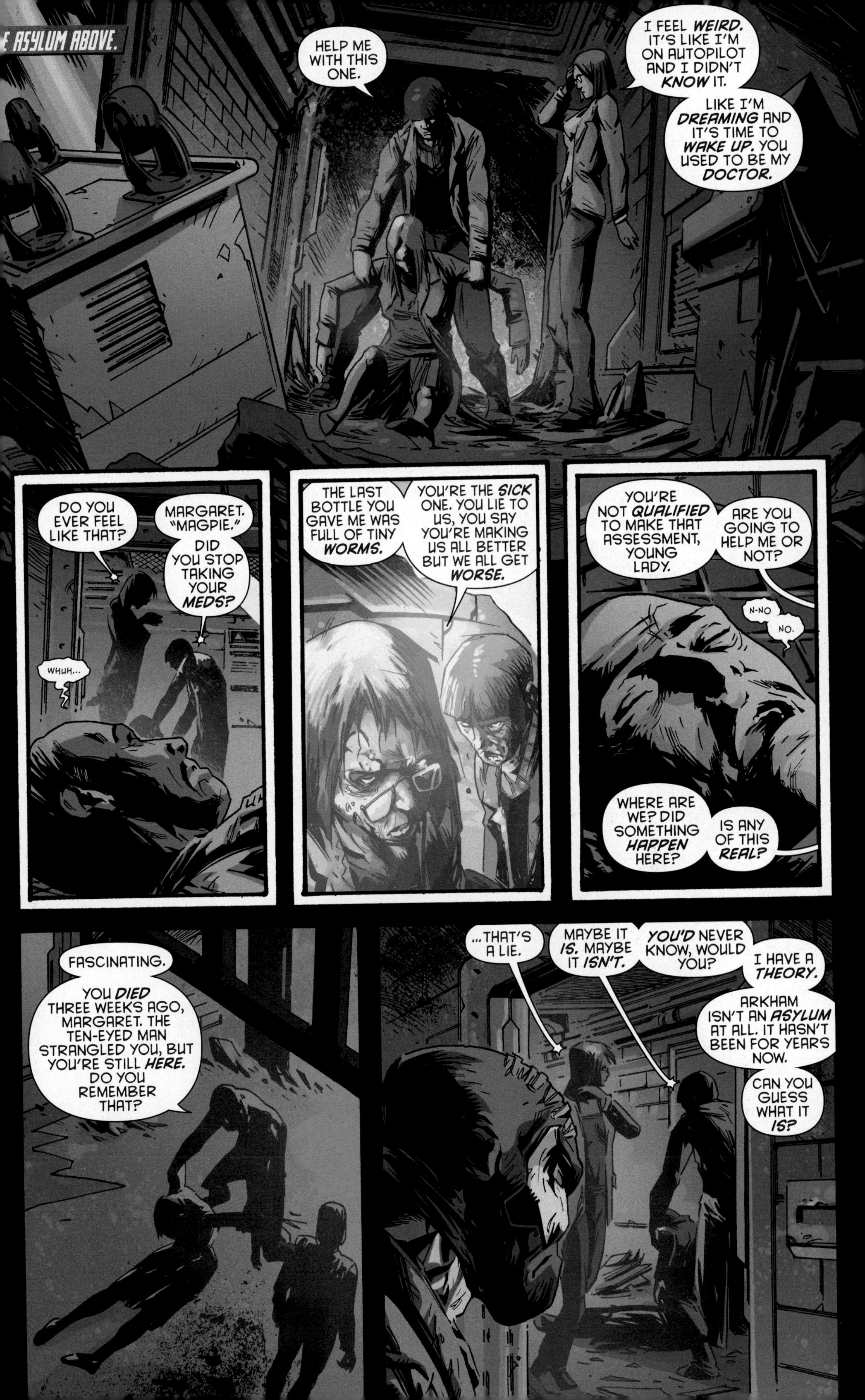

E ASYLUM ABOVE.
HELP ME WITH THIS ONE.
I FEEL WEIRD. IT'S LIKE I'M ON AUTOPILOT AND I DIDN'T KNOW IT.
LIKE I'M DREAMING AND IT'S TIME TO WAKE UP. YOU USED TO BE MY DOCTOR.
DO YOU EVER FEEL LIKE THAT?
MARGARET. "MAGPIE."
DID YOU STOP TAKING YOUR MEDS?
WHUH...
THE LAST BOTTLE YOU GAVE ME WAS FULL OF TINY WORMS.
YOU'RE THE SICK ONE. YOU LIE TO US, YOU SAY YOU'RE MAKING US ALL BETTER BUT WE ALL GET WORSE.
YOU'RE NOT QUALIFIED TO MAKE THAT ASSESSMENT, YOUNG LADY.
ARE YOU GOING TO HELP ME OR NOT?
N-NO
NO.
WHERE ARE WE? DID SOMETHING HAPPEN HERE?
IS ANY OF THIS REAL?
FASCINATING.
YOU DIED THREE WEEKS AGO, MARGARET. THE TEN-EYED MAN STRANGLED YOU, BUT YOU'RE STILL HERE. DO YOU REMEMBER THAT?
...THAT'S A LIE.
MAYBE IT IS. MAYBE IT ISN'T.
YOU'D NEVER KNOW, WOULD YOU?
I HAVE A THEORY.
ARKHAM ISN'T AN ASYLUM AT ALL. IT HASN'T BEEN FOR YEARS NOW.
CAN YOU GUESS WHAT IT IS?

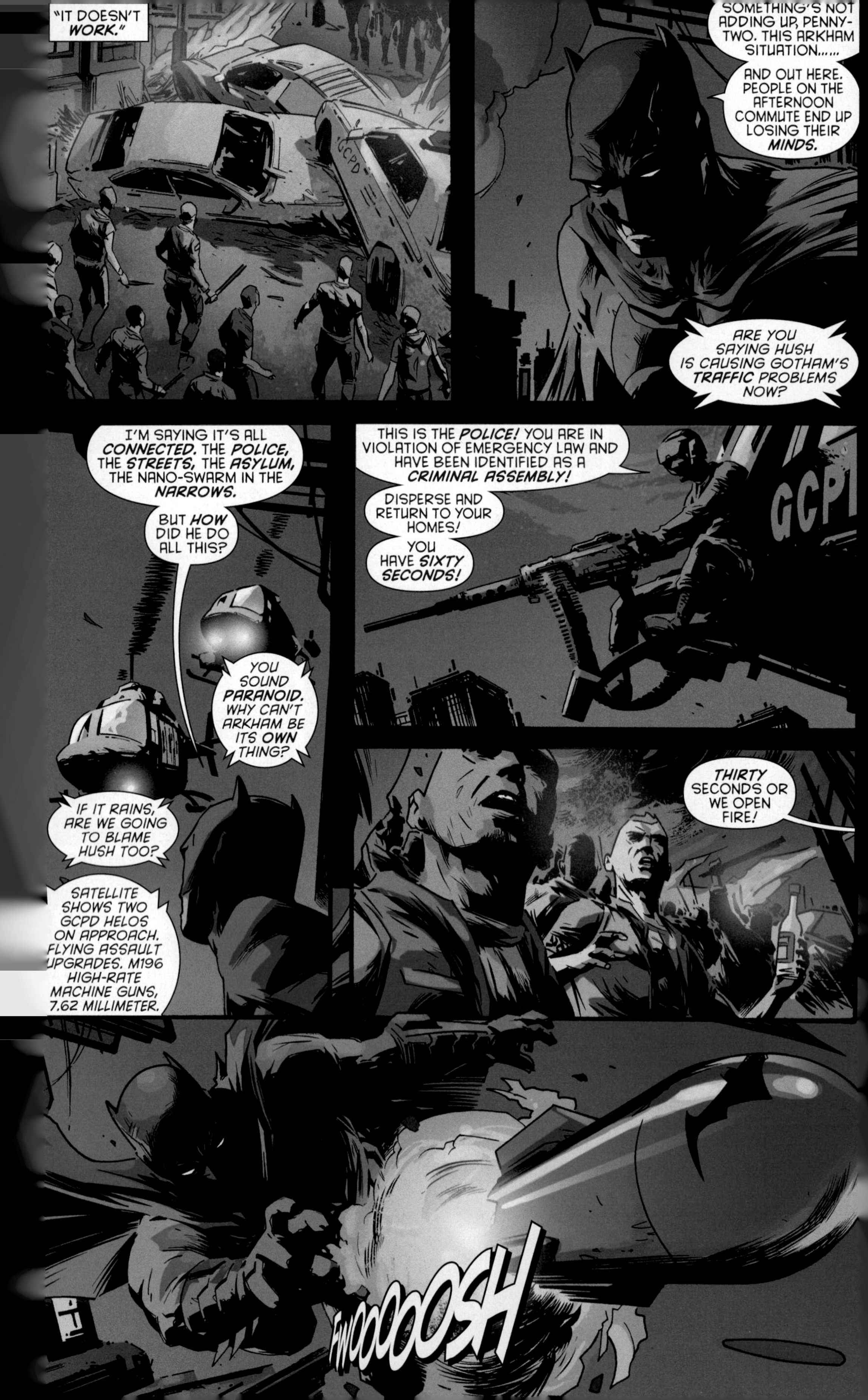
"IT DOESN'T WORK."
SOMETHING'S NOT ADDING UP, PENNY-TWO. THIS ARKHAM SITUATION......
AND OUT HERE. PEOPLE ON THE AFTERNOON COMMUTE END UP LOSING THEIR MINDS.
ARE YOU SAYING HUSH IS CAUSING GOTHAM'S TRAFFIC PROBLEMS NOW?
I'M SAYING IT'S ALL CONNECTED. THE POLICE, THE STREETS, THE ASYLUM, THE NANO-SWARM IN THE NARROWS.
BUT HOW DID HE DO ALL THIS?
YOU SOUND PARANOID. WHY CAN'T ARKHAM BE ITS OWN THING?
IF IT RAINS, ARE WE GOING TO BLAME HUSH TOO?
SATELLITE SHOWS TWO GCPD HELOS ON APPROACH. FLYING ASSAULT UPGRADES. M196 HIGH-RATE MACHINE GUNS, 7.62 MILLIMETER.
THIS IS THE POLICE! YOU ARE IN VIOLATION OF EMERGENCY LAW AND HAVE BEEN IDENTIFIED AS A CRIMINAL ASSEMBLY!
DISPERSE AND RETURN TO YOUR HOMES!
YOU HAVE SIXTY SECONDS!
THIRTY SECONDS OR WE OPEN FIRE!
FWOOOOOSH

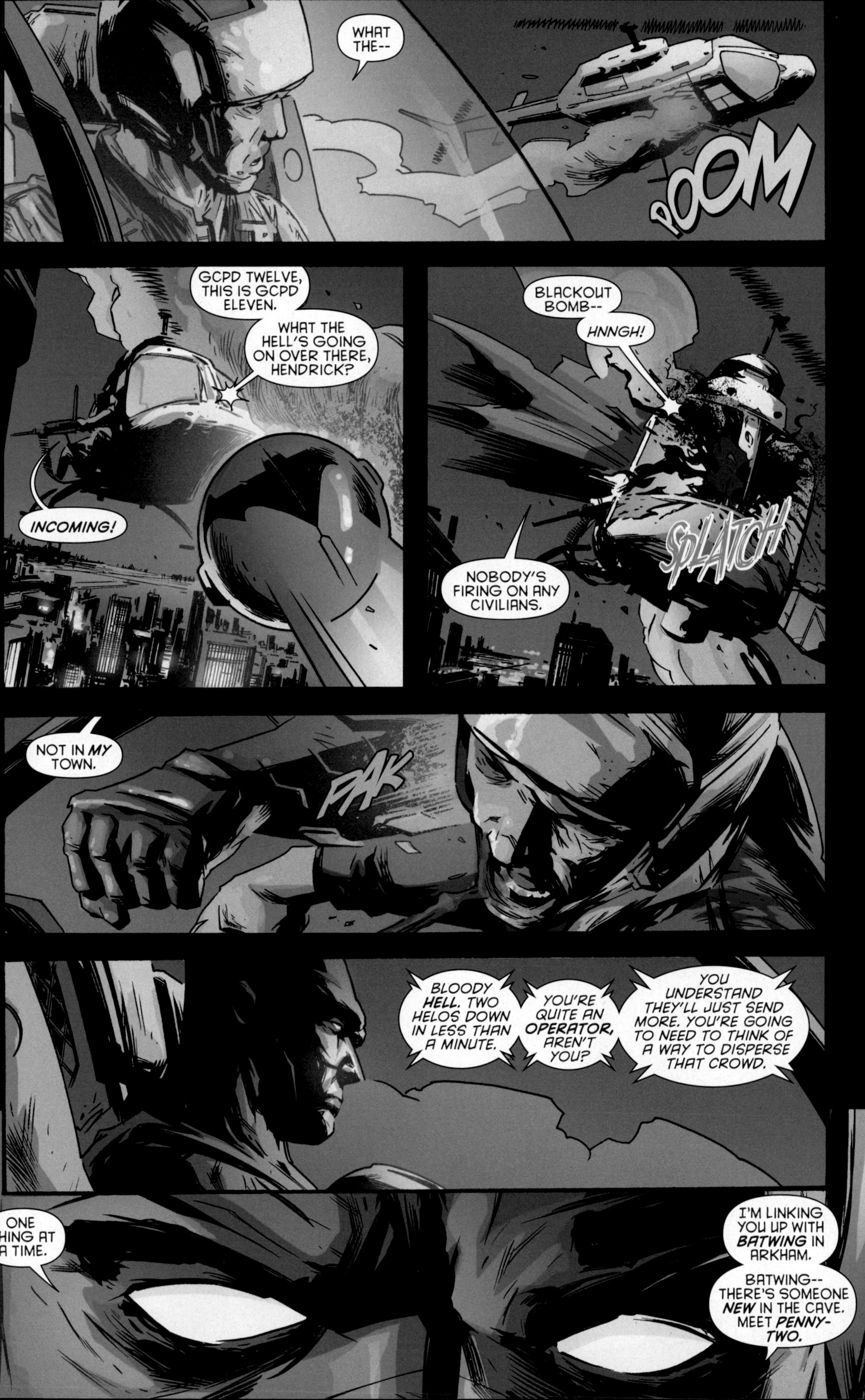
WHAT THE--
POOM
GCPD TWELVE, THIS IS GCPD ELEVEN.
WHAT THE HELL'S GOING ON OVER THERE, HENDRICK?
INCOMING!
BLACKOUT BOMB--
HNNGH!
SPLATCH
NOBODY'S FIRING ON ANY CIVILIANS.
NOT IN MY TOWN.
PAK
BLOODY HELL. TWO HELOS DOWN IN LESS THAN A MINUTE.
YOU'RE QUITE AN OPERATOR, AREN'T YOU?
YOU UNDERSTAND THEY'LL JUST SEND MORE. YOU'RE GOING TO NEED TO THINK OF A WAY TO DISPERSE THAT CROWD.
ONE THING AT A TIME.
I'M LINKING YOU UP WITH BATWING IN ARKHAM.
BATWING-- THERE'S SOMEONE NEW IN THE CAVE. MEET PENNY-TWO.

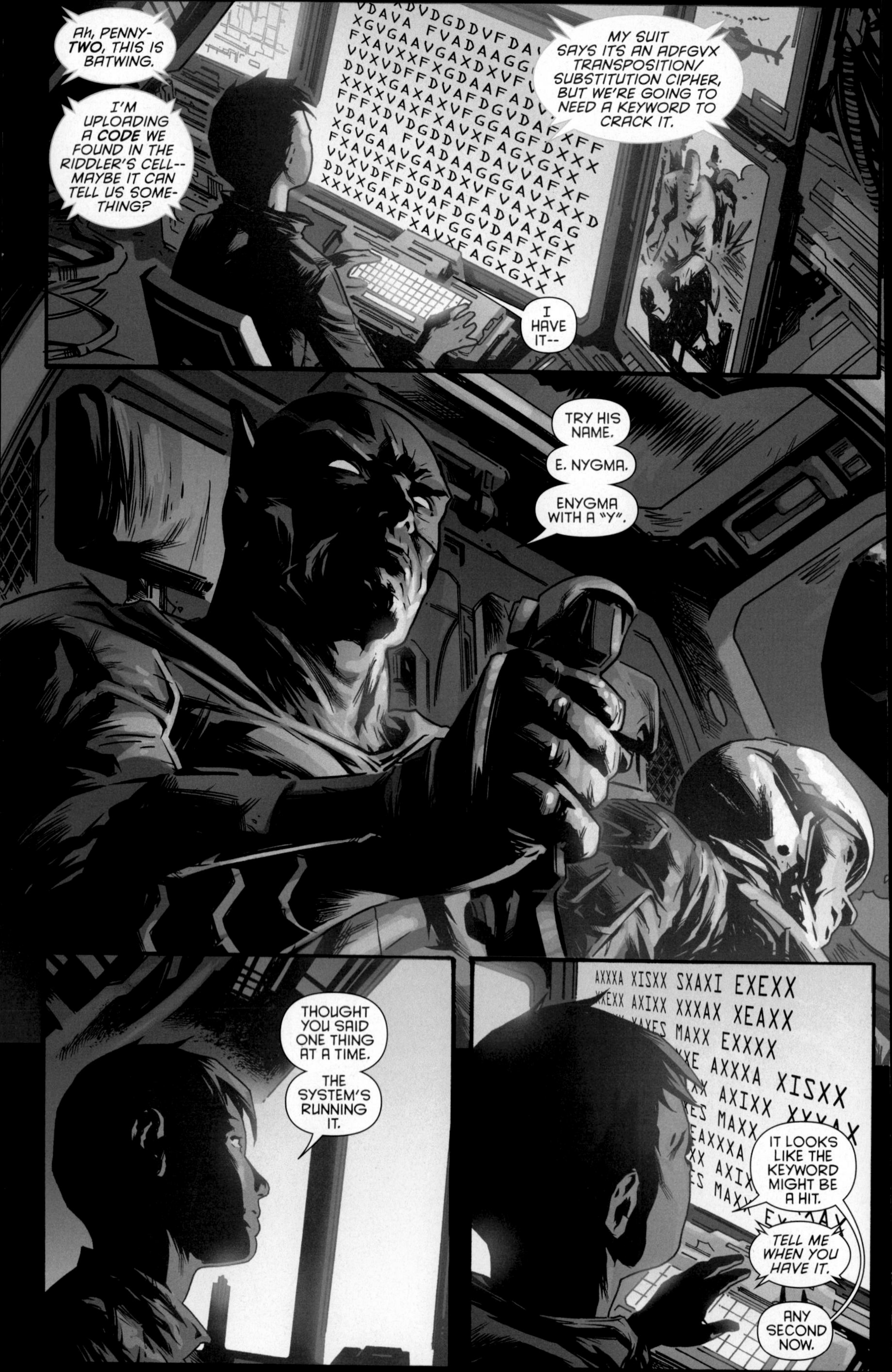
Ah, PENNY-TWO, THIS IS BATWING.
I'M UPLOADING A CODE WE FOUND IN THE RIDDLER'S CELL--MAYBE IT CAN TELL US SOMETHING?
MY SUIT SAYS ITS AN ADFGVX TRANSPOSITION/SUBSTITUTION CIPHER, BUT WE'RE GOING TO NEED A KEYWORD TO CRACK IT.
I HAVE IT--
TRY HIS NAME.
E. NYGMA.
ENYGMA WITH A "Y".
THOUGHT YOU SAID ONE THING AT A TIME.
THE SYSTEM'S RUNNING IT.
IT LOOKS LIKE THE KEYWORD MIGHT BE A HIT.
TELL ME WHEN YOU HAVE IT.
ANY SECOND NOW.

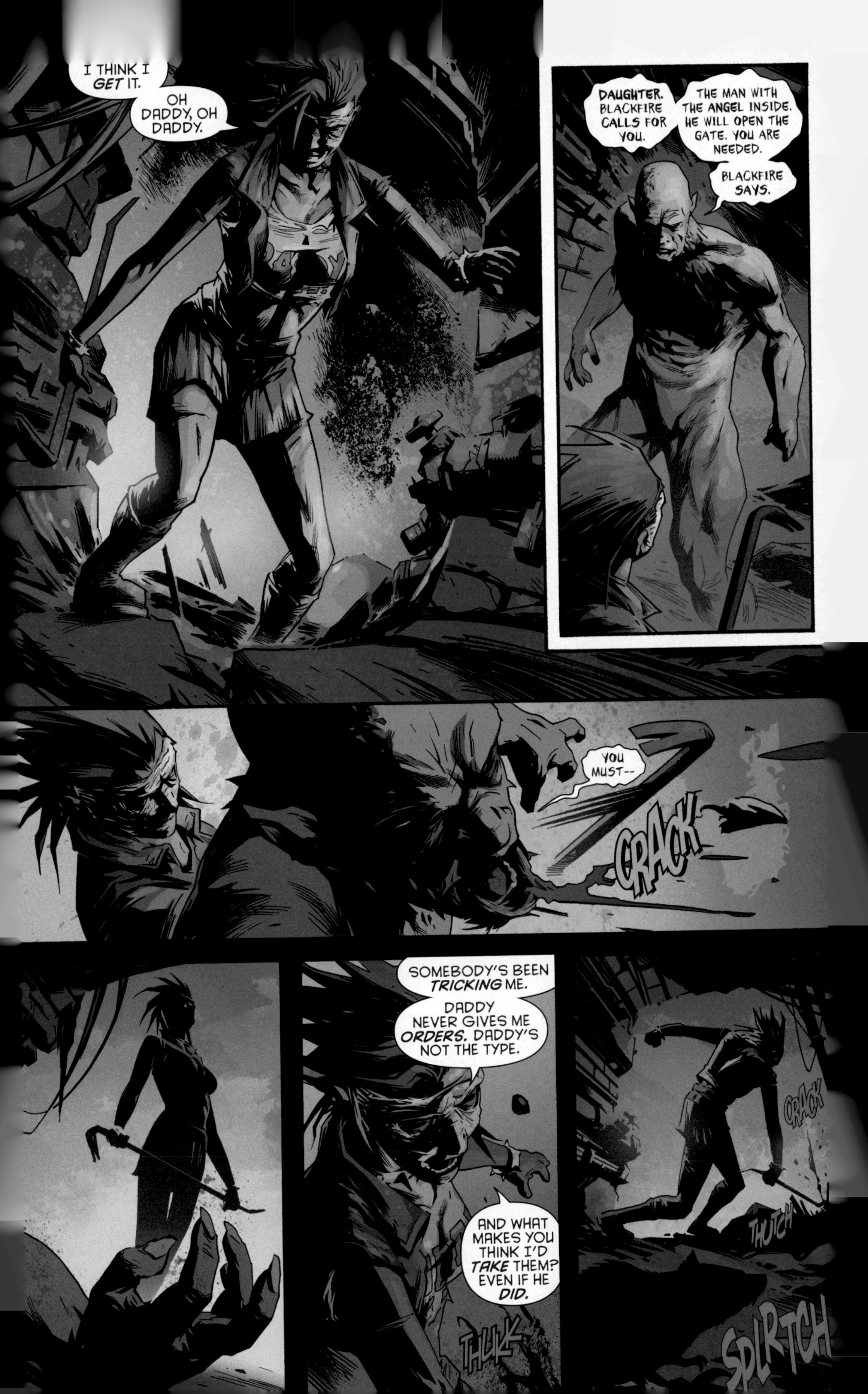
I THINK I GET IT.
OH DADDY, OH DADDY.
DAUGHTER. BLACKFIRE CALLS FOR YOU.
THE MAN WITH THE ANGEL INSIDE. HE WILL OPEN THE GATE. YOU ARE NEEDED.
BLACKFIRE SAYS.
YOU MUST--
CRACK
SOMEBODY'S BEEN TRICKING ME.
DADDY NEVER GIVES ME ORDERS. DADDY'S NOT THE TYPE.
AND WHAT MAKES YOU THINK I'D TAKE THEM? EVEN IF HE DID.
THUK
CRACK
THUTCH
SPLRTCH

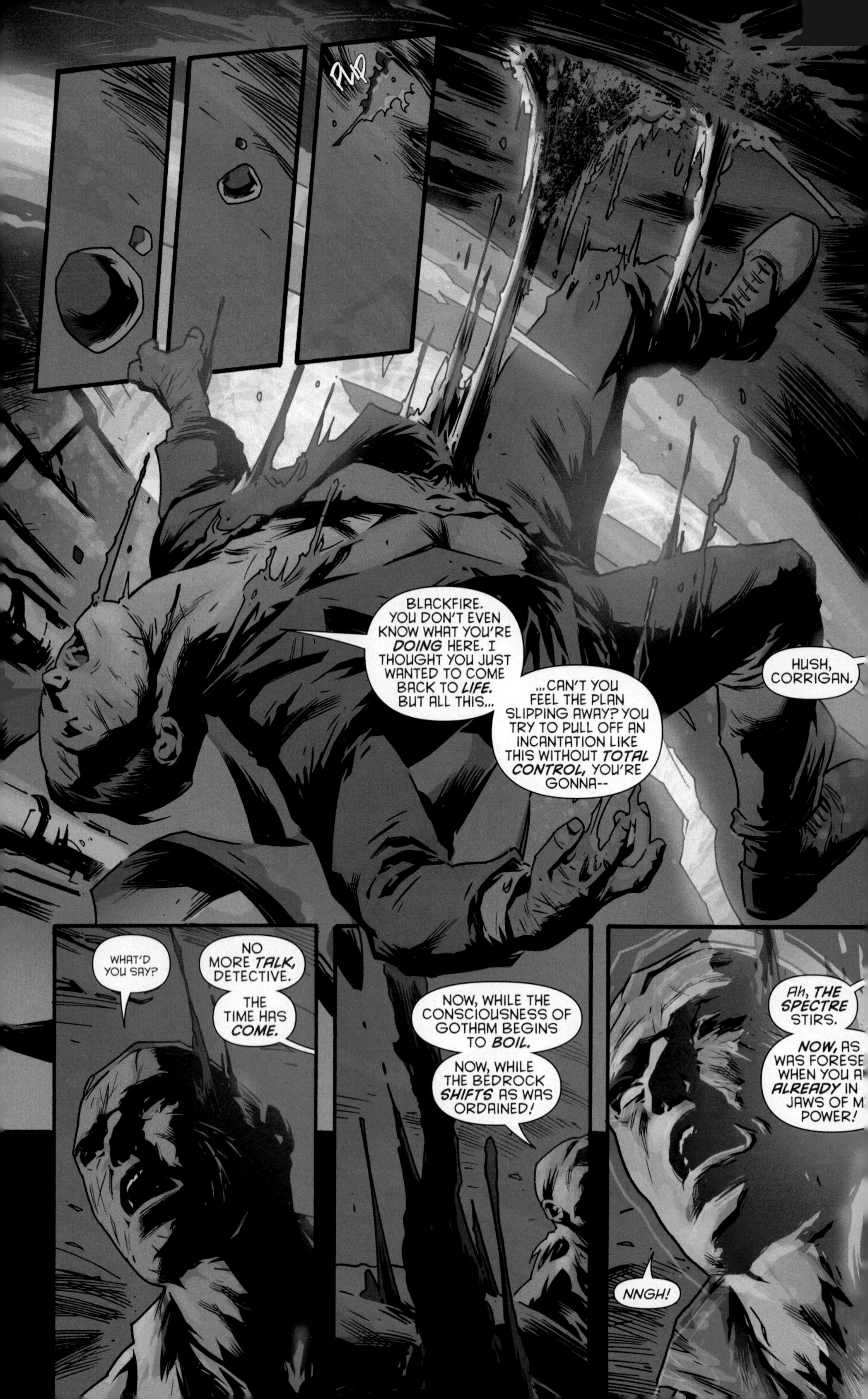
PLIP
BLACKFIRE. YOU DON'T EVEN KNOW WHAT YOU'RE DOING HERE. I THOUGHT YOU JUST WANTED TO COME BACK TO LIFE. BUT ALL THIS...
...CAN'T YOU FEEL THE PLAN SLIPPING AWAY? YOU TRY TO PULL OFF AN INCANTATION LIKE THIS WITHOUT TOTAL CONTROL, YOU'RE GONNA--
HUSH, CORRIGAN.
WHAT'D YOU SAY?
NO MORE TALK, DETECTIVE.
THE TIME HAS COME.
NOW, WHILE THE CONSCIOUSNESS OF GOTHAM BEGINS TO BOIL.
NOW, WHILE THE BEDROCK SHIFTS AS WAS ORDAINED!
Ah, THE SPECTRE STIRS.
NNGH!

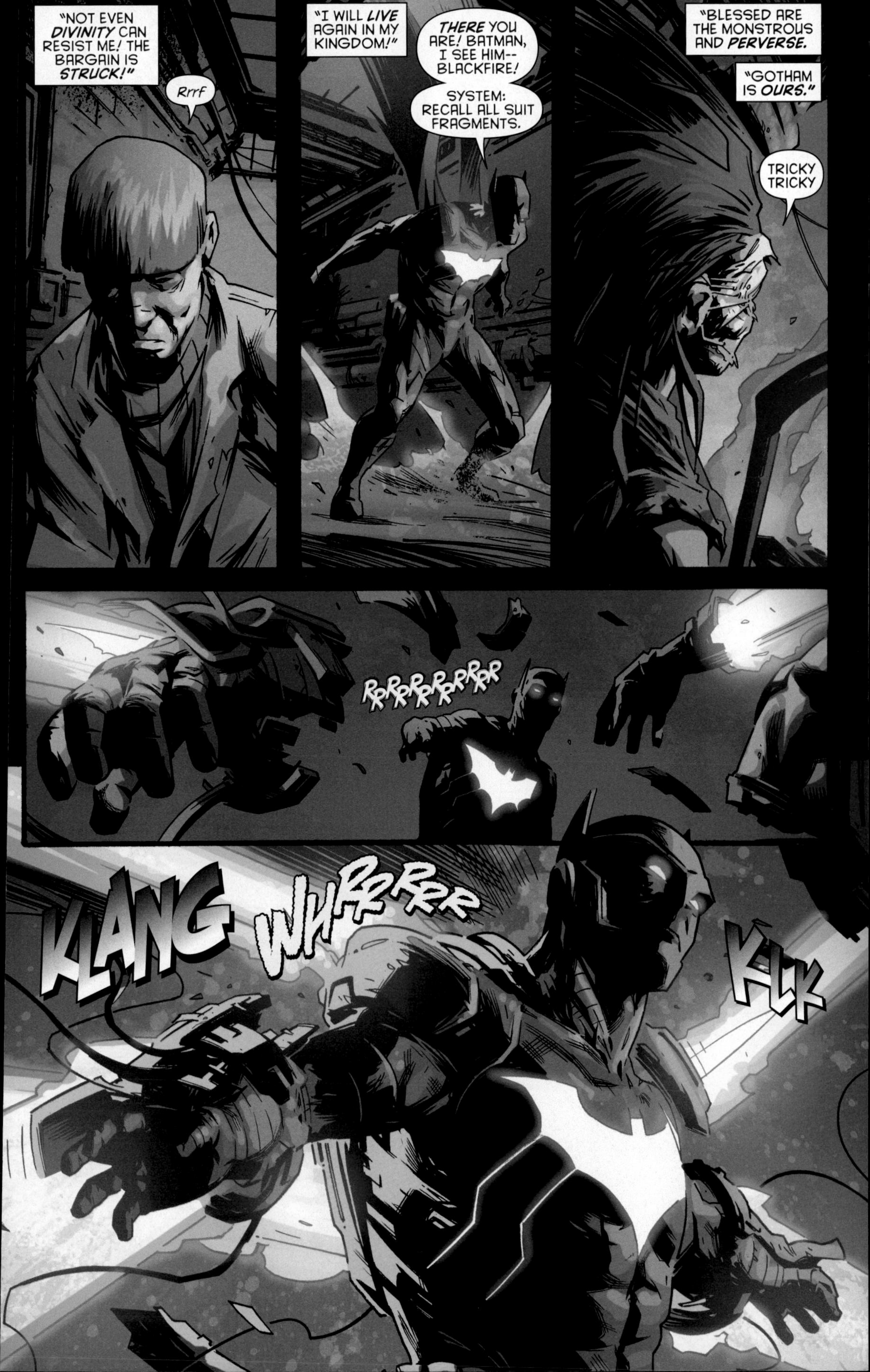
"NOT EVEN DIVINITY CAN RESIST ME! THE BARGAIN IS STRUCK!"
Rrrf
"I WILL LIVE AGAIN IN MY KINGDOM!"
THERE YOU ARE! BATMAN, I SEE HIM-- BLACKFIRE!
SYSTEM: RECALL ALL SUIT FRAGMENTS.
"BLESSED ARE THE MONSTROUS AND PERVERSE.
"GOTHAM IS OURS."
TRICKY TRICKY
RRRRRRRRRR
KLANG
WHRRRRR
KLK

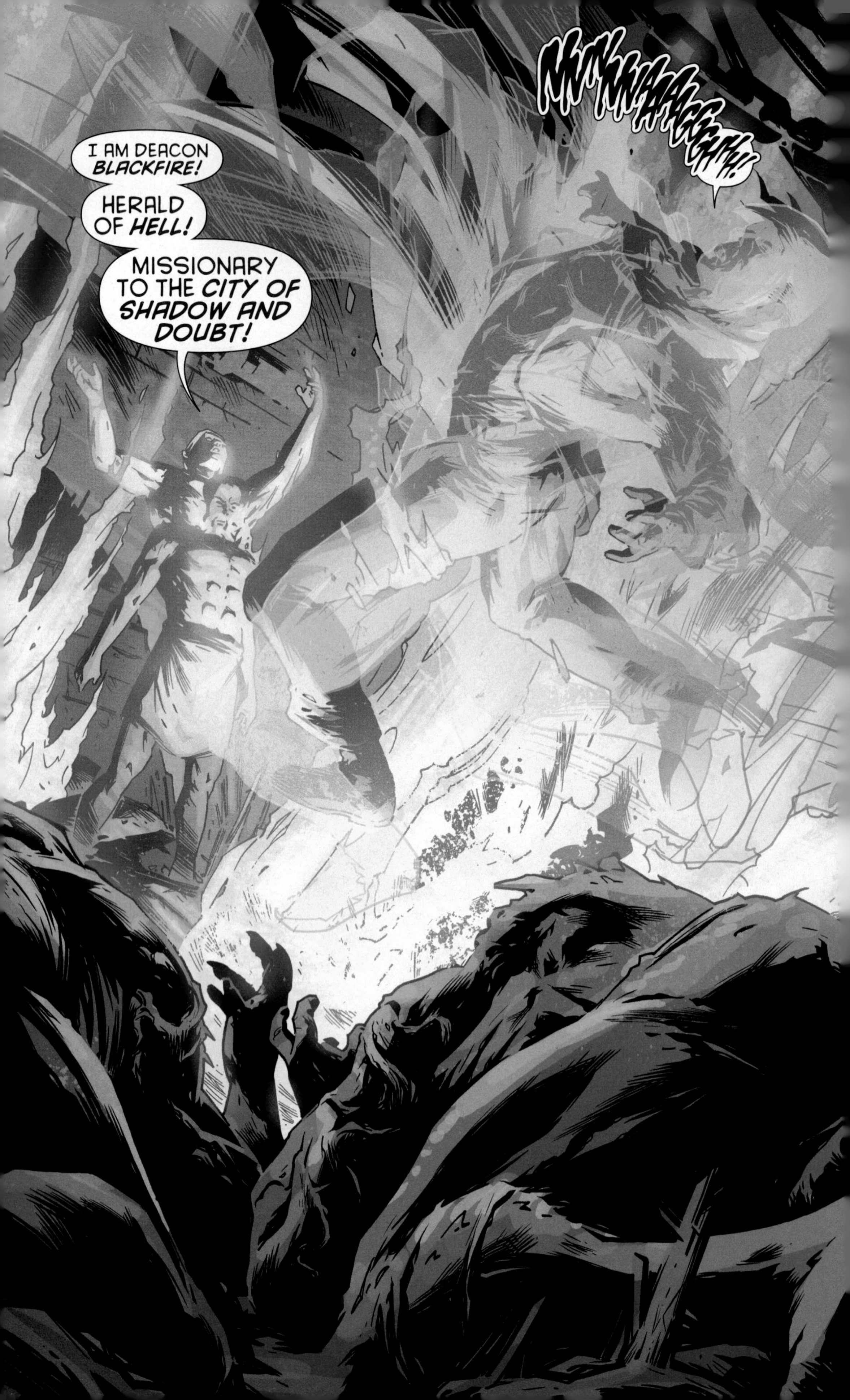
I AM DEACON BLACKFIRE!
HERALD OF HELL!
MISSIONARY TO THE CITY OF SHADOW AND DOUBT!

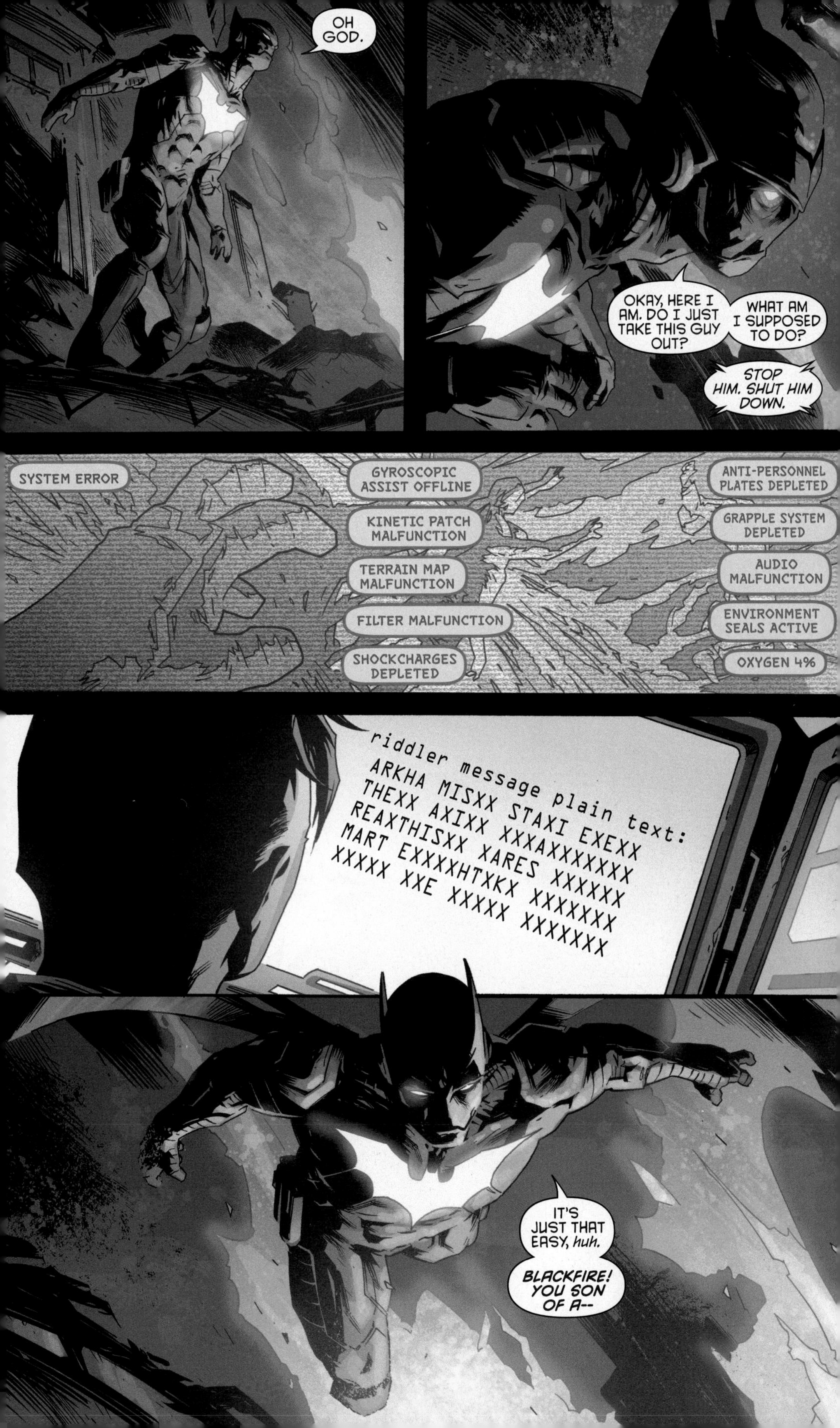
OH GOD.
OKAY, HERE I AM. DO I JUST TAKE THIS GUY OUT?
WHAT AM I SUPPOSED TO DO?
STOP HIM. SHUT HIM DOWN.
SYSTEM ERROR
GYROSCOPIC ASSIST OFFLINE
KINETIC PATCH MALFUNCTION
TERRAIN MAP MALFUNCTION
FILTER MALFUNCTION
SHOCKCHARGES DEPLETED
ANTI-PERSONNEL PLATES DEPLETED
GRAPPLE SYSTEM DEPLETED
AUDIO MALFUNCTION
ENVIRONMENT SEALS ACTIVE
OXYGEN 4%
riddler message plain text:
ARKHA MISXX STAXI EXEXX
THEXX AXIXX XXXAXXXXXXX
REAXTHISXX XARES XXXXXX
MART EXXXXHTXKX XXXXXXX
XXXXX XXE XXXXX XXXXXXX
IT'S JUST THAT EASY, *huh.*
BLACKFIRE! YOU SON OF A--

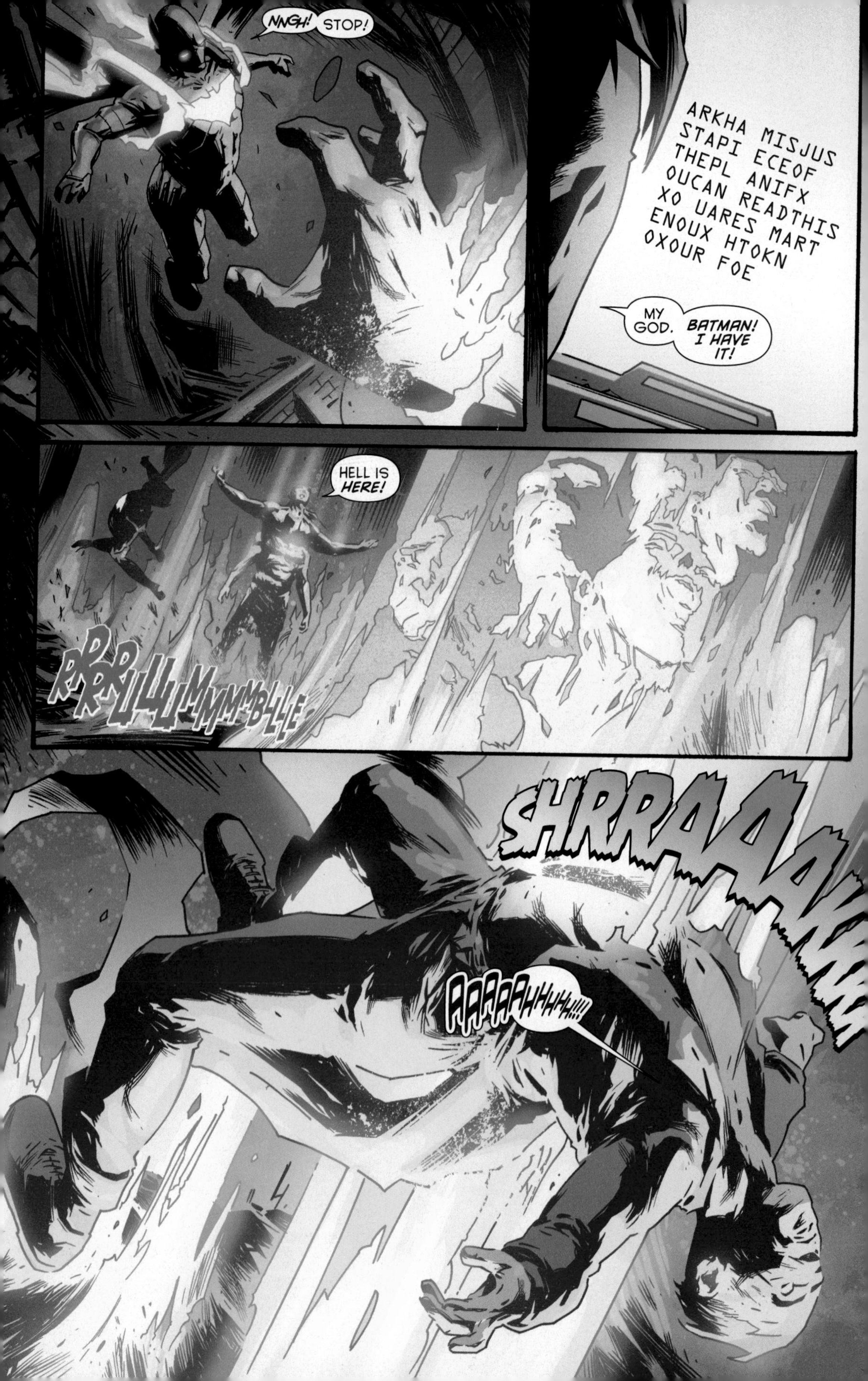
NNGH!
STOP!
ARKHA MISJUS
STAPI ECEOF
THEPL ANIFX
OUCAN READTHIS
XO UARES MART
ENOUX HTOKN
OXOUR FOE
MY GOD.
BATMAN! I HAVE IT!
HELL IS HERE!
RRRRRUUUMMMMBLLE
SHRRAAAKKK
AAAAAHHHH!!!

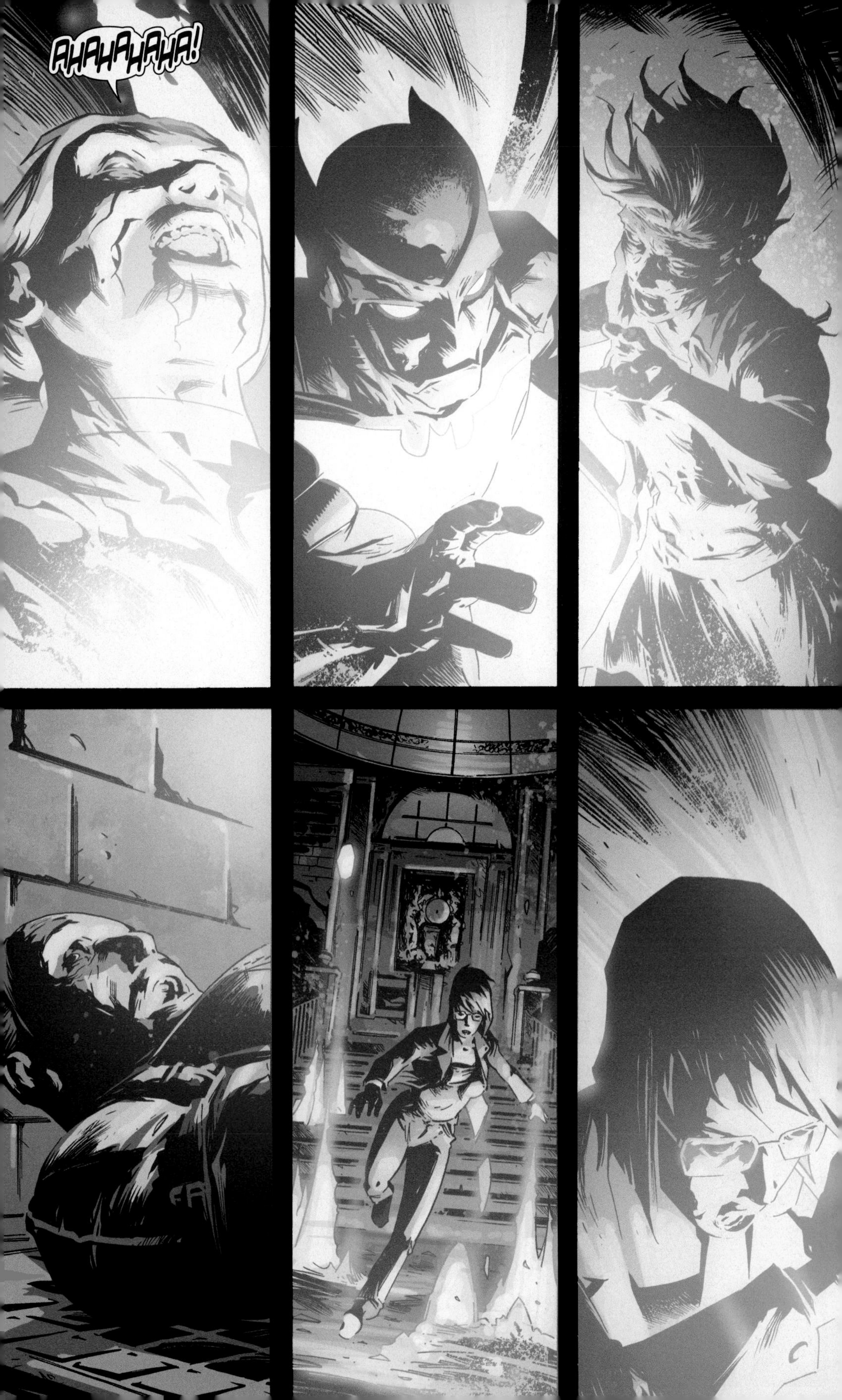
AHAHAHAHA!

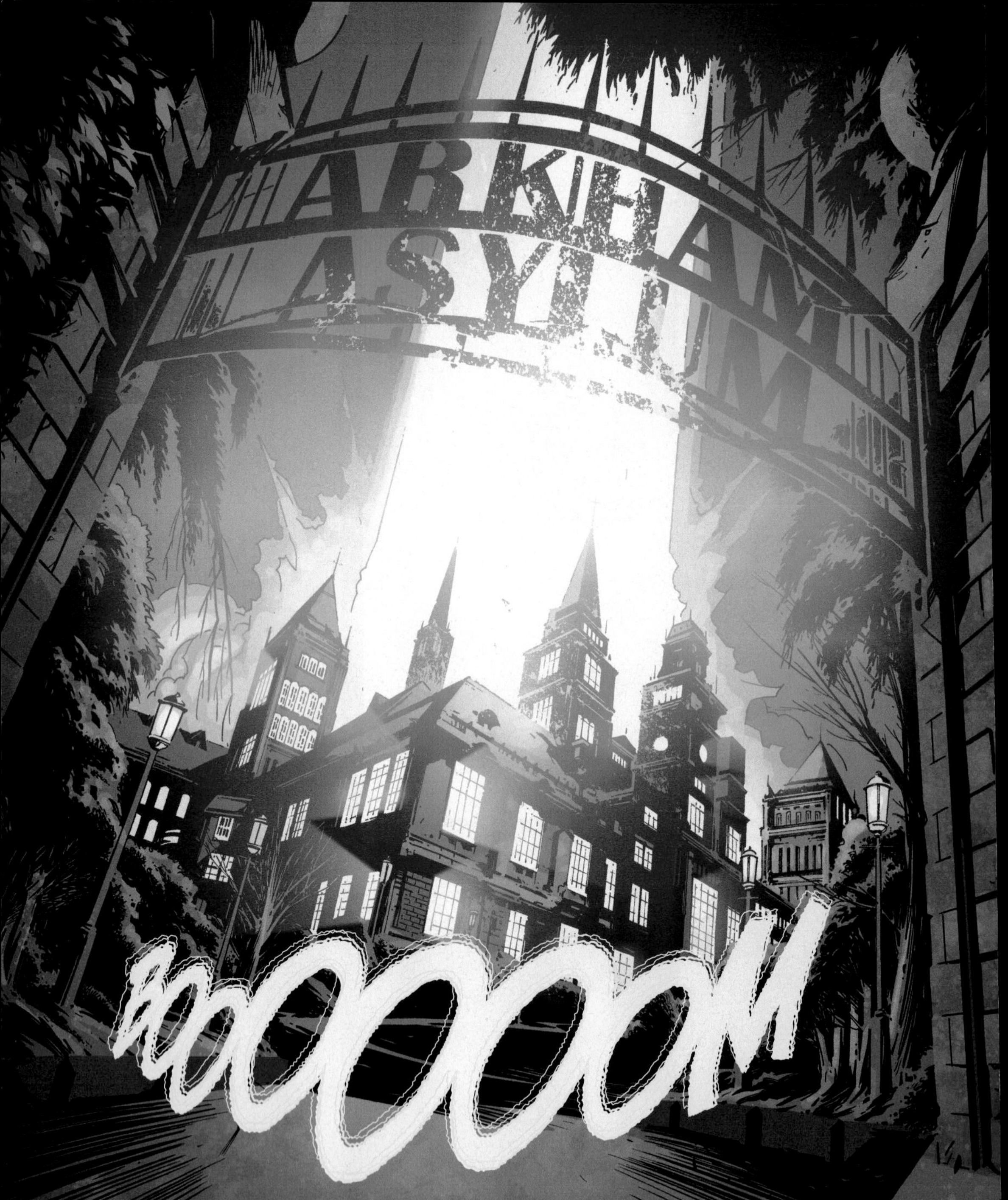
ARKHAM ASYLUM
BOOOOOM

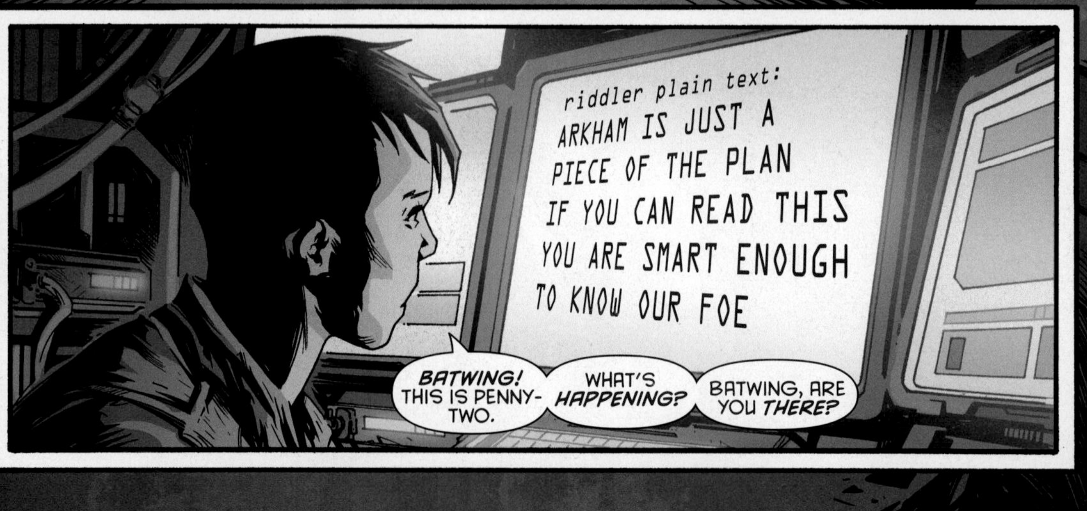
riddler plain text:
ARKHAM IS JUST A PIECE OF THE PLAN IF YOU CAN READ THIS YOU ARE SMART ENOUGH TO KNOW OUR FOE
BATWING! THIS IS PENNY-TWO.
WHAT'S HAPPENING?
BATWING, ARE YOU THERE?

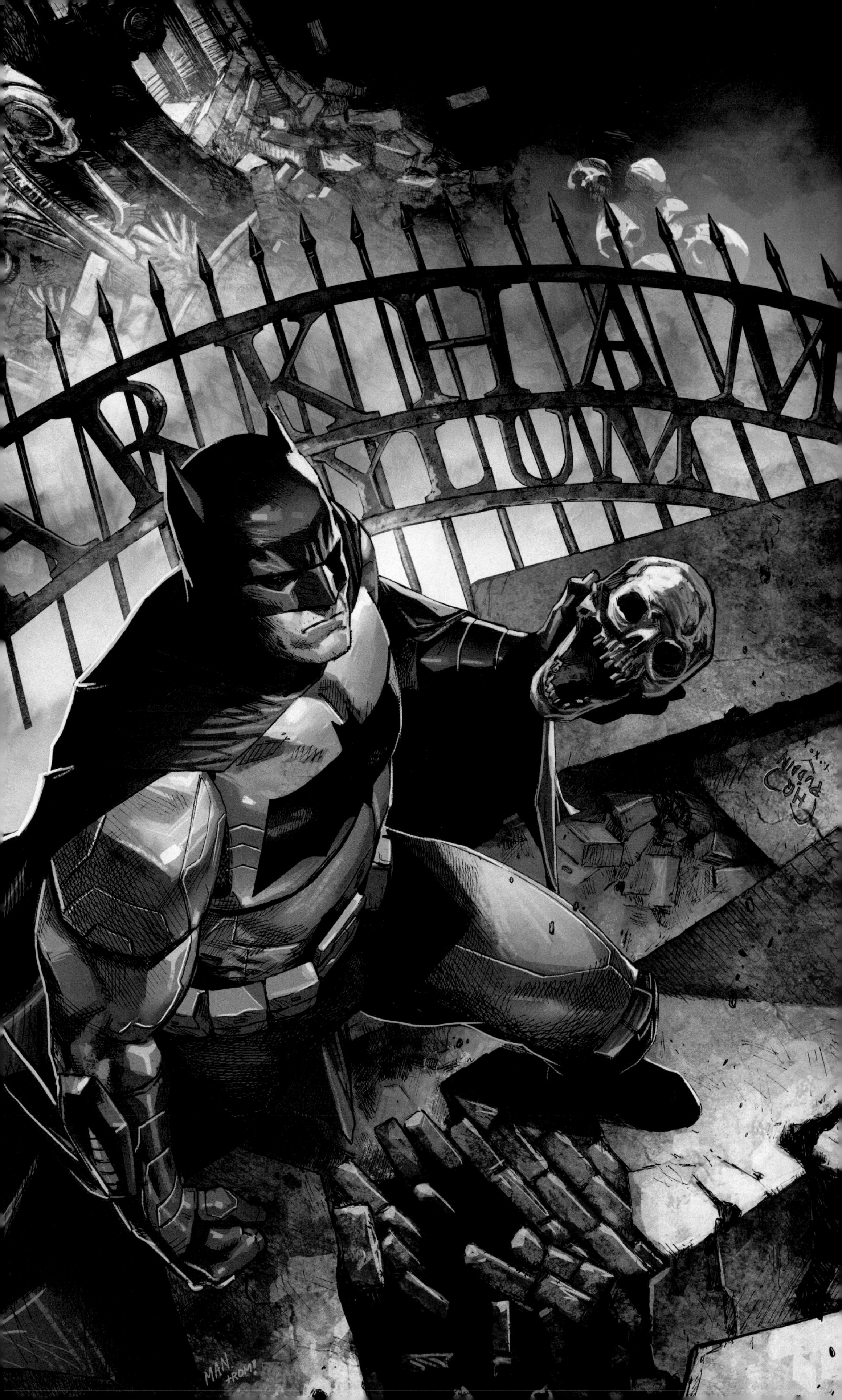

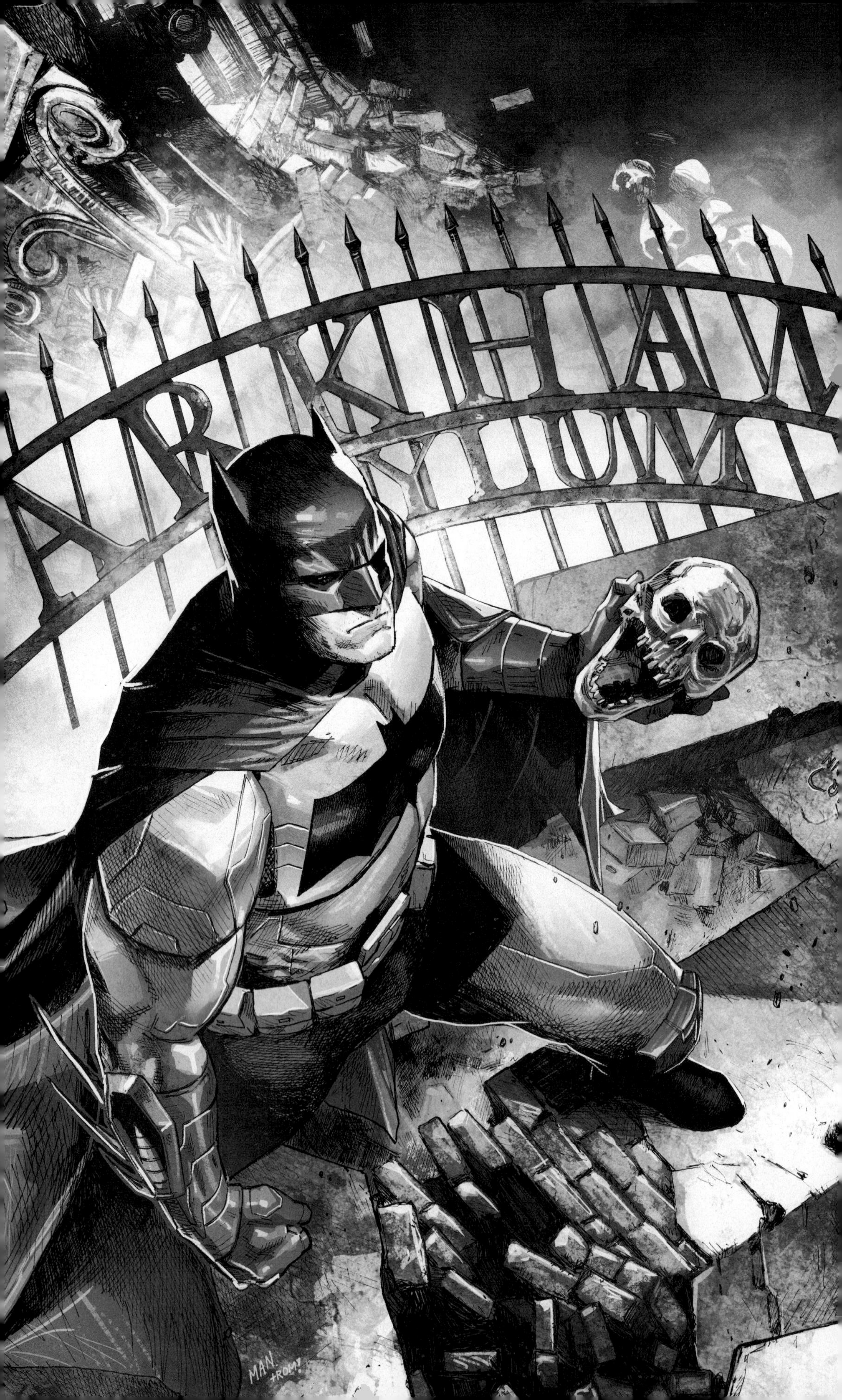
ARKHAM
YLUM

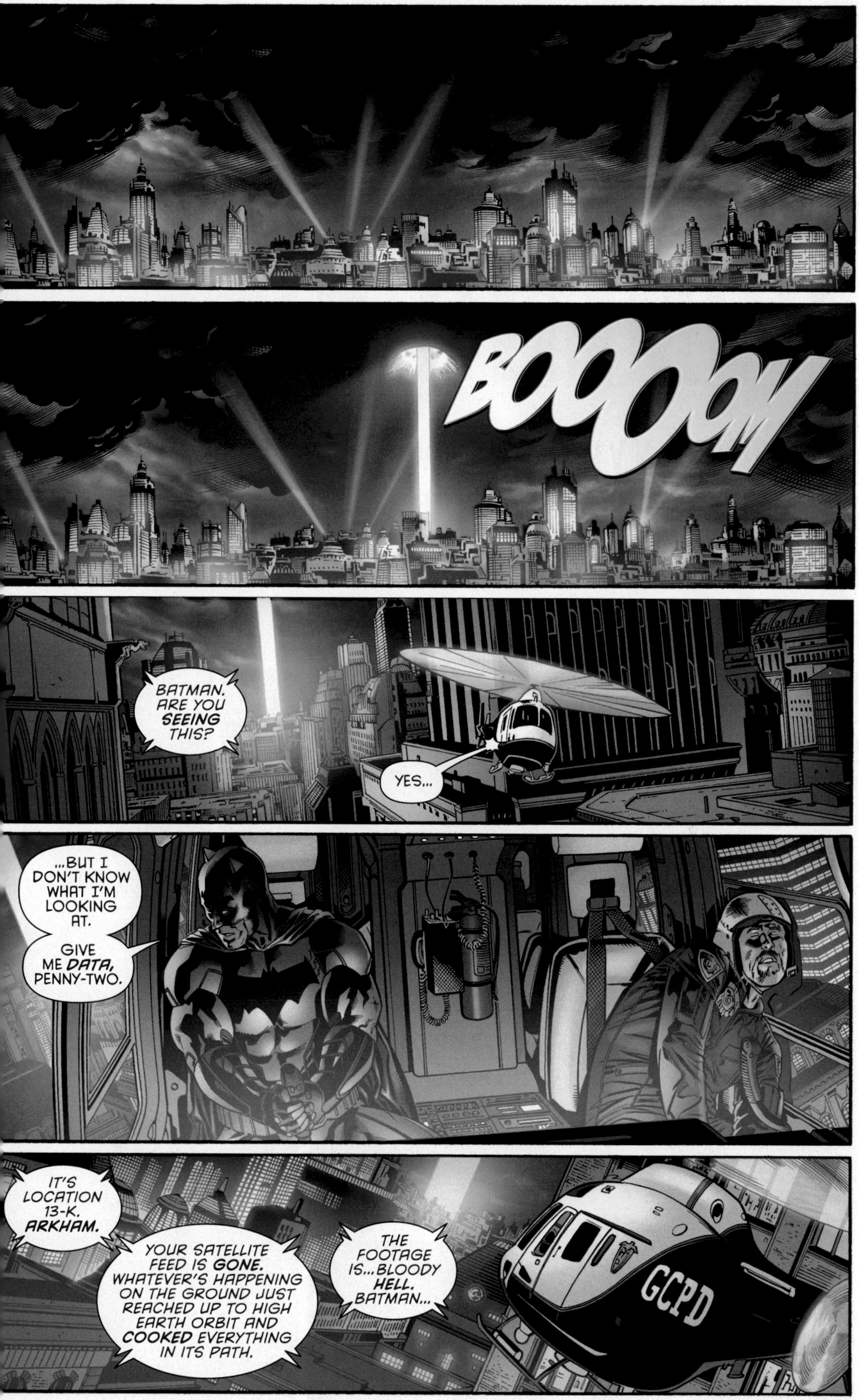
BOOOOM
BATMAN. ARE YOU SEEING THIS?
YES...
...BUT I DON'T KNOW WHAT I'M LOOKING AT.
GIVE ME DATA, PENNY-TWO.
IT'S LOCATION 13-K. ARKHAM.
YOUR SATELLITE FEED IS GONE. WHATEVER'S HAPPENING ON THE GROUND JUST REACHED UP TO HIGH EARTH ORBIT AND COOKED EVERYTHING IN ITS PATH.
THE FOOTAGE IS...BLOODY HELL, BATMAN...
GCPD

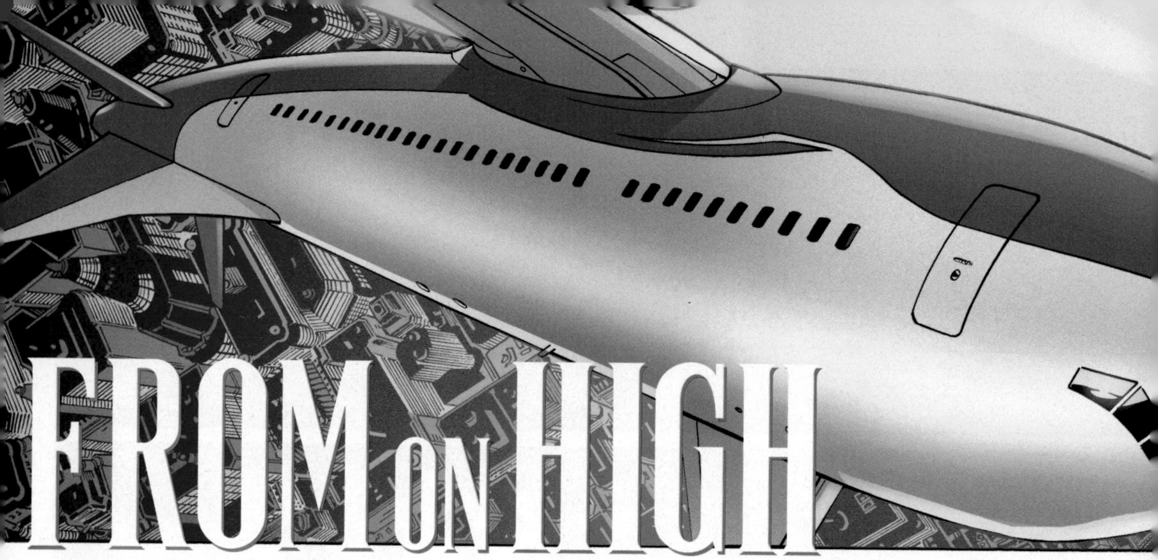

# FROM ON HIGH

SCOTT SNYDER & JAMES TYNION IV STORY
RAY FAWKES SCRIPT
KYLE HIGGINS & TIM SEELEY CONSULTING WRITERS

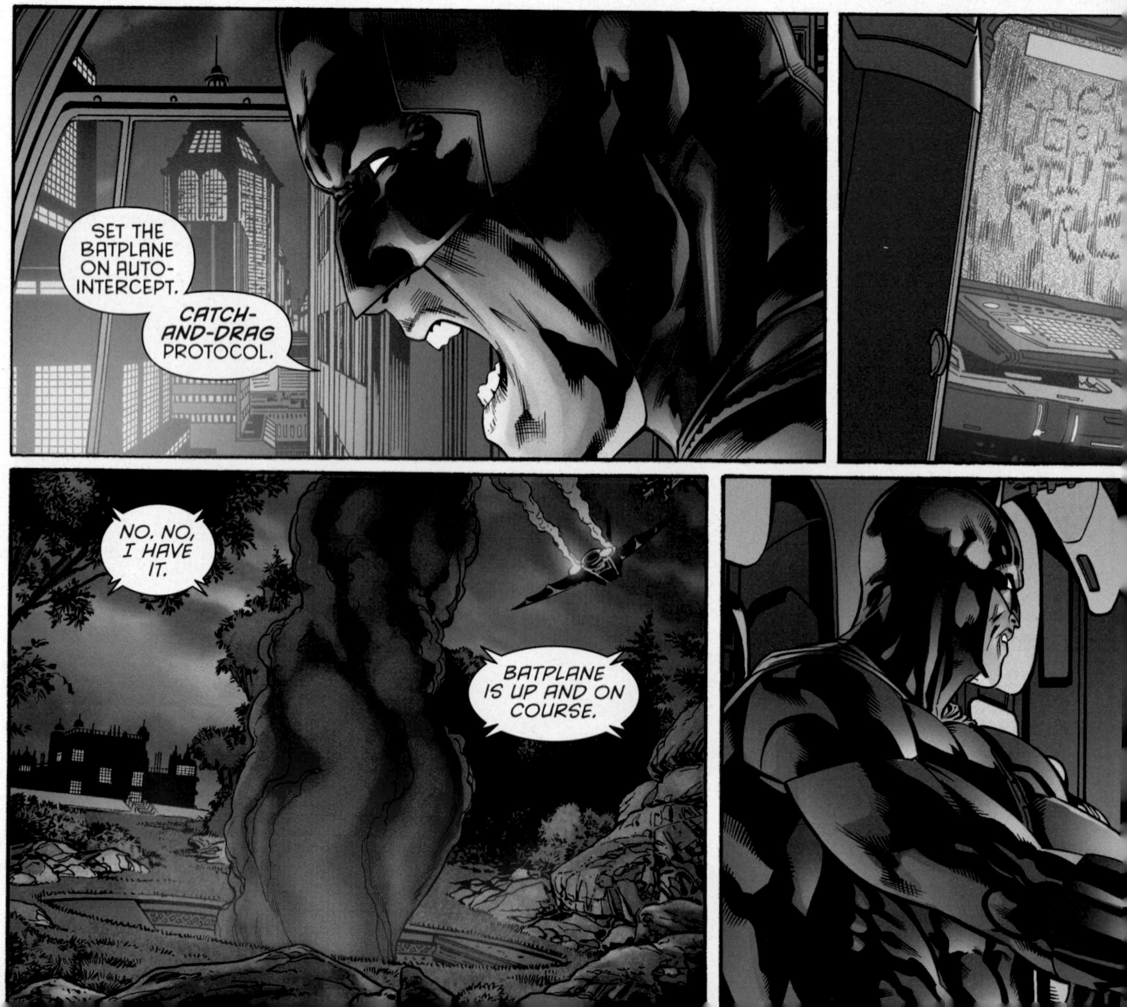
SET THE BATPLANE ON AUTO-INTERCEPT.
CATCH-AND-DRAG PROTOCOL.
NO. NO, I HAVE IT.
BATPLANE IS UP AND ON COURSE.

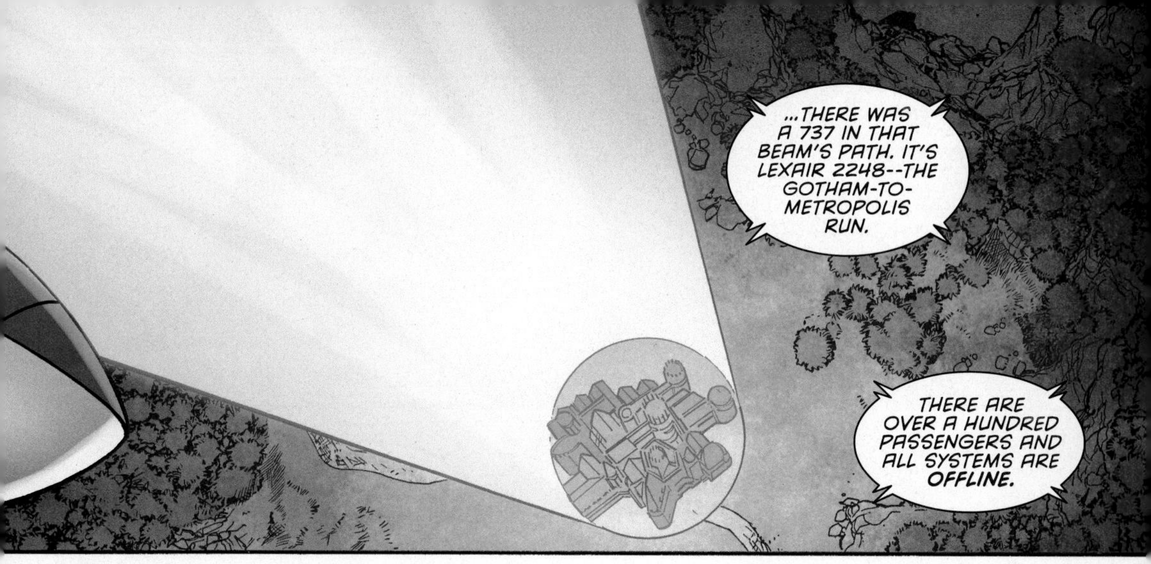
...THERE WAS A 737 IN THAT BEAM'S PATH. IT'S LEXAIR 2248--THE GOTHAM-TO-METROPOLIS RUN.
THERE ARE OVER A HUNDRED PASSENGERS AND ALL SYSTEMS ARE **OFFLINE.**

**FERNANDO PASARIN** PENCILS **MATT RYAN** INKS
**BLOND** COLORS **STEVE WANDS** LETTERS
**CLAY MANN** AND **ROMULO FAJARDO, JR.** COVER

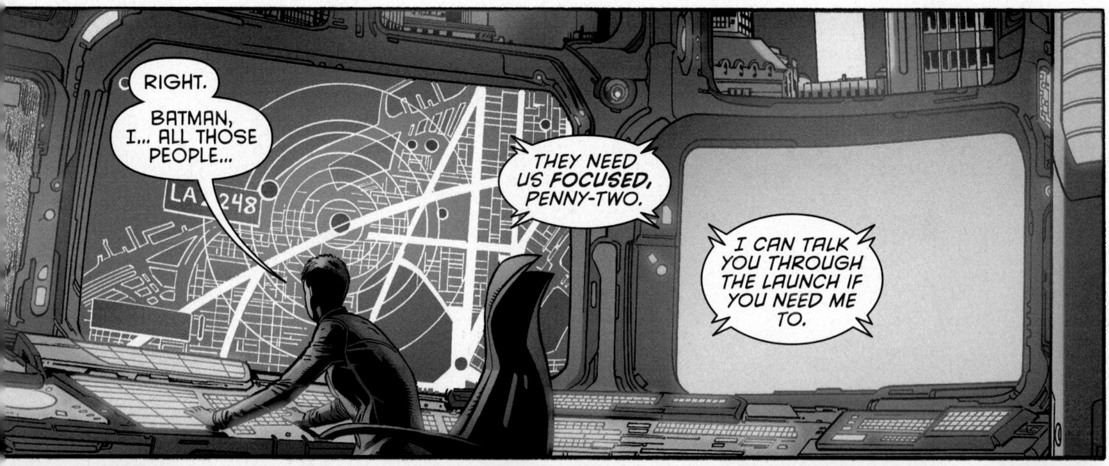
RIGHT.
BATMAN, I... ALL THOSE PEOPLE...
THEY NEED US **FOCUSED,** PENNY-TWO.
I CAN TALK YOU THROUGH THE LAUNCH IF YOU NEED ME TO.

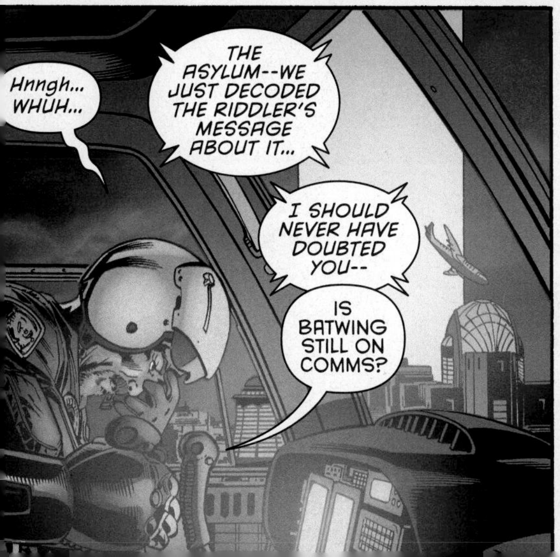
Hnngh... WHUH...
THE ASYLUM--WE JUST DECODED THE RIDDLER'S MESSAGE ABOUT IT...
I SHOULD NEVER HAVE DOUBTED YOU--
IS BATWING STILL ON COMMS?

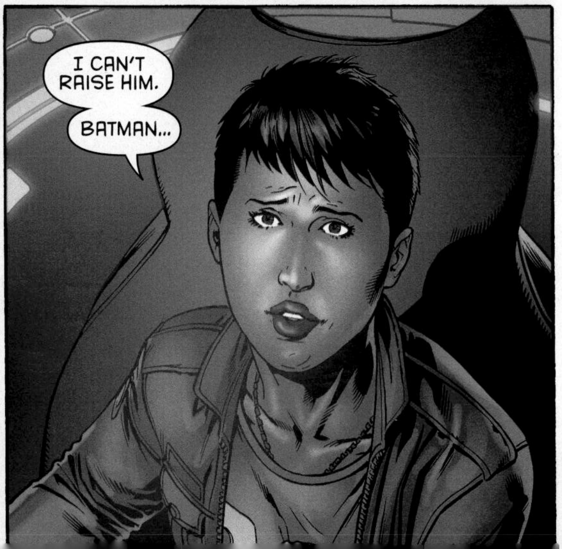
I CAN'T RAISE HIM.
BATMAN...

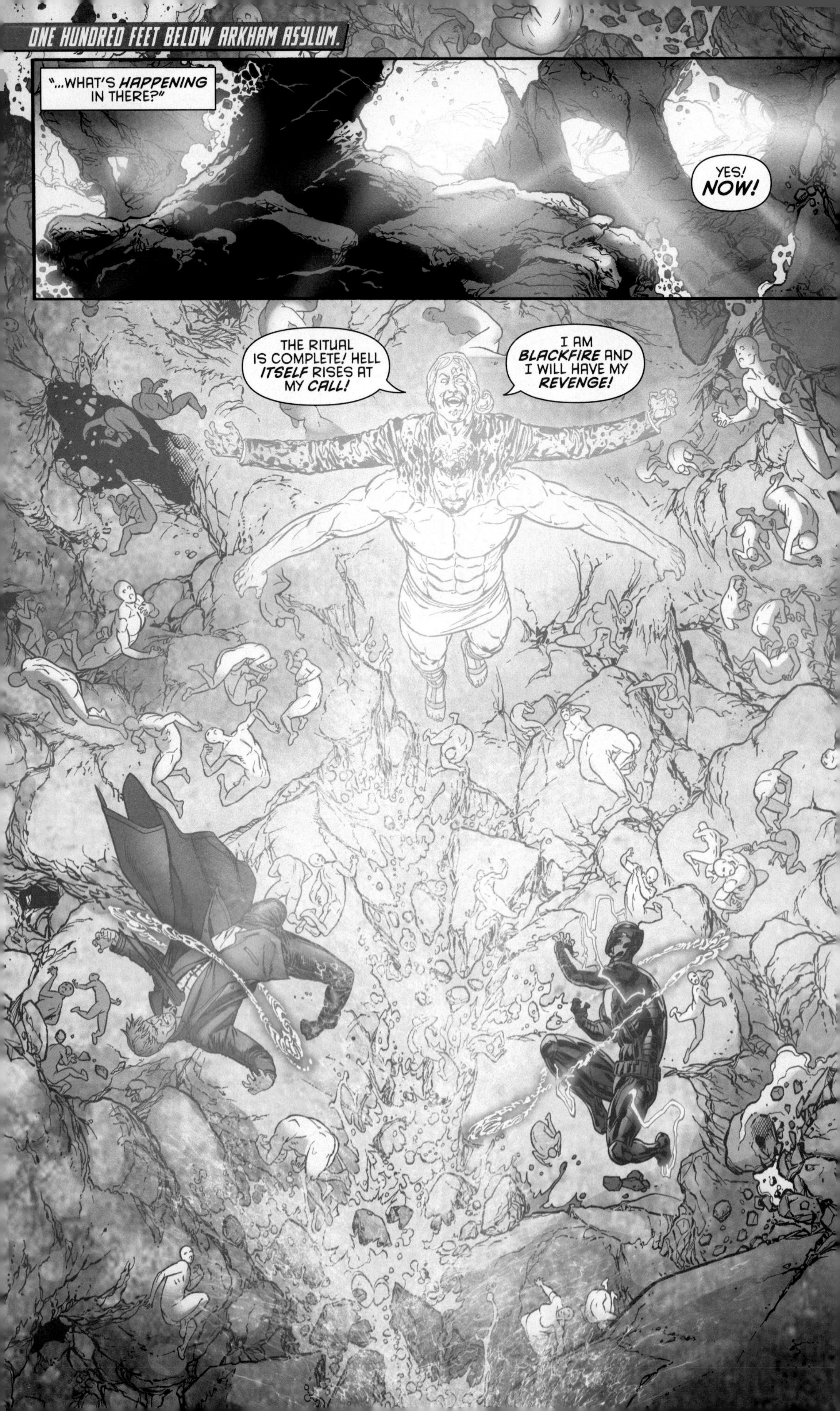
ONE HUNDRED FEET BELOW ARKHAM ASYLUM.
"...WHAT'S HAPPENING IN THERE?"
YES! NOW!
THE RITUAL IS COMPLETE! HELL ITSELF RISES AT MY CALL!
I AM BLACKFIRE AND I WILL HAVE MY REVENGE!

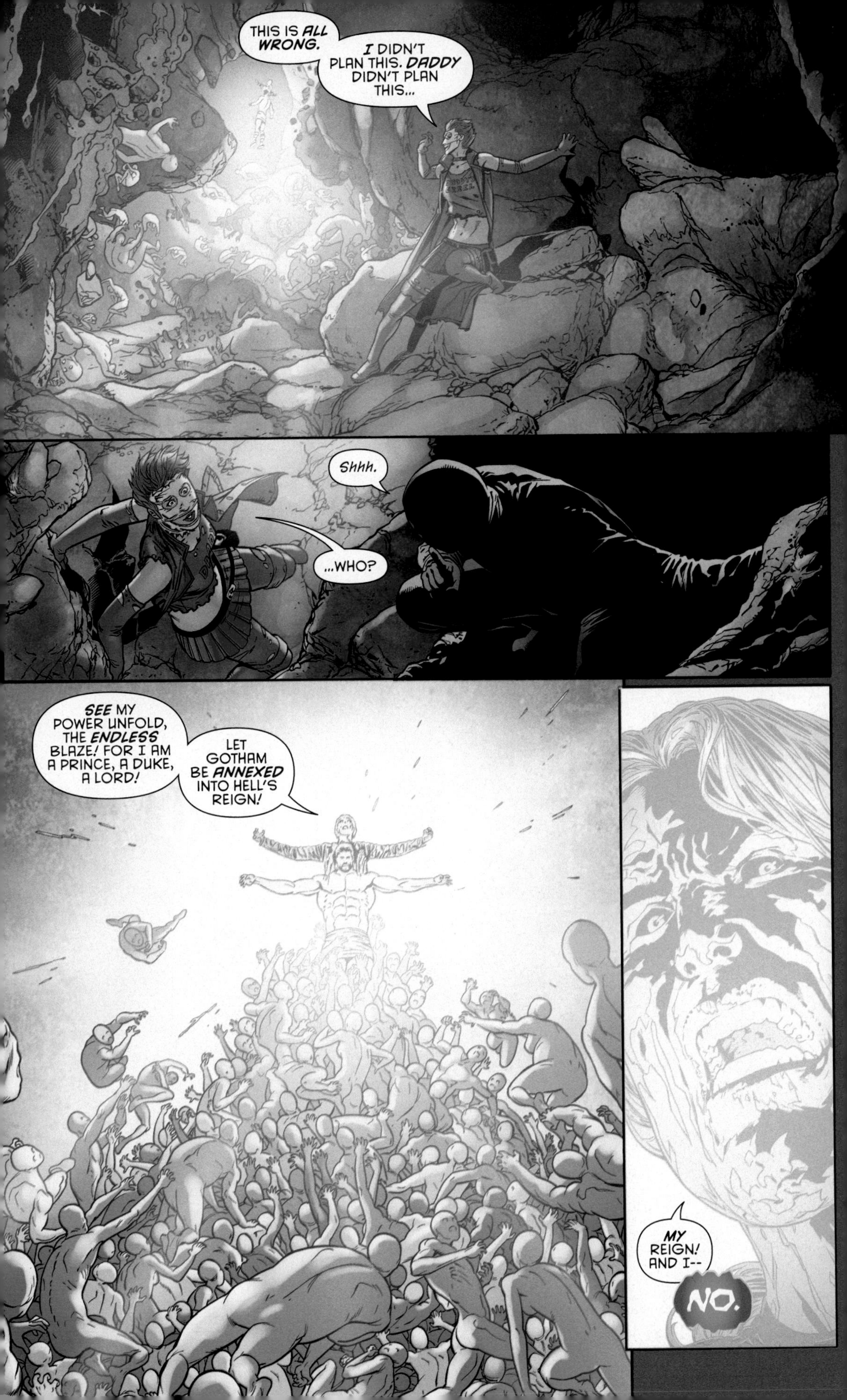
THIS IS ALL WRONG.
I DIDN'T PLAN THIS. DADDY DIDN'T PLAN THIS...
Shhh.
...WHO?
SEE MY POWER UNFOLD, THE ENDLESS BLAZE! FOR I AM A PRINCE, A DUKE, A LORD!
LET GOTHAM BE ANNEXED INTO HELL'S REIGN!
MY REIGN! AND I--
NO.

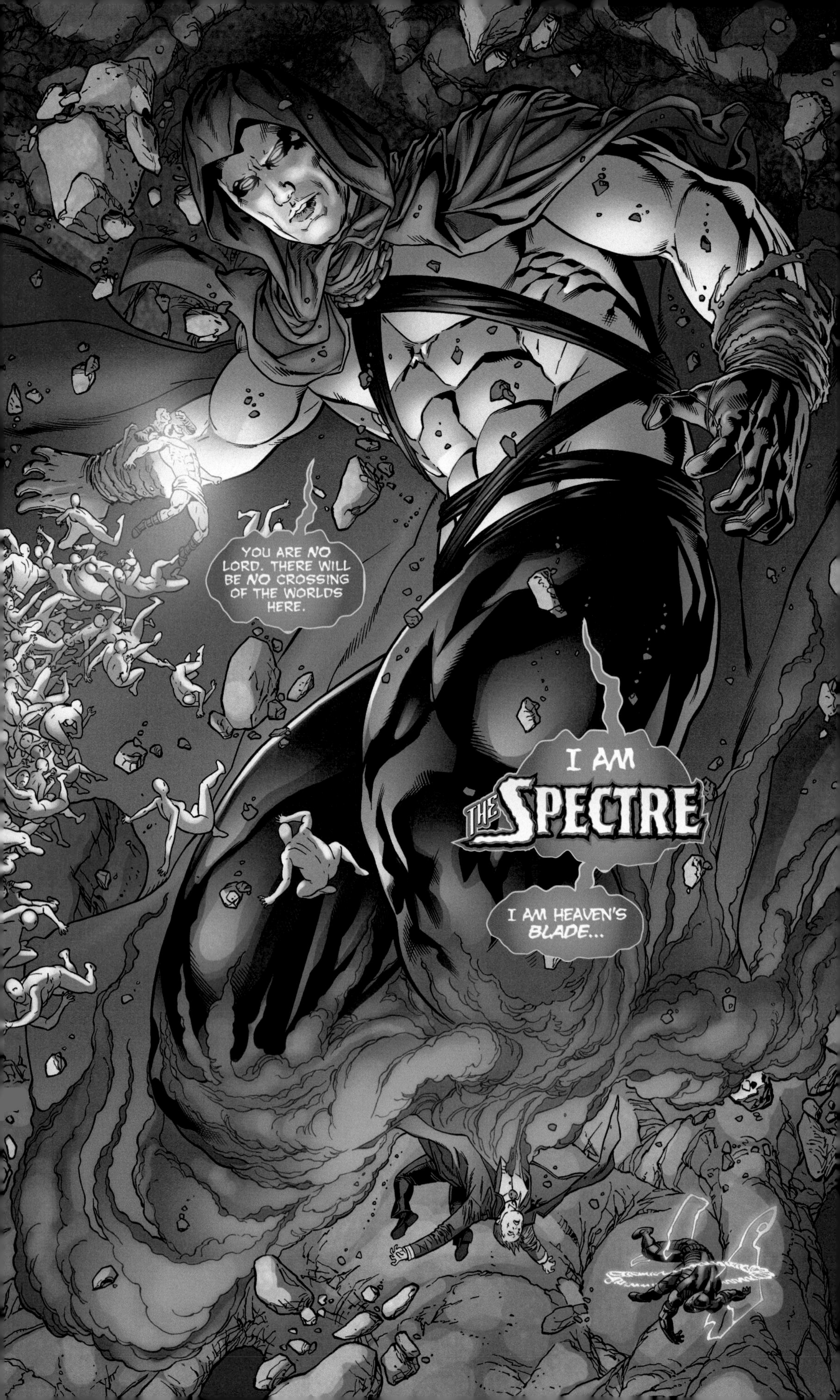
YOU ARE NO LORD. THERE WILL BE NO CROSSING OF THE WORLDS HERE.
I AM THE SPECTRE
I AM HEAVEN'S BLADE...

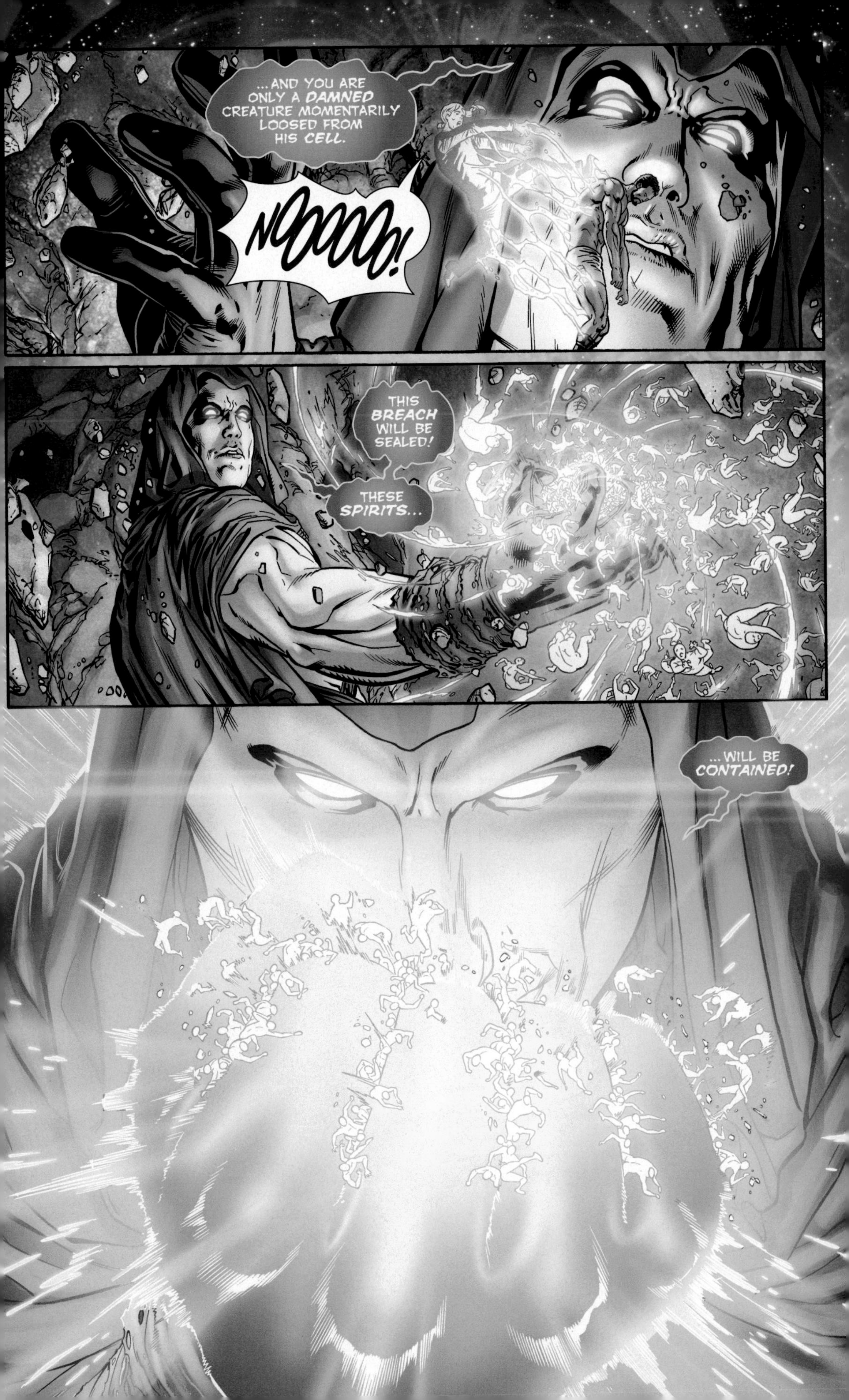
...AND YOU ARE ONLY A DAMNED CREATURE MOMENTARILY LOOSED FROM HIS CELL.
NOOOOO!
THIS BREACH WILL BE SEALED!
THESE SPIRITS...
...WILL BE CONTAINED!

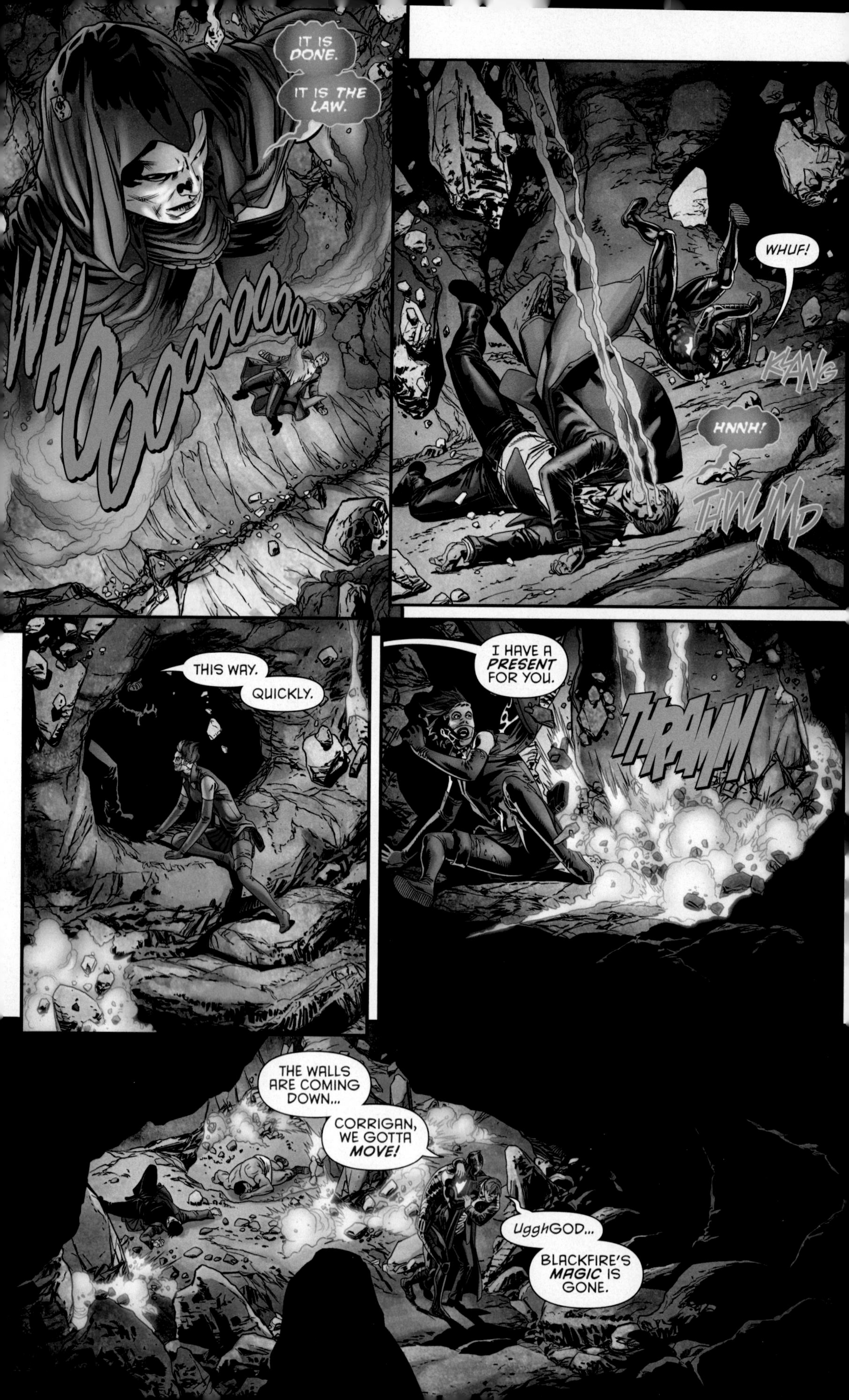
IT IS DONE.
IT IS THE LAW.
WHOOOOOOOOOOM
WHUF!
KLANG
HNNH!
THWUMP
THIS WAY.
QUICKLY.
I HAVE A PRESENT FOR YOU.
THRAMM
THE WALLS ARE COMING DOWN...
CORRIGAN, WE GOTTA MOVE!
UgghGOD...
BLACKFIRE'S MAGIC IS GONE.

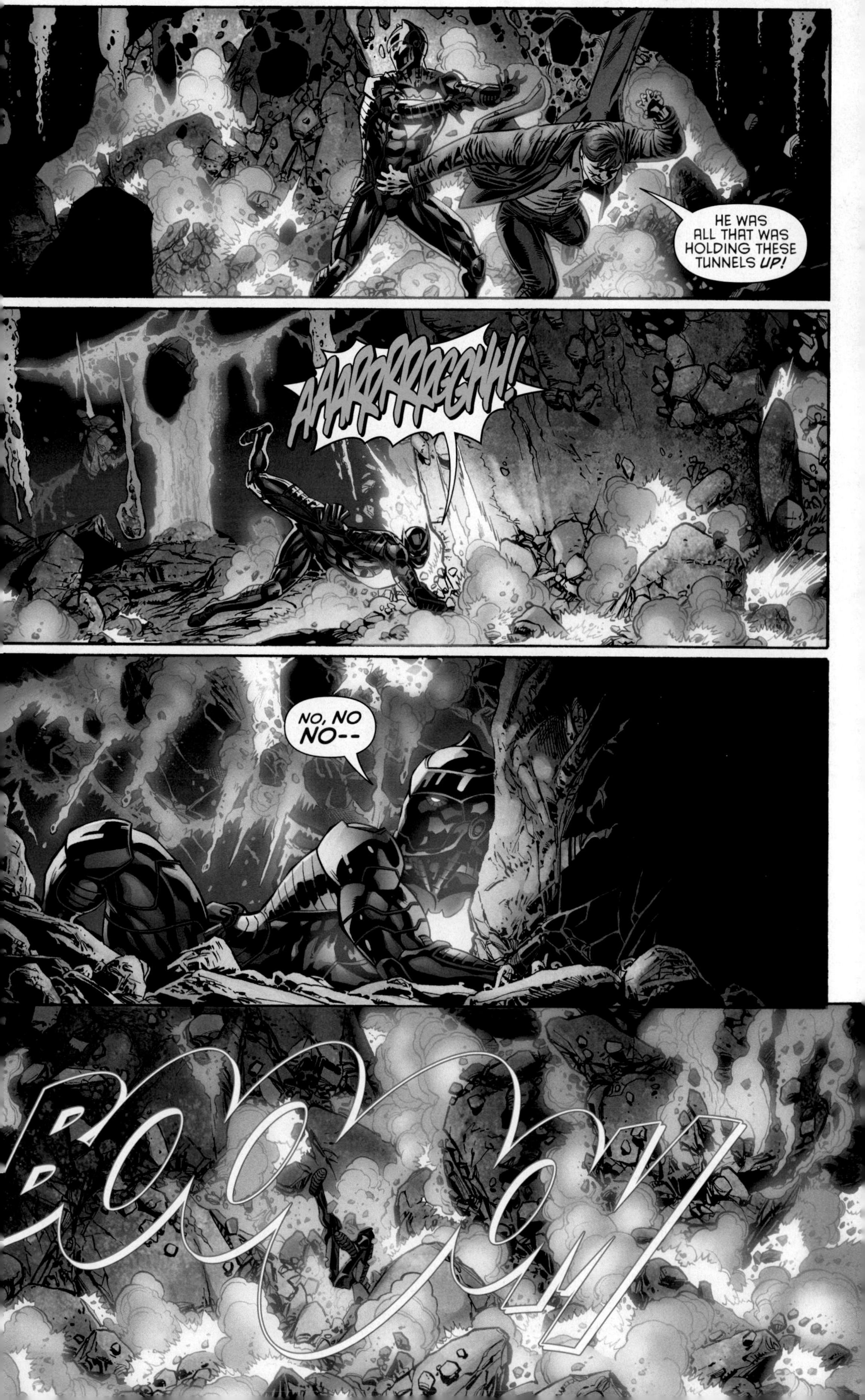
HE WAS ALL THAT WAS HOLDING THESE TUNNELS UP!
AAARRRRGGHH!
NO, NO NO--

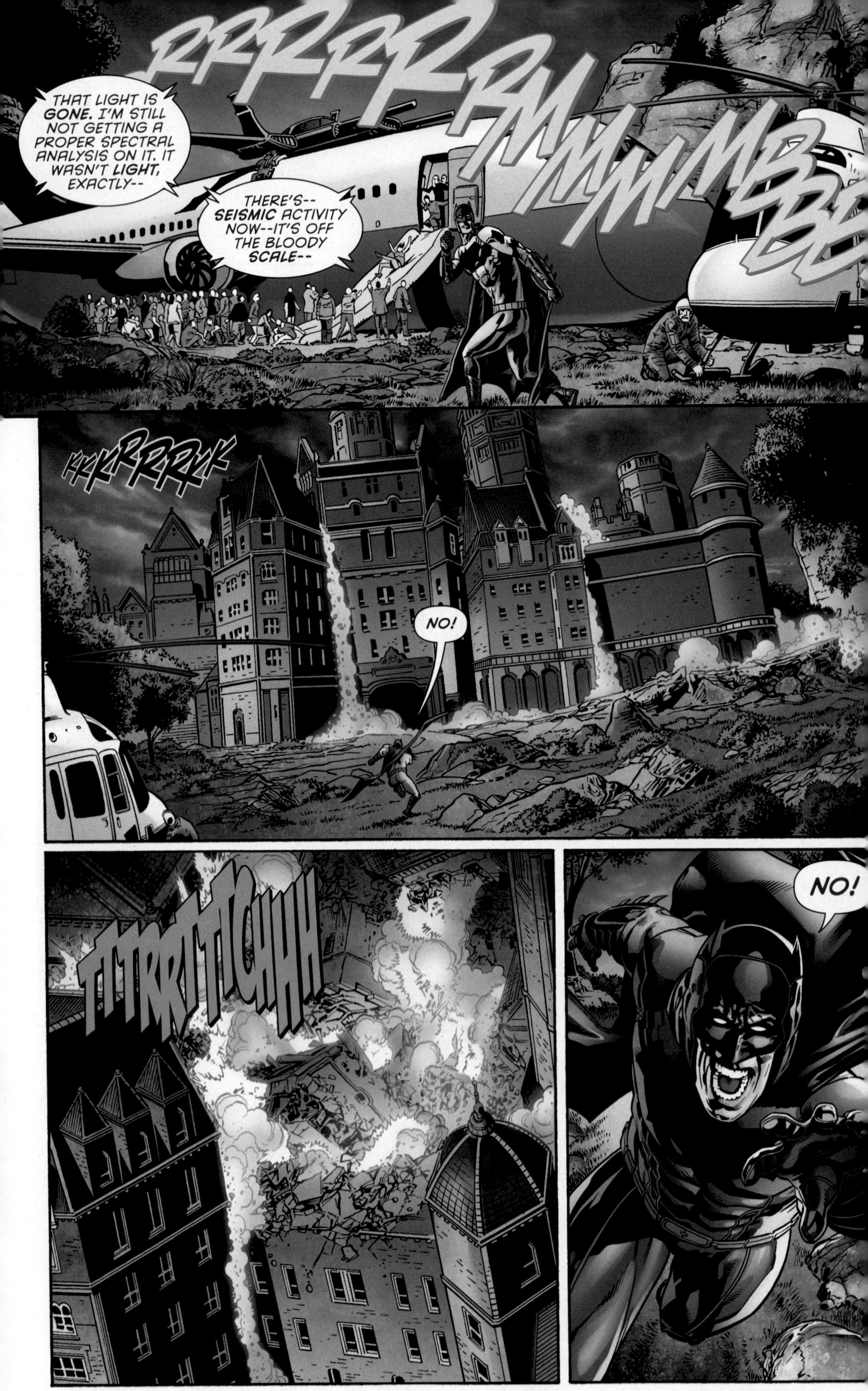
RRRRRRRMMMMMMBBB
THAT LIGHT IS GONE. I'M STILL NOT GETTING A PROPER SPECTRAL ANALYSIS ON IT. IT WASN'T LIGHT, EXACTLY--
THERE'S-- SEISMIC ACTIVITY NOW--IT'S OFF THE BLOODY SCALE--
KKKRRRRK
NO!
TTTRRTTCHHH
NO!

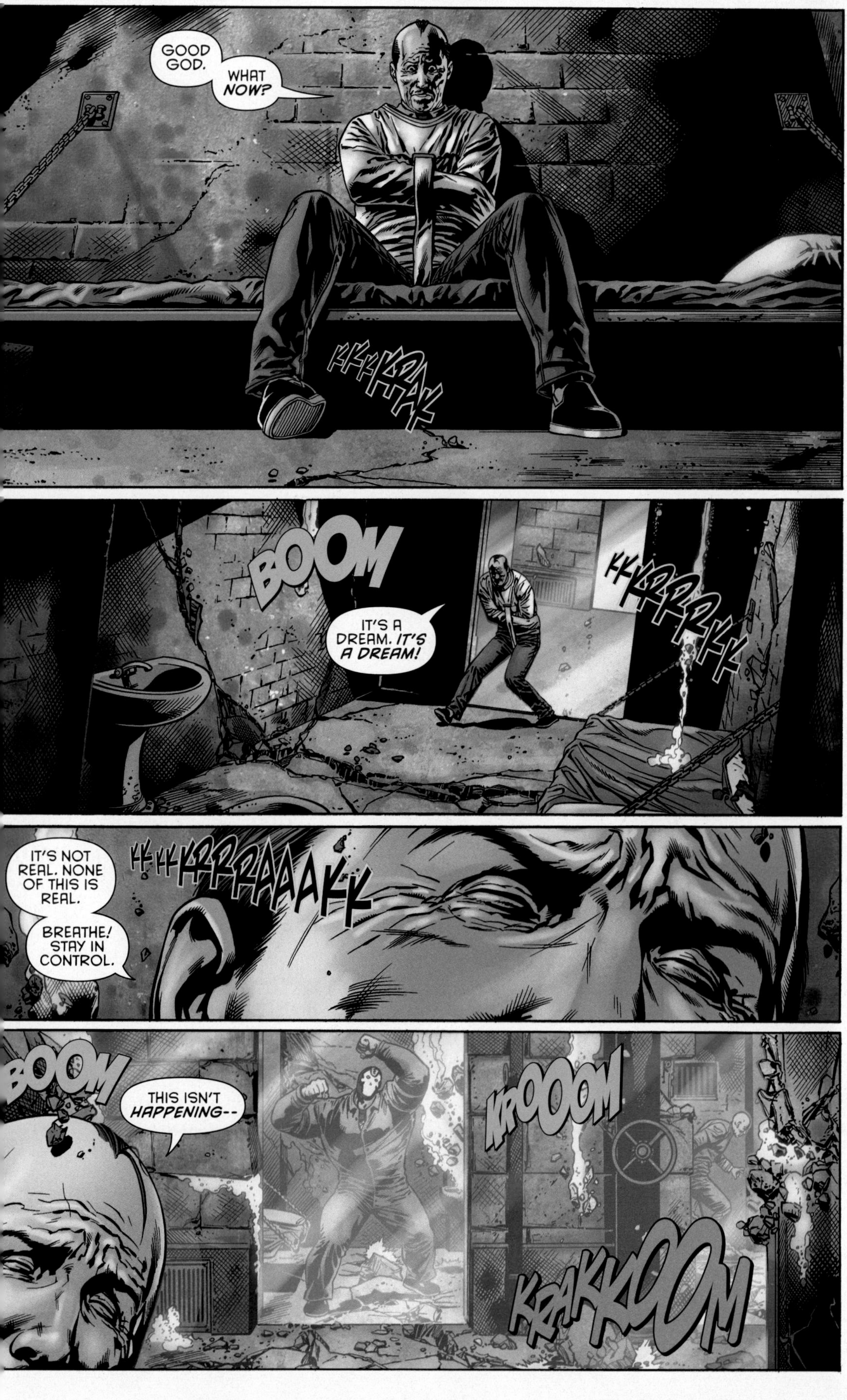
GOOD GOD.
WHAT NOW?
KKKKRAK
BOOM
IT'S A DREAM. IT'S A DREAM!
KKKRRRKK
IT'S NOT REAL. NONE OF THIS IS REAL.
BREATHE! STAY IN CONTROL.
KKKKKRRRAAAKK
BOOM
THIS ISN'T HAPPENING--
KROOOM
KRAKKOOM

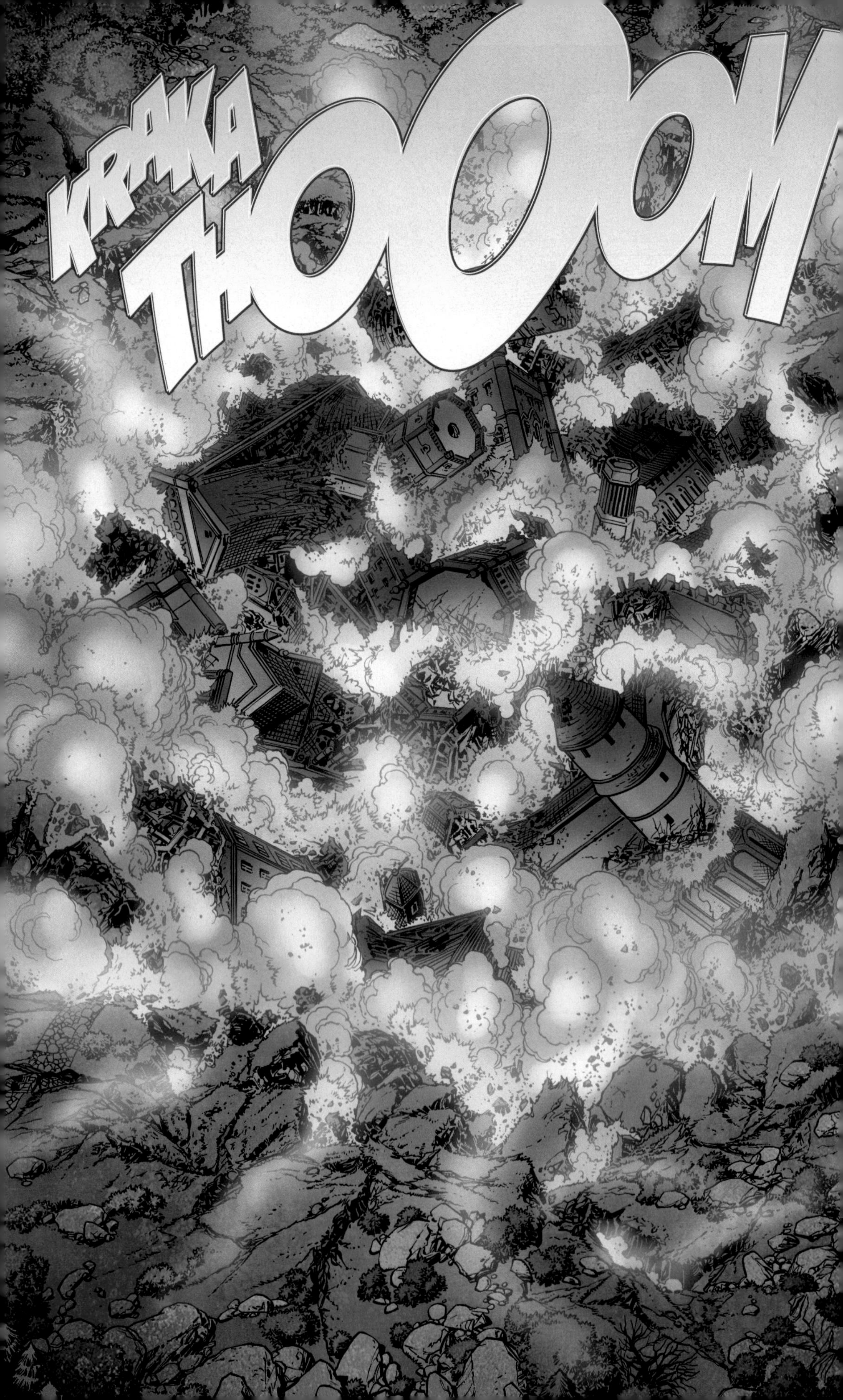
KRAKA
THOOOM

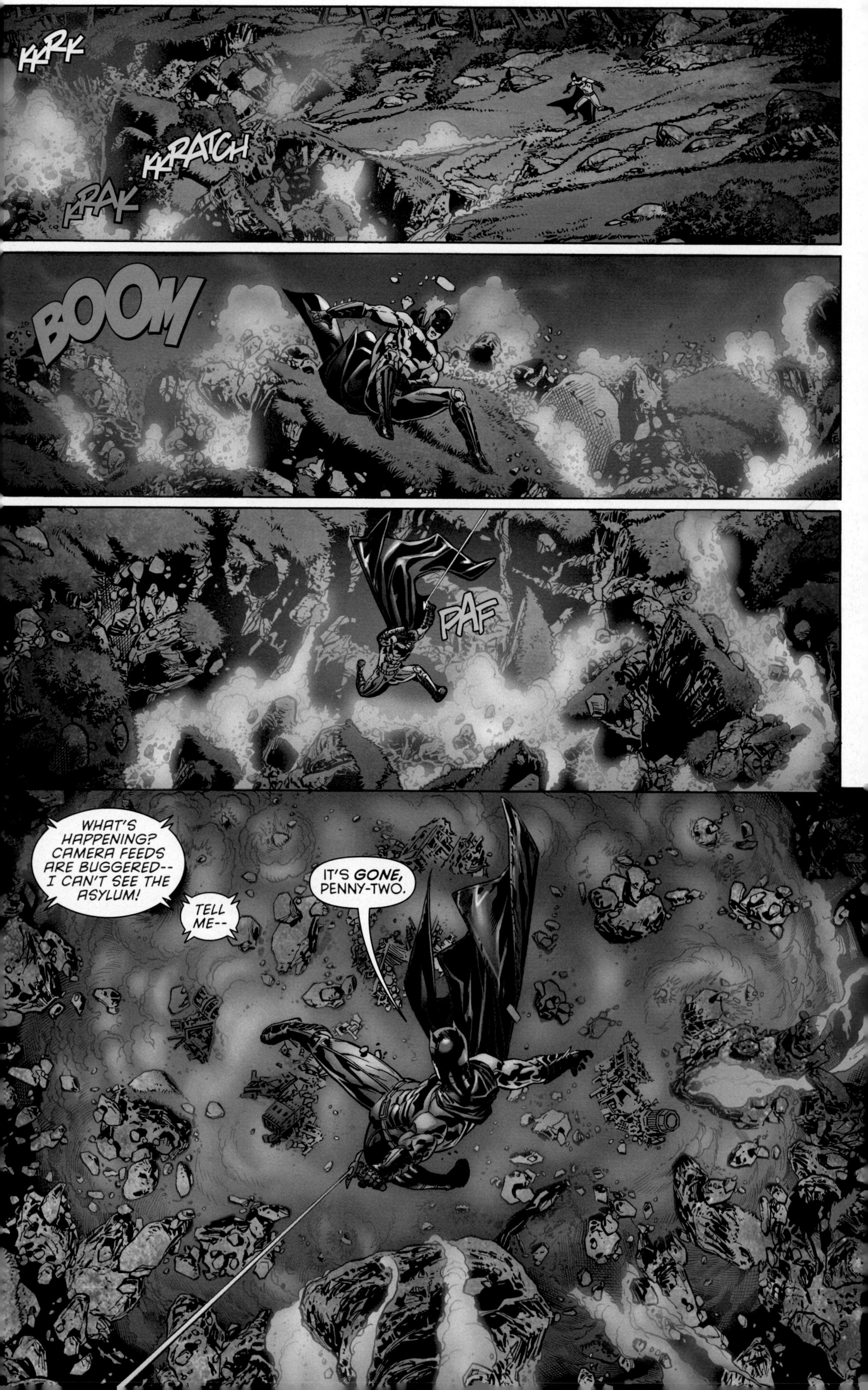
KKRK
KKRATCH
KRAK
BOOM
PAF
WHAT'S HAPPENING? CAMERA FEEDS ARE BUGGERED-- I CAN'T SEE THE ASYLUM!
TELL ME--
IT'S GONE, PENNY-TWO.

IT'S ALL GONE.

COLLAPSED.

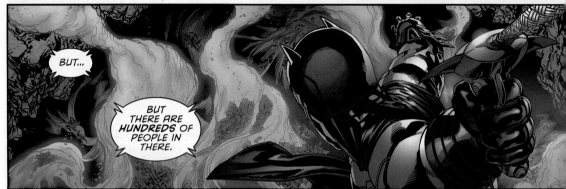

BUT...

BUT THERE ARE *HUNDREDS* OF PEOPLE IN THERE.

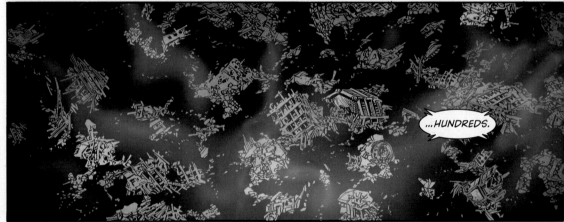

...HUNDREDS.

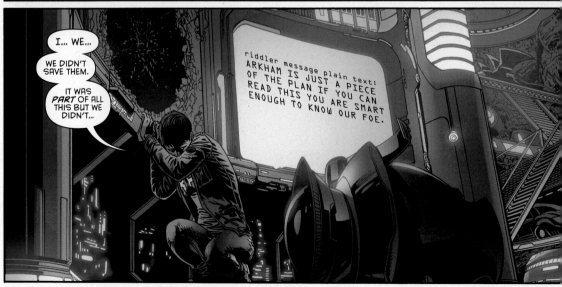

I... WE...

WE DIDN'T SAVE THEM.

IT WAS *PART* OF ALL THIS BUT WE DIDN'T...

riddler message plain text:
ARKHAM IS JUST A PIECE OF THE PLAN IF YOU CAN READ THIS YOU ARE SMART ENOUGH TO KNOW OUR FOE.

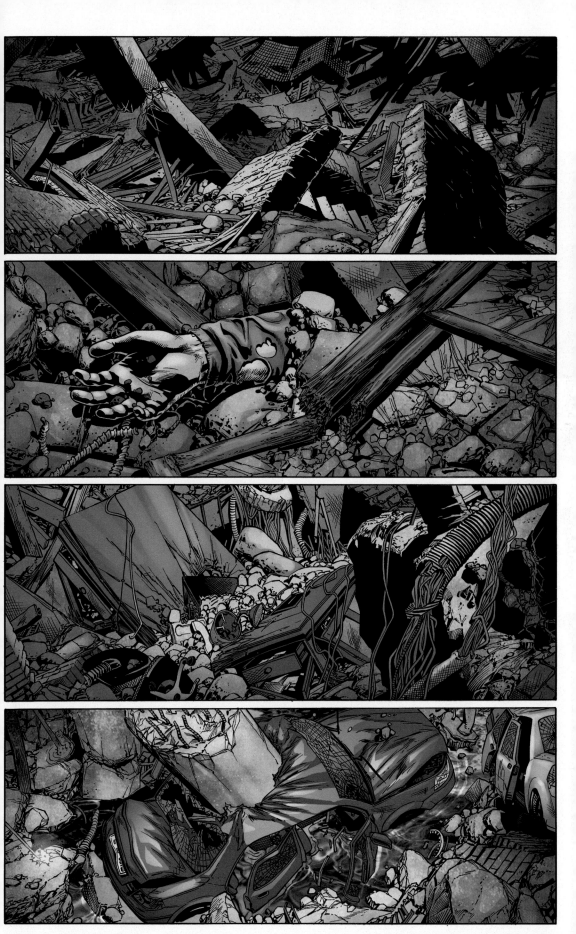

SOMEBODY. HEY...

BATMAN. CAN YOU HEAR ME?

PENNY-TWO? I'M TRAPPED, MY...MY ARMS ARE PINNED.

ARMOR'S HOLDING, BUT I'M LOSING...

...POWER...

I THINK I'M GOING INTO...

...SHOCK...

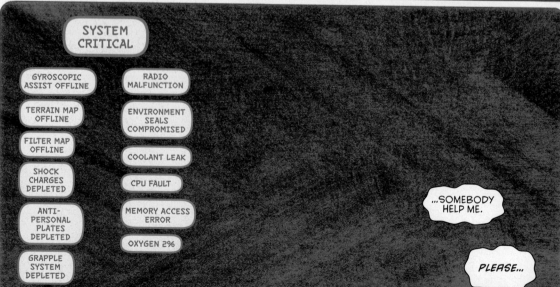

**SYSTEM CRITICAL**

GYROSCOPIC ASSIST OFFLINE

RADIO MALFUNCTION

TERRAIN MAP OFFLINE

ENVIRONMENT SEALS COMPROMISED

FILTER MAP OFFLINE

COOLANT LEAK

SHOCK CHARGES DEPLETED

CPU FAULT

ANTI-PERSONAL PLATES DEPLETED

MEMORY ACCESS ERROR

GRAPPLE SYSTEM DEPLETED

OXYGEN 2%

...SOMEBODY HELP ME.

*PLEASE...*

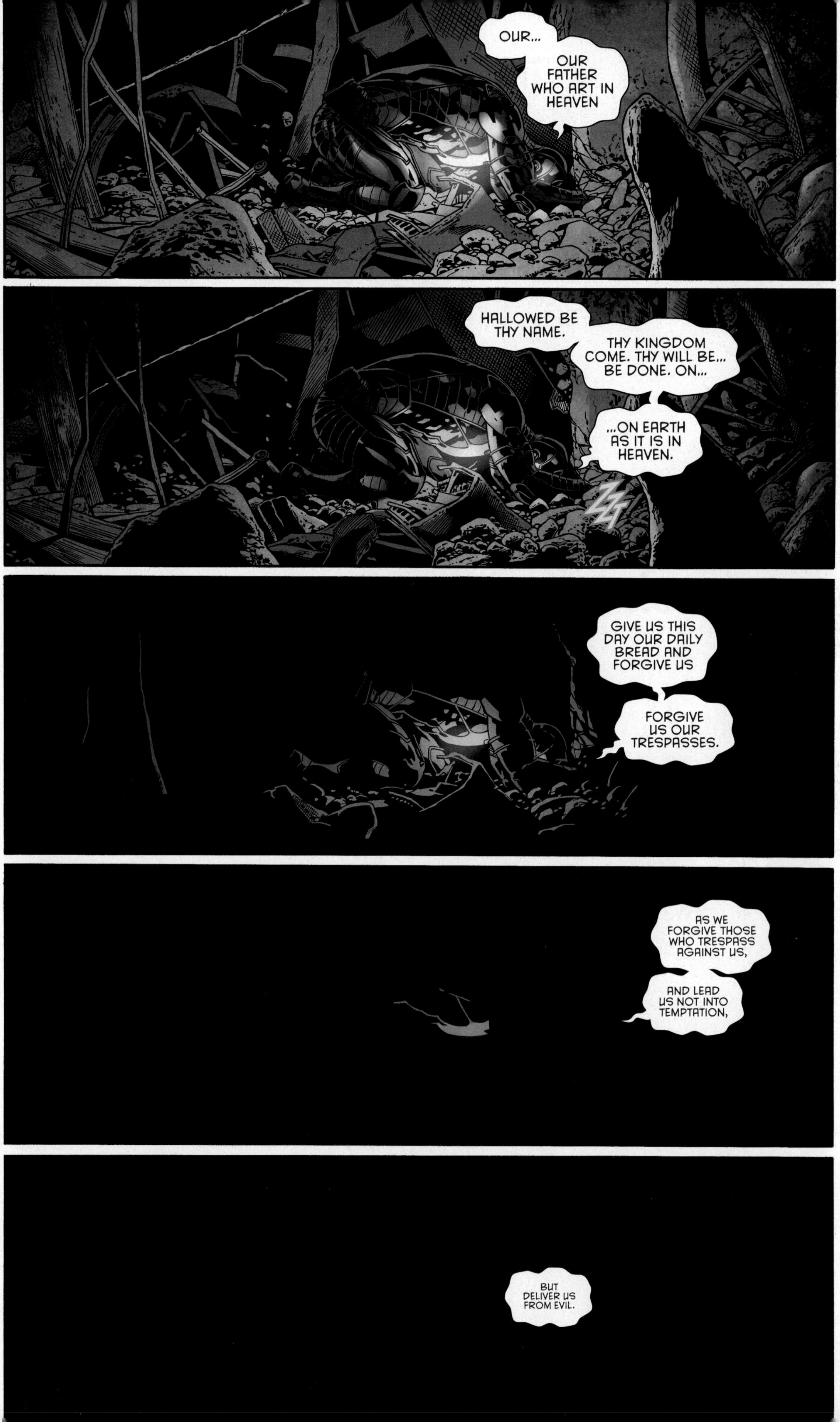
OUR...
OUR FATHER WHO ART IN HEAVEN
HALLOWED BE THY NAME.
THY KINGDOM COME. THY WILL BE... BE DONE. ON...
...ON EARTH AS IT IS IN HEAVEN.
ZZT
GIVE US THIS DAY OUR DAILY BREAD AND FORGIVE US
FORGIVE US OUR TRESPASSES.
AS WE FORGIVE THOSE WHO TRESPASS AGAINST US,
AND LEAD US NOT INTO TEMPTATION,
BUT DELIVER US FROM EVIL.

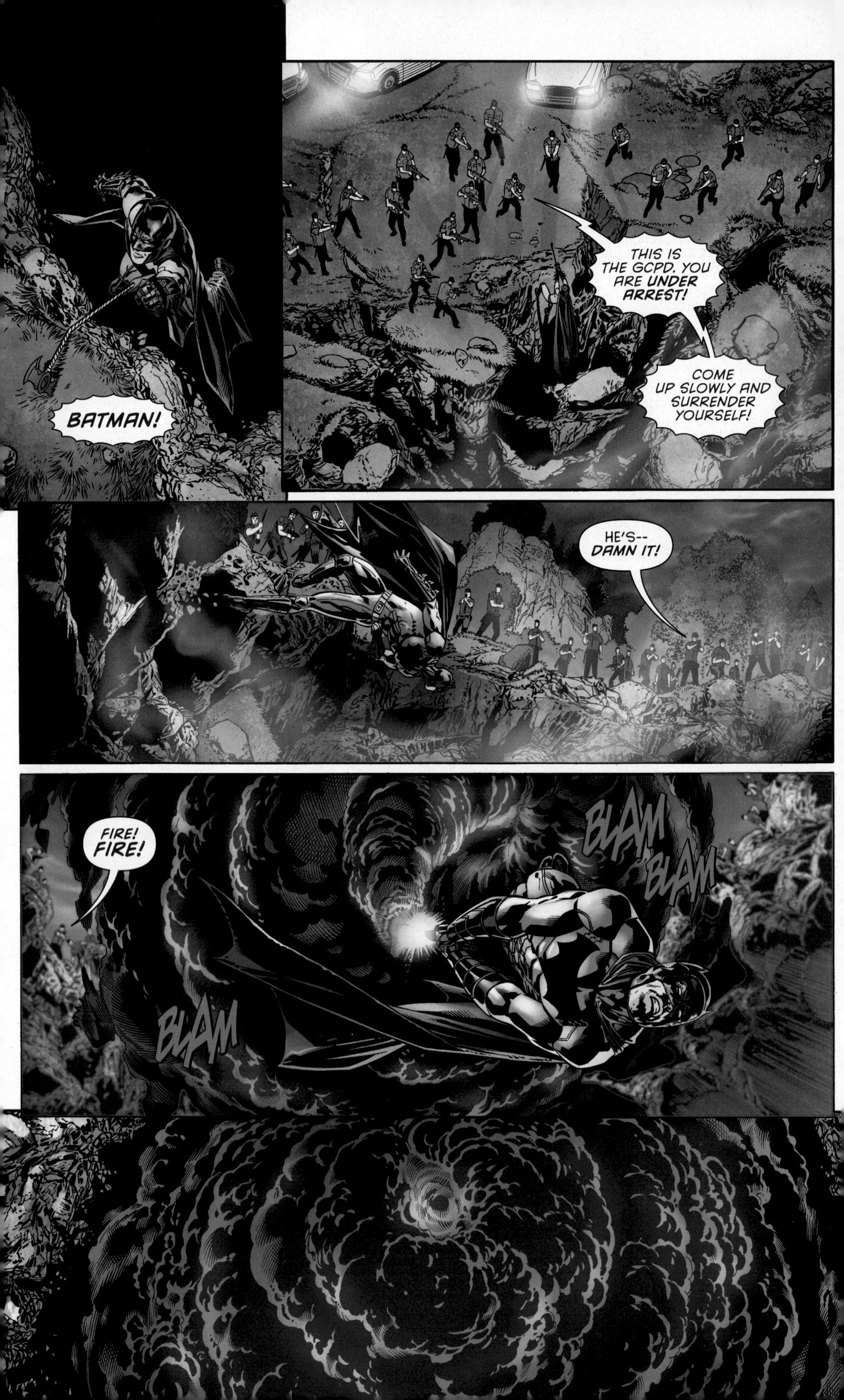
BATMAN!
THIS IS THE GCPD. YOU ARE UNDER ARREST!
COME UP SLOWLY AND SURRENDER YOURSELF!
HE'S-- DAMN IT!
FIRE! FIRE!
BLAM
BLAM
BLAM

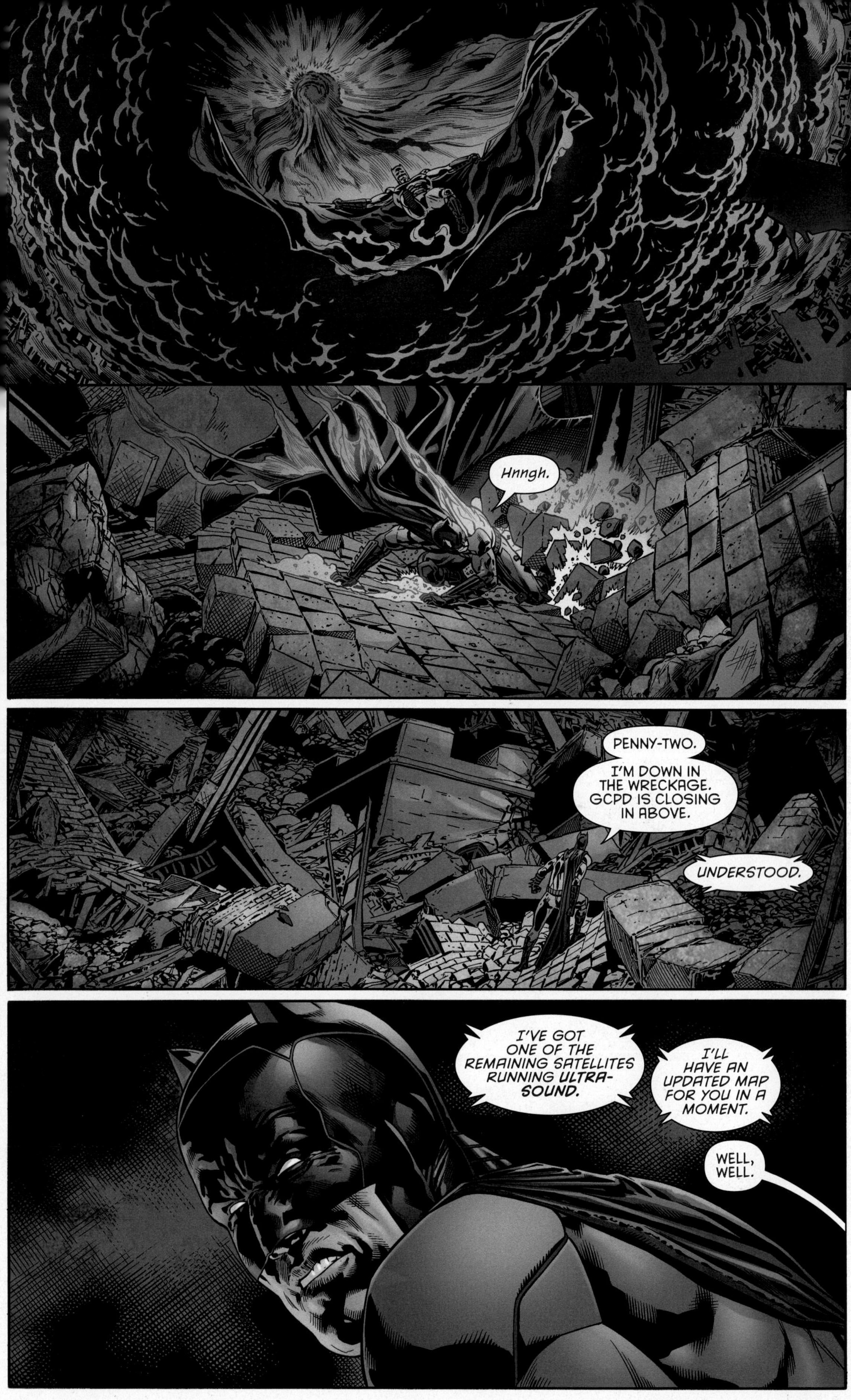
Hnngh.
PENNY-TWO.
I'M DOWN IN THE WRECKAGE. GCPD IS CLOSING IN ABOVE.
UNDERSTOOD.
I'VE GOT ONE OF THE REMAINING SATELLITES RUNNING ULTRA-SOUND.
I'LL HAVE AN UPDATED MAP FOR YOU IN A MOMENT.
WELL, WELL.

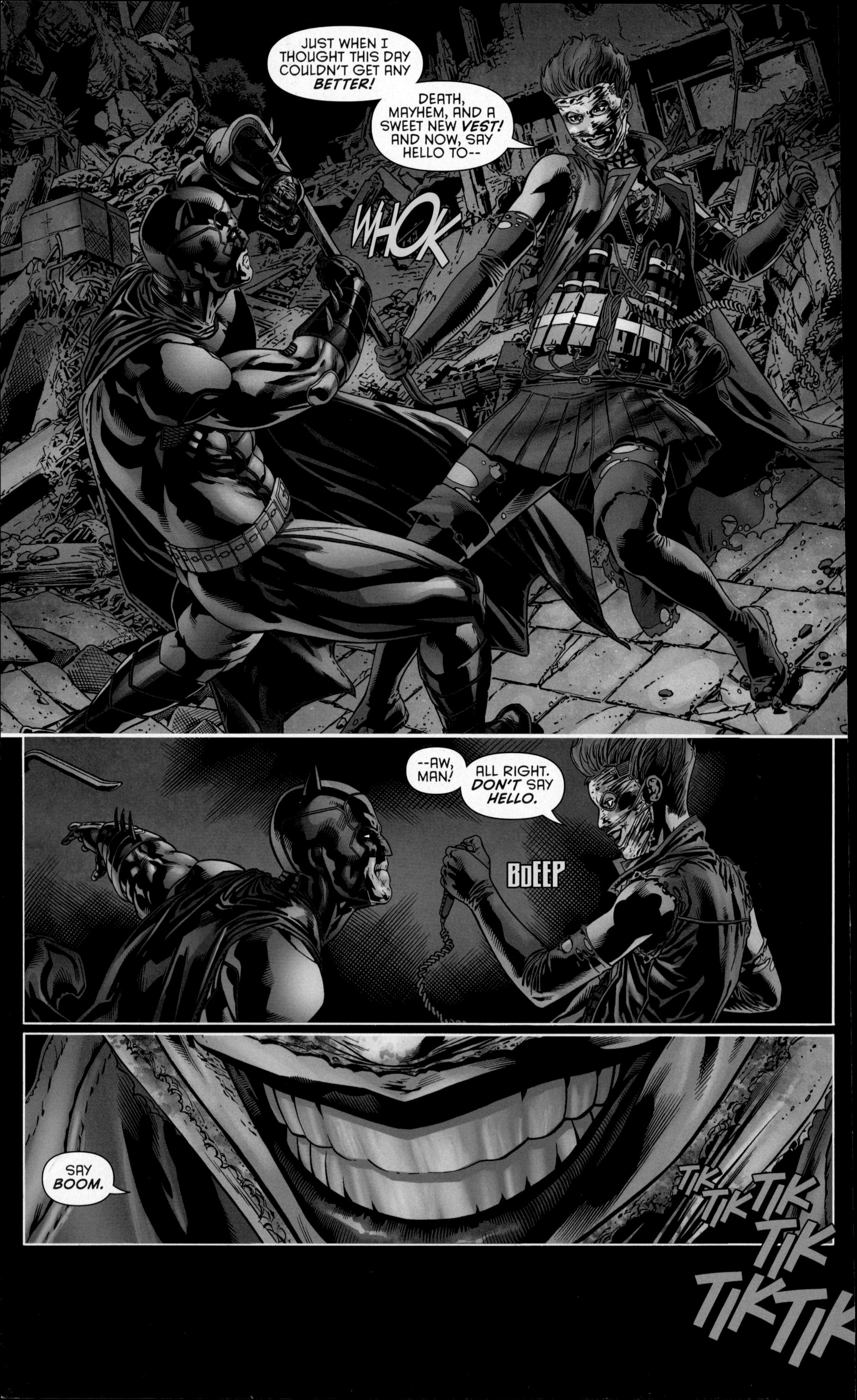
JUST WHEN I THOUGHT THIS DAY COULDN'T GET ANY *BETTER!*
DEATH, MAYHEM, AND A SWEET NEW *VEST!* AND NOW, SAY HELLO TO--
WHOK
--AW, MAN!
ALL RIGHT. *DON'T* SAY *HELLO.*
BDEEP
SAY *BOOM.*
TIK TIK TIK TIK TIK TIK

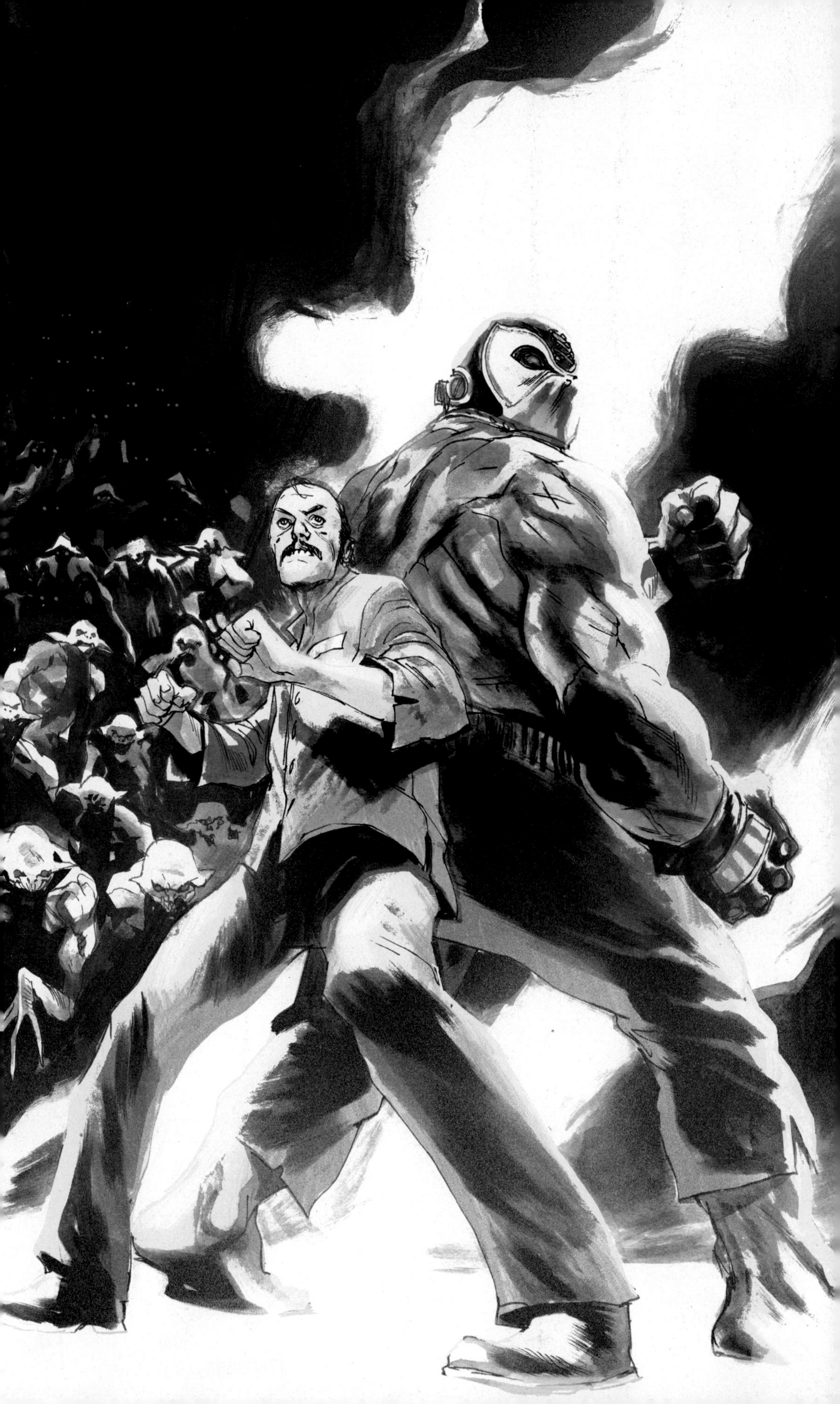

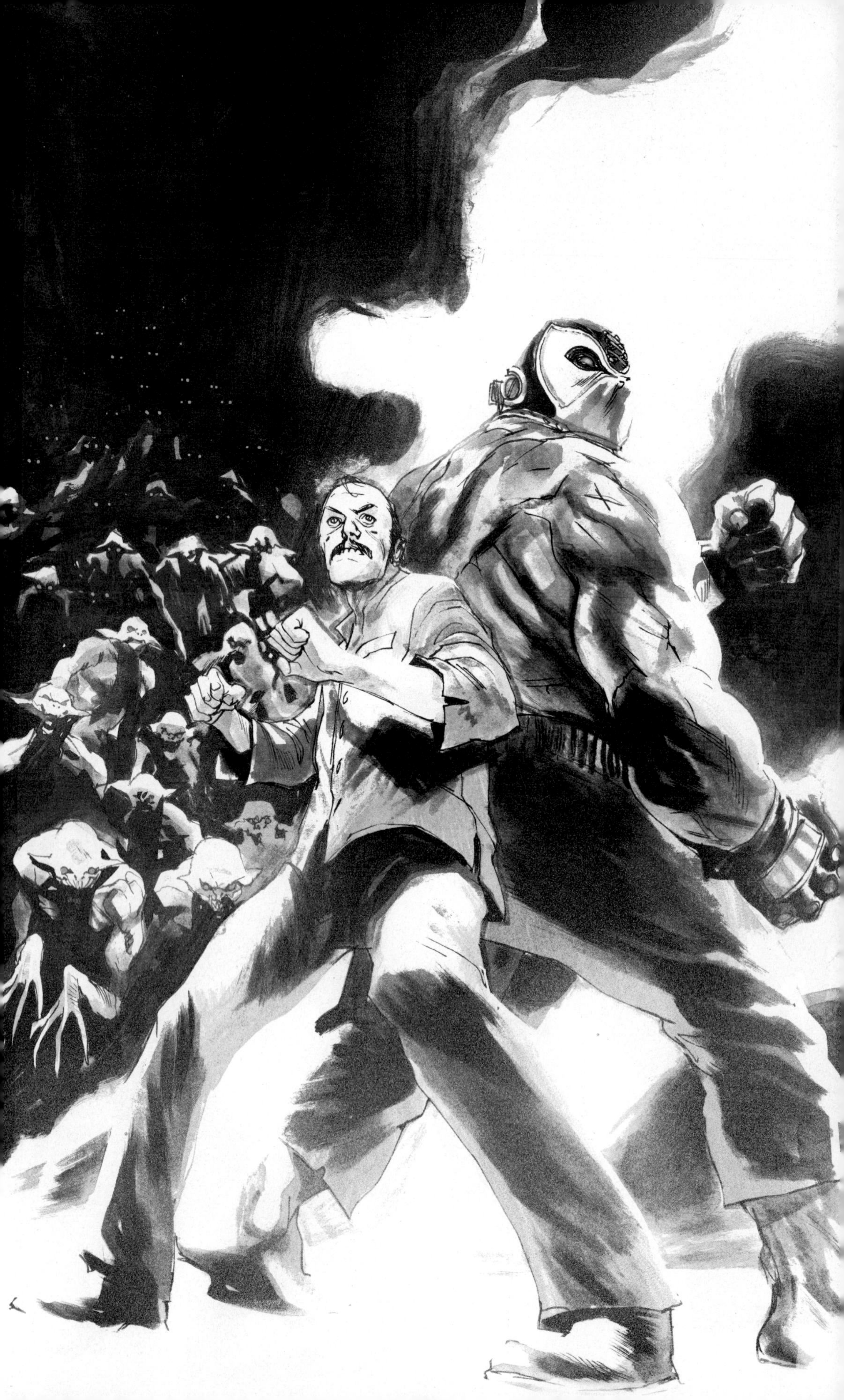

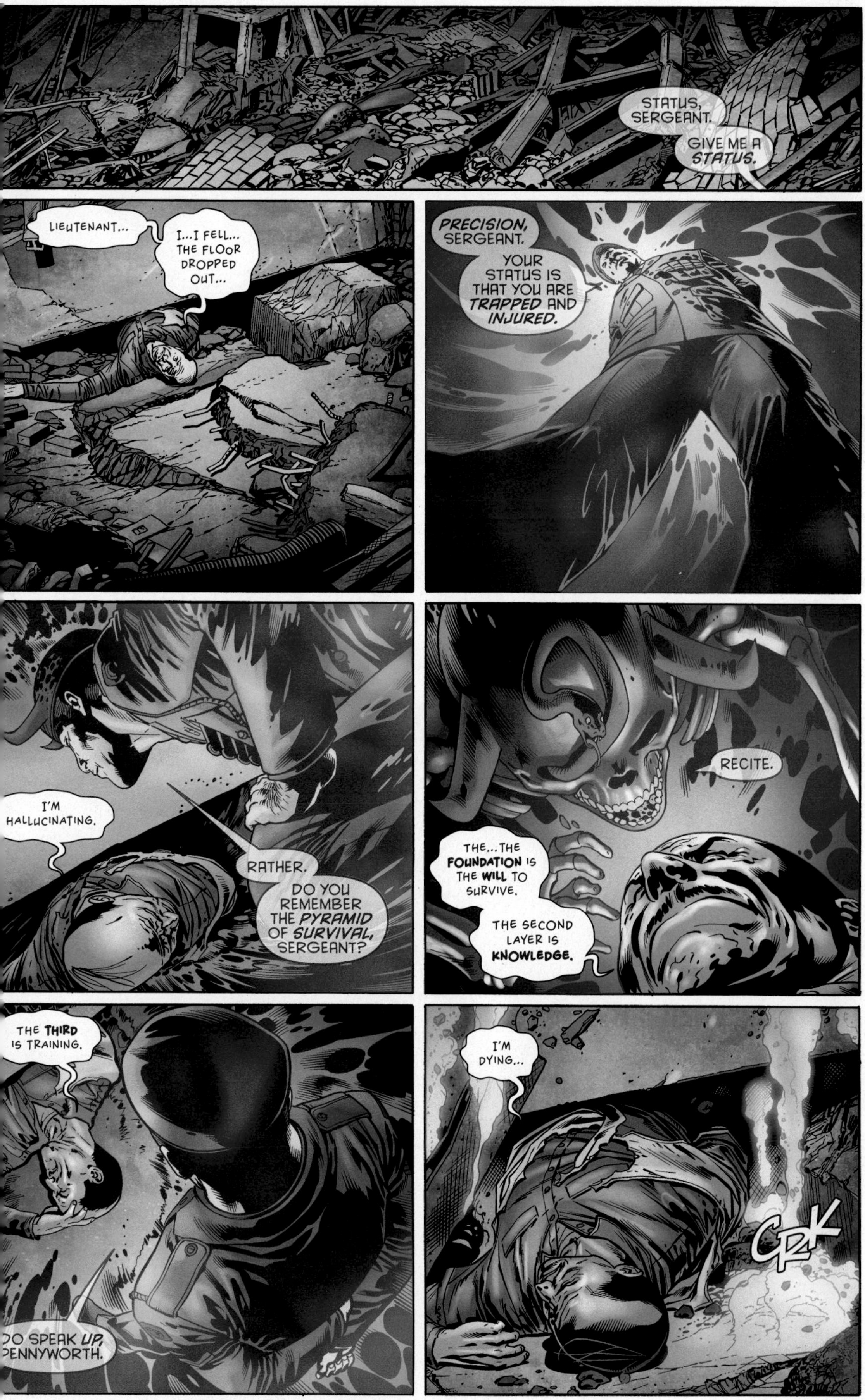
STATUS, SERGEANT.
GIVE ME A STATUS.
LIEUTENANT...
I...I FELL... THE FLOOR DROPPED OUT...
PRECISION, SERGEANT.
YOUR STATUS IS THAT YOU ARE TRAPPED AND INJURED.
I'M HALLUCINATING.
RATHER.
DO YOU REMEMBER THE PYRAMID OF SURVIVAL, SERGEANT?
RECITE.
THE...THE FOUNDATION IS THE WILL TO SURVIVE.
THE SECOND LAYER IS KNOWLEDGE.
THE THIRD IS TRAINING.
DO SPEAK UP, PENNYWORTH.
I'M DYING...
CRK

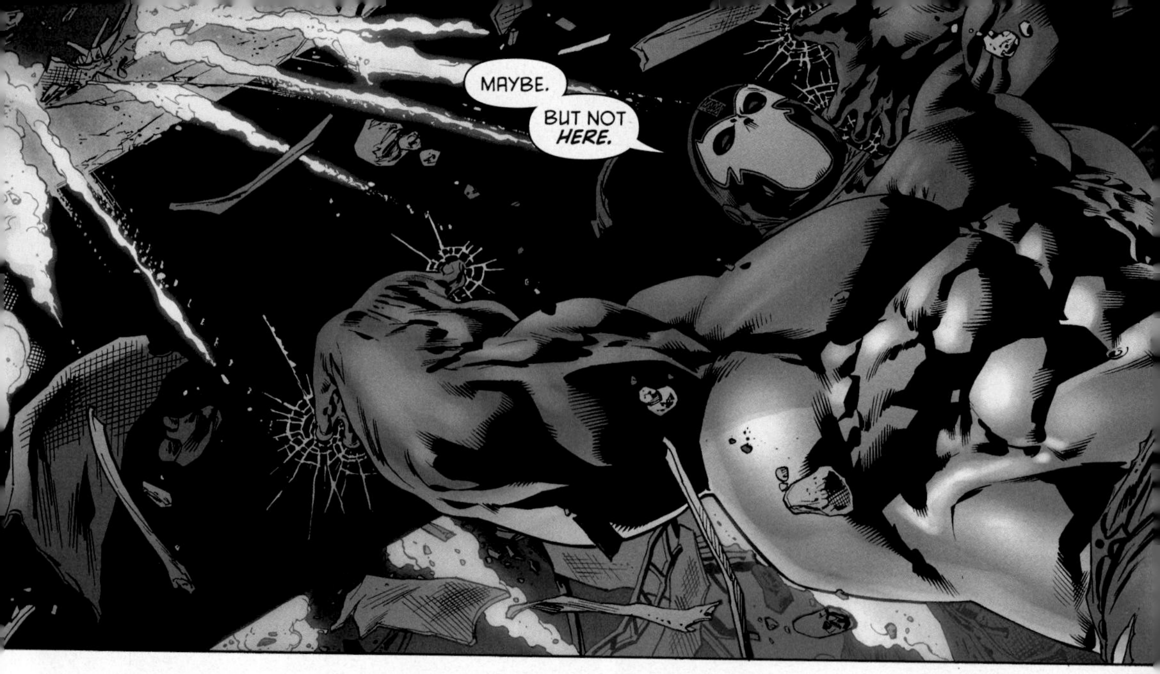
MAYBE.
BUT NOT *HERE.*

# BURIED DEEP

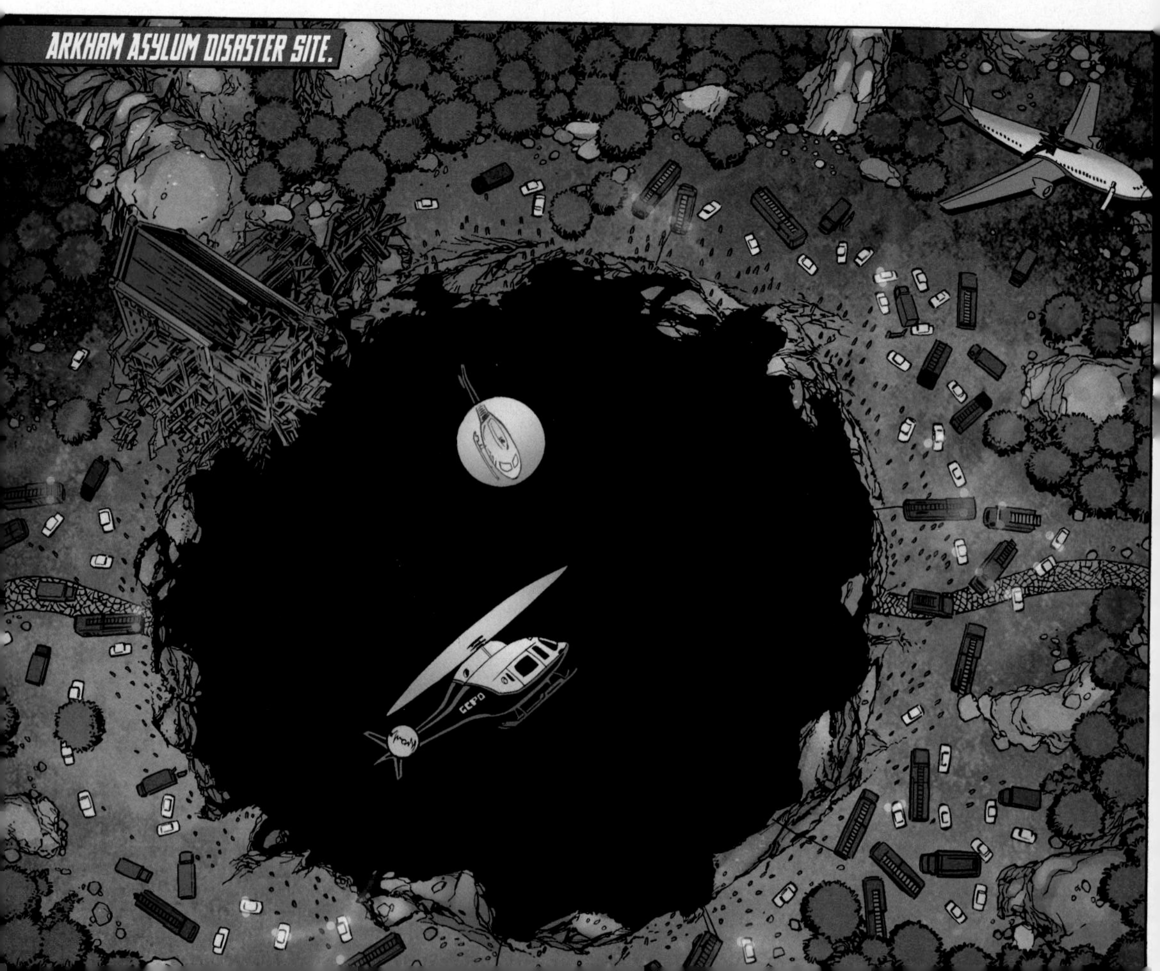
ARKHAM ASYLUM DISASTER SITE.
GCPD

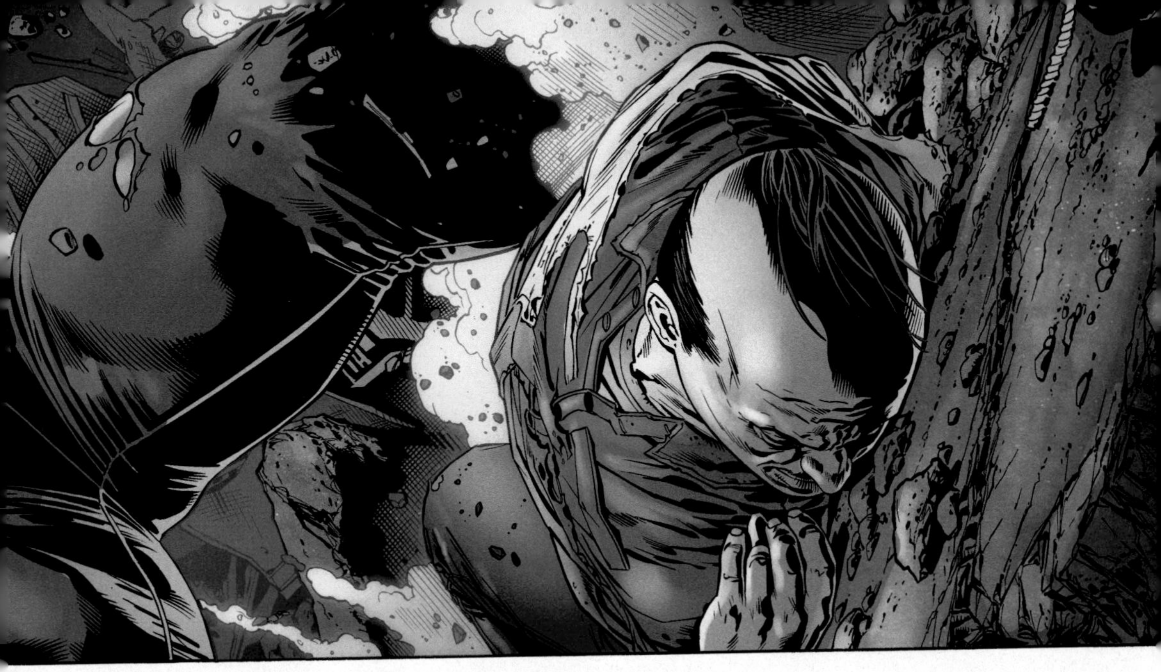

SCOTT SNYDER & JAMES TYNION IV STORY RAY FAWKES SCRIPT
KYLE HIGGINS & TIM SEELEY CONSULTING WRITERS FERNANDO PASARIN PENCILS
MATT RYAN INKS BLOND COLORS TAYLOR ESPOSITO LETTERS RAFAEL ALBUQUERQUE COVER

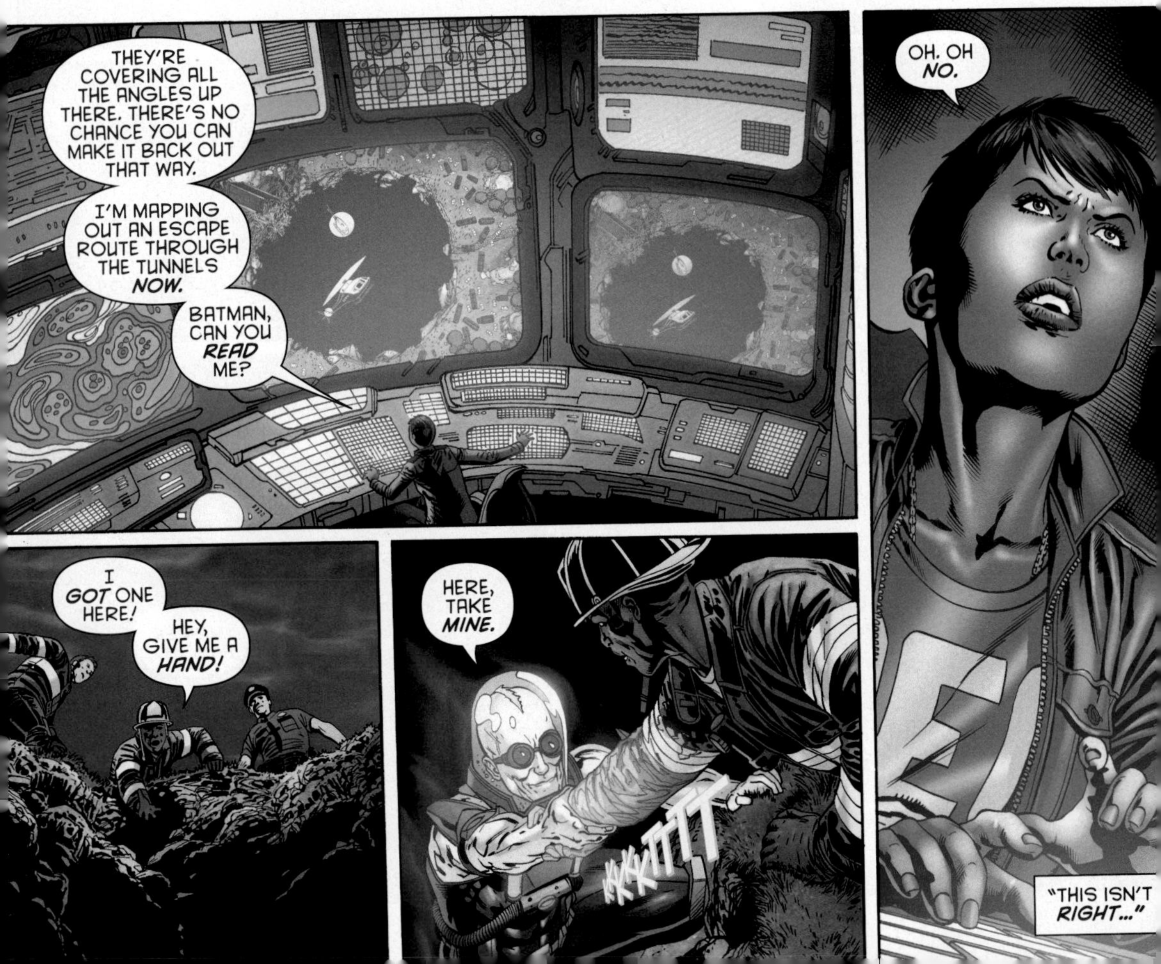
THEY'RE COVERING ALL THE ANGLES UP THERE. THERE'S NO CHANCE YOU CAN MAKE IT BACK OUT THAT WAY.
I'M MAPPING OUT AN ESCAPE ROUTE THROUGH THE TUNNELS *NOW.*
BATMAN, CAN YOU *READ* ME?
OH. OH *NO.*
I *GOT* ONE HERE!
HEY, GIVE ME A *HAND!*
HERE, TAKE *MINE.*
"THIS ISN'T *RIGHT...*"

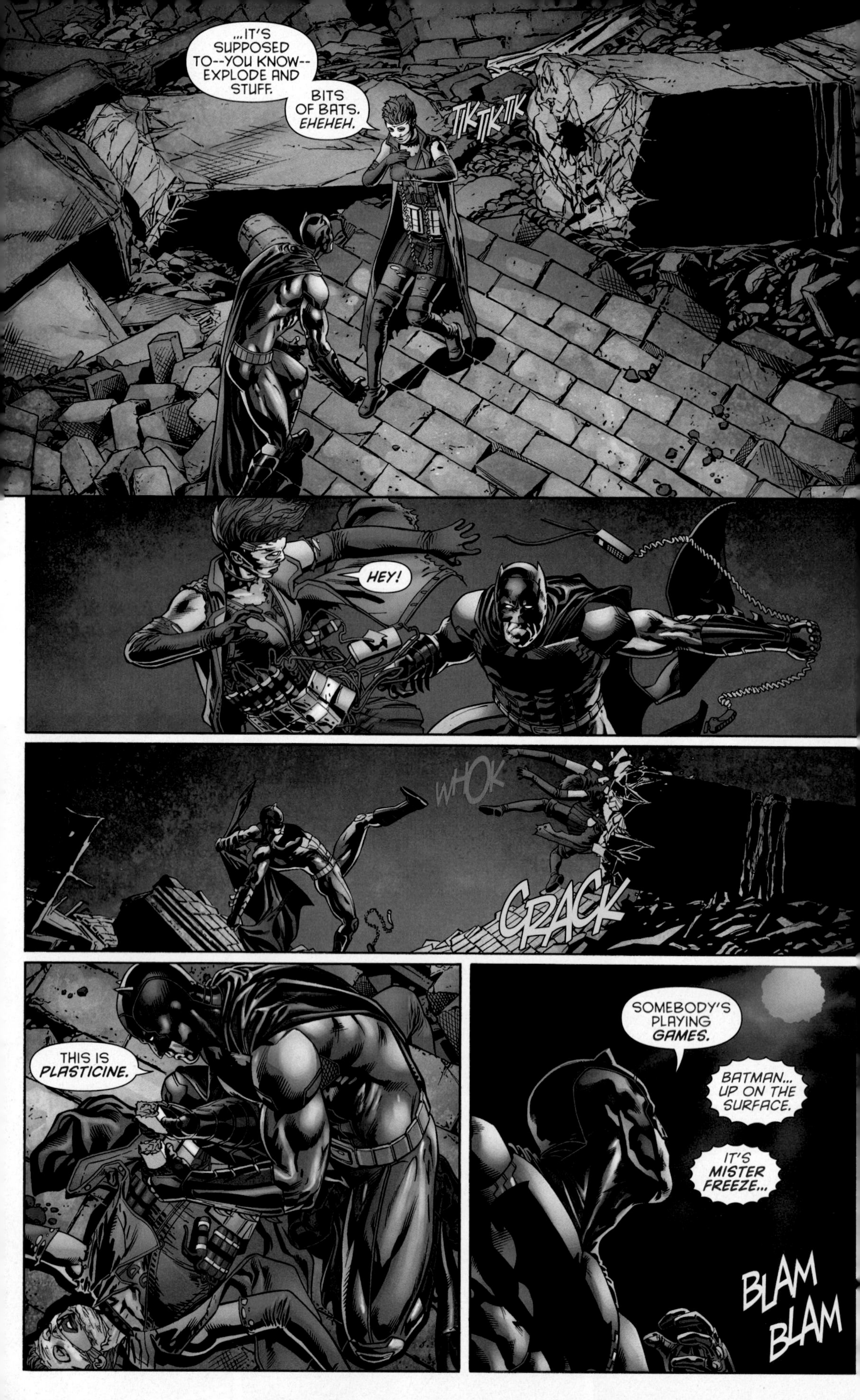
...IT'S SUPPOSED TO--YOU KNOW--EXPLODE AND STUFF.
BITS OF BATS. EHEHEH.
TIK TIK TIK
HEY!
WHOK
CRACK
THIS IS PLASTICINE.
SOMEBODY'S PLAYING GAMES.
BATMAN... UP ON THE SURFACE.
IT'S MISTER FREEZE...
BLAM BLAM

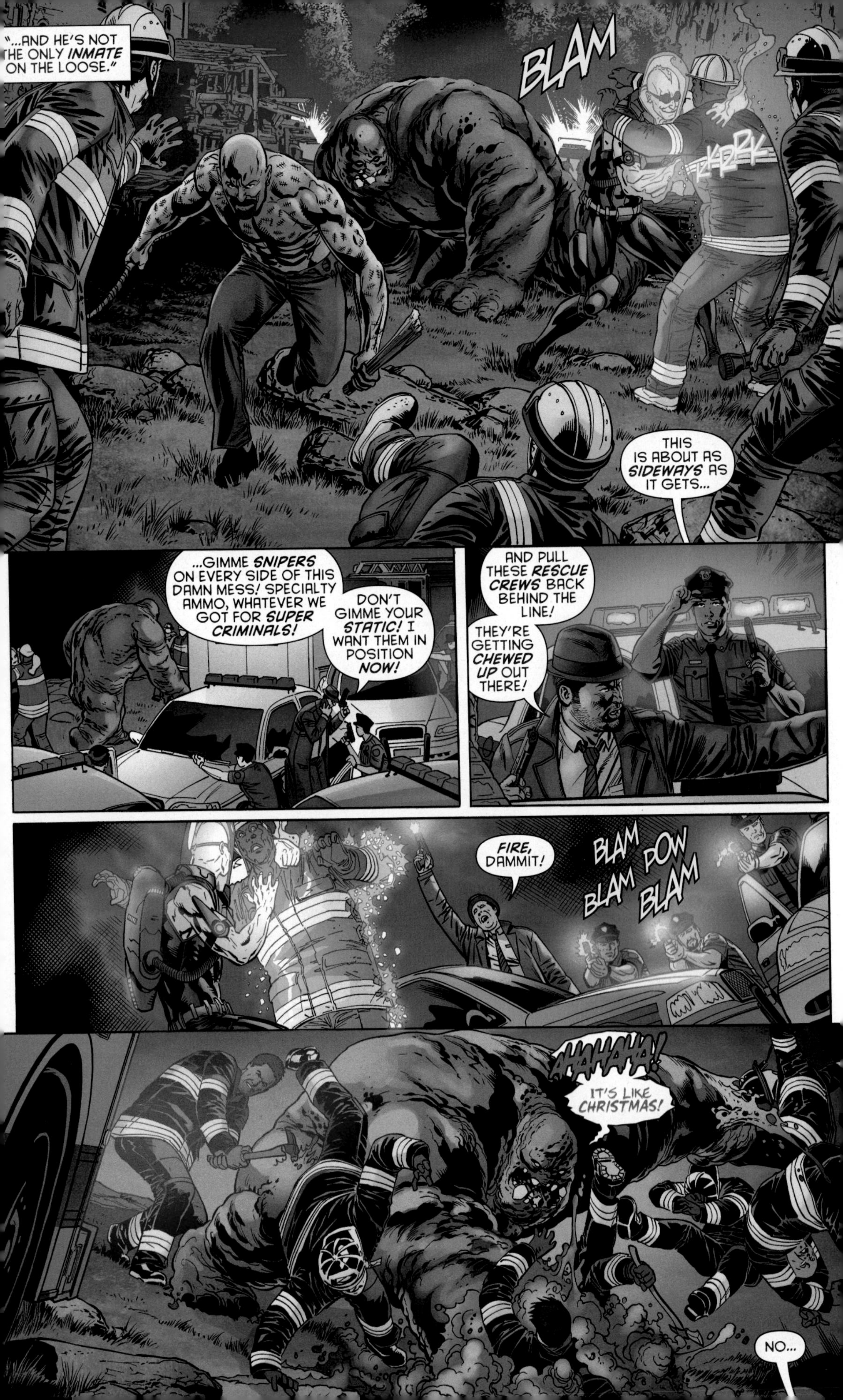
"...AND HE'S NOT THE ONLY *INMATE* ON THE LOOSE."
BLAM
KRRK
THIS IS ABOUT AS *SIDEWAYS* AS IT GETS...
...GIMME *SNIPERS* ON EVERY SIDE OF THIS DAMN MESS! SPECIALTY AMMO, WHATEVER WE GOT FOR *SUPER CRIMINALS!*
DON'T GIMME YOUR *STATIC!* I WANT THEM IN POSITION *NOW!*
AND PULL THESE *RESCUE CREWS* BACK BEHIND THE LINE!
THEY'RE GETTING *CHEWED UP* OUT THERE!
*FIRE,* DAMMIT!
BLAM
BLAM POW
BLAM
AHAHAHA!
IT'S LIKE *CHRISTMAS!*
NO...

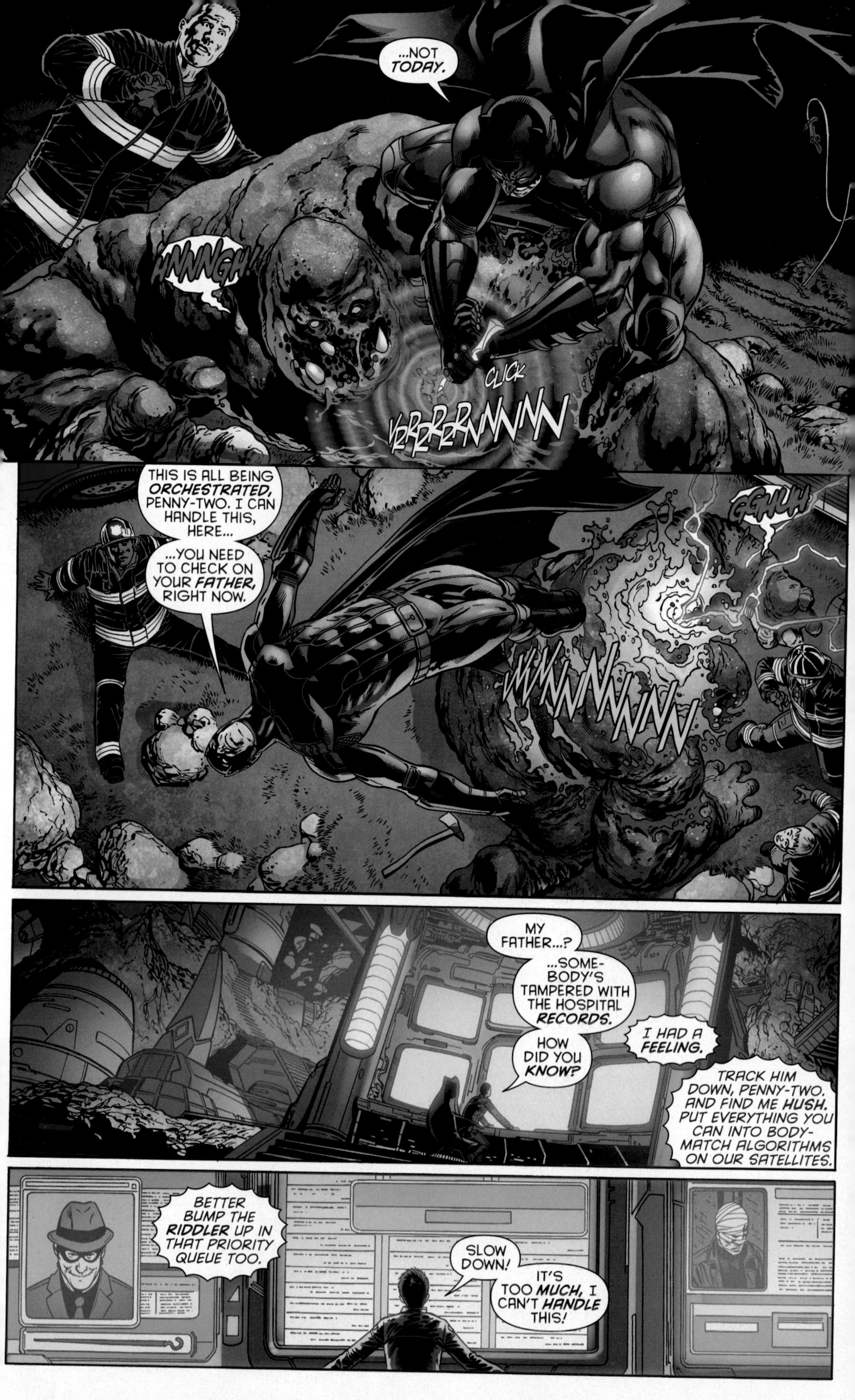

...NOT TODAY.
HNNNGH!
CLICK
VRRRRRRNNNNN
THIS IS ALL BEING ORCHESTRATED, PENNY-TWO. I CAN HANDLE THIS, HERE...
...YOU NEED TO CHECK ON YOUR FATHER, RIGHT NOW.
GGHUH
WNNNNNNN
MY FATHER...?
...SOMEBODY'S TAMPERED WITH THE HOSPITAL RECORDS.
HOW DID YOU KNOW?
I HAD A FEELING.
TRACK HIM DOWN, PENNY-TWO. AND FIND ME HUSH. PUT EVERYTHING YOU CAN INTO BODY-MATCH ALGORITHMS ON OUR SATELLITES.
BETTER BUMP THE RIDDLER UP IN THAT PRIORITY QUEUE TOO.
SLOW DOWN!
IT'S TOO MUCH, I CAN'T HANDLE THIS!

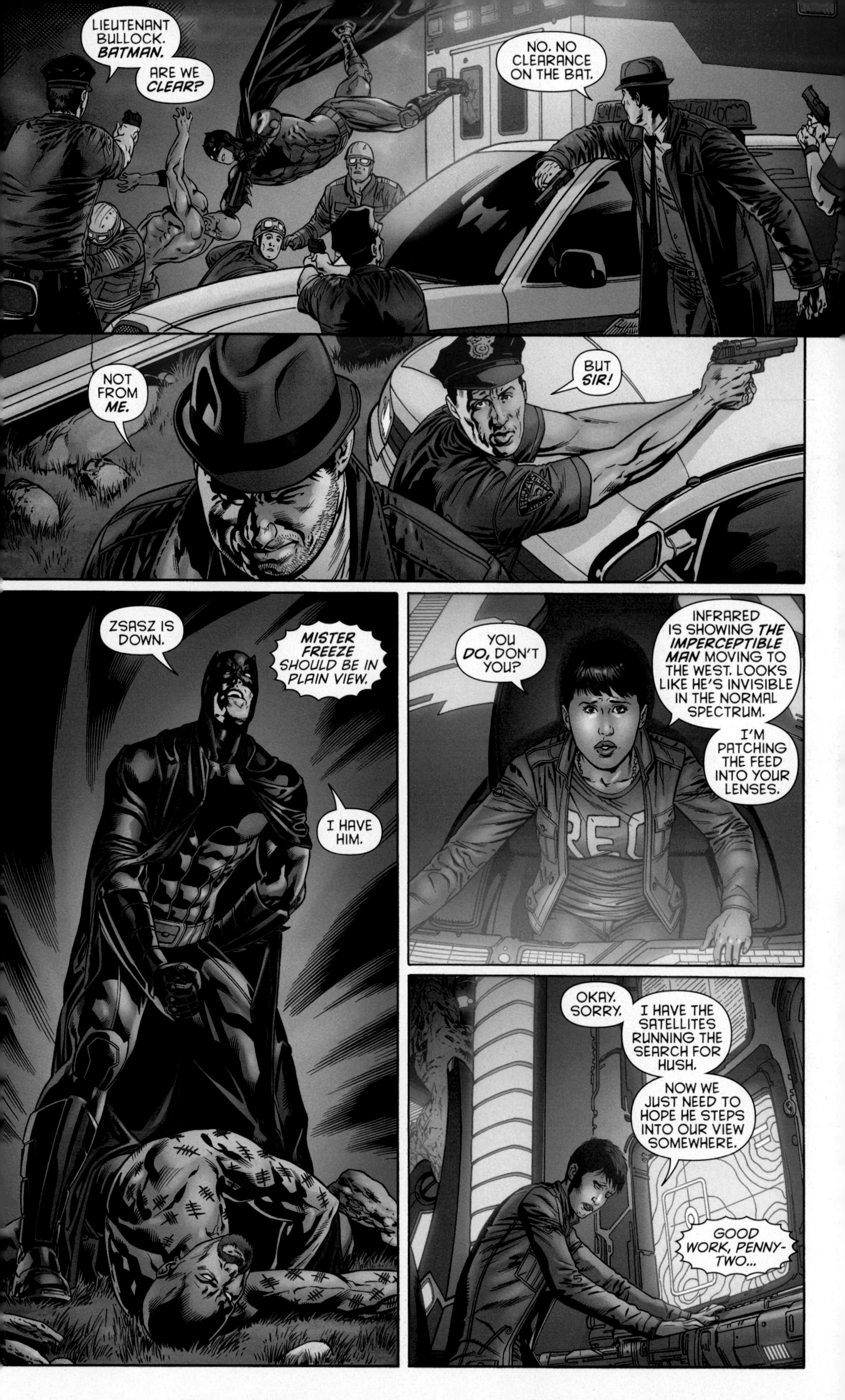
LIEUTENANT BULLOCK. BATMAN.
ARE WE CLEAR?
NO. NO CLEARANCE ON THE BAT.
NOT FROM ME.
BUT SIR!
ZSASZ IS DOWN.
MISTER FREEZE SHOULD BE IN PLAIN VIEW.
I HAVE HIM.
YOU DO, DON'T YOU?
INFRARED IS SHOWING THE IMPERCEPTIBLE MAN MOVING TO THE WEST. LOOKS LIKE HE'S INVISIBLE IN THE NORMAL SPECTRUM.
I'M PATCHING THE FEED INTO YOUR LENSES.
OKAY. SORRY.
I HAVE THE SATELLITES RUNNING THE SEARCH FOR HUSH.
NOW WE JUST NEED TO HOPE HE STEPS INTO OUR VIEW SOMEWHERE.
GOOD WORK, PENNY-TWO...

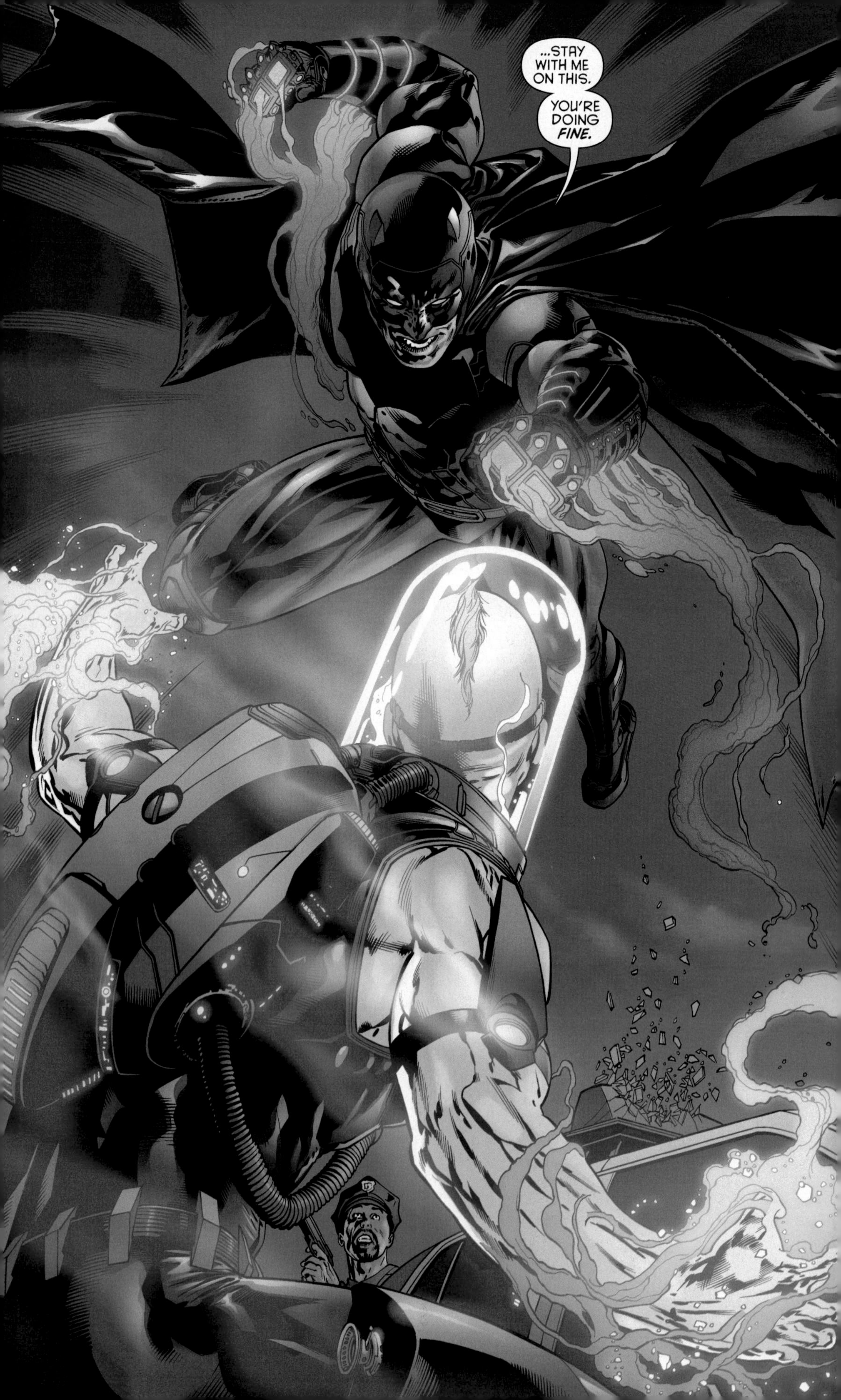
...STAY WITH ME ON THIS.
YOU'RE DOING *FINE.*

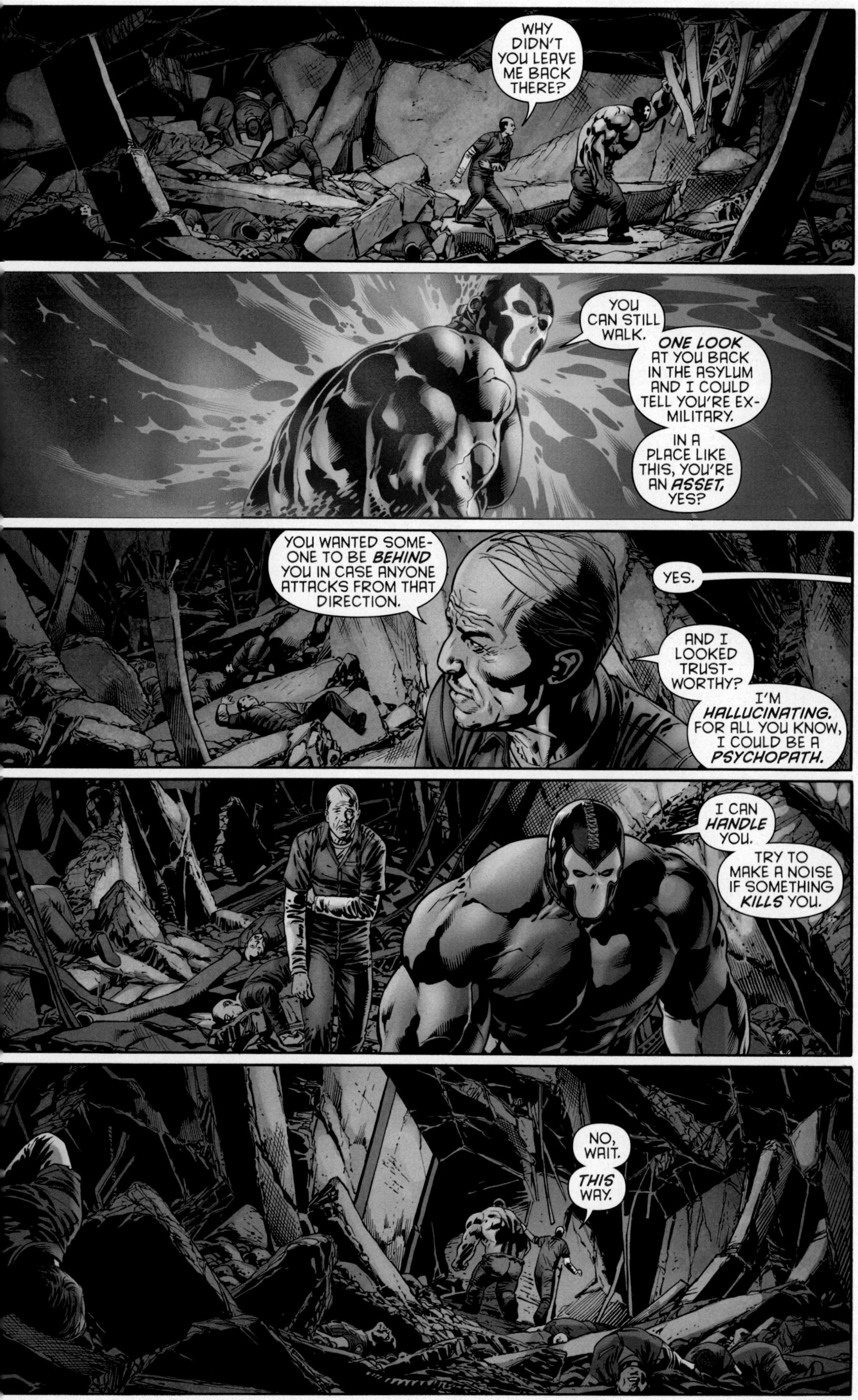
WHY DIDN'T YOU LEAVE ME BACK THERE?
YOU CAN STILL WALK. ONE LOOK AT YOU BACK IN THE ASYLUM AND I COULD TELL YOU'RE EX-MILITARY.
IN A PLACE LIKE THIS, YOU'RE AN ASSET, YES?
YOU WANTED SOME-ONE TO BE BEHIND YOU IN CASE ANYONE ATTACKS FROM THAT DIRECTION.
YES.
AND I LOOKED TRUST-WORTHY?
I'M HALLUCINATING. FOR ALL YOU KNOW, I COULD BE A PSYCHOPATH.
I CAN HANDLE YOU.
TRY TO MAKE A NOISE IF SOMETHING KILLS YOU.
NO, WAIT.
THIS WAY.

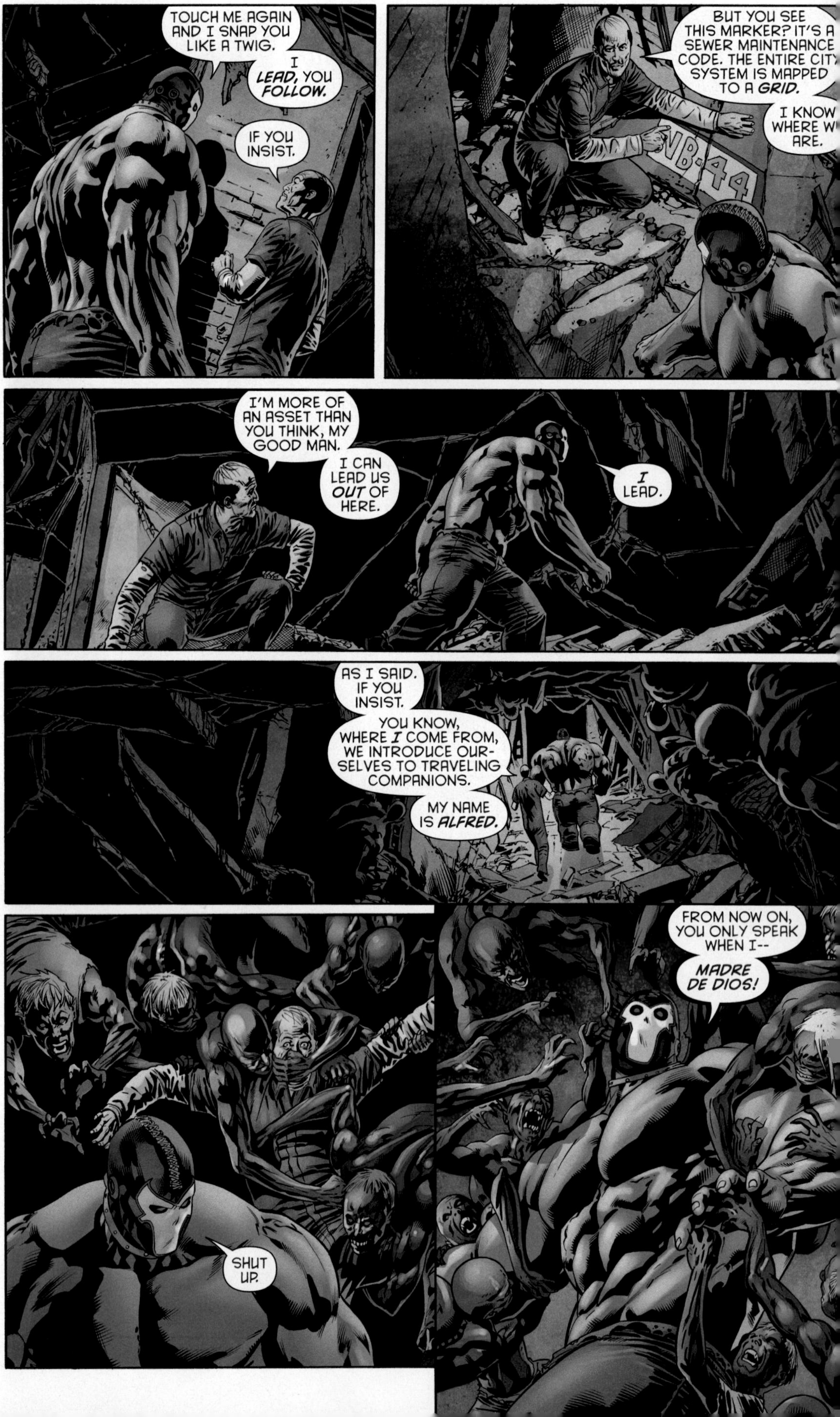
TOUCH ME AGAIN AND I SNAP YOU LIKE A TWIG.
I *LEAD*, YOU *FOLLOW*.
IF YOU INSIST.
BUT YOU SEE THIS MARKER? IT'S A SEWER MAINTENANCE CODE. THE ENTIRE CITY SYSTEM IS MAPPED TO A *GRID*.
I KNOW WHERE WE ARE.
VB-44
I'M MORE OF AN ASSET THAN YOU THINK, MY GOOD MAN.
I CAN LEAD US *OUT* OF HERE.
*I* LEAD.
AS I SAID. IF YOU INSIST.
YOU KNOW, WHERE *I* COME FROM, WE INTRODUCE OUR-SELVES TO TRAVELING COMPANIONS.
MY NAME IS *ALFRED*.
SHUT UP.
FROM NOW ON, YOU ONLY SPEAK WHEN I--
*MADRE DE DIOS!*

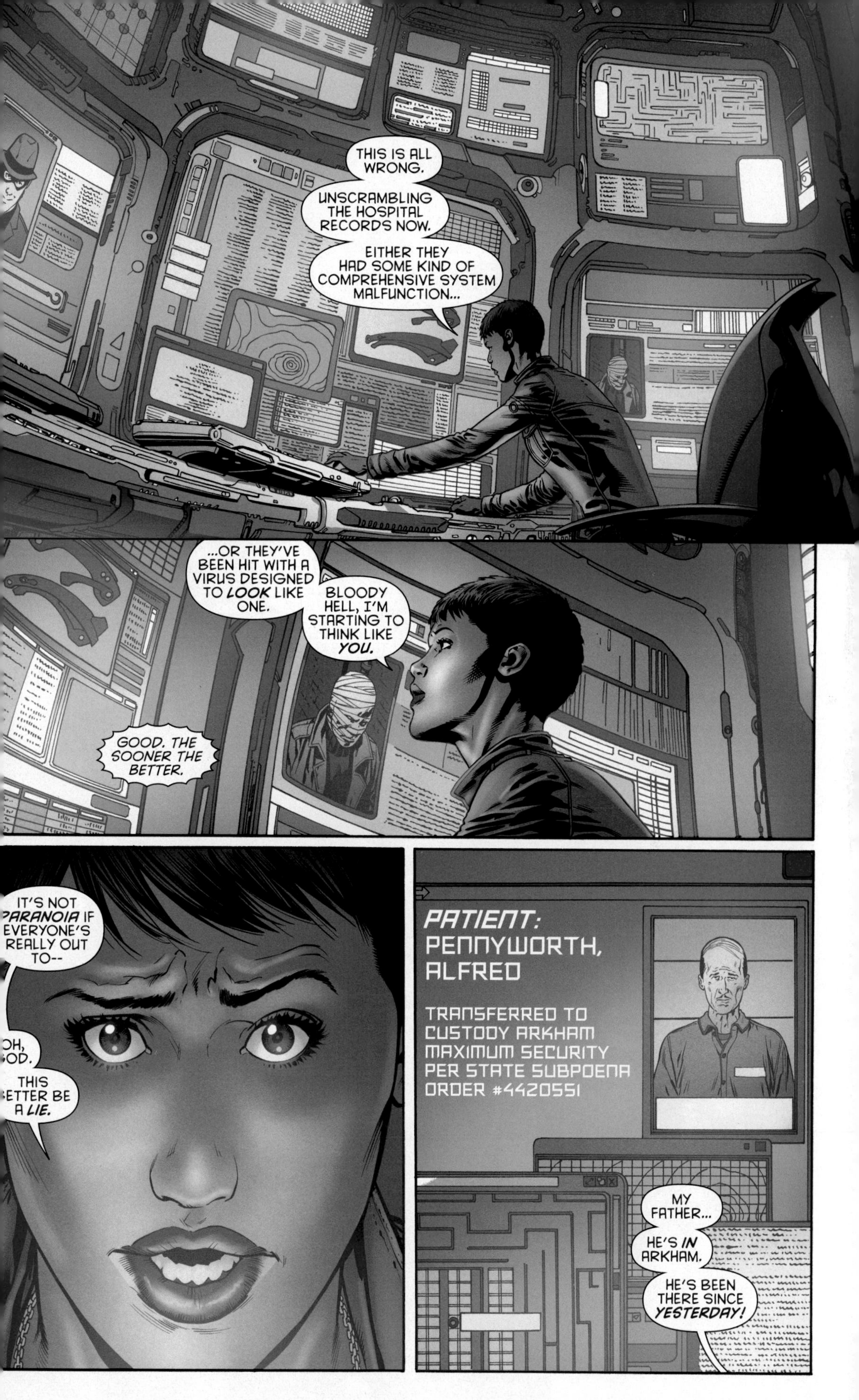

THIS IS ALL WRONG.
UNSCRAMBLING THE HOSPITAL RECORDS NOW.
EITHER THEY HAD SOME KIND OF COMPREHENSIVE SYSTEM MALFUNCTION...
...OR THEY'VE BEEN HIT WITH A VIRUS DESIGNED TO LOOK LIKE ONE.
BLOODY HELL, I'M STARTING TO THINK LIKE YOU.
GOOD. THE SOONER THE BETTER.
IT'S NOT PARANOIA IF EVERYONE'S REALLY OUT TO--
OH, GOD.
THIS BETTER BE A LIE.
PATIENT: PENNYWORTH, ALFRED
TRANSFERRED TO CUSTODY ARKHAM MAXIMUM SECURITY PER STATE SUBPOENA ORDER #4420551
MY FATHER...
HE'S IN ARKHAM.
HE'S BEEN THERE SINCE YESTERDAY!

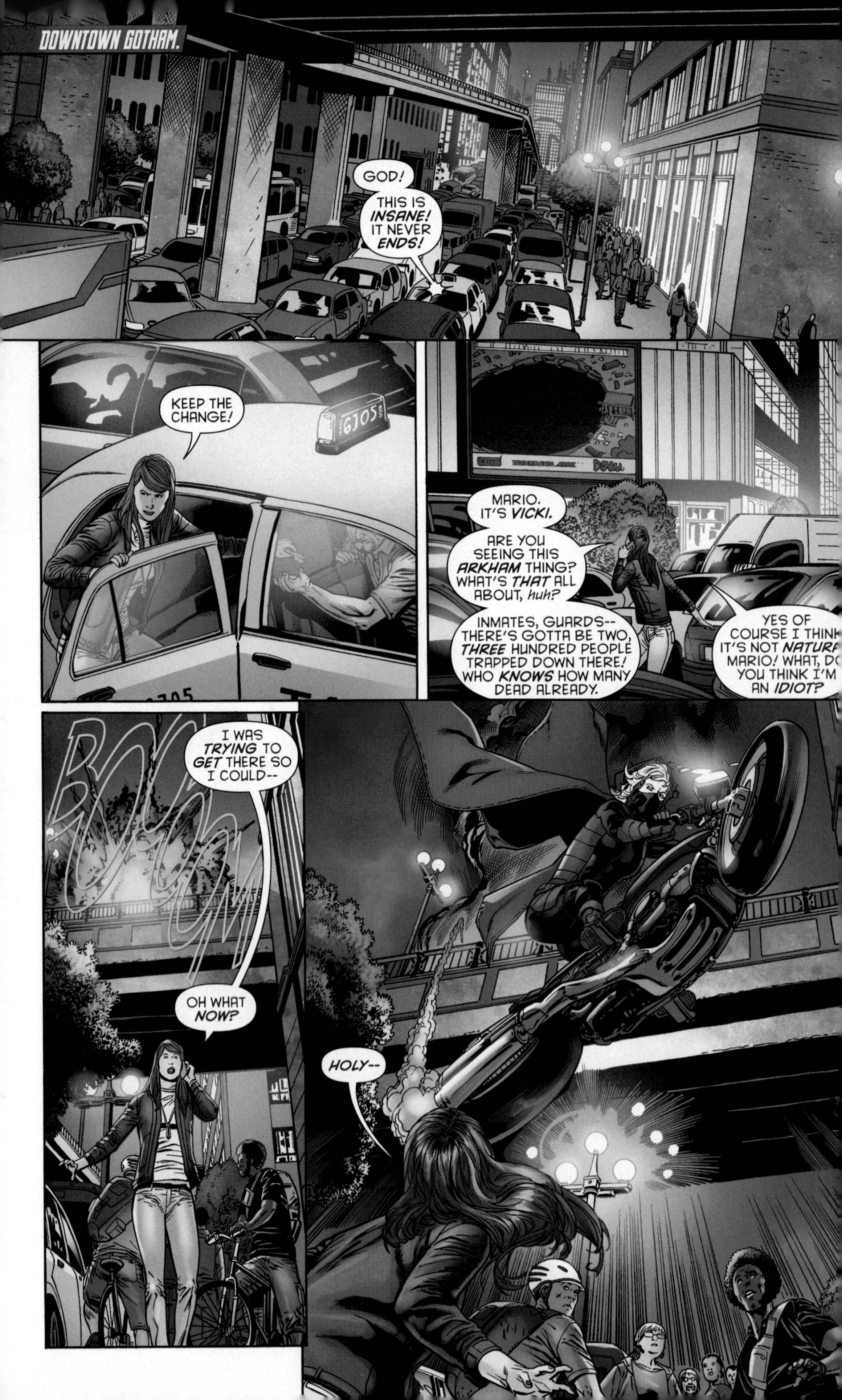
DOWNTOWN GOTHAM.
GOD!
THIS IS INSANE! IT NEVER ENDS!
KEEP THE CHANGE!
MARIO. IT'S VICKI.
ARE YOU SEEING THIS ARKHAM THING? WHAT'S THAT ALL ABOUT, huh?
INMATES, GUARDS-- THERE'S GOTTA BE TWO, THREE HUNDRED PEOPLE TRAPPED DOWN THERE! WHO KNOWS HOW MANY DEAD ALREADY.
YES OF COURSE I THINK IT'S NOT NATURA MARIO! WHAT, DO YOU THINK I'M AN IDIOT?
BOOOOM
I WAS TRYING TO GET THERE SO I COULD--
OH WHAT NOW?
HOLY--

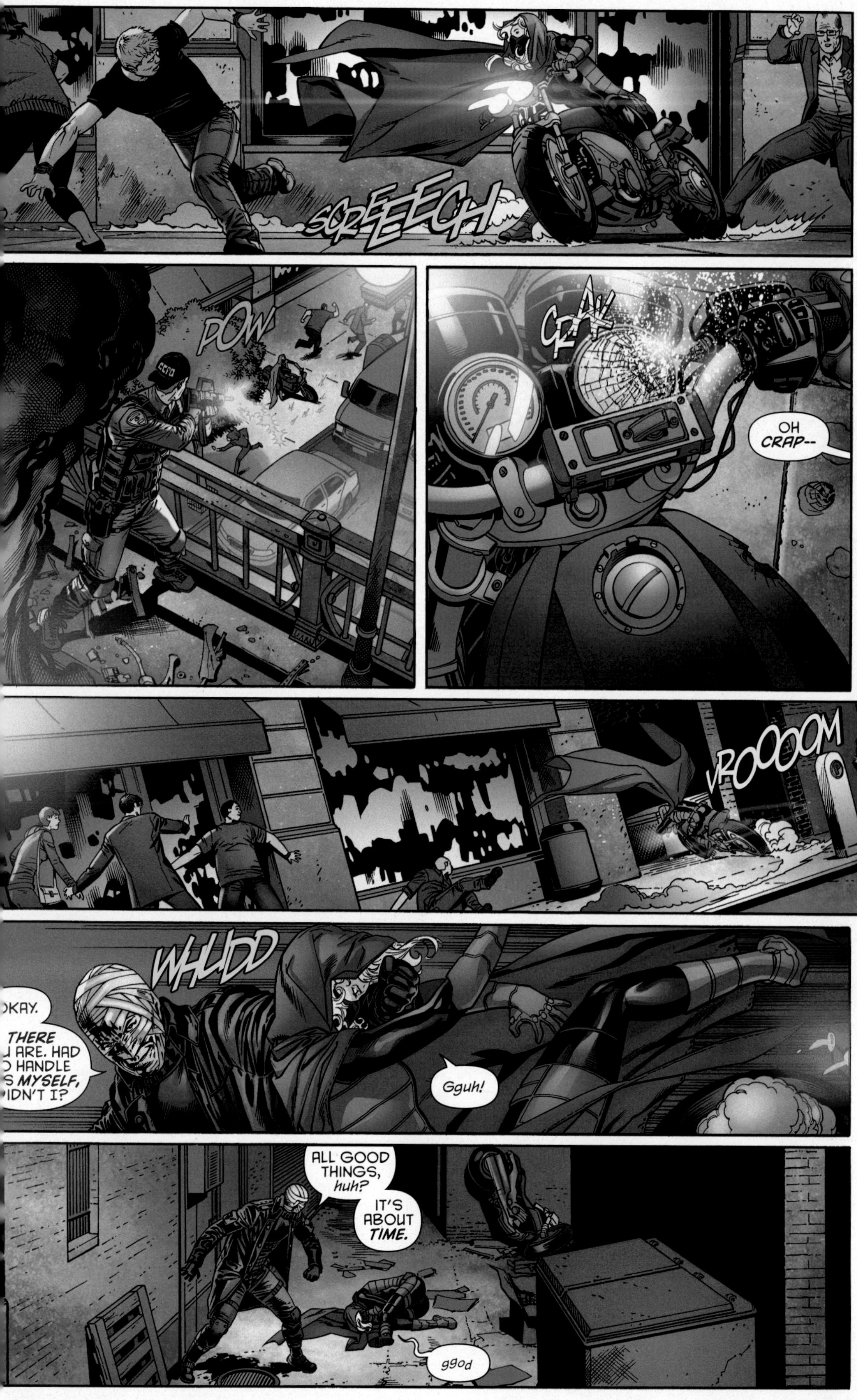
SCREEEECH
POW
CRAK
OH CRAP--
VROOOOOM
WHUDD
OKAY.
THERE U ARE. HAD O HANDLE S MYSELF, IDN'T I?
Gguh!
ALL GOOD THINGS, huh?
IT'S ABOUT TIME.
ggod

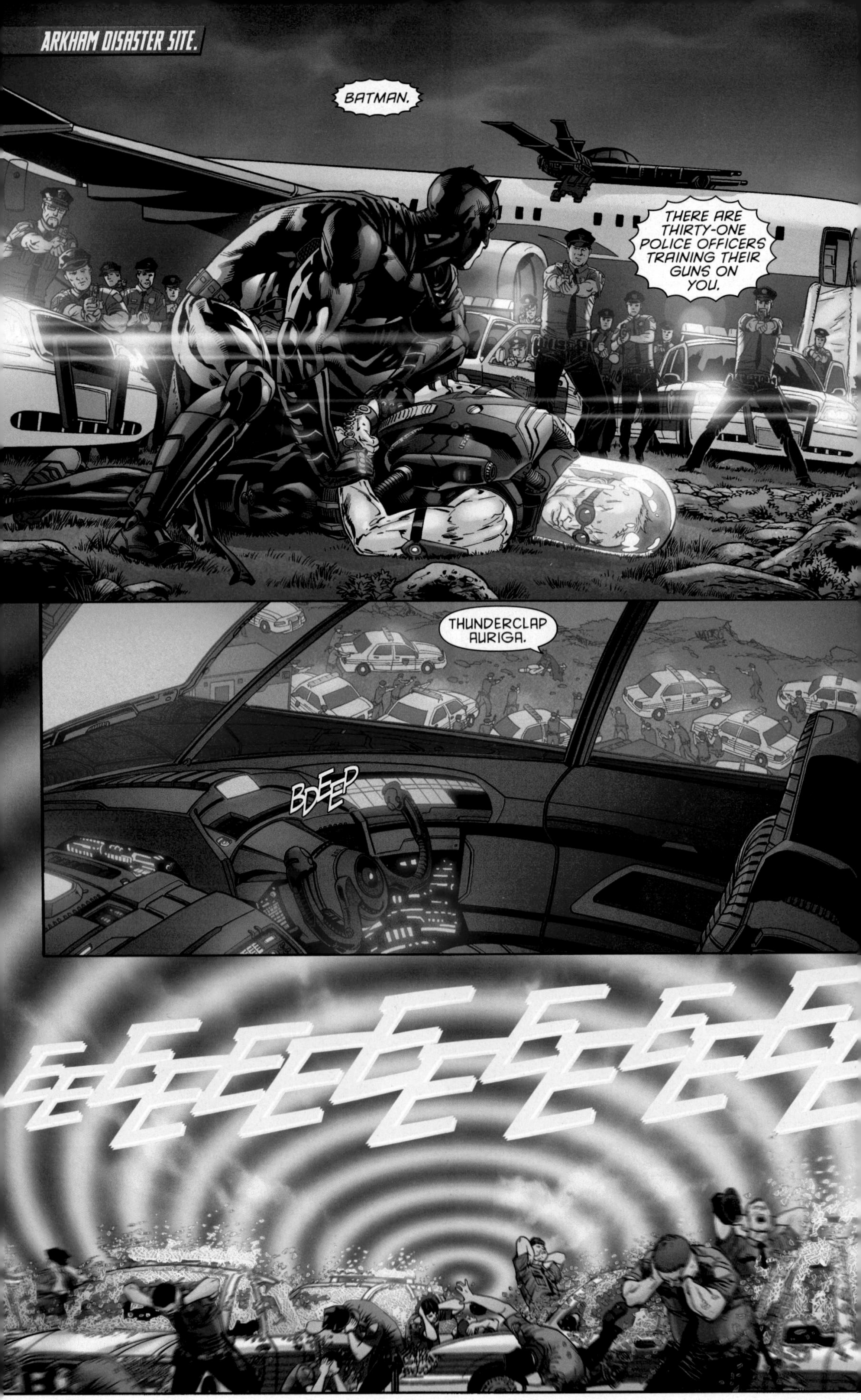
ARKHAM DISASTER SITE.
BATMAN.
THERE ARE THIRTY-ONE POLICE OFFICERS TRAINING THEIR GUNS ON YOU.
THUNDERCLAP AURIGA.
BDEEEP
EEEEEEEEEEEEEEEEEE

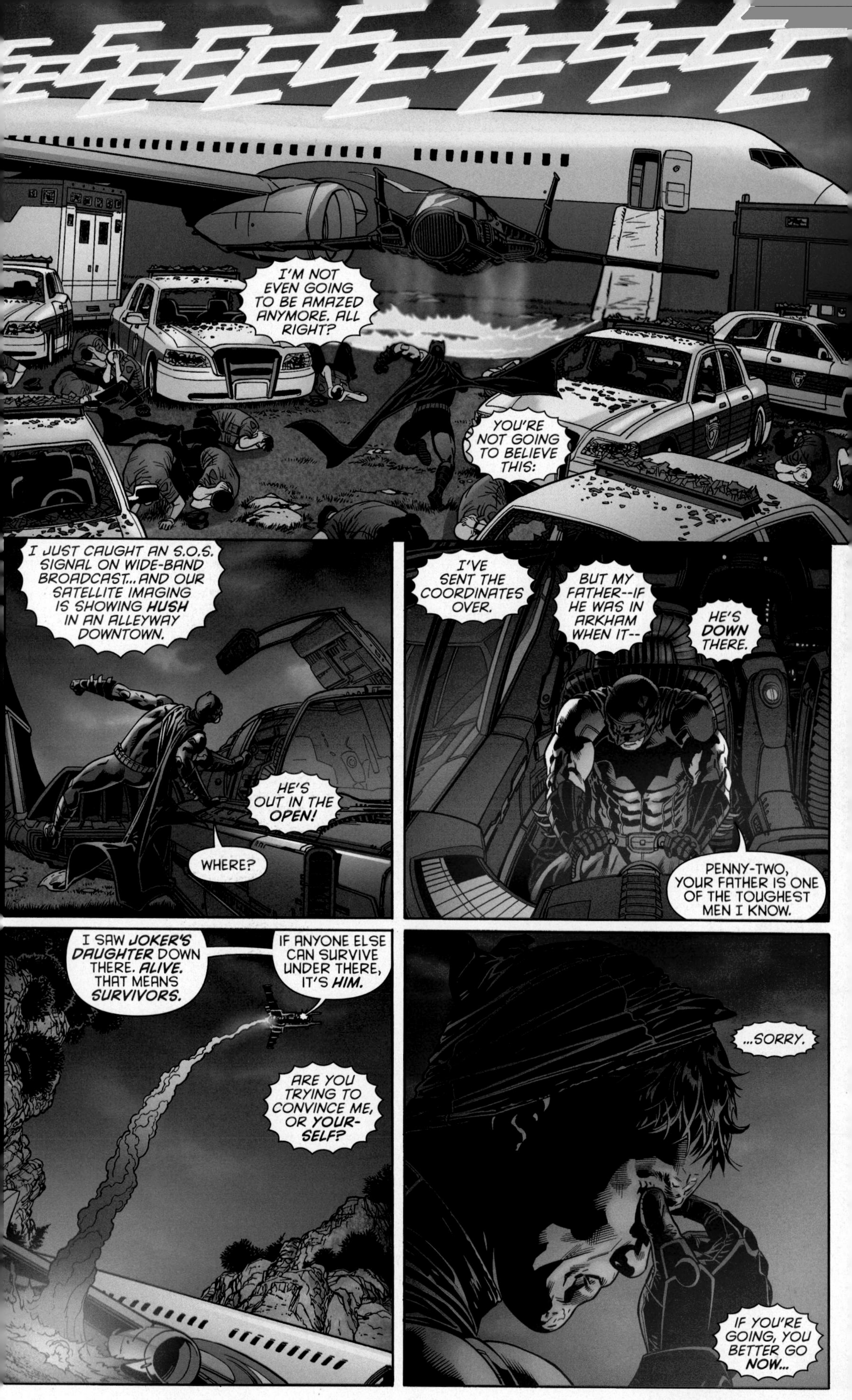
EEEEEEEEEEEEEEEE
I'M NOT EVEN GOING TO BE AMAZED ANYMORE. ALL RIGHT?
YOU'RE NOT GOING TO BELIEVE THIS:
I JUST CAUGHT AN S.O.S. SIGNAL ON WIDE-BAND BROADCAST...AND OUR SATELLITE IMAGING IS SHOWING HUSH IN AN ALLEYWAY DOWNTOWN.
HE'S OUT IN THE OPEN!
WHERE?
I'VE SENT THE COORDINATES OVER.
BUT MY FATHER--IF HE WAS IN ARKHAM WHEN IT--
HE'S DOWN THERE.
PENNY-TWO, YOUR FATHER IS ONE OF THE TOUGHEST MEN I KNOW.
I SAW JOKER'S DAUGHTER DOWN THERE. ALIVE. THAT MEANS SURVIVORS.
IF ANYONE ELSE CAN SURVIVE UNDER THERE, IT'S HIM.
ARE YOU TRYING TO CONVINCE ME, OR YOURSELF?
...SORRY.
IF YOU'RE GOING, YOU BETTER GO NOW...

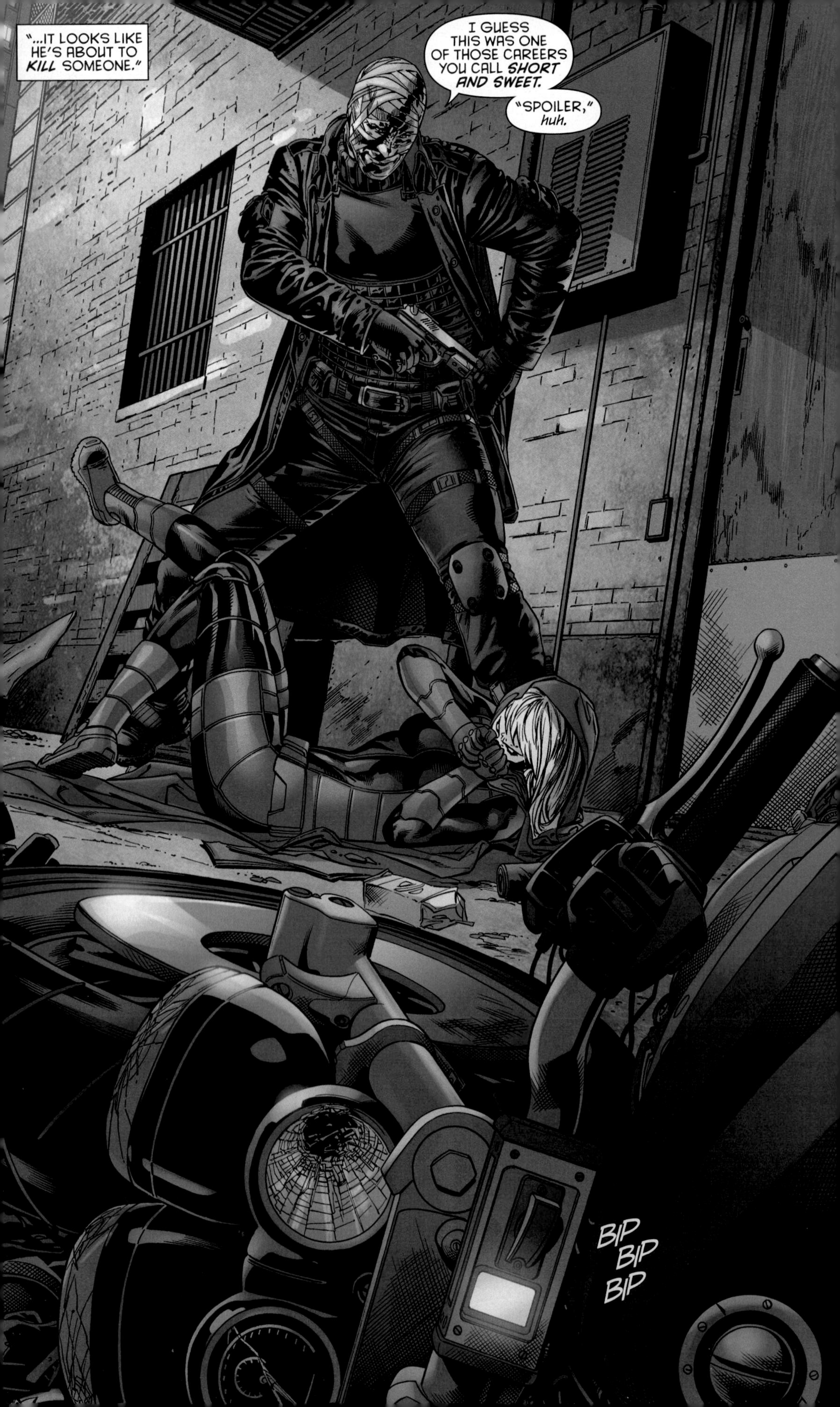
"...IT LOOKS LIKE HE'S ABOUT TO *KILL* SOMEONE."
I GUESS THIS WAS ONE OF THOSE CAREERS YOU CALL **SHORT AND SWEET.**
"SPOILER," *huh.*
BIP BIP BIP

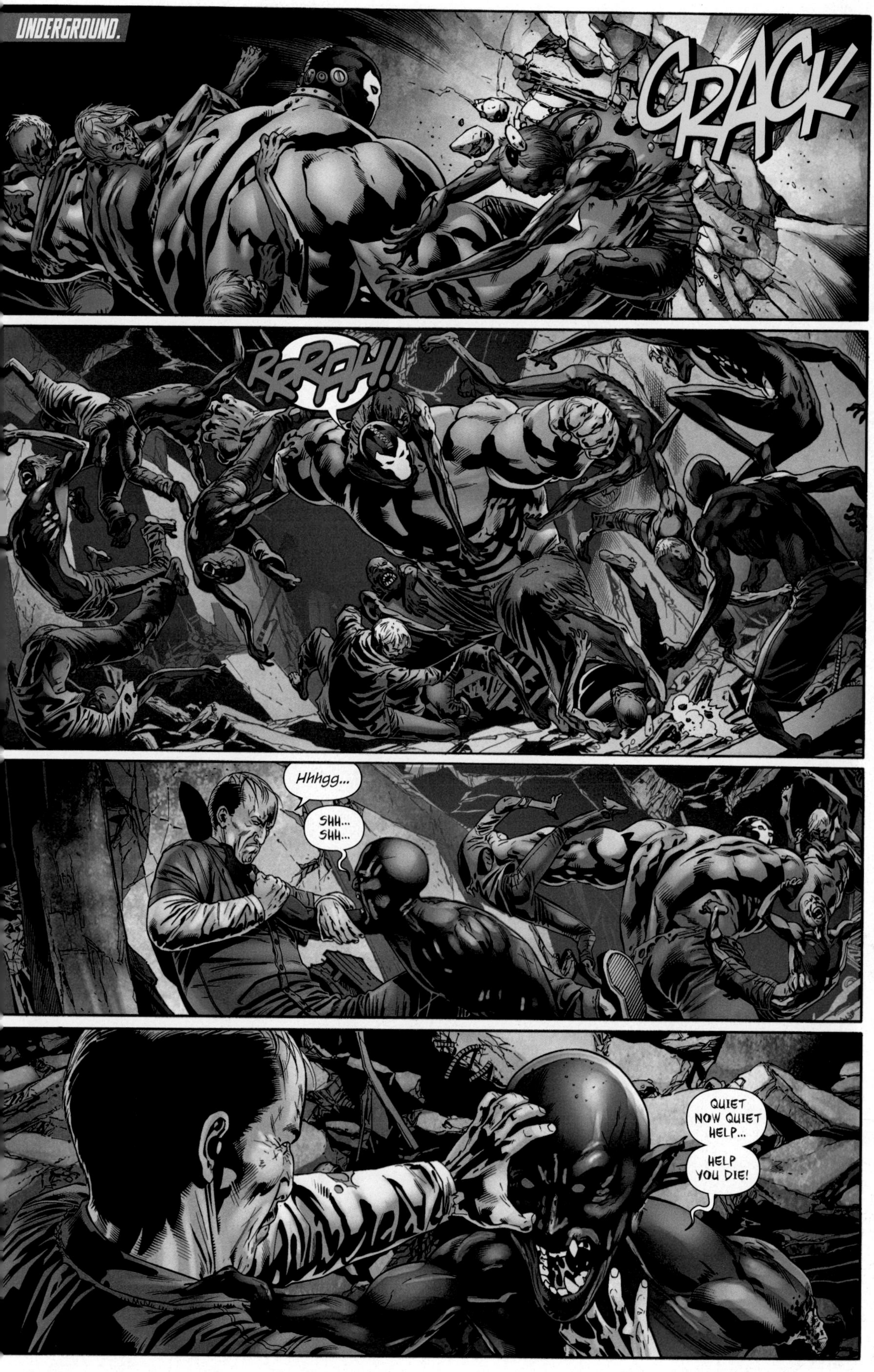
UNDERGROUND.
CRACK
RRRAH!
Hhhgg...
SHH... SHH...
QUIET NOW QUIET HELP...
HELP YOU DIE!

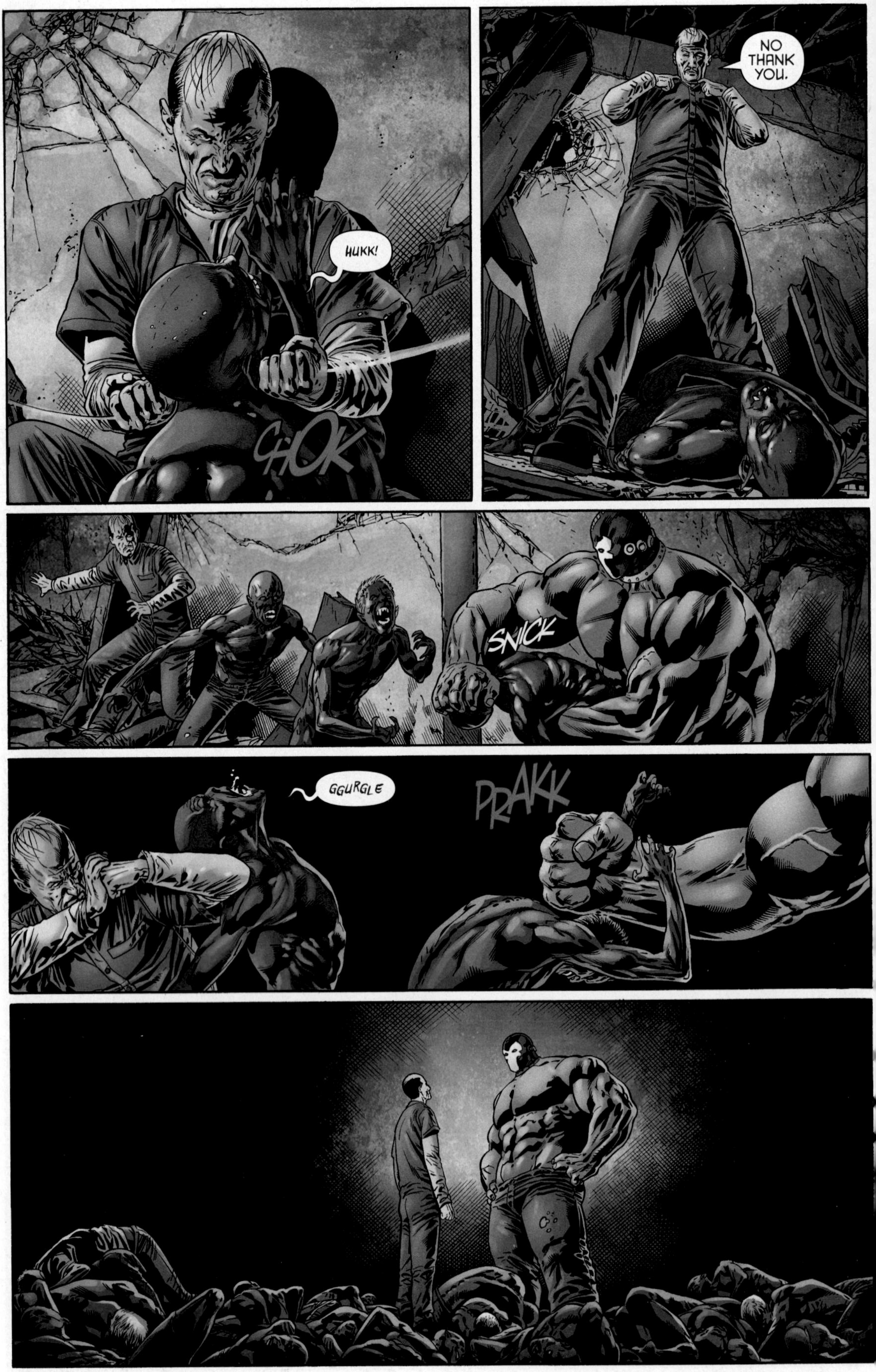
HUKK!
CHOK
NO THANK YOU.
SNICK
GGURGLE
PRAKK

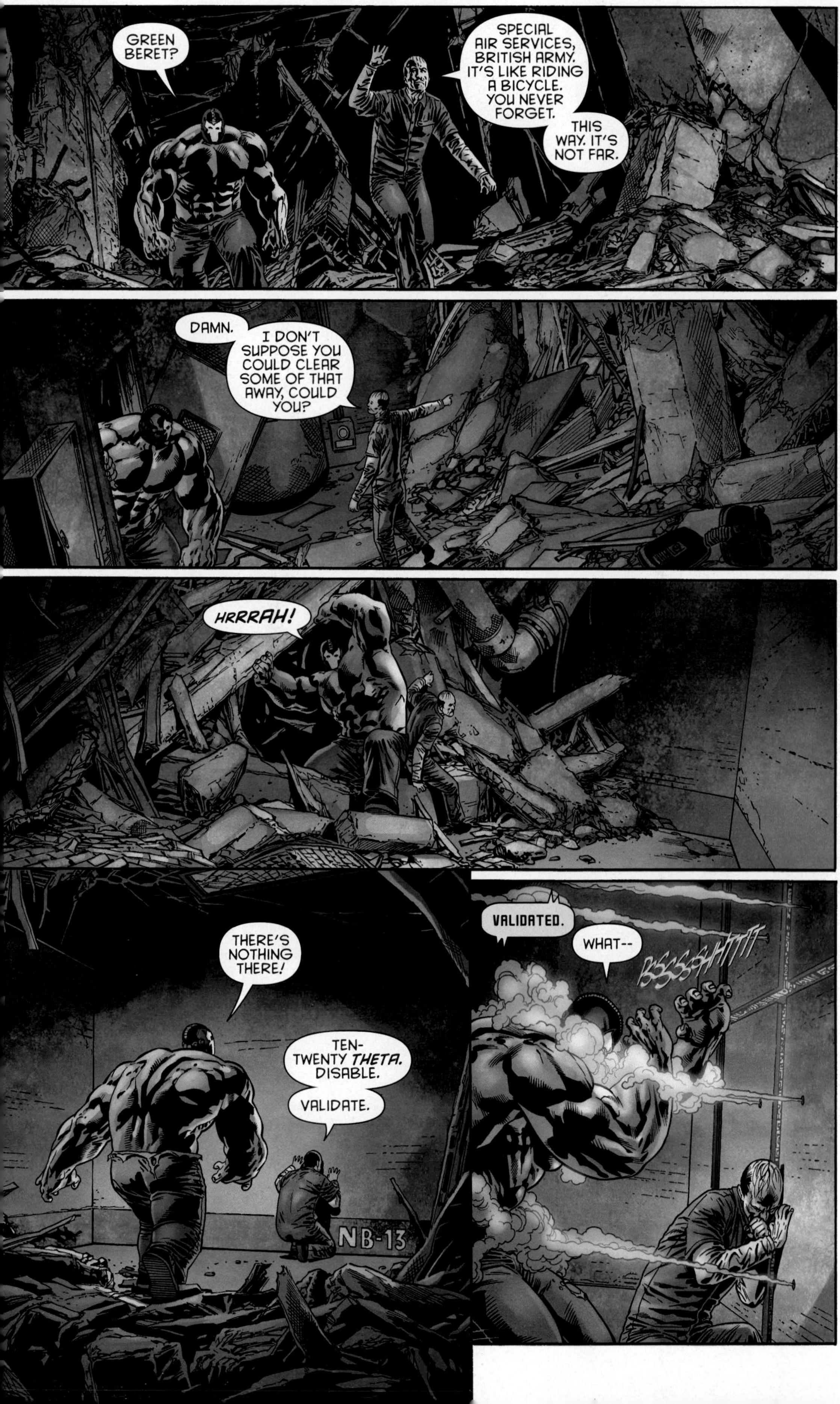
GREEN BERET?
SPECIAL AIR SERVICES, BRITISH ARMY. IT'S LIKE RIDING A BICYCLE. YOU NEVER FORGET.
THIS WAY. IT'S NOT FAR.
DAMN.
I DON'T SUPPOSE YOU COULD CLEAR SOME OF THAT AWAY, COULD YOU?
HRRRAH!
THERE'S NOTHING THERE!
TEN-TWENTY THETA. DISABLE.
VALIDATE.
NB-13
VALIDATED.
WHAT--
BSSSSHHTTTT

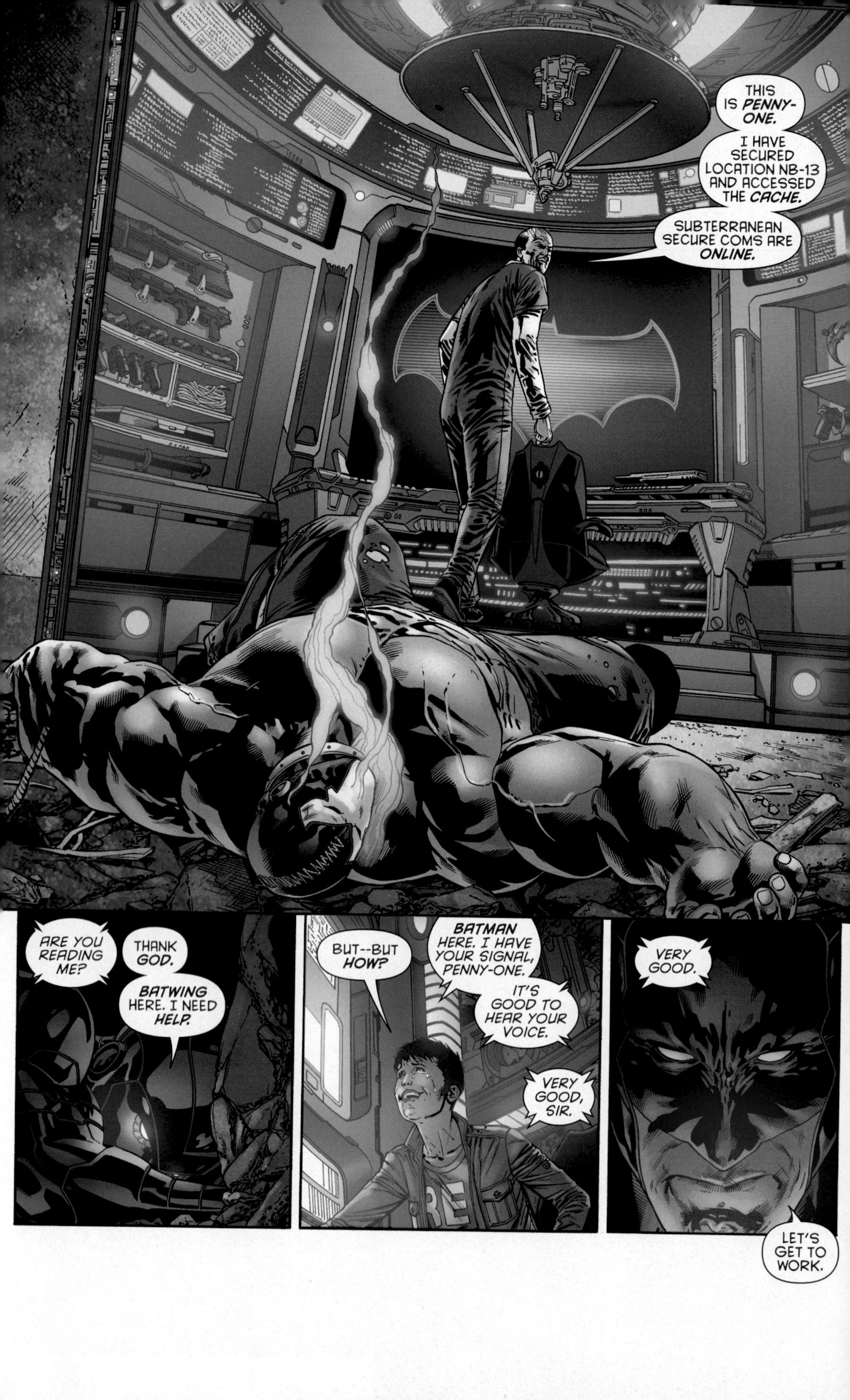

THIS IS PENNY-ONE.
I HAVE SECURED LOCATION NB-13 AND ACCESSED THE CACHE.
SUBTERRANEAN SECURE COMS ARE ONLINE.
ARE YOU READING ME?
THANK GOD.
BATWING HERE. I NEED HELP.
BUT--BUT HOW?
BATMAN HERE. I HAVE YOUR SIGNAL, PENNY-ONE.
IT'S GOOD TO HEAR YOUR VOICE.
VERY GOOD, SIR.
VERY GOOD.
LET'S GET TO WORK.

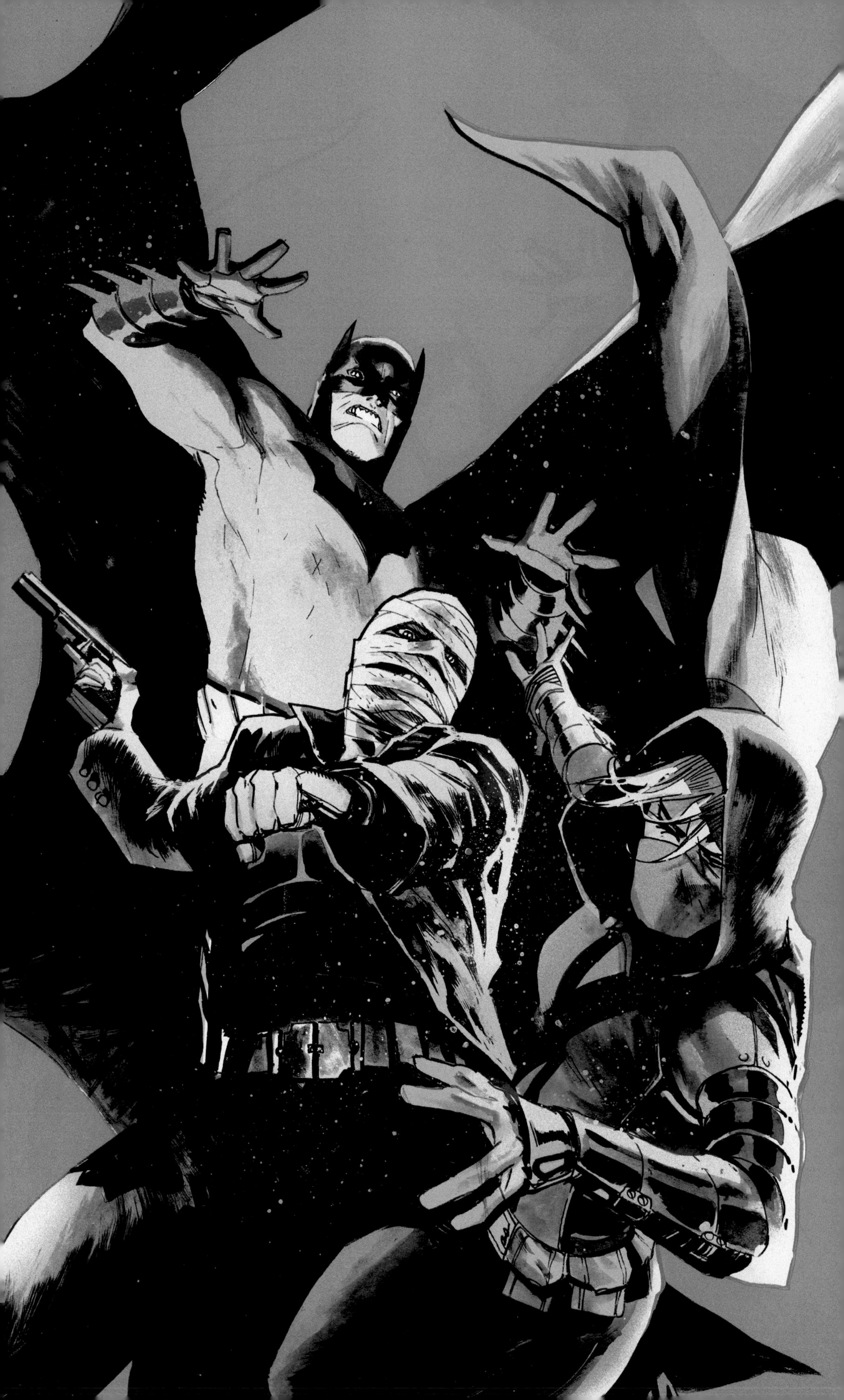

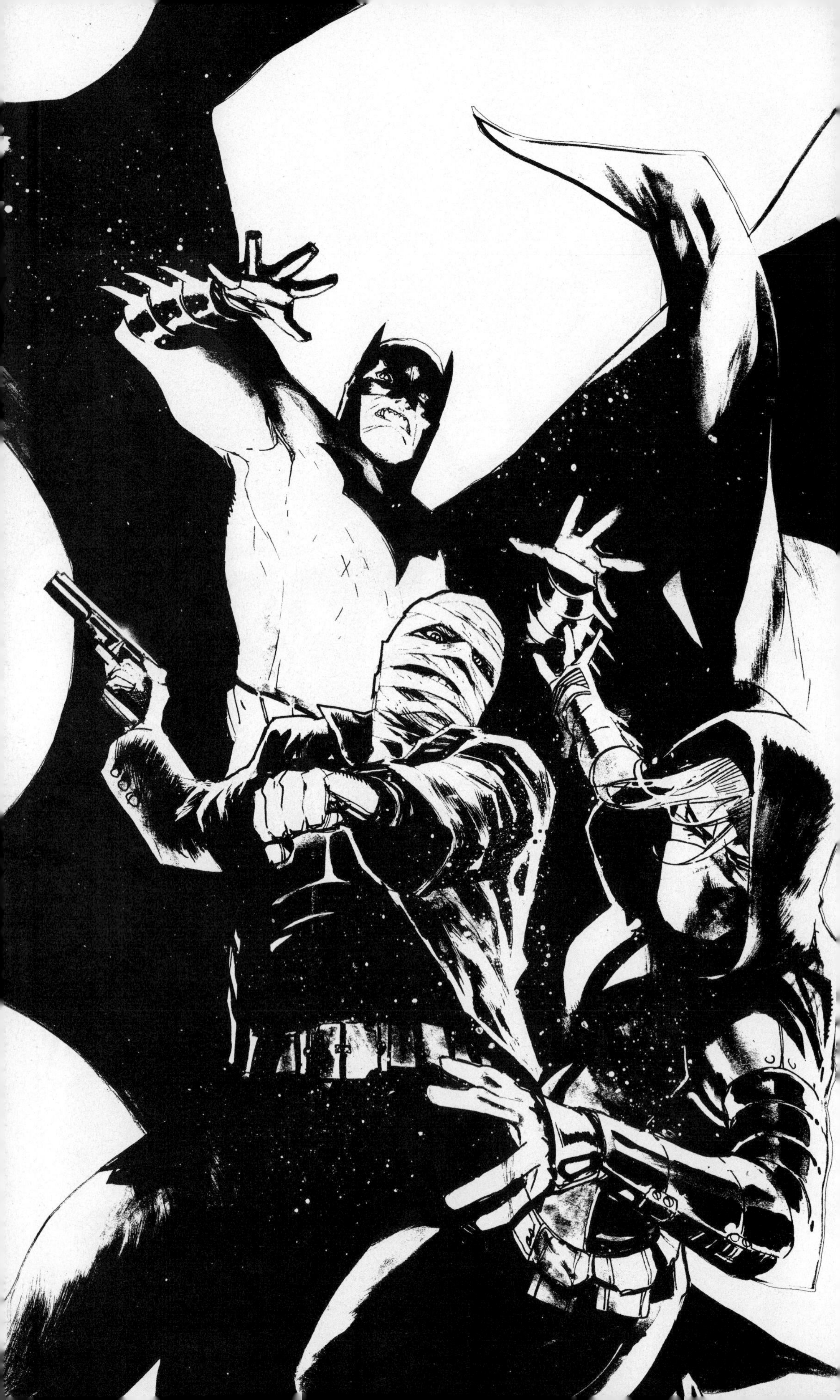

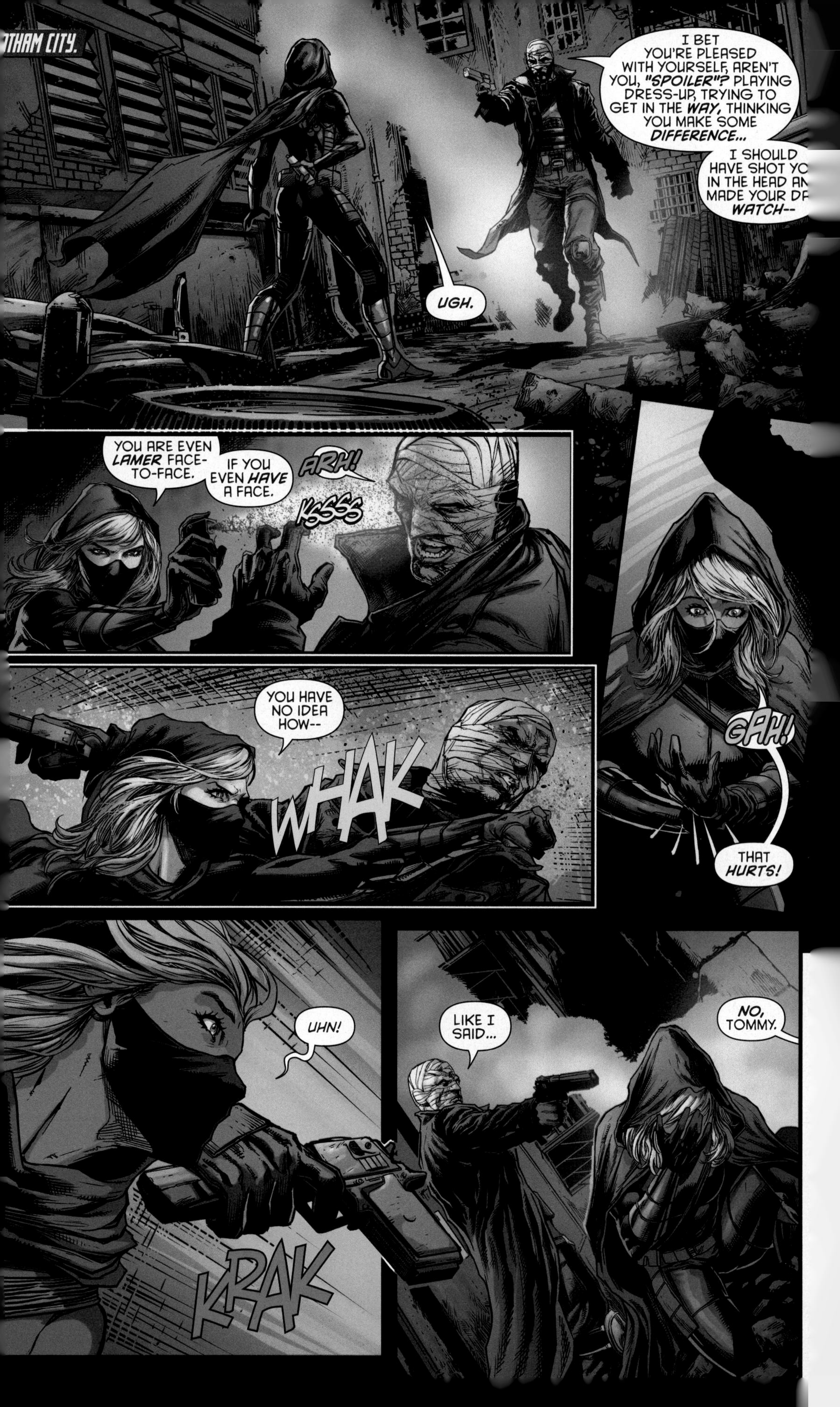

...THAM CITY.
I BET YOU'RE PLEASED WITH YOURSELF, AREN'T YOU, "SPOILER"? PLAYING DRESS-UP, TRYING TO GET IN THE WAY, THINKING YOU MAKE SOME DIFFERENCE...
I SHOULD HAVE SHOT YO IN THE HEAD AN MADE YOUR D WATCH--
UGH.
YOU ARE EVEN LAMER FACE-TO-FACE.
IF YOU EVEN HAVE A FACE.
ARH!
KSSSS
YOU HAVE NO IDEA HOW--
WHAK
GAH!
THAT HURTS!
UHN!
KRAK
LIKE I SAID...
NO, TOMMY.

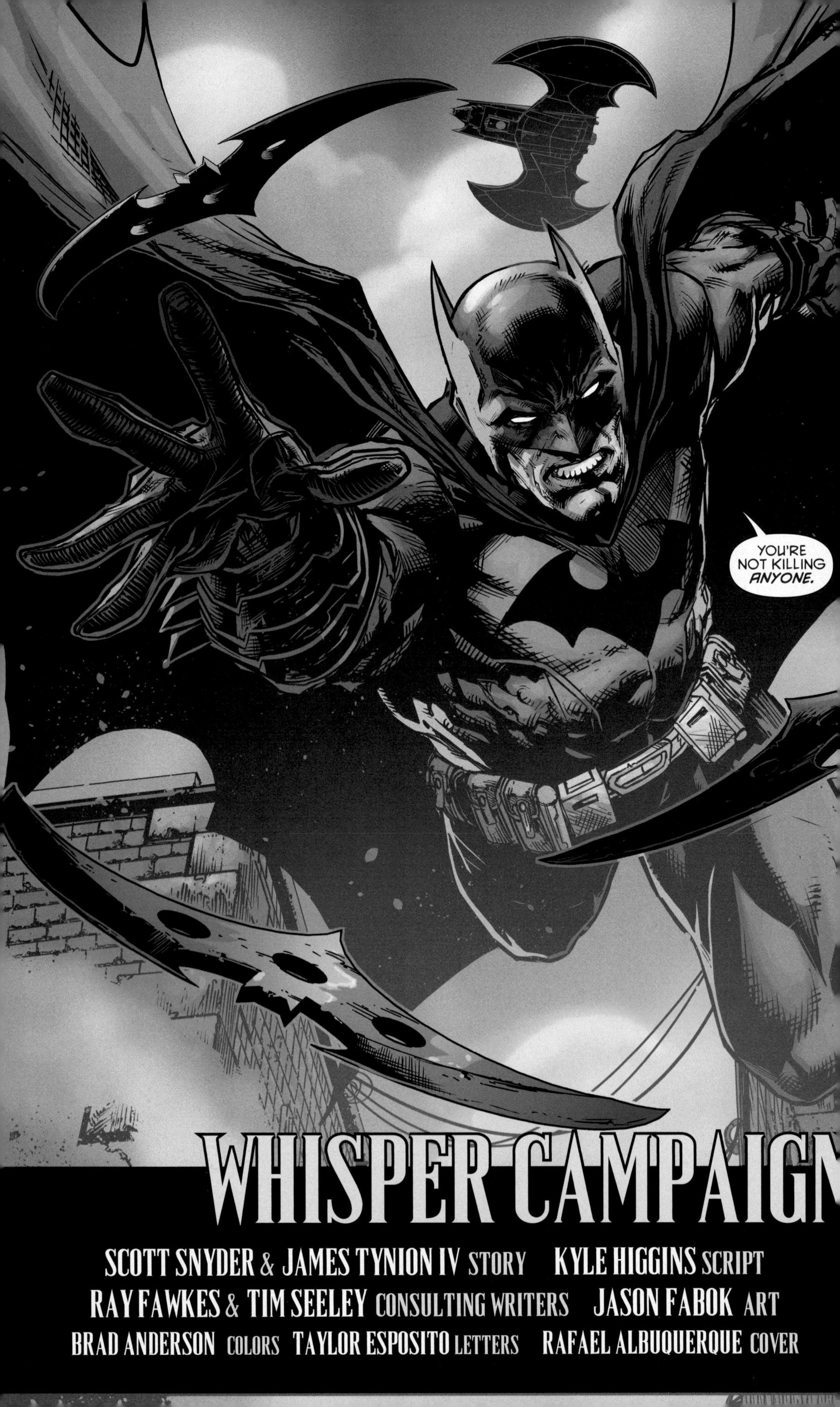
YOU'RE NOT KILLING *ANYONE.*

# WHISPER CAMPAIGN

SCOTT SNYDER & JAMES TYNION IV STORY KYLE HIGGINS SCRIPT
RAY FAWKES & TIM SEELEY CONSULTING WRITERS JASON FABOK ART
BRAD ANDERSON COLORS TAYLOR ESPOSITO LETTERS RAFAEL ALBUQUERQUE COVER

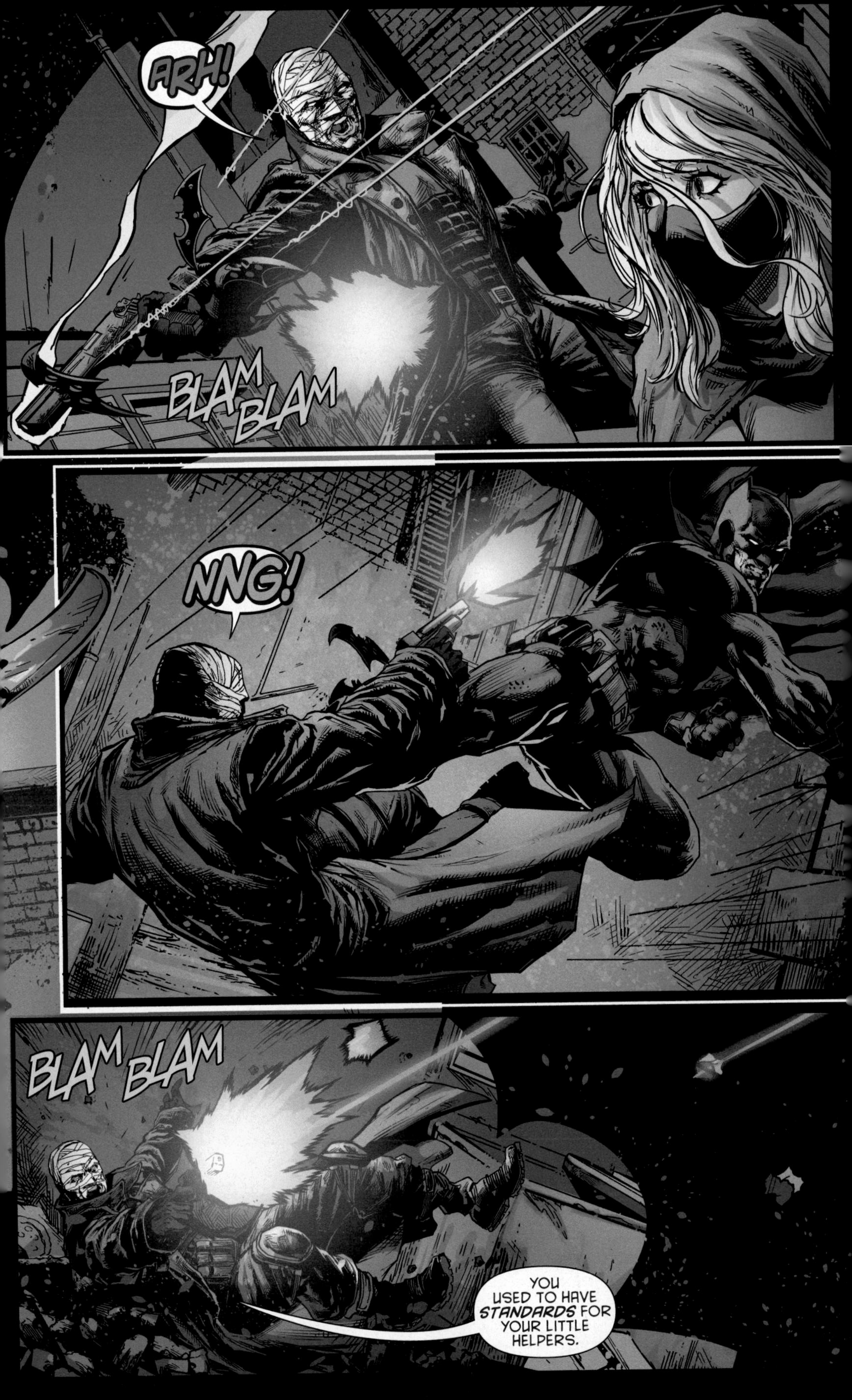
ARH!
BLAM BLAM
NNG!
BLAM BLAM
YOU USED TO HAVE *STANDARDS* FOR YOUR LITTLE HELPERS.

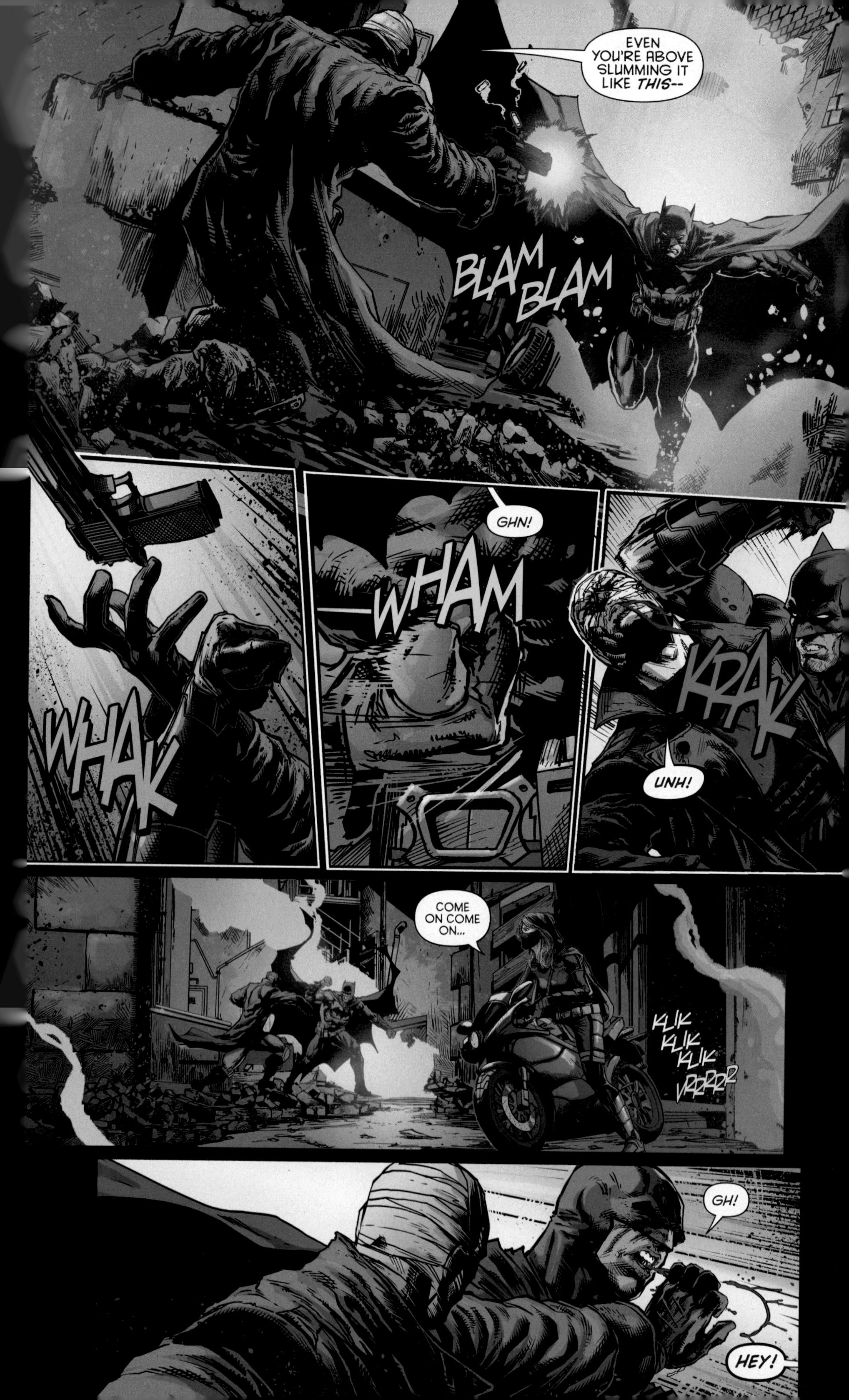

EVEN YOU'RE ABOVE SLUMMING IT LIKE THIS--
BLAM BLAM
WHAK
GHN!
WHAM
KRAK
UNH!
COME ON COME ON...
KLIK KLIK KLIK VRRRRR
GH!
HEY!

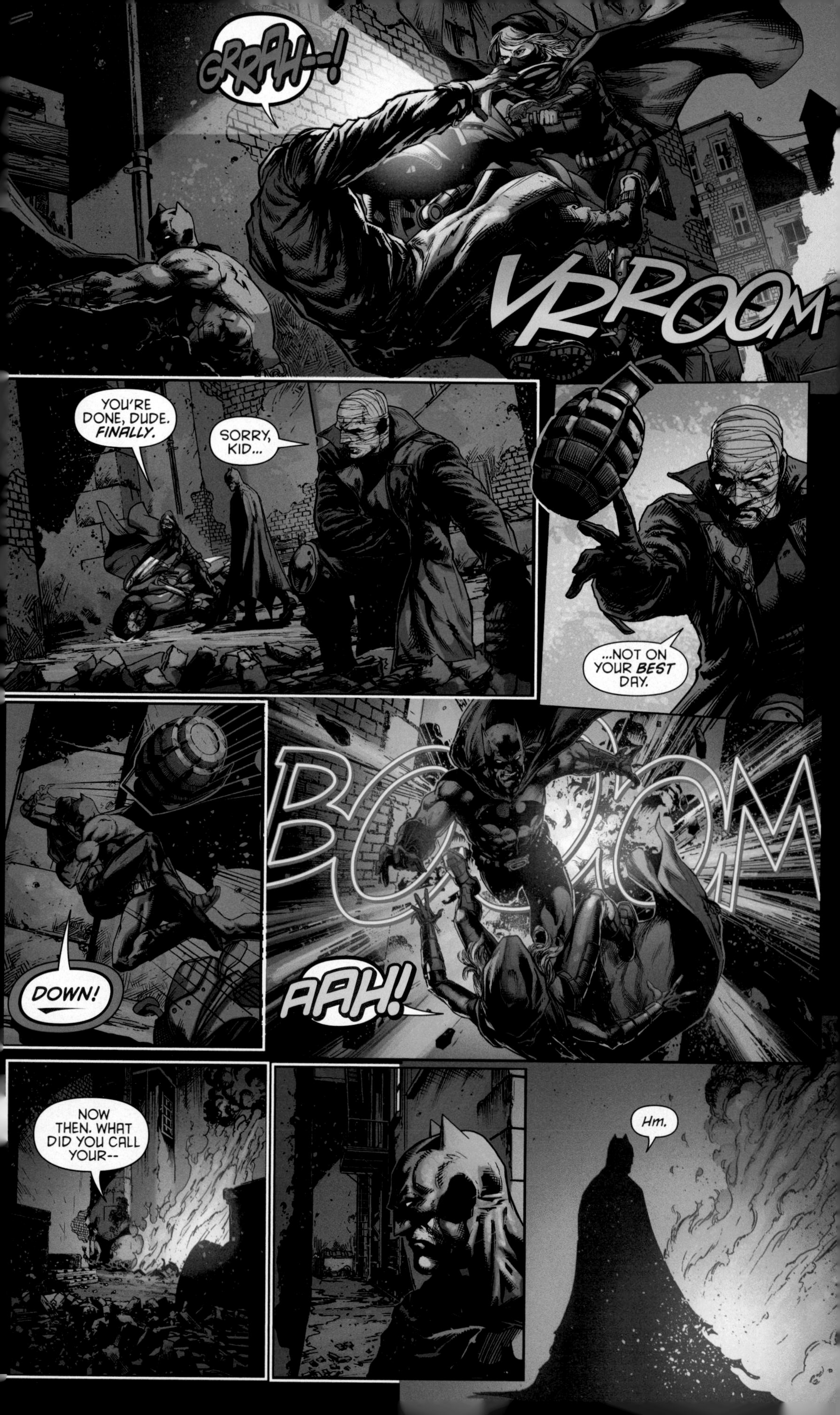

GRRAH--!
VRROOM
YOU'RE DONE, DUDE. *FINALLY.*
SORRY, KID...
...NOT ON YOUR *BEST* DAY.
DOWN!
BOOOM
AAH!
NOW THEN. WHAT DID YOU CALL YOUR--
Hm.

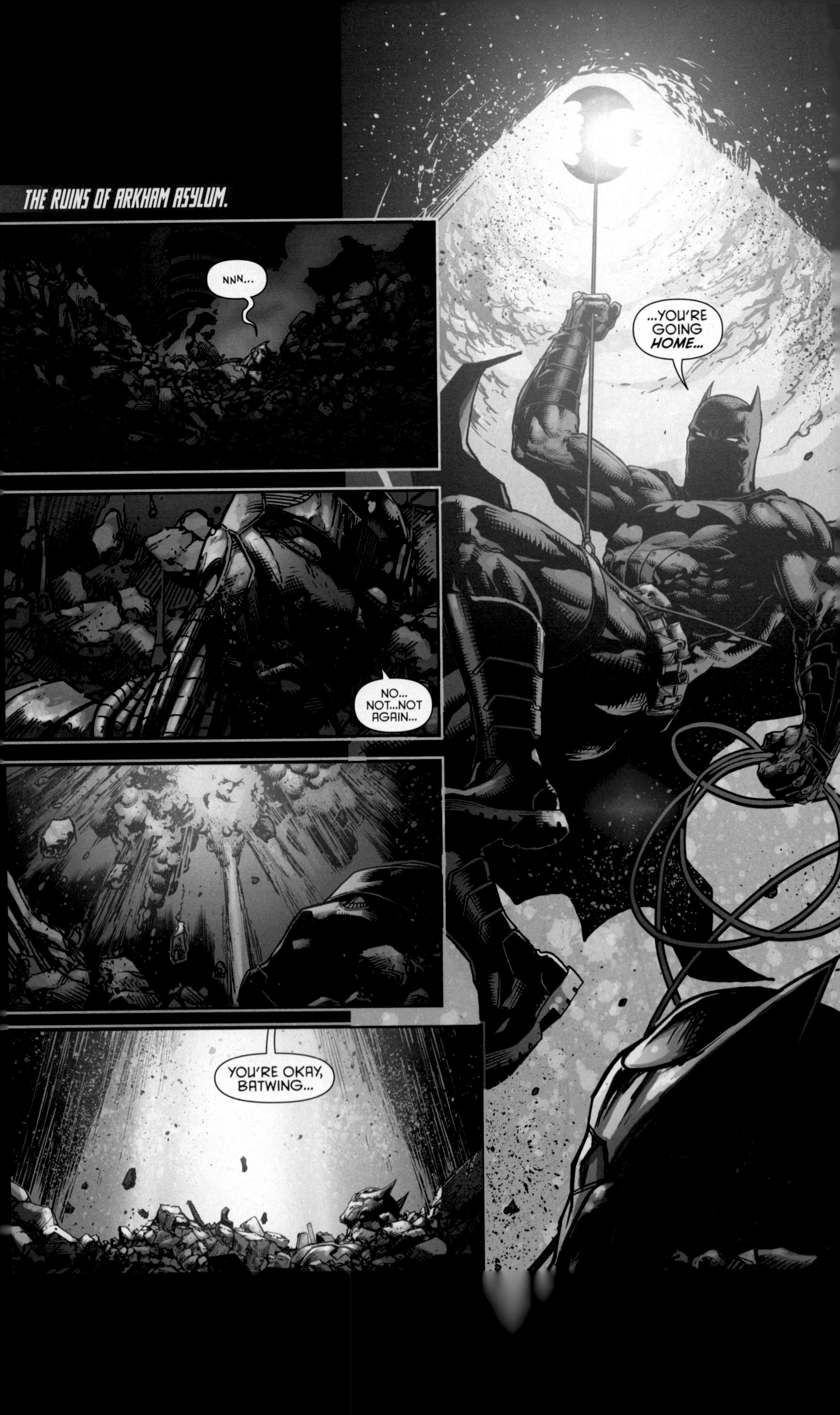
THE RUINS OF ARKHAM ASYLUM.
NNN...
NO... NOT...NOT AGAIN...
YOU'RE OKAY, BATWING...
...YOU'RE GOING HOME...

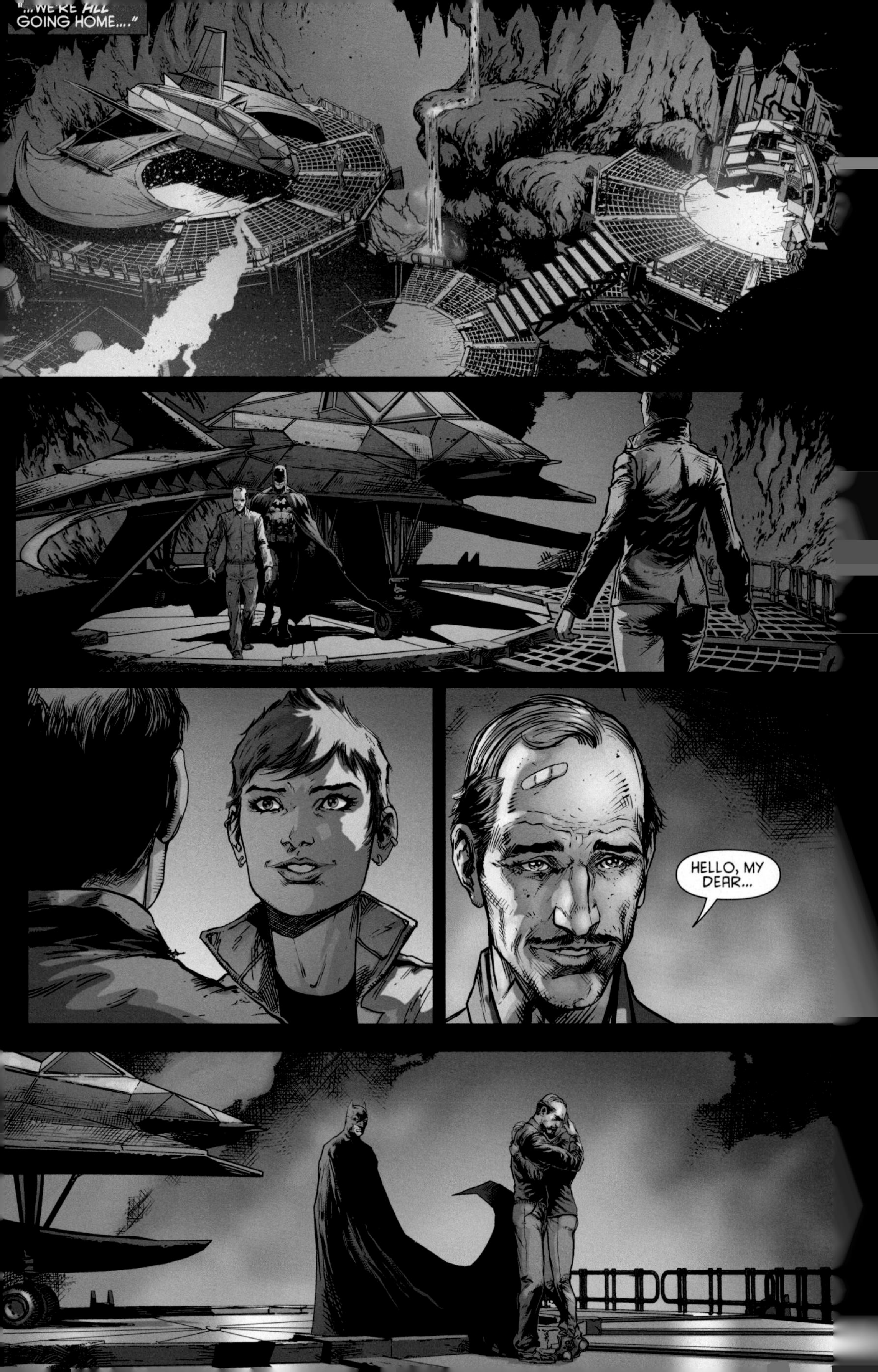
"...WE'RE ALL GOING HOME...."
HELLO, MY DEAR...

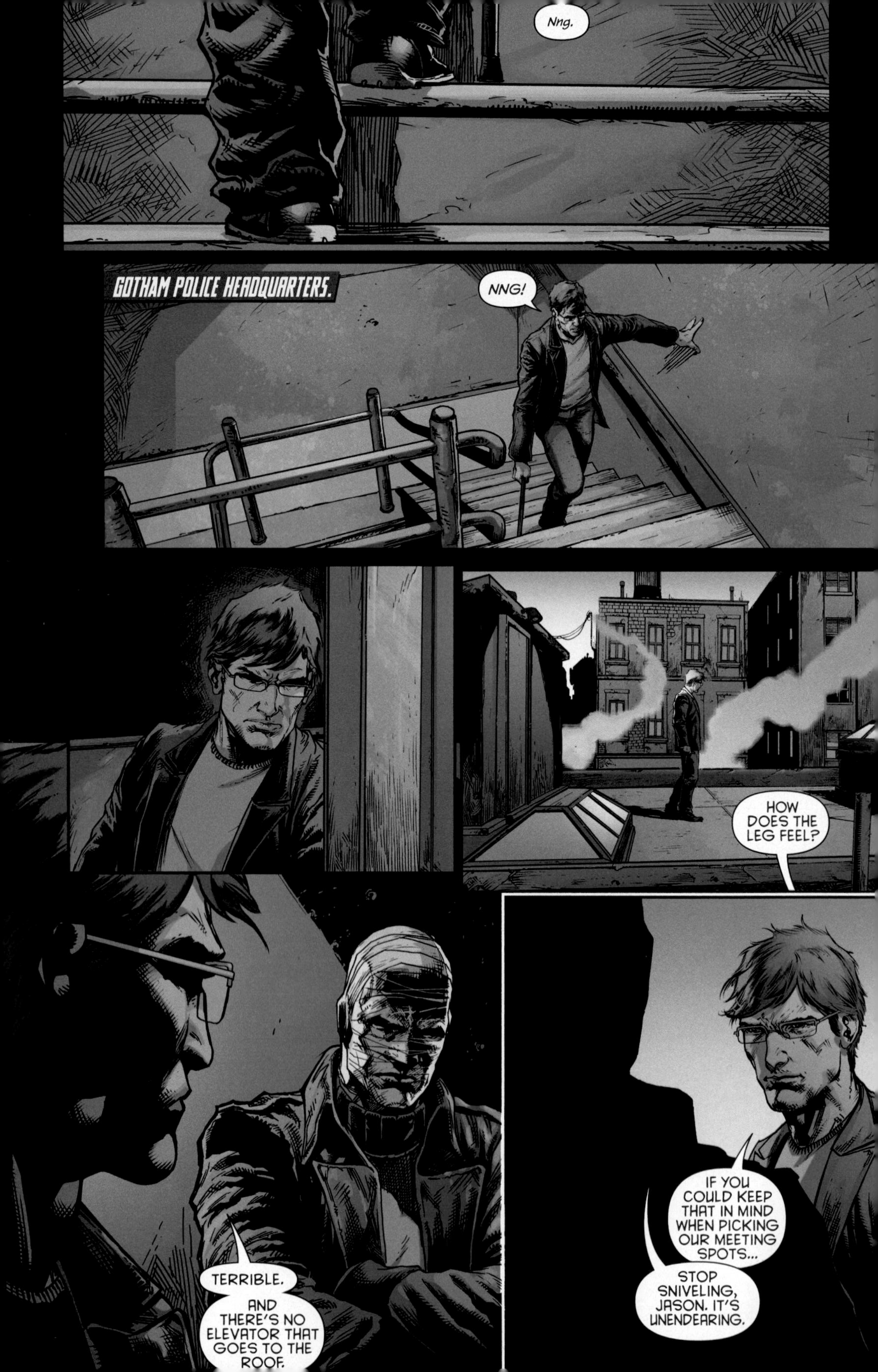
Nng.
GOTHAM POLICE HEADQUARTERS.
NNG!
HOW DOES THE LEG FEEL?
TERRIBLE.
AND THERE'S NO ELEVATOR THAT GOES TO THE ROOF.
IF YOU COULD KEEP THAT IN MIND WHEN PICKING OUR MEETING SPOTS...
STOP SNIVELING, JASON. IT'S UNENDEARING.

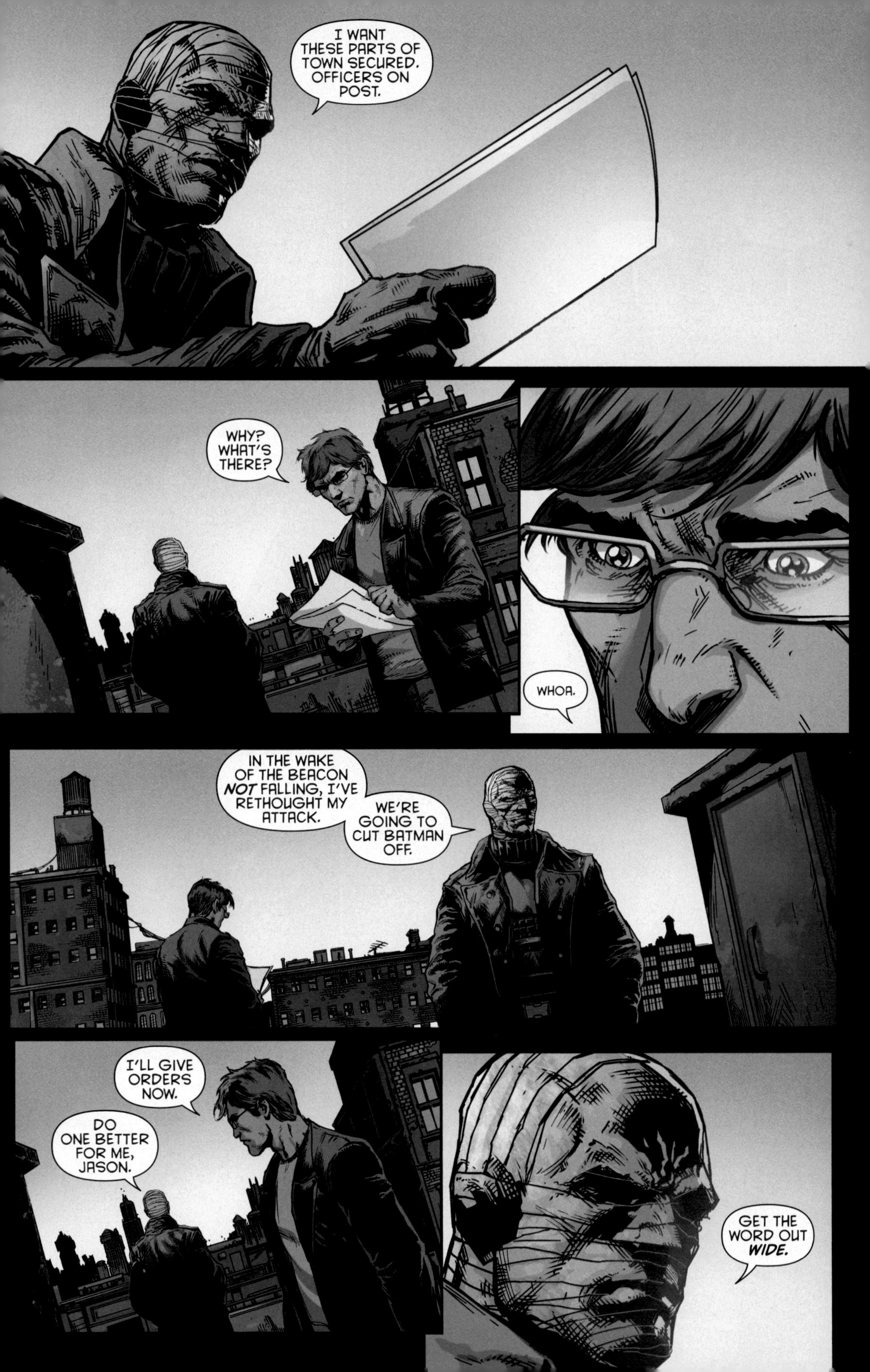

I WANT THESE PARTS OF TOWN SECURED. OFFICERS ON POST.
WHY? WHAT'S THERE?
WHOA.
IN THE WAKE OF THE BEACON *NOT* FALLING, I'VE RETHOUGHT MY ATTACK.
WE'RE GOING TO CUT BATMAN OFF.
I'LL GIVE ORDERS NOW.
DO ONE BETTER FOR ME, JASON.
GET THE WORD OUT *WIDE.*

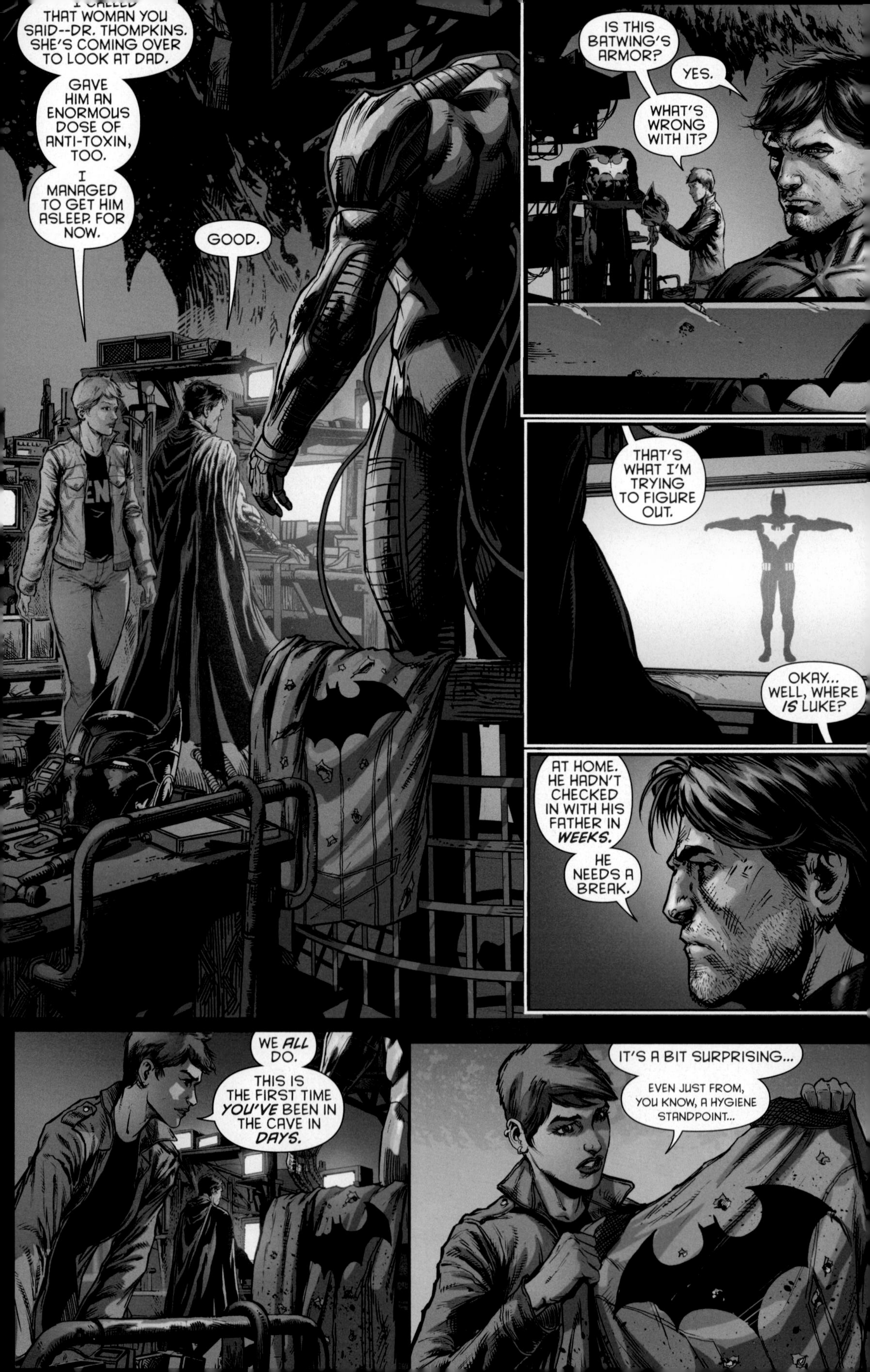
I CALLED THAT WOMAN YOU SAID--DR. THOMPKINS. SHE'S COMING OVER TO LOOK AT DAD.
GAVE HIM AN ENORMOUS DOSE OF ANTI-TOXIN, TOO.
I MANAGED TO GET HIM ASLEEP. FOR NOW.
GOOD.
IS THIS BATWING'S ARMOR?
YES.
WHAT'S WRONG WITH IT?
THAT'S WHAT I'M TRYING TO FIGURE OUT.
OKAY... WELL, WHERE *IS* LUKE?
AT HOME. HE HADN'T CHECKED IN WITH HIS FATHER IN *WEEKS.*
HE NEEDS A BREAK.
WE *ALL* DO.
THIS IS THE FIRST TIME *YOU'VE* BEEN IN THE CAVE IN *DAYS.*
IT'S A BIT SURPRISING...
EVEN JUST FROM, YOU KNOW, A HYGIENE STANDPOINT...

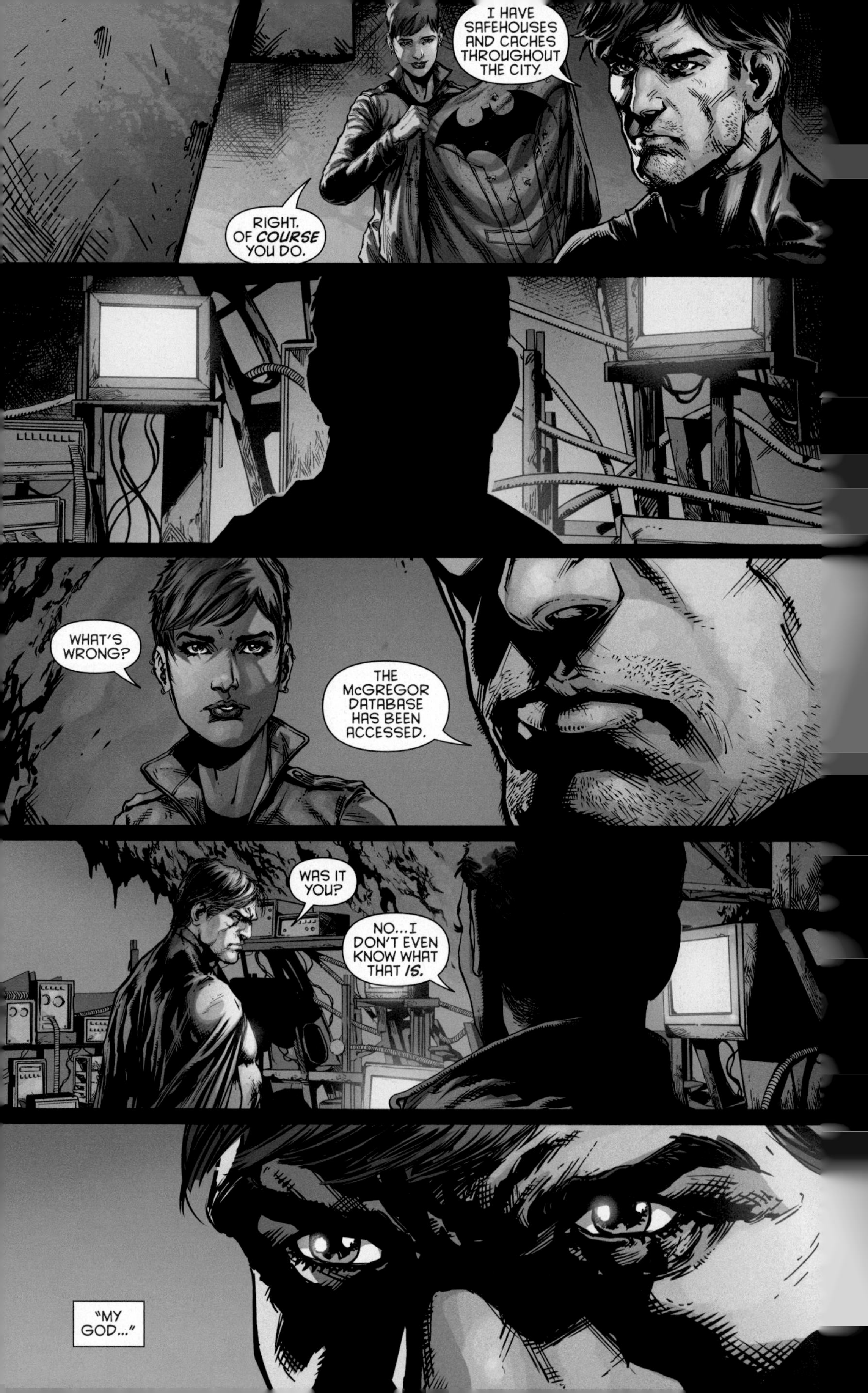
I HAVE SAFEHOUSES AND CACHES THROUGHOUT THE CITY.
RIGHT. OF COURSE YOU DO.
WHAT'S WRONG?
THE McGREGOR DATABASE HAS BEEN ACCESSED.
WAS IT YOU?
NO...I DON'T EVEN KNOW WHAT THAT IS.
"MY GOD..."

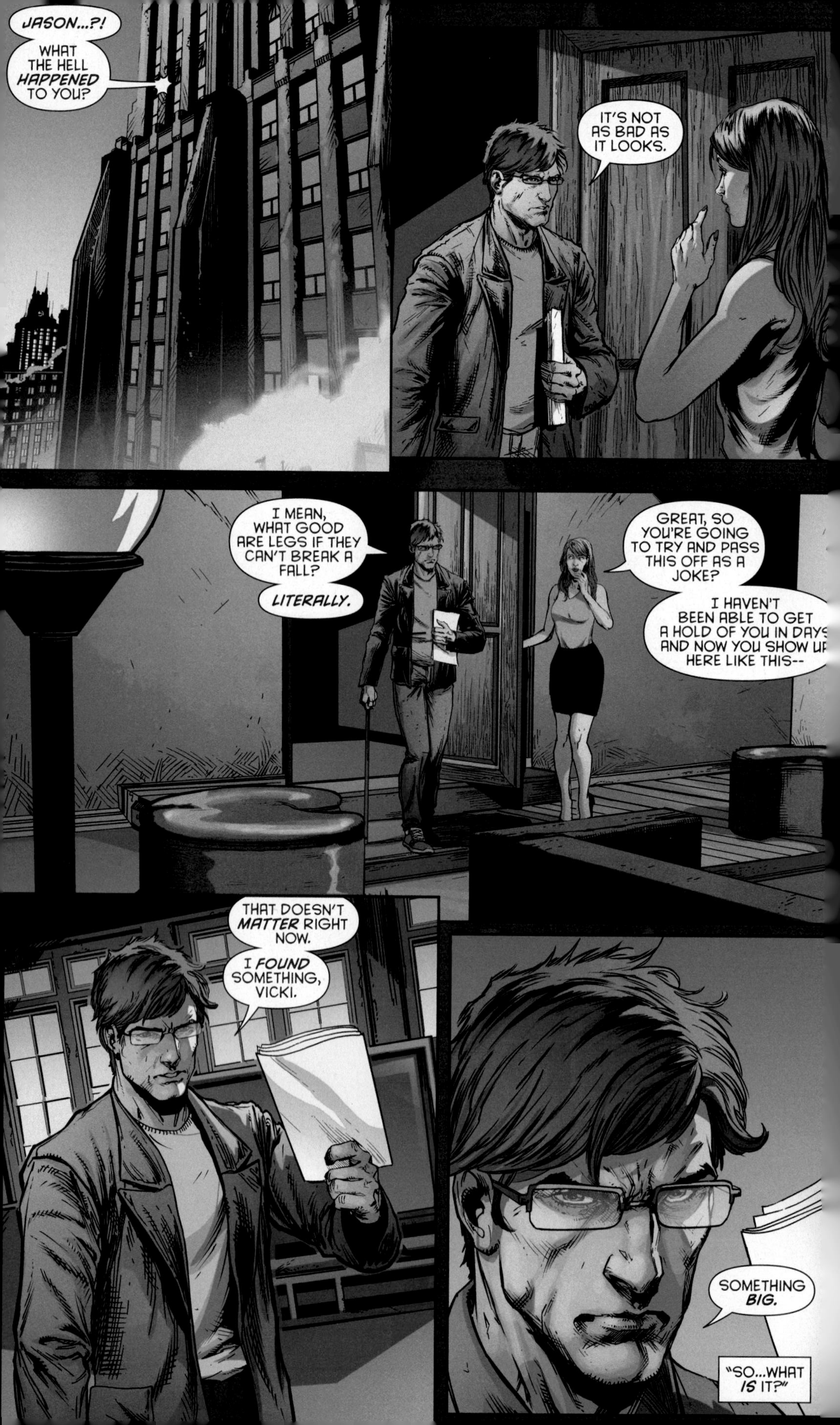
JASON...?!
WHAT THE HELL HAPPENED TO YOU?
IT'S NOT AS BAD AS IT LOOKS.
I MEAN, WHAT GOOD ARE LEGS IF THEY CAN'T BREAK A FALL?
LITERALLY.
GREAT, SO YOU'RE GOING TO TRY AND PASS THIS OFF AS A JOKE?
I HAVEN'T BEEN ABLE TO GET A HOLD OF YOU IN DAYS AND NOW YOU SHOW UP HERE LIKE THIS--
THAT DOESN'T MATTER RIGHT NOW.
I FOUND SOMETHING, VICKI.
SOMETHING BIG.
"SO...WHAT IS IT?"

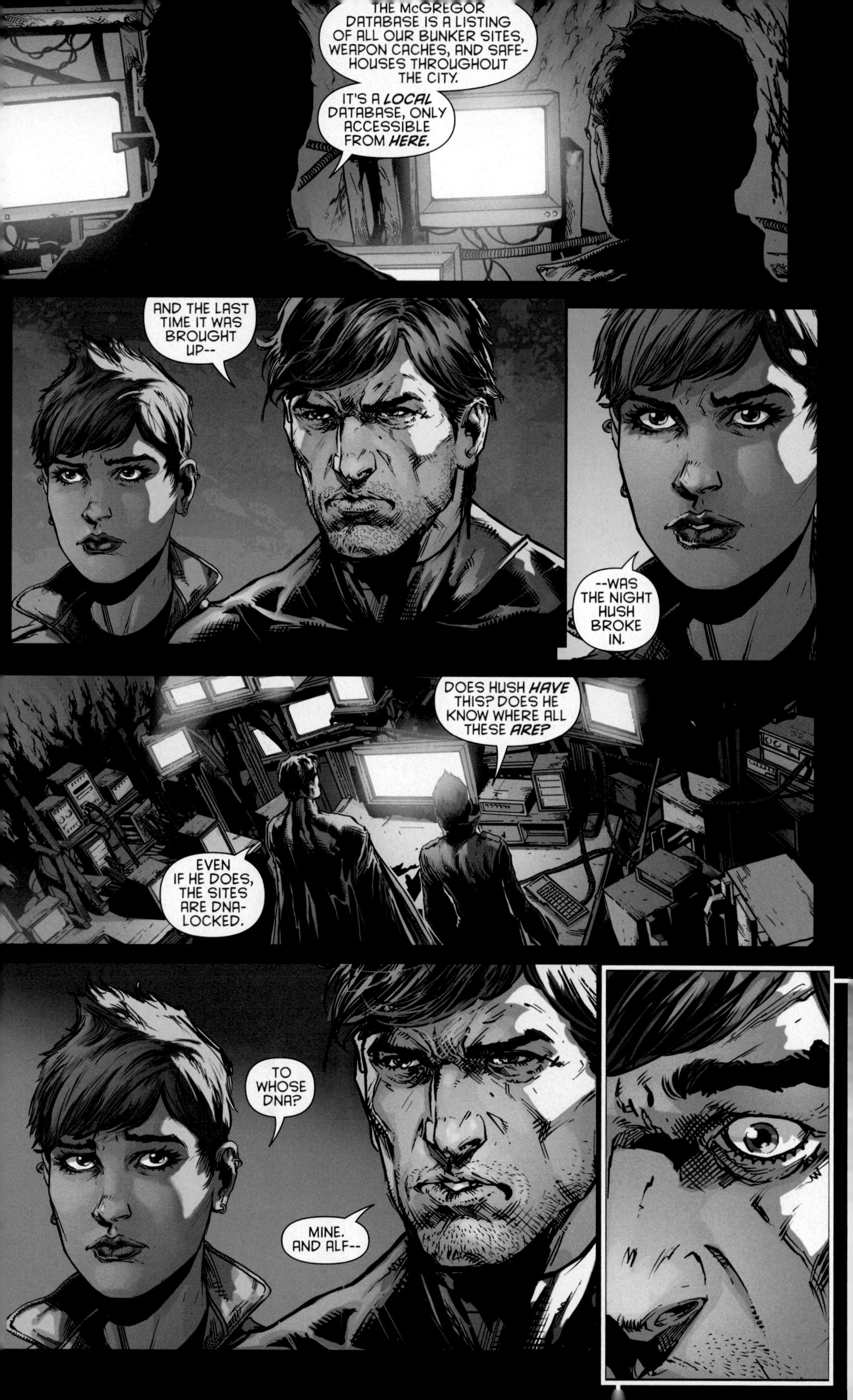
THE McGREGOR DATABASE IS A LISTING OF ALL OUR BUNKER SITES, WEAPON CACHES, AND SAFE-HOUSES THROUGHOUT THE CITY.
IT'S A *LOCAL* DATABASE, ONLY ACCESSIBLE FROM *HERE.*
AND THE LAST TIME IT WAS BROUGHT UP--
--WAS THE NIGHT HUSH BROKE IN.
DOES HUSH *HAVE* THIS? DOES HE KNOW WHERE ALL THESE *ARE?*
EVEN IF HE DOES, THE SITES ARE DNA-LOCKED.
TO WHOSE DNA?
MINE. AND ALF--

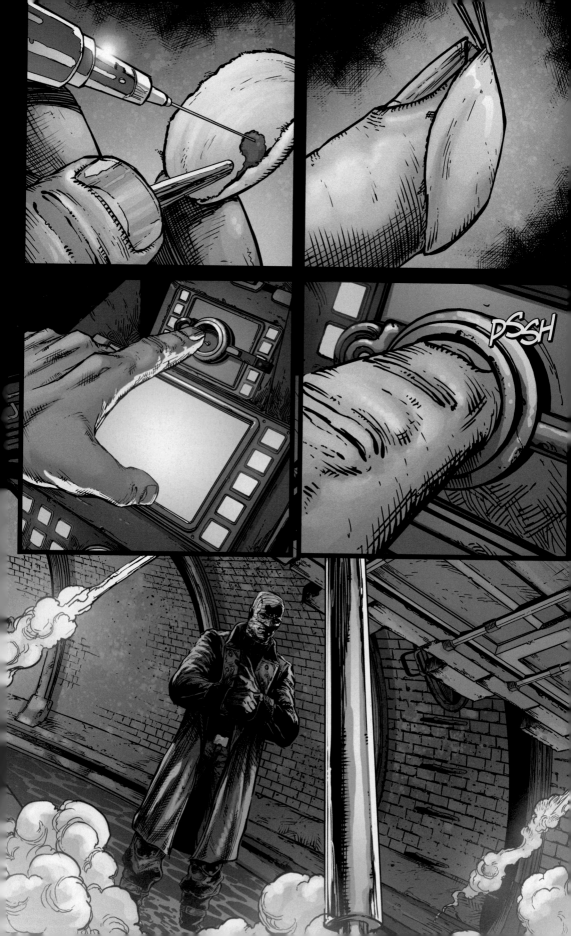

PSSH

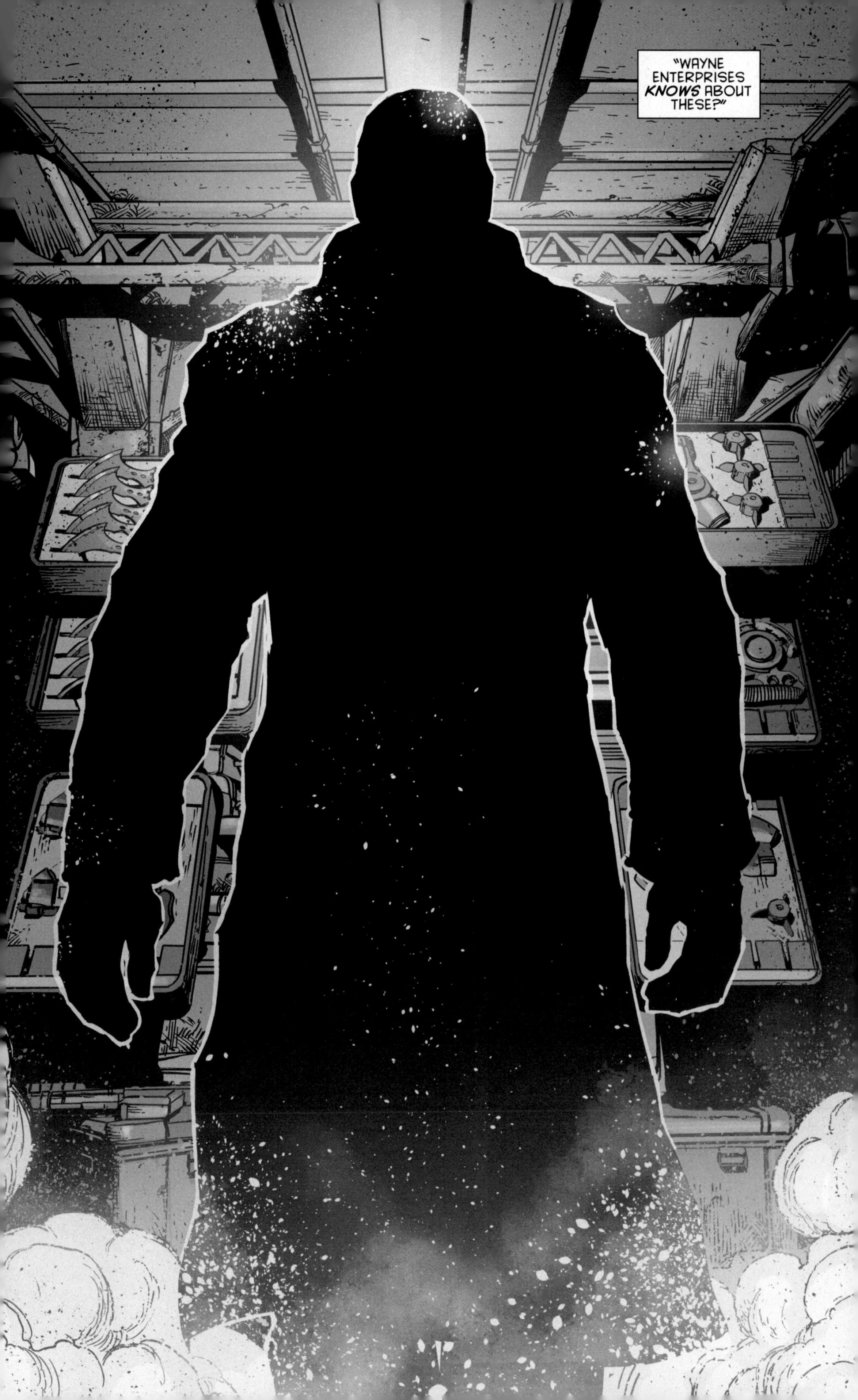
"WAYNE ENTERPRISES KNOWS ABOUT THESE?"

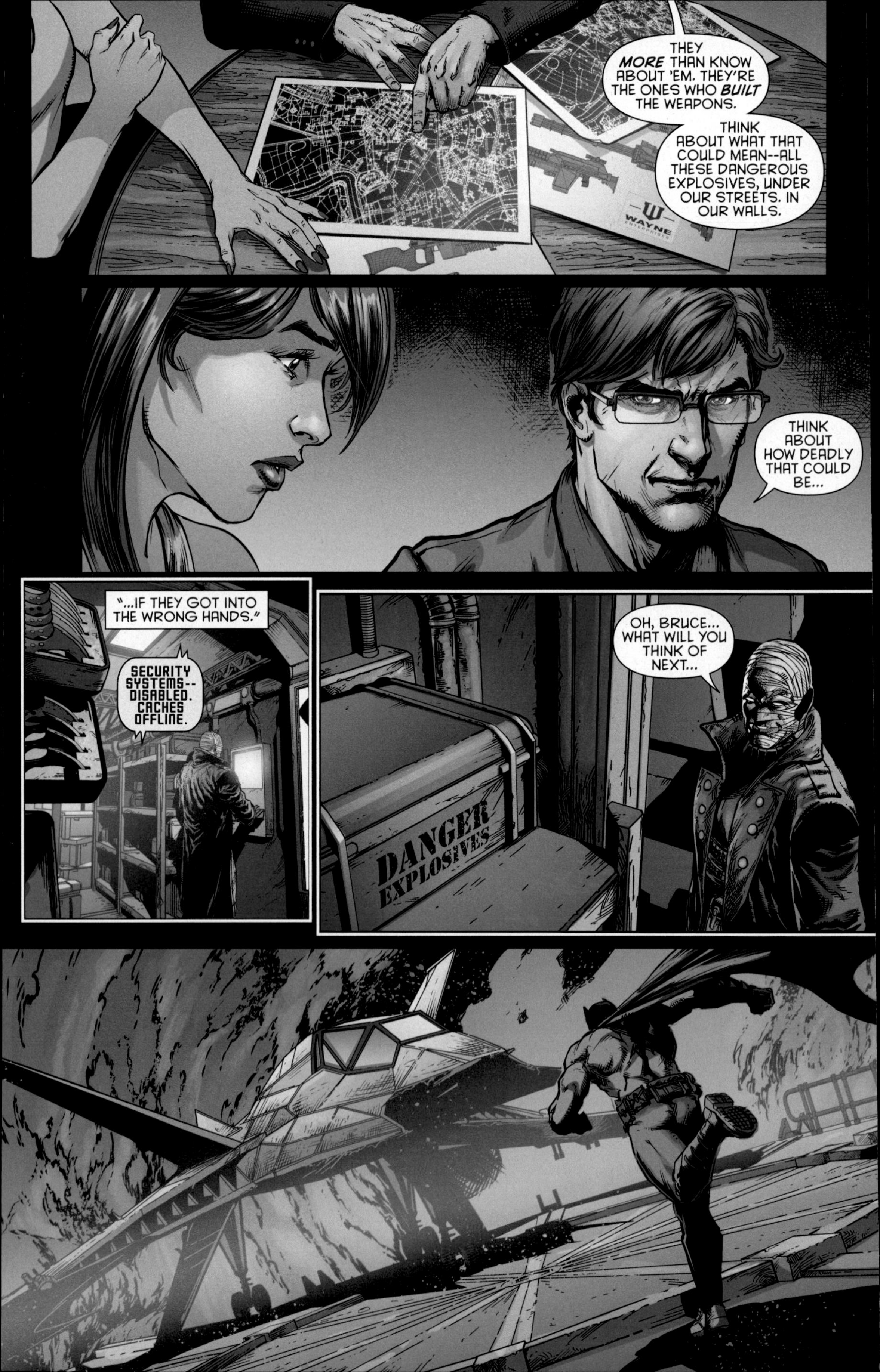
THEY MORE THAN KNOW ABOUT 'EM. THEY'RE THE ONES WHO BUILT THE WEAPONS.
THINK ABOUT WHAT THAT COULD MEAN--ALL THESE DANGEROUS EXPLOSIVES, UNDER OUR STREETS. IN OUR WALLS.
WAYNE ENTERPRISES
THINK ABOUT HOW DEADLY THAT COULD BE...
"...IF THEY GOT INTO THE WRONG HANDS."
SECURITY SYSTEMS-- DISABLED. CACHES OFFLINE.
OH, BRUCE... WHAT WILL YOU THINK OF NEXT...
DANGER EXPLOSIVES

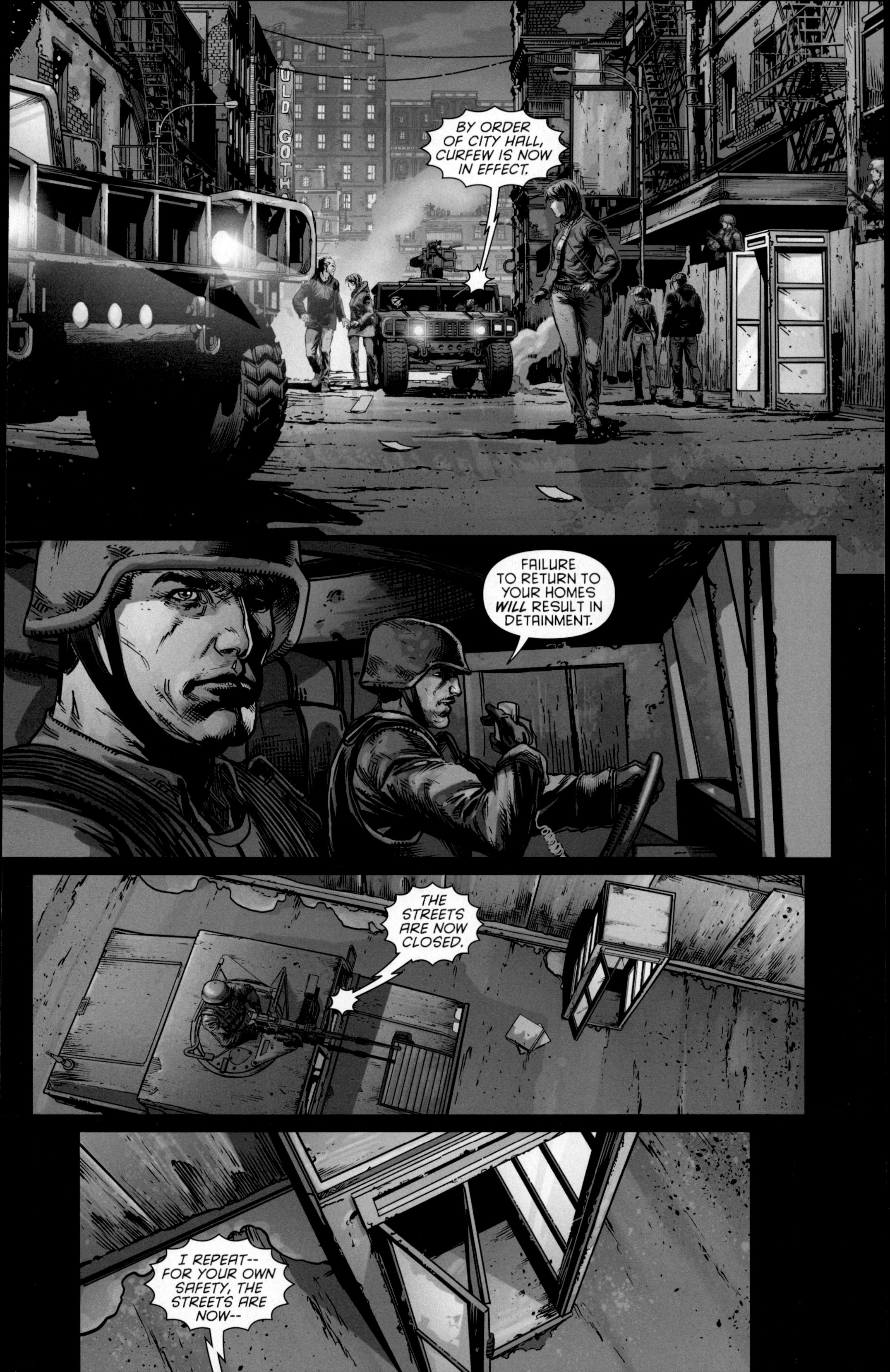
ULD GOTH
BY ORDER OF CITY HALL, CURFEW IS NOW IN EFFECT.
FAILURE TO RETURN TO YOUR HOMES WILL RESULT IN DETAINMENT.
THE STREETS ARE NOW CLOSED.
I REPEAT-- FOR YOUR OWN SAFETY, THE STREETS ARE NOW--

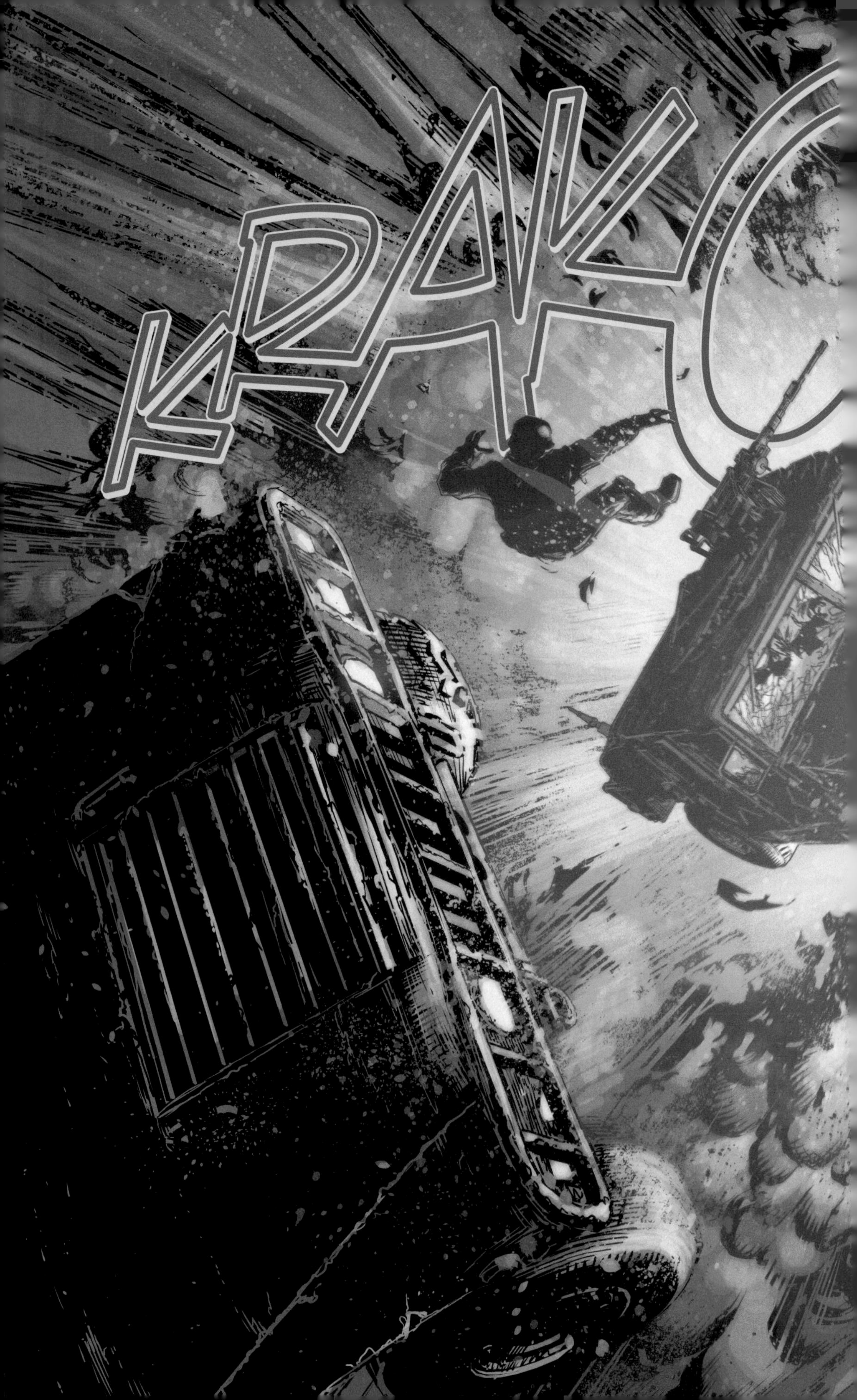

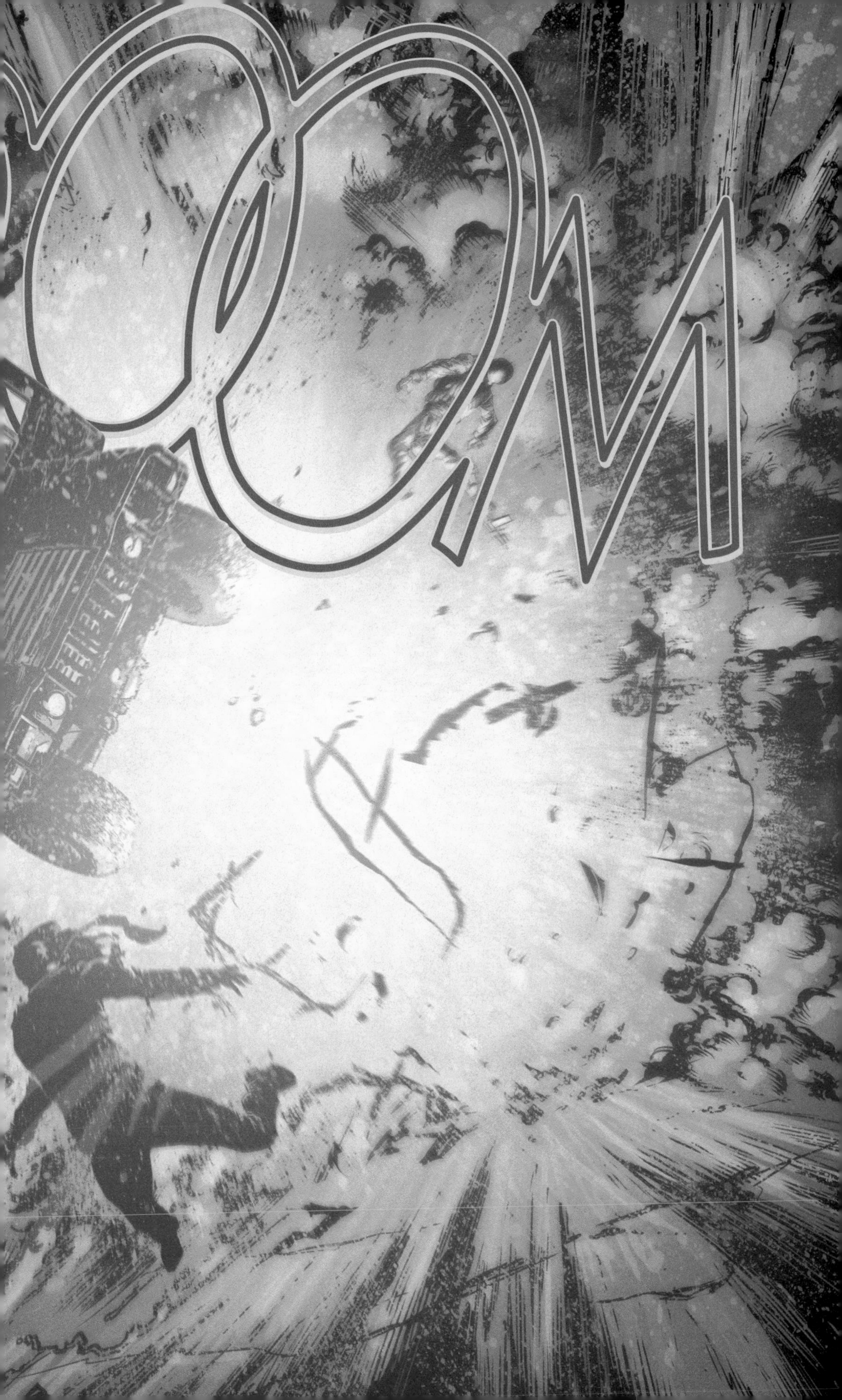
OOM

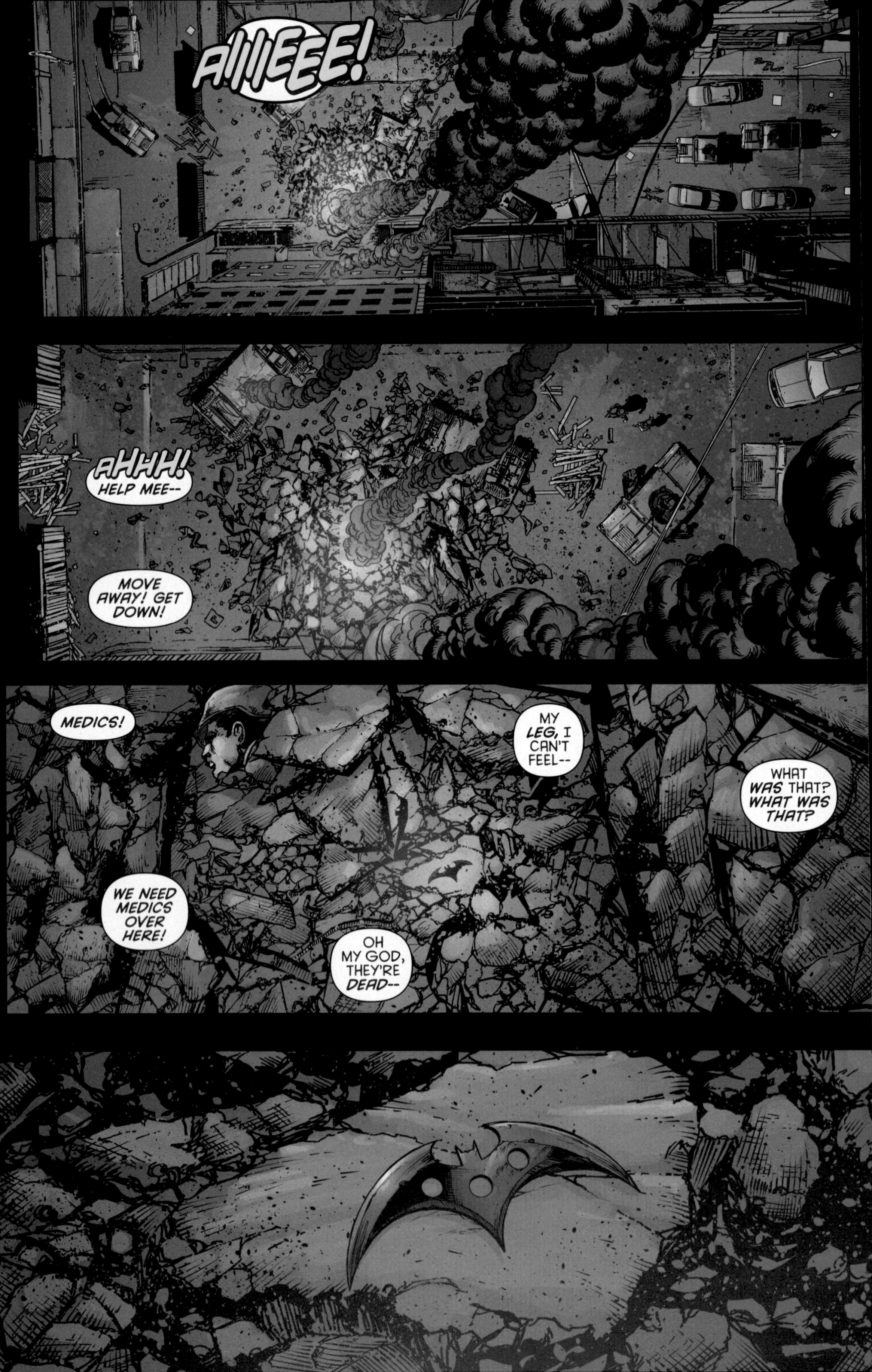

AIIIEEE!
AHHH! HELP MEE--
MOVE AWAY! GET DOWN!
MEDICS!
MY LEG, I CAN'T FEEL--
WHAT WAS THAT? WHAT WAS THAT?
WE NEED MEDICS OVER HERE!
OH MY GOD, THEY'RE DEAD--

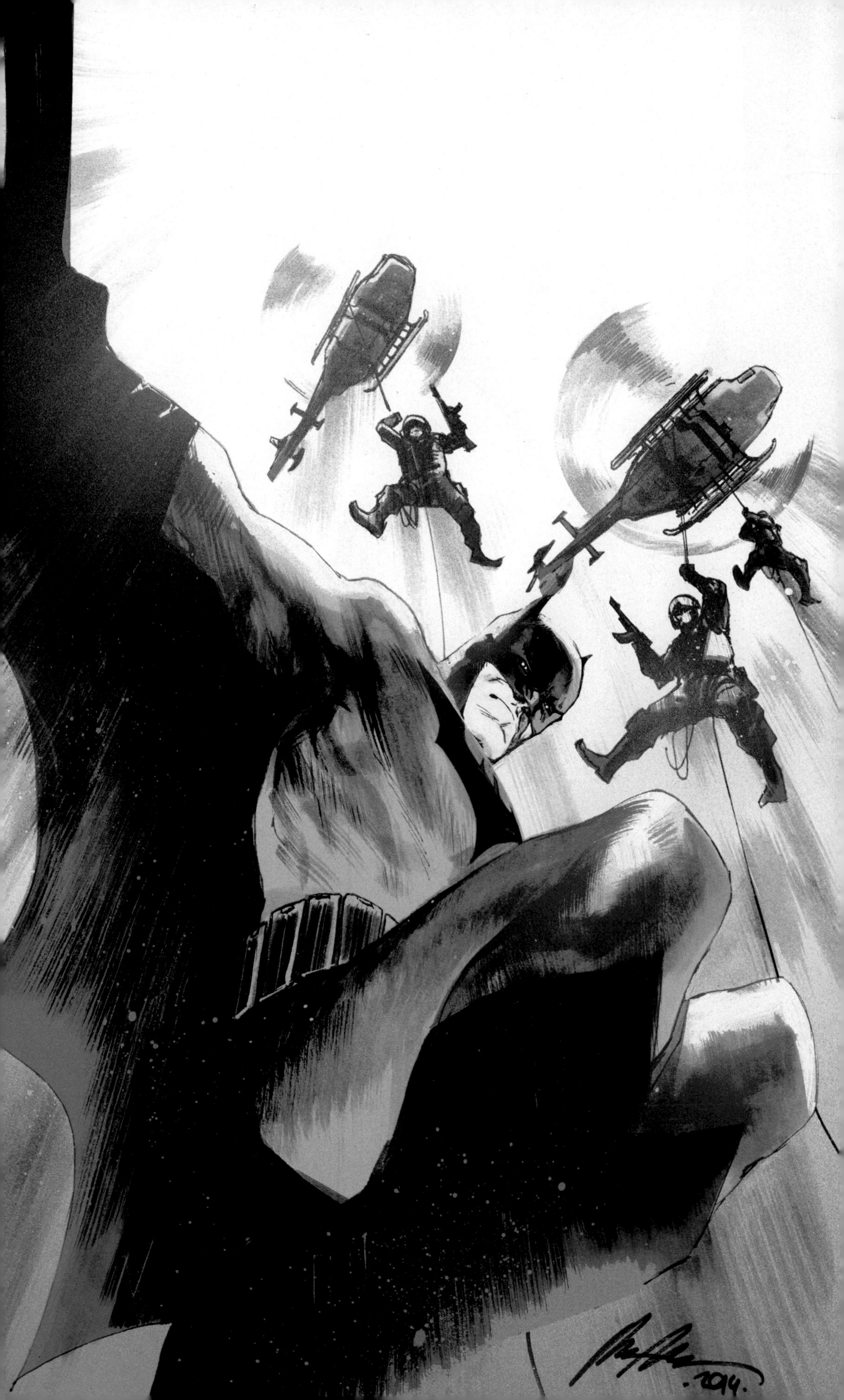

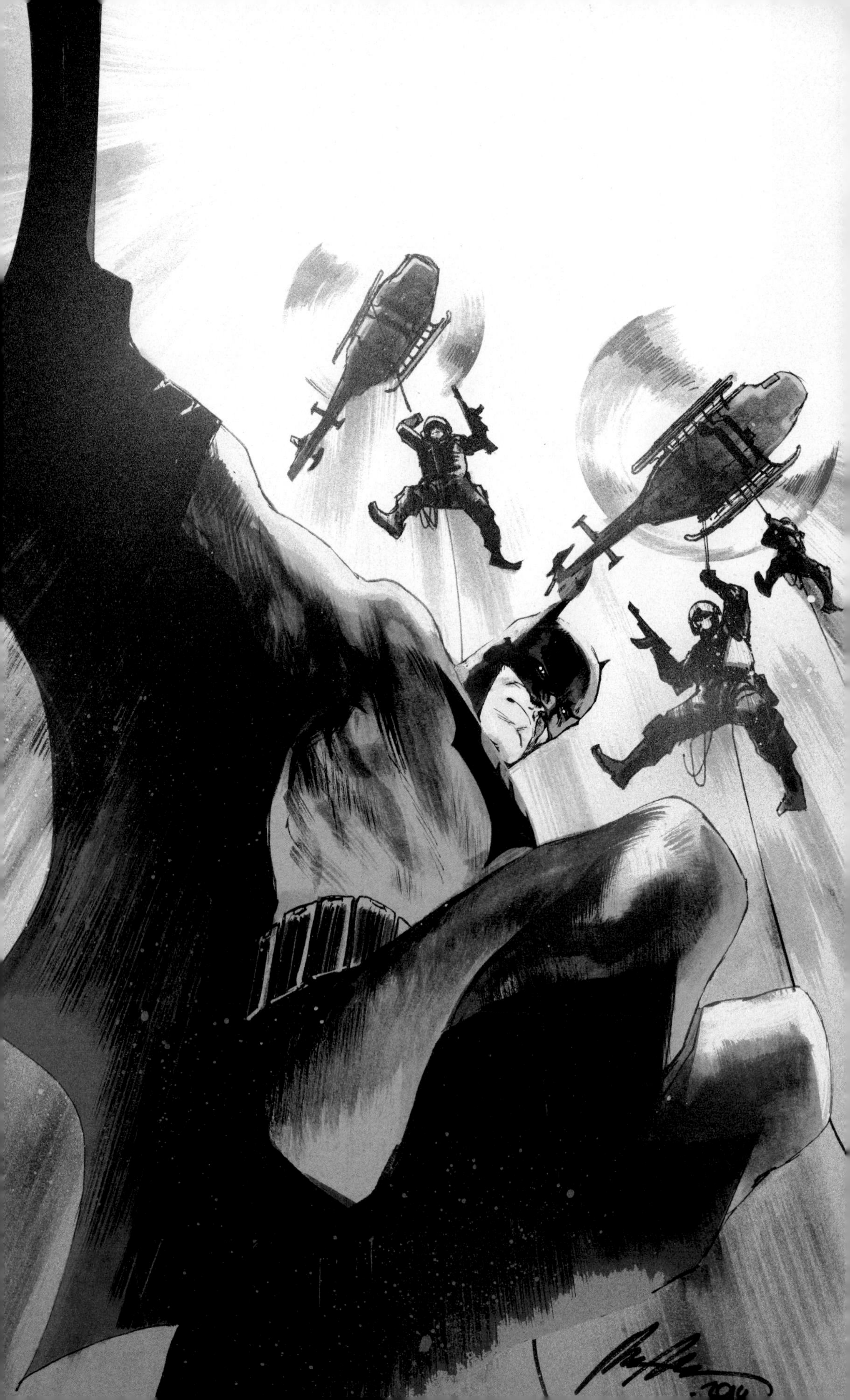

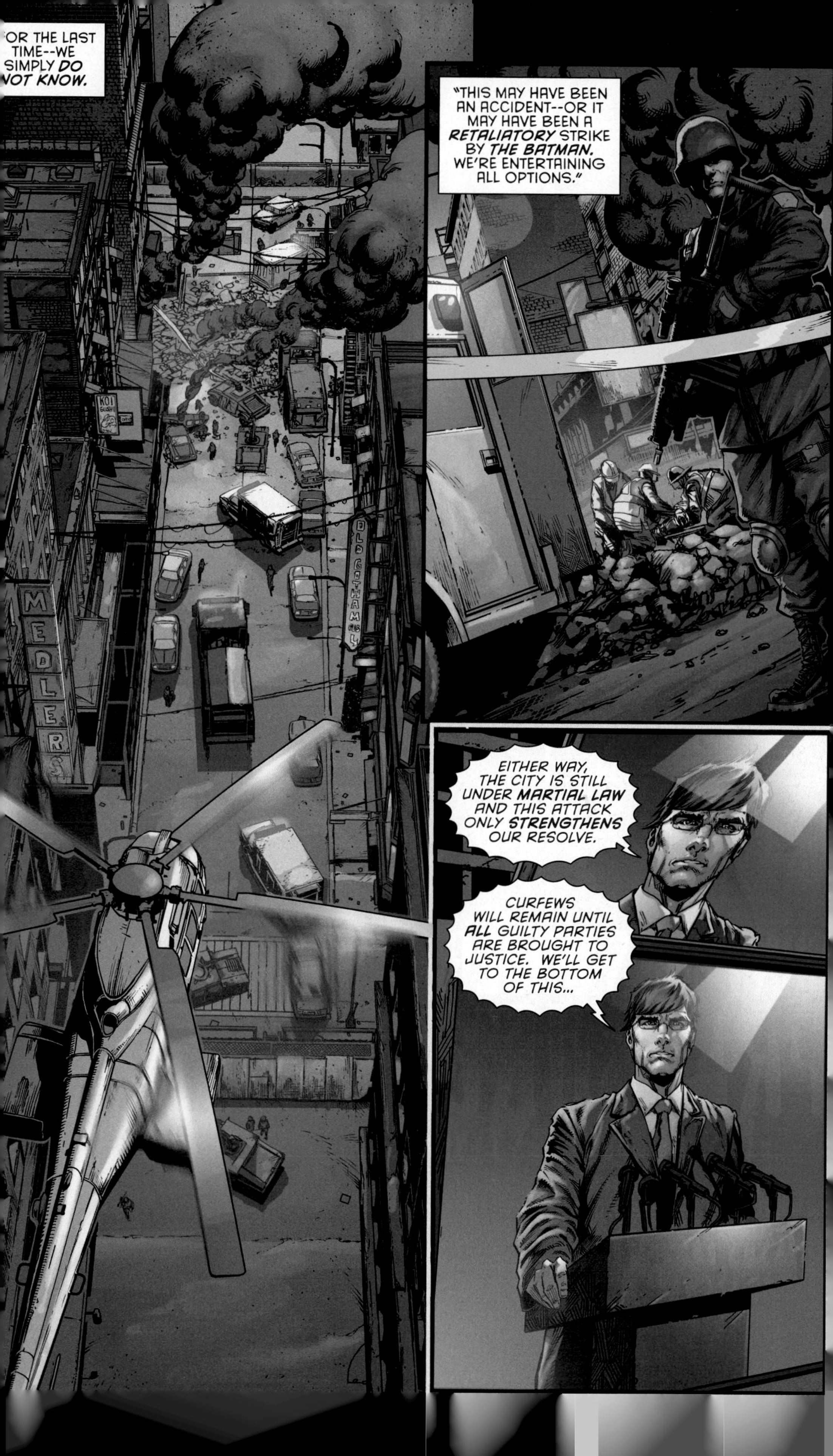

OR THE LAST TIME--WE SIMPLY DO NOT KNOW.
KOI SUSHI
MEDLERS
OLD GOTHAM
"THIS MAY HAVE BEEN AN ACCIDENT--OR IT MAY HAVE BEEN A RETALIATORY STRIKE BY THE BATMAN. WE'RE ENTERTAINING ALL OPTIONS."
EITHER WAY, THE CITY IS STILL UNDER MARTIAL LAW AND THIS ATTACK ONLY STRENGTHENS OUR RESOLVE.
CURFEWS WILL REMAIN UNTIL ALL GUILTY PARTIES ARE BROUGHT TO JUSTICE. WE'LL GET TO THE BOTTOM OF THIS...

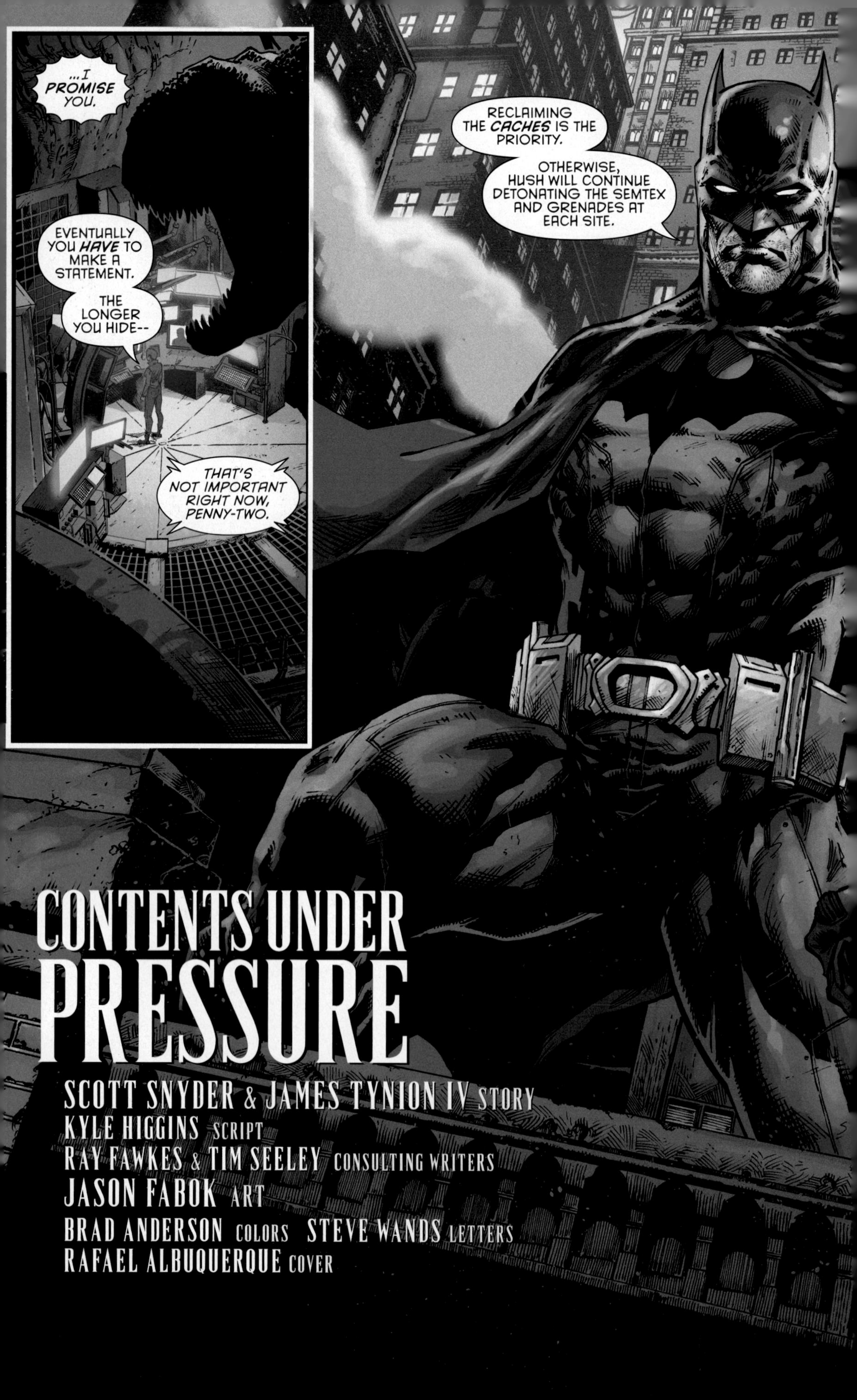
...I PROMISE YOU.
EVENTUALLY YOU HAVE TO MAKE A STATEMENT.
THE LONGER YOU HIDE--
THAT'S NOT IMPORTANT RIGHT NOW, PENNY-TWO.
RECLAIMING THE CACHES IS THE PRIORITY.
OTHERWISE, HUSH WILL CONTINUE DETONATING THE SEMTEX AND GRENADES AT EACH SITE.
CONTENTS UNDER PRESSURE
SCOTT SNYDER & JAMES TYNION IV STORY
KYLE HIGGINS SCRIPT
RAY FAWKES & TIM SEELEY CONSULTING WRITERS
JASON FABOK ART
BRAD ANDERSON COLORS STEVE WANDS LETTERS
RAFAEL ALBUQUERQUE COVER

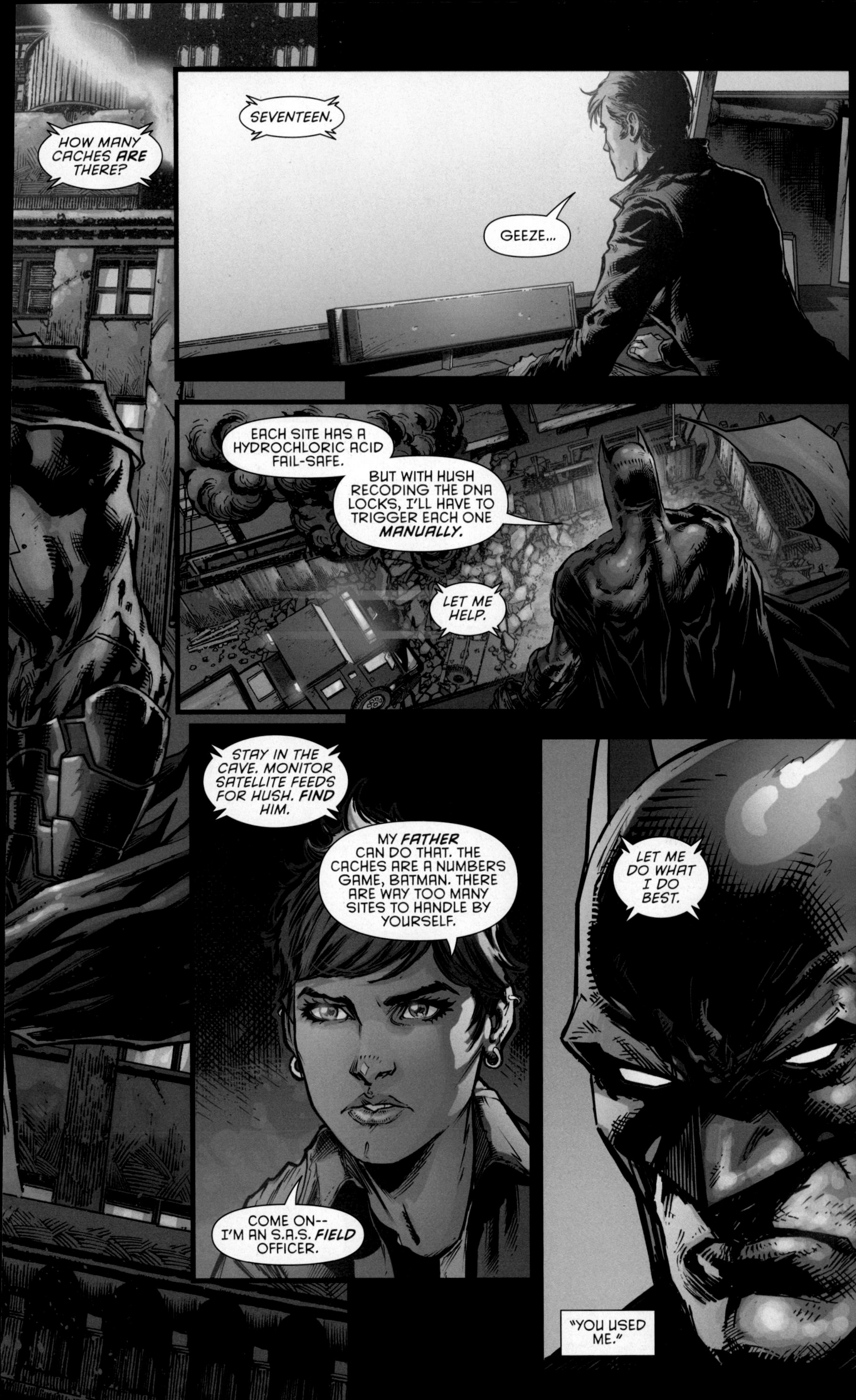
HOW MANY CACHES ARE THERE?
SEVENTEEN.
GEEZE...
EACH SITE HAS A HYDROCHLORIC ACID FAIL-SAFE.
BUT WITH HUSH RECODING THE DNA LOCKS, I'LL HAVE TO TRIGGER EACH ONE MANUALLY.
LET ME HELP.
STAY IN THE CAVE. MONITOR SATELLITE FEEDS FOR HUSH. FIND HIM.
MY FATHER CAN DO THAT. THE CACHES ARE A NUMBERS GAME, BATMAN. THERE ARE WAY TOO MANY SITES TO HANDLE BY YOURSELF.
COME ON-- I'M AN S.A.S. FIELD OFFICER.
LET ME DO WHAT I DO BEST.
"YOU USED ME."

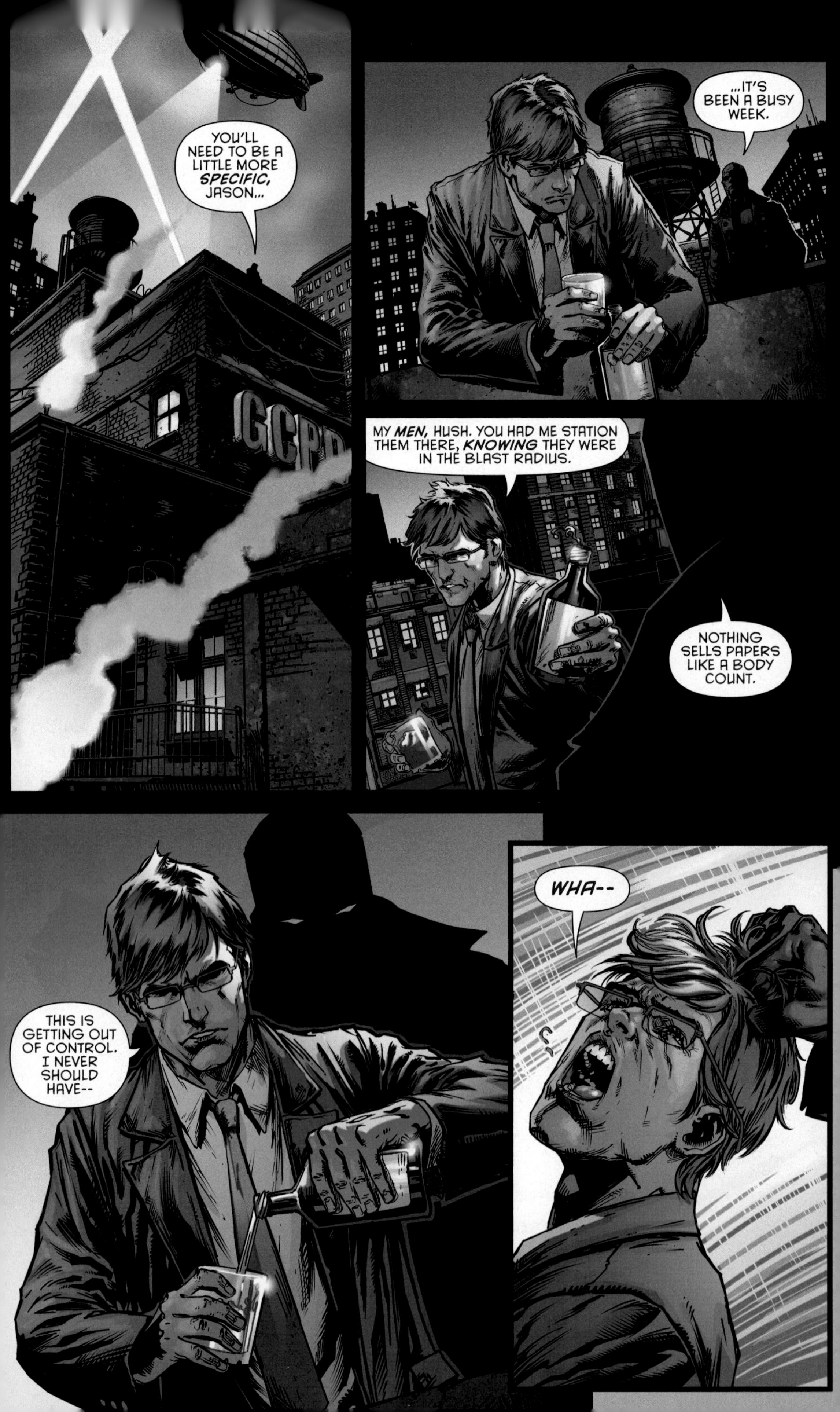
YOU'LL NEED TO BE A LITTLE MORE SPECIFIC, JASON...
...IT'S BEEN A BUSY WEEK.
MY MEN, HUSH. YOU HAD ME STATION THEM THERE, KNOWING THEY WERE IN THE BLAST RADIUS.
NOTHING SELLS PAPERS LIKE A BODY COUNT.
GCPD
THIS IS GETTING OUT OF CONTROL. I NEVER SHOULD HAVE--
WHA--

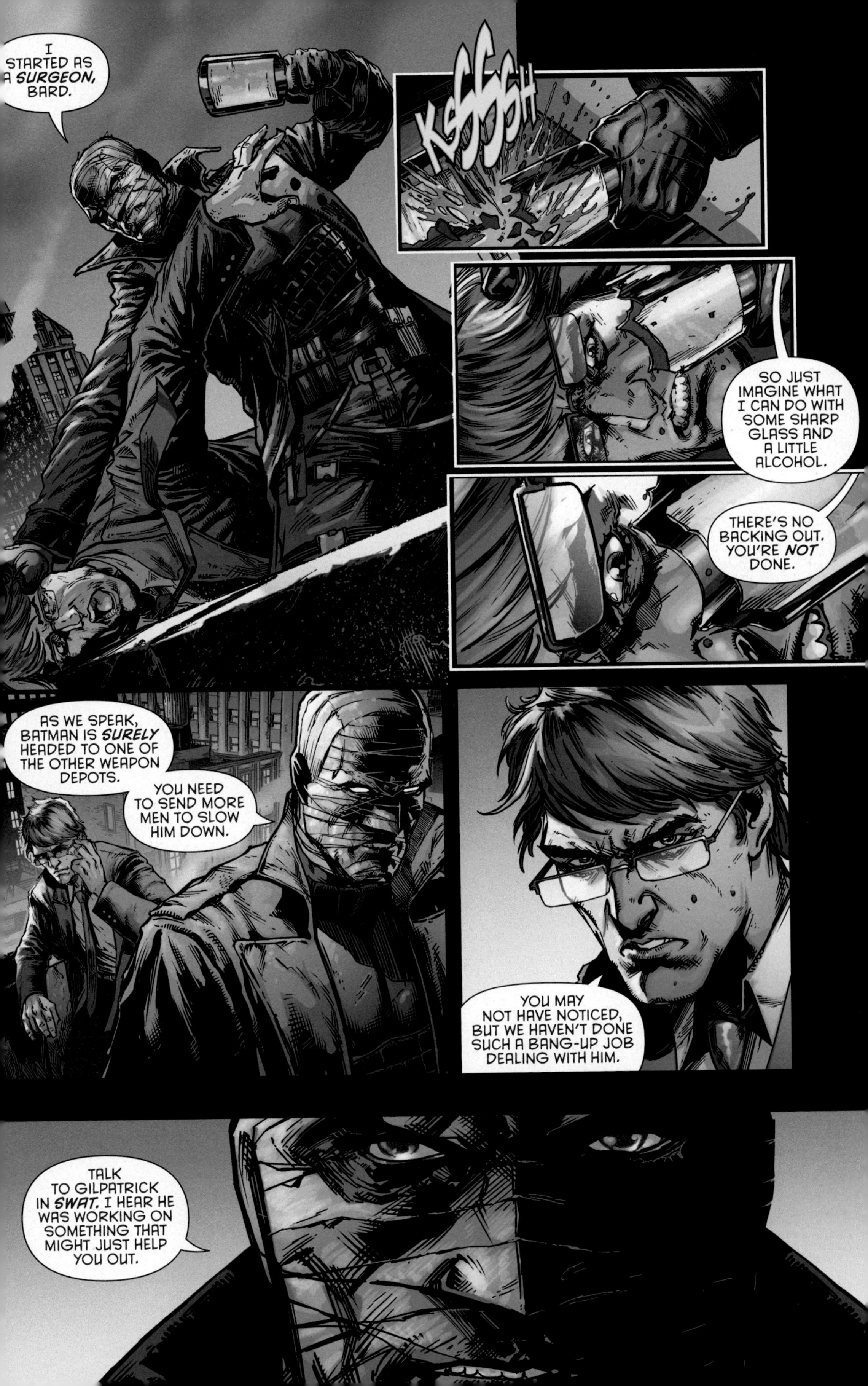

I STARTED AS A SURGEON, BARD.
KSSSSH
SO JUST IMAGINE WHAT I CAN DO WITH SOME SHARP GLASS AND A LITTLE ALCOHOL.
THERE'S NO BACKING OUT. YOU'RE NOT DONE.
AS WE SPEAK, BATMAN IS SURELY HEADED TO ONE OF THE OTHER WEAPON DEPOTS.
YOU NEED TO SEND MORE MEN TO SLOW HIM DOWN.
YOU MAY NOT HAVE NOTICED, BUT WE HAVEN'T DONE SUCH A BANG-UP JOB DEALING WITH HIM.
TALK TO GILPATRICK IN SWAT. I HEAR HE WAS WORKING ON SOMETHING THAT MIGHT JUST HELP YOU OUT.

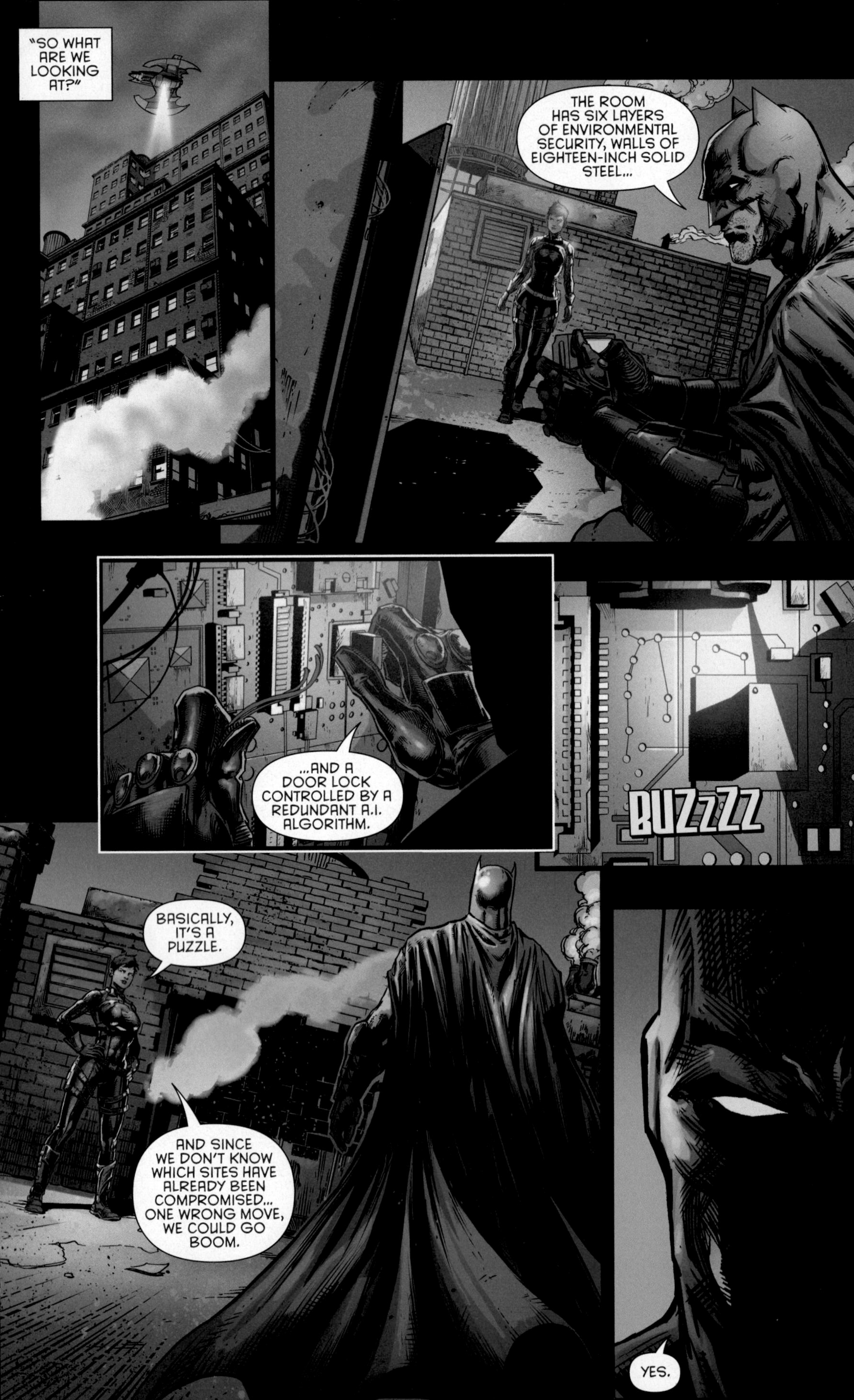
"SO WHAT ARE WE LOOKING AT?"
THE ROOM HAS SIX LAYERS OF ENVIRONMENTAL SECURITY, WALLS OF EIGHTEEN-INCH SOLID STEEL...
...AND A DOOR LOCK CONTROLLED BY A REDUNDANT A.I. ALGORITHM.
BUZZZZ
BASICALLY, IT'S A PUZZLE.
AND SINCE WE DON'T KNOW WHICH SITES HAVE ALREADY BEEN COMPROMISED... ONE WRONG MOVE, WE COULD GO BOOM.
YES.

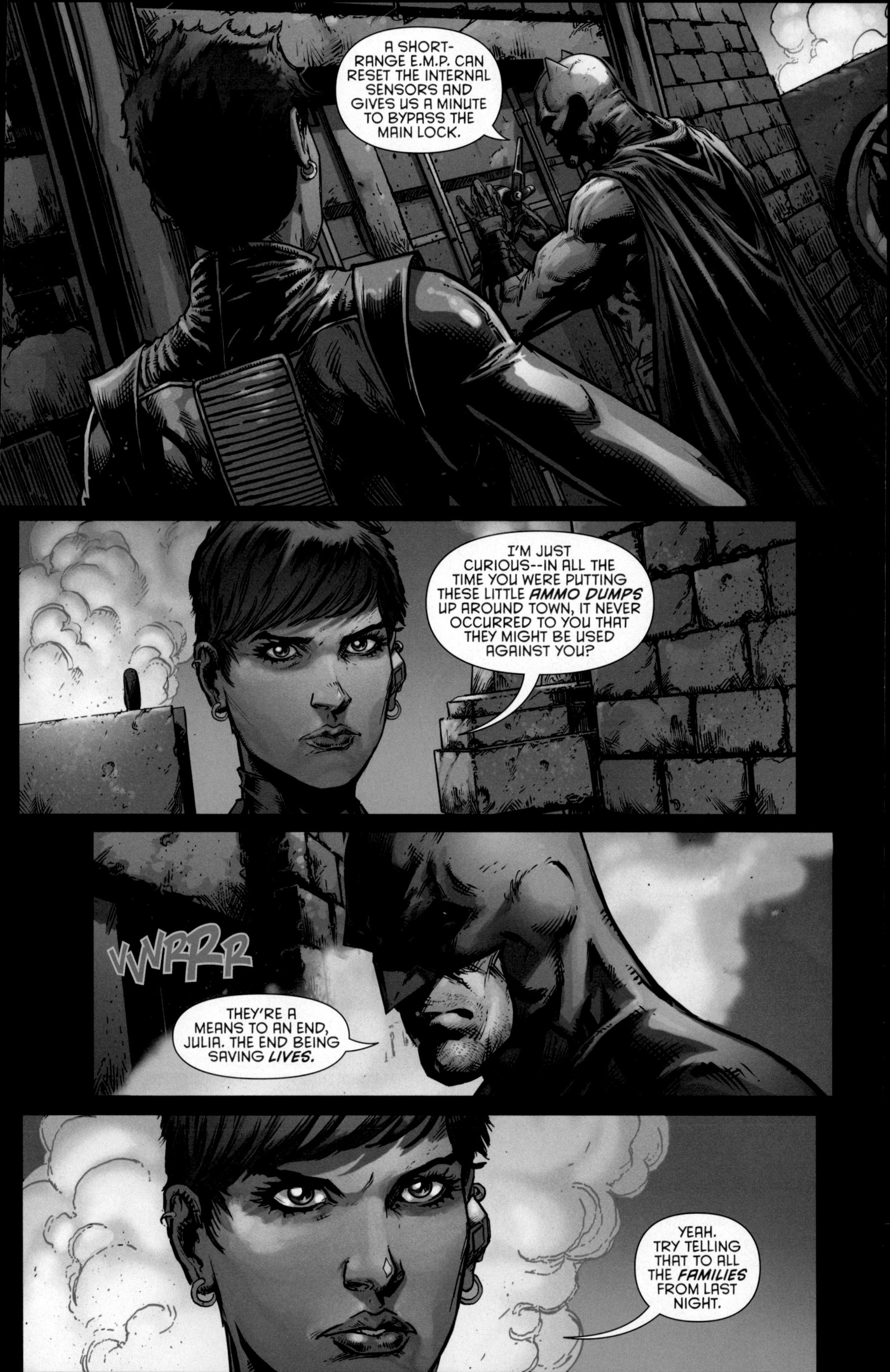
A SHORT-RANGE E.M.P. CAN RESET THE INTERNAL SENSORS AND GIVES US A MINUTE TO BYPASS THE MAIN LOCK.
I'M JUST CURIOUS--IN ALL THE TIME YOU WERE PUTTING THESE LITTLE *AMMO DUMPS* UP AROUND TOWN, IT NEVER OCCURRED TO YOU THAT THEY MIGHT BE USED AGAINST YOU?
VWRRR
THEY'RE A MEANS TO AN END, JULIA. THE END BEING SAVING *LIVES.*
YEAH. TRY TELLING THAT TO ALL THE *FAMILIES* FROM LAST NIGHT.

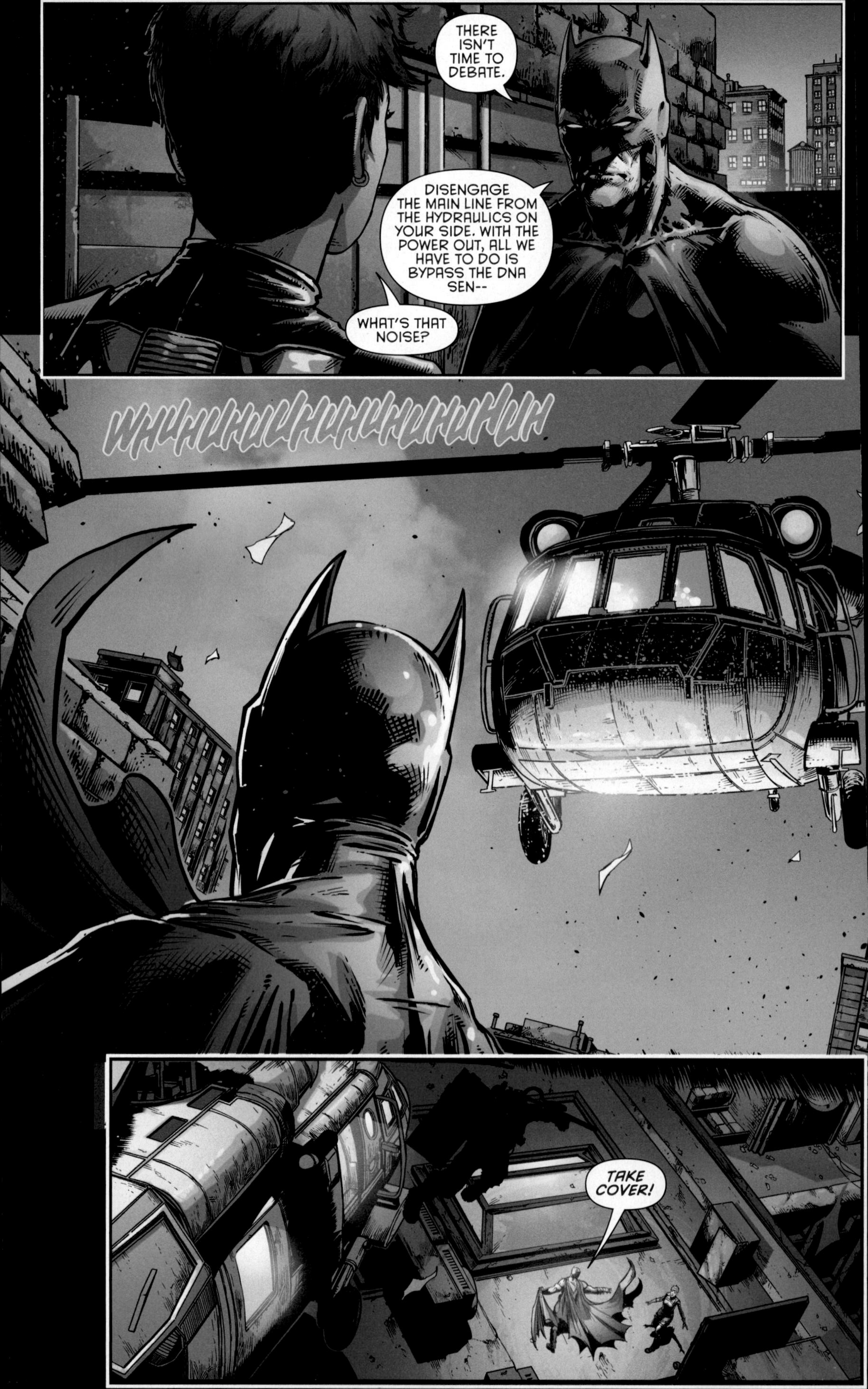
THERE ISN'T TIME TO DEBATE.
DISENGAGE THE MAIN LINE FROM THE HYDRAULICS ON YOUR SIDE. WITH THE POWER OUT, ALL WE HAVE TO DO IS BYPASS THE DNA SEN--
WHAT'S THAT NOISE?
WHUHUHUHUHUHUHUHUHUH
TAKE COVER!

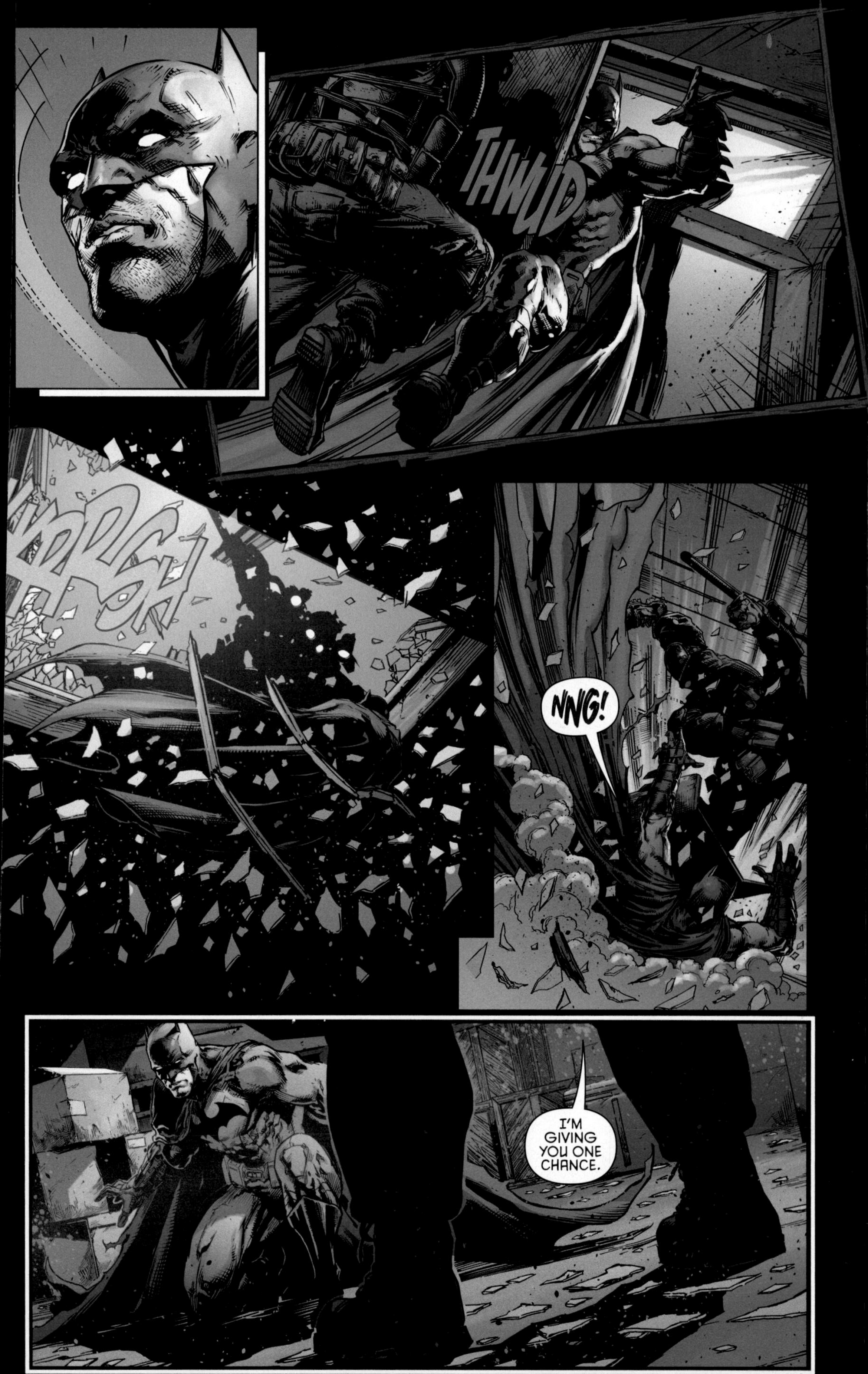
THWUD
NNG!
I'M GIVING YOU ONE CHANCE.

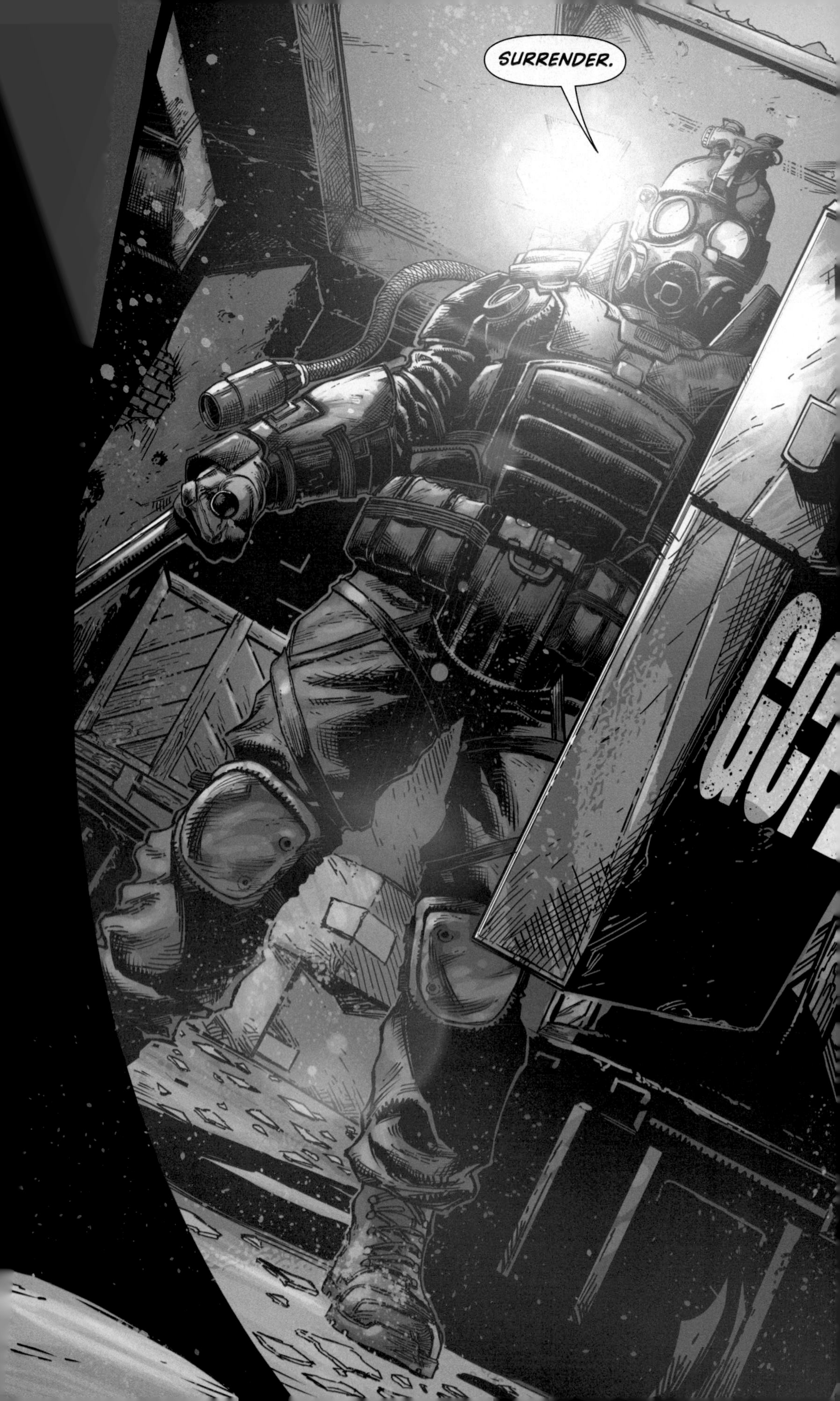
SURRENDER.

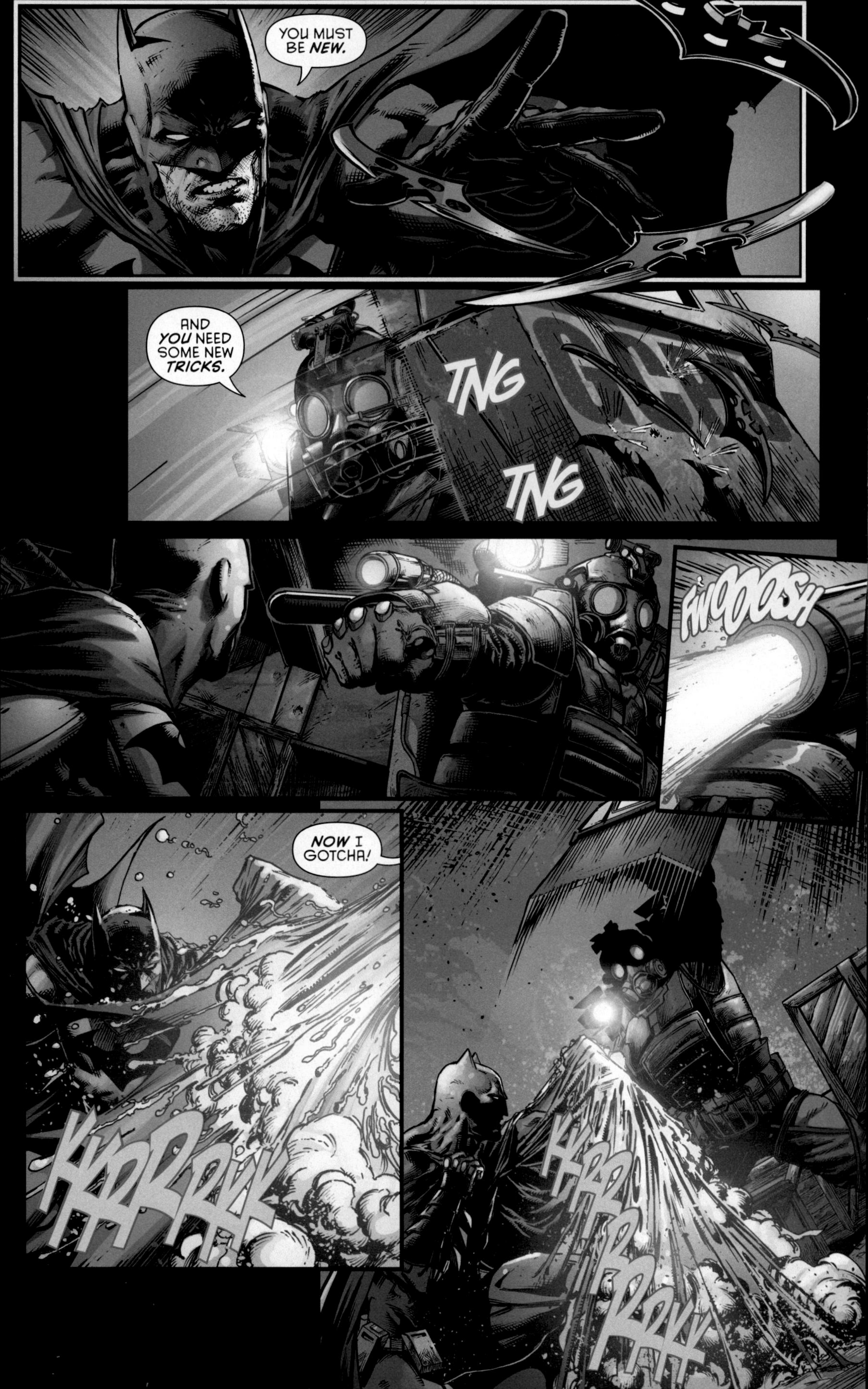
YOU MUST BE NEW.
AND YOU NEED SOME NEW TRICKS.
TNG
TNG
FWOOOOSH
NOW I GOTCHA!
KRRRAK

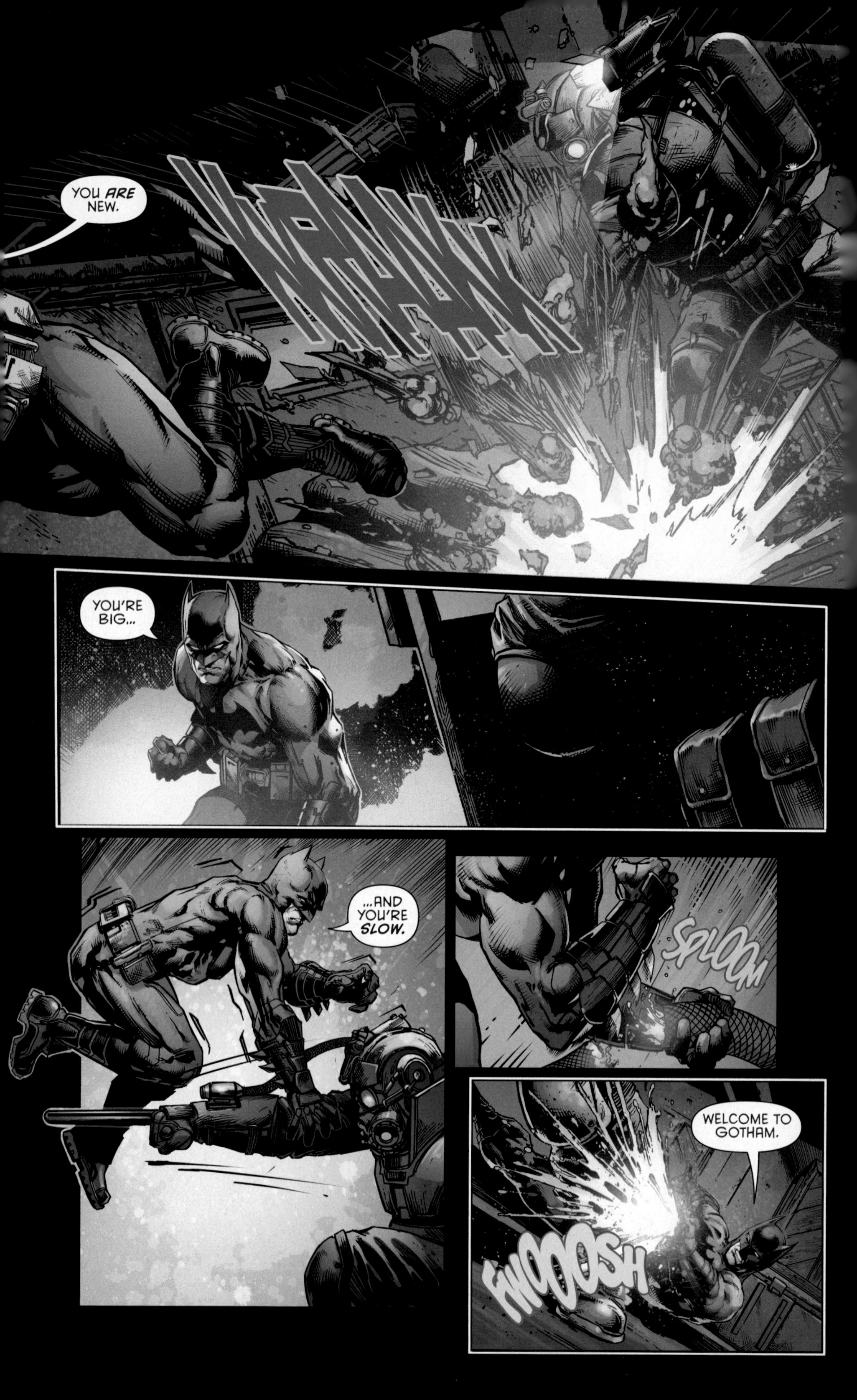
YOU ARE NEW.
KRAKKK
YOU'RE BIG...
...AND YOU'RE SLOW.
SPLOOM
WELCOME TO GOTHAM.
FWOOOSH

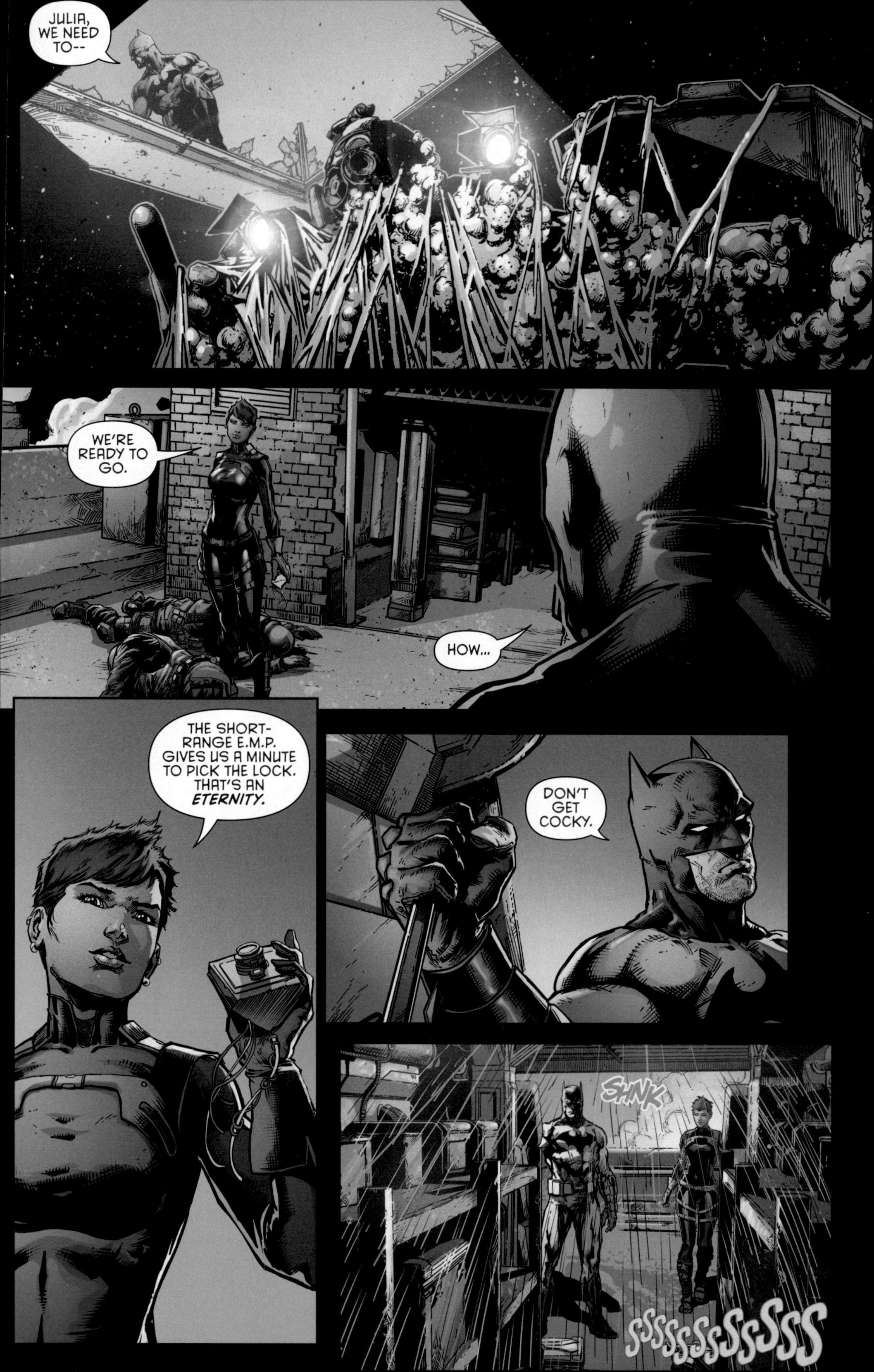
JULIA, WE NEED TO--
WE'RE READY TO GO.
HOW...
THE SHORT-RANGE E.M.P. GIVES US A MINUTE TO PICK THE LOCK. THAT'S AN *ETERNITY.*
DON'T GET COCKY.
SHNK
SSSSSSSSSSSS

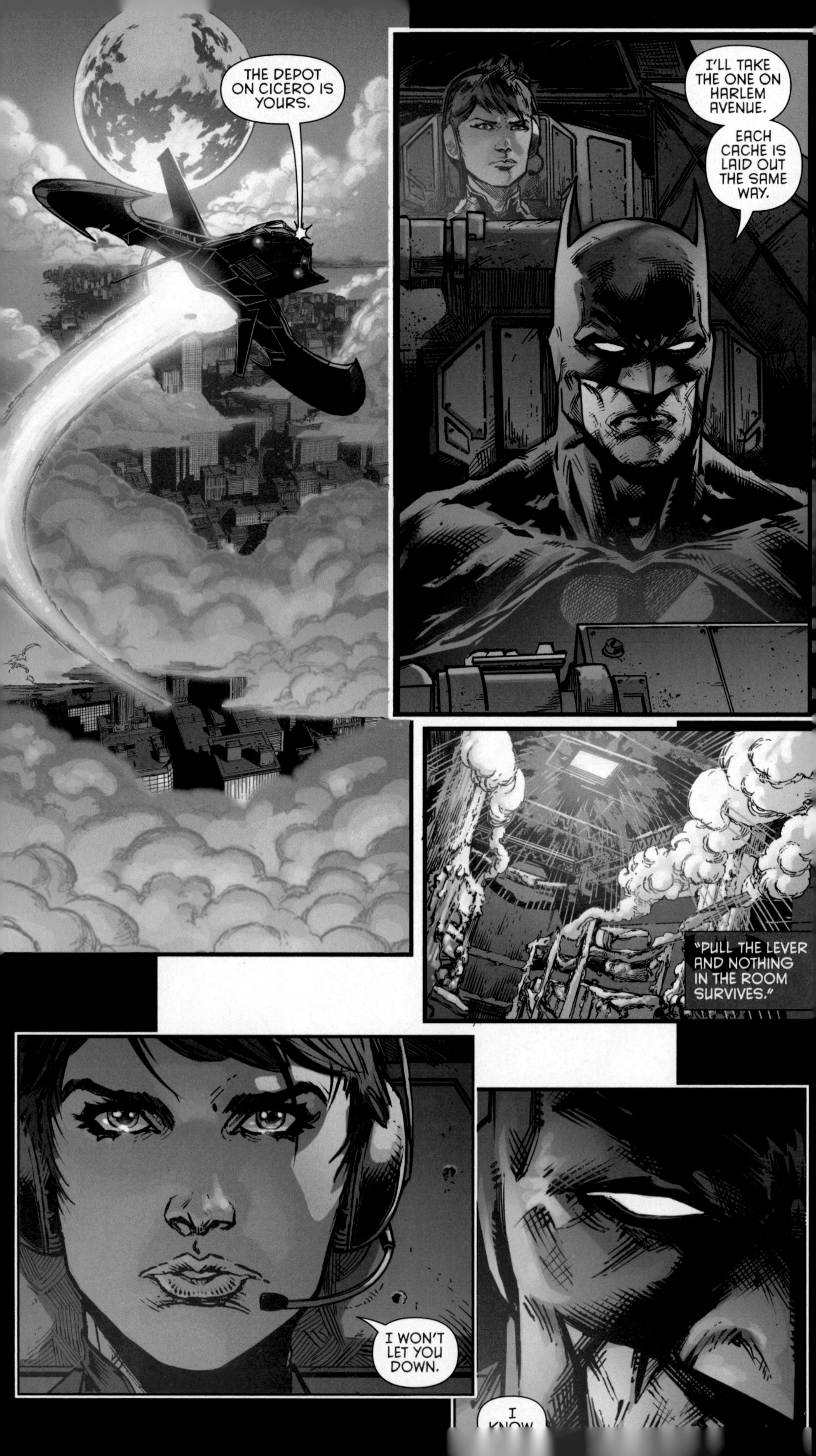
THE DEPOT ON CICERO IS YOURS.
I'LL TAKE THE ONE ON HARLEM AVENUE.
EACH CACHE IS LAID OUT THE SAME WAY.
"PULL THE LEVER AND NOTHING IN THE ROOM SURVIVES."
I WON'T LET YOU DOWN.
I

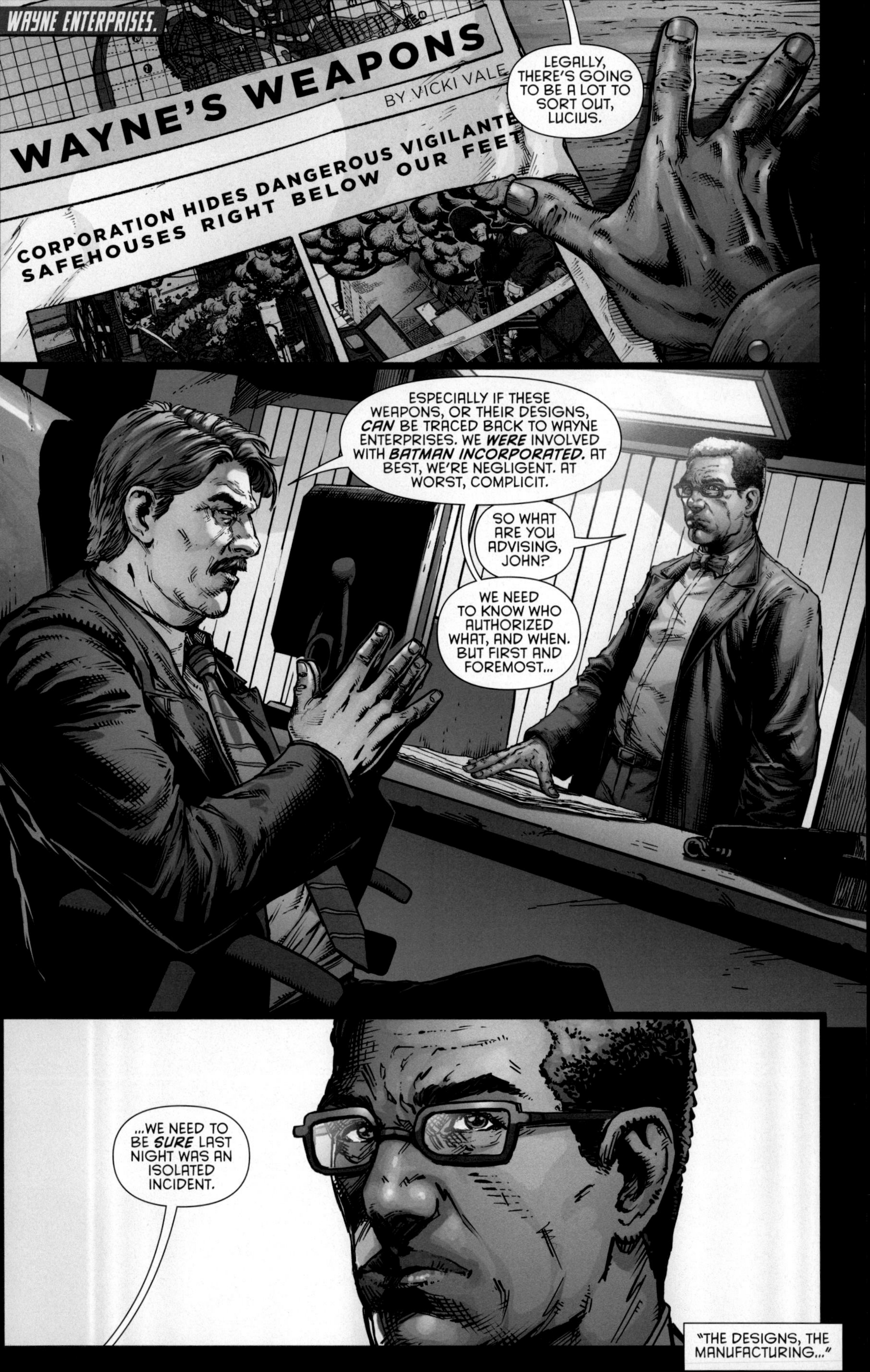
WAYNE ENTERPRISES.
WAYNE'S WEAPONS
BY VICKI VALE
CORPORATION HIDES DANGEROUS VIGILANTE SAFEHOUSES RIGHT BELOW OUR FEET
LEGALLY, THERE'S GOING TO BE A LOT TO SORT OUT, LUCIUS.
ESPECIALLY IF THESE WEAPONS, OR THEIR DESIGNS, CAN BE TRACED BACK TO WAYNE ENTERPRISES. WE WERE INVOLVED WITH BATMAN INCORPORATED. AT BEST, WE'RE NEGLIGENT. AT WORST, COMPLICIT.
SO WHAT ARE YOU ADVISING, JOHN?
WE NEED TO KNOW WHO AUTHORIZED WHAT, AND WHEN. BUT FIRST AND FOREMOST...
...WE NEED TO BE SURE LAST NIGHT WAS AN ISOLATED INCIDENT.
"THE DESIGNS, THE MANUFACTURING..."

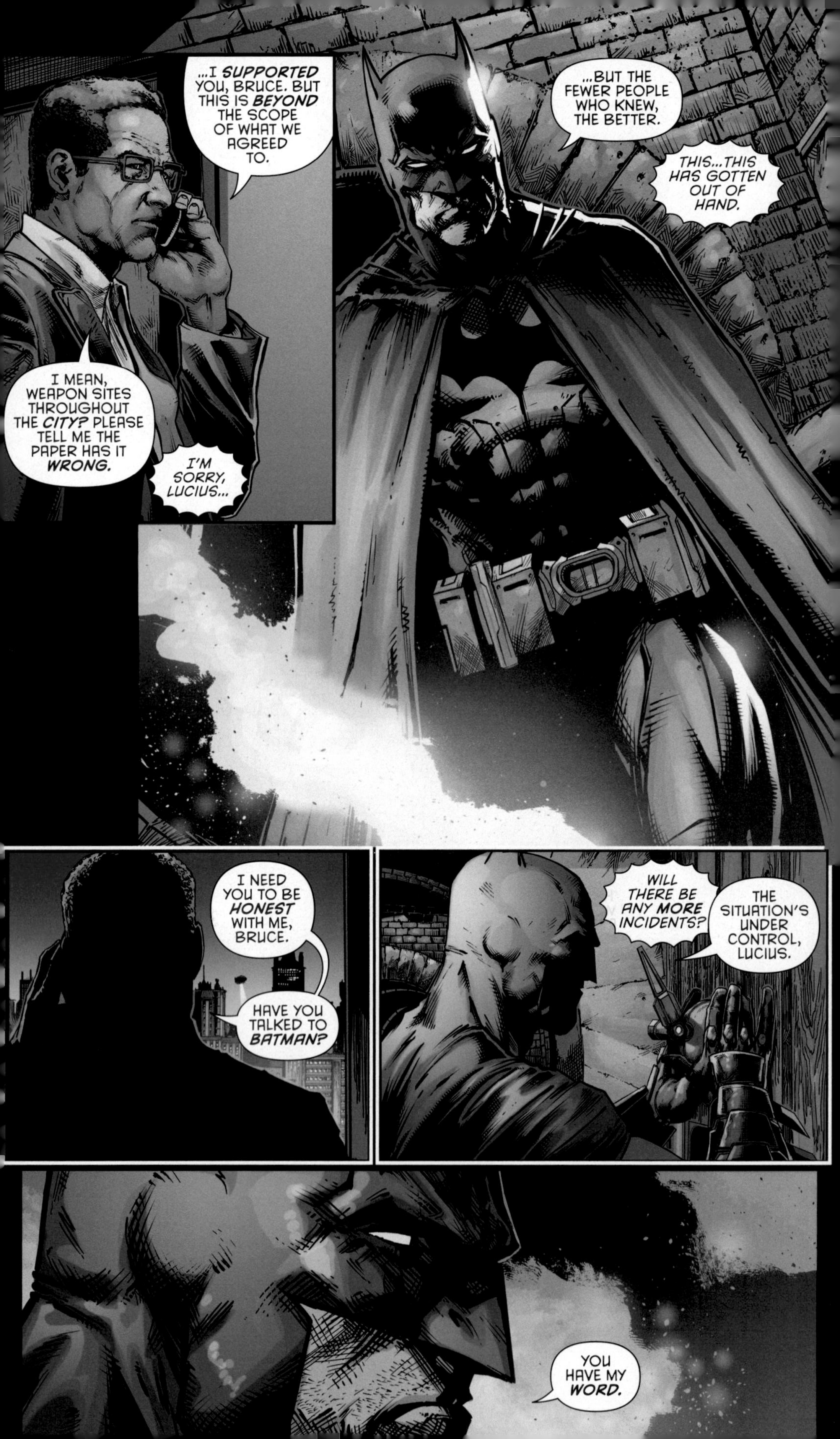
...I SUPPORTED YOU, BRUCE. BUT THIS IS BEYOND THE SCOPE OF WHAT WE AGREED TO.
I MEAN, WEAPON SITES THROUGHOUT THE CITY? PLEASE TELL ME THE PAPER HAS IT WRONG.
I'M SORRY, LUCIUS...
...BUT THE FEWER PEOPLE WHO KNEW, THE BETTER.
THIS...THIS HAS GOTTEN OUT OF HAND.
I NEED YOU TO BE HONEST WITH ME, BRUCE.
HAVE YOU TALKED TO BATMAN?
WILL THERE BE ANY MORE INCIDENTS?
THE SITUATION'S UNDER CONTROL, LUCIUS.
YOU HAVE MY WORD.

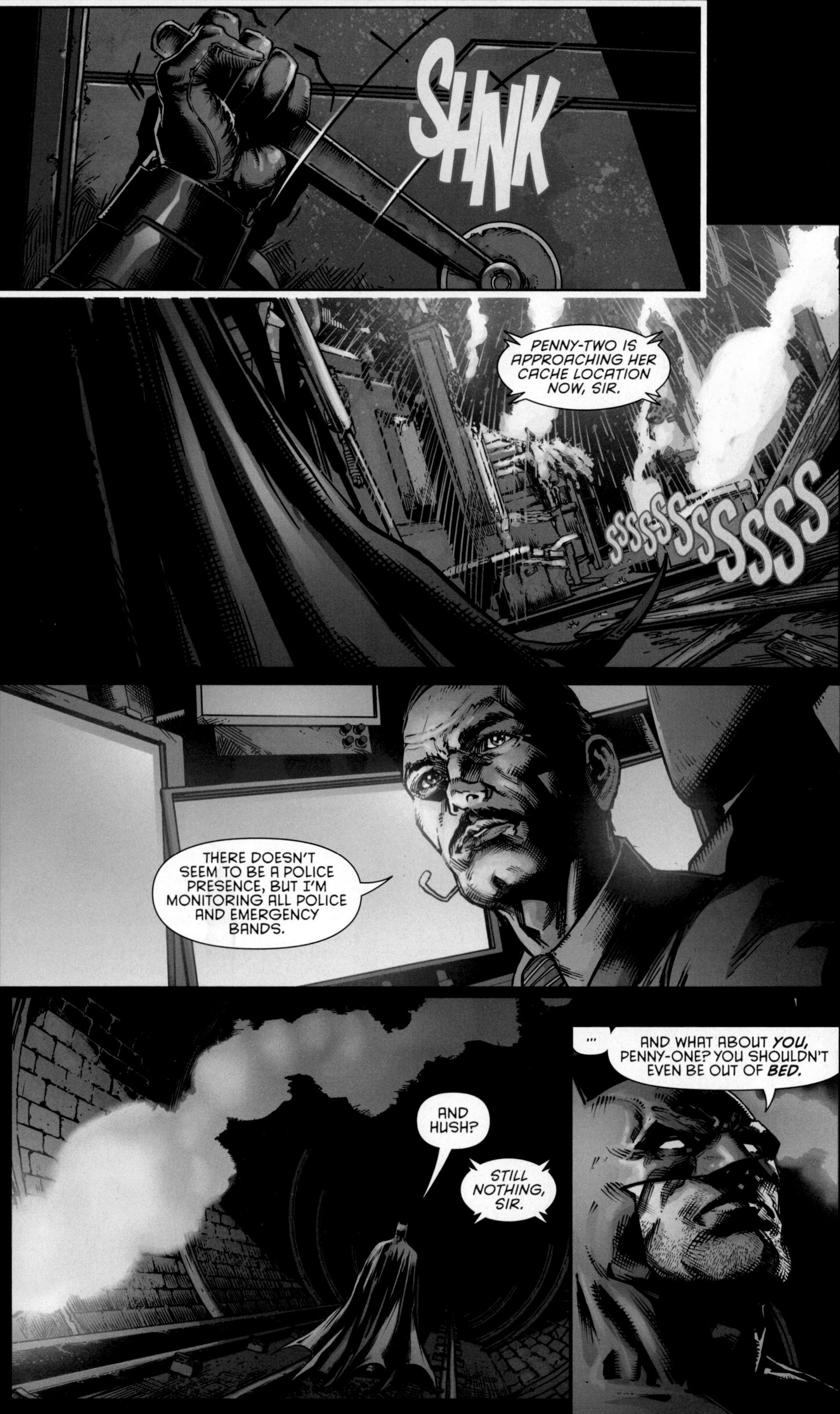
SHNK
PENNY-TWO IS APPROACHING HER CACHE LOCATION NOW, SIR.
SSSSSSSSSS
THERE DOESN'T SEEM TO BE A POLICE PRESENCE, BUT I'M MONITORING ALL POLICE AND EMERGENCY BANDS.
AND HUSH?
STILL NOTHING, SIR.
...
AND WHAT ABOUT *YOU*, PENNY-ONE? YOU SHOULDN'T EVEN BE OUT OF *BED*.

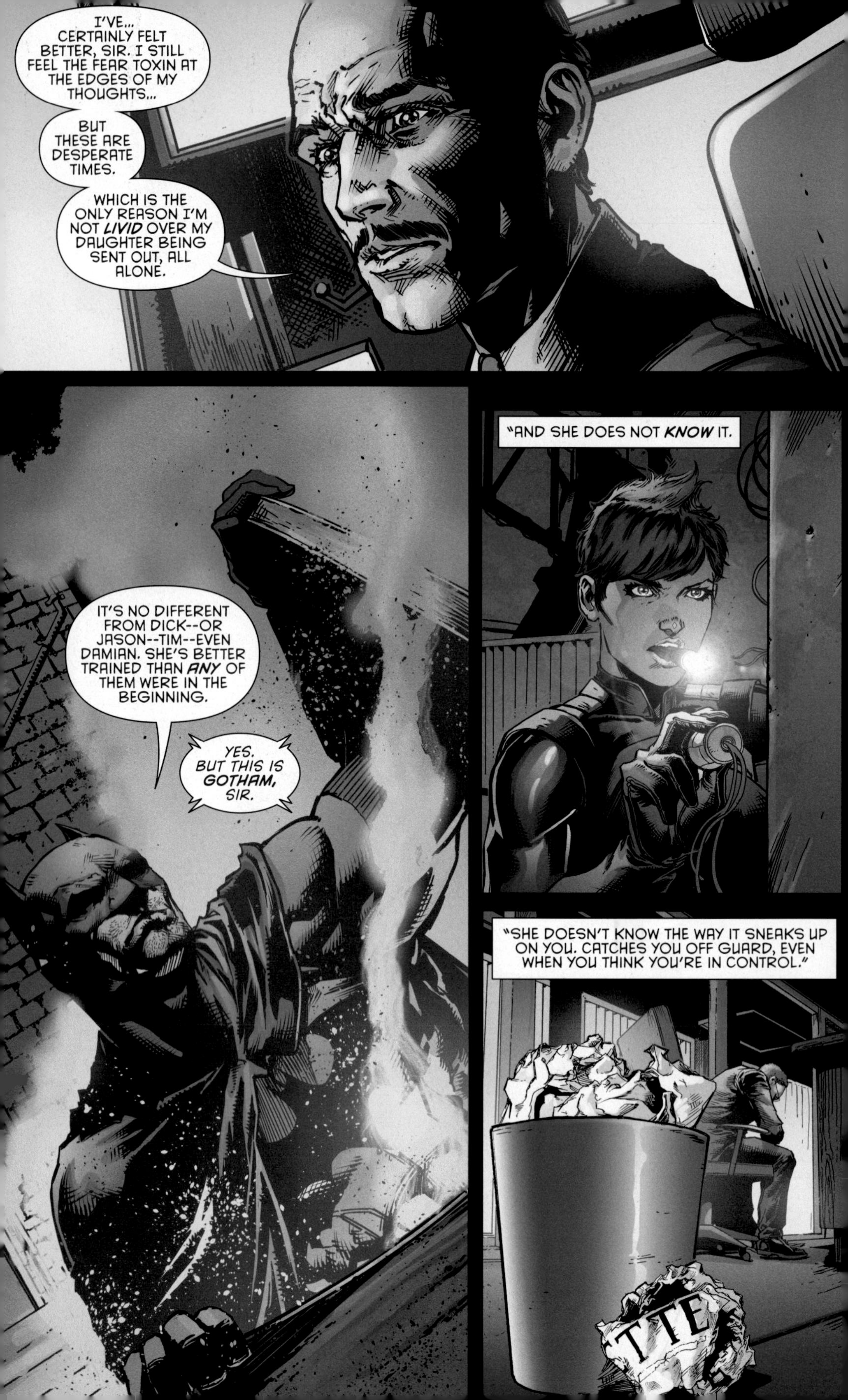
I'VE... CERTAINLY FELT BETTER, SIR. I STILL FEEL THE FEAR TOXIN AT THE EDGES OF MY THOUGHTS...
BUT THESE ARE DESPERATE TIMES.
WHICH IS THE ONLY REASON I'M NOT *LIVID* OVER MY DAUGHTER BEING SENT OUT, ALL ALONE.
IT'S NO DIFFERENT FROM DICK--OR JASON--TIM--EVEN DAMIAN. SHE'S BETTER TRAINED THAN *ANY* OF THEM WERE IN THE BEGINNING.
YES. BUT THIS IS ***GOTHAM,*** SIR.
"AND SHE DOES NOT ***KNOW*** IT.
"SHE DOESN'T KNOW THE WAY IT SNEAKS UP ON YOU. CATCHES YOU OFF GUARD, EVEN WHEN YOU THINK YOU'RE IN CONTROL."
TTE

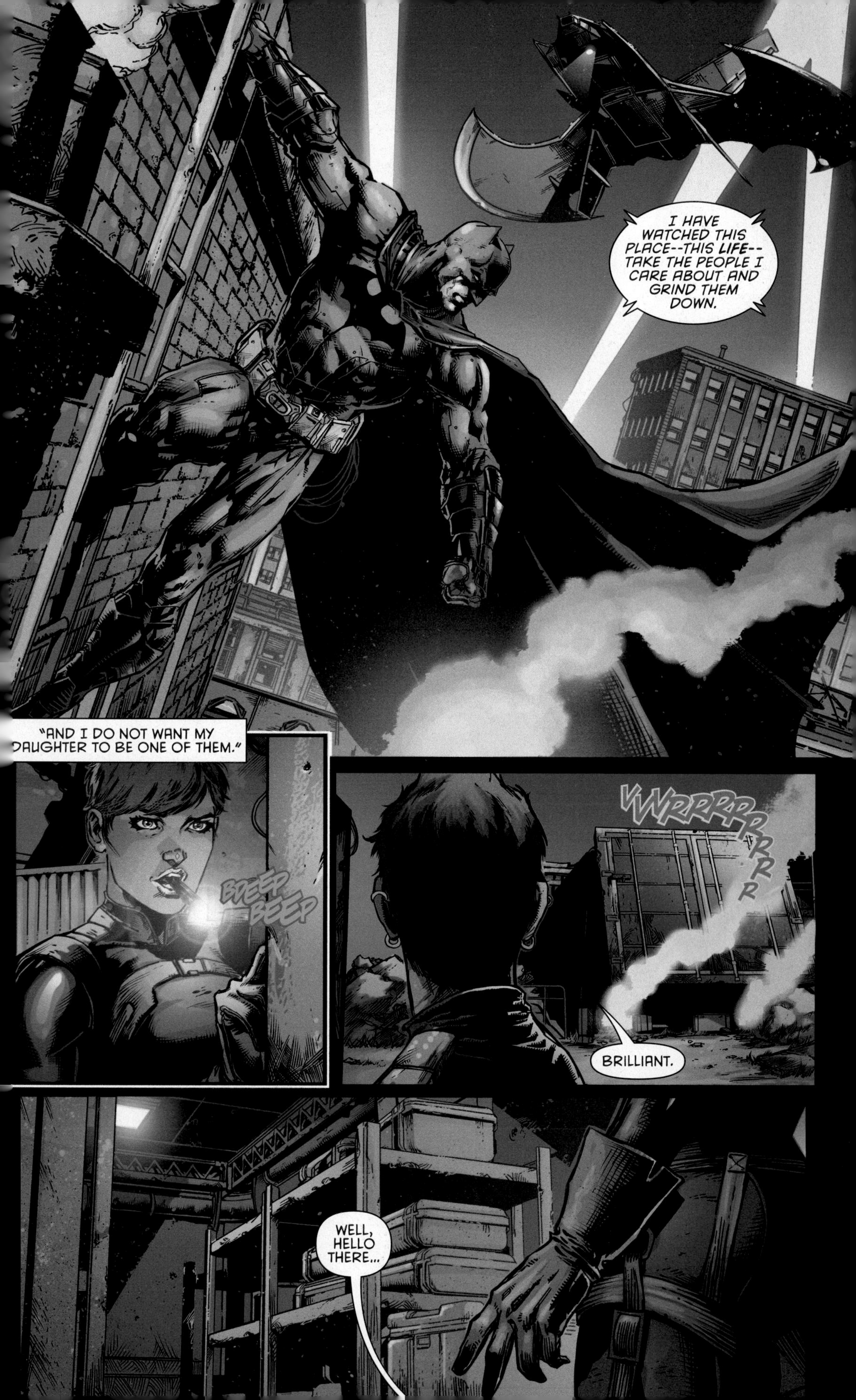
I HAVE WATCHED THIS PLACE--THIS LIFE--TAKE THE PEOPLE I CARE ABOUT AND GRIND THEM DOWN.
"AND I DO NOT WANT MY DAUGHTER TO BE ONE OF THEM."
BEEP BEEP
VVRRRRRRRRR
BRILLIANT.
WELL, HELLO THERE...

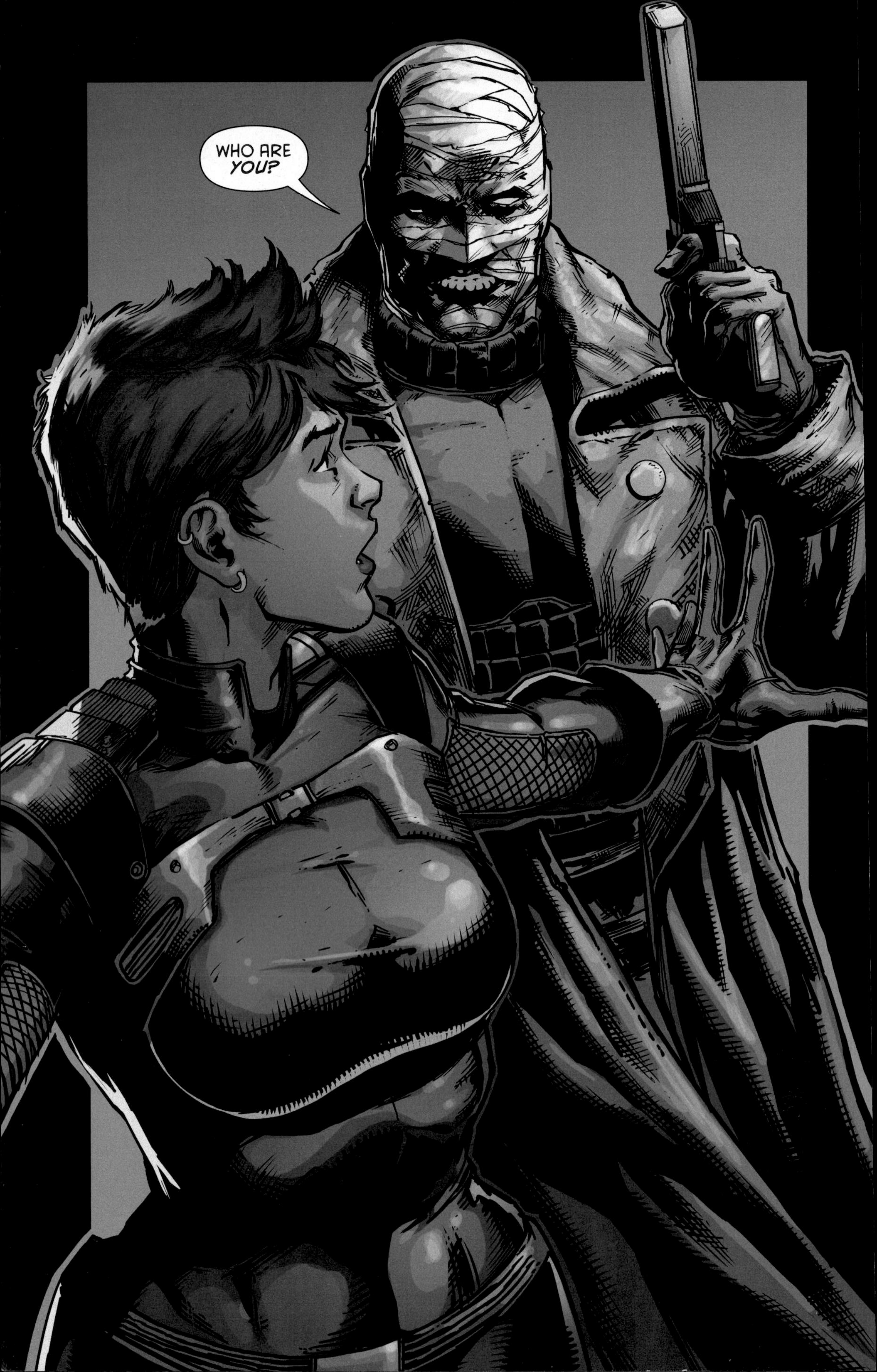
WHO ARE *YOU?*

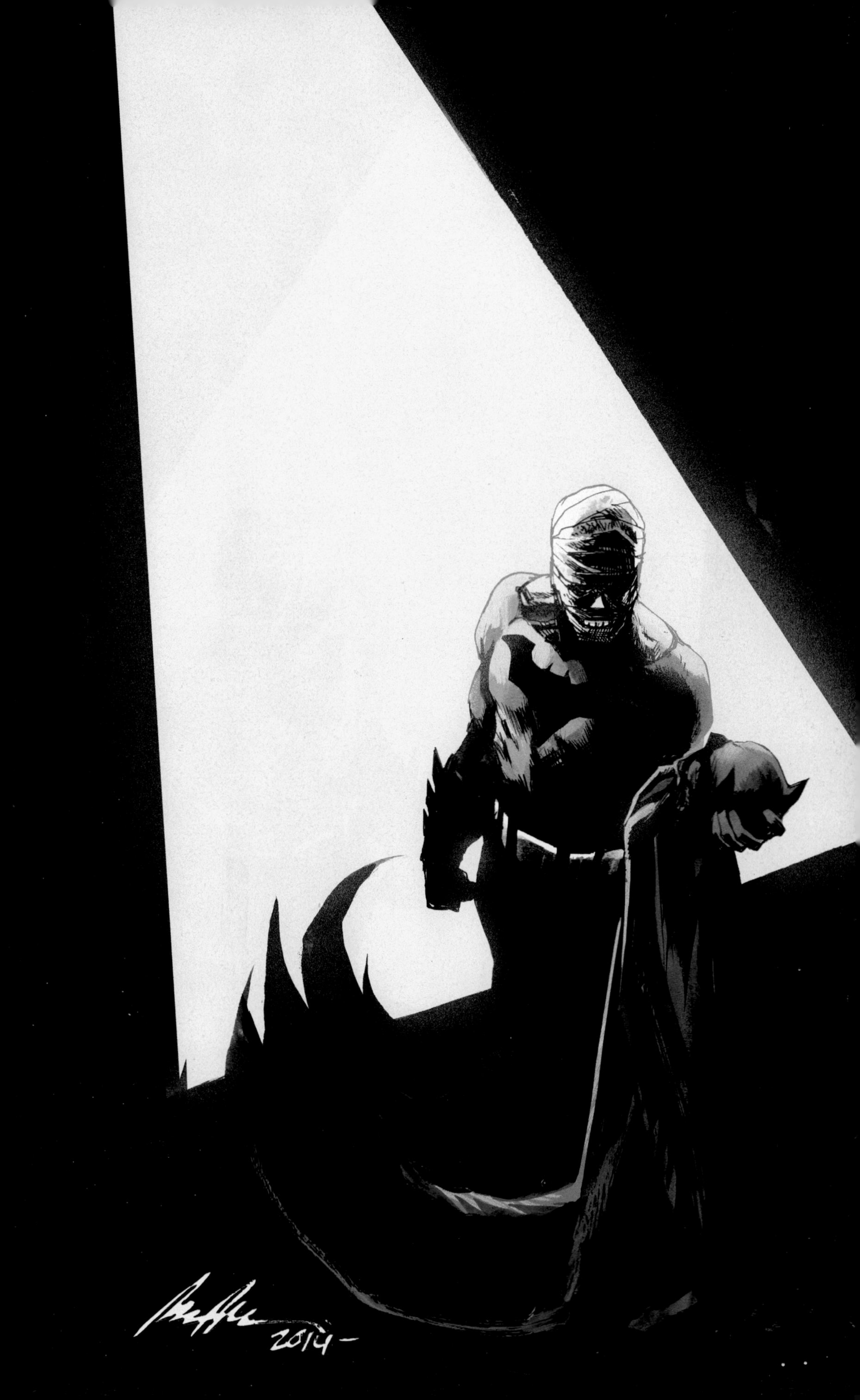

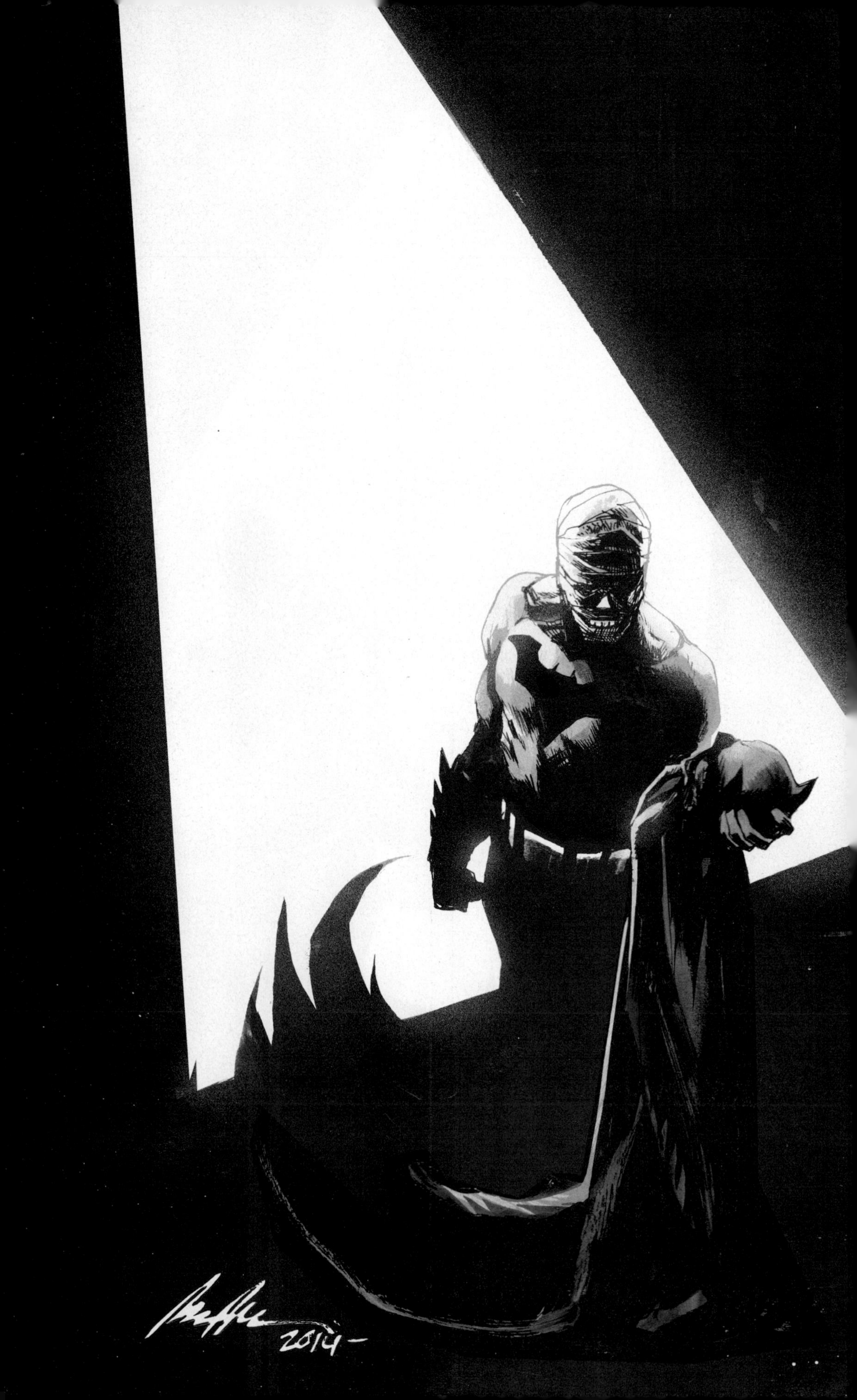

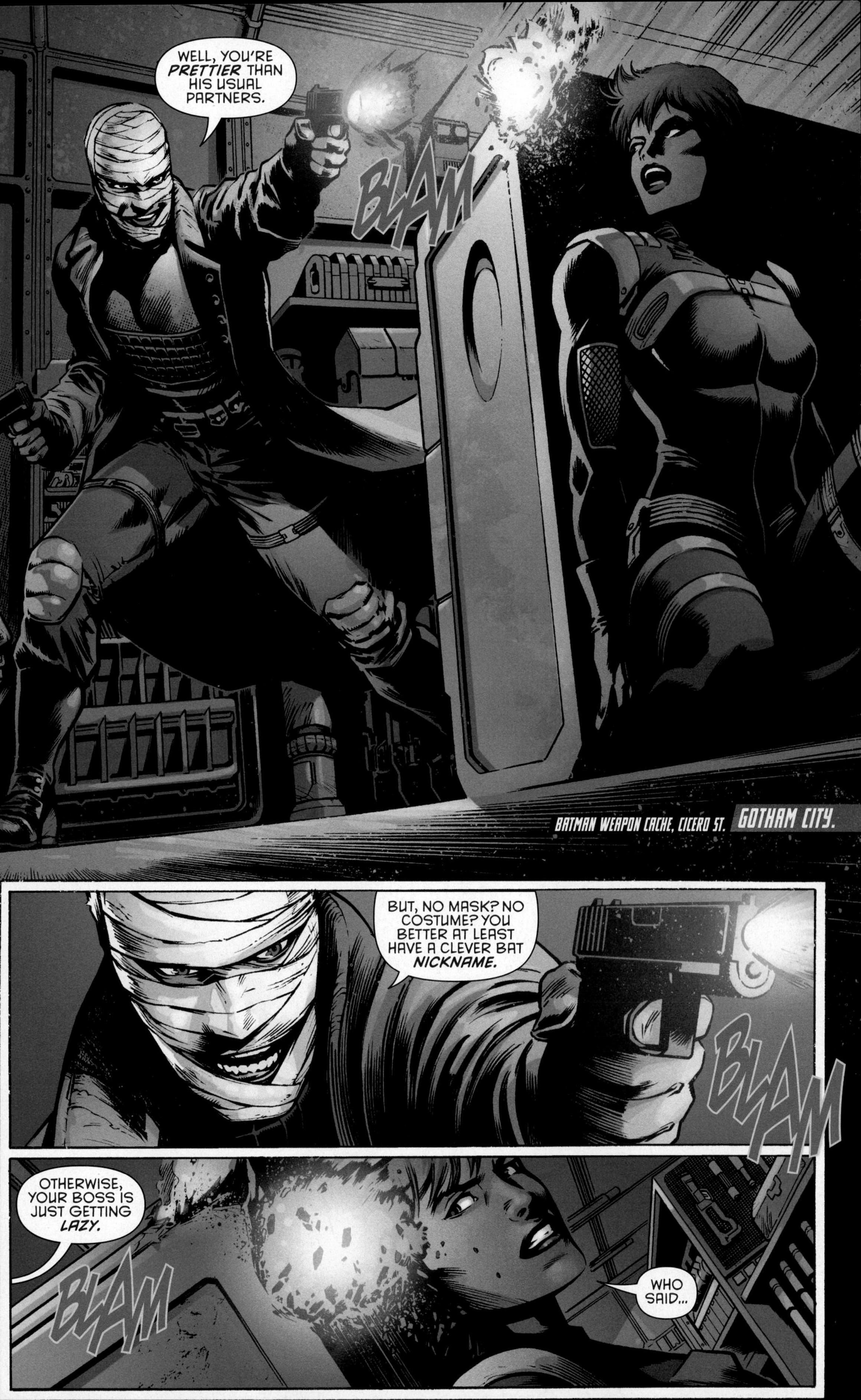
WELL, YOU'RE PRETTIER THAN HIS USUAL PARTNERS.
BLAM
BATMAN WEAPON CACHE, CICERO ST. GOTHAM CITY.
BUT, NO MASK? NO COSTUME? YOU BETTER AT LEAST HAVE A CLEVER BAT NICKNAME.
BLAM
OTHERWISE, YOUR BOSS IS JUST GETTING LAZY.
BLAM
WHO SAID...

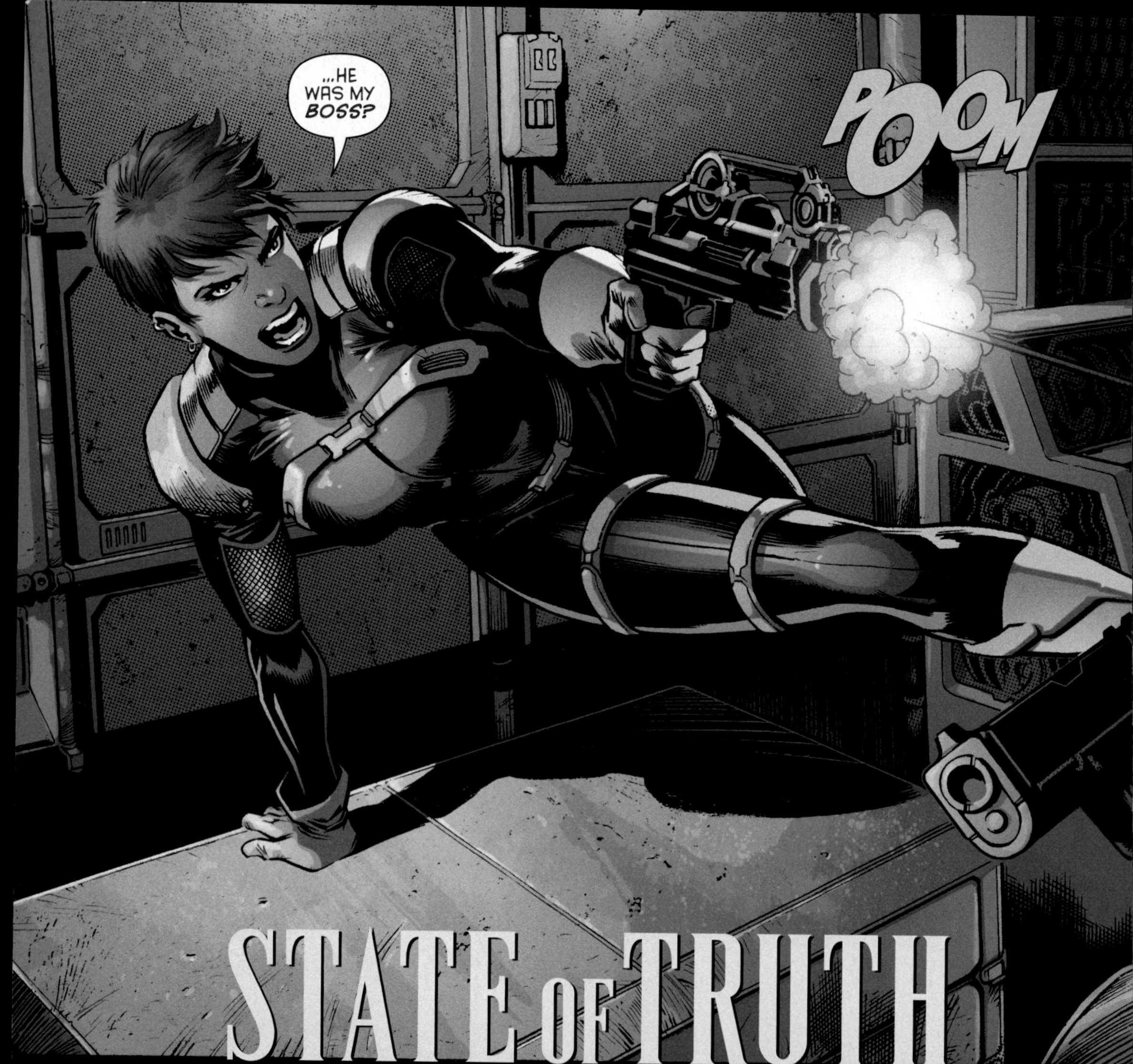
...HE WAS MY BOSS?
POOM

# STATE OF TRUTH

SCOTT SNYDER & JAMES TYNION IV STORY
KYLE HIGGINS SCRIPT
RAY FAWKES & TIM SEELEY CONSULTING WRITERS

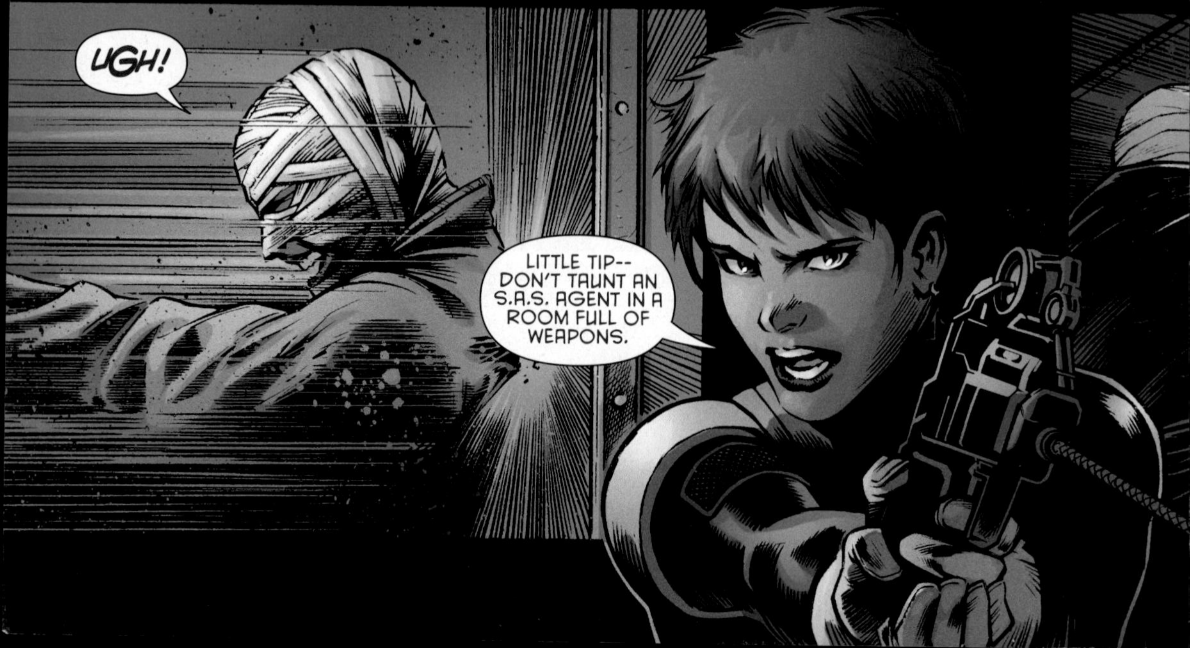
UGH!
LITTLE TIP-- DON'T TAUNT AN S.A.S. AGENT IN A ROOM FULL OF WEAPONS.

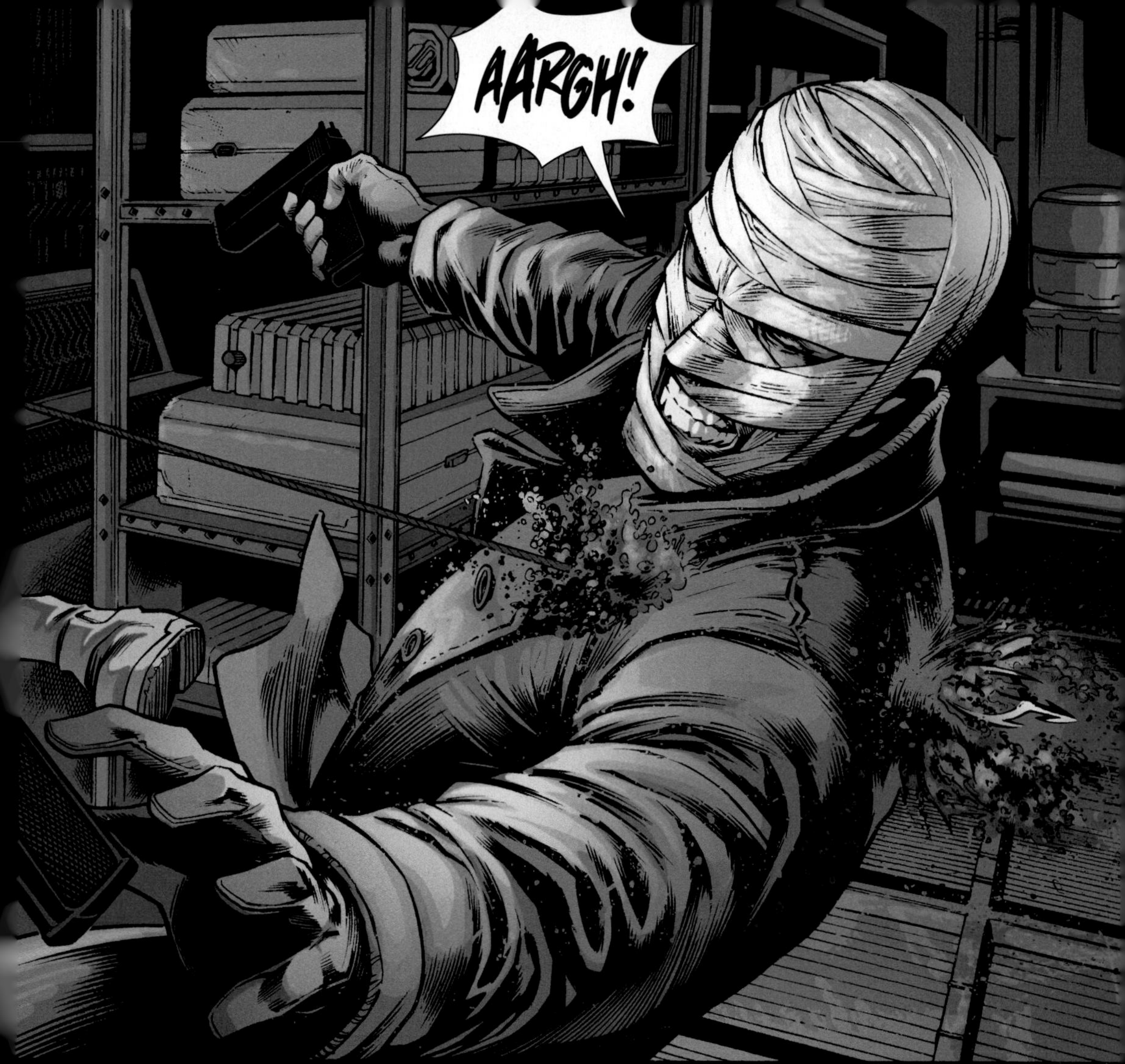
AARGH!

ALVARO MARTINEZ PENCILS RAUL FERNANDEZ INKS
BRAD ANDERSON COLORS STEVE WANDS LETTERS
RAFAEL ALBUQUERQUE COVER

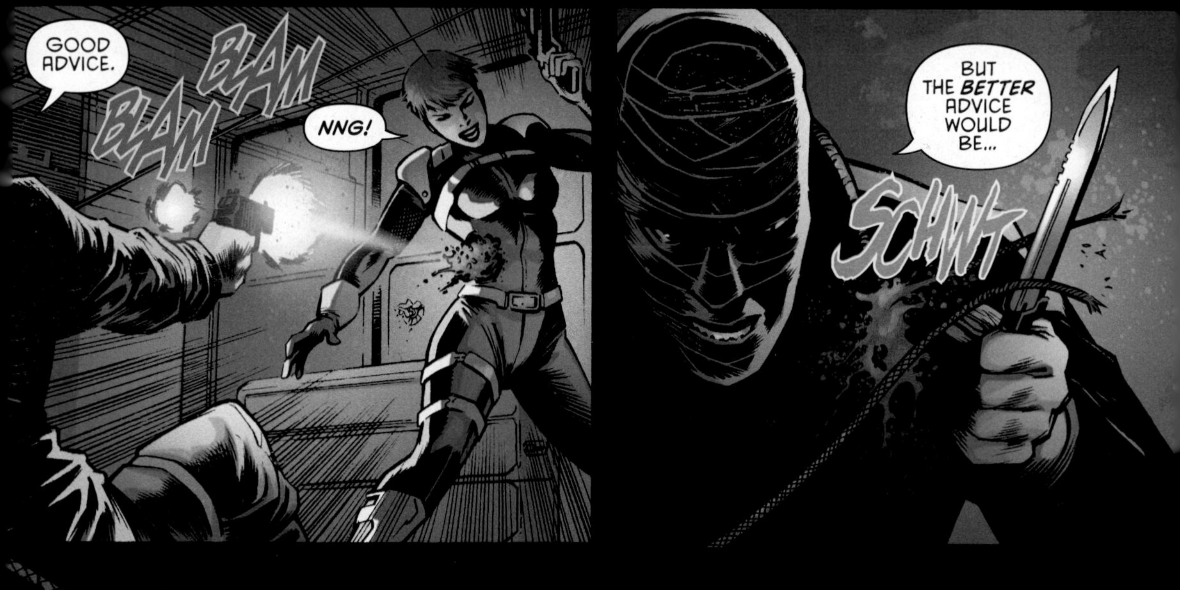
GOOD ADVICE.
BLAM
BLAM
NNG!
BUT THE *BETTER* ADVICE WOULD BE...
SCHWT

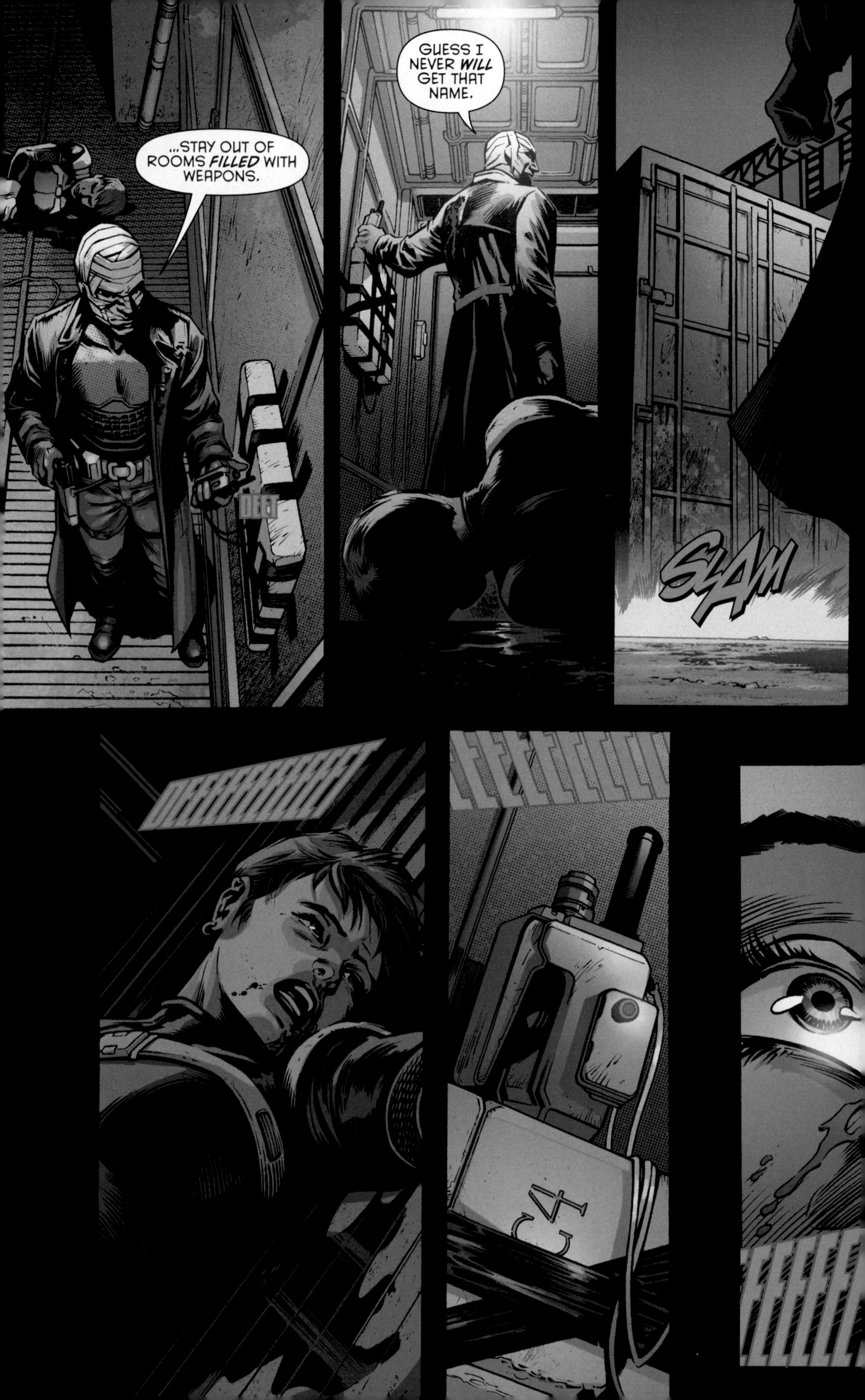
...STAY OUT OF ROOMS FILLED WITH WEAPONS.
DEET
GUESS I NEVER WILL GET THAT NAME.
SLAM
DEEEEEEEEEET
EEEEEEEEE
EEEEEE
C4

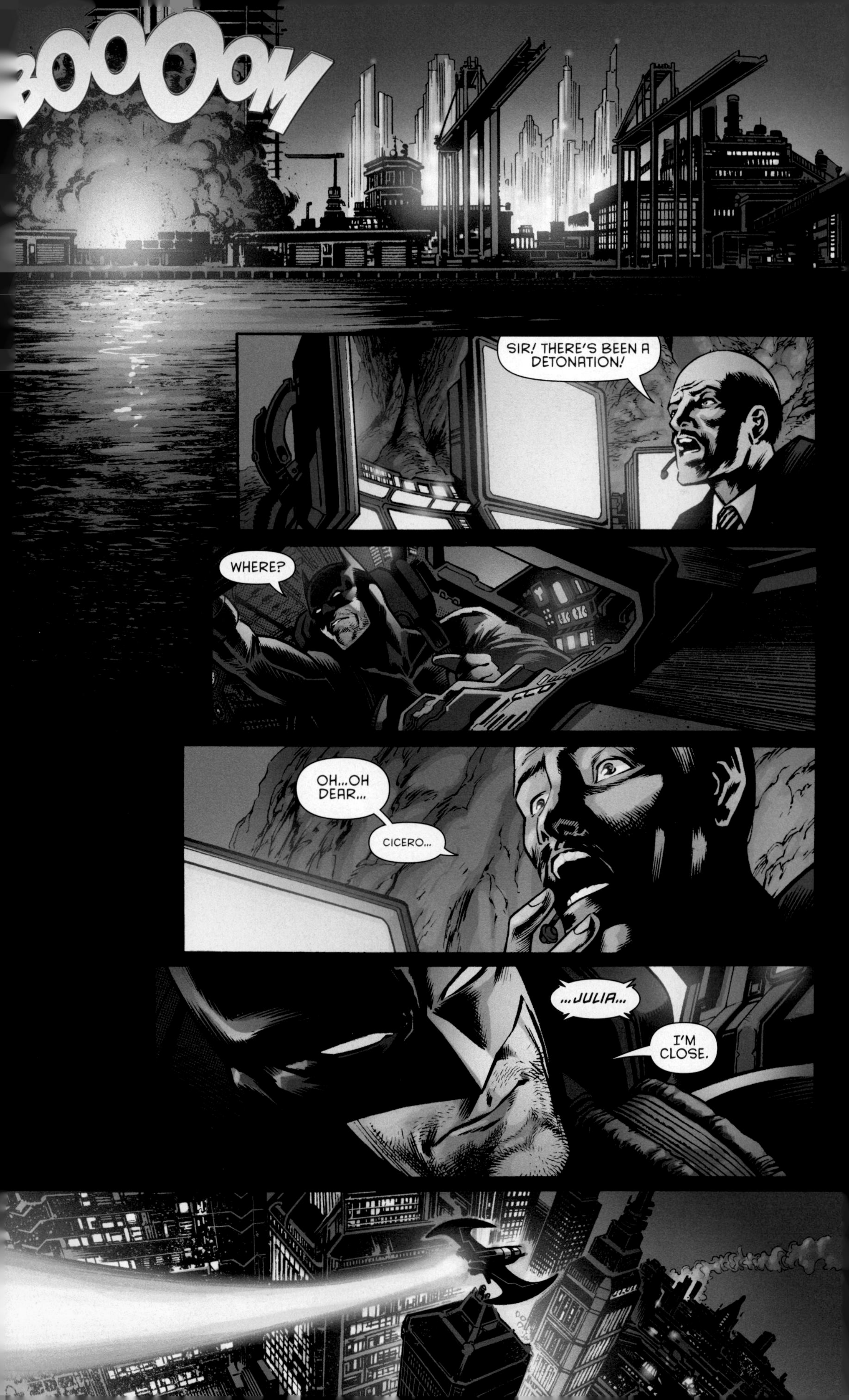
BOOOOM
SIR! THERE'S BEEN A DETONATION!
WHERE?
OH...OH DEAR...
CICERO...
...JULIA...
I'M CLOSE.

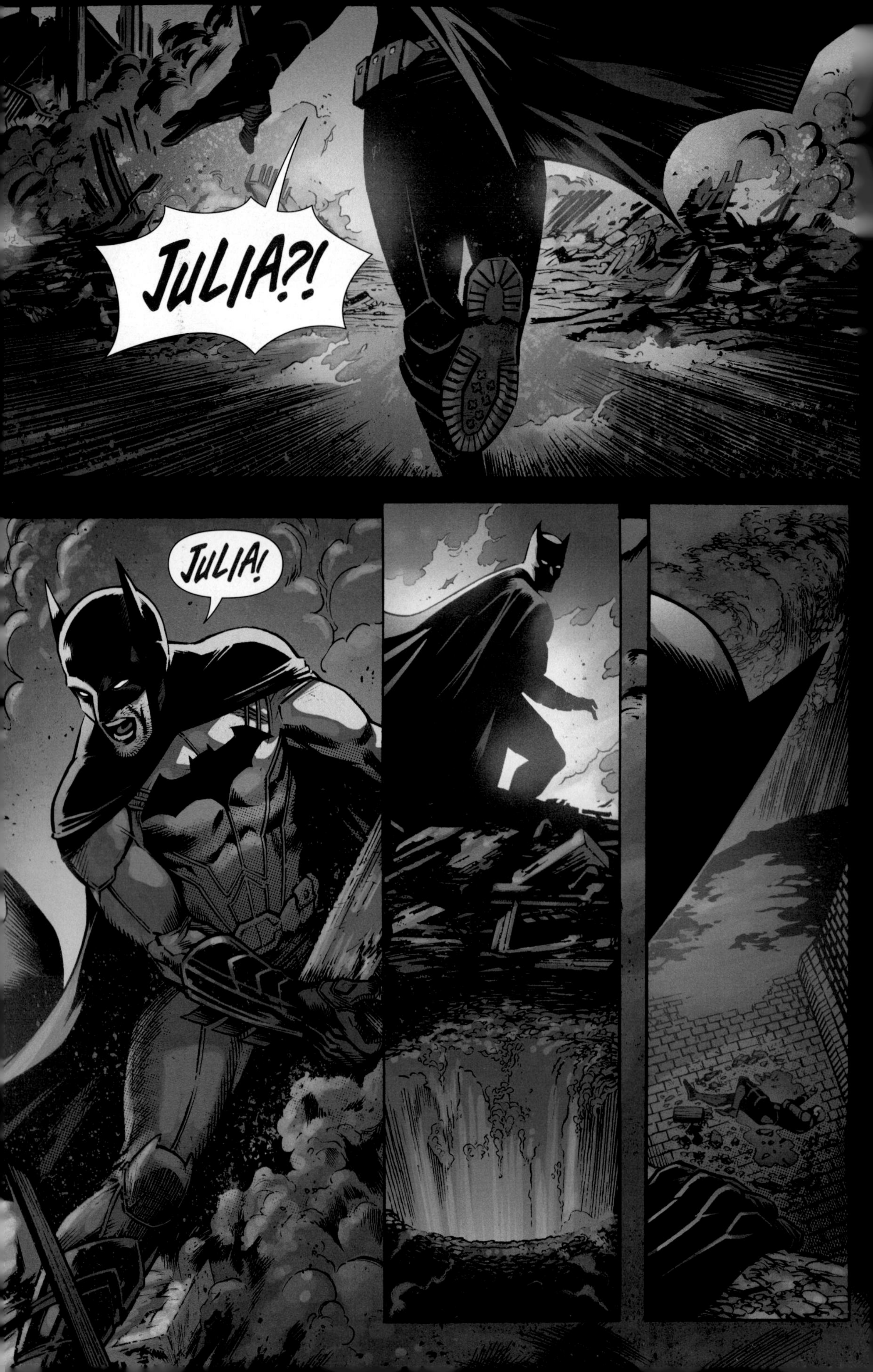
JULIA?!
JULIA!

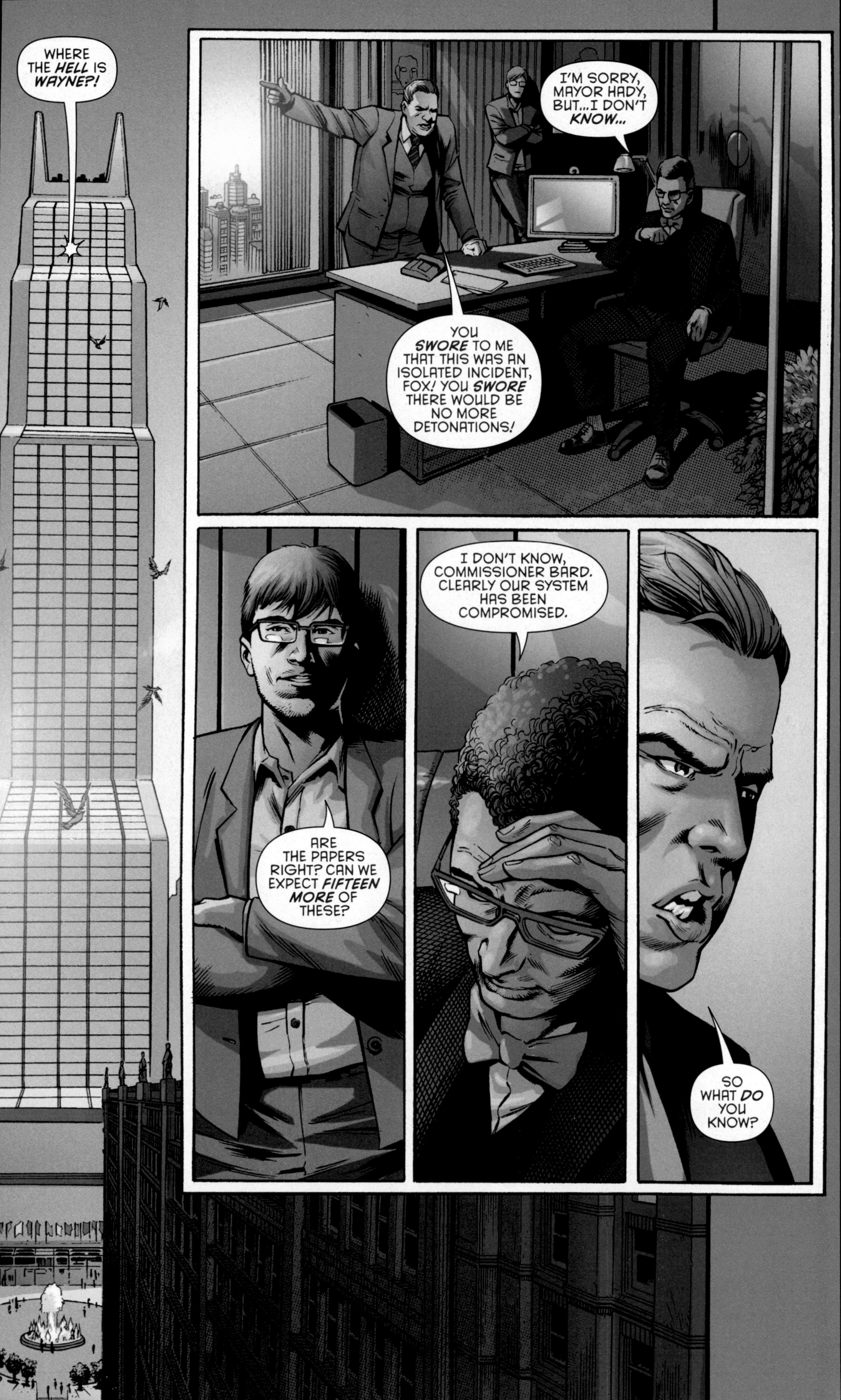

WHERE THE HELL IS WAYNE?!
I'M SORRY, MAYOR HADY, BUT...I DON'T KNOW...
YOU SWORE TO ME THAT THIS WAS AN ISOLATED INCIDENT, FOX! YOU SWORE THERE WOULD BE NO MORE DETONATIONS!
ARE THE PAPERS RIGHT? CAN WE EXPECT FIFTEEN MORE OF THESE?
I DON'T KNOW, COMMISSIONER BARD. CLEARLY OUR SYSTEM HAS BEEN COMPROMISED.
SO WHAT DO YOU KNOW?

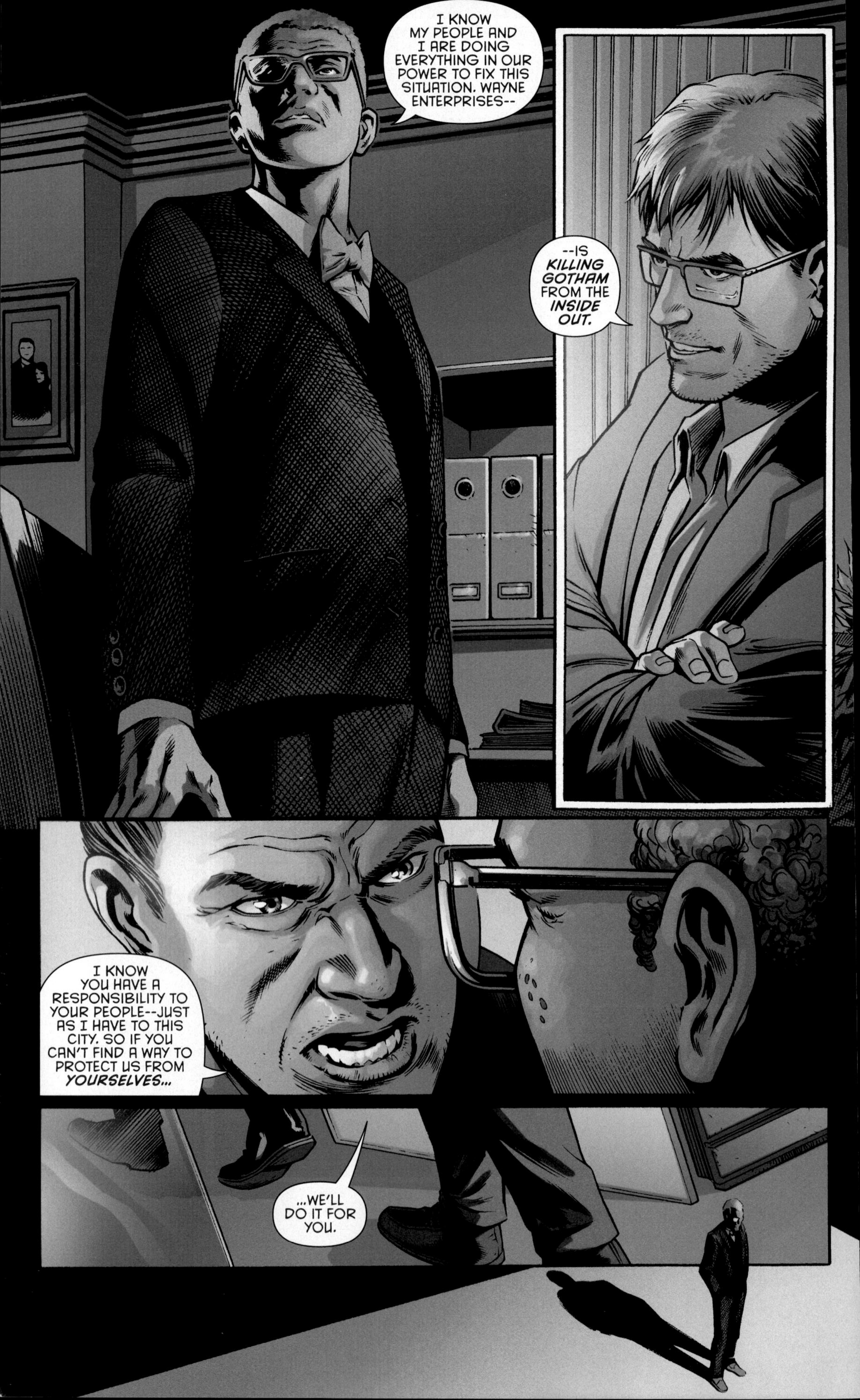
I KNOW MY PEOPLE AND I ARE DOING EVERYTHING IN OUR POWER TO FIX THIS SITUATION. WAYNE ENTERPRISES--
--IS *KILLING GOTHAM* FROM THE *INSIDE OUT.*
I KNOW YOU HAVE A RESPONSIBILITY TO YOUR PEOPLE--JUST AS I HAVE TO THIS CITY. SO IF YOU CAN'T FIND A WAY TO PROTECT US FROM *YOURSELVES...*
...WE'LL DO IT FOR YOU.

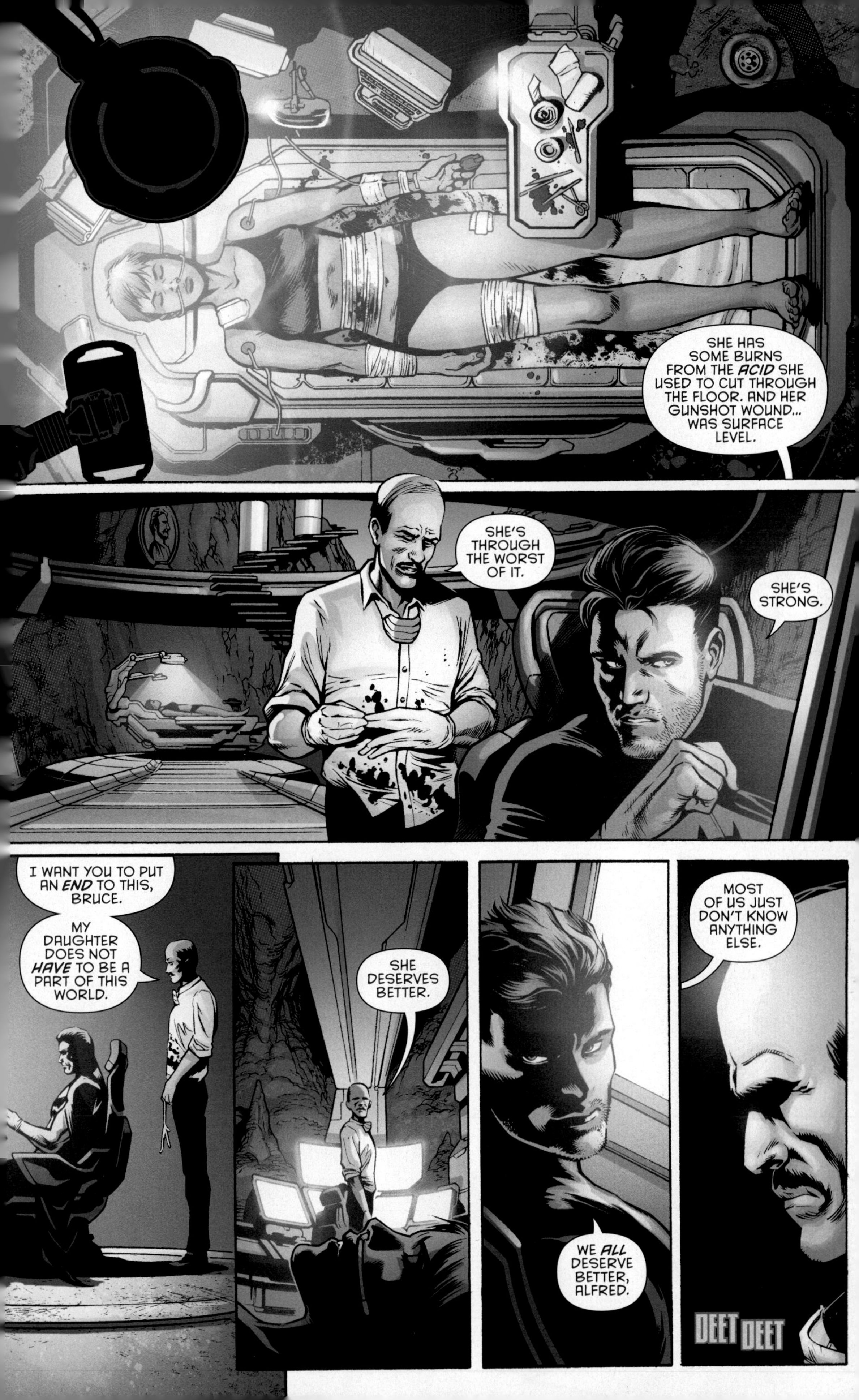
SHE HAS SOME BURNS FROM THE ACID SHE USED TO CUT THROUGH THE FLOOR. AND HER GUNSHOT WOUND... WAS SURFACE LEVEL.
SHE'S THROUGH THE WORST OF IT.
SHE'S STRONG.
I WANT YOU TO PUT AN END TO THIS, BRUCE.
MY DAUGHTER DOES NOT HAVE TO BE A PART OF THIS WORLD.
SHE DESERVES BETTER.
WE ALL DESERVE BETTER, ALFRED.
MOST OF US JUST DON'T KNOW ANYTHING ELSE.
DEET DEET

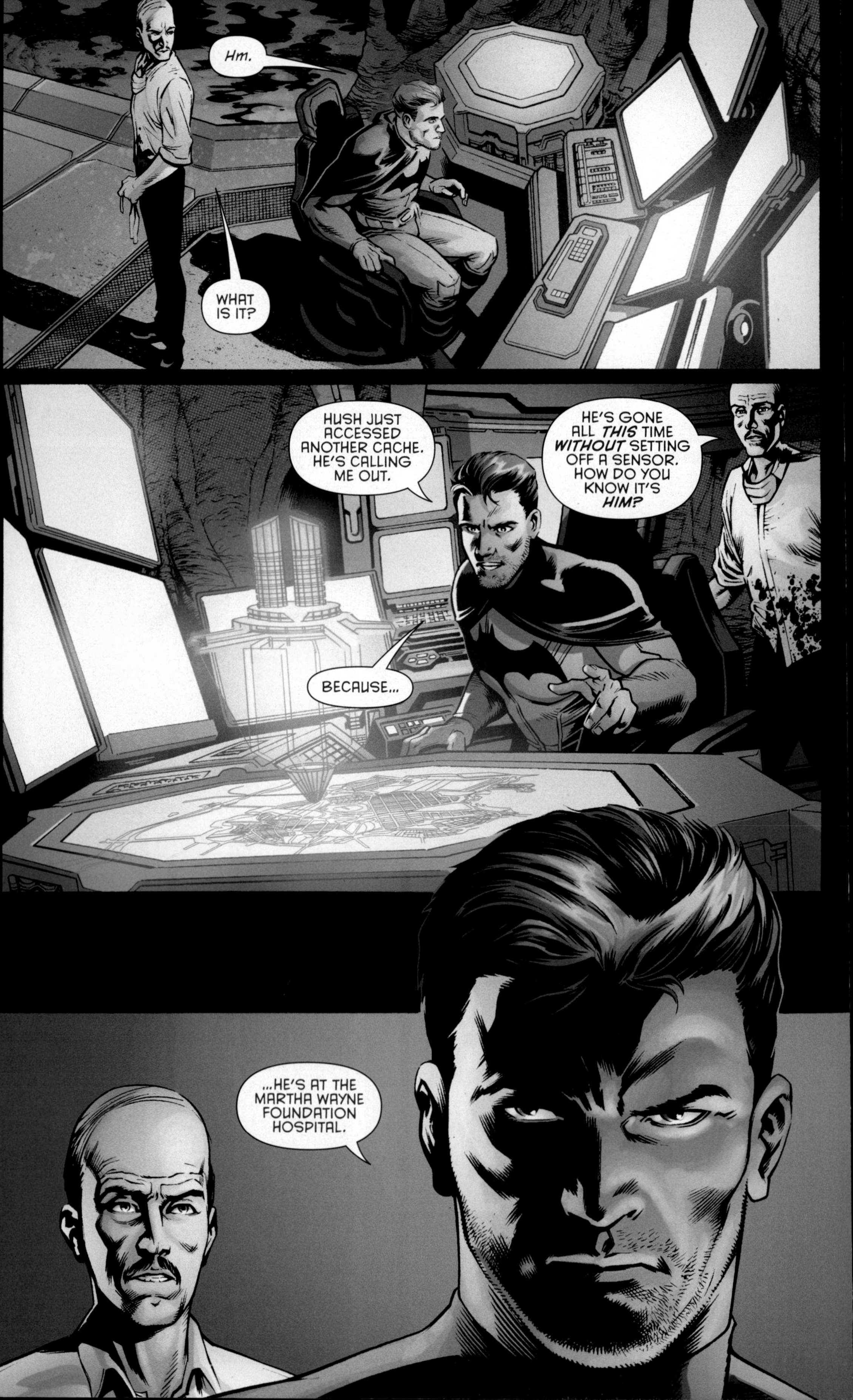
Hm.
WHAT IS IT?
HUSH JUST ACCESSED ANOTHER CACHE. HE'S CALLING ME OUT.
HE'S GONE ALL *THIS* TIME *WITHOUT* SETTING OFF A SENSOR. HOW DO YOU KNOW IT'S *HIM?*
BECAUSE...
...HE'S AT THE MARTHA WAYNE FOUNDATION HOSPITAL.

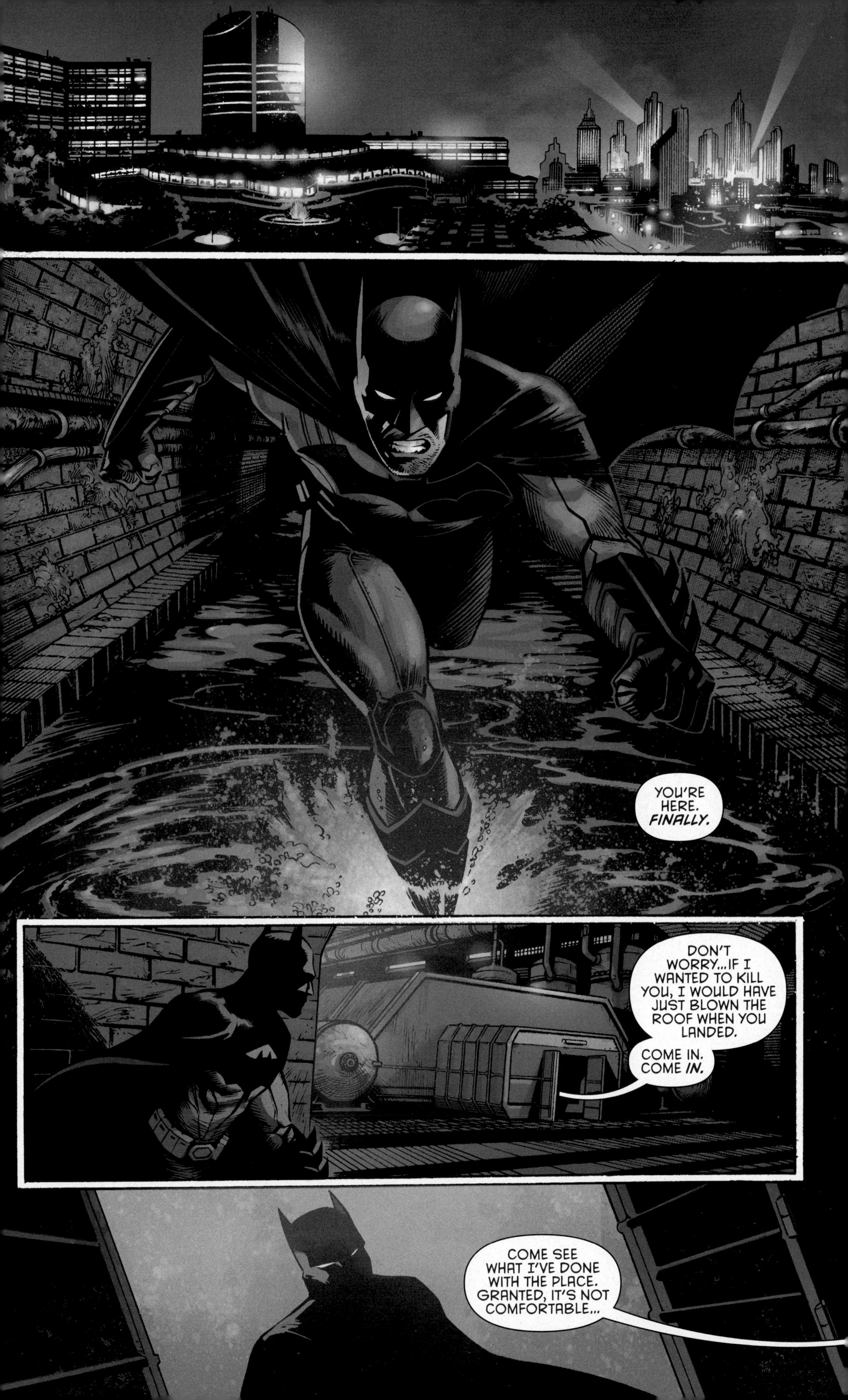
YOU'RE HERE. *FINALLY.*
DON'T WORRY...IF I WANTED TO KILL YOU, I WOULD HAVE JUST BLOWN THE ROOF WHEN YOU LANDED.
COME IN. COME *IN.*
COME SEE WHAT I'VE DONE WITH THE PLACE. GRANTED, IT'S NOT COMFORTABLE...

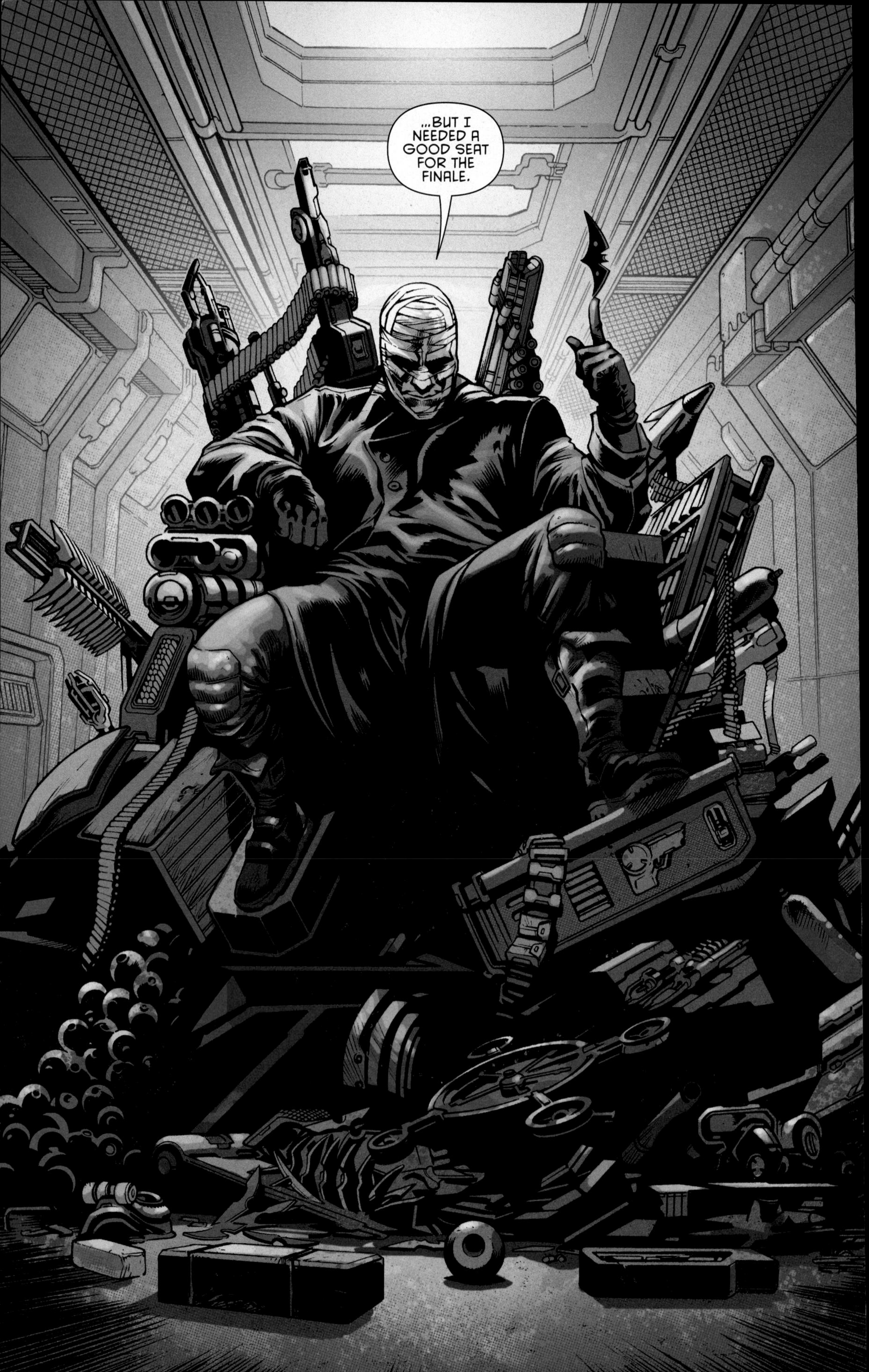
...BUT I NEEDED A GOOD SEAT FOR THE FINALE.

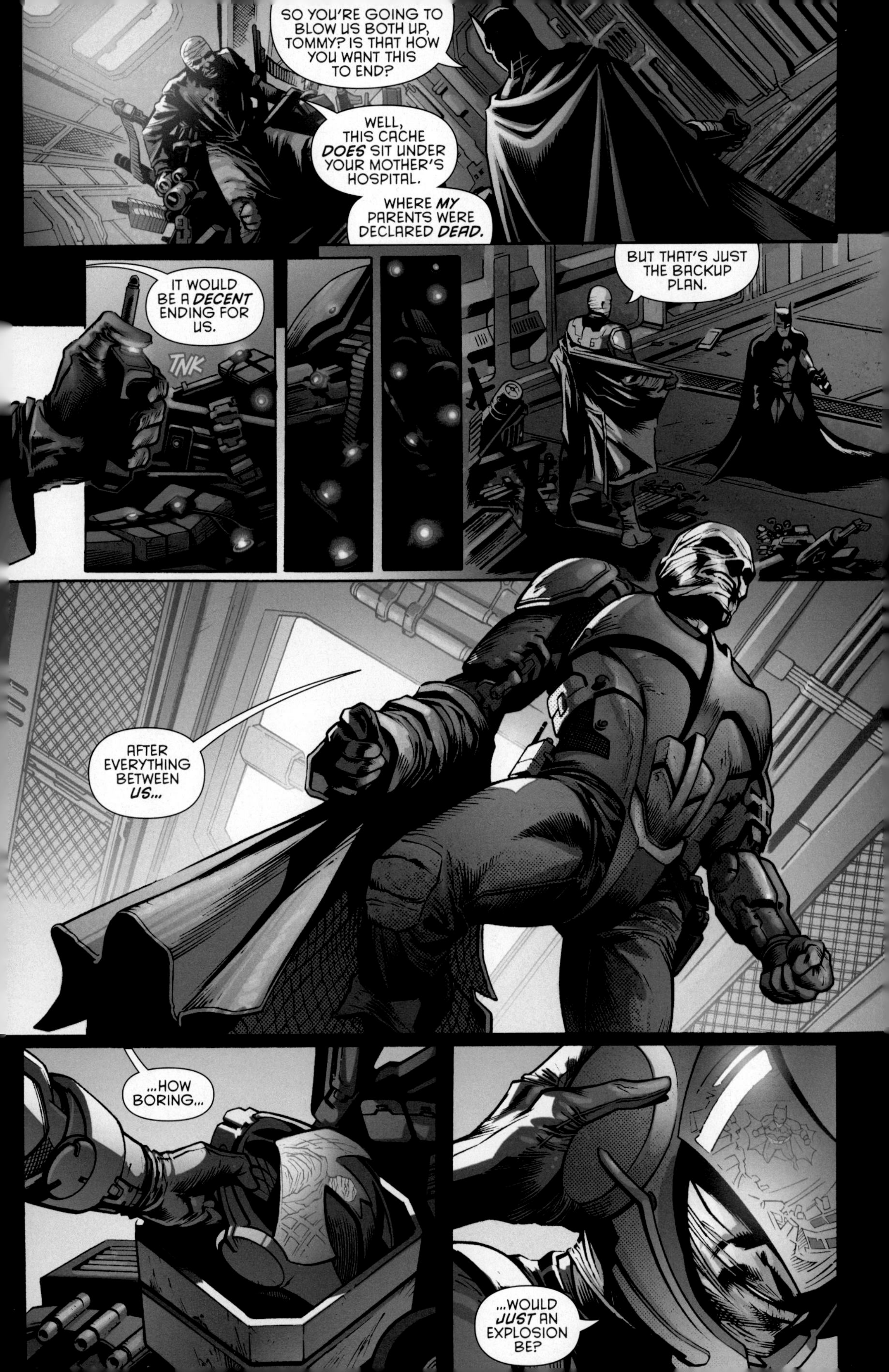
SO YOU'RE GOING TO BLOW US BOTH UP, TOMMY? IS THAT HOW YOU WANT THIS TO END?
WELL, THIS CACHE DOES SIT UNDER YOUR MOTHER'S HOSPITAL.
WHERE MY PARENTS WERE DECLARED DEAD.
IT WOULD BE A DECENT ENDING FOR US.
TNK
BUT THAT'S JUST THE BACKUP PLAN.
AFTER EVERYTHING BETWEEN US...
...HOW BORING...
...WOULD JUST AN EXPLOSION BE?

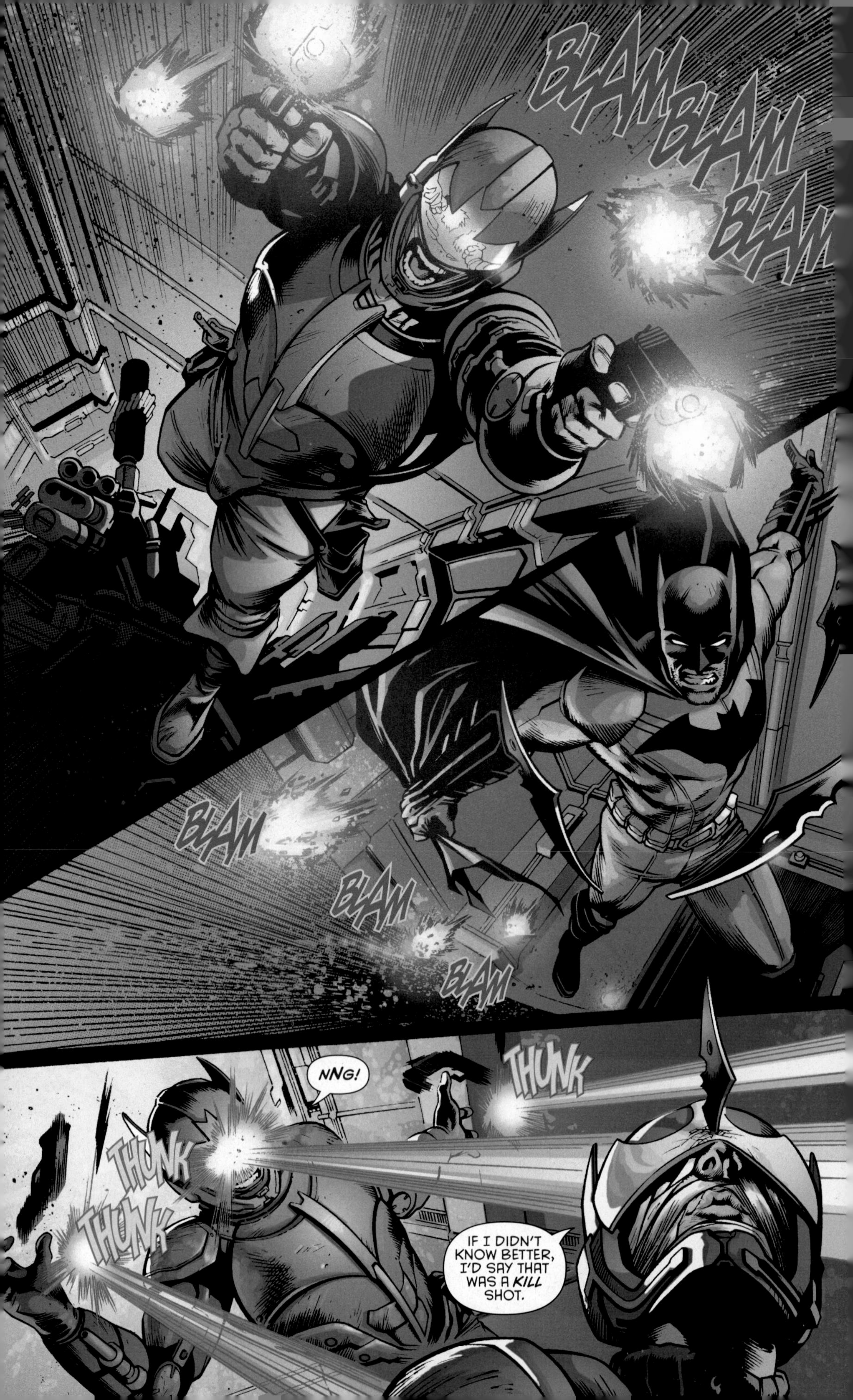
BLAM BLAM BLAM
BLAM
BLAM
BLAM
THUNK
NNG!
THUNK
THUNK
IF I DIDN'T KNOW BETTER, I'D SAY THAT WAS A *KILL* SHOT.

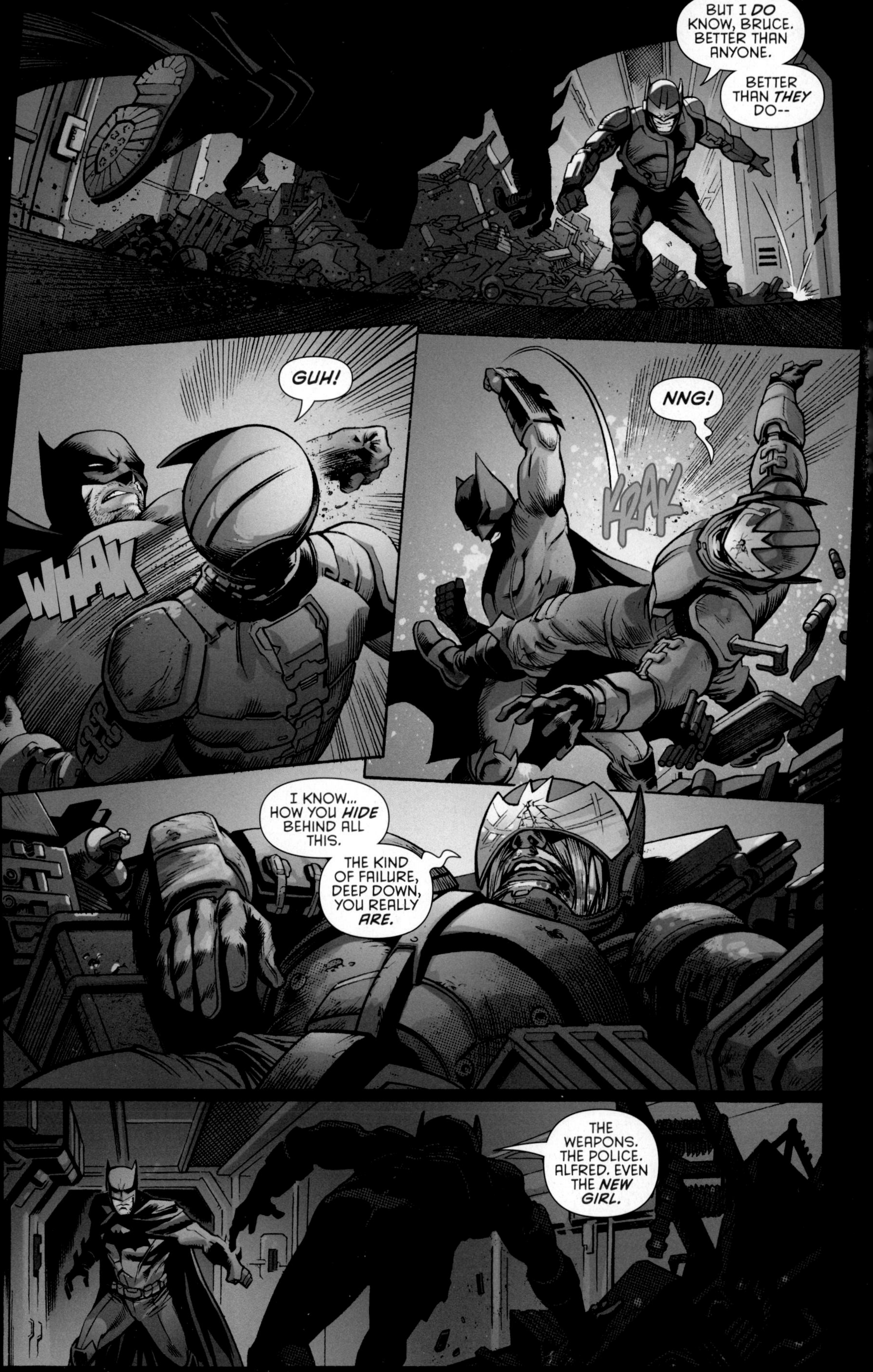

BUT I DO KNOW, BRUCE. BETTER THAN ANYONE.
BETTER THAN THEY DO--
GUH!
WHAK
NNG!
KRAK
I KNOW... HOW YOU HIDE BEHIND ALL THIS.
THE KIND OF FAILURE, DEEP DOWN, YOU REALLY ARE.
THE WEAPONS. THE POLICE. ALFRED. EVEN THE NEW GIRL.

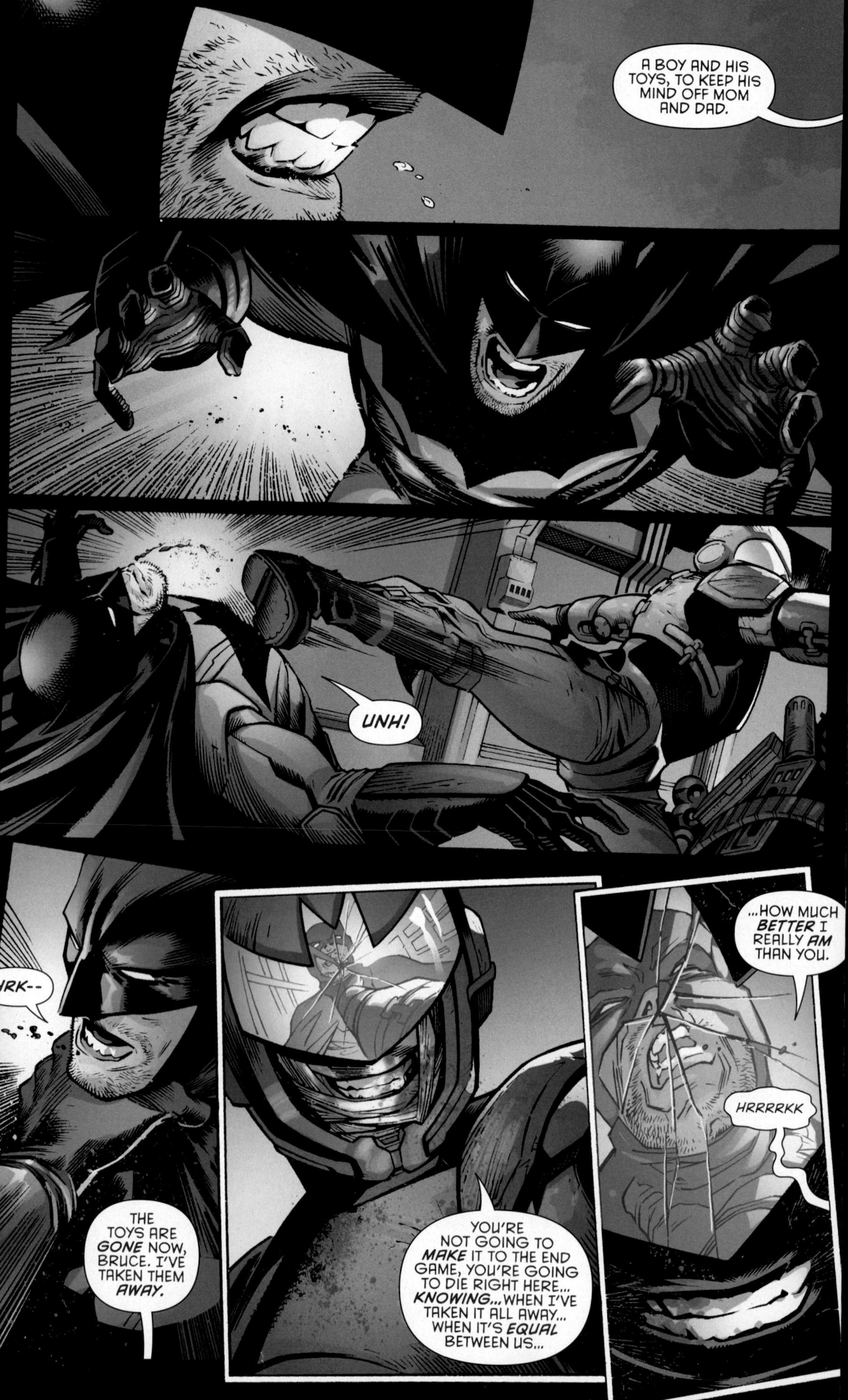
A BOY AND HIS TOYS, TO KEEP HIS MIND OFF MOM AND DAD.
UNH!
HRK--
THE TOYS ARE *GONE* NOW, BRUCE. I'VE TAKEN THEM *AWAY.*
YOU'RE NOT GOING TO *MAKE* IT TO THE END GAME, YOU'RE GOING TO DIE RIGHT HERE... *KNOWING...* WHEN I'VE TAKEN IT ALL AWAY... WHEN IT'S *EQUAL* BETWEEN US...
...HOW MUCH *BETTER* I REALLY *AM* THAN YOU.
HRRRRKK

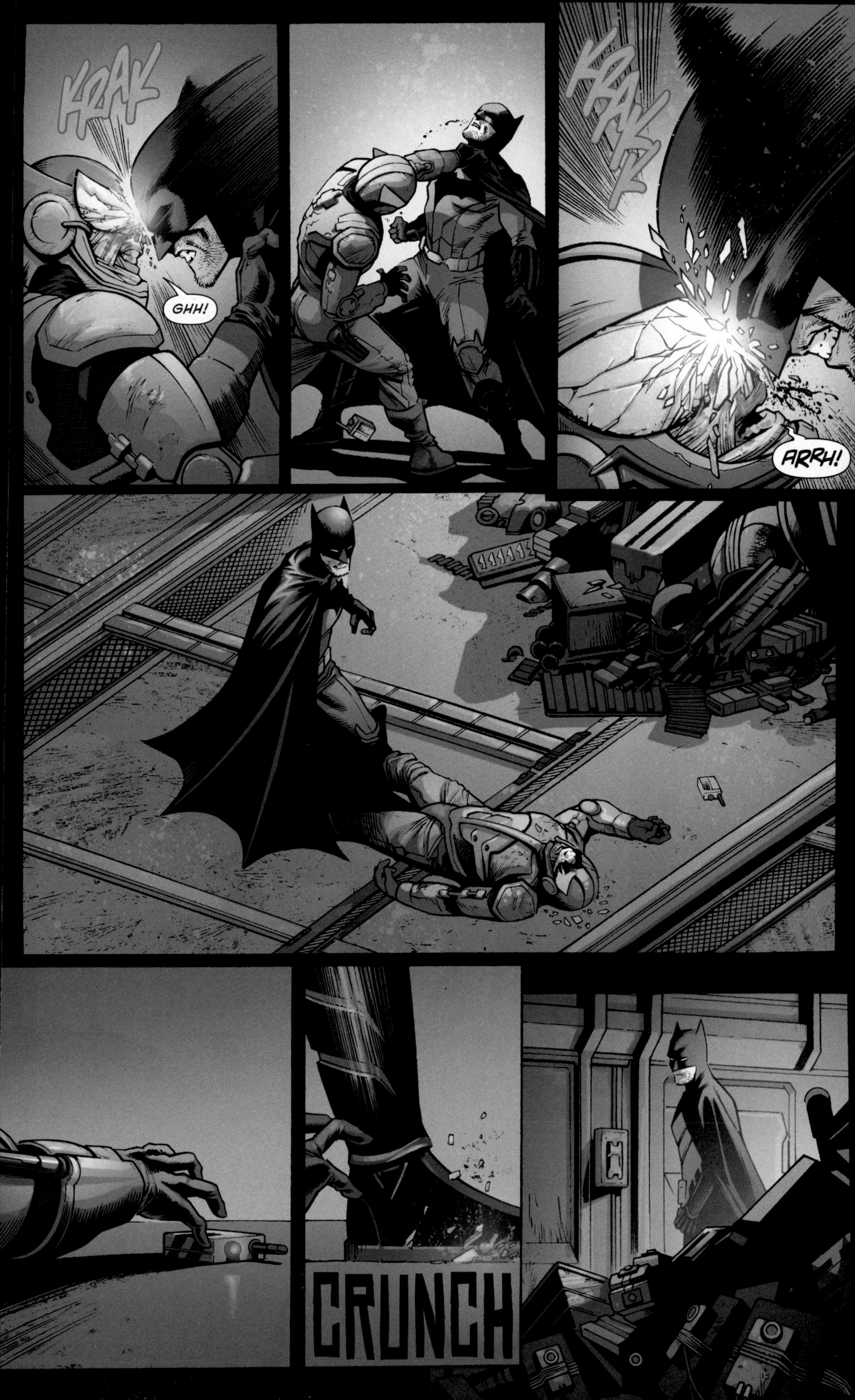
KRAK
GHH!
KRAK
ARRH!
CRUNCH

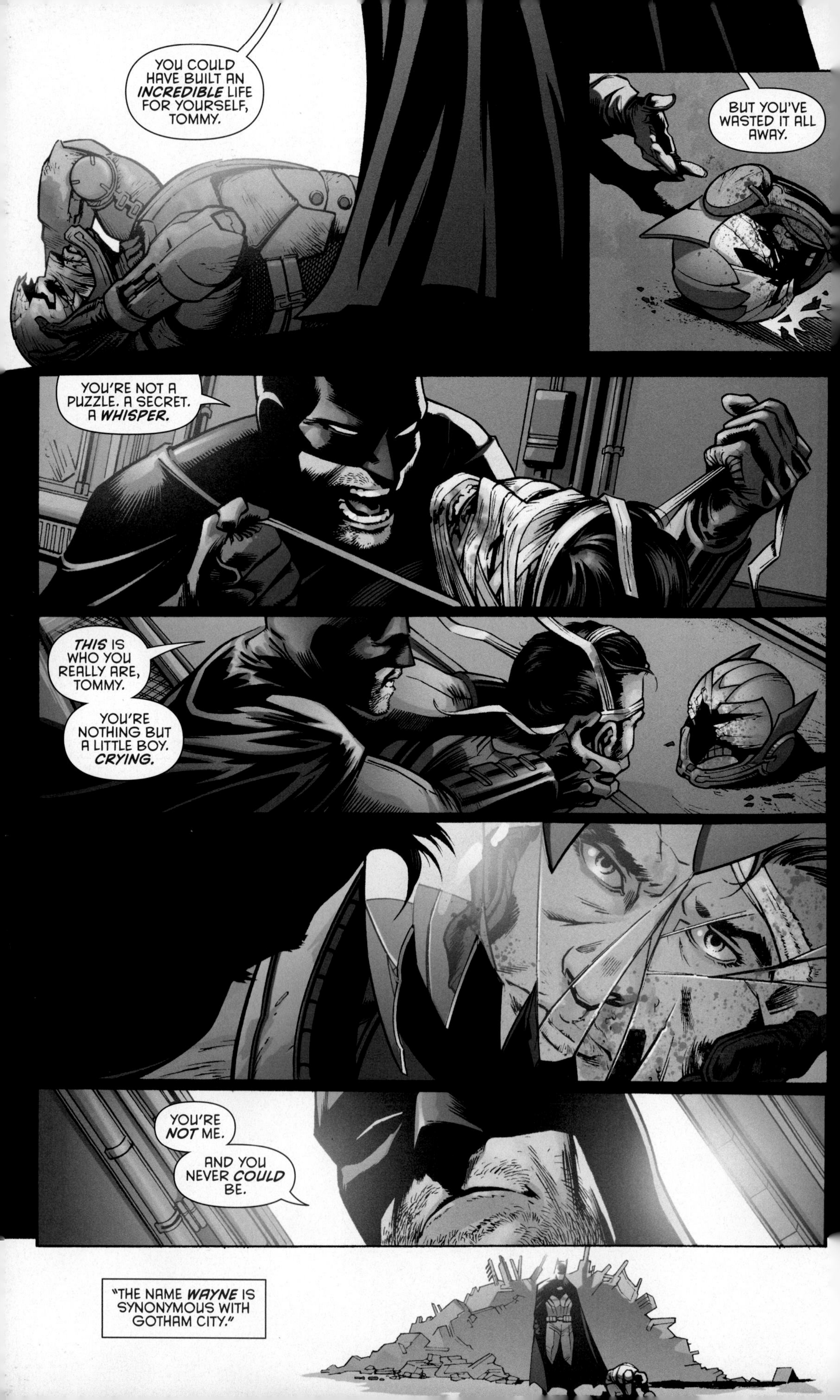
YOU COULD HAVE BUILT AN INCREDIBLE LIFE FOR YOURSELF, TOMMY.
BUT YOU'VE WASTED IT ALL AWAY.
YOU'RE NOT A PUZZLE. A SECRET. A WHISPER.
THIS IS WHO YOU REALLY ARE, TOMMY.
YOU'RE NOTHING BUT A LITTLE BOY. CRYING.
YOU'RE NOT ME.
AND YOU NEVER COULD BE.
"THE NAME WAYNE IS SYNONYMOUS WITH GOTHAM CITY."

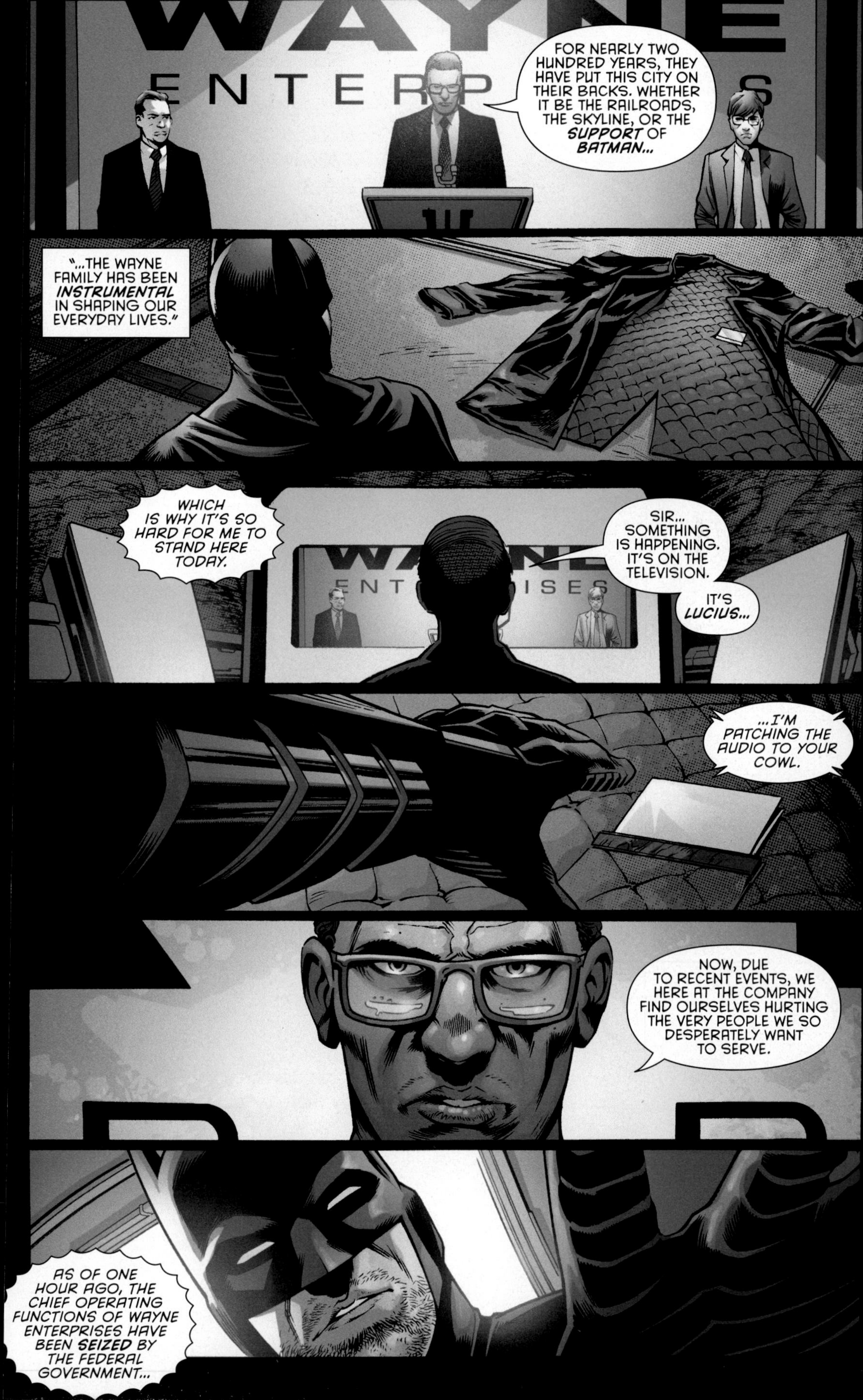
WAYNE
ENTERPRISES
FOR NEARLY TWO HUNDRED YEARS, THEY HAVE PUT THIS CITY ON THEIR BACKS. WHETHER IT BE THE RAILROADS, THE SKYLINE, OR THE ***SUPPORT*** OF ***BATMAN...***
"...THE WAYNE FAMILY HAS BEEN ***INSTRUMENTAL*** IN SHAPING OUR EVERYDAY LIVES."
*WHICH IS WHY IT'S SO HARD FOR ME TO STAND HERE TODAY.*
SIR... SOMETHING IS HAPPENING. IT'S ON THE TELEVISION.
*IT'S* ***LUCIUS...***
*...I'M PATCHING THE AUDIO TO YOUR COWL.*
NOW, DUE TO RECENT EVENTS, WE HERE AT THE COMPANY FIND OURSELVES HURTING THE VERY PEOPLE WE SO DESPERATELY WANT TO SERVE.
AS OF ONE HOUR AGO, THE CHIEF OPERATING FUNCTIONS OF WAYNE ENTERPRISES HAVE BEEN ***SEIZED*** BY THE FEDERAL GOVERNMENT...

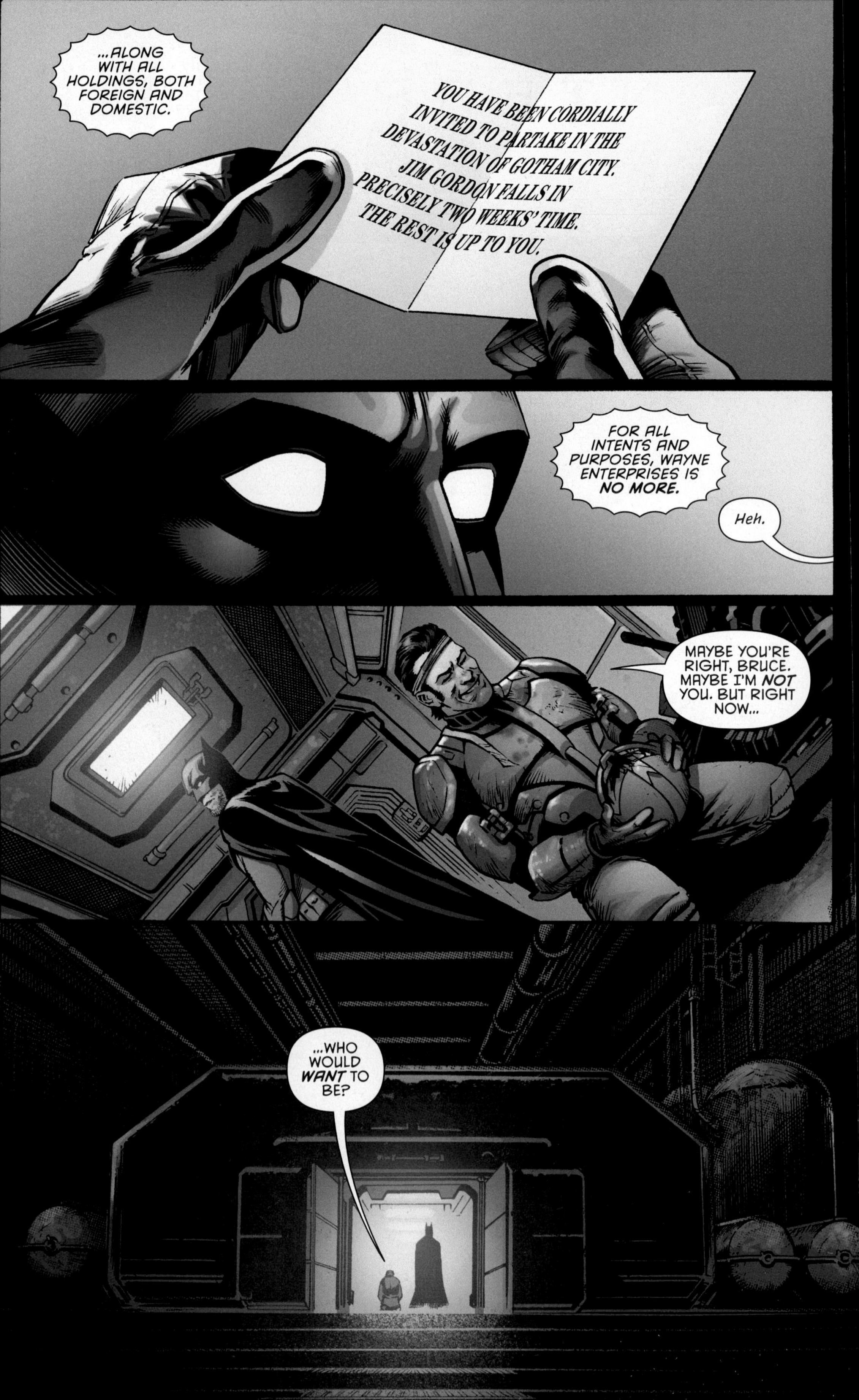
...ALONG WITH ALL HOLDINGS, BOTH FOREIGN AND DOMESTIC.
YOU HAVE BEEN CORDIALLY INVITED TO PARTAKE IN THE DEVASTATION OF GOTHAM CITY. JIM GORDON FALLS IN PRECISELY TWO WEEKS' TIME. THE REST IS UP TO YOU.
FOR ALL INTENTS AND PURPOSES, WAYNE ENTERPRISES IS NO MORE.
Heh.
MAYBE YOU'RE RIGHT, BRUCE. MAYBE I'M NOT YOU. BUT RIGHT NOW...
...WHO WOULD WANT TO BE?

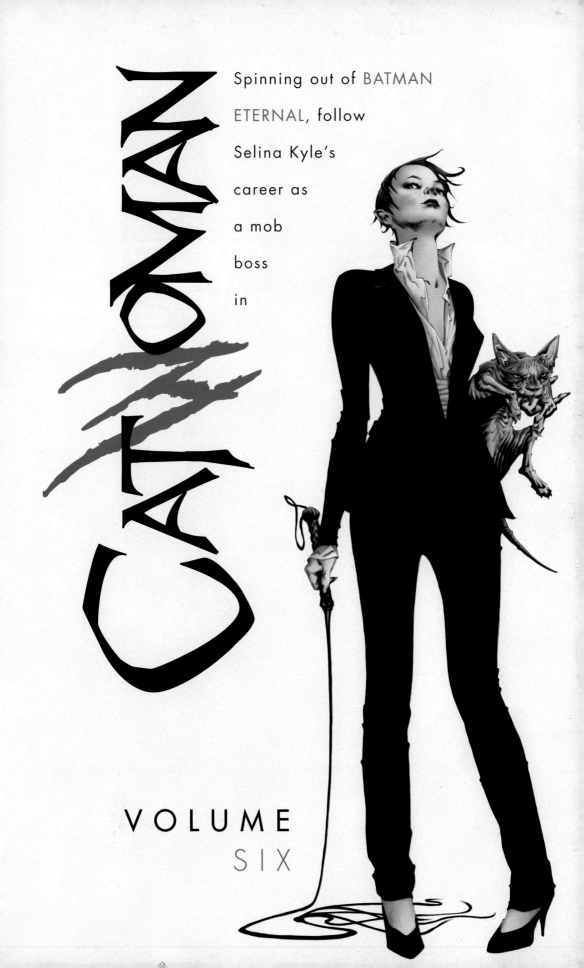

Spinning out of BATMAN
ETERNAL, follow
Selina Kyle's
career as
a mob
boss
in

# CATWOMAN

# VOLUME
## SIX

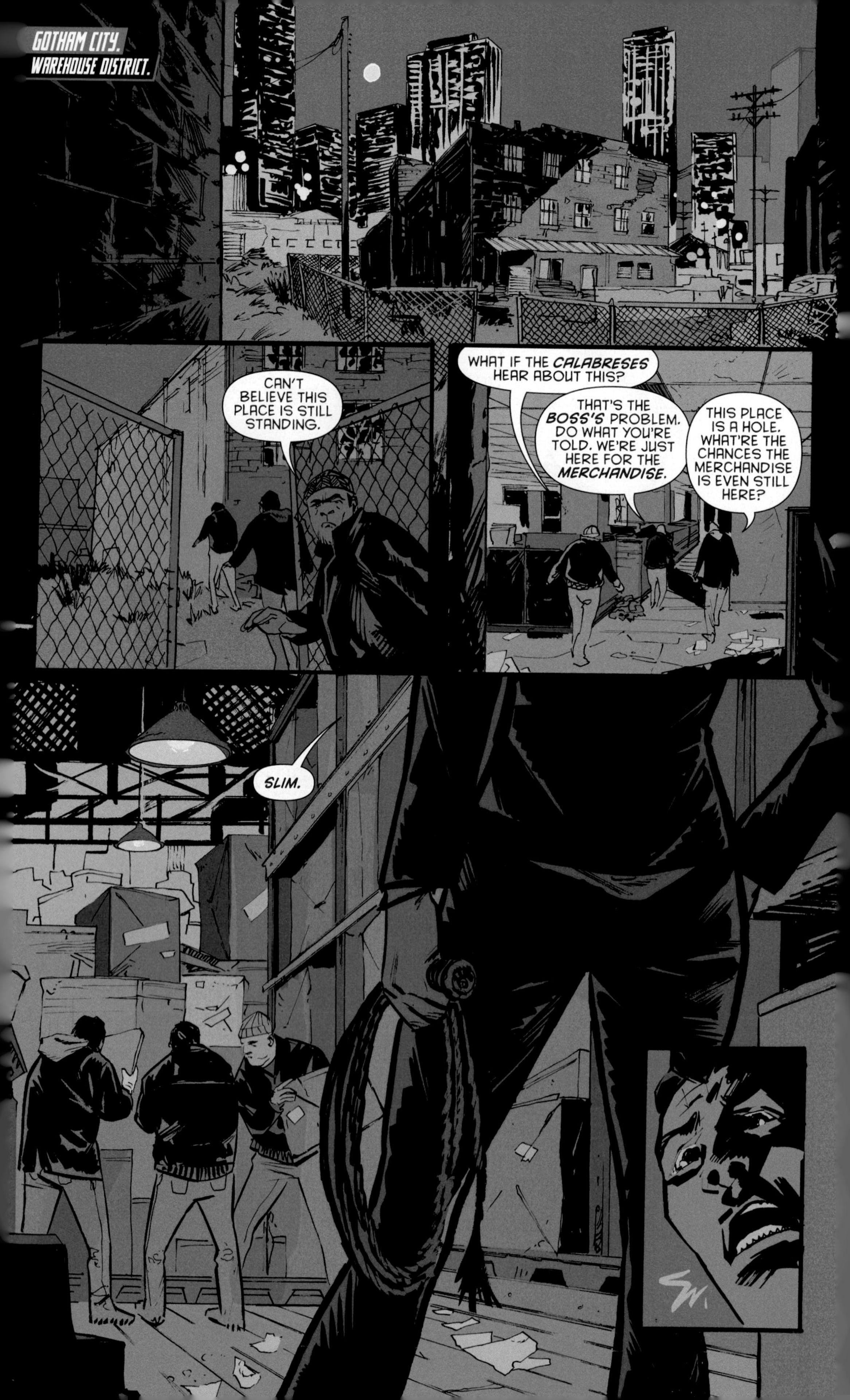
GOTHAM CITY.
WAREHOUSE DISTRICT.
CAN'T BELIEVE THIS PLACE IS STILL STANDING.
WHAT IF THE CALABRESES HEAR ABOUT THIS?
THAT'S THE BOSS'S PROBLEM. DO WHAT YOU'RE TOLD. WE'RE JUST HERE FOR THE MERCHANDISE.
THIS PLACE IS A HOLE. WHAT'RE THE CHANCES THE MERCHANDISE IS EVEN STILL HERE?
SLIM.

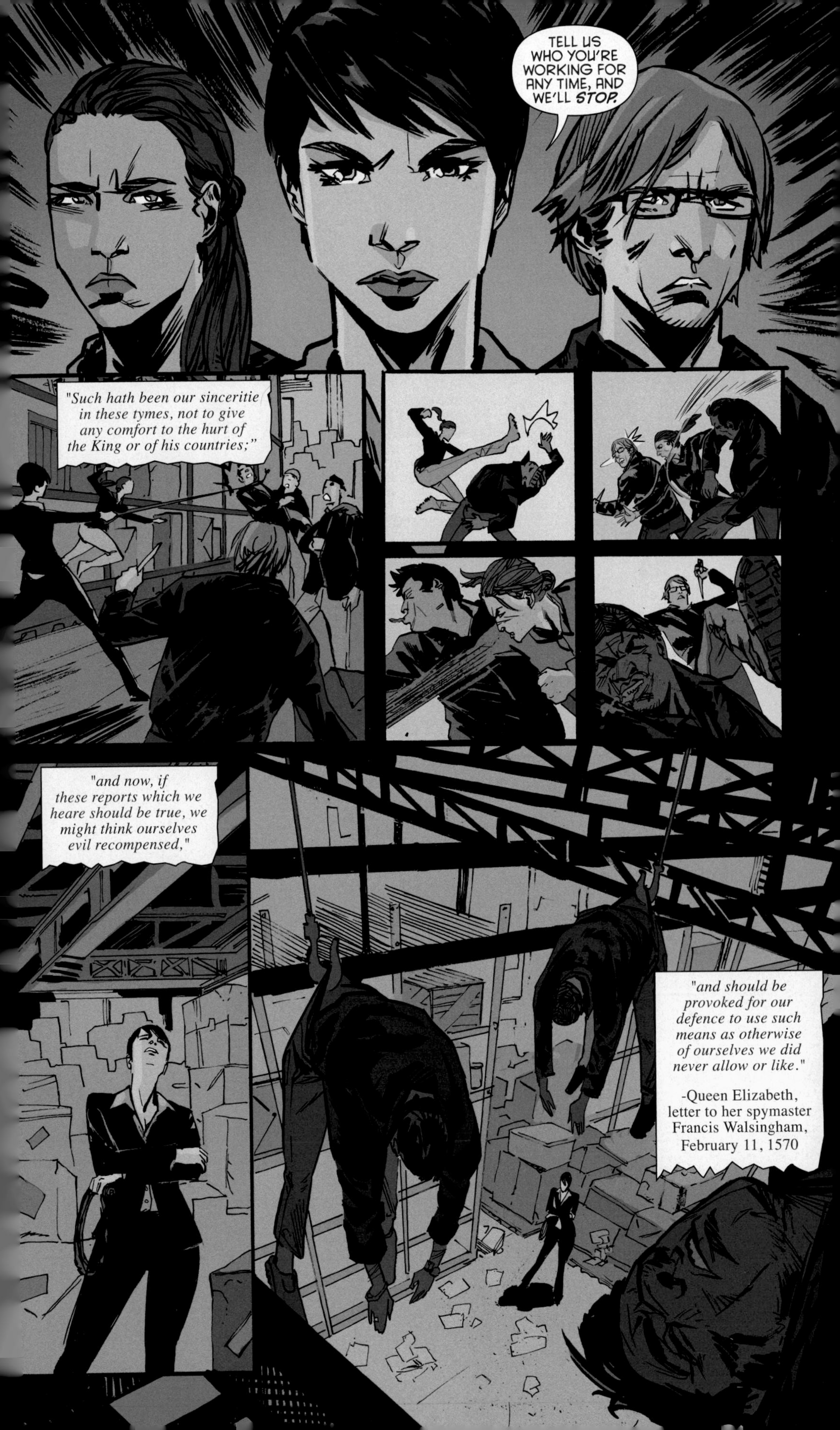
TELL US WHO YOU'RE WORKING FOR ANY TIME, AND WE'LL STOP.
"Such hath been our sinceritie in these tymes, not to give any comfort to the hurt of the King or of his countries;"
"and now, if these reports which we heare should be true, we might think ourselves evil recompensed,"
"and should be provoked for our defence to use such means as otherwise of ourselves we did never allow or like."
-Queen Elizabeth, letter to her spymaster Francis Walsingham, February 11, 1570

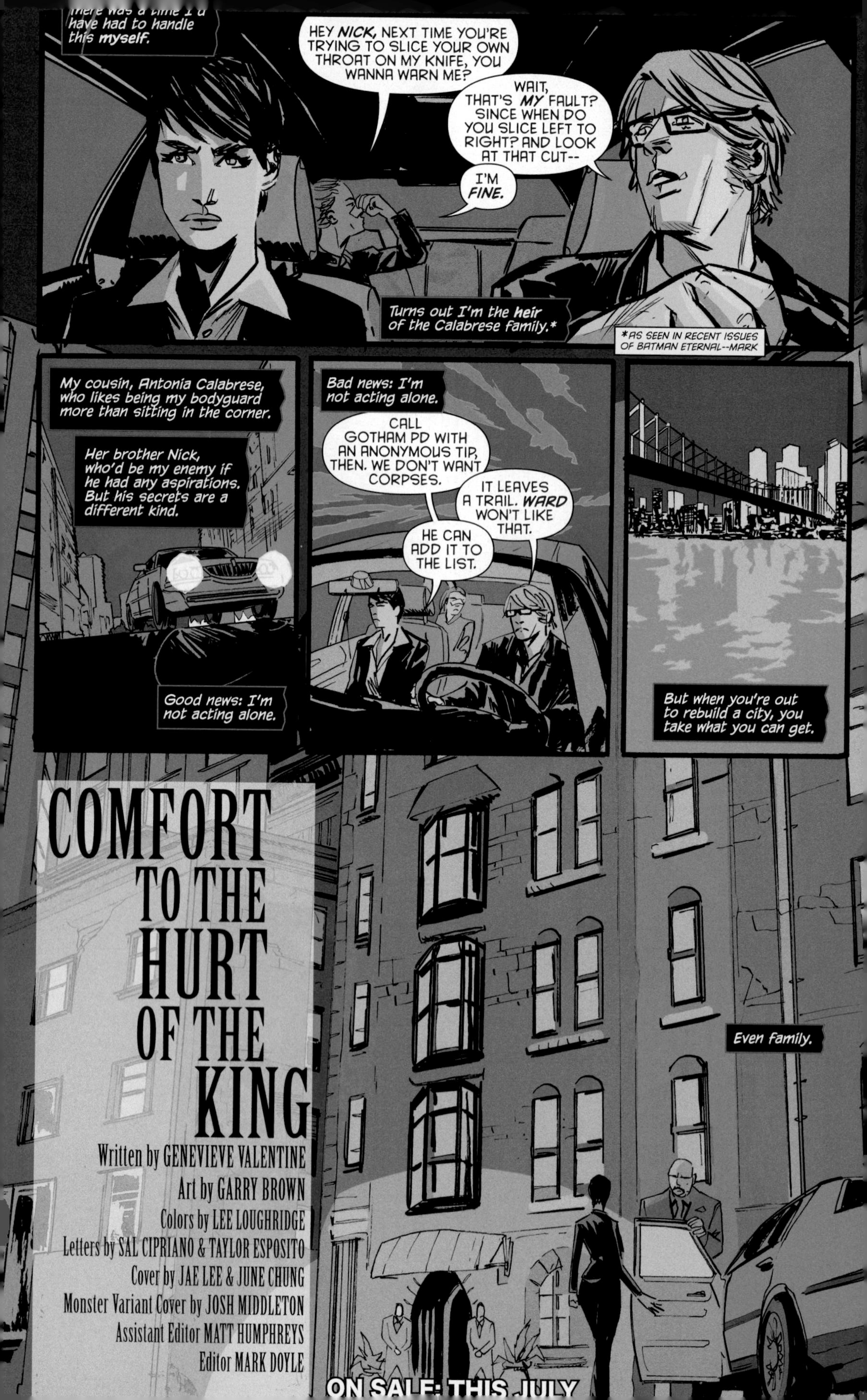

have had to handle this myself.
HEY NICK, NEXT TIME YOU'RE TRYING TO SLICE YOUR OWN THROAT ON MY KNIFE, YOU WANNA WARN ME?
WAIT, THAT'S MY FAULT? SINCE WHEN DO YOU SLICE LEFT TO RIGHT? AND LOOK AT THAT CUT--
I'M FINE.
Turns out I'm the heir of the Calabrese family.*
*AS SEEN IN RECENT ISSUES OF BATMAN ETERNAL--MARK
My cousin, Antonia Calabrese, who likes being my bodyguard more than sitting in the corner.
Her brother Nick, who'd be my enemy if he had any aspirations. But his secrets are a different kind.
Good news: I'm not acting alone.
Bad news: I'm not acting alone.
CALL GOTHAM PD WITH AN ANONYMOUS TIP, THEN. WE DON'T WANT CORPSES.
IT LEAVES A TRAIL. WARD WON'T LIKE THAT.
HE CAN ADD IT TO THE LIST.
But when you're out to rebuild a city, you take what you can get.
Even family.
COMFORT TO THE HURT OF THE KING
Written by GENEVIEVE VALENTINE
Art by GARRY BROWN
Colors by LEE LOUGHRIDGE
Letters by SAL CIPRIANO & TAYLOR ESPOSITO
Cover by JAE LEE & JUNE CHUNG
Monster Variant Cover by JOSH MIDDLETON
Assistant Editor MATT HUMPHREYS
Editor MARK DOYLE
ON SALE: THIS JULY

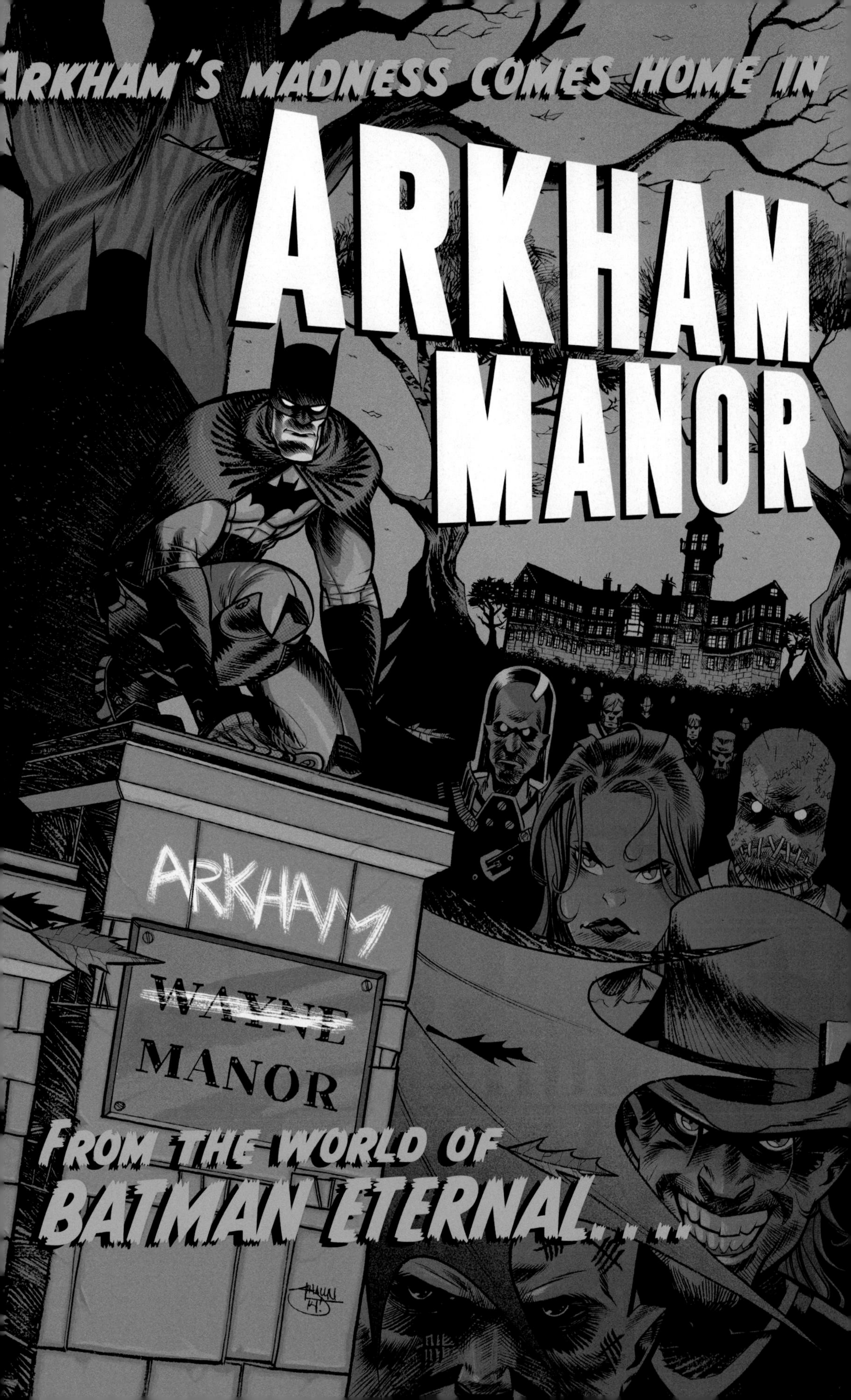
ARKHAM'S MADNESS COMES HOME IN
ARKHAM MANOR
ARKHAM
~~WAYNE~~
MANOR
FROM THE WORLD OF
BATMAN ETERNAL....

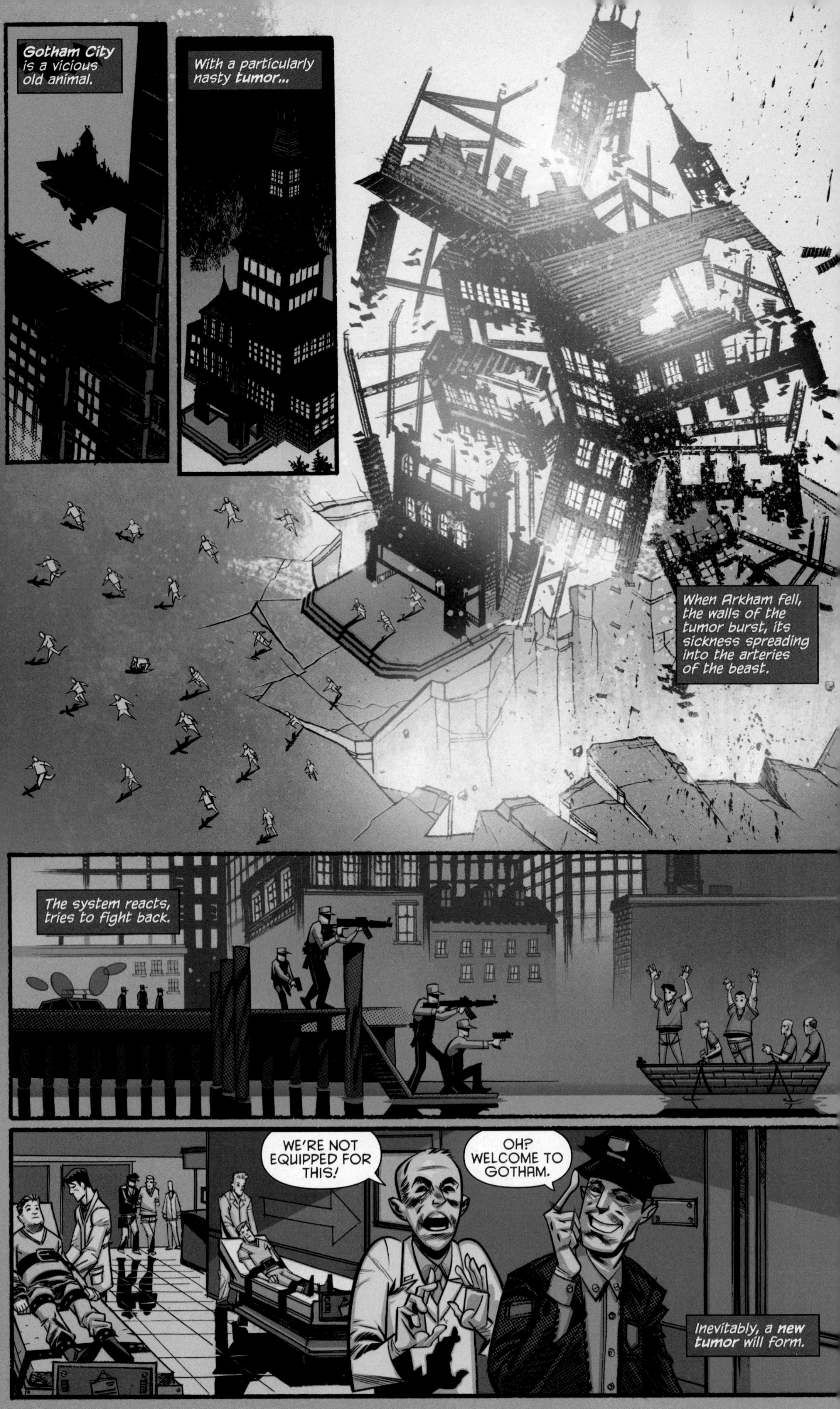
Gotham City is a vicious old animal.
With a particularly nasty tumor...
When Arkham fell, the walls of the tumor burst, its sickness spreading into the arteries of the beast.
The system reacts, tries to fight back.
WE'RE NOT EQUIPPED FOR THIS!
OH? WELCOME TO GOTHAM.
Inevitably, a new tumor will form.

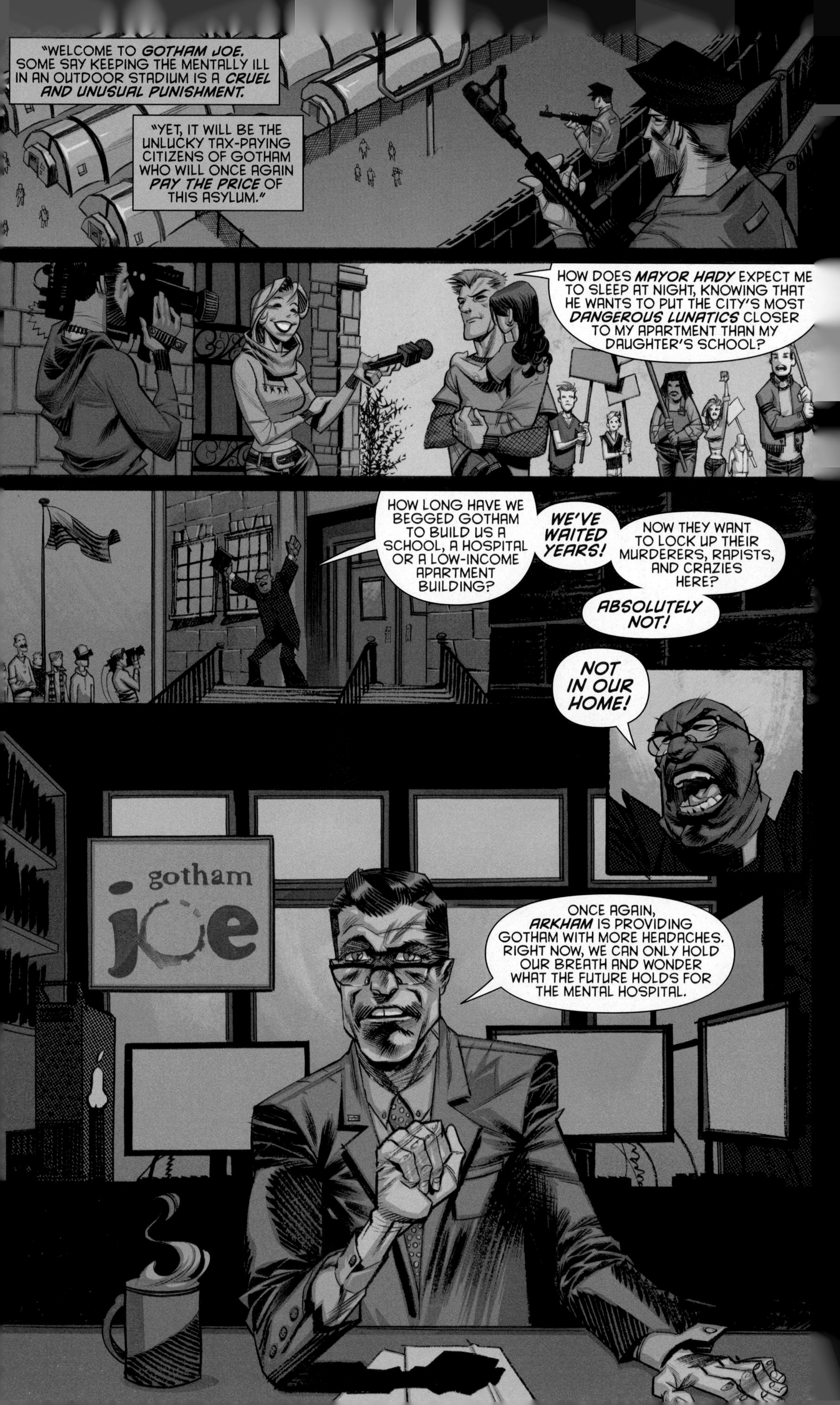
"WELCOME TO GOTHAM JOE. SOME SAY KEEPING THE MENTALLY ILL IN AN OUTDOOR STADIUM IS A CRUEL AND UNUSUAL PUNISHMENT.
"YET, IT WILL BE THE UNLUCKY TAX-PAYING CITIZENS OF GOTHAM WHO WILL ONCE AGAIN PAY THE PRICE OF THIS ASYLUM."
HOW DOES MAYOR HADY EXPECT ME TO SLEEP AT NIGHT, KNOWING THAT HE WANTS TO PUT THE CITY'S MOST DANGEROUS LUNATICS CLOSER TO MY APARTMENT THAN MY DAUGHTER'S SCHOOL?
HOW LONG HAVE WE BEGGED GOTHAM TO BUILD US A SCHOOL, A HOSPITAL OR A LOW-INCOME APARTMENT BUILDING?
WE'VE WAITED YEARS!
NOW THEY WANT TO LOCK UP THEIR MURDERERS, RAPISTS, AND CRAZIES HERE?
ABSOLUTELY NOT!
NOT IN OUR HOME!
gotham joe
ONCE AGAIN, ARKHAM IS PROVIDING GOTHAM WITH MORE HEADACHES. RIGHT NOW, WE CAN ONLY HOLD OUR BREATH AND WONDER WHAT THE FUTURE HOLDS FOR THE MENTAL HOSPITAL.

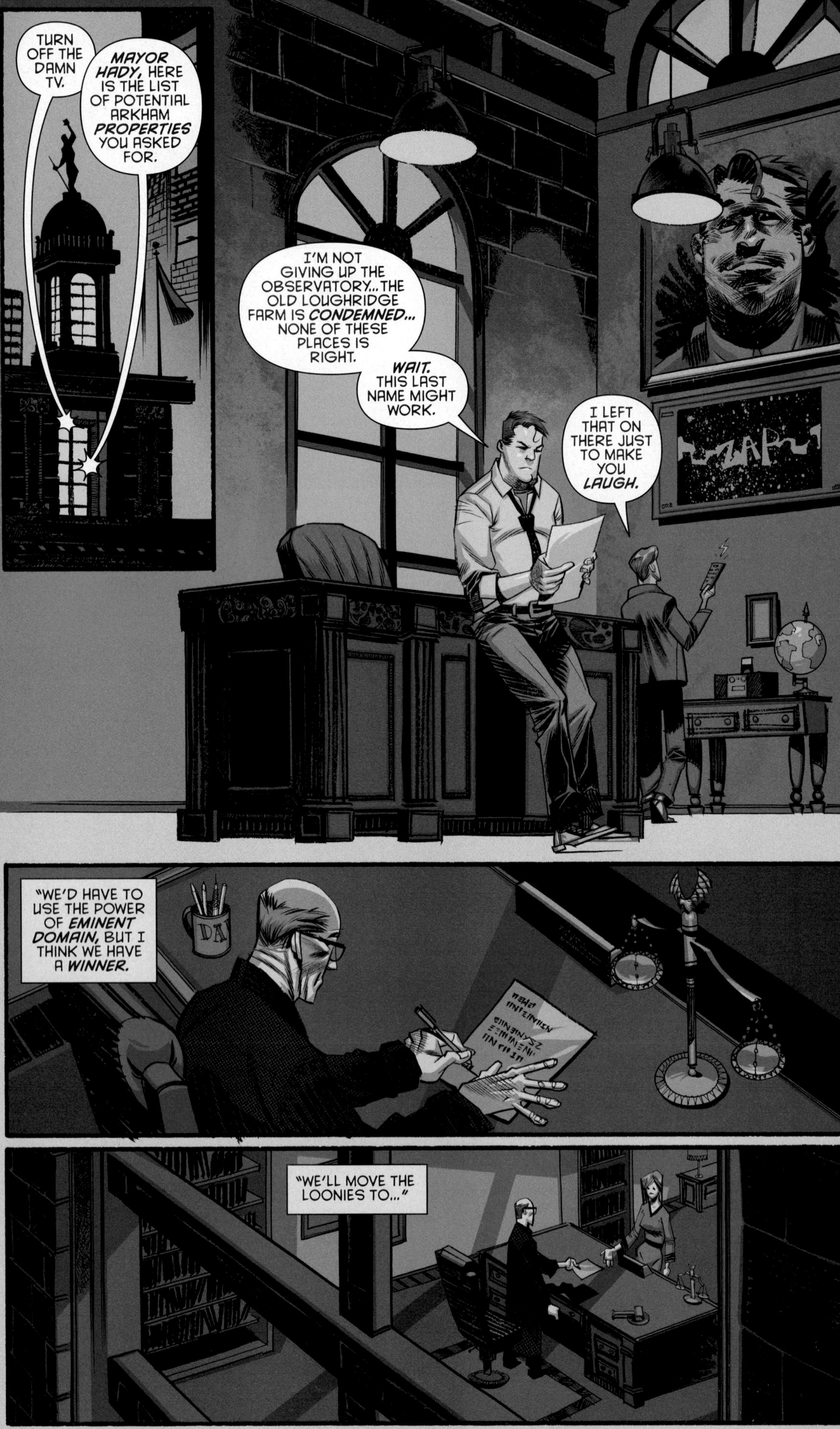

TURN OFF THE DAMN TV.
MAYOR HADY, HERE IS THE LIST OF POTENTIAL ARKHAM PROPERTIES YOU ASKED FOR.
I'M NOT GIVING UP THE OBSERVATORY... THE OLD LOUGHRIDGE FARM IS CONDEMNED... NONE OF THESE PLACES IS RIGHT.
WAIT. THIS LAST NAME MIGHT WORK.
I LEFT THAT ON THERE JUST TO MAKE YOU LAUGH.
ZAP
"WE'D HAVE TO USE THE POWER OF EMINENT DOMAIN, BUT I THINK WE HAVE A WINNER.
"WE'LL MOVE THE LOONIES TO..."

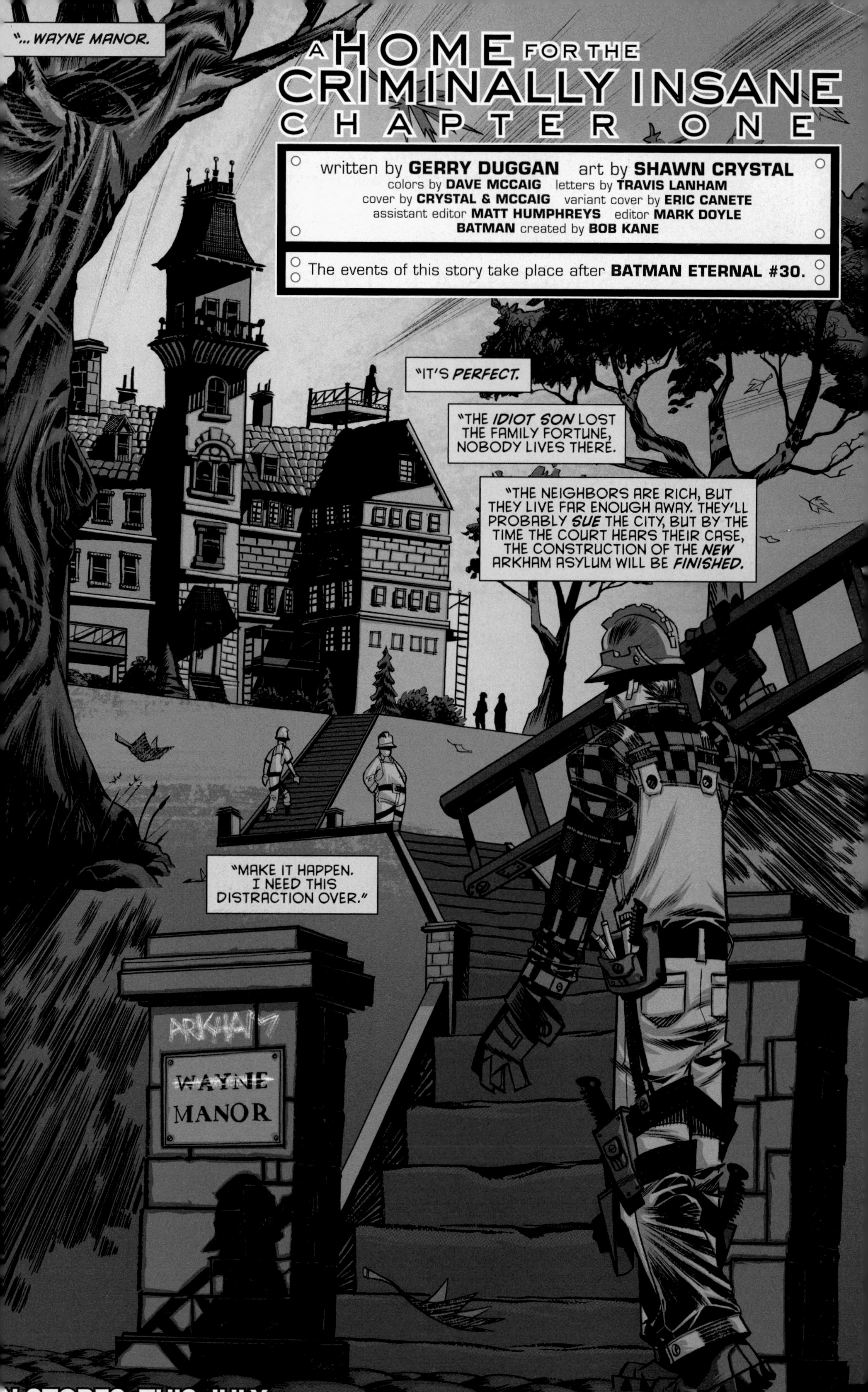
"...WAYNE MANOR.
A HOME FOR THE CRIMINALLY INSANE
CHAPTER ONE
written by GERRY DUGGAN art by SHAWN CRYSTAL
colors by DAVE MCCAIG letters by TRAVIS LANHAM
cover by CRYSTAL & MCCAIG variant cover by ERIC CANETE
assistant editor MATT HUMPHREYS editor MARK DOYLE
BATMAN created by BOB KANE
The events of this story take place after BATMAN ETERNAL #30.
"IT'S PERFECT.
"THE IDIOT SON LOST THE FAMILY FORTUNE, NOBODY LIVES THERE.
"THE NEIGHBORS ARE RICH, BUT THEY LIVE FAR ENOUGH AWAY. THEY'LL PROBABLY SUE THE CITY, BUT BY THE TIME THE COURT HEARS THEIR CASE, THE CONSTRUCTION OF THE NEW ARKHAM ASYLUM WILL BE FINISHED.
"MAKE IT HAPPEN. I NEED THIS DISTRACTION OVER."
ARKHAM
WAYNE
MANOR


N STORES: THIS JULY

# START AT THE BEGINNING!

# BATMAN VOLUME 1: THE COURT OF OWLS

**BATMAN VOL. 2: THE CITY OF OWLS**

with SCOTT SNYDER and GREG CAPULLO

**BATMAN VOL. 3: DEATH OF THE FAMILY**

with SCOTT SNYDER and GREG CAPULLO

**BATMAN: NIGHT OF THE OWLS**

with SCOTT SNYDER and GREG CAPULLO

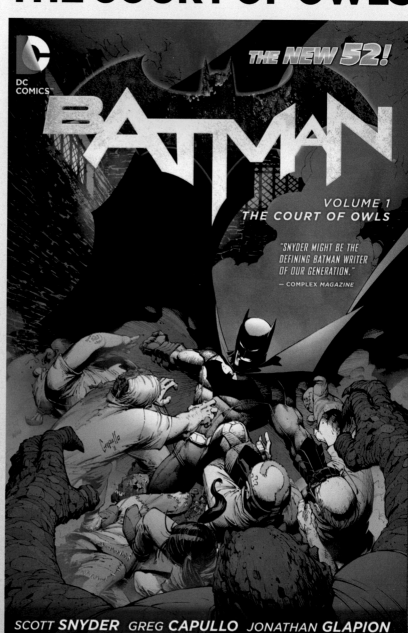

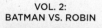

# GRANT MORRISON
## with FRANK QUITELY & PHILIP TAN

**VOL. 2:
BATMAN VS. ROBIN**

**VOL. 3: BATMAN &
ROBIN MUST DIE!**

**DARK KNIGHT VS.
WHITE KNIGHT**

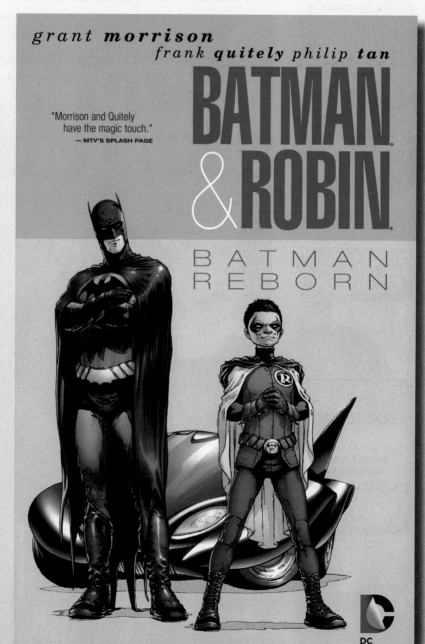

# DC COMICS™

FROM THE *NEW YORK TIMES* BEST-SELLING WRITERS

# ED BRUBAKER
# & GREG RUCKA
## with MICHAEL LARK

**GOTHAM CENTRAL
BOOK TWO:
JOKERS AND MADMEN**

**GOTHAM CENTRAL
BOOK THREE:
ON THE FREAK BEAT**

**GOTHAM CENTRAL
BOOK FOUR:
CORRIGAN**

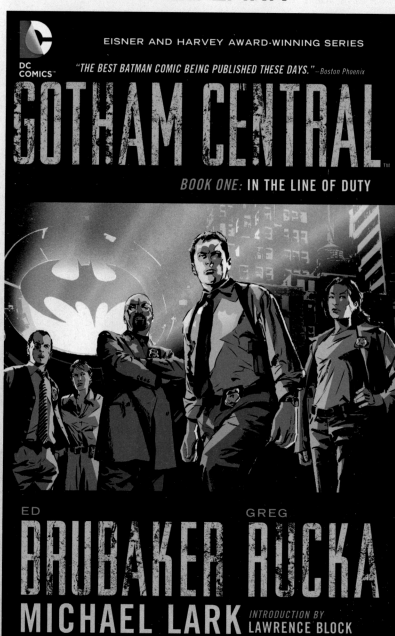